Contemporary Readings in
Literacy Education

Contemporary Readings in
Literacy Education

Marva Cappello
San Diego State University

Barbara Moss
San Diego State University

Editors

Contemporary
Readings Series

Los Angeles | London | New Delhi
Singapore | Washington DC

For information:

SAGE Publications, Inc.
2455 Teller Road
Thousand Oaks, California 91320
E-mail: order@sagepub.com

SAGE Publications Ltd.
1 Oliver's Yard
55 City Road
London EC1Y 1SP
United Kingdom

SAGE Publications India Pvt. Ltd.
B 1/I 1 Mohan Cooperative Industrial Area
Mathura Road, New Delhi 110 044
India

SAGE Publications Asia-Pacific Pte. Ltd.
33 Pekin Street #02-01
Far East Square
Singapore 048763

Printed in the United States of America

Library of Congress Cataloging-in-Publication Data

Contemporary readings in literacy education/edited by Marva Cappello, Barbara Moss.

    p. cm.

Includes bibliographical references and index.

ISBN 978-1-4129-6591-0 (pbk.)

  1. Reading. 2. Language arts. 3. Literacy. I. Cappello, Marva. II. Moss, Barbara, 1950-

LB1573.C55624 2010
372.6—dc22   2009029110

This book is printed on acid-free paper.

09 10 11 12 13 10 9 8 7 6 5 4 3 2 1

Acquisitions Editor:	Diane McDaniel
Editorial Assistant:	Ashley Conlon
Production Editor:	Carla Freeman
Typesetter:	C&M (P) Digitals Ltd.
Proofreader:	Scott Oney
Indexer:	Jeanne R. Busemeyer
Cover Designer:	Glenn Vogel
Marketing Manager:	Helen Salmon

CONTENTS

Read this article in full-text pdf at http://www.sagepub.com/cappello/

Read this article in full-text pdf at http://www.sagepub.com/cappello/

Read this article in full-text pdf at http://www.sagepub.com/cappello/

ARTICLE ABSTRACTS

Article 1

Pearson, P. D. (2004). The Reading Wars. *Educational Policy, 18*(1), 216–252.

This article's fundamental argument is that the reading instruction and reading research have been shaped by political forces desiring to privilege particular approaches to instruction or particular combinations of methodological and epistemological perspectives on research. The swings in both dominant pedagogies and dominant research paradigms are analyzed in terms of these determining forces. The article concludes by championing balance and compatibility across both instructional approaches and research methods in hopes of arresting the pendulum swings that have characterized the field for too many decades.

Article 2

Powell, R., McIntyre, E., & Rightmyer, E. (2006). Johnny Won't Read and Susie Won't Either: Reading Instruction and Student Resistance. *Journal of Early Childhood Literacy, 6*(1), 5–31.

Why are children off task? What is going on in classrooms where a majority of children are off task? In this study, the authors analyzed primary-grade classroom literacy instruction in which there was considerable off-task behavior. Using Turner and Paris's frame for understanding student motivation in the classroom, 73 activity settings were analyzed in which students were off task at least 25% of the time for instructional characteristics positively associated with student motivation: choice, challenge, control, collaboration, constructing meaning, and consequences. Student off-task behavior was prevalent in classrooms where few of these six variables were present and instructional tasks were characterized as "closed," that is, where the products and processes were predetermined. Where there was indication of a high degree of off-task behavior, a disproportionately high number (23 of the 28 data sets) were from classrooms that used scripted literacy instructional programs. Findings are interpreted using both psychological and critical frameworks.

Article 3

Fisher, D., & Frey, N. (2008). Releasing Responsibility. *Educational Leadership, 66*(3), 32–37.

We must transfer responsibility for learning to our students gradually—and offer support at every step. There is no shortage of teachers assigning students responsibility for their own learning. But these "busywork" examples are not exemplars of true independent learning, which is a major goal of education. How can we set students on a path to true independent learning? According to Fisher and Frey, one way is to purposefully yet gradually release responsibility for learning from teacher to student. To make this transfer of responsibility, we must give students supports that they can hold on to as they take the lead—not just push them onto the path and hope they find their way. These supports include models of the kind of thinking students will need to do, access to academic language, peer collaboration, and guided instruction.

Article 4

Guskey, T. R. (2003). How Classroom Assessments Improve Learning. *Educational Leadership, 60*(5), 6–11.

This article describes how to use quizzes, tests, writing assignments, and other assessments to improve instruction and help students learn. It suggests that instead of teaching to the test, teachers test what they teach and follow assessments with corrective instruction. This article also discusses the benefits of assessments.

Article 5

Johnston, P., & Costello, P. (2005). Principles for Literacy Assessment. *Reading Research Quarterly, 40*(2), 256–267.

"What gets assessed is what gets taught" is a common assertion whose meaning is often underestimated. It is not just what gets assessed, but how it is assessed that has implications for what is learned. When a child who is asked the meaning of his report card grades responds, "If I knew that I'd be the teacher," he is saying something about the relationships of authority learned in the process of assessment. When a teacher wishes out loud that her faculty "could discuss retention and realistic expectations for grade levels without the nastiness and accusations," she is also reporting on the relational aspect of assessment practices (Johnston, 2003, p. 90). The goal in this article is to offer a framework for understanding literacy assessment that incorporates these dimensions and reminds us of the broader picture of literacy assessment of which we often lose sight.

Article 6

Valencia, S. W., & Riddle Buly, M. (2004). Behind Test Scores: What Struggling Readers *Really* Need. *The Reading Teacher, 57*(6), 520–530.

In this article, we draw from the results of an empirical study of students who failed a typical fourth-grade state reading assessment (see Riddle Buly & Valencia, 2002, for a full description of the study). Specifically, we describe the patterns of performance that distinguish different groups of students who failed to meet standards. We also provide suggestions for what classroom teachers need to know and how they might help these children succeed. These 108 students constituted approximately 10% of failing students in the district. None of them was receiving supplemental special education or English as a Second Language (ESL) services. We wanted to understand the "garden variety" (Stanovich, 1988) test failure—those students typically found in the regular classroom who are experiencing reading difficulty but have not been identified as needing special services or intensive interventions. Classroom teachers, not reading specialists or special education teachers, are solely responsible for the reading instruction of these children and, ultimately, for their achievement.

Article 7

Clark, K. F. (2004). What Can I Say Besides "Sound It Out"? Coaching Word Recognition in Beginning Reading. *The Reading Teacher, 57*(5), 440–449.

Coaching is a highly effective instructional technique in which teachers craft instructional cues that enable students to apply their developing reading skills and knowledge of strategies as they attempt to complete a task. The article describes interactions that illustrate a highly effective instructional technique: coaching. In the interactions, knowledgeable teachers have crafted just the right cues for readers to apply their developing knowledge of word recognition strategies. In doing so, the teachers have incrementally fostered students' ability to become strategic and independent readers. The purpose of this article is to describe the technique of coaching word recognition. I review the reading process, elaborate on coaching, present examples of coaching, share elements to consider when preparing to coach, discuss implications for practice, and offer conclusions about the nature of effective coaching.

Article 8

Joseph, L. M. (2002). Helping Children Link Sound to Print. *Intervention in School and Clinic, 37*(4), 217–221.

Word boxes and word sorts are two phonic approaches that help children make connections between sound and print by gaining an awareness of the phonological and orthographic features of words. This article provides step-by-step procedures for using these approaches in small-group and whole-class settings. The use of peer tutors is discussed.

Article 9

Manyak, P. (2008). Phonemes in Use: Multiple Activities for a Critical Process. *The Reading Teacher, 61*(8), 659–662.

Several decades of research have established the critical role of phonemic awareness in the development of beginning reading. In particular, phonemic awareness makes early phonics instruction useful for children and facilitates their abilities to blend letter sounds while decoding words, to learn sight words reliably, and to spell phonetically. A key finding in phonemic awareness research is that instruction involving segmenting and blending phonemes combined with a focus on the letters that represent those phonemes contributes greatly to success in beginning reading and spelling. The author found that students benefit greatly from a variety of activities combining phoneme segmenting and blending with letter-sound instruction. This variety allows children to develop a robust ability to apply phonemic awareness to tasks of reading and writing and supports students who may struggle with this critical process. In this article, the author describes five "phonemes-in-use" activities and practical ideas for implementing them in the classroom.

Article 10

Graham, S., et al. (2008). Teaching Spelling in the Primary Grades: A National Survey of Instructional Practices and Adaptations. *American Educational Research Journal, 45*(3), 796–825.

Primary grade teachers randomly selected from across the United States completed a survey ($N = 168$) that examined their instructional practices in spelling and the types of adaptations they made for struggling spellers. Almost every teacher surveyed reported teaching spelling, and the vast majority of respondents implemented a complex and multifaceted instructional program that applied a variety of research-supported procedures. Although some teachers were sensitive to the instructional needs of weaker spellers and reported making many different adaptations for these students, a sizable minority of teachers (42%) indicated they made few or no adaptations. In addition, the teachers indicated that 27% of their students experienced difficulty with spelling, calling into question the effectiveness of their instruction with these children.

Article 11

Pikulski, J. J., & Chard, D. J. (2005). Fluency: Bridge Between Decoding and Reading Comprehension. *The Reading Teacher, 58*(6), 510–519.

Fluency has sometimes been viewed as essentially an oral reading phenomenon. The National Reading Panel defined reading fluency as "the ability to read text quickly, accurately, and with proper expression" (National Institute of Child Health and Human Development, 2000, p. 3–5). Definitions that emphasize the oral aspect of fluency may, at least in part, account for why fluency has not historically received much attention. The importance of oral reading pales dramatically in comparison to that of silent reading comprehension. Most readers spend a minuscule amount of time doing oral reading as compared to silent reading. A definition of fluency needs to encompass more than oral reading. *The Literacy Dictionary: The Vocabulary of Reading and Writing* defined fluency as "freedom from word identification problems that might hinder comprehension" (Harris & Hodges, 1995, p. 85). This definition enlarges our understanding of reading fluency to include comprehension. Samuels (2002), a pioneer in research and theory in reading fluency, cited this expanded definition as a major force in elevating the importance of fluency in the field of reading.

Article 12
Therrien, W. J., & Kubina, R. M., Jr. (2006). Developing Reading Fluency With Repeated Reading. *Intervention in School and Clinic, 41*(3), 156–160.

Repeated reading has gained popularity as a technique for helping students achieve reading fluency. It is widely implemented and can be used for students with and without disabilities. Repeated reading has several components that make it more efficient. This article shares those components and provides a framework for setting up and using repeated reading in the classroom.

Article 13
Kuhn, M., & Stahl, S. (2003). Fluency: A Review of Developmental and Remedial Practices. *Journal of Educational Psychology, 95*(1), 3–21.

The authors review theory and research relating to fluency instruction and development. They found that fluency instruction is generally effective; assisted approaches seem to be more effective than unassisted approaches; repetitive approaches do not seem to hold a clear advantage over nonrepetitive approaches; and effective fluency instruction moves beyond automatic word recognition to include rhythm and expression.

Article 14
Bromley, K. (2007). Nine Things Every Teacher Should Know About Words and Vocabulary Instruction. *Journal of Adolescent and Adult Literacy, 50*(7), 528–537.

Vocabulary knowledge contributes to comprehension, fluency, and student achievement. The goal of vocabulary instruction should be to build students' independent word-learning strategies. This article provides research and theory in support of nine key ideas about words and vocabulary instruction. These ideas are important for middle and secondary teachers to know and understand in order to provide sound vocabulary teaching across the content areas. Topics discussed include (1) the English language and the consistency of its rules, (2) how language competence grows from oral to written, (3) how words are learned, (4) multiple meanings, (5) multisyllabic words, and (6) the importance of teachers' modeling word consciousness, and their own excitement about learning new words. For each key idea, the author provides several practical suggestions for classroom instruction, including strategies for individuals, small groups, and the whole class. Several websites for developing vocabulary as well as professional resources for teachers are suggested.

Article 15
Yopp, R., & Yopp, H. (2007). Ten Important Words Plus: A Strategy for Building Word Knowledge. *The Reading Teacher, 61*(2), 157–160.

In this strategy, students individually select and record 10 important words on self-adhesive notes as they read a text. Then, students build a group bar graph displaying their choices, write a sentence that summarizes the content, and respond to prompts that ask them to think about words in powerful ways. Several prompts are suggested, each emphasizing the meaning, manipulation, or application of selected words in various contexts. This strategy is based on principles of effective vocabulary instruction, as it involves repeated exposure to words, active engagement with words, and study of words with instructional potential. This strategy fosters word knowledge as well as comprehension of text with its focus on word meanings and important ideas in text.

Article 16

Pearson, P. D., Hiebert, E. H., & Kamil, M. L. (2007). Vocabulary Assessment: What We Know and What We Need to Learn. *Reading Research Quarterly, 42*(2), 282–296.

The authors assert that in order to teach vocabulary more effectively and better understand its relation to comprehension, we need first to address how vocabulary knowledge and growth are assessed. They argue that "vocabulary assessment is grossly undernourished, both in its theoretical and practical aspects—that it has been driven by tradition, convenience, psychometric standards, and a quest for economy of effort rather than a clear conceptualization of its nature and relation to other aspects of reading expertise, most notably comprehension."

Article 17

Zwiers, J. (2007). Teacher Practices and Perspectives for Developing Academic Language. *International Journal of Applied Linguistics, 17*(1), 93–116.

This study investigates the ways in which middle school teachers in the United States develop academic language in intermediate-level English learners who attend mainstream content classes. Analysis of field notes, transcripts, and student work show that (a) academic language and higher-order thinking skills are closely linked, and (b) classroom discourse patterns and activities both develop and impede language growth. The teachers used four principle communication strategies: questioning, gestures, connecting to background knowledge with examples and analogies, and personifying. The results suggest that students, despite growth in certain dimensions of cognition and language, also learn counterproductive "rules of school." This research is intended to benefit the millions of "nonmainstream" students worldwide who struggle in schools that have been created and shaped to serve mainstream purposes.

Article 18

Pardo, L. S. (2004). What Every Teacher Needs to Know About Comprehension. *The Reading Teacher, 58*(3), 272–280.

This article presents a model of comprehension to support classroom teachers as they engage their students in making meaning from text. Four areas contribute to the comprehension process: the reader, the context, the text, and the transaction, which is described as the intersection of the reader and text situated within a specific context. This model is used to describe research-based, practical applications for teachers as they provide support for comprehension in grades K–6. Teachers support the reader by teaching decoding skills, helping children build fluency, building and activating students' background knowledge, teaching vocabulary skills, motivating students, and engaging students in personal response to text. Teachers support the text by teaching text structures, modeling appropriate text selection, and providing regular independent reading time. Teachers create and support a sociocultural context that values reading and writing, contains a wide variety of texts, allows students to take risks, and provides time for reading aloud independently. Teachers support transaction by providing explicit instruction of comprehension strategies, teaching children to monitor and repair, using multiple strategy approaches, scaffolding support, and making reading and writing connections visible to students.

Article 19

   Clark, K. F., & Graves, M. F. (2005). Scaffolding Students' Comprehension of Text. *The Reading Teacher, 58*(6), 570–580.

In this article, the authors explore the concept of instructional scaffolding as it applies to facilitating students' reading comprehension. They argue that scaffolding is a highly flexible and adaptable model of instruction that supports students as they acquire both basic skills and higher order thinking processes, allows for explicit instruction within authentic contexts of reading and writing, and enables teachers to differentiate instruction for students of diverse needs. The authors hope to help professionals gain a broader perspective of the different roles they can play in using various forms of scaffolding in the reading program, so that they will employ scaffolding more frequently in their classrooms and thereby improve their students' reading comprehension. Several definitions of scaffolding are considered, foundations of the scaffolding concept are reviewed, and reasons that scaffolding is an effective technique are discussed. Three general types of scaffolding are addressed: moment-to-moment scaffolding, instructional frameworks that foster content learning, and instructional procedures for teaching reading comprehension strategies. For each type, the authors provide two examples of instruction. Finally, they discuss things to consider when making decisions about scaffolding.

Article 20

   Moss, B. (2004). Teaching Expository Text Structures Through Information Trade Book Retellings. *The Reading Teacher, 57*(8), 710–718.

While most teachers are very familiar with the power of narrative retellings to improve student comprehension, they are less experienced with expository retellings. Involving students in retelling information trade books represents a promising means not only for engaging students with outstanding literature but also for improving their understanding of expository text. This article describes how teachers can use information trade book retellings to improve student comprehension of expository text structures. First, the author provides background information about retellings, expository text structure, and teaching these text patterns through information trade books. The second part of the article describes instructional strategies and procedures for teaching the various text structures through large-group, small-group, and paired retellings. The final section of the article describes how teachers can assess individual student retellings.

Article 21

   Wood, K. D. (2003). New Dimensions of Content Area Literacy: Not Just for Secondary Teachers Anymore. *California Reader, 36,* 12–17.

The promotion of content area reading, helping students comprehend the textbooks for their courses, has been taking place for decades. However, in recent years, the term *content area reading* has been supplanted by the term *content area literacy*. This new concept involves integrating the communication process (of reading, writing, listening, speaking, and viewing) across all subject areas. This article discusses the broader range of emphasis that comes with the new terminology.

Article 22

   Blanton, W. E., Wood, K. D., & Taylor, D. B. (2007). Rethinking Middle School Reading Instruction: A Basic Literacy Activity. *Reading Psychology, 28*(1), 75–95.

Research on subject matter instruction across the 20th century (e.g., Bellack, 1966; Gall, 1970; Hoetker & Ahlbrand, 1969; Langer, 1999; Mehan, 1979; Nystrand, 1997; Stevens, 1912) reveals a preponderance of teacher-directed lecture, recitation, and round-robin reading of text in place of instruction that focuses on reading-to-learn, thinking, and transforming information into meaning and understanding (Blanton & Moorman, 1990; Durkin, 1978–1979; Langer, 1999; Wood & Muth, 1991). This kind of instruction persists despite the fact that observations of higher-performing schools have indicated the tendency to organize instruction around meaningful learning communities with extensive interactive discussion of material read (Langer, 1999; Myers, 1996; Wenglinsky, 2000, 2004). The purpose of this essay is twofold: (1) to argue that a great deal of reading instruction fails to meet the multiple and complex literacy needs of most middle school students, and (2) to propose a new orientation for thinking about middle school reading instruction. The authors begin with a discussion of research findings on classroom reading instruction, followed by an exploration of issues central to the problem. Next is proposed what the authors have titled *the basic literacy activity,* a conceptual tool for thinking about and arranging middle school reading instruction. The article ends with an overview of selected instructional strategies that exemplify the characteristics of basic literacy activity.

Article 23
   Fisher, D., & Ivey, G. (2006). Evaluating the Interventions for Struggling Adolescent Readers. *Journal of Adolescent & Adult Literacy, 50*(3), 180–189.

Struggling adolescent readers need interventions that provide them with opportunities to read more and to read better. The authors examine two case studies of interventions at work and propose criteria on which to evaluate intervention programs. Their review of the evidence on these programs for struggling adolescent readers suggests that at least five factors must be present for the intervention to matter: (1) The teacher should play a critical role in assessment and instruction; (2) the intervention should reflect a comprehensive approach to reading and writing; (3) reading and writing in the intervention should be engaging; (4) interventions should be driven by useful and relevant assessments; and (5) interventions should include significant opportunities for authentic reading and writing.

Article 24
   Cappello, M. (2005). Supporting Independent Writing: A Continuum of Writing Instruction. *California Reader, 39*(2), 38–46.

Every teacher knows the ultimate goal of education is student independence. Contemporary understandings of the teaching and learning process highlight the multiple roles teachers enact in their classrooms to support their students' journey toward independence (e.g., coach, facilitator, model, informant). This article presents a structure to help teachers promote the writing independence of their students. The framework presented organizes classroom writing instruction to meet individual needs using varying degrees of teacher support.

Article 25
   Whitney, A., et al. (2008). Beyond Strategies: Teacher Practice, Writing Process, and the Influence of Inquiry. *English Education, 40*(3), 201–232.

With respect to the writing process in particular, a now well-established body of research demonstrates that process-oriented writing instruction benefits student achievement in writing. Process-oriented terms and concepts have entered the material environment of America's schools, in textbooks and curricula even where the theoretical bases underlying those materials might appear to conflict with it, such as materials in which priority is placed on rhetorical modes, form, or grammatical correctness. Even in settings where no one would explicitly claim to embrace a "process pedagogy," classrooms exhibit some of its markers: Students and teachers use words like "drafts," "pre-writing," and "revision" in commonplace speech. Yet, though it is now difficult to imagine any language arts teacher at any grade level not knowing about "the writing process," many teaching practices employed in classrooms in the name of "the writing process" suggest that teachers may have different understandings about what the writing process entails as a model of writing and learning to write, conceptually or epistemologically. What "pre-writing" means in classrooms, for example, may differ. Most teachers know about different strategies for pre-writing, but differences appear in how teachers and school programs construct their own understanding of what pre-writing means. This article presents and discusses case studies of two teachers, drawn from a larger study, who represent different ways of envisioning and enacting a process-influenced pedagogy, one who worked with the South Coast Writing Project in an inquiry-oriented inservice program and one who did not. These two teachers work in similar school settings with similar kinds of students and similar (in some instances identical) district-provided writing curricula, yet their differing approaches to the "same" classroom strategies suggest how National Writing Project (NWP)-influenced professional development might continue to influence even basic practice in the teaching of writing.

Article 26

Juzwik, M. M., et al. (2006). Writing Into the 21st Century: An Overview of Research on Writing, 1999 to 2004. *Written Communication, 23*(4), 451–476.

This study charts the terrain of research on writing during the 6-year period from 1999 to 2004, asking "What are current trends and foci in research on writing?" In examining a cross-section of writing research, the authors focus on four issues: (1) What are the general problems being investigated by contemporary writing researchers? Which of the various problems dominate recent writing research, and which are not as prominent? (2) What population age groups are prominent in recent writing research? (3) What is the relationship between population age groups and problems under investigation? and (4) What methodologies are being used in research on writing? Based on a body of refereed journal articles ($N = 1,502$) reporting studies about writing and composition instruction that were located using three databases, the authors characterize various lines of inquiry currently undertaken. Social context and writing practices, bi- or multilingualism and writing, and writing instruction are the most actively studied problems during this period, whereas writing and technologies, writing assessment and evaluation, and relationships among literacy modalities are the least studied problems. Undergraduate, adult, and other postsecondary populations are the most prominently studied population age group, whereas preschool-aged children and middle and high school students are least studied. Research on instruction within the preschool through 12th grade (PreK–12) age group is prominent, whereas research on genre, assessment, and bi- or multilingualism is scarce within this population. The majority of articles employ interpretive methods. This indicator of current writing research should be useful to researchers, policymakers, and funding agencies, as well as to writing teachers and teacher educators.

Article 27

Krashen, S. (2008). Language Education: Past, Present, and Future. *RELC Journal, 39*(2), 178–187.

The recent past in language teaching has been dominated by the Skill-Building Hypothesis, the view that we learn language by first learning about it, and then practicing the rules we learned in output. The present is marked by the emergence of the Comprehension Hypothesis, the view that we acquire language when we understand messages, and is also characterized by the beginning stages of its applications: comprehensible-input-based teaching methods, sheltered subject matter teaching, and the use of extensive reading for intermediate language students. The author's hope is that the future will see a clearer understanding of the Comprehension Hypothesis, and the profession taking more advantage of it.

Article 28

Goldenberg, C. N. (2008). Teaching English Language Learners: What the Research Does—and Does Not—Say. *American Educator, 32*(2), 8–42.

It's time to move beyond charged debates and all-too-certain answers. What students need is for educators and policymakers to take a more in-depth look, starting with what existing research does—and does not—say. In this article, Claude Goldenberg walks us through the major findings of two recent reviews of the research on educating ELLs. Given all the strong opinions one sees in newspaper op-eds, readers may be surprised to discover how little is actually known. What is certain is that if we conducted more research with ELLs, and paid more attention to the research that exists, we would be in a much better position.

Article 29

Manyak, P. C. (2007). A Framework for Robust Literacy Instruction for English Learners. *The Reading Teacher, 61*(2), 197–199.

This column from the English Learners department outlines a framework for robust literacy instruction for English learners—instruction that addresses the cognitive challenges of acquiring literacy, accounts for English learners' special language needs and abilities, and includes their unique cultural experiences. The framework consists of four complementary elements: explicit code and comprehension instruction, language-rich instruction, socioculturally informed instruction, and additive-literacy instruction. Drawing on key research findings and successful classroom interventions, the author provides a brief rationale for each of these elements.

Article 30

Verdugo, R. R., & Flores, B. (2007). English Learners: Key Issues. *Education and Urban Society, 39*(2), 167–193.

Since its inception, America's system of public education has faced many challenges. One of its more important challenges has been how to teach children from diverse backgrounds and cultures. As a society that prides itself on a democratic ideology, cultural diversity and schooling are not trivial issues. One of the more significant diversity topics has been the presence of English-language learners (ELL) in American public schools. This article introduces the topic of ELL students and the education and education-related issues surrounding ELL students. For researchers and policymakers deeply steeped in the issues surrounding ELL students, the issues and concerns raised in this article are familiar. However, for the vast majority of other researchers and policymakers, these issues are not familiar and may have an important impact on their own research agendas.

Article 31

Tomlinson, C. A. (2000). Reconcilable Differences? Standards-Based Teaching and Differentiation. *Educational Leadership, 58*(1), 6–11.

For many teachers, curriculum has become a prescribed set of academic standards, instructional pacing has become a race against the clock to cover the standards, and the sole goal of teaching has been reduced to raising student test scores on a single test. Teachers are admonished to attend to students' differences, but they must ensure that every student becomes competent in the same subject matter. To examine the dichotomy between standards-based teaching and differentiation—the philosophy that student differences impact what they need in order to learn—this article asks questions about how standards influence the quality of teaching and learning. It assesses ways in which standards-based approaches can make an impact on students whose abilities are outside the usual norms of achievement.

Article 32

Hoover, J. J., & Patton, J. R. (2004). Differentiating Standards-Based Education for Students With Diverse Needs. *Remedial and Special Education, 25*(2), 74–78.

The need to differentiate or adapt curriculum and instruction to meet special needs continues to challenge educators of students with high-incidence disabilities. The current emphasis on teaching and assessing standards requires knowledge and skills to differentiate standards-based education to successfully meet diverse needs in the classroom.

Article 33

Knobel, M., & Lankshear, C. (2006). Discussing New Literacies. *Language Arts, 84*(1), 78–86.

The authors' research explores and analyzes youth practices with new media, and their vision of new literacies offers educators and researchers unprecedented pathways for thinking about texts, media, youth, and relations of power in the 21st century. The format for this article grew out of a set of questions posed to Colin and Michele via e-mail. The editors asked them to:

- Describe the ideas that have informed their thinking over the past decade
- Elaborate on their definition of new literacies
- Discuss tensions between new media experimentation and learning contexts
- Address the concerns adults and youth might have about the content and potentially predatory nature of online voices and images
- Walk readers through an example of the social networking possibilities of meaning making with new media

Article 34

Hassett, D. D., & Schieble, M. B. (2007). Finding Space and Time for the Visual in K–12 Literacy Instruction. *English Journal, 97*(1), 62–68.

Dawnene D. Hassett and Melissa B. Schieble contend that literacy instruction must include attention to the multiple ways in which print and visual images work together. They propose ways to update accepted reading strategies "with visual texts and new literacies in mind." Using examples from picture books and graphic novels, they expand our understanding of how readers extend three cueing systems—graphophonic, semantic, and syntactic—to negotiate multiple levels of meaning in visual texts.

Article 35

Cappello, M., & Hollingsworth, S. (2008). Literacy Inquiry and Pedagogy Through a Photographic Lens. *Language Arts, 85*(6), 442–449.

This paper explores the potential of photography for teaching, learning, and studying literacy in elementary school classrooms. The authors examine the ways shifting between communication systems (photography, oral language, and writing) impact students' abilities to problem solve and create rich texts. Specifically, they explore the roles photography plays in mediating and representing meaning and find that photography can be used as an effective tool for inquiry in education—and for the pedagogy of writing instruction.

Article 36

Jewitt, C. (2008). Multimodality and Literacy in School Classrooms. *Review of Research in Education, 32,* 241–267.

The characteristics of contemporary societies are increasingly theorized as global, fluid, and networked. These conditions underpin the emerging knowledge economy as it is shaped by the societal and technological forces of late capitalism. These shifts and developments have significantly affected the communicational landscape of the 21st century. A key aspect of this is the reconfiguration of the representational and communicational resources of image, action, sound, and so on in new multimodal ensembles. The terrain of communication is changing in profound ways and extends to schools and ubiquitous elements of everyday life, even if these changes are occurring to different degrees and at uneven rates. It is against this backdrop that this critical review explores school multimodality and literacy and asks what these changes mean for being literate in this new landscape of the 21st century. The two key arguments in this article are that it is not possible to think about literacy solely as a linguistic accomplishment and that the time for the habitual conjunction of language, print literacy, and learning is over. This review, organized in three parts, does not provide an exhaustive overview of multimodal literacies in and beyond classrooms. Instead, it sets out to highlight key definitions in an expanded approach to new literacies, then to link these to emergent studies of schooling and classroom practice. The first part outlines the new conditions for literacy and the ways in which this is conceptualized in the current research literature. In particular, it introduces three perspectives: New Literacies Studies, multiliteracies, and multimodality. Contemporary conceptualizations of literacy in the school classroom are explored in the second part of the chapter. This discussion is organized around themes that are central to multimodality and multiliteracies. These include multimodal perspectives on pedagogy, design, decisions about connecting with the literacy worlds of students, and the ways in which representations shape curriculum knowledge and learning. Each theme is discussed in turn, drawing on a range of examples of multimodal research. The third and final part of the article discusses future directions for multiple literacies, curriculum policy, and schooling.

PREFACE

his book was written to support beginning teachers and literacy support providers in understanding contemporary issues in literacy education. This collction of readings and their companion strategies represent a wide range of relevant topics concerning teaching and learning literacy in K–12 classrooms.

We created the sections based on the abundance of ideas that have appeared in recent professional journals, as well as the domains identified on the RICA (Reading Instruction Competence Assessment), the California literacy assessment for multiple subject candidates. The specific articles were selected to provide a balance between readings that focus on key theoretical concerns and readings that suggest classroom applications of those guiding principals.

This text is organized into sections that represent important contemporary literacy concerns that all teachers must familiarize themselves with. Each section leads off with an overview of the topic, which is designed to serve as a pre-reading introduction. We have also included an instructional strategy chosen specifically to help readers negotiate the articles. Just as Fisher and Frey (2008) suggest in their article, we believe we must "transfer responsibility for learning to our students [and readers] gradually and offer support at every step" (Article 3, p. 43). We also agree with Pearson's (2004) call for a balanced approach to literacy that "would carve out scaffolded instructional activities to spotlight necessary skills and strategies" (Article 1, p. 22).

Therefore, we have designed the text sections to include literacy strategies as scaffolds for reading and understanding the articles in each section. Each strategy was chosen to connect to the topic (e.g., a vocabulary strategy for the vocabulary section) and promote overall comprehension. In addition, we hope you will use these instructional strategies as models that are useful for your own teaching and classrooms.

We close the text with an annotated list of "Internet Resources" to help readers more fully explore the literacy education issues introduced in these pages.

Please note that some of these articles in this reader are located online only. Our goal is to provide as many articles as possible, while keeping the cost and length of the book reasonable. We placed several of the longer journal articles published by SAGE on our website, and they can be easily downloaded at http://www.sagepub.com/cappello/.

ACKNOWLEDGMENTS

We thank the following reviewers for their contributions to the development of *Contemporary Readings in Literacy Education:*

Pat Antonacci
Iona College

Sara Ann Beach
University of Oklahoma

Esther Berkowitz
St. Joseph's College, Brooklyn Campus

Andrew Johnson
Minnesota State University, Mankato

Mary Ellen Levin
Manhattanville College

Michael Moore
Georgia Southern University

Stephen Wellinski
Eastern Michigan University

ADVISORY BOARD

Section I

PLANNING AND ORGANIZING LITERACY INSTRUCTION

OVERVIEW

The articles in this section were chosen to offer the reader an exploration of the nature of literacy tasks in school curriculum as well as the role of the teacher and learner in literacy education. By examining these salient features of literacy instruction, we hope you will be better prepared to organize for literacy instruction in your classrooms.

Pearson (2004) reviews the history of "The Reading Wars" and discusses the ways politics shapes what we do in reading research and instruction. He calls for a balanced approach to literacy instruction that moves beyond "simple answers" about how best to teach reading. In their article, "Johnny Won't Read, and Susie Won't Either: Reading Instruction and Student Resistance," Powell, McIntyre, and Rightmyer (2006) explore the reasons students were off task and unmotivated during literacy lessons and found that "one of the primary reasons students were unmotivated was due to the characteristics of the tasks in which they were invited to participate."

In "Releasing Responsibility," Fisher and Frey (2008) capitalize on these ideas to help teachers organize for instruction, gradually releasing responsibility for task completion from teacher to student so they are situated to learn from independent engagements. The authors suggest that this model for instruction "promotes lasting ownership of learning."

STRATEGY

There is much educational research that recognizes "highly effective teachers are those who are capable of sustaining students' involvement with meaningful literacy tasks" (Powell et al., "Johnny Won't Read"). Use Burke's (2007) "Conversational Roundtable" to guide your thinking about the role of the teacher in each of the articles in this section. The Conversational Roundtable will help you and your colleagues organize a response to the text.

CONVERSATIONAL ROUNDTABLE

(Burke, 2007)

DIRECTIONS

As you read, take notes in the first quadrant of the graphic organizer. After you read, meet with three colleagues to discuss the reading and take notes on their comments in each of the other quadrants. Finally, write a summary answering the guiding question: What is the role of the literacy teacher in each of the articles in this section?

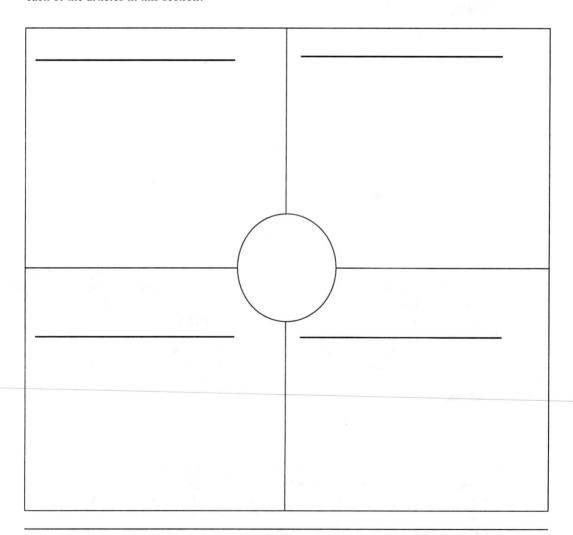

SOURCE: Burke, J. (2007). *The English Teacher's Companion* (3rd ed.). Portsmouth, NH: Heinemann.

Article 1

THE READING WARS[1]

P. DAVID PEARSON

This article's fundamental argument is that reading instruction and reading research have been shaped by political forces desiring to privilege particular approaches to instruction or particular combinations of methodological and epistemological perspectives on research. The swings in both dominant pedagogies and dominant research paradigms are analyzed in terms of these determining forces. The article concludes by championing balance and compatibility across both instructional approaches and research methods in hopes of arresting the pendulum swings that have characterized the field for too many decades.

Keywords: reading; reading research; reading policy; history of reading; reading curriculum

Writing about the politics of reading some 15 years ago (Pearson, 1989), I wondered whether the *whole-language movement*, which was the centerpiece of the reading field's foray into constructivist pedagogy, was capable of maintaining the mantle of "conventional wisdom," a status that at that time, it was on the brink of achieving. I questioned its enduring leadership capacity because of the curricular, philosophical, and political ground on which it stood. Curricularly, I expected that its guiding principles of authenticity (in texts, tasks, and tests) and curricular integration—both within the language arts (across reading, writing, speaking, and listening) and between the language arts and other curricular areas—would run afoul of the powerful publishing lobbies in the United States. Philosophically, it is built on epistemologies of interpretation rather than realism, rejecting the idea of an external reality that we will eventually find if we just look hard enough; as such, leaders of the whole

SOURCE: Pearson, P. D. (2004). The Reading Wars. *Educational Policy, 18*(1), 216–252. Reprinted by permission of Sage Publications, Inc.

language movement would have been thrilled to find provisional and situation-specific answers to burning policy questions such as, What is the best way to teach beginning reading? Those views would not sit well, I thought, in congressional or state legislative milieus or school board chambers, places where truth and simple answers to policy questions are serious goals. Politically, I predicted that its commitment to grassroots decision making—a commitment requiring that everything must be done to preserve as much power and prerogative for individual teachers (who must, in turn, offer genuine choices to individual students)—would doom it as a policy initiative. In an atmosphere in which accountability systems driven by externally mandated high-stakes tests lay just over the horizon, I wondered whether policy makers, or parents for that matter, would be willing to cede that level or prerogative to a profession that in terms of its capacity to deliver achievement, seemed to be asleep at the wheel. My overarching question was whether whole language could withstand the pressure of curricular leadership, with implicit responsibility for whatever trends in achievement ensued. My suspicion was that it was better situated as a guerilla-like movement that made occasional sorties into the policy world to snipe at those in curricular power.

In reflecting on those wonderments some 15 years later, it is clear that whole language, along with its close constructivist cousins—literature-based reading, process writing, and integrated language-arts instruction—did not experience a long tenure in the seat of curricular power, at least in the form in which it and its relations existed in the late 1980s and early 1990s. Whether the seeds of its demise were internal shortcomings, as I wondered in 1989, or external political forces of the sort that dominate the policy conversation today, or some combination of the two, is a question that I return to at the end of this article after reviewing the important developments in policy and practice that have shaped events and interpretations in the interim.

THE GOLDEN YEARS OF WHOLE-LANGUAGE INFLUENCE

Whole language did not suddenly emerge on the reading scene in the 1980s. Its roots (Y. Goodman, 1989) are in Deweyian-inspired, child-centered pedagogy and the integrated curriculum movements popular in England, Australia, and New Zealand (e.g., Holdaway, 1984). It also owes part of its heritage to earlier American movements, such as individualized reading (Veatch, 1959) and language experience (Stauffer, 1980). But it was the incredible shift in the scholarly paradigms that undergirded our views of reading acquisition that in my view, really laid the groundwork for its ascendancy (see Pearson & Stephens, 1993, for an account of these developments). The psycholinguistically oriented work of Roger Brown (1970), Frank Smith (1971), and Kenneth Goodman (1965, 1969) sent the message that reading was more a language than it was a perceptual process. The work in reading comprehension inspired by the cognitive revolution in psychology (see Anderson & Pearson, 1984) established meaning as the core, not the residual outcome, of reading. Advances in sociolinguistic theory in the 1980s (Bloome & Green, 1984; Heath, 1983) and critical literacy in the 1990s (Gee, 1989; Luke, 1995) established the understanding that all language and, hence, all literacy learning is grounded in the material motives of human interaction, with all of its social, political, and economic faces (however endearing or ugly they might be) intact.

When whole language emerged as a movement in the 1980s, it challenged the conventional wisdom of basals and questioned the unqualified support for early code emphases that had grown between 1967 and the early 1980s. One of the great ironies of whole language is that its ascendancy into curricular prominence is best documented by its influence on the one curricular tool it has most consistently and most vehemently opposed, the basal reader. Basals changed dramatically in the early 1990s, largely, I am confident, in response to the groundswell of support within the teaching profession for whole language and its close curricular allies, literature-based reading and process writing.

Vocabulary control, already weakened during the 1970s in response to Chall's (1967) admonitions, was virtually abandoned in the early 1990s in deference to attempts to incorporate more literature, this time in unexpurgated form (i.e., without the practices of adaptation and excerpting that had characterized the basals of the 1970s and 1980s) into the Grade 1 program (Hoffman et al., 1995). Phonics, along with other skills, was backgrounded, and literature moved to center stage.

Basal programs appropriated or, as some whole-language advocates have argued, "basalized" the activities and tools of whole language. Thus, in the basals of the early 1990s, each unit might have a writing process component in which the rhetoric if not the reality of some version of process writing was presented to teachers and students. In the 1980s, comprehension questions, probably following a story line, might have sufficed for the guided reading section of the manual (the part that advises teachers on how to read and discuss the story), but in the 1990s, questions and tasks that supported deep probes into students' responses to literature became more prevalent. Another concession to literature-based reading was the creation and marketing of classroom libraries—boxed sets of books, usually thematically related to each unit, that teachers could use to extend their lessons and units "horizontally" and enrich children's literary opportunities.

Basals also repositioned their "integrated language arts" and "integrated curriculum" strands. Dating back even to the 1920s and 1930s, basals had provided at least a "token" section in which teachers were encouraged to extend the themes or skills of the basal story into related writing (e.g., rewriting stories), oral language (e.g., transforming a story into a play and dramatizing it),

or cross-curricular activities (e.g., conducting community surveys, tallying the results, and reporting them), but these forays were regarded as peripheral rather than core. In the basals of the early 1990s, as skills moved into the background, these integrated language-arts activities were featured more prominently as core lesson components.[2]

These changes can, I believe, be traced to the prominent position of whole language as a curricular force during this period (Pearson, 1992). Publishers of basals accomplished this feat of appropriation not by ridding their programs of the skills of previous eras but by subtle repositioning—foregrounding one component while backgrounding another, creating optional components or modules (e.g., an intensive phonics kit or a set of literature books) that could be added to give the program one or another spin. Unsurprisingly, this created bulkier teachers' manuals and more complex programs.

Acceptance of whole language was not universal. To the contrary, there was considerable resistance to whole language and literature-based reading throughout the country.[3] In many places, whole language never really gained a foothold. In others, what was implemented in the name of whole language was not consistent with the philosophical and curricular principles of the movement; California, whole-language advocates would argue, is a case in point. Whole language got conflated with whole-class instruction and was interpreted to mean that all kids should get the same literature, even if teachers had to read it to them.[4]

Nor was there a single voice within the whole-language movement. Whole-language scholars and practitioners differed, and still differ, on a host of issues such as the role of skills, conventions, and strategies within a language-arts program. Some said, if we can just be patient, skills will emerge from meaningful communication activities; others spur things on by taking advantage of spontaneous opportunities for minilessons; still others were willing to spur spontaneity a bit with minilessons and other transparently instructional routines.

Even so, it is fair to conclude that by the early 1990s, whole language had become the conventional wisdom, the standard against which all else was referenced. The rhetoric of professional articles belies this change. As late as the mid-1980s, articles were written with the presumption of a different conventional wisdom—a world filled with skills, contrived readers, and workbooks. By 1991–1992, they were written with the presumption that whole-language reforms, although not fully ensconced in America's schools, were well on their way to implementation. The arguments in the 1990s were less about first principles of whole language and more about fine-tuning teaching repertoires. The meetings of the Whole Language Umbrella grew to be larger than most large state conventions and regional conferences of the International Reading Association. By 1995, whole language was no longer a collection of guerrilla sorties into the land of skills and basals that characterized it through the mid-1980s. It had become the conventional wisdom, in rhetoric if not in reality.

THE DEMISE OF WHOLE LANGUAGE

Toward century's end, just when it appeared as if whole language, supported by its intellectual cousins (process writing, literature-based reading, and integrated curriculum), was about to assume the position of conventional wisdom for the field, the movement was challenged seriously, and the pendulum of the pedagogical debate began to swing back toward the skills end of the curriculum and instruction continuum. Several factors converged to make the challenge credible, among them (a) unintended curricular casualties of whole language; (b) questionable applications of whole language; (c) the growth of balanced literacy as a mediating force in the debate; (d) a paradigm shift in the ideology of

reading research; (e) increasing politicization of the reading research and policy agenda; (f) increasing pressure for educators of all stripes, especially reading educators, to produce measurable results; and (g) loss of the moral high ground. All of these forces, but especially those delineated above as *d* through *f*, came together in one place—the reading first component of the No Child Left Behind Act of 2001 (NCLB, 2002). By the time this article was submitted for publication, in mid-2003, reading first had assumed the role of conventional wisdom in reading instruction, albeit by mandate rather than groundswell, and only a few traces of whole language, which seemed so dominant only 7 years earlier, could be found in our schools and curricula. How did this remarkable political transformation occur? That is the subject of this article.

Unintended Curricular Consequences

In its ascendancy, whole language changed the face of reading instruction and in the process, left behind some curricular casualties, few of which were intended by those who supported whole language. Those, including many curricular moderates, who supported practices that were discarded in the rise of whole language had difficulty supporting the whole-language movement even though they might have been philosophically and curricularly sympathetic to many of its principles and practices (see Pearson, 1996). This lack of enthusiasm from curricular moderates meant that whole language failed to build a base of support that was broad enough to survive even modest curricular opposition, let alone the political onslaught that it would experience at century's turn.

There were four casualties: skills instruction, strategy instruction, an emphasis on text structure, and reading in the content areas. Earlier, I suggested that one of the consequences of whole language was the relegation of skills to the "appendices" of instructional programs. In accepting whole language, we tacitly accepted the premise that skills are better caught in the act of reading and writing genuine texts for authentic purposes than taught directly and explicitly by teachers. The argument is the same for phonics, grammar, text conventions, and structural elements. These entities may be worthy of learning, but they are unworthy of teaching. This position presents us with a serious conundrum as a profession. Admit, for the sake of argument, that the skills instruction of the 1970s and earlier, with decontextualized lessons and practice on "textoids" in workbook pages, deserved the criticism accorded to it by whole-language advocates (and scholars from other traditions). But a retreat from most skills instruction into a world of "authentic opportunity" did not provide a satisfactory answer for teachers and scholars who understood the positive impact that instruction can have. Many young readers do not "catch" the alphabetic principle by sheer immersion in print or by listening to others read aloud. For some it seems to require careful planning and hard work by dedicated teachers who are willing to balance systematic skills instruction with authentic texts and activities (see Hiebert & Taylor, 1994, for a description of many of the interventions designed to accomplish just this balanced goal).

Strategy instruction (intentional attempts to equip students with meta-cognitive routines for understanding text, monitoring comprehension, and fixing things up when they go awry) was another casualty. This loss was particularly difficult for scholars who spent the better part of the 1980s convincing basal publishers and textbook authors that the thoughtful teaching of flexible strategies for making and monitoring meaning was a viable alternative to ubiquitous skill instruction, where skills were taught as though they were only ever to be applied to workbook pages and end-of-unit tests. But the strategy lessons that filled basals in the mid- to late 1980s were virtually nonexistent in the basals of the early to mid-1990s. Although there is no inherent bias in whole language or literature-based reading against the learning and use of a whole range of cognitive strategies, there is, as with phonics and grammar, a serious question about whether direct, explicit instruction in how to use them will help. The advice is to let them emerge from attempts to solve real reading problems and puzzles, the kind students meet in genuine encounters with authentic texts.

Structural emphasis was also suspect within whole language. This suspicion extended to formal grammars, story grammars, rhetorical structures, and genre features of texts. As with skills and strategies, whole-language reformers did not claim that students should not learn and develop control over these structural tools; they simply claimed that like skills, they are best inferred from reading and writing authentic texts in the process of making meaning. So, the advocates are comfortable in adopting Smith's (1983) admonition to encourage kids to read like a writer (meaning to read the text with a kind of critical eye toward understanding the tools and tricks of the trade that the author uses to make points and achieve his or her effects on readers), but they would likely reject a systematic set of lessons designed to teach and assess children's control of story grammar elements (such as plot, characterization, style, mood, or theme) or some system for dealing with basic patterns of the various genres of expository text. As with skills and strategies, many in the field sought a compromise alternative to both the formulaic approach of the early 1980s and the "discovery" approach of the new reforms—dealing with these structural elements as they emanate from stories that a group is currently reading can provide some guidance and useful tools for students and teachers.

Content area reading also suffered during the ascendancy of whole language and literature-based reading. Content area texts—expository texts in general, but especially textbook-like entries—were not privileged in a world of literature-based reading. There is a certain irony in this development, for it is competence with expository reading, not narrative reading, that most concerns educators and future employers. The cost here has been very dear. Concerned that students either cannot or will not read textbook assignments, most high school teachers have chosen either to read the text to students or even more likely, to tell students what they would have encountered had they or could they have read it. Although understandable, this approach is ultimately counterproductive. There comes a time in the lives of students—either when they go to college or enter the world of work—when others expect them to read and understand informational texts on their own and in printed form rather than through oral or video transformation.[5]

Because whole language did not go out of its way to accommodate these structural- and content-focused curricular practices, those who were sympathetic with whole language but also champions of one or another approach were not available to help whole language respond to the criticism leveled at it in the late 1990s. Building allies across boundaries of curricular political divides was not, as it turned out, a strength of the movement.

Questionable Applications of Whole Language

One of the dilemmas faced by any curricular initiative is sustaining the integrity of the movement without imposing the very sorts of controls it is trying to eliminate. Whole language did not find a way to manage this dilemma, and it suffered as a consequence. Many schools, teachers, and institutions appropriated the whole-language label without honoring its fundamental principles of authenticity, integration, and empowerment. Basal-reader publishers made the most obvious and widespread appropriation, some even positioning their basal series as "whole-language" programs. The most egregious misapplication was the conflation of whole language with whole-class instruction. Nowhere was this conflation more extreme than in the implementation of the California literature framework. The logic that prevailed in many classrooms was that it was better to keep the entire class together, all experiencing the same texts, even if it meant that the teacher had to read the text to those children who lacked the skills to read it on their own. Implicit in this practice are two interesting assumptions: (a) that getting the content of the stories is the most important goal for reading

instruction, and (b) that the skills and processes needed to read independently will emerge somehow from this environment in which many students are pulled through texts that far exceed their grasp, given the sophistication of their current skills repertoire. Needless to say, whole language had enough on its hands dealing with its own assumptions and practices; these philosophical and curricular misapplications exposed the movement to a whole set of criticisms that derived from practices not of its own making.

A plausible explanation for the misapplication of whole language was its lack of an explicit plan for professional development. Given its grassroots political assumptions, it is not surprising that whole language gave teachers a wide berth for making curricular and instructional decisions. It assumed that teachers who are empowered, sincere, and serious about their work would be able to tailor programs and activities to the needs and interests of individual children. Such an approach makes sense only when teacher knowledge is widely and richly distributed in our profession. To offer these prerogatives in the face of narrow and shallow knowledge is to guarantee that misguided practices, even perversions of the very intent of the movement, will be widespread. The puzzle, of course, is where to begin the reform—by ensuring that the knowledge precedes the prerogative, or by ceding the prerogative to teachers as a way of leveraging their motivation for greater knowledge. Similar arguments have been made for the reform movements in mathematics (i.e., that the reforms got out ahead of the professional knowledge base); interestingly the reform movement in mathematics has experienced a fate similar to that of the whole-language movement (see Good & Braden, 2000; Schoenfeld, 2004.)

Balanced Literacy

Although it has reached its peak in the past 5 years, concern about extreme positions, be they extremely child centered (such as the more radical of whole-language approaches) or extremely curriculum centered (such as highly structured, unswerving phonics programs), is not new. Voices from the middle, extolling balanced approaches or rationalizing the eclectic practices of teachers, began to be heard even in the earliest days of whole language's ascendancy.[6] Scholars and teachers raised a number of concerns about the assumptions and practices of the whole-language movement. Most important, they expressed concern about the consequences of whole language outlined earlier in this article. They questioned the assumption that skills are best "caught" during the pursuit of authentic reading activity rather than "taught" directly and explicitly. They also questioned the insistence on authentic texts and the corollary ban on "instructional" texts written to permit the application of skills within the curriculum. They questioned the zeal and commitment of the movement qua movement, with its strong sense of insularity and exclusivity. Finally, they worried that the press toward the use of authentic literature and literature-based reading would eradicate, albeit unintentionally, what little progress had been made toward the use of informational texts and teaching reading in the content areas (Pearson, 1996).

Ironically, in the past few years, these voices from the middle have found themselves responding not to those who hold a radical whole-language position but to those who hold steadfastly to the phonics first position. Even so, the fact that those with centrist positions were not inclined to defend whole language when the political campaign against it began in the middle 1990s undoubtedly hastened the demise of whole language as the pretender to the title of conventional wisdom.

Changing Research Paradigms

Prior to the 1980s, qualitative research in any form had little visibility within the reading research community. Among the array of qualitative efforts, only miscue analysis[7] and some early forays into sociolinguistic and anthropological accounts of literacy had achieved much in the way of archival status.[8] However, all that changed in the 1980s and early 1990s. Qualitative research more generally, along with more specific lines of inquiry taking a critical perspective on literacy as a social and pedagogical phenomenon, became more widely accepted as part of the mainstream archival literature.[9] Treatises pointing out the shortcomings of traditional forms of quantitative inquiry, especially experimental research, appeared frequently in educational research journals.[10] Much of the research that undergirds whole language comes from this more qualitative, more interpretive, more critical tradition. Thus, the credibility of this type of research increased in concert with the influence of whole language as a curricular movement.

Somewhere in the mid-1990s, the discourse of literacy research began to take a new turn. Stimulated by research supported by the National Institute for Child Health and Human Development, a "new" brand of experimental work began to appear, beginning in the mid-1980s and gathering momentum steadily since that time (Lyon, 1995; Lyon & Chhaba, 1996). This is experimentalism reborn from the 1950s and 1960s, with great emphasis placed on "reliable, replicable research," large samples, random assignment of treatments to teachers and/or schools, and tried and true outcome measures.[11] It finds its aegis in the experimental rhetoric of science and medicine and in the laboratory research that has examined reading as a perceptual process.[12] Although it was not broadly accepted by the reading education community when it first appeared, this work found a very sympathetic ear in the public policy arena.[13]

The political positioning of this research is important, but so is its substance. Two themes from this work have been particularly important in shaping a new set of instructional practices—phonemic awareness and phonics instruction.

The absolutely critical role played by phonemic awareness (the ability to segment the speech stream of a spoken word, e.g., /cat/ into component phonemes /cuh + ah + tuh/ and/or to blend separately heard sounds, e.g., /cuh + ah + tuh/ into a normally spoken word /cat/) in the development of the ability to decode and to read for meaning has been well documented in the past decade and a half (Adams, 1990; Juel, 1988; Snow, Burns, & Griffin, 1998). Irrespective of mode of instruction, the overwhelming evidence suggests that phonemic awareness is a necessary but not a sufficient condition for the development of decoding and reading. First, children who possess high degrees of phonemic awareness in kindergarten or early in first grade are very likely to be good readers throughout their elementary school careers (Juel, 1988). Second, almost no children who are successful readers at the end of Grade 1 exhibit a low level of mastery of phonemic awareness. On the other hand, a substantial proportion of unsuccessful end-of-Grade-1 readers possess better than average phonemic awareness; this evidence is the critical piece in establishing that phonemic awareness is a necessary but not a sufficient condition for reading success. Although we can be confident of its critical role in learning to read, we are less sure about the optimal way to enhance its development. Many scholars have documented the efficacy of teaching it directly, but they also admit that it is highly likely to develop as a consequence of learning phonics, learning to read, or especially learning to write, especially when teachers encourage students to use invented spellings (see Adams, 1990; Juel, 1991). Research in whole-language classrooms (Clarke, 1988; Winsor & Pearson, 1992) suggests that writing is the medium through which both phonemic awareness and phonics knowledge develop—the former because students have to segment the speech stream of spoken words to focus on a phoneme and the latter because there is substantial transfer value from the focus on sound-symbol information in spelling to symbol-sound knowledge in reading.

The second consistent thread in the new experimentalism of the 1990s was the emphasis on the code in the early stages of learning to read. Reminiscent of Chall's (1967) earlier conclusions, scholars in this tradition advocated phonics first, fast, and simple.[14] Less well documented, and surely less well agreed on, is the optimal course of instruction to facilitate phonics development. Even Gough (Gough & Hillinger,

1980), a classic bottom-up theorist, while arguing that what distinguishes the good reader from the poor reader is swift and accurate word identification, suggested that an early insistence on reading for meaning may be the best way to develop such decoding proficiency. Both Juel (1991) and Gough are convinced that students can learn how to read when they have *cryptoanalytic intent* (a disposition to decipher the specific letter-to-sound codes), phonemic awareness, an appreciation of the alphabetic principle (i.e., regardless of the numerous exceptions, letters do stand for sounds), and "data" (some texts to read and someone to assist when the going gets tough).

After reviewing available instructional evidence, two of the most respected scholars in this tradition, Marilyn Adams and Connie Juel, independently concluded that children can and should learn the "cipher" through a combination of explicit instruction in phonemic awareness and letter-sound correspondences, a steady insistence on invented spellings as the route to conventional spellings in writing activities, and lots of opportunity to read connected text (especially when the texts contain enough decodable words to allow students to apply the phonics information they are learning through explicit instruction). Both of these reviewers, known for their sympathies toward instruction in the code, are quick to add that rich experiences with language, environmental print, patterned stories, and "big books" should also be a staple of effective early reading instruction (Adams, 1990; Juel, 1991).[15]

This new research paradigm became officially codified by the appearance, in rapid succession, of two research syntheses—the publication of the report of the National Academy of Science's Committee on Preventing Reading Difficulties (Snow et al., 1998) and the report of the National Reading Panel (NRP) (2000). These are very different documents, and they have exerted very different influences on the reading field, particularly on reading policy. The *Preventing Reading Difficulties* report was conducted in the tradition of "best evidence" syntheses: well-established scholars meet, decide on the issues, the domain of relevant research, and some subdivision of labor, do the work, write up the results, and turn the manuscript over to a set of editors to bring some synthetic clarity to the entire effort. As such, it considered a range of studies conducted within very different research traditions using very different research methods. The result was an apology for a balanced view of reading instruction, but with a special nod to phonemic awareness and phonics first and fast. A solid piece of scholarship many of us thought, but not much news (Pearson, 1999).

Authorized by congressional mandate, the NRP report used the most "scientific" review approaches (i.e., meta-analysis, at least wherever they could) available to them to distill from existing research what we knew about the efficacy of teaching phonemic awareness, phonics, fluency (instantiated as either guided reading instruction or independent reading), comprehension, and vocabulary; in addition, they investigated the status of the research base on teacher education and professional development and attempted to review research on technology and literacy. It is interesting to note that according to Catherine Snow (2001), one of the lead authors of the *Preventing Reading Difficulties* report, officials such as G. Reid Lyon and Duane Alexander from the National Institute for Child Health and Human Development, one of the sponsoring agencies of the NRP, were concerned about the *Preventing Reading Difficulties* report because it was vague and did not discriminate between trustworthy and untrustworthy research. The NRP report is noteworthy on a number of grounds. First, the actual conclusions in the main report are consistent with earlier attempts to summarize the knowledge base on these key issues, such as *Becoming a Nation of Readers* (Anderson, Hiebert, Scott, & Wilkinson, 1984) and *Preventing Reading Difficulties* (Snow et al., 1998), and point to a balanced approach to teaching reading. Second, although the vote of confidence in teaching phonics and phonemic awareness was strong and direct, it was moderated by important caveats that limit the applicability of these important instructional tools. For

example, phonics was found to be a useful instructional approach, but only in a particular time frame (Grades K–1); it was not effective for older students. Moreover, although the analysis privileged systematic phonics, nothing in the analysis implicated a particular approach (e.g., synthetic or letter-by-letter phonics vs. analytic phonics), nor was there any explicit support for decodable text. Also, the authors of the NRP report were careful, in their conclusions, to suggest that phonics by itself was not the total reading program: "Finally, it is important to emphasize that systematic phonics instruction should be integrated with other reading instruction to create a balanced reading program. Phonics instruction is never a total reading program " (NRP, 2000, p. 2-135).

Third, the authors of the NRP report were very clear about which topics and studies would be included. It would review only those topics for which there existed a sufficiently large pool of "potentially viable" experimental studies. Hence issues of grouping, the relationship of reading to writing, the role of texts in reading acquisition—just to name a few of the more obvious issues that schools and teachers must address in crafting local reading programs—are not addressed at all. Regarding specific studies, they would include only those that met minimal criteria: employ an experimental or quasi-experimental design with an identifiable comparison group, measure reading as an outcome, describe participants, interventions, study methods, and outcome measures in sufficient detail to "contribute to the validity of any conclusions drawn." Natural experiments of the sort found in large-scale evaluation efforts or epidemiological investigations of relationships between methods and outcomes were excluded.

Vis-à-vis whole language, the point is straightforward: The changes in the dominant paradigm meant that the research base on which whole language was grounded (all of those close ethnographies of individual classrooms and teacher action stories) was no longer privileged in official conversations about "research"-based practice. Numbers, not compelling stories, were the order of a new day; and it was not clear whether there was a place for constructivist pedagogy in general or whole language in particular, in these new conversations.

Politicization of the Reading Research and Policy Agenda

From its beginnings, one of the great hopes of educational research (and those who conduct it) has been that policy makers will take research seriously when they establish policy at a local, state, or national level. After all, the improvement of educational practice is the ultimate goal of educational research, and policy is our society's most transparent tool for educational improvement. Historically, however, research has been regarded as one among many information sources consulted in policy formation—including expert testimony from practitioners, information about school organization and finance, and evaluations of compelling cases. In the past half decade, research, at least selective bits of research, has never been taken more seriously. Several laws in California make direct references to research. For example, in 1998, California Assembly Bill 1086 prohibited the use of Goals 2000: Educate America Act of 1994 money for professional developers who advocated the use of context clues over phonics or supported the use of "inventive [sic] spellings" in children's writing. The federally sponsored Reading Excellence Act of 1998, which allocated U.S.$240,000,000 for staff development in reading, required that both state and local applications for funding base their programs on research that meets scientifically rigorous standards. The *scientifically rigorous* phrase was a late entry; in all but the penultimate version of the bill, the phrase was *reliable, replicable research*, which had been interpreted as a code word for experimental research. As of early 1999, "phonics bills" (bills mandating either the use of phonics materials or some sort of teacher training to acquaint teachers with knowledge of the English sound-symbol system and its use in teaching) had been passed or were pending in 36 states.[16]

The NCLB made this goal of "evidence-based practice" even more explicit, with the phrase *scientifically based reading research* appearing more than 110 times in the Reading First portion of this act reauthorizing Title I.

Policy makers like to shroud mandates and initiatives in the rhetoric of science, and sometimes that practice results in strained, if not indefensible, extrapolations from research. This has happened consistently in the reading policy arena in the past decade. Three examples make the point vividly. First, California Assembly Bill 1086, with its prohibition on context clues and invented spelling, represents an ironic application of research to policy. The irony stems from the fact that many of the advocates of a return to code emphasis, such as Marilyn Adams, read the research as supporting the use of invented spellings in the development of phonemic awareness and phonics (Adams, 1990). Second, the mandate in several states calling for the use of decodable text (usually defined as text consisting of words that could be sounded out using a combination of the phonics rules taught up to that point in the program plus some instant recognition of a few highly frequent "sight" words) is based on the thinnest of research bases. The idea is that children will learn to use their phonics better, faster, and more efficiently if the texts they read permit facile application of the principles they are learning. Although it all sounds very logical, there is precious little research evidence to support the systematic and exclusive use of decodable text.[17] This lack of evidence, however, does not seem to have deterred advocates who, on the phonics issues, championed scientific evidence as the gold standard for policy implementation.

The third example comes from the state of California's application for Reading First funds. The Reading First provision of NCLB requires that all elements of a program's application—instructional materials, assessments, and professional development—be supported by scientifically based reading research. *Scientifically based professional development* was defined in the California application as the professional development required to help teachers implement the two state-adopted commercial reading programs; the proposal was accepted by federal officials without objection to this definition. This development was convenient in a financially troubled state that could ill afford to pay for the professional development for its new adoptions entirely on its own hook. The irony here, of course, is that the two commercially adopted programs in California, although they might be able to trace 15% to 20% of their practices to scientific research, are no more research based, let alone scientifically based (i.e., they have not regularly used randomized trials to test their efficacy) than the average run-of-the-mill commercial program. They are now, of course, officially blessed as scientific.

When research moves into the policy arena, one of two outcomes are most likely. If the research is widely accepted by members of the profession from which it comes, widespread acceptance and implementation usually follows. This often occurs in medical, pharmaceutical, or agricultural research. If widespread consensus on what the research says about practice is not reached, then research-based policy initiatives are likely to sharpen and deepen the schisms that already exist and the whole enterprise is likely to be regarded as a "war" among balkanized factions within the field. The latter scenario appears to characterize the reading field. The entry of science into the reading research community, and its accompanying blessing of particular approaches to teaching reading, has met with considerable resistance, some overt and some quiet, within the reading research community. The most vocal and prominent voices in the resistance have been Elaine Garan, Denny Taylor, and Richard Allington. Soon after the publication of the report of the Committee on Preventing Reading Difficulties of the National Academy of Science in 1998, D. Taylor (1998) published her treatise unveiling the "spin doctors of science." Essentially, D. Taylor attempted to show how the conservatives involved in promoting the "new-phonics" agenda had used public relations techniques rather than science to

accomplish two goals: (a) to convince policy makers and the general public that the answer to teaching reading was more phonics earlier, and (b) to discredit public education more generally. Garan's (2001, 2002) critique focused on the report of the NRP, and essentially, she offers two types of critique: internal and external. The internal critique holds the methodology of meta-analysis to its own standards, and she tried to show that the NRP effort was a fundamentally flawed approach to meta-analysis. For example, a principle of meta-analysis (Salkind, 2000) is that although the outcome measures need not be identical from one study to another, they should represent the same underlying construct; the NRP phonics analysis, Garan argued, fails this standard. She pointed out the many internal contradictions in method: for one group, eight studies are too few to move ahead with the meta-analysis whereas for another, nine is enough. However, perhaps most important, Garan pointed out that the statements included in the executive summary of the report are often inconsistent with comparable statements in the more elaborated reports of the various subgroups (on phonics, comprehension, and the like). I could not agree more with this last critique; as I will point out later, these discrepancies with the elaborated report only worsen when we examine the more "popular" version of the report written for general consumption and the headlines distilled by reporters for headlines and newspaper articles. Allington (2002) took a third approach. He enlisted the help of several colleagues in his edited volume to make the case that for the past 30 years, a conservative lobby has been trying to manipulate several policy levers (standards, assessment, professional development, and evidence-based practice) to shape a national reading policy that privileges basic skills for students and limits teacher education to training rather than educative practices. The case he made could be characterized as a sort of "skill the kids and de-skill the teachers" approach (my words, not his).

Interestingly, the debate, accompanied by its warlike metaphors, appears to have more life in the public and professional press than it does in our schools. Reporters and scholars revel in keeping the debate alive and well, portraying clearly divided sides and detailing a host of differences of a philosophical, political, and pedagogical nature (see Manzo, 1997, 1998a, 1998b). Teachers, by contrast, often talk about, and more important enact, more balanced approaches. For example, several scholars, in documenting the practices of highly effective, highly regarded teachers, found that these exemplary teachers employed a wide array of practices, some of which appear decidedly whole language in character (e.g., process writing, literature groups, and contextualized skills practice) and some of which appear remarkably skills oriented (explicit phonics lessons, sight word practice, and comprehension strategy instruction). Exemplary teachers (e.g., Pressley et al., 2001; B. M. Taylor, Pearson, Clark, & Walpole, 2000; Wharton-MacDonald, Pressley, & Hampton, 1998) appear to find an easier path to balance than either scholars or policy pundits.

Producing Measurable Results

Evaluation has always posed a conundrum for whole-language supporters. First, some advocates oppose the use of any sort of externally mandated or administered assessments as a matter of principle, holding that assessment is ultimately the responsibility of a teacher in collaboration with a student and his or her parents. Second, even those supporters who are open to external forms of accountability, or at least reporting outside the boundaries of the classroom or school, often claim that standardized tests, state assessments, and other external measures of student accomplishment do not provide sensitive indicators of the goals of curricula based on whole-language principles. Most appealing would be assessments that are classroom based and individualized in nature, with the option of aggregating these sorts of data at the classroom and school levels when accountability comes knocking. During the 1990s, many felt that the increased emphasis on performance assessment and portfolios would fill this need.[18]

In an age of high expectations, explicit standards, and school- and classroom-level accountability, none of these options is a good fit with the views and desires of policy makers and the public. Both of these constituents seem quite uneasy about the quality of our schools and our educational system, so uneasy that leaving assessment in the hands of our teachers seems an unlikely outcome. It is not at all clear to me that the proponents of at least strong versions of whole language can, or will be willing to, hold themselves accountable to the sorts of measures that the public and policy makers find credible.

Loss of the Moral High Ground

One other factor, although difficult to document, seems to be operating in the rhetoric of the field in the first years of the 21st century. Whole language, and constructivist approaches generally, has always privileged the role of the teacher as the primary curriculum decision maker. Teachers, the argument goes, are in the best position to serve this important role because of their vast knowledge of language and literacy development, their skills as diagnosticians (they are expert "kid watchers"), and the materials and teaching strategies they have at their disposal. And in the arguments against more structured approaches, this is exactly the approach whole-language advocates have taken: "Don't make these decisions at the state, district, or even the school level. Arm teachers with the professional prerogative (and corollary levels of professional knowledge) they need in order to craft unique decisions for individual children." Although this may seem a reasonable, even admirable position, it has recently been turned into an apology for a self-serving teacher ideology.[19] The counter argument suggests that the broad base of privilege accorded to teachers may come at the expense of students and their parents. Thus, those who advocate a strong phonics-first position often take the moral high ground: "We are doing this for America's children (and for YOUR child!)—so that they have the right to read for themselves." Even if one opposes this rhetorical move, it is hard not to appreciate the clever repositioning on the part of those who want to return to more phonics and skills.

The Net Effect

Taken together, these factors created a policy environment in which whole language, or any other constructivist movement for that matter, was unlikely to flourish as the mainstream approach to teaching reading and writing. In the final analysis, however, I believe that the reluctance to own up to the "measurable results" standards was the Achilles' heel of whole language. If whole-language advocates had been willing to play by the rules of external accountability, to assert that students who experience good instruction based on solid principles of progressive pedagogy will perform well on standardized tests and other standards of performance, they would have stood a better chance of gaining a sympathetic ear with the public and with policy makers. And as long as the criteria for what counts as evidence for growth and accomplishment are vague or left to individual teachers, the public could question the movement and wonder whose interests were being served by an unwillingness to commit to common standards.

LOOKING AHEAD

So where has this journey left us? And where will it take us next? I want to divide my analysis of the future of reading policy into two strands, research and curriculum, because these two faces of reading policy, although often joined at the hip, occasionally privilege different themes and issues. I will close by bringing them back together.

Research Policy

Complementarity as a Scientific Value

In the current research context, literacy scholars find themselves between a rock and a hard place. The official views of research promulgated by the federal government in its research programs administered within the Department of Education are weighted toward quantitative and experimental work. At the same time, the work of many, perhaps even most, literacy researchers and doctoral students in research training programs is decidedly qualitative, narrative, and/or ethnographic in character. An impending crisis? A confrontation of the immovable object and the irresistible force? Or just the exclusion of a wide array of literacy scholars from federally funded research efforts? I would bet on the exclusion, but I hope and argue for a rapprochement among methods and even epistemologies.

Regarding science, my fundamental claim is that reading research can never be truly rigorous, indeed truly scientific, until and unless it privileges all of the empirical and theoretical methodologies that characterize the scientific disciplines. Included among those methodologies would surely be experimentation and of course randomized field trials of the sort that are being proposed for several federally sponsored programs, but the range of scientific methods would extend to:

- careful descriptions of phenomena in their natural settings (just like Darwin did and just like today's environmental scientists);

- examinations of natural correlations among variables in an environment, just to see what goes with what;

- natural experiments in which we take advantage of the differences that serendipity and the normal course of events have created between two or more settings that are otherwise remarkably similar—the most common form of this effort in education being outlier studies and the even more common approach in public health's epidemiological studies;

- data gathered in the name of theory building and evaluation—just to see if we can explain the nature of things;

- design experiments in which we adopt a planful, incremental approach to knowledge refinement, with each successive step building carefully on what was learned in the last; and

- the use of qualitative tools such as ethnography and discourse analysis in concert with randomized experiments to describe what is really going on inside those randomly assigned treatments, so that we can explain why a treatment worked or did not work, or whether the range of variation in treatments is so great across sites that it is doubtful that it can really be called the same intervention across sites, or what the consequences, especially the unintended consequences, of an intervention might be.

As good as randomized experiments are for determining the overall efficacy of interventions, they are very short on details about the interventions, such as why, how, for whom, and under what conditions interventions work. For that we need complementary methods, and this is where qualitative methods come into play. Donald Campbell (1984), one of the foremost design methodologists of the 20th century and the coauthor of the infamous book on quasi experiments (Campbell & Stanley, 1963), the classic treatment of threats to internal and external validity, recognized this need for complementarity:

> To rule out plausible rival hypotheses we need situation-specific wisdom. The lack of this knowledge (whether it be called ethnography, program history, or gossip) makes us incompetent estimators of program impacts, turning out conclusions that are not only wrong, but are often wrong in socially destructive ways. . . .
>
> There is the mistaken belief that quantitative measures replace qualitative knowledge. Instead, qualitative knowing is absolutely essential as a prerequisite for quantification in any science. Without competence at the qualitative level, one's computer printout is misleading or meaningless. (pp. 141–142)

We hear a lot of talk about randomized field trials in medical and pharmaceutical research, and we are advised to follow their lead. I agree. But if we follow medicine and pharmacology, then we should follow them all the way down the road of science. Let us remember that before researchers in those fields get to the last 10% of the journey, which is when they invoke randomized field trials in anticipation of advocacy and

policy recommendations, they have already used a much wider range of methodologies, including much observation, description, examinations of relationships, and just plain messing around (that is a technical term used by scientists to describe what they spend most of their time doing) to travel the first 90% of that journey. So let us talk about complementarities and convergence among methods rather than competition and displacement of one worldview with another. This is the message of the recent report on educational research by a committee empanelled by the National Academy of Science (Shavelson & Towne, 2002), a message I heartily endorse.

If we rush too soon to the last 10% of the journey and enamor ourselves of randomized field trials for their own sake, we are likely to end up conducting expensive experiments on interventions that were not worth evaluating in the first place. A drug company would never think of conducting a randomized field trial on a new drug that had not gone through a thorough basic research phase in which biochemical theories, tryouts on nonhuman organisms, correlational research on chemical components of the drug in the natural environment, and probably some serendipitous case studies of individual subjects who volunteered to use the drug out of desperation all played a key role. We should ask no less of educational interventions and programs. An intervention that is based on bad theory or no theory is not likely to yield a significant contribution to practice in the long run. To know that something worked without a clue about how and why it worked does not advance either our scientific or professional understanding of an educational issue. We cannot afford blind experimentation and horse races with interventions of unknown theoretical characteristics. As our candidates for randomized field trials, we want treatments and interventions that have gone through these various stages of scientific development.

I fear that as a profession we have fallen into a methodological trap. We have become so attached to our methodologies and to their epistemological (some would say ideological) underbellies that we, as individuals, are likely to begin our work by looking for a question that fits our methodological preferences rather than the other way around. This does not serve our profession well, for it allows us to address questions that may or may not be of great relevance to policy and practice. We must return to the ethic of insisting that just as form follows function in language, so methods must follow questions in research. And if we do not, as individuals, possess the range of methodological expertise to address different sorts of questions, then we ought to align ourselves with scholarly communities in which such expertise is distributed among its members.

As a curious and ironic footnote, I would point out that complementarity across methods is consistent with the definition of *scientifically based reading research* in the Reading First portion of NCLB; the definition includes these standards:

- employs systematic, empirical methods that draw on observation and experiment;

- involves rigorous data analyses that are adequate to test the stated hypotheses and justify the general conclusions;

- relies on measures that provide valid data across observers and occasions; and

- is published in peer-reviewed journals (or reviewed by a duly constituted panel).

The Complexity of Research in Education

Complexity in the policy arena is always a double-edged sword. To assert that educational research is complex is to imply that there is something categorically different about educational research in comparison to research in agriculture, physics, chemistry, medicine, or even psychology. Usually the complexity is attributed to the human factor and the variation introduced by human activity:

- that individuals differ from one another;

- that they live and work in groups;

- that the members of the group influence what others do, how they act, and what they believe; and

- that when humans are involved, things change in unpredictable ways.

David Berliner (2002), in a persuasive article in a recent issue of *Educational Researcher*, puts forward just such a view. And there is much truth in the argument. I know this all too well from my own experience in trying to do large-scale research on best practices (B. M. Taylor, Pearson, Peterson, & Rodriguez, 2003). We tried to do an outlier analysis of schools that beat the odds predicted by their demographics. However, we found that high poverty/high performance status is not a static characteristic. Some schools that entered the study with a record of high achievement foundered; some with reputations as failing the mark changed their ways. Had we not collected a wide array of student outcomes (which allowed us to build post hoc indicators of who was and was not beating the odds) and an even wider array of indicators of school reform efforts and teacher practices, we would not have been able to unearth program and instructional characteristics that explain variation in achievement growth. Moreover, we found that a combination of quantitative and qualitative approaches were absolutely essential in teasing out important relationships between programs and outcomes.

We continue to find, in our more recent work (B. M. Taylor et al., 2003) with low-income, low-performing, aspiring schools, that things are not always what they appear to be—that there is incredible variability among our intervention schools in the degree to which the intervention is actually implemented, both across schools and across classrooms within schools. We also find that the degree of fidelity to the intervention, not to a set of specific instructional practices but to a set of broad principles outlining the process to be followed and the issues to be addressed, is a good predictor of achievement growth, again both across schools and across classrooms within schools. My point is simple—no matter how well planned an intervention might be, things happen and variation will occur. In many studies, the variation within treatments is often equal to the variation between treatments. Thus, it is critical in research involving programmatic and instructional reform, to document carefully the nature of the actual practices across schools and classrooms. And there is no better tool to do this than ethnographic descriptions of classroom instruction and professional development meetings. In short, we need all the tools we can muster to address the inherent complexity of research involving human beings who live and work in groups.

The final question about randomized field trials is whether we will be willing to pay the price tag. It is one thing to randomly assign college freshmen who happen to have the misfortune to be enrolled in Psychology 1-A to different treatments. It is quite another to randomly assign teachers, classrooms, and even schools to a particular treatment. In the psychology class, I test 30 subjects and I get 30 data points for my analysis. In the classroom, I test 30 students and get one data point—the classroom mean. That is one cost factor. But there are others: For example, if we want to know if the treatment generalizes across types of students and types of schools, then we will either have to draw very large samples or very carefully shaped selective samples.

The Treacherous Road From Research to Policy

The road from research to policy is fraught with many dangers—potholes, blind corners, road hogs, and detours that can frustrate even the most thoughtful traveler. Both researchers and policy makers must be aware of these threats as they do their best to draw valid inferences from research for practice and policy. Let me unpack some of the dangers and some guidelines for minimizing risk to students, parents, and teachers.

When research travels to the land of policy, often only the headlines make the journey, leaving the details and the nuance behind. The consequences of this fact of policy life are depicted with real examples of the discrepancy in Table 1.1.

I am not sure the journalists are to blame; the reporting of educational research probably does not differ much from the reporting of medical, pharmaceutical, agricultural, or public health research. Lest we think that education is different, compare these two headlines, one composed by a staff writer of the *New York Times* and the other by a staff writer of the *Washington Post* in reporting the findings from an article released by the *New England Journal of Medicine* about the relative effectiveness of surgery versus benign neglect in treating prostate cancer in men:[20]

From the *New York Times* on September 12, 2002: "Prostate Cancer Surgery Found to Cut Death Risk" (Kolata, 2002)

From the *Washington Post* on September 12, 2002: "Prostate Cancer Therapies About Equal" (D. Brown, 2002)

One glass is half full; the other half empty. A person contemplating surgery would much rather be reading the *Times*! The point is that as a society we must find a way to cope with the persistent problem of interpretation that tends toward oversimplification, whether it occurs in the press, the Congress, or our statehouses. Perhaps we should require that policy makers (or members of their staffs) be required to read beyond the headlines of educational reports before setting policy in concrete. Nuance may not make things simple, but nuance is a fact of life in most policy contexts, including public health and medicine.

Research is often used in a selective, uneven, and opportunistic manner by policy makers. An unfortunate corollary of this surface-level approach to summarizing research for policy purposes is the uneven use of the research card in setting policy. The danger is that those who set policy will choose to play that card when the evidence swings in their favor; and when it does not, they will appeal to common sense, the conventional wisdom of practice, or authoritative opinion. So, for example, when the NRP report blessed the systematic teaching of phonics,

Table 1.1   Headlines Versus Details in the Reporting of Reading Research

Headline	Source	Digging Deeper Into the Actual Report
Systematic, Explicit, Synthetic Phonics Improves Reading Achievement	Foorman, Francis, Fletcher, Schatschneider, and Mehta (1998)	When a program includes systematic, synthetic phonics among many other elements (lots of writing, lots of reading of a whole range of texts, and lots of supplementary activities), a small but robust effect for a subset of the population is found on a measure that requires kids to read lists of pseudowords.
Phonemic Awareness Improves Later Reading Achievement	National Reading Panel (2000)	Phonemic awareness helps . . . • If taught early (K–1); • Mostly on measures of word identification; • If taught with letter-sound instruction; • If limited in scope (from 18 to 20 hours).
Phonics Wins	National Reading Panel (2000)	Phonics helps . . . • If it is taught early (not great beyond Grade 1); • More on word recognition than comprehension; • If it is systematic and explicit (no evidence for one approach over another); • If it is embedded in a rich curriculum; • If caveats are recognized, for example, that there is no evidence for decodable text.
Independent Reading Does Not Help—If You Want to Do It, Assign It as Homework	National Reading Panel (2000)	The National Reading Panel did not study independent reading but rather the impact on fluency of instructional interventions designed to increase the amount of independent reading done in classrooms. From the paltry array of studies they were able to assemble, they concluded that the research on the efficacy of such interventions was inconclusive.

basic-skills advocates were quick to point to the scientific evidence underlying their policy initiatives. But the use of decodable text in conjunction with those programs, which could not be justified by the available evidence, was rationalized as a commonsense adjunct to a systematic approach to teaching phonics. In a similar vein, the Los Angeles Unified School District has

mandated that all high schools use a remedial program with the ironic title of *Language* for all of its low-performing secondary students. *Language* is a decodable text ("Dan can fan Nan") throwback to the linguistic readers of the mid-1960s. The noteworthy aspect of its adoption is it was adopted not by appealing to the evidence (the NRP could not document the use of phonics for readers in that age range) but by appealing to common sense (these kids clearly missed out on phonics the first time around so let's go back to square one and do it right). Allington and Woodside-Jiron (1998) have documented similar enactments of selective attention to research in noting the widespread adoption of decodable texts in state textbook standards.

Some science is more important than other science. Another corollary of this uneven use of research is a kind of first among equals conspiracy of good intentions. And it applies to the use of the NRP report in setting policy. The chapters on comprehension and vocabulary in the NRP are laudatory in their praise for the work in these areas (although they eschewed meta-analysis in favor of a best evidence synthesis on the grounds of too few studies) and enthusiastic in recommendations for renewed attention to strategy instruction and ambitious vocabulary teaching. Moreover, the even more recent Rand report (Snow, 2002) advocates a renaissance in research in comprehension instruction and assessment. But I have not witnessed a groundswell in advocacy for comprehension and vocabulary instruction as the fundamental solution to America's literacy problems. There seems to be a kind of "first things first" ethic, suggesting that "of course we'll get to comprehension and vocabulary . . . , but first let's make sure we have the basics in place." The same could be said for the section on teacher education and professional development in the comprehension chapter of NRP; we get glowing recommendations for the efficacy of professional-education models to increase teacher capacity to teach comprehension but little action on the policy and "scientifically based" professional development fronts. One of the other ironies of professional development in NCLB is that what it means to conduct evidence-based professional development is that the content of the professional development sessions must be based on scientifically based reading research about how young children learn to read, but need not attend at all to the substantial body of research documenting the optimal ways

to promote teacher learning. We know from a host of studies (see Richardson & Placier, 2002; Wilson & Berne, 1999) that professional learning is at its best when teachers have a voice in its design, when it is long term and school based, when it is focused on analyses of teaching and student learning, and most important, when the focus is on establishing learning-sustained communities. Yet NCLB, as committed as it is to science, is moot on the point of how professional development (itself to be based on scientifically based reading research) ought to be organized or delivered.

When we do not have definitive research to answer a question about policy or practice, we can easily slip over the line and privilege ideology and belief over evidence. The gold standard in research leading to policy implementation is surely the randomized field trial (see Mosteller & Baruch, 2002, for a series of articles extolling the virtues and assessing the limitations of the randomized field trial). Other things being equal, it is better to have experimental evidence to support a claim or validate a practice. But what are educators, especially school- and district-based educators, to do when they must establish curricular practices or forge new programs without the benefit of randomized experiments? Do we go straight from randomized trials to personal beliefs? Or do we establish a principle that requires us to use the best evidence available to us in any situation? If there are no randomized field trials, can we rely on the evidence from quasi experiments? Natural experiments? Correlational research? Best-practice research? They are all quantitative, but they cannot easily rule out rival hypotheses. How about case studies? Ethnographies? They are both empirical- and data-driven but they have a different set of evidentiary rules and a different notion of generalizability (Firestone, 1987). And when do we resort to professional consensus, the wisdom of experience, and personal belief? As a profession, we have not established any sort of hierarchy of evidentiary sources (Peirce, 1885, as cited in Hartshorne, Weiss, & Burks, 1931–1958).

Perhaps it is time we did. It is my personal conviction that it is our moral and ethical obligation to use the best evidence we can muster for making policy decisions of consequence. Further, when we have no evidence, we must fess up to that fact and make it clear that we are basing policy on values, beliefs, and hunches. If we followed some sort of evidentiary guidelines, we would not have so many intensive phonics programs for older students, so much decodable text in our commercial programs, or so little time for independent reading.

The independent reading issue is particularly troubling because it took a double hit. First, the NRP chose to examine it even though there were precious few studies that could pass through the eye of the needle imposed by their standards for inclusion. When they did, they stated their conclusion in a way that allowed readers to move from what they did say, "There is no evidence to support the efficacy of school-based programs that promote independent reading," to what some wanted to hear, "Independent reading is a waste of time."

Second, the NRP did not look at anything but experiments, thus eliminating some powerful evidence documenting the importance of everyday reading. Had the NRP examined a wider array of research, including several experiments conducted in other countries for second-language learners (e.g., Elley, 1998), a few smaller scale experiments (e.g., B. Taylor, Frye, & Maruyama, 1990), some impressive naturalistic studies conducted in an epidemiological tradition (e.g., Anderson, Wilson, & Fielding, 1988), and a wide array of best-practice research (e.g., B. M. Taylor, Pearson, et al., 2000; Wharton-MacDonald et al., 1998), they would have reached a very different conclusion about the efficacy of just plain reading. And in a situation in which the experimental research is moot, that would have been the high road to take on such a key professional issue.

Curricular Policy

Many recent developments suggest that we are retreating to a more familiar, more comfortable paradigm of basic skills in which phonics, skills, and controlled text dominate our practices. Other developments suggest that we are on the verge of a new paradigm, a hybrid that weds some of the principles of whole language (integrated instruction and authentic texts and tasks) with some of the traditions of earlier eras (explicit attention to skills and strategies, some vocabulary control of early readers, and lots of early emphasis on the code) in an "ecologically balanced" approach to reading instruction.[21] The most cynical among us might even argue that we are just riding the natural swing of a pendulum that will, if we have the patience, take us back to whole language, or whatever its pedagogically constructivist, child-centered descendant turns out to be, in a decade or so. Before making a prediction about the direction the field will take, let me play out the first two scenarios: phonics first and balanced reading instruction.

Two Different Worlds

If those who have advocated most strongly for a return to phonics and a heavy skills orientation have their way—if they are able to influence federal, state, and local policy as well as the educational publishing industry—we will experience even bigger shifts in the very earliest stages of learning to read—preschool, kindergarten, and Grade 1. They suggest explicit instruction on phonemic awareness and phonics, with a strong preference for decodable texts in the early grades. When it comes to writing, literature, response, and comprehension, the phonics-first advocates seem quite content to cede curricular authority to the practices that emerged during the 1980s and early 1990s, those associated with whole language, literature-based reading, and process writing (see Adams & Bruck, 1995; Fletcher & Lyon, 1998). Thus, looking broadly at the entire elementary reading curriculum (the range of materials and the range of pedagogical practices), things might on the surface look similar to the early 1990s, with some retreat to the 1980s, especially in terms of skill and strategy instruction.

But beneath that curricular surface, major changes would have occurred. For example, the role of the teacher and the learner would have reverted to what they were before the ascendancy of constructivist teaching reforms, such as whole language. The role of the teacher would be to transmit the received knowledge of the field, as reflected in research-based curricular mandates, to students. Students would eventually be regarded as active meaning makers, but only after they had received the tools of decoding from their teachers. The greatest changes of all would have taken place in the underlying model of reading and reading acquisition. The simple view of reading (that reading comprehension is the simple product of decoding prowess and listening comprehension) would have returned in full force, and the job of young readers would be to acquire the decoding knowledge they lack when they begin to learn to read.

If those who are pushing for ecological balance carry the day, the field will experience less dramatic shifts. A balanced approach will privilege authentic texts and tasks, a heavy emphasis on writing, literature, response, and comprehension, but it will also call for an ambitious program of explicit instruction for phonics, word identification, comprehension, spelling, and writing. A balanced approach is likely to look like some instantiations of whole language from the early 1990s, but recalibrated to redress the unintended curricular consequences outlined earlier in this chapter. Major differences between a balanced approach and the new phonics are likely to manifest themselves most vividly in kindergarten and Grade 1, where a rich set of language and literacy experiences would provide the context from which teachers would carve out scaffolded instructional activities to spotlight necessary skills and strategies—phonemic awareness, letter-sound knowledge, concepts of print, and conceptual development. Thus instruction, although focused and explicit, would retain the highly contextualized patina of whole language.

Beneath the curricular surface, balanced approaches seem to share slightly more in common, at least on a philosophical plane, with whole-language than with new-phonics approaches. The teacher is both facilitator and instructor. The teacher facilitates learning by establishing authentic activities, intervening where necessary to provide the scaffolding and explicit instruction required to help students take the next step toward independence. The student is, as in whole language, an active meaning maker from day one of preschool. Reading is a process of constructing meaning in response to texts encountered in a specific context, and the emergent literacy metaphor, not the readiness metaphor, characterizes the acquisition process.

An Ecologically Balanced Approach

Just in case my personal bias has not emerged, let me declare it unequivocally. I favor the conceptual map of the ecologically balanced approach, both for research and curricular policy.

I hope my reasons for supporting ecological balance—or as Howe and Eisenhart (1990) have characterized it, compatabalism—in research methods are transparent. The problems we face are too vexing to limit ourselves to a single methodology or epistemology. Multiplicity in the tradition of Spiro's (Spiro & Jehng, 1990) cognitive flexibility theory is what is needed now. We surely need to know what works, but we also need to know why it works, for whom, and under what conditions; interestingly, this sort of approach is appealing to many research policy leaders, including those who have led the charge toward more experimental approaches (see Lyon, 2003; Whitehurst, 2001). For example, in testifying to Congress, Lyon (1999) expressed just the sort of complementarity I have argued for:

> In order to develop the most effective instructional approaches and interventions, we must clearly define what works, the conditions under which it works, and what may not be helpful. This requires a thoughtful integration of experimental, quasi-experimental, and qualitative/descriptive methodologies.

To paraphrase Spiro and his colleagues, neither simplemindedness nor muddleheadedness will serve our interests, or those of the nation, well.

There are several reasons for favoring an ecologically balanced, or comprehensive, stance toward curriculum. First, my reading of the reading research points to the balanced-curricular position, not to the new-phonics position or the whole-language position, and it does so on both a theoretical and a pedagogical plane. I do not see much support for the simple view of reading that underlies the new phonics; readers do construct meaning, they do not just find it lying there in the text. Regarding pedagogical research, my reading requires me to side with Chall's (1967) view that although some sort of early, focused, and systematic emphasis on the code is called for, no particular approach can be singled out. Even the recent report of the NRP (2000) took exactly that position. And although I readily accept the findings of the phonemic awareness research, I do not read them as supporting drill and practice approaches to this important linguistic understanding; to the contrary, highly embedded approaches, such as invented spelling, are equally as strongly implicated in the research (see Clarke, 1988; NRP, 2000; Winsor & Pearson, 1992).

Second, an ecologically balanced approach is more respectful of the entire range of research in our field. It does not have to exclude major research paradigms or methodological approaches to sustain its integrity.

Third, an ecologically balanced approach also respects the wisdom of practice. It is no accident that studies of exemplary teachers, those who are respected by their peers and nurture high student achievement, consistently find that they exhibit a balanced repertoire of instructional strategies. Teachers who are faced with the variations in achievement, experience, and aptitude found in today's classrooms need, and deserve, a full toolbox of pedagogical practices.

Finally, an ecologically balanced approach respects our professional history. It retains the practices that have proved useful from each era but transforms and extends them, rendering them more effective, more useful, and more supportive of teachers and students. And it may represent our only alternative to the pendulum-swing view of our pedagogical history that seems to have plagued the field of reading for most of the 20th century. A transformative rather than a cyclical view of progress would be a nice start for a new century.

P. David Pearson is professor and dean within the Graduate School of Education at the University of California, Berkeley, where he pursues a program of scholarship in reading pedagogy, assessment, and policy analysis.

Article 2

JOHNNY WON'T READ, AND SUSIE WON'T EITHER

Reading Instruction and Student Resistance

REBECCA POWELL, ELLEN MCINTYRE, AND ELIZABETH RIGHTMYER

Abstract Why are children off task? What is going on in classrooms where a majority of children are off task? In this study we analyzed primary-grade classroom literacy instruction in which there was considerable off-task behavior. Using Turner and Paris's frame for understanding student motivation in the classroom, we analyzed 73 activity settings where students were off task at least 25 percent of the time for instructional characteristics positively associated with student motivation: choice, challenge, control, collaboration, constructing meaning, and consequences. Student off-task behavior was prevalent in classrooms where few of these six variables were present and instructional tasks were characterized as "closed," i.e., where the products and processes were predetermined. Where there was indication of a high degree of off-task behavior, a disproportionately high number (23 of the 28 data sets) were from classrooms that used scripted literacy instructional programs. Findings are interpreted using both psychological and critical frameworks.

Keywords motivation; reading; scripted reading programs; struggling readers

SOURCE: Powell, R., McIntyre, E., and Rightmyer, E. (2006). Johnny Won't Read, and Susie Won't Either: Reading Instruction and Student Resistance. *Journal of Early Childhood Literacy, 6*(1), 5–31. Reprinted by permission of SAGE Publications, Ltd.

The students (most of them) are on the floor looking at the teacher. They are playing with their pencils, so she takes them up. Teacher: "We are going to get started now. We have a new sound. My turn; listen as I make the sound for 'X.'" (The teacher makes [the sound] two or three times.) The students are making "sounds," not really paying attention to the teacher. Teacher: "Eyes up here, please—everybody ready." The students make the sounds as she points to the letters. Two boys are talking and not taking part. Teacher tries to correct behavior; students still talking and moving. Teacher: "Sound out these words." The teacher points to the words as the students say them. They don't really sound them out. Teacher: "Max and Stephen, do you have something you want to share?" Teacher: "Michael, sound it out." Michael reads "toy"—he didn't really sound it out, just said the word. Teacher takes sweater from someone. Teacher: "Get ready to read this word the fast way." (They just say the words when it is the fast way.) Teacher starts passing out the books. The students are still on the floor. Teacher: "No talking. Turn to page 69." One boy had to go to the bathroom. Some students are talking, not really into the story and group. "Everyone on page 69. Max and Stephen, do you have something you want to share with us?" Teacher instructs students to read the story to themselves. They don't really read. Teacher: "Cheryl, move up—don't move back. What is the story about?" (They continue with round robin reading.) Teacher: "Cheryl, get your hand off his book and let him read."

At this point, the observer is having difficulty hearing some of the children read because the group is making too much noise. The lesson continues to deteriorate from this point on. Cheryl rocks on the floor and does not pay attention; the teacher waits for Max to find the page before he can read; one boy lies on the floor and begins rolling around. The field notes end with this comment from the observer: "One boy said things that were not very nice."

This scenario took place in a first-grade pull-out program that was designed to assist students who were having difficulty with reading. As researchers studying classroom reading instruction for young children, it was painful for us to witness such instruction. Why were the children so off task? Is it something about the children themselves, or the teacher? Is it something about the instruction? Until educators have a clearer sense of what precipitates off-task behavior, it is impossible to "fix" the problem. In this article, we attempt to answer these questions and draw conclusions about appropriate instruction for young children. In doing so, we describe similar scenarios that occurred during our observations in primary classrooms in which we analyzed instructional tasks for characteristics of motivating factors. We then examine our findings using a psychological and critical theoretical framework.

THEORETICAL FRAMEWORKS

In conceptualizing our data, we argue that there are three primary lenses through which we might view literacy instruction. The first lens looks at student achievement. Most government-endorsed research is designed to see literacy through this lens by examining which instructional practices result in the highest achievement scores. Literacy instruction, therefore, serves primarily instrumental purposes in that it is designed to help students perform well on certain predetermined measures (Broughton and Fairbanks, 2002). While this is one useful way of evaluating instructional practices, we suggest that it is also limited in that other essential ways of examining literacy instruction are ignored.

The second lens, which we are choosing to call the psychological lens because it evolves from the field of psychology, encourages us to look at motivation and attribution variables linked to literacy learning. That is, while students might be acquiring the intended achievement outcomes, this lens asks us to consider the impact of literacy instructional practices on variables such as students' sense of self-efficacy, on their inclination to remain cognitively engaged, and on their willingness to take risks as they read. These questions are essential to eventual student success and move us beyond looking at data solely in terms of achievement scores.

The third lens—what we are calling the sociopolitical lens—takes us into the critical domain. That is, it asks us to address questions relating to social and cultural differences in literacy and language use, and how literacy might be taught so as to penetrate and disrupt societal inequities. This lens causes us to question the instrumental uses of literacy that are currently in vogue, e.g. literacy for the workplace, or to maintain our national competitive stance. Rather, the sociopolitical lens leads us to recognize that democracy is not static, but is continually being challenged, and hence is never really assured. Looking at literacy instruction through this lens would indicate the most important variable in literacy instruction would be enhancing student empowerment so as to promote the goals of a multicultural, democratic state.

In this article, we look at instruction in classrooms with high student disengagement primarily through psychological and sociopolitical lenses. We argue that one of the primary reasons students were unmotivated was due to the characteristics of the tasks in which they were invited to participate. We further suggest that student off-task behavior should be thought of in terms of student resistance (the sociopolitical lens) rather than merely boredom or frustration (a psychological lens). That is, students were not merely passive recipients of the instruction in their classrooms, but at times they actively resisted the literacy instruction that they were receiving.

RESEARCH ON COGNITIVE ENGAGEMENT

Research shows that there is a positive relationship between "engaged time"—or time

where students are actively attending to the learning task—and student achievement. (See Cotton, 2001 for a comprehensive summary of this research.) Research that focuses specifically on literacy achievement similarly suggests that the best teachers of reading and writing are those who are capable of engaging students in literacy learning for sustained periods of time (Pressley et al., 1998). Bohn et al. write that "in an effective primary-grades classroom students are academically engaged and working productively. This contrasts with other classrooms where academic engagement is often much lower" (2004: 269–70). Students who read widely often tend to outscore their peers by 10–15 percent on standardized tests (Guthrie and Anderson, 1999), and engaged readers perform better on measures of text comprehension and reading achievement (Guthrie et al., 2001).

It is important to recognize that lack of engagement can be a sign of student resistance. Research shows that students often tend to perceive the educational process as uncaring, irrelevant, or contrary to their home cultures (Deyhle, 1996; Peshkin, 1997; Valenzuela, 1999). When instruction lacks real-world validity for students, and school values (such as competition and upward mobility) contradict the values of students' cultural communities, they often will be only minimally engaged in school. Similarly, when students experience a lack of control over their own learning or when they perceive that a task might lead to failure and subsequent embarrassment, they tend to engage in resistant behaviors.

During the past two years, we have been involved in analyzing classroom observation and student achievement data that were collected over a 2-year period. This larger research study was designed to examine the effects of various literacy programs selected for use in first, second and third grades by school districts throughout our state. As we met as a research team to read and discuss field and interview notes, we were struck by the wide variability in student engagement in the classrooms in which we had observed. In some classrooms, students appeared highly motivated and involved, whereas in others, students were frequently off-task and even non-compliant. We began to get a sense that there were factors affecting student involvement that went beyond classroom management and discipline policies, that were related directly to the ways in which literacy was being taught. Thus, a number of interesting questions emerged. One such question provides the focus for this article: what is the nature of literacy instructional tasks in classrooms with a high percentage of off-task behavior?

EFFECTIVE TEACHERS OF LITERACY = HIGH STUDENT ENGAGEMENT

In recent years, there have been several studies that have examined the variables associated with effective teachers of literacy. One factor that remains constant throughout this research is that highly effective teachers are those who are capable of sustaining students' involvement in meaningful literacy tasks (Allington et al., 2002; Bohn et al., 2004; Morrow and Tracey, 1997). For instance, Allington et al. claim that "Exemplary teachers created classrooms that engaged their students in learning to read, write, and think about important topics, themes, and issues" (2002: 466). In this section, we summarize the research on students' cognitive engagement as it relates to literacy instruction. It should be noted that cognitive engagement—or students' intrinsic motivation for engaging in literacy tasks—can be determined through a variety of factors, such as students' willingness to persist in applying various reading strategies, their propensity to choose to read during leisure time, and their tendency to remain immersed in literacy experiences. Thus, time on task is only one measure of students' cognitive engagement.

In a study of reading growth in high-poverty classrooms, Taylor et al. (2003) classified literacy activities as those that required either active or passive responses from students. Examples of passive responding included reading turn-taking (round robin reading and other oral turn-taking tasks) or listening to the teacher—activities requiring essentially mechanistic or routine cognitive processing. Examples of active responding were reading, writing, and manipulating that required more strategic (versus mechanical) cognitive processes, such as discussing ideas with a partner and responding in journals to higher-level questions. In this study, passive responding was negatively related to students' growth in reading comprehension, whereas active responding was positively related. Similarly, teacher coaching and involving students in active reading (in contrast to passive turn-taking) were linked to gains in fluency in grades 2–5. The researchers concluded that effective literacy teachers "actively involve students in literacy activities, often giving them responsibility for holding their own discussions about text, and they maintain high pupil involvement" (2003: 24).

A recent study of effective primary-grade teachers supports these findings. Bohn et al. (2004) documented the differences in student engagement between highly effective and less effective primary teachers. Engagement was determined through classroom observations by calculating the percentage of students who were working attentively at several points during the observation. The authors share that student engagement was highest in the classrooms of the effective teachers. Literacy instruction in these classrooms was characterized by appropriately challenging tasks (e.g. "just-right" books for children), peer collaboration, student choice, and self-regulation (e.g. independent application of reading strategies). In contrast, literacy instruction in the less effective teachers' classrooms was characterized by adherence to procedures, tasks that were either too difficult or too easy, and lack of student self-regulation. The authors concluded that the effective teachers "let students know that they had choices, that they owned the classroom too" (2004: 281). They further state that "this was in decided contrast to the other four [less effective] teachers. For example, teacher B even dictated the colors students were to use during coloring, and teacher F restricted the words students could use during writing" (2004: 281).

Morrow and Tracey (1997) examined the inclusion of motivational characteristics in phonics and phonemic awareness instruction. Their research consisted of observations of phonics instructional lessons in preschool, kindergarten, and grades 1 and 2. Three categories emerged from their research: (1) explicit instruction that incorporated direct instructional techniques controlled by the teacher (e.g. phonics books and worksheets); (2) authentic instruction that integrated phonics instruction within meaningful contexts (e.g. morning message, storybook reading); and (3) a balanced approach that combined explicit and authentic instruction (that is, instruction was embedded in authentic contexts, but was planned and explicit). The researchers found that the most commonly used strategy was explicit instruction. Further, these lessons typically had fewer motivating features, such as student choice of activities, self-direction and self-pacing, peer collaboration, and authentic literacy experiences. The authentic and balanced lessons included more of these motivating features (Tracey and Morrow, 1998).

The differences between tasks that engaged students (e.g. those involving choices [Bohn et al., 2004] or involving peer collaboration and authentic literacy [Morrow and Tracey, 1997), and those tasks that did not engage students, can be characterized as either "open" or "closed" (Turner and Paris, 1995). In a study of early reading tasks and student motivation, researchers examined how young children's behaviors were affected by the instructional context (Turner, 1995; Turner and Paris, 1995). Three aspects of motivational behavior were assessed: (1) students' use of reading strategies, (2) students' persistence in solving problems and trying out new strategies, and (3) students' volitional control, that is, their willingness and ability to use various control strategies to carry a particular task to fruition. These three behaviors involve students' propensity to invest time and effort in learning to read, and were selected because they have been shown through research to be related to motivation and literacy achievement. Instructional tasks were categorized as either "closed" or "open." Tasks were categorized as "closed" when

outcomes were predetermined and students were required to use specified information to reach those outcomes. Examples of "closed" activities were practice activities and worksheets, where the children were directed to use particular information (such as rhyming words) to arrive at a single, correct solution. Tasks were categorized as "open" when the children could select the information required to complete the task and choose how to use that information. Examples of "open" activities were self-selected reading and partner reading. Turner found that motivational behaviors were more likely to occur when the children were engaged in open tasks.

Turner and Paris (1995) further suggest that there were six critical features of open tasks that seemed to affect students' engagement with literacy. They refer to these features as the "six Cs": choice, challenge, control, collaboration, constructive comprehension (also referred to as "constructing meaning") and consequences. *Choice* allows students to select tasks and texts that they are interested in or that they find personally relevant, which encourages students to set goals and take responsibility for their own literacy development. *Challenge* provides tasks that scaffold student learning and that show students their capabilities without frustrating them. Challenging tasks are those that enable students to use their competencies to solve problems, versus those that require only a single answer. *Control* enables students and teachers to share in the decision-making process, giving students ownership of their learning. *Collaboration* encourages social interaction, where students learn from one another and support each other's efforts. *Constructing meaning* helps students make sense of what they are learning by using literacy to solve problems, to entertain, to inform. Instruction that supports the construction of meaning also helps students to develop important metacognitive abilities. Finally, *consequences*—or outcomes—can influence students' motivation for literacy learning by providing either positive or negative feelings about achievement. Those tasks that allow students to maintain a belief in their ability to be successful are more motivating than closed tasks that have correct responses or require single, narrow strategies for success. (See also Wigfield, 2000; Tracey and Morrow, 1998.)

Together, Turner and Paris (1995) found that these six variables—all associated with "open" tasks—create a context that positively affects students' motivation for literacy. The authors conclude that "Tasks that provided opportunities for students to use reading and writing for authentic purposes . . . that conveyed the value of literacy for communication and enjoyment, and that allowed students to be actively involved in constructing meaning and metacognitions about literacy, were most successful in motivating students" (1995: 664). In the present study, we use the frame established by Turner and Paris to examine instructional tasks in low-engagement activity settings of different instructional models in an attempt to find patterns of instructional tasks that relate to student engagement.

RESEARCH ON RESISTANT STUDENT BEHAVIORS

It is possible to link the variables noted above—choice, challenge, control, collaboration, constructing meaning, and consequences—to the classic study of Jean Anyon (1996), who conducted observations in fifth-grade public school classrooms in five different schools. These schools were located in neighborhoods that varied in affluence. Anyon refers to these schools as working class, middle class, affluent professional, and executive elite.

In the two working-class schools in which she observed, students primarily were involved in mechanical, rote tasks and had very little choice or control in their learning. Students were required to follow the rules and were told to copy the steps and procedures for completing assignments as they were listed on the board. For instance, in science, the teacher demonstrated the experiment to the whole class and the children copied the directions from the science book. After the experiment, the teacher wrote the results on the board and the children copied the results in their notebooks.

Language arts instruction primarily consisted of acquiring writing mechanics (punctuation, capitalization, etc.), and did not involve creative writing. Anyon reports that occasionally assignments were given that required extended writing, but these were generally in the form of questions to which students had to respond.

Skills worksheets required a single correct response. When reviewing math and language arts skills sheets, the teacher "fired the questions rapidly"; Anyon writes that "the scene reminded the observer of a sergeant drilling recruits" (1996: 189).

It is clear that these classrooms seemed to be characterized by a lack of the "six Cs". That is, students had no choice of activities and little control; tasks were generally rote, unchallenging, and allowed for little meaning construction. One can assume that within this controlling environment, there was little student collaboration, and most tasks potentially led to negative consequences as they typically involved a single accurate response.

As a result, Anyon writes that "The control that the teachers have is less than they would like . . . They [the children] do not directly challenge the teachers" authority, but they make indirect attempts to sabotage and resist the flow of assignments" (1996: 189). In fact, Anyon found that teachers assigned work that was less challenging because such work led to less student resistance.

These findings are consistent with those of Linda McNeil (1988), who examined student resistance in high school social studies classrooms. McNeil found that teachers engaged in what she calls "defensive teaching," using instructional methods that they believed would lead to the least student resistance. These defensive tactics included reducing complex topics to a series of disjointed facts to be memorized, and "mystification"—the tendency to limit discussion on certain topics and issues. McNeil writes that "*Their patterns of knowledge control were, according to their own statements in taped interviews, rooted in their desire for classroom control*" (1988: 159, emphasis in original). Such tactics led to student passivity, whereby students learned only enough to get by. Thus, McNeil found that teacher control of knowledge was directly linked to a lack of student engagement.

In her interviews with second-grade students, Angela Spaulding (2000) found that even young children admit to intentional resistance and are able to articulate the reasons that they resist particular activities. For instance, one child used the resistance strategy of "interruption" by interrupting the teacher as she was instructing two other students to ask if he could give water to the classroom gerbil instead of reading. The reasons he stated for the interruption were a lack of reading choice and control: "I didn't want to read. I get tired of reading. I like it sometimes (reading) but not some stories and not doing it for so long" (2000: 10). Similarly, students occasionally used the resistance strategy of changing topics, and stated in the interviews that "We change the topic because it's hard and we didn't understand it so we talked about something we understood better, like contractions" (2000: 13).

Spaulding found that students occasionally demonstrated aggressive resistance when they had an intense dislike for the activity and they lacked choice and control. For instance, one student protested loudly when the teacher required him to include illustrations in the book he had created. The child explained that "I don't like to draw and I wasn't gonna do it" (2000: 19).

Children reported that they particularly disliked tasks where they had difficulty comprehending the activity (that is, the task was not appropriately challenging) and where they feared failure (that is, they believed they might experience negative consequences). Thus, tasks in which the children had limited control and choice and those in which they feared negative consequences resulted not merely in disengagement, but in behaviors that even the children themselves characterized as resistance.

DATA COLLECTION AND ANALYSIS

This study was part of a larger study of literacy instruction and student achievement conducted to determine the effectiveness of various literacy instructional models being implemented in first- through third-grade classrooms which serve children aged 5–8. Researchers were trained by the project director by observing classroom lessons on videotape, using the instruments described below to record instruction, and then negotiating and refining interpretations. Details of these steps follow.

Participants

The larger study included teachers in 13 schools and 46 classrooms. We invited schools that had recently received a grant to implement one of the reading models. We invited teachers to participate in a study of classroom literacy instruction through contacting the principals, asking them to recommend teachers who were particularly successful at implementing the instructional model for at least one year. At the time, we had not specifically anticipated an analysis of specific tasks through a lens of motivation with a sociopolitical stance.

Data Collection Procedures

We collected data on the instructional models in three ways: (1) by observing the teachers and taking field notes, (2) by interviewing the teachers about their practices, and (3) by completing an observation instrument after leaving the site (which required reflection and quantification of what was observed). We visited each teacher four times and observed between 60 and 180 minutes during each visit, depending on how long "literacy instruction" was conducted in that classroom. Researchers sat in the room and recorded what the teacher said and did in the form of field notes. We noted the instructional activities, classroom interactions, apparent focus of instruction, amount of time children spent reading connected text, and other issues that seemed to affect achievement outcomes (distractions, etc.). Following each observation, teachers were interviewed to determine the degree to which they felt the observation was typical of their instructional practices and what else occurred regularly that we did not observe.

After exiting the field site, the researcher used the field notes and interview to complete the observation instrument that summarized and quantified instructional patterns. This instrument was used to provide information on the observer's sense of the focus of the lesson and the quality of the instruction. Observers noted such items as the activities in which the children were involved, the percentage of time the children spent reading connected text, the percentage of time that children were working on isolated skills, the percentage of time that children appeared to be off task, and so on. When students appeared bored or when there was a significant amount of off-task behavior, observers frequently noted it both in the field notes and on the observation instrument. An excerpted section of the instrument relevant to this analysis is included in the Appendix. The instrument, the field notes, and the interview made a "data set" for analysis.

In the larger study, we analyzed 75 completed data sets. Of these 75 sets, 38 (51%) came from classrooms with "scripted" instructional programs, e.g. SRA Corrective Reading and Open Court Direct Instruction. "Scripted programs" are defined here as programs used for literacy instruction that have specific, predetermined procedures the teacher must follow and language the teacher must use. The other 37 sets (49%) came from classrooms that used what we referred to as "balanced" literacy models: Four Blocks, Early Intervention (based on Taylor et al., 1994), Early Success, Together We Can (a locally developed model), and Breakthrough to Literacy.

Unit of Analysis

In the larger study, we used "activity setting" as the unit of analysis for our documentation of patterns across instructional sites (Miles and Huberman, 1994). An activity setting was defined as "an activity bounded by a beginning and ending that has a particular purpose." An activity setting is a specific segment of instruction that is delimited by a particular focus,

instructional objective, participants, and setting (Tharp and Gallimore, 1993). So, for instance, a literacy event in which a teacher reads a storybook aloud would be designated as one activity setting; when the class switches to small group guided reading instruction, this would signal the start of a new activity setting. In the larger study, we examined each activity setting for patterns of activities, instructional tasks, how time was spent, and the teacher's apparent instructional focus. This content analysis (Miles and Huberman, 1994) led us to more specific analyses such as the one presented in this article.

To understand the motivational features as described by Turner (1995) in settings in which children were off task, we first determined the activity settings with considerable off-task behavior. That is, we isolated all activity settings where the observer had checked on the observation report that the children were off task at least 25 percent of the time. From this subset of data, we selected only those field notes for analysis where there was clear evidence of off-task behavior. These field notes—those where the observer indicated at least 25 percent off-task behavior and where there was also evidence of this in the qualitative data through field notes—were subsequently analyzed for motivational features.

Out of the 75 complete data sets in the larger study, 28 fell into the "low engagement" category, using our conservative inclusion criteria just described. From the 28 data sets that were analyzed for this study, 23 (82%) were from scripted models (SRA and Direct Instruction), and 5 (18%) were not (Four Blocks and Early Intervention). From these 28 data sets, a total of 73 activity settings were coded and analyzed. The activity settings ranged from 5 minutes to 55 minutes, with the average being approximately 20 minutes long. Table 2.1 summarizes the data we analyzed.

Coding

In coding the data, we used the framework reported by Turner and Paris (1995) described above. We explain the data analysis categories,

Table 2.1   Data for inclusion in study

Larger study

13 schools, 46 classrooms

75 completed data sets from 46 classrooms

38 sets from scripted and 37 from non-scripted models (51% scripted, 49% non-scripted)

Current analysis

28 "low-engagement" data sets from 75 completed data sets of larger study

23 data sets from scripted models, 5 data sets from non-scripted models (82% scripted, 18% non-scripted)

73 activity settings delineated from the 28 "low engagement" data sets

Activity settings lasted 5–55 minutes with an average of approximately 20 minutes

---

and then provide specific examples from the classrooms we observed.

Choice. A task was coded positively (+) for choice if it allowed students to select activities or texts that they were interested in or that they found personally relevant. An example came from learning centers. A task was coded negatively (–) if it did not allow for student choice in texts or activities. Examples from our data include whole class skill instruction and mandatory worksheets. A third category, "neutral," was checked if the task allowed students to select from a narrow range of options (e.g. forming a sentence using a word they had selected from a list).

Challenge. A task was coded positively (+) if the task was determined to be appropriately challenging in that students' knowledge was scaffolded, and they could demonstrate competence without being frustrated. Examples from our data included some guided reading lessons (when the text was clearly appropriate), some choral reading sessions, some discussions of literature. A task was coded negatively (–) if it was either too difficult or too easy for some children in the group, causing students to be frustrated or bored. Examples from our data include when children were expected to complete sentences in choral fashion, when they were asked to create oral sentences with simple words, when students were asked to repeatedly

pronounce words. A task was coded as "neutral" if the appropriateness of the level of challenge could not be determined from field notes.

Control. A task was coded positively (+) for control when students had some autonomy and ownership in the task. Examples often came from writing time or center time. It was coded negatively (–) when students had no decision-making authority, when responses were controlled, and/or when there was only a single correct response. Examples often came from whole class skill lessons. A task was coded "neutral" when we were unable to determine the degree of student autonomy from the data.

Collaboration. A task was coded positively (+) for collaboration when peer social interaction was an integral part of the activity. An example came during time in learning centers in one classroom, and another during writing time in one classroom. A task was coded negatively (–) for collaboration when the task did not allow for peer interaction and individual response was required. Examples usually came from direct lessons and independent work time. A task was coded as "neutral" when students worked together but it was not encouraged or was not a part of the task, or when we were unable to determine the degree of collaboration from the data.

Constructing Meaning. A task was coded positively (+) for constructing meaning if it enabled students to use literacy for authentic purposes, and/or skills instruction was embedded in meaningful contexts. Examples came from book discussions, learning centers, writing time, and some reading lessons. A task was coded negatively (–) for constructing meaning if literacy was not used for authentic purposes and/or skills were taught in isolation, such as repeatedly spelling words. A task was considered "neutral" when there was a limited attempt to link instruction to a meaningful context, or when we were unable to determine the meaningfulness of a task from the data.

Consequences. A task was coded positively (+) if it allowed students to believe in their ability to be successful. Examples from our data included some choral response sessions and book discussions. A task was coded negatively (–) if the task had the potential to create failure. Examples usually came from lessons in which the discourse followed the traditional initiation, response, evaluation (IRE) pattern (Cazden, 1988) in which only one response was the correct one. A task was coded as "neutral" when we were unable to determine potential consequences from the data.

These variables provided the conceptual framework for coding the activity settings in our data where there was determined to be a high degree of off-task behavior. Because the field notes and observation reports in the larger data set did not provide the specificity necessary to determine classrooms where there was an exceptionally high degree of on-task behavior, we chose to limit our analysis to off-task behavior activity settings. Two of the authors were involved in coding the data. To determine reliability, nine activity settings were coded separately and results were compared. This procedure yielded a reliability of 0.81.

FINDINGS

First, in classroom reading instructional models where there is a high degree of off-task behavior,

academic tasks were often determined to be "closed." Second, there was a disproportionately high percentage of off-task behavior in classrooms using scripted models. That is, 51 percent of the analyzed data sets from the larger study were from scripted models, while 82 percent of the low-engagement data sets were from scripted models. The whole class scripted models appeared to contribute to the off-task behavior, making the examination of the nature of literacy tasks critical for determining its value beyond short term achievement.

To present these findings, we first describe the tasks we analyzed through Turner and Paris's coding scheme. Then, we show patterns across the codes with examples from inside these classrooms. Finally, we discuss these findings using both a psychological and a sociopolitical framework for looking at classroom instruction.

Closed Tasks = Low Engagement

Our original research question was: "What is the nature of literacy instructional tasks in classrooms with a high percentage of off-task behavior?" For each of the six Cs from Turner and Paris's (1995) frame, we find that closed tasks mean students will often be off task.

Choice. Only one of the tasks was coded positive for choice: 94.5 percent were coded as negative; 4 percent were determined to be neutral. In these low-engagement settings, choice was almost non-existent. The only low-engagement activity setting coded as positive on *choice* was in one classroom where the teacher had established learning centers.

Challenge. Approximately 11 percent of the tasks were found to be positive on challenge; approximately 68.5 percent of the tasks were found to be negative; 20.5 percent were coded as neutral. Often the activity settings were coded as "neutral" in *challenge* because we did not know the students well enough to ascertain whether the task was too easy, too difficult, or appropriately challenging. Many lessons were easily coded, however, and "challenge" was based on students' responses. For example, when children easily and quickly answered all questions asked or when very simplistic responses were elicited and accepted, we coded the task as too easy. We also coded instances such as coloring worksheets as negative. Other times, the setting was coded as negative when students were off task because they didn't seem to know what to do or how to do it, indicating the task was too challenging.

Control. Four percent of the tasks allowed for student control; 77 percent of the tasks did not provide any student autonomy; 19 percent were coded as neutral. Nearly all low-engagement activity settings where a determination was possible were coded as negative on *control.* Students had virtually no ownership or autonomy in most of these activity settings. The few exceptions were usually when teachers allowed students to write on self-selected topics, allowing for control but not choice (since the students still had to write).

Collaboration. Two of the tasks were coded as positive (3%); 93 percent were coded as negative; 4 percent were coded as neutral. In these settings, students almost never had a chance to work with one another. The scripted programs did not appear to invite collaboration. The only tasks we observed regularly in which children did something together involved choral reading and responding; however, these were eventually coded as negative as there was no exchange of ideas and/or peer assistance.

Constructing Meaning. Approximately 16 percent of the tasks were determined to focus on meaning; 75 percent were determined to consist of non-authentic activities and/or isolated skills; approximately 8 percent were coded as neutral. Activity settings coded as "neutral" in constructing meaning included reading lessons in which students were told to read silently, but there was

no follow-up discussion or the discussion included only low-level questions. Sometimes these limited "discussions" consisted of questions to which the students were asked to respond chorally, or choral sentence completion tasks (e.g. "And the wolf and pig became . . .?" and children responded with "Friends!"). The few activity settings coded as positive in constructing meaning occurred either during reading lessons, or more commonly during read alouds, when there was evidence that some children (not all, due to the low-engagement rating) were responding to the story as if they were constructing meaning.

Consequences. Approximately 12 percent of the tasks were coded as positive; 80 percent of the tasks were coded as negative; 8 percent of the tasks were coded as neutral. Settings coded negatively for *consequences* were often those in which teachers asked low-level questions with one right answer, and the students had to answer in public, indicating a less than emotionally safe environment. Or, students had to fill in worksheets or spell words, again with a single correct answer. Those with a positive coding for this category were usually related to the few writing tasks that involved choice. Table 2.2 provides a summary of the various assigned codes.

Patterns Across Codes: Negative Codes and Scripted Models

Those activity settings that were characterized by "closed" tasks and had a preponderance of negative codes were often phonics lessons with no follow-up reading or writing; reading lessons which focused exclusively or primarily on round robin reading, often conducted in whole class settings; or work time in which students had no choice in the work, the task was seemingly meaningless, or the students were told to work independently. As will be shown later in more detail, some activity settings were coded negatively for all six Cs.

As noted earlier, 23 of the 28 data sets (82%) where there was indication of a high degree of

Table 2.2 Number of positive, negative, neutral codes of low-engagement activity settings

	Positive	*Negative*	*Neutral*
Choice	1	69	3
Challenge	8	50	15
Control	3	56	14
Collaboration	2	68	3
Constructing meaning	12	55	6
Consequences	9	58	6

off-task behavior were from schools that had adopted scripted programs (SRA Reading Mastery and Open Court Direct Instruction), and five (18%) were from schools that had adopted balanced instructional programs (Four Blocks and Early Intervention). We argue that this disproportionate number comes directly from the tasks within the scripted models. Students had few opportunities for choice, control, and collaboration if their teachers implemented the models as they were intended to be implemented. Another feature of these scripted programs was that they tended to have a "one-size-fits-all" approach, so that tasks were frequently coded negatively for "challenge" because some students appeared bored, while others were frustrated. Further, the scripted models had accompanying materials that delimited what the teacher was to say or do, making them non-responsive to students who do not follow the script.

Further evidence for this pattern comes from one scripted classroom in which the observer reported multiple incidences when the children were off task, to the degree that one sensed a lack of control. These same children, however, were quite engaged in the computer lab, where they had more control over the literacy events, they were appropriately challenged, and they were able to experience success (positive consequences). Because the computer lab teacher was absent on the day of the observation and the classroom teacher accompanied

the group to the lab, it was apparent that students' improved behavior was linked to the task and not to other factors such as the teacher's management style.

A Look Inside Classrooms

What follows are three classroom scenarios that typify instruction and behavior in the off-task classrooms. Each scenario constitutes one activity setting. Following each example, we discuss how we analyzed the data and explain our reasoning for assigning the codes.

Example One

The whole class is in the back of the room on the floor surrounding the teacher. The teacher has a [name of program] instruction book in his hand that he holds up so the whole class can see. The page he is showing has about 10 words on it. He points to each word and reads from the script at the side of the book. The students say/read each word, spell it, and then say it again. When they come to a word that causes some confusion, the teacher stops and asks "What is this word again?" The teacher says, "That's right. Were. Who can use 'were' in a sentence?" A girl says "There were three dogs." The teacher nods his head [yes] and asks a boy to use it in a sentence. The boy says, "There were six cats."

This activity setting continues with students reading individual words accompanied by teacher explanation. Students then read columns of words individually. The observer noted that children were off task during this activity setting at least 25 percent of the time. In her interpretation of the observation, she stated that the children "got restless" and that the "children in the back tended to lose focus fast."

This activity setting was coded as "negative." for all six variables. Students had no choice of activity; the task was not challenging (e.g., use "were" in a sentence); the task did not involve collaboration and was not authentic; and the task had the potential to create failure due to the limited number of acceptable responses. Such activities can be referred to as "exercises" whereby the task and its outcomes are strictly controlled (Edelsky, 1991). Such exercises do not constitute "real" reading.

Unfortunately, in some classrooms there seemed to be a negative cycle that evolved as students and teachers experienced elevated levels of frustration. The next two activity settings illustrate this phenomenon.

Example Two

Teacher [says] "Everyone's finger on item 1. We are going to read this the 'fast' way." The kids scramble to get pens/pencils. The teacher helps and to hurry them along. Again [the teacher says] "Everyone's finger. We are going to read this the 'fast' way." (He says this often throughout the workbook lesson.) The teacher collects pens/pencils when students begin working ahead. The workbook asks basic comprehension questions from the story they just read. Teacher snaps his fingers and children read the sentence together. One kid (with sunglasses on) gets smart with the teacher on a few occasions and with the other students as well. The teacher says "Everyone get ready. Be quiet." Kids are getting fidgety and restless. Teacher snaps fingers again and kids say answer to next question (some get it wrong). Teacher snaps again and this time they all get it right.

Next, the children work on workbook pages independently. When the students finish, the teacher begins to hand them word searches to complete. The teacher tells one student that this is to "keep you busy." Five minutes later, the field notes read:

Busy work continues. Teacher brings more busy work out. Kids fight over the sheets. Teacher disciplines the sunglass boy who is taunting others. Teacher looks boy in the eye and takes his pencil and says, "We don't need to hear that." Teacher gives back the pencil . . . Kids are now coloring their sheets, talking to each other, and Trevor is reading his agenda book. Kristin is drawing a picture. Martin is just sitting, tapping his pencil on his mouth.

This activity setting was coded as negative on choice. It was coded as neutral on challenge as it was difficult to tell whether the tasks were appropriate or not. It was also coded as negative on collaboration, meaningfulness, and consequences as these sorts of "fast-paced" reading lessons often appeared to move at a pace not conducive for real thinking. The questions asked required specified answers that had to be answered quickly.

In this classroom, we were struck by the disrespectful behavior of some of the students. While there are undoubtedly many variables that contribute to these negative environments, it appears that when students have little control over their own learning, the opportunity for such behavior escalates.

In the following example, the researcher's field notes (elaborated later with parentheses) illustrate another lesson from one of the scripted classrooms and the students' responses to the lesson. We think it is significant that the observer spends much of her time writing about the children.

Example Three

The teacher has children turn to [the] skills lesson in their basal reader. Hands go up to show her they are ready when they are on the right page. "Touch under the first word in column A," says the teacher. Children then say all of the words aloud in each column (8 columns of about 6 words each). They have trouble with the word "probably" and so the teacher stops them to pronounce it again together. They still have trouble, so the teacher says it. They go on to the next word. James isn't saying words. He is fidgeting with his pencil, pushing the chair across from him with his feet. Teacher calls on James to say those words again. Teacher reprimands James. He doesn't know where they are so the teacher asks the class to read that column again. Growls of frustration are heard from some of the kids. The teacher discusses the words "lawn" and "foist." She asks for examples of what they mean. (I don't catch.) The teacher then calls on individual children to read a column. Maxine gets stuck on "probably" and says "probly". The teacher asks everyone to say it. Again. Again. It's a hard word to say correctly.

[Another boy begins to read.] The boy reading the words is obviously upset about something—home or reading aloud or who knows. He is covering his eyes with his hand as he reads. When he is finished he wipes his eyes with his other hand. The teacher doesn't take notice of this or she doesn't want to draw attention to the boy because she goes on to the next child. Each child is called on to read words out loud individually. Some kids are fidgety and restless. The teacher stops to discipline children. Maxine reads her column again. The teacher calls on those who didn't read words without mistakes. She praises them for not missing any words.

Not surprisingly, this setting was also coded negatively on all Cs, for reasons apparent from the two previous examples. It appears from these field notes that the primary aim of this instructional event was to get through the scripted materials. At times the script created conditions where even a child's pronunciation of words like "probably" was viewed as a literacy problem. Clearly, instruction in many of the scripted programs in our study did not allow for student choice, control, or social interaction. We sensed in many of these classrooms that the children were simply bored. Yet, we also sensed that often, student behavior could be characterized not simply as boredom or frustration, but outright resistance. We explore this notion further in the discussion that follows.

DISCUSSION

Current literacy research efforts focus primarily on instrumental literacy, that is, literacy that is designed to promote higher achievement on standardized tests. In looking at literacy instruction through this lens, research clearly shows that skills instruction is an important part of a balanced literacy program, and direct, explicit teaching of phonics and phonemic awareness is linked to reading achievement (Report of the National Reading Panel, 2000). But, at what cost is achievement of this sort made? There are other equally important determinants of a quality literacy program. Looking at literacy instruction through a psychological and sociopolitical lens, we would suggest that *how* skills are taught in primary classrooms ought to be a major consideration in decisions about instruction. For it is also clear that not all instructional tasks are equally motivating to young learners, nor are they equally empowering.

In this study, we examined the motivational variables that have been found to correlate with high student involvement in literacy: student choice, appropriate challenge, student control, peer collaboration, meaning construction, and positive consequences. We found that in classrooms where there was a high degree of student off-task behavior, all or most of these six variables were absent. Thus, this study supports the findings of previous studies on student motivation that suggest that learning tasks are motivating when they are purposeful to students, when they involve peer collaboration and real-world experiences, when they provide opportunities for student choice, when they provide challenge and stimulate curiosity, and when basic skills are taught in the context of meaningful themes or topics (Freppon and McIntyre, 1999; McCarthey et al., 1999; McCombs, 1996; Tracey and Morrow, 1998; Turner, 1995; Turner and Paris, 1995).

Looking at literacy instruction through a psychological lens, it would seem that instructional tasks that do little to promote motivation for reading might ultimately hinder children's literacy development and their perceptions of themselves as readers. Turner writes that "the tasks that teachers select to foster important literacy goals represent to students what literacy is, why it is important, and what it can do" (1995: 415). Research on student engagement in reading indicates that there is a complex interplay between metacognition, motivation, and the social context within which the learning event occurs (Baker et al., 2000). Even students' use of reading strategies is linked to motivation in that students must be willing to expend the effort to try them out and to actively monitor their use (Paris and Paris, 2001; Turner, 1995). Thus, it would seem that motivational variables ought to be at least as important as achievement variables in assessing quality literacy instruction.

As we read the field notes of classroom observations, however, we were challenged to view the data not merely through a psychological lens, but also through a sociopolitical one. Some of the children's behaviors appeared to be attempts to actively resist the instruction they were receiving. Edelsky (1991) observes that much of our literacy instruction positions students as "objects," in that they have little control and ownership of their learning. Similarly, McNeil (1988) suggests that students become relegated to the role of "clients" as they are forced to learn essentially meaningless information. We suggest that the role of "object" or "client" leads to a minimal investment in literacy learning, and also denies the cultural knowledge that students bring with them to school (Powell, 1999).

Literacy learning is both social and cultural and collaborative literacy experiences tend to promote student engagement (Gambrell and Almasi, 1996; Gambrell et al., 2000; Oldfather, 1993). Further, when the social and cultural dimensions of literacy instruction are ignored, students often fail to see the significance of literacy for their lives. When "school literacy" becomes distinct from "real literacy," literacy instruction can negatively affect individuals' perceptions of themselves as readers— particularly among those students whose "funds of knowledge" (Moll, 2001) have historically been marginalized or devalued in schools.

When "school literacy" is viewed as irrelevant and students assume the role of "object," students typically respond either by becoming apathetic, or by engaging in subversive action (Anyon, 1996; Finn, 1999; Kohl, 1995; Kohn, 1993; Powell, 1999; Willis, 1977). Our data remind us of the subversive student behaviors that Anyon (1996) reports in her study of working class schools discussed earlier, where students were subjected to constant control and were never asked to think beyond a very basic level. The children in the fifth grade classrooms in which she observed were not only disengaged, but also actively resisted by breaking pencils, falling out of their chairs, and so on. These behaviors are not unlike those we saw in the primary classrooms in which we observed. Some children responded to their "client" role by engaging in behaviors that wasted time and that got them out of doing the task: going to the bathroom, rolling around on the floor, coloring, covering up the pages of their books, losing their place. Others merely became restless and inattentive and responded by pushing the chair in front of them, or talking to a friend. Others simply cried.

We argue that all of these behaviors need to be conceptualized as acts of resistance to instrumental literacy practices that demean and dehumanize. When students are subjected to instruction that is irrelevant and that devalues their language and cultural knowledge, they tend to resist in various ways, sometimes even by sabotaging their own learning. Instructional literacy practices such as those we observed in this study are designed to teach children to follow and to conform—to accept and adapt to the status quo (Anyon, 1996)—rather than to lead, to challenge, to be "critical agents in the act of knowing" (Shor and Freire, 1987: 33). Yet children are not that malleable; they are not "products" that can be molded to fit a predetermined agenda. Anyon (1996: 200) writes that "the children [that she observed] in the working-class schools are not learning to be docile and obedient in the face of present or future degrading conditions or financial exploitation. They are developing abilities and skills of resistance."

LIMITATIONS OF THE STUDY

We acknowledge that this research is limited in that only one aspect that affects students' motivation for literacy engagement was investigated, i.e. the educational context. We concur with Tracey and Morrow when they state that "Motivation to read . . . is more than effortful activity or time spent on the task, and is reflected in how children think about themselves as readers and how they think about reading tasks and activities" (1998: 342). It was not possible to determine from the data other factors that might have impinged upon students' off-task behavior, such as students' self-efficacy and sense of their own competence, and students' perceptions of the meaningfulness of the various literacy tasks in which they were engaged. It was also difficult to determine from the data other variables that might affect student effort, such as the classroom management structure. Determining the effect of these various factors would require more sustained and focused classroom observations than were undertaken here. It would have also been instructive to analyze instructional tasks in classrooms in which there was a high degree of student engagement so that we might compare these data to those in low engagement classrooms. As noted above, we were unable to identify the high-engagement classrooms with any degree of sophistication.

CONCLUSION

Over 40 years ago, in his "A Talk to Teachers," James Baldwin stated that:

> The purpose of education, finally, is to create in a person the ability to look at the world for himself, to make his own decisions, to say to himself this is black or this is white, to decide for himself whether there is a God in heaven or not . . . But no society is really anxious to have that kind of person around. What societies really, ideally, want is a citizenry which will simply obey the rules of society. If a society succeeds in this, that society is about to perish. (1988: 4)

Our current obsession with testing has resulted in a reductionist notion of literacy that equates reading with the mastery of a narrow range of skills. Absent is the notion that literacy can, and ought to be, used for liberating ends: to critique, to empower, to transform. Scripted literacy programs force both teachers and children to "obey the rules," to accept a lack of autonomy as necessary in exchange for higher test scores. Yet we would argue that such programs are not neutral or innocent, but rather can have potentially detrimental consequences for students' engagement with literacy and for their ability to see the importance of literacy in their lives.

In his book *Phonics Exposed* (2002), Richard Meyer reports on the changes that Karen, a primary teacher, was forced to make in her classroom as she followed the scripted phonics program mandated by her school. Noting the off-task behaviors of the children during these lessons, he writes that Karen "could *make* them sit politely" (2002: 66). Yet she also realized that accepting a certain amount of student misbehavior during this time helped to preserve the teacher–student relationship.

It was the erosion of this relationship that we found to be particularly problematic in these classrooms in which we observed. The children resisted, the teachers reacted to their resistance, and a cycle of negativity evolved. Absent were meaningful literacy experiences that would enable teachers to affirm students' cultural experiences and to develop more supportive and nurturing relationships—experiences such as personal writing, engaging in real discussion about books, and so on. Absent, too, were literacy experiences that positioned students as "subjects" so that they might understand the power of literacy for their lives. Thus, we argue that scripted programs are problematic not only because of the off-task student behavior that ensues, but also because they erode the student–teacher relationship and obscure the potential of literacy for agency and critique.

The questions that we pose as researchers determine what we see. When we only see literacy instruction through an instrumental lens and the sole objective of our investigation is achievement on standardized reading tests, then we must ask what other, perhaps more significant questions are ignored—questions such as: are there particular ways of teaching literacy that affirm the cultural identities of historically marginalized students? Are there particular ways of teaching literacy that better prepare students to participate in a democracy? Are there particular ways of teaching literacy that promote creative, higher-order thinking and problem-solving? Are there particular ways of teaching literacy that enhance, rather than erode, the critical relationship between teachers and students? The fact that there is little discussion or concern for teaching literacy for empowerment—for helping students to see the power of reading and writing for individual and societal transformation—reveals how far we have come in viewing literacy solely in technical or instrumental terms (Edelsky, 1999; Powell, 1999; Shannon, 1992, 1998).

This study and others that examine the motivational dimension of literacy instruction underscore the limitations of research that solely addresses student achievement. Closed instructional tasks can negatively affect students' willingness to engage in reading and to take risks, and, as we have illustrated through our research, can potentially lead to student resistance. Since the scripted, commercial programs that are currently in vogue tend to be associated with such tasks, we believe that the increased use of such programs is cause for concern, not only because of the potential impact on student achievement, but also because students may never see the value of literacy for their lives. As literacy scholars, we believe that we have an obligation to view literacy more broadly and to lead the way in seeking answers to the truly important questions, so that reading and writing, speaking and listening can once again be viewed as tools for empowerment and change.

Appendix: Relevant Excerpts From
Observation Instrument

Section 1: Demographics and Organizational Features

Date_____ Teacher_____

School_____

Observer_____

Intervention

Model _____

Setting Features_____

#Ss_____Gr_____

Organizational Features (Check all that apply)

Grouping

One-on-one_____ Small Group_____ Whole Class_____Pull-out program_____
In-class with regular T_____ In-class with asst/parent_____ Computer as T____

Time Block ——:——to——:——

Section 2: Texts Used (Check all that apply; Please write titles in notes)

Narrative Literature_____Non-fiction_____Poetry____Predictable Text_____
Decodable text_____Literature anthology_____Basals____Isolated words or phrases_____
Children's own writing____Other_____

Section 3: How Students Spend Time

How much time would you judge students were on task?

_____ 25%
_____ 50%
_____ 75%
_____ 100%

All names are pseudonyms.

Rebecca Powell, Georgetown College
Ellen McIntyre, University of Louisville
Elizabeth Rightmyer, University of Louisville

Article 3

RELEASING RESPONSIBILITY

DOUGLAS FISHER AND NANCY FREY

We must transfer responsibility for learning to our students gradually—and offer support at every step.

There is no shortage of teachers assigning students responsibility for their own learning. Who isn't familiar with the following scenarios?

- In a first-grade class, students independently complete practice pages from a workbook.

- A teacher gives her 4th graders a writing prompt and allows them 30 minutes to respond.

- Students in 8th grade are told to read Chapter 12 and answer the questions at the end.

Yes, students in these situations are responsible for their own work, but are they really learning? Students who do well in these kinds of activities are usually those who already understand the content. It's not hard to fill out a worksheet (or "shut-up sheet" as one of our colleagues calls it) when you have already mastered the information. Nor is it hard to answer end-of-chapter questions when you read well and are familiar with the genre of questions asked in textbooks.

But these "busywork" examples are not exemplars of true independent learning, which is a major goal of education. If students are to reach the high expectations we set for them, they need to be able to marshal previously learned concepts and apply them to achieve new understandings after they leave our schools.

SOURCE: From "Releasing Responsibility," by Douglas Fisher and Nancy Frey. In the November 2008 issue of *Educational Leadership*, 66(3), 32–37. © 2008 by ASCD. Used by permission. Learn more about ASCD at http//www.ascd.org.

How can we set students on a path to true independent learning? One way is to purposefully yet gradually release responsibility for learning from teacher to student (Fisher & Frey, 2008). To make this transfer of responsibility, we must give students supports that they can hold on to as they take the lead—not just push them onto the path and hope they find their way These supports include models of the kind of thinking they will need to do, access to academic language, peer collaboration, and guided instruction. We've found the following instructional routines work well for teachers who seek to promote lasting ownership of learning.

ESTABLISHING LEARNING OBJECTIVES

Teachers must clearly establish the purpose behind any activity, including what exactly students are supposed to do to successfully perform learning tasks. A coherent objective or purpose makes it easier for learners to gain access to background knowledge that they can use to build a schema for new learning. When the objective is clear and instructional tasks align with it, students can share responsibility for learning and will be motivated to do so. When the purpose for learning is muddy or students don't buy into it or perceive its relevance, they may complete many tasks but will have zero motivation and assume no responsibility. Students practically beg for an established purpose to their learning when they ask, "What do we gotta know?" and "What are we supposed to do with the information?"

The learning purposes that you provide students when they ask these guidance-seeking questions should include both content and language goals, especially for English language learners (Dong, 2004/2005; Hill & Flynn, 2006). Generally, teachers post on the wall and discuss with students exactly what is to be learned and how students should demonstrate that learning through oral or written language. Content goals should come directly from the standards. For example, in a unit focused on oceans, waves, and tides, a content goal for a given lesson might be to identify the phases of the moon.

The focus of the language goal should reflect students' needs. For example, a goal might focus on vocabulary. Students of all ages need to understand both specialized words (those that change meaning in different contexts, such as *expression*) and technical words (words rarely used outside of a specific discipline, such as *rhombus*). A vocabulary-related language goal for the study of the moon might be to use the terms *full, half, quarter,* and *new moon* to explain the phases of the moon.

Alternatively, the goal might focus on language structure, such as grammar, syntax, or sentence frames. Returning to the study of the moon, a structure-related goal might be to appropriately use sequence words (*first, next, then, last*) to explain the phases of the moon. Or the goal might be based on mastering certain functions of language, such as questioning, summarizing, explaining, or persuading. A function-related language goal might be to explain how the moon, earth, and sun move through their phases.

TEACHER MODELING

Modeling is another crucial component of releasing responsibility. Humans are hardwired to imitate other humans (Winerman, 2005). Students deserve to see an example of the kind of thinking and language a new task will require before they engage in that task independently, and teachers can provide that example. Through modeling—either by thinking aloud or by showing students their written notes—teachers reveal what goes on in their minds as they solve problems, read, write, or generate ideas. Modeling does not mean providing explanations or questioning students; it means demonstrating the way experts think as they approach problems.

Expert teachers prepare students for independent reading by focusing their modeling on comprehension, word solving, text structures, and text features (Fisher, Frey, & Lapp, 2008).

Choosing Strategies for Comprehension

Good readers deploy a number of cognitive strategies as they read, such as questioning, inferring, making connections, summarizing, and predicting. The key is to know when to use each strategy and to be able to use it automatically.

For example, predicting can help a reader create meaning when the author provides specific kinds of information, but it isn't a good strategy for understanding all texts. To model using this strategy well, a teacher might share his or her prediction when reading a certain text and then ask students to make predictions. A 9th grade English teacher we observed paused while reading the short story "Kipling and I" by Jesús Colón out loud and speculated on why the author would describe a gilt-framed poem so early in the story. "This must be an important object to the narrator," she mused. "I'll need to keep reading to find out." Later in the same story she reflected on the protagonist decision to burn the poem to keep warm:

> I wonder if this means that the inspirational message of the poem is being destroyed, too? I could understand this in two ways: that he feels the poem is inside of him and he doesn't need the object anymore, or that a dream has died. I'm going to reread that earlier section where the character describes the poem's importance to see if I missed anything that would help me understand the deeper meaning.

With enough modeling and practice, students will imitate behaviors like this and reach for appropriate strategies automatically as they read complex texts on their own.

Teaching Word Solving

Given the demands of academic vocabulary and the effect that word knowledge has on comprehension, teachers need to show students how they can figure out the meaning of unfamiliar words on their own. Students must practice this skill enough so that it becomes automatic. There are two main word-solving strategies:

- *Using context clues.* We call this an "outside the word" strategy. A teacher might pause on an unfamiliar word and model using an illustration and familiar words in the same sentence to make inferences about the mystery word's meaning. The teacher's modeling should get across the fact that context clues don't always help and may be misleading. For example, a teacher might draw students' attention to a diagram of the solar system as she notes that an elliptical orbit is shaped like an oval: "I wasn't sure at first what *elliptical* meant, but the picture helped me understand that an elliptical shape is not a perfect circle."

- *Looking "inside the word."* This strategy involves looking at prefixes, suffixes, bases, roots, or cognates of the target word for clues to meaning. For example, while reading a science text out loud, Mr. Bonine stopped at the word *carnivore* and modeled his realization that *carnivore* was related to the Spanish word *carne* (meat). He noted that this probably means *carnivore* has something to do with meat and went on to use context clues—the fact that the word was describing an animal's habits—to conclude that the word meant meat eating.

Teachers should also model using dictionaries, Internet resources, or even reliable peers to understand a word, for those times when neither context clues nor looking inside the word helps.

Highlighting Text Structures

One way readers extract meaning from texts is through recognizing common text structures. Almost all narrative texts, for example, use a "story grammar" that includes character, setting, plot, conflict, resolution, dialogue, and various literary devices. Teachers should model using these structures as a tool for understanding stories. For example, Mr. Goodwin paused in his reading of *The Outsiders* by S. E. Hinton to point out how a character's recitation of Robert Frost's poem "Nothing Gold Can Stay" at a key point in the story helps reveal the themes of loss and redemption that are central to the novel—and that using a recurring phrase or image to highlight an underlying theme is a common text structure.

Nonfiction texts also have internal structures, such as problem-solution, cause-effect, compare-contrast, and description. Noticing which text structure a particular informational text uses helps readers predict what kind of content the author might present next. It also helps people remember what they read and organize their thinking about a text.

For example, while reading a passage about the construction of the transcontinental railroad, Ms. Allen paused at the point where the author introduced the problem of pay differences between Chinese and white workers and told the class:

> Now here's a problem. I can predict that the solution to the problem will come next. That's how many authors write, by introducing a problem followed by a solution. I might even help myself remember this information by taking notes using a problem and solution chart. In many cases, the solution to one problem creates new problems. I wonder if that will be the case here.

When Ms. Allen came to the part in the text describing the Chinese workers' strike for higher wages, she pointed out that the author was following up a problem with its solution.

Explaining Text Features

Students often need help understanding the text features included with many academic readings, such as tables, charts, figures, bold and italicized words, and headings. Many students aren't even sure when they should read text features—before, during, or after the text. But a lot of essential information can be presented in these features.

Teachers should model how to thoughtfully analyze text features. For example, while looking at a table in a math textbook on the use of distance as a function of time, Ms. Burrow pointed out the column and row headings and showed students how to use them to find information. Ms. Johnson modeled how to interpret a legend on a map in the geography textbook to find the latitude and longitude of a city.

COLLABORATIVE WORK

Armed with a clear learning objective and examples of the kind of thinking and actions they should engage in, students will be ready to work—but not to work independently yet. First, they need time to try out their fledgling understandings in collaborative work with their peers. Collaborative learning transfers more responsibility to students, yet provides them with peer support.

In any content area, students learn more and retain information longer when they work in productive groups (Totten, Sills, Digby, & Russ, 1991). Students who work in collaborative groups tend to be more satisfied with their classes, complete more assignments, and generally like school better (Summers, 2006). To be productive, groups need sufficient time to interact, time lines, clear roles for everyone in the group, and tasks that truly call for interdependence. Ideal collaborative learning tasks are those that cannot be accomplished just as well by one individual; they require interaction and the natural give and take of learning.

But the real key to collaborative groups lies in accountability. Each student must be held accountable for some aspect of the work. Unfortunately that's not always the case: We can all remember group work in which one student did all the work and everyone else got the credit. This situation not only prevents some students from learning but also thwarts teachers' attempts to check for each student's understanding and link instruction with formative assessment. In addition to holding students individually accountable, teachers should hold the entire group accountable for completing tasks. Tasks can vary from something as simple as straightening up the science area after a complicated experiment to something as complex as writing a group summary of a lesson.

In her geometry class, Ms. Chen has students complete a collaborative poster for each proof they solve. Each student contributes to the poster using an individually assigned marker color. In addition, the group must ensure that each of its members can explain the proof independently. This requires a significant amount of reteaching, negotiation, support, and trust. Students assume responsibility for their learning and the learning of their peers.

GUIDED INSTRUCTION

While modeling and collaborative work provide a great start, some learners will require guided instruction to successfully assume responsibility for their own learning. Guided instruction is the strategic use of cues, prompts, or questions to facilitate student thinking. Teachers should base guided instruction on what formative assessments reveal that students need. Such instruction is most effective with small groups.

In working with a group of students who misunderstood photosynthesis, Ms. Grant used a series of questions and prompts to increase understanding.

Ms. Grant: Some of you thought that plants ate soil to grow. Do you remember the video we saw about photosynthesis? What role did soil play in that video?

Destiny: Well, it wasn't about the dirt. It was about the sun and carbon dioxide.

Andrew: And how the plants make oxygen for humans.

Ms. Grant: Plants make oxygen for humans?

Andrew: Well, I guess that they'd make oxygen even if there were no humans.

Michael: It's called a by-product. They don't make oxygen for humans. They just make oxygen.

Ms. Grant: And what is left, once they've made this oxygen?

Destiny: Carbon. They take in carbon dioxide and then give off oxygen, so carbon is left.

Ms. Grant: And what do you know about carbon?

Guided instruction gives teachers an opportunity to engage students' thinking without telling them what to think—and a chance to scaffold students' understanding before they complete tasks independently.

FROM COMPETENT NOVICE TO EXPERT

Newly (or barely) learned tasks do not make for good independent learning activities. Unfortunately, educators often ask students to assume full responsibility for their learning prematurely in the instructional cycle. In the MetLife survey about homework (Markow, Kim, & Liebman, 2007), 26 percent of secondary teachers confessed that they "very often or often" assign homework because they run out of time in class to cover material. The likelihood of a student successfully completing newly introduced tasks alone, away from fellow learners or the teacher, is slim.

Teachers should reserve independent work for review and reinforcement of concepts that have been previously taught. This phase of the instructional framework is ideal for the spiral review that most educators know their students need. In addition, it helps build connections between previously learned concepts and new ones. For example, if an independent learning task to review the (previously taught) phases of the moon coincides with new instruction on the movement of planets around the sun, the task will not only reinforce students' knowledge of the moon's phases but also deepen their understanding of patterns of movement in the sky and how planets influence one another.

Well-structured independent learning tasks are the ultimate way to build self-esteem through competence. By the time a student has reached this phase, he or she should be working at the level of competent novice; the purpose of additional work is to refine skills and become expert. Isn't this how many of us learned to be good teachers?

Douglas Fisher and Nancy Frey are Professors of Literacy at San Diego State University in California and teach English at Health Sciences High and Middle College in San Diego, California.

Section II

The Assessment/Instruction Relationship

Overview

Understanding the assessment-instruction relationship is paramount for successful planning and teaching to meet students' individual needs. The articles in this section are provided to help readers view their assessments as an integral part of the instructional process and as significant tools for helping students learn literacy. Certainly, teachers who use assessment data to plan and provide (corrective) instruction can improve their teaching and help students learn.

In "How Classroom Assessments Improve Learning," Guskey (2003) suggests that "assessments must be part of an ongoing effort to help students learn." In this article, the author helps readers understand the importance of classroom assessments that are directly related to teaching objectives. Guskey argues that when we focus on high-stakes tests, which do little more than rank schools and students, we miss the most compelling benefits of using assessments. In "Principles for Literacy Assessment," Johnston and Costello (2005) offer a framework for understanding literacy assessment that accounts for relational aspects and "reminds us of the broader picture of literacy assessment of which we often lose sight." Literacy is complex. Therefore, literacy assessment must be multidimensional and focus on more than an individual skill. In addition, the authors remind readers that assessment, like learning, is social and must be seen in context.

What do standardized test scores tell us about what struggling readers really need? This is the question Valencia and Riddle Buly tackle in their 2004 article, "Behind Test Scores." Some schools/districts are on the search for programs that might be "solutions for poor test performance," and others spend a significant amount of time preparing students to be high-stakes-test ready. The authors suggest that instead we examine the reasons underlying *why* so many of our children struggle on these assessments, and more specifically, *why* individual children fail high-stakes tests, which do not themselves provide teachers with enough information to plan instruction to meet students' needs.

STRATEGY

Although there are many purposes for assessments, we believe they are best used to improve instruction and, in turn, student learning. The articles in Section II differentiate purposes between individual and institutional assessments, as well as those that are summative and formative. Use the "Dual Entry Journal" (Barone, 1990) to organize salient quotes and structure your thinking about the purposes of assessment. Completing this strategy will help you maximize your understanding of the articles in this section.

DUAL ENTRY JOURNAL

(Barone, 1990)

DIRECTIONS

As you read the articles in this section, copy important or interesting quotes into the left column of the journal page. Reflect on the quotes in the right column, thinking about why you chose the quote, what it means to you, and how it connects to your experiences. Remember to indicate where the quote is located in text, so you may return to the text for clarification if needed.

What I Read	What's in My Head

SOURCE: Barone, D. (1990). The Written Responses of Young Children: Beyond Comprehension to Story Understanding. *The New Advocate, 3,* 49–56.

Article 4

HOW CLASSROOM ASSESSMENTS IMPROVE LEARNING

THOMAS R. GUSKEY

Teachers who develop useful assessments, provide corrective instruction, and give students second chances to demonstrate success can improve their instruction and help students learn.

Large-scale assessments, like all assessments, are designed for a specific purpose. Those used in most states today are designed to rank-order schools and students for the purposes of accountability—and some do so fairly well. But assessments designed for ranking are generally not good instruments for helping teachers improve their instruction or modify their approach to individual students. First, students take them at the end of the school year, when most instructional activities are near completion. Second, teachers don't receive the results until two or three months later, by which time their students have usually moved on to other teachers. And third, the results that teachers receive usually lack the level of detail needed to target specific improvements (Barton, 2002; Kifer, 2001).

The assessments best suited to guide improvements in student learning are the quizzes, tests, writing assignments, and other assessments teachers administer on a regular basis in their classrooms. Teachers trust the results from these assessments because of their direct relation to classroom instructions goals. Plus, results are immediate and easy to analyze at the individual student level. To use classroom assessments to make improvements, however, teachers must change both their view of assessments and their interpretation of results. Specifically, they need to see their assessments as an integral part of the instruction process and as crucial for helping students learn.

SOURCE: Guskey, T. R. (2003). How Classroom Assessments Improve Learning. *Educational Leadership, 60*(5), 6–11. Reprinted by permission of the author.

Despite the importance of assessments in education today, few teachers receive much formal training in assessment design or analysis. A recent survey showed, for example, that fewer that half the states require competence in assessment for licensure as a teacher (Stiggins, 1999). Lacking specific training, teachers rely heavily on the assessments offered by the publisher of their textbooks or instructional materials. When no suitable assessments are available, teachers construct their own in a haphazard fashion, with questions and essay prompts similar to the ones that their teachers used. They treat assessments as evaluation devices to administer when instructional activities are completed and to use primarily for assigning students' grades.

To use assessments to improve instruction and student learning, teachers need to change their approach to assessments in three important ways.

MAKE ASSESSMENTS USEFUL

For Students

Nearly every student has suffered the experience of spending hours preparing for a major assessment, only to discover that the material that he or she had studied was different from what the teacher chose to emphasize on the assessment. This experience teaches students two unfortunate lessons. First, students realize that hard work and effort don't pay off in school because the time and effort that they spent studying had little or no influence on the results. And second, they learn that they cannot trust their teachers (Guskey, 2000a). These are hardly the lessons that responsible teachers want their students to learn.

Nonetheless, this experience is common because many teachers still mistakenly believe that they must keep their assessments secret. As a result, students come to regard assessments as guessing games, especially from the middle grades on. They view success as depending on how well they can guess what their teachers will ask on quizzes, tests, and other assessments.

Some teachers even take pride in their ability to out-guess students. They ask questions about isolated concepts or obscure understandings just to see whether students are reading carefully. Generally, these teachers don't include such "gotcha" questions maliciously, but rather—often unconsciously—because such questions were asked of them when they were students.

Classroom assessments that serve as meaningful sources of information don't surprise students. Instead, these assessments reflect the concepts and skills that the teacher emphasized in class, along with the teacher's clear criteria for judging students' performance. These concepts, skills, and criteria align with the teacher's instructional activities and, ideally, with state or district standards. Students see these assessments as fair measures of important learning goals. Teachers facilitate learning by providing students with important feedback on their learning progress and by helping them identify learning problems (Bloom, Madaus, & Hastings, 1981; Stiggins, 2002).

Critics sometimes contend that this approach means "teaching to the test." But the crucial issue is, What determines the content and methods of teaching? If the test is the primary determinant of what teachers teach and how they teach it then we are indeed "teaching to the test." But if desired learning goals are the foundation of students' instructional experiences, then assessments of student learning are simply extensions of those same goals. Instead of "teaching to the test," teachers are more accurately "testing what they teach." If a concept or skill is important enough to assess, then it should be important enough to teach. And if it is not important enough to teach, then there's little justification for assessing it.

For Teachers

The best classroom assessments also serve as meaningful sources of information for teachers, helping them identify what they taught well and what they need to work on. Gathering this vital information does not require a sophisticated statistical analysis of assessment results. Teachers need only make a simple tally of how many students missed each assessment item or failed to meet a specific criterion. State assessments sometimes provide similar item-by-item information, but concerns about item security and the cost of developing new items each year usually make assessments developers reluctant to offer such detailed information. Once teachers have made specific tallies, they can pay special attention to the trouble spots—those items or criteria missed by large numbers of students in the class.

In reviewing these results, the teacher must first consider the quality of the item or criterion. Perhaps the question is ambiguously worded or the criterion is unclear. Perhaps students misinterpreted the question. Whatever the case, teachers must determine whether these items adequately address the knowledge, understanding, or skill that they were intended to measure.

If teachers find no obvious problems with the item or criterion, then they must turn their attention to their teaching. When as many as half the students in a class answer a clear question incorrectly or fail to meet a particular criterion, it's not a student learning problem—it's a teaching problem. Whatever teaching strategy was used, whatever examples were employed, or whatever explanation was offered, it simply didn't work.

Analyzing assessment results in this way means setting aside some powerful ego issues. Many teachers may initially say, "I taught them. They just didn't learn it!" But on reflection, most recognize that their effectiveness is not defined on the basis of what they do as teachers but rather on what their students are able to do. Can effective teaching take place in the absence of learning? Certainly not.

Some argue that such a perspective puts too much responsibility on teachers and not enough on students. Occasionally, teachers respond "Don't students have responsibilities in this process? Shouldn't students display initiative and personal accountability?"

Indeed, teachers and students share responsibility for learning. Even with valiant teaching efforts, we cannot guarantee that all students will learn everything excellently. Only rarely do

teachers find items or assessment criteria that every student answers correctly. A few students are never willing to put forth the necessary effort, but these students tend to be the exception, not the rule. If a teacher is reaching fewer than half of the students in the class, the teacher's method of instruction needs to improve. And teachers need this kind of evidence to help target their instructional improvement efforts.

FOLLOW ASSESSMENTS WITH CORRECTIVE INSTRUCTION

If assessments provide information for both students and teachers, then they cannot mark the end of learning. Instead, assessments must be followed by high-quality, corrective instruction designed to remedy whatever learning errors the assessment identified (see Guskey, 1997). To charge ahead knowing that students have not learned certain concepts or skills well would be foolish. Teachers must therefore follow their assessments with instructional alternatives that present those concepts in new ways and engage students in different and more appropriate learning experiences.

High-quality, corrective instruction is not the same as reteaching, which often consists simply of restating the original explanations louder and more slowly. Instead, the teacher must use approaches that accommodate differences in students' learning styles and intelligences (Sternberg, 1994). Although teachers generally try to incorporate different teaching approaches when they initially plan their lessons, corrective instruction involves extending and strengthening that work. In addition, those students who have few or no learning errors to correct should receive enrichment activities to help broaden and expand their learning. Materials designed for gifted and talented students provide an excellent resource for such activities.

Developing ideas for corrective instruction and enrichment activities can be difficult, especially if teachers believe that they must do it alone, but structured professional developing opportunities can help teachers share strategies and collaborate on teaching techniques (Guskey, 1998, 2000b). Faculty meetings devoted to examining classroom assessment results and developing alternative strategies can be highly effective. District-level personnel and collaborative partnerships with local colleges and universities offer wonderful resources for ideas and practical advice.

Occasionally, teachers express concern that if they take time to offer corrective instruction, they will sacrifice curriculum coverage. Because corrective work is initially best done during class and under the teacher's direction, early instructional units will typically involve an extra class period or two. Teachers who ask students to complete corrective work independently, outside of class, generally find that those students who most need to spend time on corrective work are the least likely to do so.

As students become accustomed to this corrective process and realize the personal benefits it offers, however, the teacher can drastically reduce the amount of class time allocated to such work and accomplish much of it through homework assignments or in special study sessions before or after school. And by not allowing minor errors to become major learning problems, teachers better prepare students for subsequent learning tasks, eventually need less time for corrective work (Whiting, Van Burgh, & Render, 1995), and can proceed at a more rapid pace in later learning units. By pacing their instructional units more flexibly, most teachers find that they need not sacrifice curriculum coverage to offer students the benefits of corrective instruction.

GIVE SECOND CHANCES TO DEMONSTRATE SUCCESS

To become an integral part of the instructional process, assessments cannot be a one-shot, do-or-die experience for students. Instead, assessments must be part of an ongoing effort to help students learn. And if teachers follow assessments with helpful corrective instruction, then students should have a second chance to demonstrate their new level of competence and understanding. This second chance helps determine the effectiveness of the corrective instruction and offers students another opportunity to experience success in learning.

Writing teachers have long recognized the many benefits of a second chance. They know that students rarely write well on an initial attempt. Teachers build into the writing process several opportunities for students to gain feedback on early drafts and then to use that feedback to revise and improve their writing. Teachers of other subjects frequently balk at the idea, however—mostly because it differs from their personal learning experiences.

Some teachers express concern that giving students a second chance might be unfair and that "life isn't like that." They point out that that a surgeon doesn't get a second chance to perform an operation successfully and a pilot doesn't get a second chance to land a jumbo jet safely. Because of the very high stakes involved, each must get it right the first time.

But how did these highly skilled professionals learn their craft? The first operation performed by that surgeon was on a cadaver—a situation that allows a lot of latitude for mistakes. Similarly, the pilot spent many hours in a flight simulator before ever attempting a landing from the cockpit. Such experiences allowed them to learn from their mistakes and to improve their performance. Similar instructional techniques are used in nearly every professional endeavor. Only in schools do students face the prospect of one-shot, do-or-die assessments, with no chance to demonstrate what they learned from previous mistakes.

All educators strive to have their students become lifelong learners and develop learning-to-learn skills. What better learning-to-learn skill is there than learning from one's mistakes? A mistake can be the beginning of learning. Some assessment experts argue, in fact, that students learn nothing from a successful performance. Rather, students learn best when their initial performance is less than successful, for then they can gain direction on how to improve (Wiggins, 1998).

Other teachers suggest that it's unfair to offer the same privileges and high grades to students who require a second chance that we offer to those students who demonstrate a high level of learning on the initial assessment. After all, these students may simply have failed to prepare appropriately. Certainly, we should recognize students who do well on the initial assessment and provide opportunities for them to extend their learning through enrichment activities. But those students who do well on a second assessment have also learned well. More important, their poor performance on the first assessment may not have been their fault. Maybe the teaching strategies used during the initial instruction were inappropriate for these students, but the corrective instruction proved more effective. If we determine grades on the basis of performance and these students have performed at a high level then they certainly deserve the same grades as those who scored well on their first try.

A comparable example is the driver's license examination. Many individuals do not pass their driver's test on the first attempt. On the second or third try, however, they may reach the same high level of performance as others did on their first. Should these drivers be restricted, for instance, to driving in fair weather only? In inclement weather, should they be required to pull their cars over and park until the weather clears? Of course not, because they eventually met the same high performance standards as those who passed on their initial attempt they receive the same privileges. The same should hold true for students who show that they, too, have learned well.

SIMILAR SITUATIONS

Using assessments as sources of information, following assessments with corrective instruction, and giving students a second chance are steps in a process that all teachers use naturally when they tutor individual students. If the student makes a mistake, the teacher stops and points out the mistake. The teacher then explains that concept in a different way. Finally, the teacher asks another question or poses a similar problem to ensure the student's understanding before going on. The challenge for teachers is to use their classroom assessments in similar ways to provide all students with this sort of individualized assistance.

Successful coaches use the same process. Immediately following a gymnast's performance on the balance beam, for example, the coach explains to her what she did correctly and what could be improved. The coach then offers specific strategies for improvement and encourages her to try again. As the athlete repeats her performance, the coach watches carefully to ensure that she had corrected the problem.

Successful students typically know how to take corrective action on their own. They save their assessments and review the items or criteria that they missed. They rework problems, look up answers in their textbooks or other resource materials, and ask the teacher about ideas or concepts that they don't understand. Less successful students rarely take such initiative. After looking at their grades, they typically crumple up their assessments and deposit them in the trash can as they leave the classroom. Teachers who use classroom assessments as part of the instructional process help all of their students do what the most successful students have learned to do for themselves.

THE BENEFITS OF ASSESSMENT

Using classroom assessment to improve student learning is not a new idea. More that 30 years ago, Benjamin Bloom showed how to conduct this process in practical and highly effective ways when he described the practice of mastery learning (Bloom, 1968, 1971). But since that time, the emphasis on assessments as tools for accountability has diverted attention from this more important and fundamental purpose.

Assessments can be a vital component in our efforts to improve education. But as long as we use them only as a means to rank schools and students, we will miss their more powerful benefits. We must focus instead on helping teachers change the way they use assessments results, improve the quality of their classroom assessments, and align their assessments with valued learning goals and state or district standards. When teachers' classroom assessments become an integral part of the instructional process and a central ingredient in their efforts to help students learn, the benefits of assessment for both students and teachers will be boundless.

Thomas R. Guskey is Professor of Education Policy Studies and Evaluation in the College of Education at the University of Kentucky.

Article 5

PRINCIPLES FOR LITERACY ASSESSMENT

PETER JOHNSTON AND PAULA COSTELLO

In a "learning society" everyone will need to become, and remain, committed to learning. If assessment potentially represents the key to achieving this, it also currently represents the biggest single stumbling block.

(Broadfoot, 2002, p. 6)

"What gets assessed is what gets taught" is a common assertion whose meaning is often underestimated. It is not just *what* gets assessed, but *how* it is assessed that has implications for what is learned. When a child who is asked the meaning of his report card grades responds, "If I knew that I'd be the teacher" he is saying something about the relationships of authority learned in the process of assessment. When a teacher wishes out loud that her faculty "could discuss retention and realistic expectations for grade levels without the nastiness and accusations," she is also reporting on the relational aspect of assessment practices (Johnston, 2003, p. 90). Our goal in this article is to offer a framework for understanding literacy assessment that incorporates these dimensions and reminds us of the broader picture of literacy assessment of which we often lose sight.

LITERACY IS A COMPLEX CONSTRUCT

Although we often think of literacy as a set of all-purpose skills and strategies to be learned, it is more complex, more local, more personal, and more social than that. Becoming literate involves developing identities, relationships, dispositions,

SOURCE: Johnston, P., & Costello, P. (2005). Principles for Literacy Assessment. *Reading Research Quarterly,* *40*(2), 256–267. Reprinted by permission of the International Reading Association.

and values as much as acquiring strategies for working with print (Brandt, 2001; Collins & Blot, 2003; Gee, 2000). Children becoming literate are being apprenticed into ways of living with people as much as with symbols. Consequently, literacy assessment must be grounded in current understandings of literacy and society (Johnson & Kress, 2003; Johnston, 1999). We have to consider what kind of literacy might benefit individuals, what kind of literate society we aspire to, and what assessment might best serve those ends.

For example, what kind of literacy assessment will enable children to live in and contribute to an increasingly democratic society? Democracy has to do with "the way persons attend to one another, care for one another, and interact with one another . . . [and] the capacity to look at things as though they could be otherwise" (Greene, 1985, p. 3), and citizens who "have the convictions and enthusiasms of their own responses, yet . . . are willing to keep an open mind about alternate points of view, and . . . to negotiate meanings and actions that respect both individual diversity and community needs" (Pradl, 1996, pp. 11–12). In other words, our literacy assessment practices must foster a literate disposition towards *reciprocity* (Carr & Claxton, 2002); that is, "a willingness to engage in joint learning tasks, to express uncertainties and ask questions, to take a variety of roles in joint learning enterprises and to take others' purposes and perspectives into account" (p. 16).

What might such assessment look like? The National Educational Monitoring Project (NEMP) in New Zealand is charged with taking stock of the nation's progress in educating a literate society. To this end, the NEMP includes items such as providing a group of children with a set of books from which they, as a class library committee, must make their best selection. Students individually justify their choices to the group before the group negotiates and justifies the final selection. The negotiation has a time limit and is videotaped for analysis of reading and literate interactions (Flockton & Crooks, 1996). This item requires children to evaluate the qualities of texts, take a stance, make persuasive arguments,

actively listen, and negotiate a collective position— all independent and interdependent literate practices central to democratic classrooms and society. The item reflects and encourages an individual and mutual disposition toward reciprocity, a foundation for a democratic literacy.

Literacy has complications that assessment must deal with. Not only is literacy complex and social but also the literate demands of the world keep changing with exponential acceleration. The apparent boundaries between spoken and written words and their conventions have been obliterated by instant messaging, book tapes, cell-phone text messaging, speech translation software, interactive hypertext, and the facility with which text and image (moving or still) are fused. Literate demands are changing so rapidly that we can't predict with certainty what kindergartners will face in adulthood. We do know however, that they will need to be resilient learners (Carr & Claxton, 2002) to maintain their literate development in the face of the increasingly rapid transformations of literacy in their communities.

Because "what is assessed is taught," literacy assessment should reflect and encourage resilience—a disposition to focus on learning when the going gets tough, to quickly recover from setbacks, and to adapt. Its opposite is brittleness—the disposition to avoid challenging tasks and to shift into ego-defensive behaviors when learning is difficult. A brittle learner believes that having difficulty with a literate task reveals a lack of "ability." A brittle disposition in children prior to first grade negatively predicts word recognition in grades 1 and 2, and is a better predictor than assessments of phonological awareness (Niemi & Poskiparta, 2002). This negative effect on learning is amplified by the pressures of competitive and overly difficult situations, particularly where ability is the primary emphasis. These are exactly the contexts produced by current testing practices.

Resilience can be assessed. For example, teachers can collect specific examples of resilience with quotes and artifacts to produce documented narratives (Carr & Claxton, 2002) for later review with the student and other stakeholders (see also

Himley & Carini, 2000). In fact, the process of generating such assessment narratives will foster a resilient literate disposition (Johnston, 2004).

We begin with these uncommon examples of literacy assessment to suggest that, although assessing literacy in its complexity can be challenging, it is possible. It is also important. Failure to keep our attention on the bigger picture might not be a problem except that, intended or not, literacy assessment instruments define literacy within the assessment activity and, particularly when the stakes are high, within instruction (Smith, 1991). The higher the stakes, the more necessary it is that assessments reflect the breadth of literacy. Alas, most assessment practices, particularly testing practices, oversample narrow aspects of literacy, such as sound-symbol knowledge (Stallman & Pearson, 1991), and undersample other aspects such as writing, any media beyond print on paper, and ways of framing texts and literacy, such as the critical literacies necessary for managing the coercive pressures of literacy.

The more an assessment focuses on a narrow sample of literate behavior, as happens in individual tests, the more undersampling occurs. Literacy assessments distorted in this way affect instruction in many subtle ways. For example, the extensive use of pencil-and-paper state tests has forced many teachers to decrease instructional use of computers, particularly for writing. This problem is most damaging in urban and poor-performing schools (Russell & Abrams, 2004). The tests simultaneously risk underestimating the writing competence of students used to writing on computers, while reducing the likelihood of students not familiar with computer writing to ever become so.

ASSESSMENT IS A SOCIAL PRACTICE

Assessment is a social practice that involves noticing, representing, and responding to children's literate behaviors, rendering them meaningful for particular purposes and audiences (Johnston & Rogers, 2001). Teacher feedback to students on their literate behavior is assessment just as much as is grading students' work, classifying students as handicapped, certifying students as being "above grade level," or establishing a school as "in need of improvement" (Black & Wiliam, 1998a; Johnston, 1993). *Testing* is a subset of assessment practices in which children's literate behavior is elicited in more controlled conditions.

Although assessment often is viewed as a technical matter of developing accurate measuring instruments, it is more centrally a set of social practices in which various tools are used for various purposes. For example, leveled books can be used as part of teaching in order to monitor children's early reading growth without the use of tests. Some books can even be kept aside specifically for assessment. The same procedure could also be used as part of holding teachers accountable for children's progress (Paris, 2002). However, this is a very different social practice and would invite greater concern about the measurement precision of the "levels" and different social action. For example, teachers would be more likely to use the assessment books for instruction and to focus the curriculum on the accuracy of word reading.

Although the instrument is the same, it has different meaning in the different social practice. In the accountability context, we worry more about the measurement qualities of the instrument in order to be fair. Fairness in the teaching context is more about ensuring that children are developing adequately, focusing instruction, and ensuring that the discourse of "levels" does not dominate the children's interactions and self-assessments. Paradoxically, though we worry more about the psychometric properties of an instrument in the accountability context, the social properties of the *use* of the instrument, such as the defensiveness it might induce, or the constriction of the curriculum, can be of far more significance.

With the realization that assessments are social practices has come the awareness that the validity of an assessment instrument cannot be established outside of its consequences in use

(Messick, 1994; Moss, 1998). Literacy assessment practices affect the constructs used to organize teaching practice and to represent children (Johnston, 1997; Moss). This is especially powerful when tests are used for purposes that attach high stakes such as teacher salaries, student retention, graduation, or classification.

Although there are occasional studies claiming that high-stakes testing has no negative effects, or even some positive effects on children's learning, there are many more studies showing the opposite and with greater specificity. For example, high-stakes accountability testing has consistently been demonstrated to undermine teaching and learning (Allington & McGill-Franzen, 1995; Morrison & Joan, 2002; Rex & Nelson, 2004; Smith, 1991; Smith & Rottenberg, 1991) particularly for lower achieving students (Harlen & Crick, 2003). It restricts the literacy curriculum, thus defeating the original intention to improve literacy learning. Teachers under threat drop from the curriculum complex literacy practices involving, for example, multimedia, research, and role-play, and at the same time their learning community is disrupted (Rex & Nelson). Increasing accountability pressure on teachers is counterproductive, especially when teachers already have an internal accountability system. It results instead in "escalating teacher outrage, diminishing moral [sic], and the exiting of committed teachers . . . from teaching" (Rex & Nelson, p. 1324).

The dictum "first do no harm" has become part of validity in theory, though rarely in assessment practice. Indeed, although high-stakes testing has lately been supported by arguments that it will reduce literacy achievement differences associated with race and poverty, there is evidence that the long-term effect of such testing is to create a curriculum that extends stratification rather than reducing it (Darling-Hammond, 2004; McNeil, 2000).

INDIVIDUAL AND INSTITUTIONAL LEARNING

Literacy assessment is part of a larger project to educate children both for their immediate and long-term benefit and for the evolution of society. The implication of this is that literacy assessment must be grounded in current understandings of individual and institutional learning. There are two general kinds of assessment—summative and formative. Summative assessments are the backward-looking assessments *of* learning, the tests we most commonly think of that summarize or judge performance as in educational monitoring, teacher and student accountability testing, and certification (Black & Wiliam, 1998a). These have not been overtly associated with current understandings of individual or institutional learning.

Indeed, the theories of learning underlying psychometric practices have largely been implicit, individualistic, and behavioristic (Shepard, 1991). For example, current accountability testing, driven by psychometrics, is based on rewarding and punishing students, teachers, and school systems. The evidence so far is that, rather than accomplishing the intended learning, these practices shift participants' goals toward avoidance of punishment, which thwarts the goal of improving the quality of literacy learning for all students and particularly for historically low-achieving students (McNeil, 2000).

Formative assessment, or assessment *for* learning, is the forward-looking assessment that occurs in the process of learning, the feedback the teacher provides to the student, and the nature of the feedback matters (Crooks, 1988). For example, rather than praise or grades, comments improve performance, though praise keeps students thinking they are doing well (Black & Wiliam, 1998a). Feedback that focuses attention on traits such as ability, smartness, or goodness, undermines resilience (Dweck, 1999).

But the *process* of formative assessment is also critical. For example, the most common assessment practices associated with comprehension involve asking for retellings or asking questions to which teachers already know the answers. These interactional patterns teach children about how literacy is done and how authority is organized (Johnston, Jiron, & Day, 2001; Nystrand, Gamoran, Kachur, & Prendergast, 1997). Arranging for children to ask the questions and selectively discuss them can provide more interesting information regarding children's understanding, while simultaneously socializing them into productive literacy practices and identities (Comeyras, 1995).

Formative assessment is specifically directed toward affecting learning. Its validity depends on its ability to do so (Crooks, 2001). This means that the validity of formative assessment rests on factors not normally considered in discussions of validity, such as trust and sensitivity, the social supports, and motivations of the classroom. Task factors will be important, such as the nature and difficulty of the task, its personal and external relevance, the articulation of task features, and performance criteria. Each of these will affect the development of self-assessment. The nature and timing of feedback will be important. But because human interactions are structured around who the participants think they are and what they think they are doing, teachers' understanding of such things as literate practice, how children learn, and cultural difference will also be important, as will their social imagination and insight on conceptual confusions.

While this is true of formative assessments, summative assessment practices affect learning too. Some, such as accountability testing, do so deliberately. Consequently, to be valid, *all* assessment practices should be grounded in current and consistent understandings of learning, including the above factors. Both summative and formative assessments participate in socializing children's and teachers' self-assessments, with implications for control of learning and the management of self-assessment to serve learning goals.

Basing assessment on current understandings about learning does not simply negate principles of psychometrics. For example, neo-Piagetian theories of learning view the process of confronting and resolving discrepancies as a primary vehicle for learning (Schaffer, 1996; Tudge & Rogoff, 1989). A self-extending literacy learning system requires children to attend to discrepancies between cue systems, for example (Clay, 1991). In a similar way, learning communities require disjunctures, such as between minority and mainstream performance, to stimulate learning.

However, as with formative assessment, the independent sources of information providing the conflict must be trusted, and measurement principles can help provide the grounds for this. The context in which such discrepancies are presented affects what is learned. The assessment activity must enable productive *engagement* of the disjunctures and foster productive use of data.

Thinking about assessment in terms of individual and institutional learning can change the way we value technical characteristics of assessment. For example, consider the role of consistent agreement among examiners (reliability). Complex authentic assessment items such as those used in the NEMP often reduce reliability (Shavelson, Baxter, & Pine, 1992). Weighty assessment practices like sorting and certifying students demand practices that ensure agreement—the higher the stakes, the more important this agreement.

Disagreements in this context are viewed as "measurement error," which leads to a reduction of complex authentic items. By contrast, in low-stakes and more formative assessment, disagreement among teachers about the meaning of particular documentation, such as portfolios, can open an important learning space by inviting discussions that lead to improvements in instruction and assessment itself. Indeed, this negotiation of values, qualities, and purposes is the most productive part of standards-based or performance-based assessments (Falk, 2001; Johnston, 1989; Moss & Schutz, 2001; Sadler, 1987). Complex and problematic examples provoke the most productive teaching-learning conversations. In other words, when the stakes are low, the less reliable the assessment is—to a point—the more likely it is to produce new learning and innovation in teaching. Because the validity of an assessment rests partly upon its consequences, improving teaching increases the validity of the assessment. In this context, imperfect reliability, contrary to psychometric theory, can increase validity.

As a concrete example, consider the NEMP test item mentioned at the beginning of this article in which children evaluate books individually and collaboratively as a library committee. The item and instrument are possible because NEMP uses a light matrix sample. Different children take a different selection of items; nationally, only a sample of children takes any items at all. The sampling system is possible because the emphasis is on the performance of the system, not of individual schools, teachers, or children. The instrument provides system information without raising individual or organizational defenses (Argyris, 1990).

Aggregate performance is published and analyzed by kind and size of school, minority percentage, community size, socioeconomic status, ethnicity, and gender, but direct institutional comparisons cannot be made. Test items are also published to reduce emphasis on abstracted numerical comparisons. The four-year assessment cycle allows time for both the construction of complex assessments and productive institutional and societal responses. At the same time, each administration of the assessment requires training a group of teachers to reliably administer the assessment. Teachers involved in the training report that it is an exceptional form of professional development that influences their own assessment and teaching competence, and that they pass this competence on to others (Gilmore, 2002).

MINDS IN SOCIETY

Children's thinking evolves from the discourses in which they are immersed. So, for example, the ways children assess themselves as literate individuals will reflect the discourse of classroom assessment practices. Consider Henry (all names are pseudonyms), for example, a fourth-grade student who describes himself as a writer (Johnston et al., 2001). Though he says writing takes him a little longer than some, he notes that he has a journal with lots of entries and can borrow ideas from other authors, among whom he includes peers whose feedback and suggestions he values. He talks about their writing in terms of the ways they can affect him as a reader. He enjoys reading, and if he wanted to learn about another person as a reader, he would ask about favorite and current books and authors.

Indeed, he describes peers first in terms of their reading interests (topic, author, genre, difficulty) and then, matter-of-factly, their reading speed. He is confident that he makes important contributions to book discussions, but he also feels he benefits from hearing other students' experiences and interpretations. He has learned to manage these discussions to maximize this learning. In his research efforts he has encountered disagreements among authors, which he ascribes to one of them not "doing his homework," and he resolves them by consulting more sources (print, personal, and electronic). Henry has a strong sense of agency and uniqueness in his literate practice, which is an important part of who he feels he is. He recognizes a range of sources of authority and that none is beyond critique. When his teacher describes Henry's literate development, it is in terms of details of his interests and engagements, what he has accomplished, how he approaches literate activities, and what he is beginning to do collaboratively or with assistance.

Henry's self-assessment, his interpretation and representation of himself as a literate person, reflects the literate practices and values of his classroom. In a different discourse community, his and his teachers' assessments could have focused more centrally on his decoding skills, what he is *un*able to do, or on his normative standing. The test used by his school district does provide a numerical quantity to represent the amount of his literacy and places him in the lower quarter of his class. But this particular teacher in this particular school and district finds that representation of little significance, and it does not enter the discourse of the classroom. Another teacher in another discursive community in which the pressures and goals are different would likely represent the child's literacy development differently.

Indeed, teachers in districts more concerned with accountability pressures tend to describe children's literacy development with less detail, with less attention to the child's interests, and with more distancing language (Johnston, Afflerbach, & Weiss, 1993). In a similar manner, the pressures of standards assessment change not only the representations but also the relationships among teacher and students, making them more authoritarian (Deci, Siegel, Ryan, Koestner, & Kauffman, 1982), a relationship that is part of the literacy that is acquired.

A corollary of the "mind in society" principle is that literate development is constructed. Mandy, for example, in the same grade in another school district, feels that she is a good writer because she "writes fast" and feels that she will get an "excellent" on her report card for writing with a comment that she "has behaved and she is nice to other classmates." She feels that the good readers are recognizable because they "are quiet and they just listen . . . and they get chapter books." However, she does not think that conversations between writers are good because they would result in other writers taking ideas and having the same stories and because feelings might get hurt.

Mandy's conception of literacy foregrounds convention, conformity, speed, and individualism (Johnston et al., 2001). Rather than acquiring similar amounts of literacy, as their test scores might suggest, Henry and Mandy have acquired different literacies. Literate development is not a matter of acquiring a series of stepping stones in a particular order. First graders are quite capable of acquiring knowledge of letters and sounds and other print conventions as part of developing a critical literacy. The conventions, however, will mean something different when acquired as part of different literacies. The fact that there are predictable sequences of development is as much a feature of our assessment and curricular imperatives as it is a feature of a natural sequence of literate subskills, or of biological or other potentials and limitations.

REPRESENTATION AND INTERPRETATION

Assessment practices are always representational and interpretive. A teacher, an administrator, and a parent are likely to make different sense of a child's literate behavior both because they bring different histories to the assessment and because they often have different goals as part of different,

if overlapping, social practices. Even a test score (a particular choice of representation) will mean different things to them. Each assessment practice is associated with distinct ways of using language that influence the interpretations made (Fairclough, 1992; Gee, 1996). A school psychologist or a speech therapist can tilt the representational language of a committee on the handicapped toward "learning disabled" or "language delayed" on the basis of the same evidence (Rueda & Mercer, 1985). A single teacher can bring different discourses to representing different children depending on the way the child has been categorized, and these representations have consequences for children's understandings of literacy, themselves, and one another as literate individuals (Arya, 2003; Johnston et al., 2001).

Representational practices in assessment perpetuate the wider cultural discourses. If our discourse offers a category called "reading disabled," then we will find assessment tools to identify members of the category and an appealing narrative of "services" and "support" (McDermott, 1993). The representational language of trait and deficit (Johnston, 1993; Mehan, 1993) within which learning narratives are set offers children, teachers, parents, and other community members problematic identities and dispositions. Once "identified," children remain caught in the problematic discursive web, partly because the problem is represented as a trait of the child rather than as in the instructional environment, partly because the identification process groups children together who share common identifications, and partly because the child is moved to a system that specializes in children's problems that often emphasizes different understandings about literacy learning (Allington & McGill-Franzen, 1989).

Although we might worry about the nature of the categories, which are surely important, the practice is about more than that. As Yalom (1989) pointed out, "If we relate to people believing that we can categorize them, we will neither identify nor nurture . . . the vital parts of the other that transcend category" (cited in Greenberg & Williams, 2002, p. 107). This is evident in casual transformations such as "He's a two, borderline three, right now and we hope that this enrichment program will put him over the edge" (Baudanza, 2001, p. 8).

PRIMACY OF TEACHERS' ASSESSMENT PRACTICES

No instrument or assessment practice can overcome the fact that the teacher is the primary agent of assessment (International Reading Association and National Council of Teachers of English Joint Task Force on Assessment, 1994). The bulk of literacy assessment occurs moment by moment as part of the activity of teaching (Black & Wiliam, 1998b; Crooks, 1988; Johnston, 1989). Consider an example. A teacher was observed introducing to a student a predictable book with the pattern "Grandpa is [verb—e.g., sitting]." The last page was "Grandpa is snoring," at which the child laughed and said that his grandpa snores too. However, when he read the book he read that page as "Grandpa is so funny." The teacher prompted the child to recall what his grandpa does and then prompted a rereading. The child reread, hesitated before *snoring,* and read it correctly.

But why *that* prompt or teaching strategy? Why not ask the child to read with his finger to emphasize the mismatch between the number of words spoken and in print? Because the teacher hypothesizes, based on her ongoing assessment of the child, that he thinks *so funny* is one word. Pointing would not prompt rethinking because he would still have a one-to-one match and an initial letter match. Why not simply provide accuracy feedback? Because she hypothesizes that the process through which the child solves the problem himself will help build a sense of literate agency. Her feedback is based on a theory of learning more than a notion of performance.

The essence of formative assessment is noticing details of literate behavior, imagining what they mean from the child's perspective, knowing what the child knows and can do, and knowing how to arrange for that knowledge and competence to be displayed, engaged, and extended. This requires a

"sensitive observer" (Clay, 1993) or "kidwatcher" (Goodman, 1978), a teacher who is "present" in the classroom—focused and receptive to noticing the children's literate behavior (Rodgers, 2002). A child's acquisition of a "reading disabled" classification (and identity) begins with the teacher's assessment, and teachers who notice less about children's literacy development refer more children to be classified than do those who notice more (Broikou, 1992). The more detailed teachers' knowledge of children's literate development, the more agency they appear to feel with respect to solving literacy learning problems.

Formative assessment requires not only noticing and making productive sense of the literate behaviors that occur but also arranging classroom literacy practices that encourage children to act in literate ways and that make their literate learning visible and audible. A child explaining how she figured out a word is not only providing this information for the teacher but also spinning an agentive narrative of her own literate competence. She is building a productive self-assessment and literate identity (Johnston, 2004).

If a classroom is arranged so that children routinely engage in literate activities that provide manageable challenges and talk about the process and experience of their literate practice, assessment information is available to the teacher and, simultaneously, strategic information is available for the students. *Play* is a particularly rich context for the display of young children's understanding of how literate practices work (Roskos & Neuman, 1993; Teale, 1991). In a similar way, collaboration demands an externalization of shared thinking, which also provides an excellent source of information.

To the extent that formative assessment is a technical matter, the "instrument" is the teacher and his or her mind and its social and textual supports. Improving performance on summative assessments requires improving formative assessment. There is research that suggests how to do this, but it also suggests that change will be slow because the practices assume active involvement on the part of students as well as changes in the ways teachers understand students, themselves, and what they are trying to accomplish (Black & Wiliam, 1998b). These changes are strongly resisted by societal assessment discourses and their sedimentation in teachers' own subjectivities, as we discuss presently.

LITERACY ASSESSMENT AND CONTEXT

Literacy is somewhat local in that people engage in literate practices differently in different contexts. Different tools and social contexts invoke different strategies and ways of thinking. Common assessment practices do not recognize this fact; instead they assume that performance on a particular task in a testing context is representative of all literate contexts. But children perform differently, for example, in more meaningful or authentic activities. The Primary Language Record (PLR) (Barrs, Ellis, Hester, & Thomas, 1989), an early literacy assessment instrument, requires the assessment community (teachers, families, administrators, and students) to recognize (and document) performance in different contexts including "collaborative reading and writing activities," "play," "dramatic play," and "drama and storying" across different social groups that include "pair," "small group," and "child with adult" (p. 38). It draws attention to what a child can do independently and with different kinds of support.

Assessing children's literate learning requires attending not only to what they know and do but also at least as much to the context in which they know and do. Indeed, as the PLR manual notes, "progress or lack of progress should always be seen in relation to the adequacy of the context" (p. 18). When a child appears to be unsuccessful at literate endeavors, we want to know the circumstances in which this happens. Such circumstances include the extent to which literate practices and the logic of participation are made visible in the classroom and valued as purposeful social activities, the extent to which materials are relevant and accessible, and the extent to which classroom discourse is supportive, specific, reflective, nonjudgmental, and values

problem solving (Allington & Johnston, 2002; Johnston & Rogers, 2001; Pressley, Allington, Wharton-MacDonald, Collins-Block, & Morrow, 2001).

Shifting the focus of assessment away from the isolated mind to the mind in a social context has begun to be recognized in the assessment of reading disabilities. For example, Clay (1987) proposed that labeling a child as reading disabled is premature without first eliminating the possibility that the child's progress is a result of poorly configured instruction. The assessment strategy of providing the best instructional intervention we can muster has proven effective in eliminating the need to classify most children (Scanlon, Vellutino, Small, & Fanuele, 2000). However, because this strategy remains in a discourse that expects individual disabilities, the handful of children who remain unsuccessful become viewed as bona fide "disabled," or "treatment resisters" (Torgeson, 2000). This need not happen. Indeed, Smith and her colleagues (Smith, 1997) rejected that discourse. Instead of locating the problem in the child, they entertained the possibility that their intervention might still be insufficiently responsive. Through collaborative self-assessment using videotapes, they refined their intervention and produced the desired acceleration in literate learning, removing the need to classify even these students. This concept of attending to the child in the learning context might be applied to large-scale assessments too. Teachers and schools do not operate in a vacuum.

ASSESSMENT DISCOURSES DISTRIBUTE POWER

Assessment discourses distribute and sustain power relationships. For example, formative assessments, while grounded in current understandings of learning, are not taken seriously as a form of assessment (Black & Wiliam, 1998a). They are referred to as "informal," as opposed to the more authoritative "formal" assessments. There are probably many reasons for their lack of institutional power aside from the fact that they don't always involve a textual record or artifact such as running records, documented events, or writing samples. They are the purview of teachers, mostly women, and they are normally not in the language of mathematics. When brought to a Committee on Special Education meeting, these assessments are easily trumped by the tests of the school psychologist.

Rogers (2003) showed how a mother, vehemently committed to protecting her daughter from assignment to special education, is reduced to passive acceptance by an assessment discourse that invokes subjectivities from her own unsuccessful history in schooled literacy. Rogers also showed how the discursive context induces this passivity just as well in those with highly successful histories of schooled literacy. The normative discourse of testing provides a powerful tool for asserting symbolic domination and intimidation of students, teachers, and parents (Bourdieu, 1991; Fennimore, 2000; Rogers, 2002). When an adult basic education student at the end of a reading lesson asks timidly, "Did I read this good?" (Rogers, 2002), she demonstrates the internalization of an oppressive assessment discourse.

It is possible to design assessment practices to alter these power arrangements. To return to the PLR, the manual describes specific ways for reducing power differences in assessment conferences with children and families. The form of the assessment also insists that members of the learning community focus attention on the child's assets and their instructional context. Because it directs attention toward differences in performance in a range of contexts and on a range of dimensions, it resists narrow and debilitating ability interpretations. At the same time it provides a language that represents literacy as centrally involving identity and engagement in practice, describing a child's development as a reader and a language user and implying a dimension of agency.

However, breaking free of more limiting assessment discourses is increasingly difficult as these discourses saturate a wider array of media. Constant reminders in the newspaper and reports from school are now supplemented through the Internet. Parents going to the Web are encouraged to obtain reading tests that they can use with their child. Like any advertising, these tests create a need and then direct parents to purchase the remedial instruction on the basis of the normative assessment and the "latest brain research" (Learning, 2002) to fulfill the need. At the same site, parents learn of the routinely massive company growth rate, its even better prospects following federal No Child Left Behind regulations (2002), and how they can profit through investment (Johnston & Rogers, 2001). By both reflecting and enforcing traditions of literate practice (including who gets to participate in what ways and in which media), assessment practices stabilize the literate society, limiting social change and adaptability.

CLASHES IN PRACTICES

Literacy assessment consumes resources, so there is a constant search for multipurpose assessments. However, each new function often has different demands, requiring difficult trade-offs and bringing different discourses. Recall the NEMP assessment described earlier. Many of the features of the NEMP were once part of the National Assessment of Educational Progress (NAEP in the United States). However, political pressures have changed the timing of the NAEP to a two-year cycle, increasing pressure for simpler computerized responses. The sampling structure has changed to enable state-by-state comparisons, and state performance has become pegged to federal funding through the No Child Left Behind legislation (2002), thus increasing the assessment stakes. These changes add up to a change in the nature of the assessment activity from educational monitoring for productive curricular conversations to instrumental control of literacy teaching and learning. This is a different assessment practice, grounded in different views of learning and literacy.

The clash of these different discourses is common in school systems as formative and summative functions are forced together, often catching teachers in the middle (Delandshere, 2001; Hill, 2004). As with the earlier example of using leveled books for accountability practices, the higher stakes assessment will generally subvert the lower stakes practice. However, it is possible to have consistency among school literacy curriculum and assessment practices.

The PLR, described earlier, was developed in London for literacy assessment in multicultural/multilingual inner-city communities. It represents a complex, contextual, and social view of literacy learning and assessment practice that involves teacher, student, and parent in collaboratively documenting the child's literacy development over time. It was deliberately designed to inform and support teaching, students, and family literacies through clear documentation and the *process* of that documentation—the assessment *activity*. Although it is a "record," its developers took seriously the educative, communicative, and relational dimensions of assessment practice. In systematic interviews, parents describe the child's home literacy and must agree on what is recorded. Because interview topics include "opportunities that might be possible for writing at home and whether the child chooses to write" (Barrs, Ellis, Hester, & Thomas, 1989, p. 16), parents simultaneously learn about possible ways to expand family literacy practices.

The representation of the child is centrally focused on documentation of what the child does and how the child does it and understands it. In context, though, it also includes numerical ratings for aggregation at the institution level and to complement the descriptive detail. Serious professional development is required for a complex assessment system like the PLR. But that has not prevented its successful adoption (Falk, 1998; Falk & Darling-Hammond, 1993). Implementation is not expected to occur overnight, and it is recommended that teachers begin by selecting a small group of students to document, expanding the group as expertise develops.

However, much of the professional development is built into the process of the assessment. In order to obtain reliable ratings, participants in the assessment community (teachers, administrators, parent representatives) regularly gather to compare their analyses of one another's assessments. The discussion around cases of disagreement is productive in clarifying the need for recording detail and the bases for judgment. The public nature of these discussions keeps teachers responsible for their assessments and requires a measure of courage. Because the assessment requires a range of literacy learning contexts and particular kinds of evidence, it helps teachers to structure their classroom practice.

We provide this example to show that more common approaches to assessment should not be thought of as "givens" that merely need tweaking. This assessment holds very different assumptions from the more standard views and has very different consequences. For example, the assumption behind current accountability testing is that schools as organizations, and the individuals within them, are not only unable to monitor their own performance but also are unlikely to provide the best instruction they can unless forced to do so annually through rewards and punishments. The successful use of the PLR suggests that this assumption, at least in some contexts, is not tenable. Instead, we might sensibly ask, "Under what circumstances can organizations and individuals productively monitor their teaching and learning as part of improving literacy learning?"

Darling-Hammond (2004), examining successful examples of assessment-driven reforms, provided some answers, concluding that consistency in assessment and curricular imperatives across the institutional learning community is essential. Other critical properties that the system provides, in a timely way, included sophisticated information that is consistent with current understandings of learning and relevant for teaching individual students. Successful assessment systems also provide information about the qualities of students' learning opportunities (the context of learning), develop productive teacher-student relationships, and are able to "leverage continuous change and improvement" through a focus on teacher quality and learning (p. 1078). She noted that relatively low stakes and consistency among the assessment and curricular imperatives are important and that institutional size is not trivial. Although Darling-Hammond focused on the testing context privileged in the United States, these emphases are exactly the design features of the PLR. This is a description of the PLR.

FINAL COMMENT

Assessment always (a) is representational and interpretive; (b) is a dynamic part of ongoing, goal-directed social activities and societal discourses; (c) reflects and imposes particular values, beliefs, relationships, and ways of being literate; and thus (d) has consequences for individuals' and communities' understandings of themselves and one another, as well as for the kinds of individuals and communities they will become. If the accelerating shifts in society will require everyone "to become, and remain, committed to learning" (Broadfoot, 2002, p. 6) and to acquire literacies that are more flexible and open, more resilient and self-directed, and more collaborative in a culturally and linguistically diverse context (Kalantzis, Cope, & Harvey, 2003), they will need to be socialized into a literacy that makes this possible, and our assessment systems are part of that socialization.

This means that learning must form the basis of our assessment practice. Current understandings show that the ability to guide and monitor one's own learning is essential to this project (Crooks, 2001). Focusing on learning in this way might incidentally accomplish other shorter term goals. For example, creating classrooms in which assessment practices socialize children into self-regulated literacy learning not only serves students' development as learners but also develops their literate achievement (Harlen & Crick, 2003; McDonald & Boud, 2003). The same principles almost certainly apply to teachers as individuals and as institutional communities. Indeed, if we are to have consistency among assessment and curricular imperatives within schools, the consistency should apply to the processes as well as the content. If literacy assessment is to serve literacy learners and society then it has to be grounded in processes that reflect current understandings of learning, literacy, and society. It also has to remain open to evolution in both literacy and assessment, which at the very least means encouraging some diversity in assessment practice.

Nearly a decade ago, Shepard and her colleagues interviewed officials from state departments across the United States and concluded that more complex and authentic forms of literacy assessment were developing and that the previous excesses and problems of assessing children, particularly young children, for high-stakes purposes like accountability and retention were largely gone (Shepard, Taylor, & Kagan, 1996). The opposite is now true, a development that has everything to do with politics and relatively little to do with research (Allington, 2002; Allington & Woodside-Jiron, 1999; Johnson & Kress, 2003; Wixson & Pearson, 1998).

Indeed, the United States has currently reached the highest volume of testing and the highest stakes testing in its history. We are reminded of a definition of fanaticism as the act of redoubling one's efforts while having forgotten what one is fighting for (de Toqueville, cited in Claxton, 1999, p. 281). Although this article is in the service of "theory and research into practice," we must not pretend that literacy assessment can be improved by simple application of either. At the very least our theory in practice has to include the fact that changing assessment practices is about changing societal discourses regarding children, literacy, and education, with all the values, relationships, identities, and resources that entails.

Peter Johnston is Professor of Education at the University at Albany–SUNY.

Paula Costello is an instructor of education at East Carolina University.

Article 6

BEHIND TEST SCORES

What Struggling Readers Really *Need*

SHEILA W. VALENCIA AND MARSHA RIDDLE BULY

Why do so many children in the United States fail state and standardized reading tests each year? This analysis is a look behind test scores at the specific reading abilities of students who failed one state reading test.

Every year thousands of U.S. students take standardized tests and state reading tests, and every year thousands fail them. With the implementation of the No Child Left Behind legislation (www.ed.gov/nclb/landing.jhtml), which mandates testing all children from grades 3 to 8 every year, these numbers will grow exponentially, and alarming numbers of schools and students will be targeted for "improvement." Whether you believe this increased focus on testing is good news or bad, if you are an educator, you are undoubtedly concerned about the children who struggle every day with reading and the implications of their test failure.

Although legislators, administrators, parents, and educators have been warned repeatedly not to rely on a single measure to make important instructional decisions (Elmore, 2002; Linn, n.d.; Shepard, 2000), scores from state tests still seem to drive the search for programs and approaches that will help students learn and meet state standards. The popular press, educational publications, teacher workshops, and state and school district policies are filled with attempts to find solutions for poor test performance. For example, some schools have eliminated sustained silent reading in favor of more time for explicit instruction (Edmondson & Shannon,

SOURCE: Valencia, S. W., & Riddle Buly, M. (2004). Behind Test Scores: What Struggling Readers *Really* Need. *The Reading Teacher*, *57*(6), 520–530. Reprinted by permission of the International Reading Association.

2002; Riddle Buly & Valencia, 2002), others are buying special programs or mandating specific interventions (Goodnough, 2001; Helfand, 2002), and some states and districts are requiring teachers to have particular instructional emphases (McNeil, 2000; Paterson, 2000; Riddle Buly & Valencia, 2002). Furthermore, it is common to find teachers spending enormous amounts of time preparing students for these high-stakes tests (Olson, 2001), even though a narrow focus on preparing students for specific tests does not translate into real learning (Klein, Hamilton, McCaffrey, & Stecher, 2000; Linn, 2000). But, if we are really going to help students, we need to understand the underlying reasons for their test failure. Simply knowing which children have failed state tests is a bit like knowing that you have a fever when you are feeling ill but having no idea of the cause or cure. A test score, like a fever, is a symptom that demands more specific analysis of the problem. In this case, what is required is a more in-depth analysis of the strengths and needs of students who fail to meet standards and instructional plans that will meet their needs.

In this article, we draw from the results of an empirical study of students who failed a typical fourth-grade state reading assessment (see Riddle Buly & Valencia, 2002, for a full description of the study). Specifically, we describe the patterns of performance that distinguish different groups of students who failed to meet standards. We also provide suggestions for what classroom teachers need to know and how they might help these children succeed.

STUDY CONTEXT

Our research was conducted in a typical northwestern U.S. school district of 18,000 students located adjacent to the largest urban district in the state. At the time of our study, 43% were students of color and 47% received free or reduced-price lunch. Over the past several years, approximately 50% of students had failed the state fourth-grade reading test that, like many

other standards-based state assessments, consisted of several extended narrative and expository reading selections accompanied by a combination of multiple-choice and open-ended comprehension questions. For the purposes of this study, during September of fifth grade we randomly selected 108 students who had scored below standard on the state test given at the end of fourth grade. These 108 students constituted approximately 10% of failing students in the district. None of them was receiving supplemental special education or English as a Second Language (ESL) services. We wanted to understand the "garden variety" (Stanovich, 1988) test failure—those students typically found in the regular classroom who are experiencing reading difficulty but have not been identified as needing special services or intensive interventions. Classroom teachers, not reading specialists or special education teachers, are solely responsible for the reading instruction of these children and, ultimately, for their achievement.

DATA COLLECTION AND ASSESSMENT TOOLS

Our approach was to conduct individual reading assessments, working one-on-one with the children for approximately two hours over several days to gather information about their reading abilities. We administered a series of assessments that targeted key components of reading ability identified by experts: word identification, meaning (comprehension and vocabulary), and fluency (rate and expression) (Lipson & Wixson, 2003; National Institute of Child Health and Human Development, 2000; Snow, Burns, & Griffin, 1998). Table 6.1 presents the measures we used and the areas in which each provided information.

To measure word identification, we used two tests from the 1989 Woodcock-Johnson Psycho-Educational Battery–Revised (WJ-R) that assessed students' reading of single and multisyllabic words, both real and pseudowords. We also scored oral reading errors students made on

Table 6.1 Diagnostic Assessments

Assessment	Word Identification	Meaning	Fluency
Woodcock-Johnson–Revised			
Letter-word identification	X		
Word attack	X		
Qualitative Reading Inventory–II			
Reading accuracy	X		
Reading acceptability	X		
Rate			X
Expression			X
Comprehension		X	
Peabody Picture Vocabulary Text Revised			
Vocabulary meaning		X	
State fourth-grade passages			
Reading accuracy	X		
Reading acceptability	X		
Rate			X
Expression			X

narrative and expository graded passages from the 1995 Qualitative Reading Inventory–II (QRI-II) and from the state test. We calculated total accuracy (percentage of words read correctly) and acceptability (counting only those errors that changed the meaning of the text). Students also responded orally to comprehension questions that accompanied the QRI-II passages, providing a measure of their comprehension that was not confounded by writing ability. To assess receptive vocabulary, we used the 1981 Peabody Picture Vocabulary Test–Revised (PPVT-R), which requires students to listen and point to a picture that corresponds to a word (scores of 85 or higher are judged to be average or above average). As with the comprehension questions, the vocabulary measure does not confound understanding with students' ability to write responses. Finally, in the area of fluency, we assessed rate of reading and expression (Samuels, 2002). We timed the readings of all passages (i.e., QRI-II and state test selections) to get a reading rate and used a 4-point rubric developed for the Oral Reading Study of the fourth-grade National Assessment of Educational Progress (NAEP) (Pinnell, Pikulski, Wixson, Campbell, Gough, & Beatty, 1995) to assess phrasing and expression (1–2 is judged to be nonfluent; 3–4 is judged to be fluent).

FINDINGS

Scores from all the assessments for each student fell into three statistically distinct and educationally familiar categories: word identification (word reading in isolation and context), meaning (comprehension and vocabulary), and fluency (rate and expression). When we examined the average scores for all 108 students in the sample, students appeared to be substantially below grade level in all three areas. However, when we analyzed the data using a cluster analysis (Aldenderfer & Blashfield, 1984), looking for groups of students who had similar patterns across all three factors, we found six distinct profiles of students who failed the test. Most striking is that the majority of students were not weak in all three areas: they were actually strong in some and weak in others. Table 6.2 indicates the percentage of students in each group and their relative strength (+) or weakness (−) in word identification, meaning, and fluency.

The Profiles

We illuminate each profile by describing a prototypical student from each cluster (see Figure 6.1) and specific suggested instructional targets for each (all names are pseudonyms). Although the instructional strategies we recommend have not been implemented with these

particular children, we base our recommendations on our review of research-based practices (e.g., Allington, 2001; Allington & Johnston, 2001; Lipson & Wixson, 2003; National Institute of Child Health and Human Development, 2000), our interpretation of the profiles, and our experiences teaching struggling readers. We conclude with several general implications for school and classroom instruction.

Cluster 1–Automatic Word Callers

We call these students Automatic Word Callers because they can decode words quickly and accurately, but they fail to read for meaning. The majority of students in this cluster qualify for free or reduced-price lunch, and they are English language learners who no longer receive special support. Tomas is a typical student in this cluster.

Tomas has excellent word identification skills. He scored at ninth-grade level when reading real words and pseudowords (i.e., phonetically regular nonsense words such as *fot*) on the WJ-R tests, and at the independent level for

Table 6.2   Cluster Analysis

Cluster	Sample Percentage	English Language Learner Percentage	Low Socioeconomic Status Percentage	Word Identification	Meaning	Fluency
1–Automatic Word Callers	18	63	89	+ +	−	+ +
2–Struggling Word Callers	15	56	81	−	−	+ +
3–Word Stumblers	17	16	42	−	+	−
4–Slow Comprehenders	24	19	54	+	+ +	−
5–Slow Word Callers	17	56	67	+	−	−
6–Disabled Readers	9	20	80	− −	− −	− −

word identification on the QRI-II and state fourth-grade passages. However, when asked about what he read, Tomas had difficulty, placing his comprehension at the second-grade level. Although Tomas's first language is not English, his score of 108 on the PPVT-R suggests that his comprehension difficulties are more complex than individual word meanings. Tomas's "proficient" score on the state writing assessment also suggests that his difficulty is in understanding rather than in writing answers to comprehension questions. This student's rate of reading, which was quite high compared with rates of fourth-grade students on the Oral Reading Study of NAEP (Pinnell et al., 1995) and other research (Harris & Sipay, 1990), suggests that his decoding is automatic and unlikely to be contributing to his comprehension difficulty. His score in expression is also consistent with students who were rated as "fluent" according to the NAEP rubric, although this seems unusual for a student who is demonstrating difficulty with comprehension.

The evidence suggests that Tomas needs additional instruction in comprehension and most likely would benefit from explicit instruction, teacher modeling, and think-alouds of key reading strategies (e.g., summarizing, self-monitoring, creating visual representations, evaluating), using a variety of types of material at the fourth- or fifth-grade level (Block & Pressley, 2002; Duke & Pearson, 2002). His comprehension performance on the QRI-II suggests that his literal comprehension is quite strong but that he has difficulty with more inferential and critical aspects of understanding. Although Tomas has strong scores in the fluency category, both in expression and rate, he may be reading too fast to attend to meaning, especially deeper meaning of the ideas in the text. Tomas's teacher should help him understand that the purpose for reading is to understand and that rate varies depending on the type of text and the purpose for reading. Then, the teacher should suggest that he slow down to focus on meaning. Self-monitoring strategies would also help Tomas check for understanding and encourage him to think about the ideas while he is reading. These and other such strategies may help him learn to adjust his rate to meet the demands of the text.

Figure 6.1 The Profiles

Prototypical Students From Each Cluster					
Cluster 1–Automatic Word Callers (18%)			**Cluster 4–Slow Comprehenders (24%)**		
Word identification	Meaning	Fluency	Word identification	Meaning	Fluency
+ +	–	+ +	+	+ +	–
Tomas			Martin		
Word identification = ninth grade (WJ-R) > fourth grade (QRI-II) = 98% (state passages)			Word identification = sixth grade (W-R) > fourth grade (QRI-II) = 100% (state passages)		
Comprehension = second/third grade			Comprehension = > fourth grade		
Vocabulary = 108			Vocabulary = 103		
Expression = 3			Expression = 2.5		
Rate = 155 words per minute			Rate = 61 words per minute		
Writing = proficient			Writing = proficient		

(Continued)

(Continued)

Cluster 2–Struggling Word Callers (15%)			Cluster 5–Slow Word Callers (17%)		
Word identification	Meaning	Fluency	Word identification	Meaning	Fluency
–	–	+ +	+	–	–
Makara			Andrew		
Word identification = fourth grade (WJ-R) < second grade (QRI-II) = 75% (state passages)			Word identification = seventh grade (WJ-R) > fourth grade (QRI-II) = 98% (state passages)		
Comprehension = < second grade			Comprehension = second grade		
Vocabulary = 58			Vocabulary = 74		
Expression = 2.5			Expression = 1.5		
Rate = 117 words per minute			Rate = 62 words per minute		
Writing = below proficient			Writing = not proficient		
Cluster 3–Word Stumblers (17%)			Cluster 6–Disabled Readers (9%)		
Word identification	Meaning	Fluency	Word identification	Meaning	Fluency
–	+	–	–	–	–
Sandy			Jesse		
Word identification = second grade (WJ-R) = second-grade accuracy/third-grade acceptability (QRI-II) = 80% accuracy/99% acceptability (state passages)			Word identification = first grade (WJ-R) < first grade (QRI-II) < 50% (state passages)		
Comprehension = fourth grade			Comprehension = < first grade		
Vocabulary = 135			Vocabulary = 105		
Expression = 1.5			Writing = not proficient		
Rate = 77 words per minute					
Writing = proficient					

Tomas would also likely benefit from additional support in acquiring academic language, which takes many years for English-language learners to develop (Cummins, 1991). Reading activities such as building background; developing understanding of new words, concepts, and figurative language in his "to-be-read" texts; and acquiring familiarity with genre structures found in longer, more complex texts like those found at fourth grade and above would provide important opportunities for his language and conceptual development (Antunez, 2002; Hiebert, Pearson, Taylor, Richardson, & Paris, 1998). Classroom read-alouds and discussions as well as lots of additional independent reading would also help Tomas in building language and attention to understanding.

Cluster 2—Struggling Word Callers

The students in this cluster not only struggle with meaning, like the Automatic Word Callers in Cluster 1, but they also struggle with word identification. Makara, a student from Cambodia, is one of these students. Like Tomas, Makara struggled with comprehension. But unlike Tomas, he had substantial difficulty applying word identification skills when reading connected text (QRI-II and state passages), even though his reading of isolated words on the WJ-R was at a fourth-grade level. Such word identification difficulties would likely contribute to comprehension problems. However, Makara's performance on the PPVT-R, which placed him below the 1st percentile compared with other students his age, and his poor performance on the state writing assessment suggest that language may contribute to his comprehension difficulties as well—not surprising for a student acquiring a second language. These language-related results need to be viewed with caution, however, because the version of the PPVT-R available for use in this study may underestimate the language abilities of students from culturally and linguistically diverse backgrounds, and written language takes longer than oral language to develop. Despite difficulty with meaning, Makara read quickly—117 words per minute. At first glance, this may seem unusual given his difficulty with both decoding and comprehension. Closer investigation of his performance, however, revealed that Makara read words quickly whether he was reading them correctly or incorrectly and didn't stop to monitor or self-correct. In addition, although Makara was fast, his expression and phrasing were uneven and consistent with comprehension difficulties.

Makara likely needs instruction and practice in oral and written language, as well as in constructing meaning in reading and writing, self-monitoring, and decoding while reading connected text. All this needs to be done in rich, meaningful contexts, taking into account his background knowledge and interests. Like Tomas, Makara would benefit from teacher or peer read-alouds, lots of experience with independent reading at his level, small-group instruction, and the kinds of activities aimed at building academic language that we described earlier, as well as a more foundational emphasis on word meanings. Makara also needs instruction in self-monitoring and fix-up strategies to improve his comprehension and awareness of reading for understanding. Decoding instruction is also important for him, although his teacher would need to gather more information using tools such as miscue analysis or tests of decoding to determine his specific decoding needs and how

they interact with his knowledge of word meanings. Makara clearly cannot be instructed in fourth-grade material; most likely, his teacher would need to begin with second-grade material that is familiar and interesting to him and a good deal of interactive background building. At the same time, however, Makara needs exposure to the content and vocabulary of grade-level texts through activities such as teacher read-alouds, tapes, and partner reading so that his conceptual understanding continues to grow.

Cluster 3—Word Stumblers

Students in this cluster have substantial difficulty with word identification, but they still have surprisingly strong comprehension. How does that happen? Sandy, a native English speaker from a middle class home, is a good example of this type of student. Sandy stumbled on so many words initially that it seemed unlikely that she would comprehend what she had read, yet she did. Her word identification scores were at second-grade level, and she read the state fourth-grade passages at frustration level. However, a clue to her strong comprehension is evident from the difference between her immediate word recognition accuracy score and her acceptability score, which takes into account self-corrections or errors that do not change the meaning. In other words, Sandy was so focused on reading for meaning that she spontaneously self-corrected many of her decoding miscues or substituted words that preserved the meaning. She attempted to read every word in the reading selections, working until she could figure out some part of each word and then using context clues to help her get the entire word. She seemed to over-rely on context because her decoding skills were so weak (Stanovich, 1994). Remarkably, she was eventually able to read the words on the state fourth-grade reading passages at an independent level. But, as we might predict, Sandy's rate was very slow, and her initial attempts to read were choppy and lacked flow—she spent an enormous amount of time self-correcting and rereading. After she finally self-corrected or figured out unknown words, however, Sandy reread phrases with good expression and flow to fit with the meaning. Although Sandy's overall fluency score was low, her primary difficulty does not appear in the area of either rate or expression; rather, her low performance in fluency seems to be a result of her difficulty with decoding.

With such a strong quest for meaning, Sandy was able to comprehend fourth-grade material even when her decoding was at frustration level. No doubt her strong language and vocabulary abilities (i.e., 99th percentile) were assets. As we might predict, Sandy was more than proficient at expressing her ideas when writing about her experiences. She understands that reading and writing should make sense, and she has the self-monitoring strategies, perseverance, and language background to make that happen.

Sandy needs systematic instruction in word identification and opportunities to practice when reading connected text at her reading level. She is clearly beyond the early stages of reading and decoding, but her teacher will need to determine through a more in-depth analysis precisely which decoding skills should be the focus of her instruction. At the same time, Sandy needs supported experiences with texts that will continue to feed and challenge her drive for meaning. For students like Sandy, it is critical not to sacrifice intellectual engagement with text while they are receiving decoding instruction and practice in below-grade-level material. Furthermore, Sandy needs to develop automaticity with word identification, and to do that she would benefit from assisted reading (i.e., reading along with others, monitored reading with a tape, or partner reading) as well as unassisted reading practice (i.e., repeated reading, reading to younger students) with materials at her instructional level (Kuhn & Stahl, 2000).

Cluster 4—Slow Comprehenders

Almost one fourth of the students in this sample were Slow Comprehenders. Like other students in this cluster, Martin is a native English speaker and a relatively strong decoder, scoring above fourth-grade level on all measures of decoding. His comprehension was at the instructional level on the fourth-grade QRI-II selections, and his vocabulary and writing ability were average for his age. On the surface, this

information is puzzling because Martin failed the fourth-grade state test.

Insight about Martin's reading performance comes from several sources. First, Martin was within two points of passing the state assessment, so he doesn't seem to have a serious reading problem. Second, although his reading rate is quite slow and this often interferes with comprehension (Adams, 1990), results of the QRI-II suggest that Martin's comprehension is quite strong, in spite of his slow rate. This is most likely because Martin has good word knowledge and understands that reading should make sense, and neither the QRI-II nor the state test has time limits. His strong score in expression confirms that Martin did, indeed, attend to meaning while reading. Third, a close examination of his reading behaviors while reading words from the WJ-R tests, QRI-II, and state reading selections revealed that he had some difficulty reading multisyllabic words, although, with time, he was able to read enough words to score at grade level or above. It appears that Martin has the decoding skills to attack multisyllabic words, but they are not yet automatic.

The outstanding characteristic of Martin's profile is his extremely slow rate combined with his relatively strong word identification abilities and comprehension. Our work with him suggests that, even if Martin were to get the additional two points needed to pass the state test, he would still have a significant problem with rate and some difficulty with automatic decoding of multisyllabic words, both of which could hamper his future reading success. Furthermore, with such a lack of automaticity and a slow rate, it is unlikely that Martin enjoys or spends much time reading. As a result, he is likely to fall further and further behind his peers (Stanovich, 1986), especially as he enters middle school where the amount of reading increases dramatically. Martin needs fluency-building activities such as guided repeated oral reading, partner reading, and Readers Theatre (Allington, 2001; Kuhn & Stahl, 2000; Lipson & Wixson, 2003). Given his word identification and comprehension abilities, he most likely could get that practice using fourth-grade material where he will also encounter multisyllabic words.

It is important to find reading material that is interesting to Martin and that, initially, can be completed in a relatively short time. Martin needs to develop stamina as well as fluency, and to do that he will need to spend time reading short and extended texts. In addition, Martin might benefit from instruction and practice in strategies for identifying multisyllabic words so that he is more prepared to deal with them automatically while reading.

Cluster 5—Slow Word Callers

The students in this cluster are similar to Tomas, the Automatic Word Caller in Cluster 1. The difference is that Tomas is an automatic, fluent word caller, whereas the students in this cluster are slow. This group is a fairly even mix of English-language learners and native English speakers who have difficulty in comprehension and fluency. Andrew is an example of such a student. He has well-developed decoding skills, scoring at the seventh-grade level when reading words in isolation and at the independent level when reading connected text. Even with such strong decoding abilities. Andrew had difficulty with comprehension. We had to drop down to the second-grade QRI-II passage for Andrew to score at the instructional level for comprehension, and, even at that level, his retelling was minimal. Andrew's score on the PPVT-R, corresponding to first grade (the 4th percentile for his age), adds to the comprehension picture as well. It suggests that Andrew may be experiencing difficulty with both individual word meanings and text-based understanding when reading paragraphs and longer selections. Like Martin, Andrew's reading rate was substantially below rates expected for fourth-grade students (Harris & Sipay, 1990; Pinnell et al., 1995), averaging 62 words per minute when reading narrative and expository selections. In practical terms, this means he read just one word per second. As we might anticipate from his slow rate and his comprehension difficulty, Andrew did not read with expression or meaningful phrasing.

The relationship between meaning and fluency is unclear in Andrew's case. On the one hand, students who realize they don't understand would be wise to slow down and monitor meaning. On the other hand, Andrew's lack of automaticity and slow rate may interfere with comprehension. To disentangle these factors, his teacher would need to experiment with reading materials about which Andrew has a good deal of background knowledge to eliminate difficulty with individual word meanings and overall comprehension. If his reading rate and expression improve under such conditions, a primary focus for instruction would be meaning. That is, his slow rate of reading and lack of prosody would seem to be a response to lack of understanding rather than contributing to it. In contrast, if Andrew's rate and expression are still low when the material and vocabulary are familiar, instruction should focus on both fluency and meaning. In either case, Andrew would certainly benefit from attention to vocabulary building, both indirect building through extensive independent reading and teacher read-alouds as well as more explicit instruction in word learning strategies and new words he will encounter when reading specific texts (Nagy, 1988; Stahl & Kapinus, 2001).

It is interesting that 50% of the students in this cluster scored at Level 1 on the state test, the lowest level possible. State guidelines characterize these students as lacking prerequisite knowledge and skills that are fundamental for meeting the standard. Given such a definition, a logical assumption would be that these students lack basic, early reading skills such as decoding. However, as the evidence here suggests, we cannot assume that students who score at the lowest level on the test need decoding instruction. Andrew, like others in this cluster, needs instruction in meaning and fluency.

Cluster 6—Disabled Readers

We call this group Disabled Readers because they are experiencing severe difficulty in all three areas—word identification, meaning, and fluency. This is the smallest group (9%), yet, ironically, this is the profile that most likely comes to mind when we think of children who fail state reading tests. This group also includes one of the lowest numbers of second-language learners. The most telling characteristic of students in this cluster, like Jesse, is their very limited word identification abilities. Jesse had few decoding skills beyond initial consonants, basic consonant-vowel-consonant patterns (e.g., *hat, box*), and high-frequency sight words. However, his knowledge of word meanings was average, like most of the students in this cluster, which suggests that receptive language was not a major problem and that he does not likely have limited learning ability. With decoding ability at the first-grade level and below, it is not surprising that Jesse's comprehension and fluency were also low. He simply could not read enough words at the first-grade level to get any meaning.

As we might anticipate, the majority of students in this cluster were not proficient in writing and scored at the lowest level, Level 1, on the state fourth-grade reading test. It is important to remember, however, that children who were receiving special education intervention were not included in our sample. So, the children in this cluster, like Jesse, are receiving all of their instruction, or the majority of it (some may be getting supplemental help), from their regular classroom teachers.

Jesse clearly needs intensive, systematic word identification instruction targeted at beginning reading along with access to lots of reading material at first-grade level and below. This will be a challenge for Jesse's fifth-grade teacher. Pedagogically, Jesse needs explicit instruction in basic word identification. Yet few intermediate-grade teachers include this as a part of their instruction, and most do not have an adequate supply of easy materials for instruction or fluency building. In addition, the majority of texts in other subject areas such as social studies and science are written at levels that will be inaccessible to students like Jesse, so alternative materials and strategies will be needed. On the social-emotional front, it will be a challenge to keep Jesse engaged in learning and to provide opportunities for him to succeed in the classroom, even if he is referred for additional reading support. Without that engagement and desire to learn, it is unlikely he will be motivated to put

forth the effort it will take for him to make progress. Jesse needs a great deal of support from his regular classroom teacher and from a reading specialist, working together to build a comprehensive instructional program in school and support at home that will help him develop the skill and will to progress.

CONCLUSIONS AND IMPLICATIONS

Our brief descriptions of the six prototypical children and the instructional focus each one needs is a testimony to individual differences. As we have heard a thousand times before, and as our data support, one-size instruction will not fit all children. The evidence here clearly demonstrates that students fail state reading tests for a variety of reasons and that, if we are to help these students, we will need to provide appropriate instruction to meet their varying needs. For example, placing all struggling students in a phonics or word identification program would be inappropriate for nearly 58% of the students in this sample who had adequate or strong word identification skills. In a similar manner, an instructional approach that did not address fluency and building reading stamina for longer, more complex text or that did not provide sufficient reading material at a range of levels would miss almost 70% of the students who demonstrated difficulty with fluency. In addition to these important cautions about overgeneralizing students' needs, we believe there are several strategies aimed at assessment, classroom organization and materials, and school structures that could help teachers meet their students' needs.

First and most obvious, teachers need to go beneath the scores on state tests by conducting additional diagnostic assessments that will help them identify students' needs. The data here demonstrate quite clearly that, without more in-depth and individual student assessment, distinctive and instructionally important patterns of students' abilities are masked. We believe that informal reading inventories, oral reading records, and other individually tailored assessments provide useful information about all students. At the same time, we realize that many teachers do not have the time to do complete diagnostic evaluations, such as those we did, with every student. At a minimum, we suggest a kind of layered approach to assessment in which teachers first work diagnostically with students who have demonstrated difficulty on broad measures of reading. Then, they can work with other students as the need arises.

However, we caution that simply administering more and more assessments and recording the scores will miss the point. The value of in-depth classroom assessment comes from teachers having a deep understanding of reading processes and instruction, thinking diagnostically, and using the information on an ongoing basis to inform instruction (Black & Wiliam, 1998; Place, 2002; Shepard, 2000). Requiring teachers to administer grade-level classroom assessments to all their students regardless of individual student needs would not yield useful information or help teachers make effective instructional decisions. For example, administering a fourth-grade reading selection to Jesse, who is reading at first-grade level, would not provide useful information. However, using a fourth- or even fifth-grade selection for Tomas would. Similarly, assessing Jesse's word identification abilities should probably include assessments of basic sound/symbol correspondences or even phonemic awareness, but assessing decoding of multisyllabic words would be more appropriate for Martin. This kind of matching of assessment to students' needs is precisely what we hope would happen when teachers have the knowledge, the assessment tools, and the flexibility to assess and teach children according to their ongoing analysis. Both long-term professional development and time are critical if teachers are to implement the kind of sophisticated classroom assessment that struggling readers need.

Second, the evidence points to the need for multilevel, flexible, small-group instruction (Allington & Johnston, 2001; Cunningham & Allington, 1999; Opitz, 1998). Imagine, if you will, teaching just the six students we have

described, who could easily be in the same class. These students not only need support in different aspects of reading, but they also need materials that differ in difficulty, topic, and familiarity. For example, Tomas, Makara, and Andrew all need instruction in comprehension. However, Tomas and Andrew likely can receive that instruction using grade-level material, but Makara would need to use easier material. Both Makara and Andrew need work in vocabulary, whereas Tomas is fairly strong in word meanings. As second-language learners, Tomas and Makara likely need more background building and exposure to topics, concepts, and academic vocabulary as well as the structure of English texts than Andrew, who is a native English speaker. Furthermore, the teacher likely needs to experiment with having Tomas and Makara slow down when they read to get them to attend to meaning, whereas Andrew needs to increase his fluency through practice in below-grade-level text.

So, although these three students might be able to participate in whole-class instruction in which the teacher models and explicitly teaches comprehension strategies, they clearly need guided practice to apply the strategies to different types and levels of material, and they each need attention to other aspects of reading as well. This means the teacher must have strong classroom management and organizational skills to provide small-group instruction. Furthermore, he or she must have access to a wide range of books and reading materials that are intellectually challenging yet accessible to students reading substantially below grade level. At the same time, these struggling readers need access to grade-level material through a variety of scaffolded experiences (i.e., partner reading, guided reading, read-alouds) so that they are exposed to grade-level ideas, text structures, and vocabulary (Cunningham & Allington, 1999). Some of these students and their teachers would benefit from collaboration with other professionals in their schools, such as speech and language and second-language specialists, who could suggest classroom-based strategies targeted to the students' specific needs.

The six clusters and the three strands within each one (word identification, meaning, fluency) clearly provide more in-depth analysis of students' reading abilities than general test scores. Nevertheless, we caution that there is still more to be learned about individual students in each cluster, beyond what we describe here, that would help teachers plan for instruction. Two examples make this point. The first example comes from Cluster 1, Automatic Word Callers. Tomas had substantial difficulty with comprehension, but his scores on the vocabulary measure suggested that word meanings were likely not a problem for him. However, other students in this cluster, such as Maria, did have difficulty with word meanings and would need not only comprehension instruction like Tomas but also many more language-building activities and exposure to oral and written English. The second example that highlights the importance of looking beyond the cluster profile is Andrew, our Slow Word Caller from Cluster 5. Although we know that in-depth assessment revealed that Andrew had difficulty with comprehension and fluency, we argue above that the teacher must do more work with Andrew to determine how much fluency is contributing to comprehension and how much it is a result of Andrew's effort to self-monitor. Our point here is that even the clusters do not tell the entire story.

Finally, from a school or district perspective, we are concerned about the disproportionate number of second-language students who failed the test. In our study, 11% of the students in the school district were identified as second-language learners and were receiving additional instructional support. However, in our sample of students who failed the test, 43% were second-language learners who were *not* receiving additional support. Tomas and Makara are typical of many English-language learners in our schools. Their reading abilities are sufficient, according to school guidelines, to allow them to exit supplemental ESL programs, yet they are failing state tests and struggling in the classroom. In this district, as in others across the state, students exit supplemental programs when they score at the 35th percentile or above on a norm-referenced reading test—hardly sufficient to thrive, or even survive, in a mainstream classroom without additional help. States, school districts, and schools need to rethink the support they offer English-language learners both in terms of providing more sustained instructional support over time and of scaffolding their integration into the regular classroom. In addition, there must be a concerted effort to foster academically and intellectually rigorous learning of subject matter for these students (e.g., science, social studies) while they are developing their English-language abilities. Without such a focus, either in their first language or in English, these students will be denied access to important school learning, will fall further behind in other school subjects, and become increasingly disengaged from school and learning (Echevarria, Vogt, & Short, 2000).

Our findings and recommendations may, on one level, seem obvious. Indeed, good teachers have always acknowledged differences among the students in their classes, and they have always tried to meet individual needs. But, in the current environment of high-stakes testing and accountability, it has become more of a challenge to keep an eye on individual children, and more difficult to stay focused on the complex nature of reading performance and reading instruction. This study serves as a reminder of these cornerstones of good teaching. We owe it to our students, their parents, and ourselves to provide struggling readers with the instruction they *really* need.

Sheila W. Valencia teaches at the University of Washington in Seattle.

Marsha Riddle Buly teaches at Western Washington University in Bellingham.

Section III

WORD RECOGNITION

OVERVIEW

This section includes articles that address a range of approaches to word recognition, including phonemic awareness, phonics, and spelling. There is no denying the importance of word recognition to the development of students' reading and writing. Phonemic awareness has been heralded as one of the best predictors of later reading success. Knowledge of the alphabetic principle is considered paramount for making sense of text. Therefore, it is critical that teachers develop a range of activities and approaches to meet the needs of our students.

Reading is a meaning-centered endeavor; however, the words get in the way. Experts agree that word recognition is insufficient for reading, but struggles in this area can prevent comprehension of text. Word recognition presents a significant challenge for many young students. As Clark (2004) notes in her article "What Can I Say Besides 'Sound It Out'?": "While they work to construct meaning, they must devote considerable attention to activating, coordinating and applying their developing knowledge of word-recognition strategies."

The articles in this section were collected to give readers a brief overview of word recognition theory situated in a range of instructional approaches that may be useful in your classrooms. This section will also help readers think about how to differentiate approaches and activities for word study so they may better meet the needs of individual students.

In his article, "Phonemes in Use: Multiple Activities for a Critical Process," Manyak (2008) helps readers understand the difference between phonemic awareness and phonics and then combines them in a set of activities that focus on what he calls "phonemes in use." These brief student-centered activities are designed to help students "use phonemic awareness within the context of reading and writing words." Like Manyak, Joseph (2002) advocates approaches in which students manipulate materials as they make connections between sound and print. His article, "Helping Children Link Sound to Print: Phonics Procedures for Small-Group or Whole-Class Settings," appropriates word boxes and word sorts, typically individual activities, and makes them available for teachers to use in whole- and small-group instructional settings.

Another approach to teaching word recognition is coaching. In her article, Clark (2004) describes coaching word recognition and its usefulness for helping beginning readers. As literacy coaches, teachers interact with students by providing prompts that guide students in using their literacy knowledge to solve a textual problem. The coaching model capitalizes on students' instructional histories and recognizes them as active learners in the process.

Another element of word recognition, spelling, can also enhance early reading and writing development. Like all other facets of teaching word recognition, Graham et al. (2008) support spelling instruction that is "responsive to children's individual needs." This article, "Teaching Spelling in the Primary Grades: A National Survey of Instructional Practices and Adaptations" (available at http://www.sagepub.com/cappello/), highlights common spelling activities and instructional approaches and also addresses the need to differentiate spelling instruction.

STRATEGY

Use "The Anticipation/Reaction Guide" (Readence, Bean, & Baldwin, 2004) to accompany the articles on word recognition in this section of the text. This strategy consists of two parts: before and after reading. For each part, you will decide whether you agree or disagree with statements related to the topic. The purpose of this strategy is to motivate your interest, activate background knowledge about key concepts, and expose any misconceptions you may have about the topic The guide is useful after reading, as it clarifies main ideas and provides closure for the activity.

ANTICIPATION/REACTION GUIDE

(Readence, Bean, & Baldwin, 2004)

DIRECTIONS

Complete the "before" column in the following Anticipation/Reaction Guide on your own. Save the "after" column to complete with your classmates once you have a chance to further discuss word recognition.

Word Recognition	Before		After	
	Agree	Disagree	Agree	Disagree
The alphabetic principal is the understanding that each letter of the alphabet represents an individual phoneme in speech.				
Mastering spelling is important to both reading and writing.				
Phonemic awareness is the ability to recognize and manipulate the smallest units of sounds in words.				
It is very important that students become equally as knowledgeable about the terms associated with orthographic patterns and phonic elements.				
Phonemic awareness is a prerequisite for phonics instruction.				
Phonics strategies may also be used to teach spelling.				
Phonemic awareness must only be taught orally. It should never be associated with print.				

SOURCE: Readence, J. E., Bean, T. W., & Baldwin, R. S. (2004) *Content Area Literacy: An Integrated Approach* (8th ed.). Dubuque, IA: Kendall/Hunt.

Article 7

WHAT CAN I SAY BESIDES "SOUND IT OUT"?

Coaching Word Recognition in Beginning Reading

KATHLEEN F. CLARK

Coaching is a highly effective instructional technique in which teachers craft instructional cues that enable students to apply their developing reading skills and knowledge of strategies as they attempt to complete a task.

It's 9:20 in the morning. Five first graders are reading *Cave Boy* (Dubowksi, 1988) with their teacher. After they read from the text, "He gets lots of presents. A rock, some wood, a fish, a bone" (p. 19), the following interaction takes place:

Student: "He gets lots of presents and. . . ." [a rock]

Teacher: And. . . .

Student: [no response]

Teacher: Let's see. Have we done everything we know how to do? We can look at the picture. We can take a running start. Think of all the things you can do.

Student: Hope? [rock]

Teacher: Can you say the sounds?

SOURCE: Clark, K. F. (2004). What Can I Say Besides "Sound It Out"? Coaching Word Recognition in Beginning Reading. *The Reading Teacher, 57*(5), 440–449. Reprinted by permission of the International Reading Association.

Student:	/r/ /o/ /k/
Teacher:	Now take a running start.
Student:	Rock.
Teacher:	Works every time.

In a classroom in another state, four second graders are reading *The Color Wizard* (Brenner, 1989) with their teacher. After they read, "'What we need around here is a little red. Red is bright!' So he painted his coach" (pp. 4–5), a similar interaction takes place:

Student:	"So he painted. . . . His . . ." [coach]
Teacher:	Good job. Now just follow your rules. What's that [coach] going to say? Follow your rules. What vowel will you hear?
Student:	[no response]
Teacher:	Will you hear the *o* or the *a?*
Student:	*o*
Teacher:	And now what does *ch* say?
Student:	/ch/
Teacher:	So what's the word? The *c* is making the hard sound.
Student:	Cuch . . . coach!
Teacher:	Coach is right! Did you see Cinderella? She had a beautiful coach. That's what this is [picture of a coach].

These interactions illustrate a highly effective instructional technique, that of coaching. In the interactions, knowledgeable teachers have crafted just the right cues for readers to apply their developing knowledge of word-recognition strategies. In doing so, the teachers have incrementally fostered students' ability to become strategic and independent readers. The purpose of this article is to describe the technique of coaching word recognition. I review the reading process, elaborate on coaching, present examples of coaching, share elements to consider when preparing to coach, discuss implications for practice, and offer conclusions about the nature of effective coaching.

THE READING PROCESS: AN OVERVIEW

Reading is a complex problem-solving process in which readers actively pursue meaning (Graves, Juel, & Graves, 2001). It is a "message-getting" activity (Clay, 1991, p. 6) in which readers draw on multiple interacting knowledge sources to construct meaning. Readers use these sources as they engage in basic (i.e., word-recognition and syntactic) and higher order (i.e., inferring and reasoning) processes (van den Broek & Kremer, 2000). As educators, we seek to develop students' knowledge of these sources and their ability to coordinate and apply them flexibly as they read.

The challenges readers face as they work to construct meaning vary with skill and experience. In early primary grade classrooms, word recognition presents a significant challenge for students. While they work to construct meaning, they must devote considerable attention to activating, coordinating, and applying their developing knowledge of word-recognition strategies. That so much attention be allocated to acquiring and refining word-recognition strategies is no insignificant matter. Word recognition is a necessary but insufficient condition for comprehension: It alone does not guarantee comprehension, but without it comprehension cannot occur (van den Broek & Kremer, 2000).

COACHING: THE CONCEPT

Coaching is a technique with roots in the work of Marie Clay. Clay (2001) viewed young readers as active learners working to construct a self-extending system—a system that "bring[s] about new forms of mediation," "alter[s] an existing working system to become more effective," and "compile[s] more effective assemblies of systems" (p. 136). One way children develop this system is through "powerful interactions with teachers" during reading (p. 136). Teachers closely observe students and intervene to support their developing strategic processes. Clay described this approach as an interactive option. Others have referred to it as coaching (Taylor, Pearson, Lark, & Walpole, 2000) and scaffolding (Pressley et al., 2001). Recent students have identified the technique as characteristic of accomplished classroom teachers (Pressley et al., 2001; Taylor et al., 2000) and Reading Recovery teachers (Rodgers, 2000) and as a technique that distinguishes more effective teachers from their less effective peers (Taylor et al.).

The following discussion is derived from my case study (Clark, 2000) of the instructional talk of a subset of teachers identified as most accomplished in a large-scale study of effective practice (Taylor et al., 2000). The case study inquiry occurred after the original study in which the teachers participated and yielded a unique data set and analysis. All teacher and student names used in this discussion are pseudonyms.

All teachers grouped their students homogenously for guided reading instruction based on their perceptions of students' abilities, and each teacher altered the composition of these groups as necessary to meet student needs. I first describe the nature of teachers' instructional cues, then I provide examples of their coaching as it occurred in context.

The Nature of Teachers' Instructional Cues

In the case study (Clark, 2000), I qualitatively analyzed teachers' instructional cues using the constant-comparison method (Glaser & Strauss, 1967). In coding the cues, I engaged in an iterative process in which categories emerged from the data. As successive transcripts were coded, and additional categories emerged and were refined, I returned to previously coded cues and adjusted my analysis. In addition, I used two independent coders to validate my structure.

Teachers' cues to students were of two broad types: generate cues to prompt thought and more focused cues to prompt specific action. The cues took the form of either questions or statements to students. The particular characteristics of these cues are as follows.

General Cues to Promote Thought

General cues to promote thought are nonspecific in nature. They prompt readers to think about their knowledge of word-recognition strategies and how to apply this knowledge to the word-recognition task (e.g., How are you going to figure that out? What can you do?). They do not, however, point readers in any one direction. The responsibility for thinking is with the reader. Examples of these cues are presented in Table 7.1.

Table 7.1 General Cues to Prompt Thought

Questions

What do you know about that?

What are you going to do to help yourself out?

If you're stuck, what can you do?

What do you think?

How are you going to figure that out?

Statements

Look for something you already know how to do.

Look and think what you need to do.

Cues to Prompt Specific Action

Cues to prompt specific action provide readers with more detailed information about the word-recognition task. They focus readers' attention on graphophonic knowledge, word-part identification strategies, and contextual supports.

Cues that focus readers' attention on grapheme-phoneme correspondences direct them to consider individual letters and sounds (e.g., It's a soft *c*. The *y* is acting like an *i*) and multiple-letter phonic elements such as blends (e.g., What does *spr-* say?), digraphs (e.g., What does *ch-* say? Remember, *gh* can make an *f* sound), and *r*-controlled vowels (e.g., Does the *-or* sound like *-or* in corn or in actor?).

Other specific cues direct readers' attention to larger word-part identification strategies. They encourage readers to locate phonograms (e.g., I see one of our word families), known smaller words (e.g., Is there a little word in there? It's a compound word: the first word is. . . .), and

inflected (e.g., Take off the *-es/-ed/-ing*) and derivational (e.g., Take off the *-ly*) endings in an unfamiliar print word.

Cues that make use of contextual supports focus readers' attention on the inappropriateness of a miscue (e.g., You said *taking* [thinking] of ways.), the possibilities given the sentence (e.g., What ___ are you counting?), and picture supports (e.g., Use pictures and words). I summarize these cues in Table 7.2 to illustrate their specific characteristics.

Table 7.2   Cues to Prompt Specific Action

Grapheme-Phoneme Correspondences	*Word-Part Identification Strategies*
The first *g* is hard; the second *g* is soft.	Is there a chunk you know?
It's a soft *c*.	Can you take something off?
Throw away the *g-h*.	Take off or cover up the ending and see what the word is.
Remember, *g-h* can make an *f* sound.	
It's a double vowel.	Look for a little word.
It's an *r*-controlled vowel.	It's a compound word. What's the first or second word?
What do you think that *e* should sound like?	
Put an /h/ sound in front of *is*.	Use of contextual supports (sentence structure or picture supports)
The *y* is acting like an *i*.	
It's a blend. I see a blend.	This is what you said: Brer Fox is taking [thinking] of ways. . . .
Does that sound right?	Let's read to the end and see what makes sense.
What ___ are you counting? What would make sense there?	Use pictures and words.
	What in the picture starts with the letter you see?

The Nature of Coaching as It Occurred in Context

The following dialogues illustrate the manner in which coaching occurred within the context of guided reading lessons. In the dialogues, teachers cue students as they apply their knowledge of word-recognition strategies during reading. The cues reflect multiple instructional focuses.

Grade 1

Mrs. Fry taught first grade in a rural school. There were 22 children in her classroom (20 European American and 2 Hispanic children). Mrs. Fry had a master's degree in elementary education and 11 years of experience, all in grade 1. Mrs. Wilson taught first grade in an urban school. There were 18 students in her classroom, all of whom were African American. She had 10 years of experience, 7 in kindergarten and 3 in first grade. She had a master's degree in curriculum and instruction.

In these teachers' classrooms, leveled texts were used. These are sets of texts that move from simpler to more complex reading and can be matched to students' abilities (Brabham & Villaume, 2002). Mrs. Fry's students read texts she believed would enable them to practice previously taught phonic elements and orthographic patterns. Mrs. Wilson's students read books that came with a reading series.

In the following example, Mrs. Fry's first graders are reading *"Not Now!" Said the Cow* (Oppenheim, 1989), when a child has difficulty recognizing the word *grunted*. The text reads, " 'I can't do that!' meowed the cat. 'Not my job!' grunted hog" (p. 24).

Student:	" 'I can't do that!' meowed the cat. 'Not my job!' grunt . . . grunt. . . .'"
Teacher:	If there were an *-ed* at the end of that word, how would you say that?
Student:	Grundable?
Teacher:	Say it again?
Student:	Grunded.
Teacher:	Okay, cover up the *-ed* and see what the word is.
Student:	Grund.
Teacher:	Is it grun*d* or grun*t?*
Student:	Grunt. . . .'" Grunted hog."

In this dialogue, the reader's first attempt to recognize *grunted* results in *grunt*. The child recognizes the root of the unfamiliar word *grunted*. Mrs. Fry prompts her to call to mind her knowledge of how to pronounce *-ed* at the end of a word. The reader responds with two inaccurate attempts, *grundable* and *grunded*, in which she has both applied incorrect word endings and replaced the /t/ with /d/. Mrs. Fry then becomes more directive. She tells the reader to cover up the confusing word part and

note the remaining word. The reader identifies the root as *grund*. Mrs. Fry repeats the inaccurate partial word identification and presents it with the correct root, emphasizing the ending consonant in each. The reader is then able to identify the correct root, *grunt*, and the unfamiliar word, *grunted*. Mrs. Fry began this coaching episode by being less directive in her cueing of the child. When the child was unsuccessful, Mrs. Fry became more directive and specific in her cueing.

In Mrs. Wilson's first-grade class, the students have difficulty decoding the word *wind* during a choral reading of *Where Does Everybody Go?* (Dodds, 1996). The text reads, "When rain falls hard and cold wind blows, where does everybody go?" (p. 2).

All:	"When rain falls hard and cold . . . wuh . . . wuh. . . ." [wind]
Teacher:	Let's look for a chunk in there.
Student 1:	Can I sound it out?
Student 2:	Here's a chunk.
Teacher:	Where's a chunk?
Student 2:	[no response]
Teacher:	What is this word right here? [Teacher frames *in* within *wind*]
All:	[chorally] in.
Student 2:	That's what I said.
All:	Wind.
Teacher:	Okay. Let's start from the beginning.
All:	"When rain falls hard and cold wind blows, where does everybody go?"

In response to the students' attempt to decode the word, Mrs. Wilson cues them to look for a known word part (Let's look for a chunk in there). When the students are unsuccessful, she frames the known word *in* within the unknown word *wind*. With these two cues of increasing support, the students are able to decode the word and continue choral reading.

Grade 2

Mrs. Green taught second grade in a suburban school. She had a master's degree in curriculum development and four years of experience, with two of those years at grade 2. There were 17 students in her classroom (16 European American and 1 Korean American). Mr. Turner taught second grade in an urban school. He had three years of experience, all at grade 2, and he was completing his master's degree. He taught 22 students, all of whom were African American.

These second-grade teachers' coaching proceeded in a similar manner. In their classrooms, leveled texts as well as more literary texts are used during guided-reading lessons.

In Mr. Turner's class, a small group of students is reading *Red Riding Hood* (Marshall, 1987). The text reads, "Beyond the forest, they came to a patch of sunflowers. 'Why not pick a few?' suggested the wolf" (p. 12). One reader has difficulty with the word *suggested*.

Student:	" 'Why not pick a few?' snuggled [suggested] the wolf."
Teacher:	Okay, try it again. Sug. . . .
Student:	[no response]
Teacher:	The first *g* is hard. The second *g* is soft. *Sug*-juh. . . .
Student:	"Suggested the wolf."

In this exchange, the reader has miscued the word *suggested*. Mr. Turner models the first part of the word, but the child is unable to use this information to recognize the word. Mr. Turner then cues the child to the different sounds the two *g*s make in the word and models each. With this support, the child is able to recognize the word and continue reading. In this dialogue, Mr. Turner models pronunciation of the first syllable. This proves insufficient, so he intervenes with very focused cues.

When another small group of Mr. Turner's students is reading *The Color Wizard* (Brenner, 1989), a reader encounters difficulty when she comes to the word *fence*. The text reads, "So he painted his castle and his fence all blue" (p. 8).

Student:	"So he painted his . . . castle blue."
Teacher:	Use your strategies.
Student:	"So he painted his castle and his. . . ." [fence]
Teacher:	Use pictures and words.
Student:	His fuh . . . fllll . . . fountain.
Teacher:	Pictures and words, *f-e-n-c-e.*
Student:	Faces.
Teacher:	Look, *f-e-n,* you all should know says *fen.* That *c,* you could either make it a /k/ or /s/. *Fenk,* is that a word?
All:	[shake heads negative]
Teacher:	So what's left? Look at the picture there [points to the picture of a fence].
All:	Fence.
All:	"So he painted his castle and his fence all blue."

In this dialogue, Mr. Turner encourages the focal reader and her groupmates to use their knowledge of graphophonic and picture cues to recognize the unfamiliar print word *fence.* The readers are unable to systematically think through the application of their developing strategic knowledge, so Mr. Turner demonstrates the process, becoming more specific in his coaching as he proceeds. He indicates their familiarity with the spelling pattern that comprises the first part of the word (Look, *f-e-n,* you all should know says *fen*). Then he highlights the two sounds the letter *c* can make (That *c,* you could either make it a /k/ or /s/) and models the incorrect choice (*Fenk,* is that a word?). He then directs their attention to the illustration (So what's left? Look at the picture there). With this support, the children are able to recognize the word.

A reader in Mrs. Green's second-grade class has difficulty decoding the word *semisalted* (a word the child reports he has never seen) when reading *My Visit to the Aquarium* (Aliki, 1993). The text reads, "In the coastal stream exhibit, we saw fish that travel. They live in fresh and salt water, and in semisalted coastal streams that lead to the sea" (p. 23).

Student: "In the coastal stream exhibit, we saw fish that travel. They live in fresh and salt water, and in . . . solt. . . ."

Teacher: [points to a word in the book and sequentially covers the word parts *semi-* and *salted* with her finger] The *i* is long. Just *s-e-m-i.* . . .

Student: Sem. . . .

Teacher: Sem . . . and then a long *i*.

Student: Semi . . . salt. . . . Semisalted.

In this interaction, Mrs. Green directs the child to break the word into two parts and cues him to the vowel sound (The *i* is long). She leads him through the process, and he decodes the first syllable. Mrs. Green confirms the partial decoding and restates the graphophonic cue (and then the long *i*). With this support, the reader is able to recognize the word. Mrs. Green began the interaction by identifying a possible strategy and cueing a relevant sound, and then she became more specific by guiding the student through the strategy.

Eliciting Student Coaching

In Mrs. Fry's classroom, students had learned to contribute cues during coaching episodes. Mrs. Fry described her rationale for student coaching and how it came to occur in her classroom.

I think you have to have everybody involved when you're just addressing one child. So one day, I just started saying, "What does everybody else think?" and "Let's give some clues. How could you help her? What are some ways we could get unstuck?" And so then they're just thinking about it. Well, I could cover up that *s*. Oh look! There's a family there. What family is it? Oh, it's the *-at* family. And so everybody just became engaged in the conversation. (Clark, 2000, p. 105)

The following dialogue is representative of such a coaching episode. The students are reading *The Carrot Seed* (Krauss, 1945). The text reads "But he still pulled up the weeds around it every day and sprinkled the ground with water" (p. 17). Multiple students join Mrs. Fry in coaching a child struggling with *every*.

Student 1: "But he . . . still pulled up the weeds around the . . . it . . . a . . . a. . . ." [every]

Teacher: What do you think? Can you please touch the letters and say those sounds for me?

Student 1: Eh . . . vuh . . . er . . . ever. . . .

Teacher: There's a little word isn't there? What's the little word?

Student 1: Ever.

Teacher: Ever. . . . Now, slide to the end.

Student 1: Oh.

Teacher: Jim [another student with raised hand] thinks he knows.

Teacher: What about the *y*? Ever . . . ever . . . What's [the original reader] going to do?

Student 2: I know.

Teacher: You know?

Student 2: The *y* acts like an *i*.

Teacher: Are you sure? Then it would say evr*i* [long *i*].

Student 3: No, *-e* [long *e*].

Teacher: E [long *e* sound].

Student 1: "Every . . . day and sprinkled the ground with water."

When the reader encounters difficulty, Mrs. Fry initially intervenes with a general cue (What do you think?) and a directive to apply a strategy (Can you please touch the letters and say those sounds for me?). With this support, the reader recognizes the first two syllables in the word. The final *y* proves difficult, however. At this point, Mrs. Fry provides a more specific cue that directs the reader's attention to a known word part (There's a little word there. What's the little word?). The reader identifies the little word (*ever*), and Mrs. Fry then gives another directive (Now, slide to the end). The child remains unsuccessful, and another child raises his hand and provides a clue, albeit an inaccurate one (The *y* acts like an *i*). Mrs. Fry highlights the inaccuracy (Then it would say evr*i* [long *i*]). In so doing, she focuses the children's attention on the sound in question and implies they should try the other sound for *y*—a strategy she has taught them to apply. Another child then identifies the correct sound, and Mrs. Fry confirms it. With this support, the focal reader recognizes the word *every* and continues reading.

Preparing to Coach Word Recognition

In coaching word recognition, a teacher crafts cues that enable readers to think to the edge of their knowledge as they attempt to recognize unfamiliar words. To coach successfully, one must be aware of the knowledge sources available for word recognition, have specific knowledge of students' word-recognition abilities, be able to analyze a word, and generate appropriate cues.

Factors to Consider

In discussing coaching, the teachers highlighted factors they considered when crafting cues:

- The sounds the vowels or vowel teams (e.g., *oa, ea, oi, ay, ou*) make in the word
- The sound the *y* makes when it is a vowel (e.g., *e* or *i*)
- The sounds consonants make, such as *c, s,* or *g*
- The presence of blends (e.g., *cr, fl, sk, spr, scr*) or digraphs (e.g., *ch, sh, th, wh, gh*)
- The presence of *r*-controlled vowels (e.g., *ur, ir, er, or, ar*)
- The presence of silent letters (e.g., *e, gh*)
- The presence of known word parts, such as phonograms (e.g., *-ake, -at, -ame*); smaller

words within a word; or affixes (e.g., *re-, un-, -ment, -ly, -ed, -ing*)
- The context in which a word occurs

Generating Cues: Two Textual Examples

The teachers all said that coaching was critical to their success in helping children learn to read, and they indicated it was a technique they acquired after completing their teacher certification programs. Intrigued by this, I now include coaching in reading methods courses I teach. Following are examples of cues my preservice teachers generated.

The first example is from *Lon Po Po* (Young, 1989). The three children menaced by the wolf in the story have climbed a gingko tree to escape and outwit the wolf. He waits below, expecting to be furnished with ginkgo nuts. The text reads, " 'But Po Po, gingko is magic only if it is plucked directly from the tree' " (p. 18).

Our hypothetical reader is unable to recognize the word *gingko*. The following cues will support the reader as he or she works to decode the word.

- Think what two sounds *g* can make (/g/ and /j/).
- What sound does *-ing* make?
- Break it into two parts (*ging* and *-ko*).

The second example is from *My Visit to the Aquarium* (Aliki, 1993). The text reads, "Turtles and other reptiles share the leafy habitat" (p. 22). Our hypothetical student is unable to recognize the word *reptiles*. The following cues might help the reader.

- Cover up the *s*.
- There is a word family (*ile*).
- The first *e* is short.
- Break it into two parts (*rep* and *-tiles*).
- What kind of animals are turtles and alligators? Think about the picture and the first part of the word (*rep*). What would make sense?

Implications for Practice

Coaching Word Recognition

Three points should be made when crafting cues to support word recognition. First, it is crucial to understand word recognition in beginning reading. While readers draw on multiple knowledge sources to understand what they read (Clay, 2001), not all knowledge sources contribute equally to word recognition. Word recognition relies heavily on graphophonic knowledge (Pressley, 1998). Further, a developmental process is involved in learning to read words, and at different stages of development children read words in qualitatively different ways (Ehri, 1991; Juel, 1991).

Juel (1991) summarized three stages of word recognition: the selective-cue stage, the spelling-sound stage, and the automatic stage. In the selective-cue stage, children recognize words by attending to the environment in which words are placed (e.g., a red hexagon) or to selected print but nonalphabetic features (e.g., the two circles in *moon*). In this stage, children rely heavily on picture and semantic context clues to recognize words; their challenge is to acquire the alphabetic principle and to learn to attend to the letters and spelling patterns in words (Lipson & Wixson, 2003).

In the spelling-sound stage (Juel, 1991), children primarily use letter-sound relationships in their word recognitions and approximations. The challenge at this stage is to fully analyze the letters in words, paying particular attention to vowels and to the spelling patterns that represent the larger parts of words (Lipson & Wixson, 2003).

In the automatic stage (Juel, 1991), children are able to recognize most words they read without conscious attention to spelling-sound relationships. This ability to read words at sight enables children to allocate more attention to higher level meaning-making processes (van den Broek & Kremer, 2000).

We must recognize these developmental differences as we craft instructional cues, and the cues we craft should support students' movement through the stages of word learning. Children at the selective-cue stage should be cued to attend to print information to build their awareness and knowledge of letter-sound relationships. Those at the spelling-sound stage should be cued to fully analyze the constituent letters and orthographic patterns in words. This is not to suggest that there is no place for syntactic and semantic cues in word-recognition instruction. Rather, such cues should follow students' initial print-driven approximations (Juel, 1991). Once children have achieved automaticity of word recognition, they are beyond the stage at which they can benefit from word-level cues. Cues should address other areas of the reading process, unless a specific word-level need arises.

Second, it is important to craft cues that reflect contemporary understandings of phonics instruction. Two teachers whose practice is shared in this discussion encouraged children to use phonic rules to recognize words. I agree with Cunningham and Allington (2003) and Stahl (2002); we should not emphasize the use of phonic rules with students. As Stahl (2002) noted, Theodore Clymer found that "only 45% of the commonly taught phonics rules worked as much as 75% of the time" (p. 65). The guidelines for exemplary phonics instruction Stahl offered in this article can guide the construction of phonic cues. Cues should be "clear and direct," should focus on "reading words, not learning rules," may "include onsets and rimes," and should develop "independent word recognition strategies, focusing attention on the internal structure of words" (Stahl, 2002, pp. 63–66).

Third, it is important to consider the language we use to convey our assistance. That is, the language of phonics and orthography need not necessarily be the language of phonics and orthographic instruction. It is critical that children develop facility with orthographic patterns and phonic elements (e.g., *ake, sh, oi*). It is much less important that they become facile with the terms associated with these patterns and elements (i.e., rime, digraph, diphthong). This is not to say discipline-specific language should not be used, merely that we should be mindful of its use. The teachers whose practice is represented in this article used specific phonic terms with students. The terms they used were consistent with their knowledge and philosophies, and they were terms they had taught and reinforced throughout the year. Other teachers may choose different terms or choose not to use specific terms at all.

Coaching Across the Reading Process

The first- and second-grade teachers in this article coached word recognition. This is not surprising; learning to recognize words is extremely important for first- and second-grade readers. However, coaching can and should be applied to other reading processes in the early primary years as well as in later years. Cunningham and Allington (2003) presented one instructional format designed specifically to support coaching across the reading process. They recommended coaching groups—small, flexible groups with whom the teacher meets for 10 to 15 minutes a few times a week to coach word recognition and comprehension strategies per students' changing needs. In the groups, students of somewhat varied abilities are coached and learn to coach themselves and others. They then apply their knowledge of coaching in other instructional contexts. These groups seem an ideal way to make coaching a part of an instructional program.

Learning to Coach

It is of note that the teachers whose practice is shared in this article reported learning to coach while engaged in professional development efforts in early reading intervention. The Early Intervention in Reading (EIR) training in which Mr. Turner, Mrs. Wilson, and Mrs. Green participated involved an initial half-day workshop, monthly meetings in which they analyzed their videotaped practice, and regular classroom visits by mentors. The Right Start training in which Mrs. Fry participated involved an initial two-day workshop, monthly meetings in which participants analyzed videotapes of their practice, and ongoing observation and support by project staff

(Hiebert & Taylor, 2000). A primary focus of these efforts was the development of a strategic stance toward reading. Coaching reflects this stance. Teachers learned to support students on a moment-to-moment basis as they applied strategic knowledge while reading connected text. The teachers completed this professional development within one (Mrs. Wilson, Mr. Turner, Mrs. Green) and five (Mrs. Fry) years of the inquiry from which this discussion is drawn.

Because coaching is such an effective technique, it would make sense to include it in university reading methods courses. This is likely happening in some teacher education programs, particularly in light of recent discussions of the importance of scaffolding students' learning (Pressley et al., 2001; Taylor et al., 2000) and of the provision of a viable model for engaging in such instruction (Cunningham & Allington, 2003). I envision instruction in which preservice teachers in methods courses invoke, build, and make explicit their understanding of our graphophonic system and English orthography, use this understanding to craft cues for words with which their students struggle, and apply these cues as they read one-on-one with students. As in the EIR and Right Start intervention efforts, ongoing analysis and discussion of taped practice are critical to development.

COACHING IS A POWERFUL TECHNIQUE

The teachers in this article are highly skilled educators. Close examination of their interactions with children led me to believe three factors contributed to their coaching effectiveness. First, the teachers had considerable explicit knowledge of phonics and English orthography. They understood the relationships between graphemes and phonemes and knew how English words are put together. Second, they maintained a conscious awareness of students' instructional histories. They kept anecdotal records of what they had taught and whom they had taught, and they referred to these records to plan instruction. Third, the teachers were aware of students' individual strengths and weaknesses. When coaching, they drew on their knowledge of phonics, orthography, instructional history, and students' abilities in a coordinated manner to provide tailored, moment-to-moment cues that helped students to identify and apply their knowledge of word-recognition strategies as they read.

Strickland (2002) stated that young readers need to view learning to read as "a problem-solving activit[y] that they are increasingly equipped to handle on their own" (p. 80). Coaching is a powerful technique that supports young readers as they problem solve during meaningful reading experiences and develop reading independence.

Kathleen F. Clark teaches in the Department of Reading and Language Arts in the School of Education and Human Service at Oakland University.

Article 8

HELPING CHILDREN LINK SOUND TO PRINT

Phonics Procedures for Small-Group or Whole-Class Settings

LAURICE M. JOSEPH

Word boxes and word sorts are two phonic approaches that help children make connections between sound and print by gaining an awareness of the phonological and orthographic features of words. Word boxes and word sort lessons are engaging because students are asked to manipulate materials and make frequent responses rather than completing paper and pencil workbook exercises. These approaches have been typically used in one-to-one instructional situations. This article provides step-by-step procedures, showing how variations of these approaches can also be used in small-group and whole-class settings.

C hildren with disabilities in reading and written expression often have difficulty grasping basic word identification and spelling skills (Aaron & Joshi, 1992) due to a limited understanding of the phonological and orthographic structures of words (Levy & Carr, 1990).

SOURCE: Joseph, L. M. (2002). Helping Children Link Sound to Print. *Interventions in School and Clinic, 37*(4), 217–221. Reprinted by permission of Sage Publications, Inc.

Moreover, even if these students may have acquired phonemic awareness and are able to recognize some words by sight, they usually have difficulty making letter-sound correspondences (Stahl, 1998). Lacking skills in making letter-sound associations often results in difficulties reading words that are new to the learner (Adams & Henry, 1997). Therefore, students with basic reading difficulties need phonics instruction that focuses explicitly on letter-sound associations.

Word boxes and word sorting are two contemporary phonic approaches that encompass critical components of effective phonics instruction. Essentially, these word-study methods help children grasp the phonological and orthographic features that are necessary for identifying and spelling words.

In the following discussion, each of these approaches is described in a step-by-step fashion.

WORD BOXES

Word boxes (Clay, 1993) consist of connected boxes that are created by dividing a drawn rectangle into sections corresponding to the number of sounds heard in words. For instance, a word that contains three distinct phonemes would be represented by a rectangle drawn with two vertical lines to create three connected boxes. Word boxes consist of three phases: segmenting sounds, matching letters to sounds, and writing letters. Often each phase of this approach is presented separately over several lessons using various words that are in students' speaking vocabulary but not yet in their reading vocabulary. These three phases can be combined during any given lesson. When that happens, students systematically segment sounds, match letters to sounds, and spell words.

Word Box Procedures

The following is a step-by-step description of how to implement the three phases of word boxes in a lesson with a small group or a classroom of students (see also Figures 8.1, 8.1a, and 8.1b).

Step 1: Segmenting Sounds

Materials needed

1. Magnetic board with a drawn rectangle divided into boxes according to the number of sounds in a presented word.

2. Small magnets for each student (round, square, or pegs) used for counters.

3. Pictures (when appropriate) representing target words.

A picture representing a word can be placed above the connected boxes on the magnetic board (in some instances, pictures cannot be used because it is difficult to represent some words pictorially). The children are given counters (small magnets) that are placed below the divided sections of the rectangle. The number of counters corresponds to the number of connected boxes. The instructor models the task by saying the word slowly and placing counters in the respective divided sections of the rectangle as each sound is articulated. Next, students place counters synchronously in respective divided sections of the drawn rectangle while the teacher says the word slowly. The students may then chorally articulate a word and place counters in the respective divided sections.

Step 2: Letter-to-Sound Matching

Materials needed

1. Same as in Step 1, except the counters are replaced with magnetic letters.

In this step the students, as a class or a small group, respond in a synchronous fashion as they simultaneously say the sounds of a word slowly and place magnetic letters in the respective sections of the divided rectangle.

Step 3: Spelling

Materials needed

1. Same as in Step 2, except the magnetic letters are replaced with magic markers.

2. Tissue paper to serve as eraser for each student.

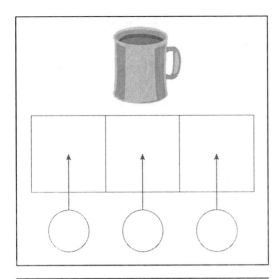

Figure 8.1 Three-step procedure for boxing words. Step 1: Children place counters in connected boxes as each sound in the word /mug/ is slowly articulated.

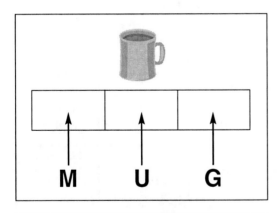

Figure 8.1a Step 2: Children place magnetic letters in connected boxes as each sound in the word /mug/ is slowly articulated.

The students write the letters of the word in the connected boxes as they say each sound slowly. Tissue paper is used to wipe the letters off the magnetic board when the task has been completed. When the students understand one-to-one correspondences between letters and sounds through writing, the sections of the rectangle are represented as drawn dotted lines to fade part of the support structure (i.e., connected boxes). Eventually, the dotted lines are removed, and students are asked to write words in the rectangle as the teacher presents them.

Students should have plenty of opportunities to practice each step on every presented word (use tissue as eraser between words). Once children complete a round of all three steps, the teacher presents another word, and the steps are repeated. Going through all three steps each word allows the children to make connections among the sounds that make up the word, the letters that correspond to those sounds, and the spelling pattern (i.e., letter sequences) of the word.

Figure 8.1b Step 3: Children write the letters in connected boxes as each sound in the word /mug/ is slowly articulated.

Word Sorting

Word sorts help children categorize words that share common phonological and orthographic components (Bear, Invernizzi, Templeton, & Johnston, 1996). Essentially, two or more sets of words that share common spelling or sound patterns are placed on note cards. One word from each set serves as a category word. The rest are to be shuffled and sorted below the appropriate category words. The number of categories can vary. You may have anywhere from two to six or more categories depending on students' functioning levels and the nature of the words being taught.

Sorting Procedures

Different kinds of sorts may be used, including sound sorts, visual (printed word) sorts, spelling sorts, and conceptual (meaning) sorts. Several types of sorts may be combined in one lesson to help children make connections between phonological and orthographic features about sets of words. The following three-step sorting procedure (see Figures 8.2, 8.2a, and 8.2b) helps children acquire phonemic awareness, recognize common and distinct spelling patterns in words, and write words that share common spelling patterns.

Step 1: Phonemic Sorts

Materials needed

1. Category words printed on note cards for each student.

2. Colored chips for each student.

3. List of words that the teacher will say orally to the students.

The printed category note cards are placed horizontally on students' desks, and each student receives a chip. The teacher says a word aloud, and the students place a chip below the category word that sounds similar to the word. The teacher checks students' responses and provides corrective feedback. Then another word is introduced. The students are asked to move the chip and place it below the appropriate category word. This process continues until at least three words for each category have been presented.

Step 2: Word Sorts

Materials needed

1. Note cards with category words used in Step 1.

2. A stack of shuffled words printed on note cards (same set of words presented orally in Step 1).

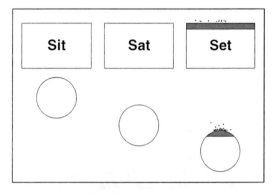

Figure 8.2   Three-step procedure for sorting words. Step 1: Children place chips below category words according to similar sound patterns.

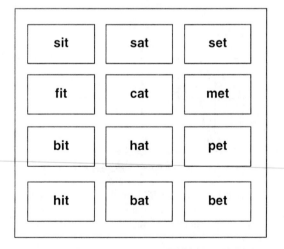

Figure 8.2a   Step 2: Children sort words printed on note cards below category words according to similar spelling patterns.

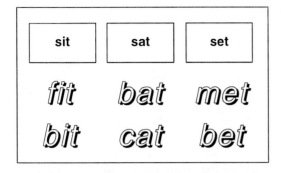

| sit | sat | set |

fit *bat* *met*
bit *cat* *bet*

Figure 8.2b Step 3: Children spell words below category words according to similar spelling and sound patterns.

Using Peer Tutors With Word Study Phonic Approaches

Classwide peer tutoring has been effective for helping children improve academically (e.g., Greenwood, 1991) and for increasing academic engaged time by providing lots of opportunities to respond (e.g., Greenwood, Delquadri, & Hall, 1984). To facilitate practice, feedback, and mastery of phonic skills, word study phonic approaches can be implemented in a peer-tutoring format.

Peer Tutoring With Word Boxes

The tutor is given a folder containing a stack of note cards with words printed on them, a scoring sheet, graph paper, and pockets labeled "stop" and "go" inserted on the inside of the folders where cards can be placed. The tutee is given counters, magnetic letters, a marker, and a magnetic board or dry erase board with a drawn rectangle divided into sections.

As the tutor articulates a word slowly from the stack of words presented on the note cards, the tutee (a) places the counters in respective divided sections, (b) places magnetic letters, and (c) finally writes the letters in the connected boxes. The tutor guides the tutee and provides corrective feedback as necessary. The process can be repeated until all words in the stack have been presented. Once the process has been completed, the tutor quizzes the tutee by having him or her read the words from the note cards or write them on a numbered sheet of paper. The tutor can record the number correct on the quizzes and, along with the tutee, graph the scores. The words that were identified and spelled correctly are placed into a pocket labeled the "stop" pocket, and the incorrect words are placed into a pocket labeled the "go" pocket. The tutor and tutee reverse their roles, switch folders, and another word box lesson takes place.

The category words are placed on the far top of desks. Students are to pick up the printed note cards and place them below the respective category words according to shared spelling patterns. After completing the task, students may read their list of words out loud. If a word is sorted incorrectly, students refer to the established categories to self-check and self-correct.

Step 3: Spelling Sorts

Materials needed

1. A pencil and a sheet of paper for each student (the same category words are printed across the top).

Using the same set of words contained in Steps 1 and 2, the teacher says a word aloud, and the students are asked to write it below the appropriate category word, which may share similar sound or spelling patterns or both. This process continues until the entire set of words has been presented.

Categories can be added to the existing categories along with a stack of words or new categories and sets of words can be presented, and the entire three-step process is repeated.

Peer Tutoring With Word Sorts

The tutor is given a folder containing a stack of note cards with words printed on them. Some of the words printed on note cards are labeled as category words. The category words are placed on the desk or table in front of the tutee. The tutee receives a chip or token. The tutor reads words printed on note cards, and the tutee places the chip below the respective category words. After the entire stack of words printed on note cards has been presented orally, it is shuffled and given to the tutee who conducts a visual sort of the word cards according to appropriate categories. The tutee is also required to read the words to the tutor. Once the tutee completes the visual sort, the cards are returned to the tutor, who provides the tutee with a sheet of paper with the category words printed across the top. The words are presented aloud by the tutor, and the tutee is asked to write them below the respective category words. Quizzes involve reading words aloud as they are presented on note cards and spelling the same words on a numbered sheet as they are presented orally. After quizzes are scored and graphed, the tutee and tutor switch roles using another folder with a different set of words.

SUMMARY

Phonic approaches that include phonemic, word recognition, and spelling components facilitate students' understandings of the connection between spoken and written language. Specifically, word boxes help students segment sounds, note letter sequences in words, and make one-to-one letter-sound correspondences. Word sorting helps students discriminate among words that share similar sound and spelling patterns from those that do not. Word boxes and word sorts can be used in small-group, whole-class, and in peer tutoring contexts.

ABOUT THE AUTHOR

Laurice M. Joseph, PhD, is an assistant professor of school psychology and special education at The Ohio State University. Her current interests include literacy interventions, learning disabilities, and academic engaged time. Address: Laurice M. Joseph, College of Education, The Ohio State University, 288 B Arps Hall, 1945 North High St., Columbus, Ohio 43210.

Article 9

PHONEMES IN USE

Multiple Activities for a Critical Process

PATRICK C. MANYAK

Several decades of research have established the critical role of phonemic awareness in the development of beginning reading. Phonemic awareness contributes centrally to children's acquisition of the alphabetic principle—the understanding that the letters of the alphabet represent phonemes in speech. This understanding makes early phonics instruction useful for children and facilitates children's ability to blend letter sounds while decoding words, to learn sight words reliably, and to spell phonetically. Given this importance, it is vital that teachers understand phonemic awareness and can teach it effectively.

Phonemic awareness is often referred to as the ability to recognize and manipulate phonemes—the individual sounds in words in oral language. While this is a practical way to talk about phonemic awareness, scholars often point out that phonemes commingle with one another in

speech and that the "individual sounds in words" are more of a hypothetical notion than a linguistic reality (Liberman, 1998). This commingling of phonemes suggests why it can be difficult for children to acquire phonemic awareness. Recent research suggests that instruction that helps children to attend to vocal gestures (the particular ways that we position our mouths as we produce phonemes) is effective in developing phonemic awareness and has a positive effect on the students' word reading (Castiglioni-Spalten & Ehri, 2003). This type of explicit attention to vocal gestures can be helpful at the beginning of phonemic awareness instruction. A second key finding in phonemic awareness research is that instruction involving segmenting and blending phonemes combined with a focus on the letters that represent those phonemes contributes greatly to success in beginning reading and spelling (National Reading Panel, 2000). This is

SOURCE: Manyak, P. (2008). Phonemes in Use: Multiple Activities for a Critical Process. *The Reading Teacher, 61*(8), 659–662. Reprinted by permission of the International Reading Association.

the type of phonemic awareness instruction that I address in this article.

For several years I have helped teachers in Wyoming meet the needs of students who enter kindergarten or first grade with little phonemic awareness or decoding ability. We have learned that after having received some basic instruction in phonemic awareness and letter–sound relationships, students benefit greatly from a variety of activities combining phoneme segmenting and blending with letter–sound instruction. As a result, we have borrowed, adapted, and invented in order to create a small set of activities focusing on what we call "phonemes in use." These activities all involve segmenting and blending phonemes within the context of reading and writing words, but each one does so in a slightly different way. This variety allows children to develop a robust ability to apply phonemic awareness to tasks of reading and writing and supports students who may struggle with this critical process. Here, I offer brief descriptions of our five phonemes-in-use activities and practical ideas for implementing them in the classroom.

BEGINNING-MIDDLE-END

We borrowed the Beginning-Middle-End activity from *Words Their Way* (Bear, Invernizzi, Templeton, & Johnston, 2003). The activity involves three steps. First, the teacher places the letters of a three- or four-letter word face down in a pocket chart so that the students cannot see them and tells the students the word (e.g., *man*). Second, the teacher and students sing the following brief song to the tune of "Are You Sleeping, Brother John?": "Beginning, middle, end; beginning, middle, end / Where is the sound? Where is the sound? / Where's the *mmm* in *man?* Where's the *mmm* in *man?* / Let's find out. Let's find out." After the song, one student comes forward, picks the position (beginning, middle, or end) that he or she believes the sound is in, and turns around the letter card. If the child reveals the letter *m* the

teacher asks the class, "Does this letter make the *mmm* sound?" and confirms, "Yes, it does, doesn't it? We hear the *mmm* sound at the beginning of *man.*" The class then repeats this process for the other two phonemes. Of course, the game is more engaging if the teacher does not ask for the phonemes in sequence. Beginning-Middle-End is useful as an extremely brief, whole-class activity. I recommend that teachers use Beginning-Middle-End one or two times each day during kindergarten and early first grade, selecting words that reinforce the letters that students are studying.

SAY-IT-AND-MOVE-IT

Say-It-And-Move-It was the cornerstone of the extremely effective phonemic awareness intervention researched by Ball and Blachman (1991) and made available to teachers in the manual *Road to the Code* (Blachman, Ball, Black, & Tangel, 2000). Say-It-And-Move-It involves moving tiles one at a time from the top of a piece of paper down to a line at the bottom, saying each corresponding phoneme while doing so (/m/, /a/, /n/) and then running a finger under the tiles while blending the phonemes to make the word (*man*). I like teachers to introduce Say-It-And-Move-It at the same time that they begin letter–sound instruction and to use the activity to reinforce the letters being taught.

Students are given a couple of blank tiles and tiles with the letters that they are currently learning (e.g., the letters *m* and *b*). The teacher then announces a two- or three-phoneme word that begins with one of those letters (e.g., *my*) and asks the students to find the tile with the letter that makes the phoneme they hear at the beginning of the word. The students put the *m* tile together with a blank tile at the top of their paper and then move the tiles down while saying each phoneme, using the *m* tile to represent /m/ and the blank tile to represent /long i/. Then they run their fingers under the letters while saying the word *my*.

At this point, the students place the tiles back at the top of the page. The teacher and students repeat this sequence with other words that either begin or end with the letters being practiced. For instance, for a session focusing on *m* and *b,* the teacher might give the following words: *my, man, ram, him, mat, be, bat, tub, bow* (using only two tiles because there are only two phonemes), and *rub.* For each of these words, the students use the *m* or *b* letter tiles to represent the /m/ and /b/ phonemes and the blank tiles for all other phonemes. It is important that the children practice hearing the target phonemes at the beginning and end of the words. The teachers that I work with like to do Say-It-And-Move-It daily in small groups as a part of a series of fast-paced letter–sound activities.

Scaffolded Spelling

As children carefully stretch out words and attempt to represent the sounds through invented spelling, they develop phonemic awareness (Richgels, 2001). Motivated by this insight, we developed the brief activity of Scaffolded Spelling as a way to increase phonemic awareness and reinforce letter–sound knowledge in the context of writing words. In simple terms, Scaffolded Spelling engages students in carefully stretching out the phonemes in simple words, writing the letters that correspond to those phonemes, and reading the words that they have written. The teacher begins by choosing three to five words that include letters that the children have or are currently learning. For instance, if a kindergarten class has just studied the phonemes represented by *m, b, s,* and *t,* the teacher might choose the following words: *man, sat, bat,* and *tab.* The teacher introduces the first word and asks the students to stretch it out and listen for the phonemes. During this step, the students put their hands to their lips and "stretch the word like bubble gum," slowly pulling their hand away from their lips while carefully articulating each

phoneme in the word. The teacher then tells the students to stretch the word again, to stop after "the first sound of the stretch," and to think about what letter makes that sound.

The students then write the letter on a white board or half sheet of paper. Next, the teacher directs the students to stretch the word again and listen for the second sound in the stretch. They then write the letter that makes that sound. The students repeat this process for the last sound in the stretch and thus complete their spelling of the word. The group repeats this process with two or three more words and then the teacher and children read the list of words that they have written two times. As children learn more letter sounds, the teacher can begin to incorporate words featuring consonant digraphs and clusters. Typically, it takes only a few minutes to write three to five words. Yet in those few minutes the children have listened for the individual phonemes in words, reinforced their knowledge of the letters that represent those phonemes, and practiced a deliberate process for invented spelling that they can use while writing independently. As with Say-It-And-Move-It, many teachers that I work with incorporate Scaffolded Spelling into a daily set of fast-paced word study activities.

Word Mapping

Efficient and reliable sight-word learning occurs when children completely map the letters in a word's spelling to the phonemes in its pronunciation, thus producing lasting bonds in memory between a word's spelling, pronunciation, and meaning (Ehri, 1998). Inspired by this principle, I developed a visual letter–phoneme mapping activity to use with high-frequency words. Word Mapping borrows a portion of Gaskins, Ehri, Cress, O'Hara, and Donnelly's (1996/1997) Word Analysis Chart. The teachers that I work with use a large laminated version of this chart (shown in Figure 9.1) for daily word mapping.

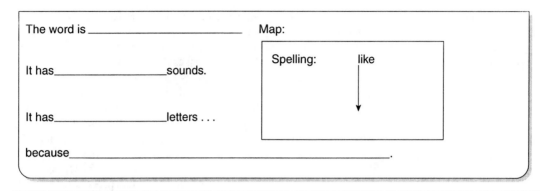

Figure 9.1   Word Mapping Chart

The teacher begins Word Mapping by announcing the high-frequency word to be mapped. The teacher and students segment the word together, counting the phonemes on their fingers. The teacher then writes the number of phonemes on the chart. Next, the teacher writes the word, asks the students to count the letters, and adds the number to the chart. The teacher maps the letters to the phonemes before filling in the "because" line. First, the teacher writes the word. Then the teacher segments the word orally, asking students what letter or letters best represent each phoneme and writing those letters below the spelling. (We continually remind the students that the proper spelling is on top and that the letters below stand for the sounds we hear in the word.) The teacher then returns to the beginning of the word, asks the students what letter or letters make each sound, and draws arrows connecting the letters to the sounds they make. When there is a consonant digraph or vowel pair in which two letters make one phoneme, we make a Y-shaped arrow to map this relationship. Silent letters have no arrow connecting them to phonemes. Finally, the teacher asks the students to use this visual map to explain any discrepancy between the number of sounds and letters (e.g., "The *th* makes one sound" or "The *e* is silent") and summarizes their explanation on the chart. If the sounds and letters are the same, then the students simply respond, "Each letter makes a sound." While the teachers use Word Mapping to introduce nearly all high-frequency words, they do not do so with a few words that contain multiple irregularities or highly unpredictable letter–sound relationships (such as *one*) that might prove to be confusing. I suggest that teachers use Word Mapping in a whole-class setting for each new high-frequency word that they introduce (one to two per day).

WORD WALL BOXES

The last activity, Word Wall Boxes, provides children with a daily review of three previously introduced high-frequency words while continuing to build their phonemic awareness. The Word Wall Boxes activity uses a sheet featuring Elkonin boxes (Figure 9.2). Popularized by Reading Recovery, Elkonin boxes provide another way for students to map the letters of a word to its phonemes. The teacher begins the high-frequency word review by asking a student to choose a word from the word wall. The teacher directs the students to the first line of boxes on their sheet and asks them to cross out any boxes beyond those required for the phonemes in the word (e.g., "How many sounds does *the* have? Two? OK, count two boxes and cross out the rest"). Then, the teacher asks the class to stretch out the word carefully and write the letter or letters that represent each phoneme in the corresponding boxes. Many teachers work along with

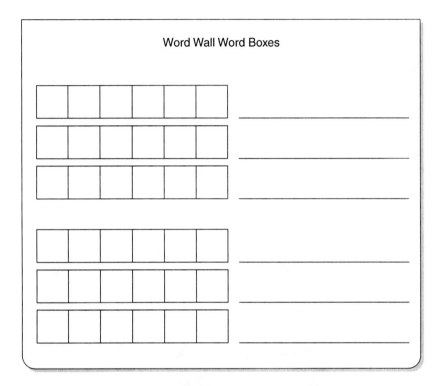

Figure 9.2   Word Wall Boxes Sheet

students on the overhead. Then the students write the word on the line beside the boxes and repeat this process with two additional words. Finally, the children read the three words written on the lines chorally and independently. As when using the word analysis chart, the teachers that I work with do not use the Elkonin boxes with a few words containing multiple irregularities or highly unpredictable letter–sound relationships. If a student chooses one of those words during the word wall review, I recommend that teachers simply review the word by talking through its irregularities with the students.

Each of the activities that I have described prompts students to use phonemic awareness within the context of reading and writing words. Used together as part of a fast-paced word study block or sprinkled throughout the day, they offer children multiple opportunities to develop and solidify this critical process in beginning reading.

Patrick Manyak teaches at the University of Wyoming, Laramie.

Article 10

Teaching Spelling in the Primary Grades

A National Survey of Instructional Practices and Adaptations

Steve Graham, Paul Morphy,
Karen R. Harris, Barbara Fink-Chorzempa,
Bruce Saddler, Susan Moran, and Linda Mason

Primary grade teachers randomly selected from across the United States completed a survey (N = 168) that examined their instructional practices in spelling and the types of adaptations they made for struggling spellers. Almost every teacher surveyed reported teaching spelling, and the vast majority of respondents implemented a complex and multifaceted instructional program that applied a variety of research-supported procedures. Although some teachers were sensitive to the instructional needs of weaker spellers and reported making many different adaptations for these students, a sizable minority of teachers (42%) indicated they made few or no adaptations. In addition, the teachers indicated that 27% of their students experienced difficulty with spelling, calling into question the effectiveness of their instruction with these children.

This article is available as a full-text PDF at http://www.sagepub.com/cappello/.

SOURCE: Graham, S., et al. (2008). Teaching Spelling in the Primary Grades: A National Survey of Instructional Practices and Adaptations. *American Educational Research Journal*, *45*(3), 796–825. Reprinted by permission of Sage Publications, Inc.

Section IV

FLUENCY

OVERVIEW

Contrary to practice in many school districts, fluency is more than simply the rate at which text is read. Research definitions of fluency include accuracy, automaticity, and prosody or the phasing and intonation in reading text. Fluent readers do not need to focus on word recognition. Indeed, fluency is necessary so that students do not exert too much emphasis and attention on decoding at the expense of comprehension. All of the articles in this section situate fluency within a comprehension-centered definition of literacy.

This section begins with Pikulski and Chard's (2005) broad definitions of fluency, specifically in relation to comprehension. In "Fluency: Bridge Between Decoding and Reading Comprehension," the authors challenge readers to move beyond oral reading definitions and focus on a "deep construct which includes accurate, efficient word recognition skills that permit a reader to construct the meaning of text." One of the strategies recommended by Pikulski and Chard is elaborated on by Therrien and Kubina (2006) in their article, "Developing Reading Fluency With Repeated Reading." The authors describe the characteristics of one effective tool for effective fluency instruction: repeated readings.

In Kuhn and Stahl's (2003) review of the literature on fluency, "Fluency: A Review of Developmental and Remedial Practices" (available at http://www.sagepub.com/cappello/), the authors provide readers with a theoretical and instructional overview with specific recommendations for classroom practice. Instructional approaches are categorized and organized for use with individuals as well as for classroom applications.

STRATEGY

The articles in this section focus on the theory and practical applications of fluency in classrooms. Complete the following "SQ3R" chart (Anderson & Armbruster, 2002) as you read the Pikulski and Chard article. The SQ3R strategy guides readers through the text using a 5-step sequence: survey, question, read, recite, and review. The purpose of this strategy is to help readers organize information in the text so they better remember the content. This strategy will help you review and remember the authors' recommendations for an instructional program based on a "deep" construct of fluency.

SQ3R STUDY STRATEGY

(Anderson & Armbruster, 2002)

DIRECTIONS

Follow the five steps (survey, question, read, recite, and review) to use the SQ3R study strategy. It will help you remember important ideas from the readings.

SURVEY: Look over Pikulski and Chard's (2005) article. Skim the title, introduction, and subtitles. Think about what you already know about fluency. Make a prediction about this article.

_____

_____

_____

_____

QUESTION	READ AND RECITE (and WRITE)
Turn each subtitle into a question. For this article, you will be focusing on the instructional recommendations.	• Read each subsection to find the answer to your question. • Recite and write the answer to each question you created.
Subtitle/Question #1: Building the graphophonic foundations for fluency	Answer #1:
Subtitle/Question #2: Oral language foundations for literacy	Answer #2:
Subtitle/Question #3: Teaching high-frequency vocabulary	Answer #3:

QUESTION	READ AND RECITE (and WRITE)
Subtitle/Question #4 Recognizing word parts and spelling patterns _____ _____ _____	Answer #4: _____ _____ _____ _____
Subtitle/Question #5: Teaching a decoding strategy _____ _____ _____	Answer #5: _____ _____ _____ _____
Subtitle/Question #6: Using appropriate texts to promote fluency _____ _____ _____	Answer #6: _____ _____ _____ _____
Subtitle/Question #7: Using repeated reading procedures _____ _____ _____	Answer #7: _____ _____ _____ _____
Subtitle/Question #8: Encouraging wide independent reading _____ _____ _____	Answer #8: _____ _____ _____ _____
Subtitle/Question #9: The assessment of fluency _____ _____ _____	Answer #9: _____ _____ _____ _____

REVIEW: Now that you have finished the article, consider the text as a whole. How do the subsections fit together? _____

_____

_____

_____

SOURCE: Anderson, T. H., & Armbruster, B. B. (2002). Studying. In P. D. Pearson (Ed.), *Handbook of Reading Research*. Mahwah, NJ: Lawrence Erlbaum.

Article 11

FLUENCY

Bridge Between Decoding and Reading Comprehension

JOHN J. PIKULSKI AND DAVID J. CHARD

As part of a developmental process of building decoding skills, fluency can form a bridge to reading comprehension.

Fluency, which has been referred to as a "neglected" aspect of reading by the National Reading Panel (National Institute of Child Health and Human Development [NICHD], 2000), currently is receiving substantial attention from researchers and practitioners. This may be because NICHD's influential *Report of the National Reading Panel* identified fluency as one of only five critical components of reading.

Fluency has sometimes been viewed as essentially an oral reading phenomenon. The National Reading Panel defined reading fluency as "the ability to read text quickly, accurately, and with proper expression" (NICHD,

2000, p. 3-5). Definitions that emphasize the oral aspect of fluency may, at least in part, account for why fluency has not historically received much attention. The importance of oral reading pales dramatically in comparison to that of silent reading comprehension. Most readers spend a minuscule amount of time doing oral reading as compared to silent reading.

A definition of fluency needs to encompass more than oral reading. *The Literacy Dictionary: The Vocabulary of Reading and Writing* defined fluency as "freedom from word identification problems that might hinder comprehension"

SOURCE: Pikulski, J. J., & Chard, D. J. (2005). Fluency: Bridge Between Decoding and Reading Comprehension. *The Reading Teacher, 58*(6), 510–519. Reprinted by permission of the International Reading Association.

(Harris & Hodges, 1995, p. 85). This definition enlarges our understanding of reading fluency to include comprehension. Samuels (2002), a pioneer in research and theory in reading fluency, cited this expanded definition as a major force in elevating the importance of fluency in the field of reading.

The correlation between fluency and comprehension was clearly established by a large-scale data analysis from the National Assessment of Educational Progress in Reading (Pinnell et al., 1995). In that study, 44% of the subjects were not fluent when reading grade-level appropriate materials; the study also showed a significant, positive relationship between oral reading fluency and reading comprehension. However, the relationship between fluency and comprehension is fairly complex. This complexity was summed up well by Stecker, Roser, and Martinez (1998) in their review of fluency research: "The issue of whether fluency is an outgrowth [of] or a contributor to comprehension is unresolved. There is empirical evidence to support both positions" (p. 300). However, in the end they concluded, "Fluency has been shown to have a 'reciprocal relationship' with comprehension, with each fostering the other" (p. 306).

A comprehensive definition, then, would relate the centrality of fluency to reading comprehension and its established dimensions. We propose the following synthesis of the definitions in the *Report of the National Reading Panel* (NICHD, 2000) and *The Literacy Dictionary* (Harris & Hodges, 1995):

> Reading fluency refers to efficient, effective word-recognition skills that permit a reader to construct the meaning of text. Fluency is manifested in accurate, rapid, expressive oral reading and is applied during, and makes possible, silent reading comprehension.

We think that the issue of a definition is not trivial but central to making important decisions about the teaching and assessment of fluency. Directly related to a definition is whether a "surface" or "deep" construct of fluency is adopted. A surface construct of fluency builds on an oral reading definition and views the development of fluency as the direct treatment of accuracy, speed, and prosody of oral reading. A surface view of fluency leads to practices such as simply urging students to read faster. On the other hand, a deep construct views fluency far more broadly as part of a developmental process of building decoding skills that will form a bridge to reading comprehension and that will have a reciprocal, causal relationship with reading comprehension. In a deep view of fluency, it becomes necessary to think about fluency as part of a child's earliest experiences with print and with the phonology that becomes associated with that print. In this view, efficient decoding is consistently related to comprehension.

HISTORICAL DEVELOPMENT OF THE CONSTRUCT OF READING FLUENCY

While an early discussion of the construct of reading fluency is found in the classic publication by Huey (1908/1968), most discussions of fluency trace their modern theoretical foundations to the 1974 seminal article by LaBerge and Samuels. These researchers argued that human beings can attend to only one thing at a time. We are able to do more than one thing at a time if we alternate our attention between two or more activities, or if one of the activities is so well learned that it can be performed automatically. Reading successfully is a complex interaction of language, sensory perception, memory, and motivation. To illustrate the role of fluency, it helps to characterize this multifaceted process as including *at least* two activities: (1) word identification or decoding and (2) comprehension, or the construction of the meaning of text. In order for reading to proceed effectively, the reader cannot focus attention on both processes. Constructing meaning involves making inferences, responding critically, and so on, and it *always* requires attention. The nonfluent reader can alternate attention between the two processes; however, this makes reading a laborious, often punishing process. If attention is drained by decoding words, little or no capacity is available for the attention-demanding process of comprehending. Therefore, automaticity of decoding—a critical component of fluency—is essential for high levels of reading achievement.

Stanovich (1986) also contributed significantly to elevating the importance of reading fluency. In his classic article, he demonstrated a clear relationship between fluency and the amount of reading in which a reader engages. Readers who achieve some fluency are likely to read more extensively than readers who lack fluency because the latter find reading difficult. Stanovich pointed out that as a result of reading more extensively, readers grow in all the skills that contribute to fluency and in fluency itself. Nonfluent readers who avoid reading fall further and further behind.

The *Report of the National Reading Panel* (NICHD, 2000) significantly elevated attention to fluency. The panel's review largely reflected the position that "fluency develops from reading practice" (p. 3-1). Therefore, much of the review was devoted to analyzing the research supporting two major approaches to providing students with reading practice: "first, procedures that emphasize repeated oral reading practice or guided repeated oral reading practice; and second, all formal efforts to increase the amounts of independent or recreational reading that students engage in" (p. 3-5). The panel concluded that there is substantial evidence to support the use of repeated reading procedures. However, they raised questions about the evidence to support wide independent reading for promoting fluency:

> There seems little reason to reject the idea that lots of silent reading would provide students with valuable practice that would enhance fluency and, ultimately, comprehension. . . . [I]t could be that if you read more, you will become a better reader; however, it also seems possible that better readers simply choose to read more. (p. 3-21)

In essence, the panel concluded that while there is very strong correlational support for independent reading contributing to fluency, there is no convincing experimental research to

show that increasing independent reading will increase fluency or reading achievement.

The previous discussion of fluency and of the related research is certainly not a comprehensive review. Many important research findings are omitted. For more comprehensive discussions of fluency, readers are encouraged to consult reviews, such as those by the National Reading Panel (NICHD, 2000), Reutzel (1996), Stecker et al. (1998), and the entire Summer 1991 (volume 30, number 3) issue of the journal *Theory Into Practice.*

While the National Reading Panel's report (NICHD, 2000) is clearly instructive for its critical review of how practice may affect fluency, the position taken in this article is that a much broader approach is warranted, one that addresses the need for systematic, long-term, explicit fluency instruction along with careful monitoring and assessment for at least some students. Rather than focus solely on how to improve fluency when it is not developing as expected, it would seem instructive to examine the elements of early literacy that contribute to fluency.

EHRI'S STAGES OF READING DEVELOPMENT AND FLUENCY

Ehri (1995, 1998) has developed a carefully researched, elegant theory of how readers systematically progress in stages to achieve fluency, which is in line with a "deep," developmental construct of fluency. We review her theory because it brings coherence to much of the research on fluency and because it offers a framework for instruction designed to promote and improve fluency. Ehri distinguished four stages of reading development.

Readers at the Pre-Alphabetic Stage have no appreciation of the alphabetic principle—the idea that, in languages like English, there is a systematic relationship between the limited number of sounds of the language and the graphic forms (letters) of the language. At the Pre-Alphabetic Stage, children attempt to translate the unfamiliar visual forms of print into familiar oral language through visual clues in the print. Children might remember the word *monkey* by associating the descending shape of the last letter with a monkey's tail. Obviously this is not a productive approach and quickly leads to confusion because *my, pony,* and many other words would also be read as *monkey.*

At the Partial Alphabetic Stage, readers have learned that letters and sounds are related, and they begin to use that insight. However, they are not able to deal with the full complexity of the sounds in words, so they aren't able to make complete use of the letter–sound relationships. Therefore, children focus on the most salient parts of a word and consequently use initial and, later, final letters as the clues to a printed word's pronunciation. If readers at this stage learn that the letter sequence *g-e-t* is *get,* they may focus just on the *g* and the sound it represents to identify the word. However, using this strategy of focusing on the first letter, the letter sequences *give, go,* and *gorilla* might also be identified as *get.* While children at this stage of development will make errors in identifying words, they can make progress toward becoming fluent because they have developed the insight that the letters of a word are clues to the sounds of the word.

As children become more familiar with letters and sounds, they move into the Fully Alphabetic Stage. Now, even though they may never have seen it in print before, if they know the sounds commonly associated with the letters *b-u-g,* they can think about the sounds for each of the letters and blend them together to arrive at the pronunciation of the word. As a result of encountering the printed word *bug* several times, as few as four times according to a widely cited study (Reitsma, 1983), children come to accurately, instantly identify the word *bug* without attending to the individual letters, sounds, or letter–sound associations. Ehri (1998) described skilled reading in the following way: "Most of the words are known by sight. Sight reading is a fast-acting process. The term *sight* indicates that sight of the word activates that word in memory, including information about its spelling, pronunciation, typical role in sentences, and meaning" (pp. 11–12). This instant, accurate, and automatic access to all

these dimensions of a printed word is the needed fluency that will allow readers to focus their attention on comprehension rather than on decoding. It is important to note that Ehri's theory and research indicate that it is the careful processing of print in the Fully Alphabetic Stage that leads to this rapid, instant recognition. Partial Alphabetic readers store incomplete representations of words and, therefore, confuse similar words, such as *were, where, wire,* and *wore.* However, once the word form is fully processed, with repeated encounters of the word, it is recognized instantly.

Readers who recognize whole words instantly have reached the Consolidated Alphabetic Stage. They also develop another valuable, attention-saving decoding skill. Not only do readers at this stage store words as units, but also repeated encounters with words allow them to store letter patterns across different words. A multiletter unit like *-ent* will be stored as a unit as a result of reading the words *went, sent,* and *bent.* Upon encountering the word *dent* for the first time, a consolidated alphabetic reader would need to connect only two units: *d* and *-ent,* rather than the four units that the Fully Alphabetic reader would need to combine. While this approach to reading a word is faster than blending the individual phonemes, it is not as fast and efficient as sight recognition of the word. Readers who have reached the Consolidated Stage of reading development are in a good position to progress toward increasingly efficient fluency; however, in addition to these advanced word-identification skills, they also need to increase their language vocabulary development in order to reach advanced levels of fluent reading.

AN INSTRUCTIONAL PROGRAM BASED ON A DEEP CONSTRUCT OF FLUENCY

Our perception is that until recently some, though certainly not all, educators took a rather simplistic approach to developing fluency that is summed up in the admonition "read, read, read." The expectation was that if students read more, they would achieve fluency. However, research and theory suggest that at least some students will need expert instruction and teacher guidance in order to progress efficiently through the stages of reading development. We propose a nine-step developmental program for improving fluency. Some of the steps, such as building the graphophonic foundation for fluency or high-frequency vocabulary, are usually accomplished in a relatively short period of time (often a year or two), while others, such as building oral language skills, are unending. Our goal in this article is to outline the rationale and the breadth of instruction needed for developing a deep construct of fluency. We give some references that offer suggestions for instructional strategies and materials, but space limitations preclude treating each of these areas in depth. The nine-step program should include

1. Building the graphophonic foundations for fluency, including phonological awareness, letter familiarity, and phonics.

2. Building and extending vocabulary and oral language skills.

3. Providing expert instruction and practice in the recognition of high-frequency vocabulary.

4. Teaching common word parts and spelling patterns.

5. Teaching, modeling, and providing practice in the application of a decoding strategy.

6. Using appropriate texts to coach strategic behaviors and to build reading speed.

7. Using repeated reading procedures as an intervention approach for struggling readers.

8. Extending growing fluency through wide independent reading.

9. Monitoring fluency development through appropriate assessment procedures.

Building the Graphophonic Foundations for Fluency

Ehri listed three prerequisite graphophonic capabilities as foundations for fluency: (1) letter familiarity, (2) phonemic awareness, and (3) knowledge of how graphemes typically represent phonemes in words.

A recent publication from the International Reading Association (Strickland & Schickedanz, 2004) offered practical, research-based approaches to developing graphophonic skills, including letter familiarity, in emergent readers. Instruction in the area of phonological awareness has been addressed widely (e.g., Adams, Foorman, Lundberg, & Beeler, 1998; O'Connor, Notari-Syverson, & Vadasy, 1998).

The importance of the three graphophonic factors is fully documented in numerous research reports (e.g., Adams, 1990; NICHD, 2000). In order to move from the Pre-Alphabetic Stage to the Partial Alphabetic and Fully Alphabetic Stages (Ehri, 1998), students need to grasp the alphabetic principle and to apply efficiently information about the relationship between the letters and sounds (phonics) to recognize words. This clearly requires a high level of familiarity with letter forms as well as the ability to segment and blend the smallest units of spoken language, phonemes.

Oral Language Foundations for Fluency

In addition to the graphophonic skills, Ehri's (1998) theory requires a foundation in language skills so that students are familiar with the syntax or grammatical function of the words and phrases they are reading and with their meanings.

Developing the oral language and vocabulary skills of children, particularly those who are learning English as a second language or those who spent their preschool years in language-restricted environments, is one of the greatest challenges facing educators. Many excellent resources exist for meeting this challenge. Recent examples include texts by Beck, McKeown, and Kucan (2002); Blachowicz and Fisher (2002); and Nagy (1988).

Ehri (1998) showed that progress in reading beyond the beginning stages is dependent on oral language development, pointing out that reading words, particularly reading them fluently, is dependent on familiarity with them in their oral form. If the syntactic and meaning aspects of the word are to be activated, they must be part of what the reader knows through oral language development. For the word-recognition process as proposed in Ehri's theory to be complete, it must connect with meaning that has been developed as another aspect of language development. Consider the following words: *zigzags* and *onychophagia* (nail biting). Mature readers have no difficulty very rapidly decoding the first word, even though it is one of the least frequent words in printed English. However, it takes mature readers much longer to arrive at a pronunciation of the second word because it not only infrequently appears in print but is also very infrequently used in speech and, therefore, is not likely to be a word in a mature reader's mental lexicon. Unless a printed word can connect with both the phonological memory for the word and also with the syntactical and meaning aspects of the word, it cannot be fluently decoded or read. It seems unfortunate that many surface discussions of fluency fail to make the point that fluency is dependent on the reader's vocabulary as well as on his or her decoding skills.

Teaching High-Frequency Vocabulary

High-frequency words are those words that appear over and over again in our language—words such as *the, of, and, at,* and *to.* If developing readers cannot instantly identify these words, they are unlikely to become fluent.

One approach to building fluent recognition of high-frequency vocabulary, exceedingly popular with primary-grade teachers, is the use of word walls where high-frequency vocabulary is posted and practiced (P. M. Cunningham, 2000). Cunningham also offered a variety of other approaches to teaching high-frequency words, as did Bear, Invernizzi, Templeton, and Johnston (1996).

Ehri's (1995, 1998) theory and research also offered important, practical teaching suggestions. High-frequency words often have been seen as a serious challenge because many of them don't lend themselves to straightforward application of decoding skills; they are, in the

jargon of reading instruction, phonically irregular—words such as *the, of, was,* and *have.* Teaching high-frequency words can be difficult. This difficulty may very well contribute to the periodic abandonment of phonics approaches and the rise of whole-word approaches to teaching beginning reading skills, with accompanying emphasis on drill using flashcards to force children to read the words as a whole. Ehri's work suggested that they also contain many letter–sound regularities, and that these regularities are the best mnemonics for developing accurate, instant recognition. For example, while the word *have* does not follow the generalization about the effect of a final *e* on a preceding vowel sound, the *h, v,* and *e* all behave as they should, and the *a* does represent a sound that it often represents. Ehri suggested that we should point out the regular elements of irregular words in order to help children gain instant recognition of them. This is a practice rarely mentioned by "experts" or used by teachers, but it might play a very important role in avoiding difficulty with such words and thus promoting the development of fluency.

Recognizing Word Parts and Spelling Patterns

Word parts and spelling patterns are combinations of letters such as *at, ell, ick,* and *op,* which are found as units in many words that appear in beginning reading texts.

Here again, P. M. Cunningham (2000) and Bear et al. (1996) are among the many resources that offer practical teaching suggestions, including a list of the most common word parts found in beginning reading materials.

Introducing students to multiple-letter units clearly helps to move them from the Fully Alphabetic to the Consolidated Alphabetic Stage. However, Ehri's (1995, 1998) research and theory offered an important instructional generalization—students should first be introduced to and made cognizant of the individual letters and sounds that constitute the rime (a Fully Alphabetic approach) in order to better recall and identify the unit.

Teaching a Decoding Strategy

There are several major ways in which words can be recognized or identified in print: instantly as units; through recognition and blending of phonic elements; through the context in which they appear, including language/sentence context and picture clues; or by checking the phonetic respellings of a dictionary or glossary. Ehri's (1995) theory is clear: The best way to recognize words is through instant recognition that drains no attention. All other approaches require attention. However, when a word is not instantly recognized, it is useful for readers to be strategic.

Ehri's (1995) theory suggested a strategic approach to dealing with words that are not instantly recognized. In kindergarten and the beginning of first grade, emphasis is on moving young readers from the Partial Alphabetic Stage to the Fully Alphabetic Stage of reading, with an emphasis on careful attention to the graphophonic characteristics of the word. By the middle of first grade, the goal is to move students increasingly into the Consolidated Alphabetic Stage. The italicized portion of the following strategy is recommended as young readers become familiar with word parts.

- Look at the letters from left to right.

- As you look at the letters, think about the sounds for the letters.

- Blend the sounds together *and look for word parts you know* to read the word.

- Ask yourself, "Is this a word I know? Does it make sense in what I am reading?"

- If it doesn't make sense, try other strategies (e.g., pronouncing the word another way or reading on).

Readers who are at the Partial Alphabetic and Fully Alphabetic Stages will need to look carefully at the word they are trying to identify, think about the sounds the letters are likely to represent, and then use the skill of phoneme blending to try to arrive at the correct decoding or pronunciation of the word. Because some words are not completely phonically regular, students should then be encouraged to ask themselves if their use of phonics results in the identification of a word that makes sense—that it is a word they have heard before and fits the context of what they are reading. As students begin to move from the Fully Alphabetic to the Consolidated Alphabetic Stage of development, in addition to using phonic elements, they should also be encouraged to look for word parts (chunks) and spelling patterns that they know, such as phonograms. The presentation of phonics and word parts, followed by use of context, appears to be, by far, the best order.

Use of context as the primary approach to identifying words has serious limitations. First, if the context is highly predictive of a word, it is likely that students will not pay attention to the graphic information in the word. Careful processing of the printed form is what eventually enables a reader to recognize that word instantly. This is a major limitation of the predictable texts that use very heavy, artificial context to allow word identification. Second, context rarely leads to the correct identification of a specific word. Ehri (1998) reviewed research suggesting that words in a text that carry the most meaning can be correctly identified by context only about 10% of the time. However, context and the other approaches to decoding words do play an important role in decoding—that of confirming the identification of words. As Ehri put it,

> As each sight word is fixated, its meaning and pronunciation are triggered in memory quickly and automatically. However, the other word reading processes do not lie dormant; their contribution is not to identify words in text but to confirm the identity already determined. Knowledge of the graphophonic system confirms that the word's pronunciation fits the spelling on the page. Knowledge of syntax confirms that the word fits into the structure of the sentence. World knowledge and text memory confirm that the word's meaning is consistent with the text's meaning up to that point. (p. 11)

Using Appropriate Texts to Promote Fluency

In order for progress in fluency to be made, students need to practice and apply their growing word-identification skills to appropriate texts. Appropriate texts are particularly critical for students having difficulty with word-identification skills. Guided reading is once again a useful way to match students and texts. Resources such as the work of Fountas and Pinnell (1996) offer guidance in selecting texts and providing appropriate instruction with those texts.

Hiebert and Fisher (in press) studied fluency development as it relates to the features of the texts used for promoting fluency. Specifically, they were interested in examining the effects of texts in which particular text features were carefully controlled. The treatment texts that Hiebert and Fisher designed had the following key features: a small number of unique words, a high percentage of most frequently used words, and often repeated critical words (those words that influence the meaning of the text most). Students in the comparison group read from texts typically associated with commercial reading programs. Students reading in the treatment texts made significant gains in fluency over their peers in the comparison condition. There also seemed to be an effect for comprehension for second-language learners. These findings suggested that the features of the texts being used to promote fluency should be carefully considered.

Using Repeated Reading Procedures

As noted earlier in this article, the *Report of the National Reading Panel* (NICHD, 2000) was unequivocal in its support of repeated reading procedures. The references described a range of procedures in sufficient detail to allow teachers to employ them with students who need extra support in developing fluency. These procedures included those described as repeated reading (Samuels, 1979), neurological impress (Heckelman, 1969), radio reading (Greene, 1979), paired reading (Topping, 1987), "and a variety of similar techniques" (p. 3-1).

A review of these approaches suggests substantial differences in the procedures used and the amount of teacher guidance offered (Chard, Vaughn, & Tyler, 2002; Kuhn & Stahl, 2000). However, as noted, the panel concluded that all appeared to have merit.

Encouraging Wide Independent Reading

For more able readers, repeated readings of the same texts may not be as necessary as they are for struggling readers. Increasing the amount of reading these able readers do may be as beneficial, and perhaps more so (Mathes & Fuchs, 1993).

The beneficial effects of wide reading appear to have been somewhat called into question by the *Report of the National Reading Panel* (NICHD, 2000), which reached the following conclusion: "Based on the existing evidence, the NRP can only indicate that while encouraging students to read might be beneficial, research has not yet demonstrated this in a clear and convincing manner" (p. 3). It is important to keep in mind that the National Reading Panel used restrictive criteria for what they included as research and also that it clearly held out the possibility of beneficial effects for wide reading.

Previous highly respected research syntheses have been far less restrained about the salutary effects of wide reading. For example, *Becoming a Nation of Readers* (Anderson, Hiebert, Scott, & Wilkinson, 1985) concluded,

> Research suggests that the amount of independent, silent reading that children do in school is significantly related to gains in reading achievement. . . . Research also shows that the amount of reading students do out of school is consistently related to gains in reading achievement. (pp. 76–77)

In her critical review of beginning reading research, Adams (1990) concluded, "Children should be given as much opportunity and encouragement as possible to practice their reading. Beyond the basics, children's reading facility, as well as their vocabulary and conceptual growth, depends strongly on the amount of text they read" (p. 127).

Stanovich and his colleagues (A. E. Cunningham & Stanovich, 1998; Nathan & Stanovich, 1991; Stanovich, 1986) have presented impressive research results and theoretical arguments for the value of wide reading. The evidence and rationale that they present, however, is that the positive relationship between reading achievement and wide reading may not be affected exclusively through the development of fluency but through the development of language and cognitive abilities as well.

If students are making adequate progress with fluency, wide reading rather than repeated readings may lead to greater improvements in vocabulary and comprehension. However, for less able readers experiencing particular difficulties with fluency, repeated readings remain an important approach to building *fluency*.

The Assessment of Fluency

As noted at the beginning of this article, fluency has been referred to as the "neglected aspect" of reading. The assessment of fluency, in particular, appears to have received very limited attention. There are few research studies that have investigated how fluency should be assessed or what criteria should be applied to determine whether or not a reader has achieved it. Perhaps it is this dearth of data that led the National Reading Panel (NICHD, 2000) to conclude,

A number of informal procedures can be used in the classroom to assess fluency: informal reading inventories, miscue analysis, pausing indices, and reading speed calculations. All these assessment procedures require oral reading of text, and all can provide an adequate index of fluency. (p. 3-9)

While few experimental studies have been conducted using these informal procedures, it may very well have been that the National Reading Panel recognized the practical need for classroom assessment, leading them to endorse procedures that may not have the strong research support they more typically require in other parts of the report.

To meet this practical need, there are many published informal inventories, such as the Qualitative Reading Inventory-III, and leveled texts, such as *Leveled Reading Passages* (Houghton Mifflin, 2001). These are just two examples of instruments that can be used to periodically and practically assess the four dimensions of fluency that are necessary for a full, deep, developmental construct of fluency: oral reading accuracy, oral reading rate, quality of oral reading, and reading comprehension.

Teachers who want to assess selective aspects of fluency can use guidelines that have been suggested for assessing oral reading rate and accuracy (e.g., Hasbrouck & Tindal, 1992; Rasinski, 2003). Likewise, procedures have been established for assessing the quality of oral reading using standardized rubrics that go beyond rate and accuracy, such as those based upon National Assessment of Educational Progress (NAEP) data (Pinnell et al., 1995).

We recommend that teachers at second grade and beyond take measures of fluency, at least at the beginning and end of a school year, to gauge progress in this important area and to check periodically through the year any students who are making doubtful progress. A more comprehensive review of the research related to fluency assessment is beyond the scope of this article.

FLUENCY IS NECESSARY

While the construct of fluency might have been neglected in the past, it is receiving much-deserved attention presently. A very strong research and theoretical base indicates that while fluency in and of itself is not sufficient to ensure high levels of reading achievement, fluency is absolutely necessary for that achievement because it depends upon and typically reflects comprehension. If a reader has not developed fluency, the process of decoding words drains attention, and insufficient attention is available for constructing the meaning of texts.

Fluency builds on a foundation of oral language skills, phonemic awareness, familiarity with letter forms, and efficient decoding skills. Ehri's (1995) description of the stages of word recognition explains how readers come to recognize words by sight through the careful processing of print.

Substantial research has also been conducted on how best to develop fluency for students who do not yet have it. While there is a dearth of experimental research studies on developing fluency through increasing the amount of independent reading in which students engage, there is substantial correlational evidence showing a clear relationship between the amount students read, their reading fluency, and their reading comprehension. However, students who are nonachieving in reading are not in a position to engage in wide reading, and they may need more guidance and support in order to develop fluency. Research shows that a variety of procedures based on repeated readings can help readers to improve their fluency.

Little research is available to guide the assessment of fluency. While more research is needed on the issues of adequate rates of fluency at various grade levels and for judging the quality of oral reading, there is good agreement that the comprehensive assessment of fluency must include measures of oral reading accuracy, rate of oral reading, and quality of oral reading. There is also growing agreement that these dimensions of fluency must be assessed within the context of reading comprehension. Fluency without accompanying high levels of reading comprehension is of very limited value.

John J. Pikulski is professor emeritus at the University of Delaware.
David J. Chard teaches at the University of Oregon at Eugene.

Article 12

DEVELOPING READING FLUENCY WITH REPEATED READING

WILLIAM J. THERRIEN AND RICHARD M. KUBINA JR.

Repeated reading has gained popularity as a technique for helping students achieve reading fluency. It is widely implemented and can be used for students with and without disabilities. Repeated reading has several components that make it more efficient. This article shares those components and provides a framework for setting up and using repeated reading in the classroom.

Reading, a complex process some have likened to rocket science (Moats, 1999), has become less of a mystery in recent years. Reports, such as that from the National Reading Panel (NRP, 2000), have highlighted extensive research that details how to best teach beginning reading. Topics in the NRP report include phonemic awareness, phonics instruction, comprehension, computer technology, and reading fluency. Fluency, in particular, has received an increasing amount of attention.

Kuhn and Stahl (2003) reviewed the literature for fluency used during developmental and remedial instruction and concluded that teachers should use fluency instruction more often because of the benefits to reading. Fluency serves as a bridge between decoding words and comprehension (Carnine, Silbert, Kame'enui, & Tarver, 2004). Moreover, oral reading fluency has been shown to predict comprehension better than such direct measures of reading comprehension as questioning, retelling, and cloze (Fuchs, Fuchs, & Hosp, 2001).

How can teachers best provide fluency instruction for their students? One answer lies in a technique called *repeated reading*. Repeated reading represents an educational strategy for building reading fluency in which

---

SOURCE: Therrien, W. J., & Kubina, R. M., Jr. (2006). Developing Reading Fluency With Repeated Reading. *Intervention in School and Clinic, 41*(3), 156–160. Reprinted by permission of Sage Publications, Inc.

a student rereads a passage until meeting a criterion level (Dahl, 1977; Samuels, 1979). Research shows that repeated reading can facilitate growth in reading fluency and other aspects of reading achievement (Adams, 1990; NRP, 2000; Therrien, 2004). We present four elements to consider when deciding whether and how to implement repeated reading.

DETERMINE IF STUDENTS HAVE THE NECESSARY PREREQUISITE SKILLS

Regardless of present grade level, repeated reading appears beneficial for students who read between a first- and third-grade instructional level. The intervention may also be useful for students who, although able to decode words above a third-grade level, read in a slow, halting manner. Repeated reading is not recommended for students who read below a first-grade level, as they have yet to acquire foundational reading skills (e.g., letter–sound correspondences, blending words).

The research base for repeated reading covers non-disabled students (Bryant et al., 2000; O'Shea, Sindelar, & O'Shea, 1985; Rasinski, Padak, Linek, & Sturtevant, 1994), students with learning disabilities (Bryant et al., 2000; Freeland, Skinner, Jackson, McDaniel, & Smith, 2000; Gilbert, Williams, & McLaughlin, 1996; Mathes & Fuchs, 1993; Mercer, Campbell, Miller, Mercer, & Lane, 2000; O'Shea, Sindelar, & O'Shea, 1987; Rashotte & Torgesen, 1985; Sindelar, Monda, & O'Shea, 1990; Vaughn, Chard, Bryant, Coleman, & Kouzekanani, 2000), high-functioning students with autism (Kamps, Barbetta, Leonard, & Delquadri, 1994), and students with low vision (Koenig & Layton, 1998). The intervention has also been used successfully with students in second (Dowhower, 1987) through eighth (Mercer et al., 2000) grades who have an instructional reading level between first (Weinstein & Cooke, 1992) and fifth grade (Homan, Klesius, & Hite, 1993).

It is instructive to think of repeated reading within the context of stages of learning. Mercer and Mercer (2001) described stages of learning as levels through which a student progresses. As the student advances through the stages of learning, the skill or behavior becomes increasingly more functional. The stages of learning progress as follows:

1. entry level,
2. acquisition,
3. proficiency,
4. maintenance,
5. generalization, and
6. adaptation.

Teachers provide instruction in the acquisition stage and help foster an accurate performance of a skill. At the proficiency stage, the aim is to develop fluency or a behavior that can be performed with both accuracy and speed (Mercer & Mercer, 2001). Thus, repeated reading can be thought of as a well-organized practice strategy resulting in sharpened decoding skills.

CHOOSE AN APPROPRIATE FORMAT FOR THE INTERVENTION

Repeated reading has been effectively implemented in a variety of formats. Interventions have been successfully conducted by teachers (Dowhower, 1987; O'Shea et al., 1987), paraprofessionals (Mercer et al., 2000), and peer tutors (Rasinski et al., 1994; Stoddard, Valcante, Sindelar, O'Shea, & Algozzine, 1993). Repeated reading has also been conducted as both a whole-class activity (Homan et al., 1993; Simmons, Fuchs, Fuchs, Mathes, & Hodge, 1995) and a pull-out program (O'Shea et al., 1985; Sindelar et al., 1990). Whole class administration can be accomplished with a peer-tutoring format. Peer-tutoring has been demonstrated to be both flexible and empirically sound (Miller, Barbetta, & Heron, 1994).

Intervention sessions should be conducted with sufficient frequency ranging from 3 to 5 times a week. Administration of repeated reading requires a time commitment between 10 to 20 min per session.

IMPLEMENT ESSENTIAL INSTRUCTIONAL COMPONENTS

Figure 12.1 shows that there are three essential instructional components to include in a repeated reading intervention (Therrien, 2004). First, passages should be read aloud to a competent tutor. Carefully selecting and preparing competent tutors is imperative because monitoring students' oral reading and providing feedback is directly tied to program success. A recent meta-analysis (Therrien, 2004) found that repeated reading interventions conducted by adults or well-trained peer tutors were, on average, three times more effective. Teachers must, therefore, ensure that all tutors are taught the skills needed to monitor tutees' oral reading and provide effective and timely feedback. Additionally, teachers should closely monitor peer groups during repeated reading sessions. If students have difficulty monitoring peers' oral reading and providing feedback, additional instruction should be given or adjustments made to the peer groupings.

The second instructional component is providing corrective feedback. Feedback on word errors and reading speed needs to be communicated to students. Depending on the type of word error, tutors should either give immediate or delayed corrective feedback. If the student hesitates on a word for 3 seconds or omits a word, error correction should be given immediately. Otherwise, error correction should be provided after the passage has been read but prior to having the tutee reread the passage. Error correction in both cases can be as simple as providing the word and asking the student to repeat it. After each passage reading, tutors should provide performance feedback to tutees on their reading speed and accuracy. For example, upon reaching the goal on the fourth reading, the tutor could say, "Great job, Sarah, You made the goal! You read 118 words and only made 1 mistake. That was 11 more

1. Passages should be read aloud to a competent tutor.	• Tutors must be trained to monitor students' oral reading and provide feedback.
2. Corrective feedback should be provided.	**Feedback on word errors**
	• Student hesitates for 3 seconds: provide word and have student repeat it.
	• Student mispronounces/omits word: provide word after reading is complete but prior to rereading.
	Performance feedback
	• Provide student with feedback on reading speed and accuracy after each passage reading.
3. Passages should be read until a performance criterion is reached.	• Read passages until student reaches a predetermined fluency level.

Figure 12.1 Repeated reading essential instructional components

words and 3 fewer errors than the last time you read it!" Providing performance feedback often motivates students as it allows them to explicitly see their progress.

The third instructional component is to reread passages until a performance criterion is reached. To ensure that students receive sufficient practice to become fluent, each passage should be reread until the student attains a performance criterion goal. An appropriate performance criterion should be selected based on the student's instructional reading level. Here are examples of performance criteria based on grade levels: second grade, 94 correct words per minute; third grade, 114 correct words per minute (Hasbrouck & Tindal, 1992). Although the use of a performance criterion is recommended, passages should, in general, be at a difficulty level where the student can achieve the goal in a reasonable amount of time. If a student consistently needs to reread passages for extended periods of time to meet the criterion, easier passages should be used. Similarly, if a tutee is consistently able to reach criterion in a few readings, more challenging passages should be used.

SELECT APPROPRIATE READING MATERIAL AND OBTAIN ADDITIONAL SUPPLIES

Three items are necessary to conduct a repeated reading intervention: instructional-level reading passages, a timer, and data-tracking sheets. Passages within students' instructional level (i.e., passages read with 85% to 95% word accuracy) that can be read by students in 1 to 2 min are preferable. Many teachers may find that their schools already have suitable reading materials. If materials are not available, teachers may purchase commercially prepared passages. A digital countdown timer or stopwatch is needed for tutors to be able to track the reading rate of the tutee. If unavailable, tutors can be taught to time readings using the classroom clock. A tracking sheet should be designed and used to record progress through the intervention (see Figure 12.2 for an example).

FOLLOW REPEATED READING INSTRUCTIONAL SEQUENCE

Repeated reading can become a routine for students each day during reading instruction. Steps involved with repeated reading may occur with a teacher or paraprofessional assuming the permanent role of tutor or following in the peer-tutor format procedure:

1. Students pair up and gather their reading material. Materials consist of the reading passage (100- to 200-word passages) at the instructional level, a copy of the passage or a transparency and dry-erase marker, and a data sheet.

2. One student begins as the reader and the other student acts as the counter. The student who is the counter may also be the timer, depending on whether the teacher starts the timing for the group or has the students time each other.

3. When the timer begins, the reader reads and the counter marks incorrect or missed words on the reading passage. Should a reader hesitate on a word for 3 s or more, the counter should provide the word and have the reader repeat it and continue reading. If using a transparency, the reader puts the transparency over her copy of the passage and places an X on missed words with the dry-erase pen.

4. After the timer or teacher indicates the 1-min interval has ended, the counter provides feedback and has the reader repeat the correct pronunciation for words she missed.

5. The counter records the number of words read, errors, and correct words per minute on the data tracking sheet.

6. The student engages in another repeated reading by rereading the passage and receiving feedback. Students can reread a passage up to 4 times per session (Rashotte & Torgesen, 1985).

7. Students switch roles, and Steps 2 through 5 are repeated.

8. The teacher and students end the repeated reading procedure on a positive note.

Figure 12.2 Sample repeated reading tracking sheet

Tutee's name: **Sarah A.**
Tutor's name: **Tasha S.**

Date	Goal	Passage #	Re-reading #	Words read	Errors	Correct words	Goal met?
5-4	114	12	1	74	10	64	no
5-4	114	12	2	87	7	80	no
5-4	114	12	3	98	4	94	no
5-4	114	12	4	118	1	117	yes

CONCLUSION

A call has been made for incorporating techniques to develop reading fluency in the classroom (Kuhn & Stahl, 2003; NRP, 2000; Rasinski, 2000). Repeated reading directly targets oral reading fluency and can easily be integrated in an existing reading program. Previous research has shown that repeated reading is effective with a variety of students, including students with disabilities. Using essential instructional components and selecting appropriate materials maximizes the effectiveness of repeated reading. Following the guidelines suggested in this article, teachers can easily incorporate repeated reading into their existing classroom routines.

William J. Therrien, PhD, is an assistant professor at Miami University. His current research interests include effective reading instruction for students with special needs and classroom management.

Richard M. Kubina Jr., PhD, is an assistant professor at The Pennsylvania State University. His current research interests include measurably effective technologies, such as precision teaching and direct instruction.

Article 13

FLUENCY

A Review of Developmental and Remedial Practices

MELANIE R. KUHN AND STEVEN A. STAHL

The authors review theory and research relating to fluency instruction and development and find that fluency instruction is generally effective; assisted approaches seem to be more effective than unassisted approaches; repetitive approaches do not seem to hold a clear advantage over non-repetitive approaches; and effective fluency instruction moves beyond automatic word recognition to include rhythm and expression.

This article is available as a full-text PDF at http://www.sagepub.com/cappello/.

SOURCE: Kuhn, M., & Stahl, S. (2003). Fluency: A Review of Developmental and Remedial Practices. *Journal of Educational Psychology, 95*(1), 3–21. Reprinted by permission of the American Psychological Association.

Section V

VOCABULARY DEVELOPMENT AND ACADEMIC LANGUAGE

OVERVIEW

Vocabulary instruction plays a key role in classroom literacy learning, as it is a major contributor to comprehension and fluency. There is no doubt that word knowledge is paramount for understanding text in all curricular areas and across all language arts (listening, speaking, reading, and writing). The articles in this section recognize vocabulary as being much more than word knowledge and therefore vocabulary instruction as much more than an immediate, local goal in a specific context. Indeed, "The goal of vocabulary instruction should be to build students' independent word learning strategies that can empower them for lifelong learning," according to Bromley (2007), in her article "Nine Things Every Teacher Should Know About Words and Vocabulary Instruction."

Like previous sections of this reader, vocabulary development and academic language are situated within the overriding goal of literacy meaning making. Bromley (2007) hypothesizes that "vocabulary development is both an outcome of comprehension and a precursor to it" and therefore "teaching vocabulary well is a key aspect of developing engaged and successful readers." In their article, "Ten Important Words Plus: A Strategy for Building Word Knowledge," Yopp and Yopp (2007) agree that word knowledge is essential for comprehension: "If students do not understand the words in a text, they have difficulty comprehending the ideas in the text." Yopp and Yopp advocate for vocabulary instruction that actively engages students with the ideas and language of the text. The "Ten Important Words Plus" strategy is offered as one tool for explicit vocabulary instruction in which students are active participants in their word learning. We recommend you use this strategy to complete the readings on vocabulary collected in this section of the reader (see below).

To more effectively *teach* vocabulary knowledge, Pearson, Hiebert, and Kamil (2007) remind us that we must effectively *assess* vocabulary knowledge. In "Vocabulary

Assessment: What We Know and What We Need to Learn," the authors present a broad definition of vocabulary, a brief history of vocabulary assessment, and suggestions for research that will create "measures that will serve us in our quest to improve both vocabulary research and, ultimately, vocabulary instruction."

One aspect of vocabulary instruction that is receiving a lot of attention is academic language. Academic language, what Zwiers (2007) refers to as the "language of schooling," is broader than content word knowledge. It includes syntactical structures, knowledge of text types, and additional characteristics of English needed to construct complex meaning. In "Teacher/Practices and Perspectives for Developing Academic Language" (available at http://www.sagepub.com/cappello), Zwiers investigates the ways traditional classroom discourse strategies—including "questioning, gestures, connecting to background knowledge with examples and analogies, and personifying"—both expand and obstruct language growth. Although his important article focuses on ways to encourage English learners, his ideas may easily be appropriate for use with all children in a wide range of academic contexts.

STRATEGY

The articles in this section focus on the importance of vocabulary instruction and academic language for comprehension. Use the "Ten Important Words Plus" strategy of Yopp and Yopp (2007) to negotiate the articles collected in this section of the reader. As you read, identify the 10 words you feel are most important for understanding the section. Record each word on a separate sticky-note to bring back to the university classroom, where your class will explore the whole group's choices. The purpose of this strategy is to help readers focus on key vocabulary for making sense of the text. Participating in the activity will also help you understand how the words are connected to the big ideas shared by the author.

TEN IMPORTANT WORDS PLUS

(Yopp & Yopp, 2007)

DIRECTIONS

As you independently read (and reread) the articles in this section, identify the 10 most important words for understanding the key concepts. Record each word on a separate sticky-note to bring back to the university classroom.

Once back in the university classroom, students will post your words on a class-created bar graph, creating columns of similar words. This part of the activity is followed by a grand conversation about the word choices. Yopp and Yopp suggest using questions to prompt the discussion:

"What words were selected by many students?"
"Why do you think these words were selected?"
"What do these words have to do with the topic of the text?"

"Why do you think these words were only selected by a few students?"
"What do they contribute to the text content?"

Section V Bar Graph

Vocabulary					
Vocabulary					
Vocabulary		Comprehension			
Vocabulary		Comprehension			
Vocabulary	Knowledge	Comprehension			
Vocabulary	Knowledge	Comprehension			
Vocabulary	Knowledge	Comprehension	Strategies		
Vocabulary	Knowledge	Comprehension	Strategies		

Now write a one-sentence summary of the vocabulary development section of the reader.

SOURCE: Yopp, R., & Yopp, H. (2007). Ten Important Words Plus: A Strategy for Building Word Knowledge. *Reading Teacher, 61*(2), 157–160.

Article 14

NINE THINGS EVERY TEACHER SHOULD KNOW ABOUT WORDS AND VOCABULARY INSTRUCTION

KAREN BROMLEY

Teaching vocabulary well is a key aspect of developing engaged and successful readers.

"There is a great divide between what we know about vocabulary instruction and what we (often, still) do" (Greenwood, 2004, p. 28). Many teachers know they need to do a better job teaching vocabulary to students who find reading difficult (Tompkins & Blanchfield, 2004). Teachers also know that one of the challenges of struggling middle school readers is their limited vocabulary and knowledge of the world (Broaddus & Ivey, 2002). While teaching vocabulary well in every curriculum area is only one aspect of developing engaged and successful readers, it is a key aspect.

Traditional vocabulary instruction for many teachers involves having students look words up in the dictionary, write definitions, and use words in sentences (Basurto, 2004). Word lists, teacher explanation, discussion, memorization, vocabulary books, and quizzes often are used in an effort to help students learn new words. But these methods ignore what research and theory tell us about word learning and sound vocabulary instruction.

Vocabulary is a principle contributor to comprehension, fluency, and achievement. Vocabulary development is both an outcome of comprehension and a precursor to it, with word meanings making up as much as 70–80% of comprehension (Davis, 1972; Nagy & Scott, 2000; Pressley, 2002). Fluent readers recognize and understand many words, and they read more quickly and

SOURCE: Bromley, K. (2007). Nine Things Every Teacher Should Know About Words and Vocabulary Instruction. *Journal of Adolescent and Adult Literacy*, *50*(7), 528–537. Reprinted by permission of the International Reading Association.

easily than those with smaller vocabularies (Allington, 2006; Samuels, 2002). Students with large vocabularies understand text better and score higher on achievement tests than students with small vocabularies (Stahl & Fairbanks, 1986).

What should middle and high school teachers understand about word learning? This article discusses nine things teachers may have forgotten (or have never known) but need to remember about words and word learning to be effective teachers of vocabulary and their content area. Suggestions for classroom practice related to each idea are provided.

1. English is a huge and unique collection of words. English is three times larger in total number of words than German and six times larger than French. Three out of every four words in the dictionary are foreign born. Many words are pronounced the same in both languages (Lederer, 1991), including *camel* (Hebrew), *zoo* (Greek), *shampoo* (Hindi), and *opera* (Italian). English grows and changes daily with neologisms (new words) from science, technology, and our culture. Things to do:

- Teach students words recently added to the Merriam-Webster's Collegiate Dictionary (2005; www.m-w.com/info/new_words.htm), such as *cybrarian* (noun)—a person who finds, collects, and manages information from the World Wide Web.

- Invite students to create their own lists of words and the definitions they think will soon be added to the dictionary. Have them find these words in our spoken language, their reading, the news, and other media.

- Give students a passage that contains words like *good, nice, said,* and *happy.* Have them work in pairs using dictionaries and thesauruses to find substitutes for these overworked words. Find an online thesaurus (e.g.,http://thesaurus.reference.com/search?r= 2&q=suggest). Then, have students rewrite the passage and share it with the class to show how they have made it more interesting and powerful.

- Have students edit one another's work using dictionaries and thesauruses to find and suggest more descriptive words.

2. The rules of English are simple and consistent compared to other languages. Despite the belief that English is a highly irregular language, it is actually quite orderly and constant (Lederer, 1991; Moats, 2005/2006). Twenty-one of 26 alphabet letters are consonants with fairly consistent pronunciations, while 5 vowels vary in the way they are said. In contrast, the Russian language has 32 alphabet letters and the Japanese and Chinese alphabets contain thousands of characters representing many more than the 44 sounds in English. Some languages such as Chinese, Thai, and Lao are tonal, and a word can be said using several different tones, with each tone changing the meaning of the word. Things to do:

- Invite an English as a second language teacher or teacher of another language to speak to your students or coteach a lesson with you to demonstrate the similarities and differences between English and another language.

- Invite students who speak another language or are learning a language to talk about the differences and similarities they notice between English and the other language.

- Teach students the prefixes, roots, and suffixes that appear most often in English and are constant in their meaning and pronunciation (Bromley, 2002) (see Table 14.1). When students know one prefix, root, or suffix, it helps unlock the meanings of other words with the same prefix, root, or suffix. For example, knowing the root *aud* means to *hear* can help students understand the meaning of *audience, auditorium, audition,* and *audible.*

3. Language proficiency grows from oral competence to written competence. Typically, the words and concepts students absorb and use as they listen and talk are the foundation for what they will read and write later. Broad word knowledge enables students to communicate in ways that

Table 14.1 The Most Frequently Appearing and Most Commonly Taught Prefixes, Roots, and Suffixes

Most Common Prefixes		
Prefix	*Definition*	*Example*
re-	again	review, revoke
un-	not	unable, untrue
in-	into or not	insight, inert
en-	in, put into	enliven, ensnare
ex-	out	exit, extinguish
de-	away, from	deflect, denounce
com-	together, with	commune, communicate
dis-	apart	dishonest, disagree
pre-	before	prevent, predict
sub-	under	submerge, submarine

Most Common Roots		
Root	*Definition*	*Example*
tract	drag, pull	tractor, distract
spect	look	inspect, spectacle
port	carry	portable, important
dict	say	diction, dictionary, prediction
rupt	break	interrupt, rupture
scrib	write	inscribe, describe, scripture
cred	believe	credit, discredit
vid	see	video, evidence
aud	hear	audience, auditorium, audible

Most Common Suffixes		
Root	*Definition*	*Example*
-ly	having the quality of	lightly, sweetly, weekly
-er	more	higher, stronger, smoother
-able/-ible	able to	believable, deliverable, incredible
-tion/-sion	a thing, a noun	invention, suspension, tension, function
-cle	small	particle
-less	without	treeless, motionless
-est	most	biggest, hardest, brightest
-ment	quality or act	contentment, excitement, basement
-ness	quality or act	kindness, wildness, softness
-arium	a place for	aquarium, terrarium
-ling	small	duckling, gosling, hatchling

are precise, powerful, persuasive, and interesting because words are tools for analyzing, inferring, evaluating, and reasoning (Vacca, Vacca, Gove, Burkey, Lenhart, & McKeon, 2005). As a result, students with large vocabularies tend to be articulate and possess the confidence that is sometimes not exhibited by students who lack vocabulary and conceptual knowledge. Things to do:

- Read literature aloud to students, stopping to explain and talk about words they may not know. Share Trelease's (2001) notion with students that the best SAT preparation course in the world is to hear literature read aloud because the richer the words student hear, the richer the words will be that they can read and give back when they speak and write.

- Play oral games with content vocabulary so students can explore pronunciations, visual display, and meanings simultaneously.

- Encourage students to ask about words they don't know. As Hahn (2002) said, "I make it a point to talk over my students' heads as much as possible. . . . It's OK to ask what a word means and it's necessary for survival in my classroom" (p. 67).

- Include small-group discussions and oral presentations in your teaching so students can listen to one another and use content area vocabulary in speaking before they use it in writing.

- Have students work together to write "paired sentences" as a way to develop their concept and word knowledge. For example, give students two terms and ask them to talk first and then write about how they are similar and how they are different.

4. Words are learned because of associations that connect the new with the known. When students store new information by linking it to their existing schema, or network of organized information, there is a better chance the new word will be remembered later (Rupley, Logan, & Nichols, 1999). Also, information about words is "dual-coded" as it is stored in memory (Paivio, 1990). It is processed in linguistic form that includes print and meaning and nonlinguistic form that includes visual and sensory images.

Learning a word's linguistic elements is enhanced by storing a nonlinguistic form or sensory image along with the linguistic image. Things to do:

- Engage students' prior knowledge and related experiences before teaching new words to introduce a chapter or content area selection. For example, before reading a selection on Communication Cyberspace, teach the word *blog,* define it (an online journal), provide the word's derivation (blog comes from web *log*), and show a picture of someone seated at a computer composing an essay or report to post on their personal website. Then, show students an actual blog (e.g., Jessamyn West's www.librarian.net/).

- Use the K-W-L strategy (know, want to know, and learned; Ogle, 1986) when you introduce a new word. First, list what students already know about the word and what they want to know about it. After you've taught the word or students have read it, make a list of what they learned about the word.

- Depending on students' abilities, either individually or in pairs, have them create three-dimensional words (Bromley, 2002). On paper (see Figure 14.1), have students include a definition, sentence, drawing, and real object to represent the word. Then have students peer teach their words to one another in small groups or to the whole class and post their work on a bulletin board for review and reference.

5. Seventy percent of the most frequently used words have multiple meanings. Students need to remember this fact (Lederer, 1991). It is especially important for struggling readers and English-language learners to understand this and learn to use context to help derive appropriate meanings for words. For example, *hand* can have many meanings (e.g., to give someone something, applause, a way of measuring a horse's height, cards dealt to someone playing a card game, or the part of the anatomy at the end of the wrist). Words such as *foot, ball,* and *java* also possess multiple meanings. Context often helps unlock the meaning of words, but when it doesn't help, students have a purpose for using the glossary, dictionary, or thesaurus. Using these references can expand vocabularies and encourage curiosity about words. Things to do:

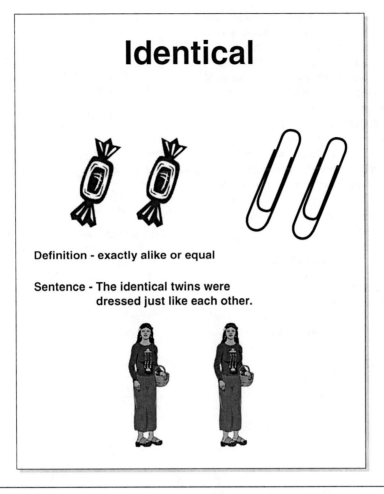

Figure 14.1   A Three-Dimensional Word

- Use a fiction or nonfiction selection to teach students how context can give clues to a word's meaning in several ways. Show students that many words have multiple meanings and explicitly teach them how to use context and references to help unlock appropriate meanings.

- Show students how to use context to figure out new words by reading to the end of a sentence or paragraph, reading a caption, analyzing a picture or graphic, or looking at a footnote. Teach students to use a picture, a phrase that defines a word, a synonym or antonym, or the position of the unknown word in a series of other words. For example, *commodity* can have several meanings (e.g., merchandise, goods, article, asset, belonging, chattel). But, the context of the following sentence suggests *merchandise* or *goods* as possible meanings and rules out *belonging* or *chattel:* Our product combines intermarket analysis and predicted moving averages to generate consistently accurate commodity forecasts.

- Challenge students to make as many words as they can from a key content term like *evaporation, ecosystem,* or *geography* (99 smaller words can be made from the word *planets*). Then teach them the multiple meanings of some of the smaller words they have created.

6. Meanings of 60% of multisyllabic words can be inferred by analyzing word parts. Students also need a mindset to alert them to this (Nagy & Scott, 2000). Knowing the meaning of a root, prefix, or suffix often gives clues to what a word means. Because much of the English language comes from Greek and Latin, we would do well to teach students the common derivatives. This is especially true in science because it contains many multisyllabic terms. Knowing just a few roots makes it much easier to figure out several other words that contain these roots. There are many dictionaries of Greek and Latin roots to help students infer meanings of difficult, multisyllabic terms. Things to do:

- Print a short dictionary of Greek and Latin roots for each of your students like the Dictionary of Greek and Latin Roots found at http://english.glendale.cc.ca.us/roots.dict.html or have them bookmark it on their computers. Encourage students to use the list as a quick way to unlock science terms like *neophyte* (little plant—*neo* means *new* and *-phyte* means *plant*) and *teleconference* (talking from far away—*tele* means *far away* and *confer* means to *talk*). This dictionary helps with meanings of everyday words, too, like *Florida,* which traces its origins to *flora* (*flower*) and helps unlock the meanings of *florid* (*gaudy*) and *floriferous* (*flowery* or *showy*).

- Help students use this type of dictionary to learn derivations of words they already know. For example, *Arctic* comes from the Greek *arktos,* which means *bear,* and Antarctica means the converse or opposite, no bears.

- Encourage students to create word trees of often-used roots (see Figure 14.2) to involve them in using dictionaries to find related multisyllabic words. In this case, print a prefix on each branch, and students can add appropriate words to each one as they find them in a dictionary or glossary, on the Web, or hear them used in the media.

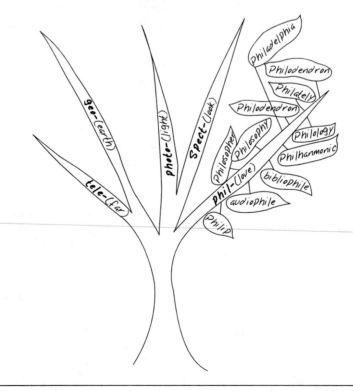

Figure 14.2   A Word Tree

7. Direct instruction in vocabulary influences comprehension more than any other factor. Although wide reading can build word knowledge, students need thoughtflul and systematic instruction in key vocabulary as well (Blachowicz & Fisher, 2004; Graves & Watts-Taffe, 2002; Nagy, 1988). Instruction that engages students in the meanings of new words and their letter, sound, and spelling patterns promotes more effective word learning than just analyzing context (Juel & Deffes, 2004). As students learn new words, they can use them to learn other new words and build independent word learning strategies (Baumann & Kame'enui, 1991; Nagy). Things to do:

- Explicitly teach students new vocabulary focusing on both meaning and word structure. Make connections with other words whenever possible because it helps build from the known to the new. For example, when you teach the word *counterrevolutionary,* relate it to *revolt, revolution, act,* and *counteract* to build on what students may already know.

- Have students keep vocabulary notebooks in which they illustrate a new word, write a paraphrased definition, and use it in a sentence. The vocabulary notebook provides a record for review before a test and a source for the correct spelling of content terms.

- Teach students to "chunk" multisyllabic words like *prestidigitation* (sleight of hand, trickery) to help them develop the habit of unlocking new words independently.

- Analyze a classroom test with students (or the practice version of a standardized test they have taken recently or will soon take). Highlight or make a list of key vocabulary from the directions and from the reading selections that students must know to answer questions. Look at specific questions that pertain directly to vocabulary knowledge and show students how to locate the word in the selection to determine its meaning in context.

- Have students creatively peer teach new words to one another in small groups before they begin a chapter or unit and encourage them to present their words in several ways (visually and verbally).

8. Teaching fewer words well is more effective than teaching several words in a cursory way. Science, math, and social studies material contain many conceptually dense terms, and most students need instruction in this technical vocabulary (Vacca et al., 2005). While it may be tempting to introduce the entire list of new vocabulary from a chapter in a content text, it is more effective to teach fewer words well rather than several words less well (Robb, 2000). Few teachers realize that they can occasionally teach vocabulary during or at the end of a lesson (Watts, 1995). Things to do:

- Teach struggling students and English-language learners no more than three to five new words at a time because they might have difficulty retaining more than that. Teach words students will need to know in the future and teach only words related to the main idea of new material.

- Call attention to important terms that appear in bold or italicized print. Show students that the meaning often follows the term or appears in the glossary at the back of the text.

- Teach most new words before reading to enhance students' comprehension. Occasionally teach new words after reading to allow students to use their own word-attack skills independently or to let you know which words they had trouble with so you can teach these words.

9. Effective teachers display an attitude of excitement and interest in words and language. Teachers who are curious and passionate about words inadvertently share their enthusiasm with students, and it becomes contagious. These teachers possess word consciousness (Graves & Watts-Taffe, 2002). They appreciate out-of-the-ordinary, powerful, and appealing word use. They are excited about words and language. They model, encourage, and engage students in wordplay, adept diction, and independent investigations into words to build students' word consciousness. Things to do:

- Reflect on your vocabulary teaching. Are you excited about language and teaching or using new words? How do you most often teach new words? Are there other, more effective ways?

- Educate yourself about best practice vocabulary teaching. Talk with colleagues about how they teach vocabulary and what works for them. Read articles and books for new ways to teach vocabulary.

- Share your excitement with students about the fascinating nature of words and language by providing students with a Word of the Day. Find these at Wordsmith (www.wordsmith.org/awad/index.html), which introduces a word a day (around a weekly theme) with definition, pronunciation, etymology, usage, and a quotation. (Students can subscribe and receive it automatically.)

- Word walls aren't just for the elementary grades. Add several new content terms each week to a word wall of science, math, or social studies to provide standard spellings for student writing. As terms are used in class discussions, visually reinforce each word by pointing it out on the word wall.

FINAL THOUGHTS

"The good intentions of conscientious teachers concerning traditional vocabulary instruction have often had pernicious side effects . . ." (Greenwood, 2004, p. 34). Overuse of dictionary hunting, definition writing, or teacher explanation can turn students off learning new words and does not necessarily result in better comprehension or learning. Word learning is a complicated process. It requires giving students a variety of opportunities to connect new words to related words, analyze word structure, understand multiple meanings, and use words actively in authentic ways. The goal of vocabulary instruction should be to build students' independent word learning strategies that can empower them for lifelong learning. This requires teachers who are passionate about words and language, who immerse their students in language, and who provide direct instruction that is thoughtful, intentional, and varied.

Karen Bromley teaches at Binghamton University.

Article 15

TEN IMPORTANT WORDS PLUS

A Strategy for Building Word Knowledge

RUTH HELEN YOPP AND HALLIE KAY YOPP

R esearch confirms what many teachers observe in their classrooms: Word knowledge is highly related to comprehension (Baumann, Kame'enui, & Ash, 2003). If students do not understand the words in a text, they have difficulty comprehending the ideas in the text. The relationship between vocabulary and comprehension is especially evident when students read informational text, which is often rich with specialized vocabulary (Chall & Conard, 1991). Vocabulary knowledge is so instrumental to reading comprehension—and to overall success in school—that it must receive focused and deliberate attention across the curriculum and throughout the school day.

The literature on vocabulary development emphasizes three primary means of enhancing students' vocabulary: wide reading, explicit instruction of words and word-learning strategies, and the establishment of an environment that promotes word consciousness. Before we briefly describe each, we address what it means

to know a word. After providing this background, we share a strategy that focuses student attention on the meanings of important words in a text.

WHAT DOES IT MEAN TO KNOW A WORD?

Take a minute to think about your own vocabulary. Certainly, there are some words you do not know at all. There are other words you recognize when you see them in print or hear them in a conversation—you have a sense of what they mean, but you do not use them yourself. Then there are words you employ comfortably in your exchanges with friends and colleagues. As Beck and McKeown (1991) stated, knowing a word is not an all-or-nothing proposition; there are gradations of word knowledge that range from no knowledge to "rich decontextualized knowledge of a word, including its relationship to other

SOURCE: Yopp, R., & Yopp, H. (2007). Ten Important Words Plus: A Strategy for Building Word Knowledge. *The Reading Teacher, 61*(2), 157–160. Reprinted by permission of the International Reading Association.

words and its extension to metaphorical uses" (p. 792). Acquiring knowledge of a word in the richest sense is a long process that involves multiple exposures in many contexts.

WIDE READING AS A MEANS OF ACQUIRING NEW WORDS

Many authorities agree that oral language experiences and wide reading influence students' word knowledge and refer to this type of word learning as "incidental word learning." In fact, they believe that the majority of new words acquired over the life span are learned incidentally (Cunningham, 2005).

As valuable as oral language experiences are, written language appears to be superior when it comes to providing students with a rich source of exposure to vocabulary. Research by Hayes and Ahrens (1988) revealed that printed texts—including children's books—contained more rare words than language used in adult and children's television programs and adult conversations. Their findings are not surprising given that oral language is embedded in a context and is accompanied by facial expressions, intonation, gestures or objects that support meaning. Because written text does not provide these kinds of support, authors are, by necessity, more specific in their language in order to convey their meanings precisely.

Thus, plentiful experiences with written language, beneficial for many reasons, play an especially important role in vocabulary development. Extensive reading presents students with exposure to rich vocabulary. Furthermore, written text typically provides multiple exposures to words (e.g., the word *bacteria* appears 22 times in the pages of Melvin Berger's 1995 book for young children, *Germs Make Me Sick!*) and the opportunity to experience words in meaningful contexts, both of which are demonstrated by research to support vocabulary growth (Kamil & Hiebert, 2005).

EXPLICIT INSTRUCTION AS A MEANS OF ACQUIRING WORDS

A number of authorities have provided guidelines for selecting target words for instruction (Beck, McKeown, & Kucan, 2002; Biemiller, 1999; Hiebert, 2005). One common guideline is that words chosen for instruction should be of sufficient frequency to be useful, yet not of such high frequency that they are likely already known, and that selected words should have instructional potential; that is, they should be "related to the selection, the content, or to a thematic unit" (Kamil & Hiebert, 2005, p. 12). Target words may be taught by explaining their meaning (e.g., "*Emaciated* means very thin"), by demonstrating their meaning (e.g., "Here's what it looks like to *amble*"), by mapping their relationship with other words (e.g., developing a semantic map for *amphibian*), and by using various other strategies (Blachowicz & Fisher, 2006). Repeated exposures to the words in rich contexts and active engagement in learning tasks are key to vocabulary instruction (National Institute of Child Health and Human Development, 2000).

Explicit instruction of vocabulary also includes teaching word parts (e.g., affixes, roots) so that students can derive the meaning of unfamiliar words. For instance, knowing that the prefix in *unable* means "not" helps students understand the words *unreliable* and *unforgivable.* Likewise, learning that the Latin root *spec* means "look" supports students' understanding of *inspect, spectacles,* and *spectacular.* In addition, providing explicit instruction in using context to determine word meanings supports the development of word knowledge. Students can be taught to look for language that can help readers understand new words. For example, the word *instead* in the following sentence signals the reader that *abate* is the opposite of *worsened:* "The storm did not abate; instead, it worsened."

ESTABLISHMENT OF AN ENVIRONMENT THAT PROMOTES WORD CONSCIOUSNESS

Scott and Nagy (2004) argued that the most effective vocabulary programs are those that foster in students the knowledge and dispositions that facilitate ongoing vocabulary development; that is, they advocate for vocabulary learning that is generative. Classrooms that promote word consciousness stimulate students' awareness of, interest in, and curiosity about words so that word learning extends beyond a particular lesson or the confines of a particular classroom. Students notice common aspects of words, explore word histories, play with words, examine expert authors' word choices, and make some of those words their own. Throughout each day, in all content areas, attention is drawn to words and students interact with words in multiple ways and make connections among them and with their lives. The teacher models an enthusiasm for words, saying, "Ah . . . interesting word" when a student uses an uncommon word or "Guess what new word I learned this morning as I was reading the newspaper?" or "What was powerful about the way the author told us about this phenomenon?" Students are part of a classroom—or better, schoolwide—culture that explicitly notices and values words.

TEN IMPORTANT WORDS PLUS

Elsewhere, we describe a strategy we call Ten Important Words (Yopp & Yopp, 2003). In this strategy, students identify the 10 (or 5 or 3, depending on the length of the selection) most important words in a text as they read an informational selection. Students focus on the meaning of the passage in order to determine which words are most important and which words are not as important. As the students read and reread, they independently choose 10 words and record each word on a separate self-adhesive note. After the students have made their selections, the teacher asks them to post their selections on a class bar graph, building columns of common words. Discussion about the word choices ensues, prompted by questions such as "What words were selected by many students? Why do you think these words were selected? What do these words have to do with the topic of the text?" and "Identify some words that were selected by only a few students. Why do you think these words were selected? What do they contribute to the text content?" Then the students write a one-sentence summary of the passage. Although not required to, they typically use several of the words from the graph.

The strategy requires students to analyze text for big ideas, to focus on words that carry important meanings, and to think about how those words are connected to the ideas in the text. The opportunity to talk about words encourages use of the words, enriches students' understanding of the words and the content, and provides students with insights into peers' perspectives about the text.

As an extension of this strategy (the "plus"), we have provided students with colored cards that contain prompts that ask them to think about and use in various ways words that appear on the class bar graph. These prompts are designed to further students' active engagement with the words in ways that promote word learning. Students think about relationships among words, use words in different contexts, explore word parts, link words to their own experiences, and so forth. For example, some students receive a pink card that says, "List synonyms or words highly related in meaning." Others receive a green card that says, "Generate several sentences in which you use the word. Make your sentences as different from one another as possible. One sentence should be directly related to the topic of the text. Other sentences should use the word in a different context." And, the remaining students receive a yellow card that says, "Think of as many other forms of the word as you can. For instance, other forms of the word *happy* include *happiness, happier,* and *unhappy.*"

The students' task is to meet with several others who have the same color card (three or four is a reasonable group size) and, given a target word selected by the teacher from the bar graph, work with one another to respond to the prompt. After sufficient opportunity for students to talk with their group mates, the teacher asks the groups to share their task and several responses. All of the groups with the same color card share first (i.e., all the pink groups share, one after the other), followed by groups with a different color. For example, given the word *communicate* selected from a graph developed while reading Mary Wallace's *The Inuksuk Book* (1999), students with the pink (synonyms/highly related words) card might share the words *talk, discuss, converse, write, chat, draw,* and *graph.* Students with the green (sentences) card might say, "Inuksuk communicate information to travelers." "She doesn't communicate well," and "I use e-mail to communicate with my out-of-state relatives." Students with the yellow (other forms) card might respond with *communication, communicator, communicating,* and *uncommunicative.* Students' responses to the prompts provide the teacher with valuable information about their understanding of the words and their use. For instance, if students misuse the target word in a sentence they have generated, the teacher can clarify the word's meaning and appropriate use immediately.

The teacher identifies another word from the graph and the students again discuss their prompt with peers. After giving the students several opportunities with the same prompt, the teacher tells them to exchange their card for one of another color. Students then engage in their new task as the teacher selects words. Thus, students have the opportunity to build some competence

in their original task before experiencing other tasks. Some words will be more difficult than others, but allowing the students to discover this and work with one another provides an interesting opportunity to talk about words. Words with multiple meanings (e.g., band, sign) or Greek or Latin roots (e.g., *astro*nomer, sym*phony*) provide the students with more sophisticated insights about the language and should be selected if they are found in the text, even if they are not included on the graph.

Other prompts we have used include

- Identify where you might expect to see or hear this word. Be specific. For example, you might expect to find the word *serene* in a travel brochure advertising a remote island hotel. Where else?

- List antonyms (or close opposites) of the word.

- Draw at least two pictures that depict the meaning of this word.

- Create a semantic map and show this word in relation to other words of your choice.

- Act out the word.

- Return to the text and find one or more sentences in which the word is used. Explain the meaning of the sentence(s) you find. Comment on any support the author provided readers to illuminate the meaning of the word.

Because the students have experienced the words in a meaningful context (i.e., through reading the book) and have participated in rich conversations with peers about the meanings of these words (i.e., through the discussion of word choices that accompanies the graphing activity), the students are likely to have acquired sufficient understanding of the words to be successful responding to the prompts. Engagement with the tasks on the cards and follow-up clarifying conversations will further develop their word knowledge.

Ruth Helen Yopp is a professor in the Department of Elementary and Bilingual Education at California State University, Fullerton.

Hallie Kay Yopp is a professor in the Department of Elementary and Bilingual Education at California State University, Fullerton.

Article 16

VOCABULARY ASSESSMENT

What We Know and What We Need to Learn

P. DAVID PEARSON, ELFRIEDA H. HIEBERT, AND MICHAEL L. KAMIL

After a nearly 15-year absence from center stage, vocabulary has returned to a prominent place in discussions of reading, and it is alive and well in reading instruction and reading research. We have no doubt that the renaissance is due, at least in part, to the salutary findings about vocabulary in the report of the National Reading Panel (NRP; National Institute of Child Health and Human Development [NICHD], 2000) and, even more important, the use of the NRP findings to shape policy and practice via the Reading First component of No Child Left Behind (2002). We regard these developments as positive, for we think

there is good reason to teach vocabulary more aggressively and even better reason to study its relation to comprehension more carefully. However, if we are going to teach it more effectively and if we are going to better understand how it is implicated in reading comprehension, we must first address the vexing question of how we assess vocabulary knowledge and, even more challenging, vocabulary growth. In this essay, we argue that vocabulary assessment is grossly undernourished, both in its theoretical and practical aspects—that it has been driven by tradition, convenience, psychometric standards, and a quest for economy of effort rather than a clear

SOURCE: Pearson, P. D., Hiebert, E. H., & Kamil, M. L. (2007). Vocabulary Assessment: What We Know and What We Need to Learn. *Reading Research Quarterly, 42*(2), 282–296. Reprinted by permission of the International Reading Association.

conceptualization of its nature and relation to other aspects of reading expertise, most notably comprehension. We hope that our essay will serve as one small step in providing the nourishment it needs.

There is no doubt that vocabulary is closely tied to comprehension (Davis, 1942; Just & Carpenter, 1987; Whipple, 1925)—in study after study, vocabulary knowledge predicts comprehension performance consistently with positive correlations typically between .6 and .8. But a correlation is not an explanation of a conceptual relation between factors. Anderson and Freebody (1985) understood this complexity well when they put forward three hypotheses to explain the ubiquitous finding of a high correlation between comprehension and vocabulary. The instrumentalist hypothesis argues that learning the words *causes* comprehension. The verbal aptitude hypothesis suggests that general verbal ability is the root cause of both vocabulary and comprehension performance. The knowledge hypothesis argues that both vocabulary and comprehension result from increases in knowledge.

More to the point, it is one thing to demonstrate a correlation and quite another to demonstrate a causal relation between vocabulary instruction or learning and comprehension. In that regard, it is worth noting the conclusions of the subgroup for vocabulary of the NRP (NICHD, 2000), which document a consistent and robust relation between learning vocabulary in specific texts and performance on experimenter-designed comprehension measures derived from those same texts. By contrast, the group found only two studies showing that vocabulary instruction transferred beyond text-specific increases in vocabulary to far transfer measures, such as norm-referenced comprehension reading tests. A question of interest raised by the NRP report is whether its conclusions are generalizable or are the artifact of some special characteristic of the ways in which the outcomes were measured in the studies they examined.

Even though experimentally documented effects of vocabulary instruction on measures of general reading comprehension are weak, at least as indexed by effects on standardized measures, vocabulary instruction has returned to a place of prominence in the reading curriculum; vocabulary serves a core role in commercial reading programs and in other curricular areas such as science, history, or foreign language. Its ubiquity and gravity are captured by the complaint, at least of science educators, that the bulk of text-centered science instruction is learning the meanings of hundreds of new scientific terms rather than experiencing the intellectual rush of hands-on inquiry (Armstrong & Collier, 1990).

There are at least three plausible explanations for the weak empirical link between vocabulary instruction and some transfer measures of reading comprehension. The first position is that there is no actual link between the two: that a vocabulary myth has clouded our reasoning and our pedagogy for centuries and that learning words does not cause comprehension. The second is that vocabulary instruction does not promote far transfer—that is, it is conceptually incapable of moving beyond the texts to which it is tied. Hence it shows up in local but not global indicators of text understanding. The third position, and the one we take up in this essay, is that our measures of vocabulary are inadequate to the challenge of documenting the relationship between word learning and global measures of comprehension. That is, it might be that our instruction is improving vocabulary learning, which might lead to improvements in general comprehension, but the instruments we use to measure vocabulary are so insensitive that they prevent us from documenting the relationship. In particular, the fact that standardized assessments do not often include types of text that are found in textbooks is an example of this potential masking of effects. The National Assessment of Educational Progress (NAEP) 2009 framework has addressed this issue by dividing what have traditionally been labeled expository texts into more explicit and descriptive subcategories (National Assessment Governing Board [NAGB], 2005). Exposition has been separated from, for example, literary nonfiction in recognition of the fact that these different genres have, at the very least, different vocabulary loads.

We don't want to dismiss the first two positions out of hand, but we want to press the measurement question so that it can be ruled in or out as the most plausible explanation for the paucity of documented transfer effects. We will never know until and unless we have developed and tested vocabulary measures that are as conceptually rich as the phenomenon (vocabulary knowledge) they are intended to measure.

We begin by defining vocabulary and offering a short historical account of vocabulary assessment. Then we examine the literature—research, common practices, and theoretical analyses—on vocabulary assessment to answer three questions:

1. What do vocabulary assessments (both past and current) measure?

2. What could vocabulary assessments measure?

3. What research will we have to conduct over the next decade in order to develop and validate measures that will serve us in our quest to improve both vocabulary research and, ultimately, vocabulary instruction?

How Is Vocabulary Defined?

Any analysis of the domain of vocabulary assessment should first consider what it means to know a word. The first definition of *vocabulary* in the *Random House Webster's Unabridged Dictionary* (Flexner, 2003) is "the stock of words used by or known to a particular people or group of persons." A subsequent definition is "the words of a language." In turn, *word* is defined as "a unit of language, consisting of one or more spoken sounds or their written representation, that functions as a principal carrier of meaning."

These dictionary definitions provide little specificity and hence little guidance to researchers who are studying vocabulary acquisition and understanding. Faced with the immediate task of reviewing the instructional research, the NRP (NICHD, 2000) was forced to establish

parameters for the types of vocabulary that were taught and learned in research studies. The NRP categorized various types of vocabulary as a function of the cognitive operations involved and the context in which vocabulary is measured. The panel asked two questions: (a) Is the use of vocabulary productive or receptive? (b) Is the mode of communication written or oral? Thus, one quickly ends up with the familiar quartet of vocabulary types: listening, speaking, reading, and writing. In general, receptive vocabulary is larger than productive vocabulary; we can understand more words through listening and reading than we use in speech or writing. This conclusion should not be surprising given the general psycholinguistic principle that comprehension normally precedes production and the recognition that additional cueing systems (various textual and contextual aids) are available to individuals during language reception, but not during production.

The assessment of vocabulary as it pertains to reading comprehension has almost exclusively emphasized the receptive dimension of vocabulary. For the most part, at least on large-scale tests, reading is the medium, but a prominent set of vocabulary assessments use the listening mode of the receptive dimension. The Peabody Picture Vocabulary Test (PPVT-III) (1997), a widely used standardized measure of vocabulary development, typifies the latter group of tests. Rarely is the productive aspect of vocabulary examined, especially as it relates to comprehension; for example, when students are taught new words in relation to new texts or topics in subject matter classes, do those words spontaneously emerge in their speaking and writing? The results of one recent analysis document substantial transfer of newly learned vocabulary to writing (an unobtrusive measure—simply looking for the spontaneous occurrence of such words) for students who had participated in an intervention where complex science vocabulary was emphasized in reading, speaking, and listening (Bravo & Tilson, 2006). Despite what we know, much needs to be learned about these complex relationships between the various modes of vocabulary learning and assessment.

What Do Vocabulary Assessments Measure?

A Brief History

The assessment of students' knowledge of word meanings, what we generally call vocabulary assessment, is as old as reading assessment itself. Vocabulary assessment dates back to at least the development of the early tests of intelligence by Binet and Thurstone (see Johnston, 1984; Pearson & Hamm, 2005) that preceded formal measures of reading comprehension. The earliest measures of reading vocabulary consisted of asking students to define or explain words that were selected because they were likely to be found in the texts they would encounter in schools; an early item might have asked a student to explain individually to an interviewer what a "fork" is used for. With the movement toward mass testing prompted by the need to test recruits for World War I (Resnick & Resnick, 1977) came the need for more efficient, easily administered, and easily scorable assessments; hence the move to standardized, multiple-choice versions of items the students read and responded to. Prototypic items are illustrated in the first row of Table 16.1.

That sort of item dominated formal vocabulary assessment until the 1970s (Read, 2000), when changes in thinking about language and reading, which emerged from the new fields of psycholinguistics and cognitive science, motivated more contextualized vocabulary assessments such as those found in the second row of Table 16.1.

The press for contextualization increased systematically, at least in the most ambitious context for vocabulary assessment, English as a Second Language (ESL; see Nation, 2001; Read, 2000), resulting in a progression of items as illustrated in the final three rows of Table 16.1.

As one can see from the progression of items in Table 16.1, the field has witnessed the increasing contextualization of vocabulary assessment during the previous quarter century. One would expect greater contextualization to increase the sensitivity of vocabulary assessment to comprehension growth precisely because increasingly contextualized formats require text comprehension as a part of the process of responding to the vocabulary items. That, however, is a claim that deserves an empirical rather than a rational test to determine its validity.

This is not to say that, because of this history, all current assessments assess vocabulary in a contextualized manner. In fact, many of the major assessments still use fairly isolated approaches. To illustrate the nature of current vocabulary assessments, we have analyzed items on four prominent vocabulary assessments that are among those identified by a national panel as fitting the criteria for use in Reading First (Kame'enui, 2002). We chose two individually administered assessments—the PPVT-III and the Woodcock Reading Mastery Test (WRMT-R) (Woodcock, 1998)—and two that are group administered—Iowa Test of Basic Skills (ITBS; 2005), and the Stanford Achievement Test (SAT-10; 2004). Items characteristic of those included in these assessments are presented in Table 16.2, except for the PPVT-III. It was difficult to portray the PPVT visually because when taking it, a student sees only pictures. The task is to identify the picture that matches the word spoken by the test administrator. If the target word was *surfing*, the picture set might include someone surfing, someone playing water polo, someone swimming, and someone driving a speedboat.

Toward a Theory of Vocabulary Assessment

Words may seem like simple entities, but they are not. Their surface simplicity belies a deeper complexity. For example, they connect with experience and knowledge, and their meanings vary depending on the linguistic contexts in which they can be found, including in a variety of literal and figurative contexts. Complexity of word knowledge is evident in Nagy and Scott's (2000) identification of five aspects of word knowledge used in reading:

Table 16.1 Sample Items of Different Eras

Time period	Sample item(s)
1915–1920: Decontextualized vocabulary assessment	Pick the word that fits in the blank: A _____ is used to eat with. saw spoon pin car Pick the best meaning for the italicized word: *glad* clever mild happy frank
1970s: Early efforts to contextualize vocabulary	Pick the best meaning for the italicized word: The farmer *discovered* a tunnel under the barn. built found searched handled
1980s: Steps toward contextualization	In a (1) *democratic* society, we presume that individuals are innocent until and unless proven guilty. (2) *Establishing* guilt is (3) *daunting*. The major question is whether the prosecution can overcome the presumption of (4) *reasonable* doubt about whether the suspect committed the alleged crime. For each item, select the choice closest in meaning to the italicized word corresponding to the number: 2. *establishing* a. attributing b. monitoring c. creating d. absolving 3. *daunting* a. exciting b. challenging c. intentional d. delightful
1995: Embedded vocabulary assessment	Among a set of comprehension items, you might find the following: In line 2, it says, "Because he was responsible for early morning chores on the farm, John was often tardy for school." The word *tardy* is closest in meaning to a. early b. loud c. ready d. late

(Continued)

Table 16.1 (Continued)

Late 1990s: Computerized format	Baseball has been a favorite American pastime for over 120 years. Each year, fans flock to diamonds all over the country to pursue this passionate hobby.
	Look at the word *hobby* in the passage. Click on the word in the text that has the same meaning.

Table 16.2   Parallel Items of Vocabulary Tasks on Three Norm-Referenced Tests

Test	Prototypical item(s)
ITBS	To *sink* in the water play rest wash go down

SAT	Item type 1:
	To *cut* is to—
	  slice bark
	  run save

	Item type 2:
	Put the money in the *safe.*
	In which sentences does the word *safe* mean the same thing as in the sentence above?
	  The puppy is *safe* from harm.
	  I am *safe* at home.
	  It is *safe* to go out now.
	  Michael opened the *safe.*

	Item type 3:
	Ron only has one hat, but he has several coats. *Several* means—
	  funny some
	  hungry large

WRMT	Subtest 1:
	Antonyms (read this word out loud and then tell me a word that means the opposite).
	  near (far)
	  dark (light)

	Subtest 2:
	Synonyms (read this word out loud and then tell me another word that means the same thing).
	  cash (money)
	  small (little)

	Subtest 3:
	Analogies (listen carefully and finish what I say [text is visible but experimenter reads the text]).
	  dark—light night—(day)
	  rain—shine wet—(dry)

ITBS = Iowa Test of Basic Skills; SAT = Stanford Achievement Test; WRMT = Woodcock Reading Mastery Test

(a) *incrementality*: knowing a word is not an all-or-nothing matter; to the contrary, each time we encounter a word and each time we use it, our knowledge becomes a little deeper and a little more precise—eventually leading to nuanced understanding and flexible use.

(b) *multidimensionality*: word knowledge consists of qualitatively different types of knowledge such as understanding nuances of meaning between words such as *glimpse* and *glance* or typical collocations of words (e.g., a *storm front* not a *storm back*).

(c) *polysemy*: many words have multiple meanings, and the more common the word, the more meanings it is likely to have; a common word like *run* may have 20 meanings, but a rare word like *geothermal* has but one.

(d) *interrelatedness*: learning or knowing a word often entails derivation or association with the meanings of related words, either in a linguistic context (dogs bark or buffaloes roam) or in one's semantic memory store (dogs are members of the canine category and related to cats because they share the attribute that they can be domesticated).

(e) *heterogeneity*: a word's meaning differs depending on its function and structure (e.g., frequency in written English, and syntactic roles). Contrast, for example, the sentences, "I spilled the cocoa, get a broom," with, "I spilled the cocoa, get a mop." Over time, by experiencing a word like *spill* in different contexts, we learn more about the range of its application.

Nagy and Scott (2000) also identified the ability to reflect on and manipulate vocabulary, or metalinguistic knowledge, as an important feature of word knowledge. Although such categories illustrate the complexity of vocabulary, few studies of vocabulary attend to these variables in any systematic fashion, especially when it comes to choosing the words for instructional interventions or for assessments (Scott, Lubliner, & Hiebert, 2006). At the present time, these distinctions are unlikely to be highly productive as filters for reviewing assessments that are commonly used in large-scale assessment. These

variables do, however, suggest important new directions for exploration in vocabulary research. They currently exist, in Nagy and Scott's work, as features of a theory of vocabulary knowledge. However, one would hope to see them eventually as a part of a theory of vocabulary instruction and assessment.

In an analysis of vocabulary assessments for ESL learners, Read (2000) identified three continua for designing and evaluating vocabulary assessments; we believe all three are useful: (a) discrete–embedded, (b) selective–comprehensive, and (c) contextualized–decontextualized. (Read actually uses the terms *context-dependent* and *context-independent* to anchor the two ends of the continuum, but we have substituted our own terminology here.) They represent dimensions that are not only conceptually interesting but also derived from careful analyses of existing tests. We discuss each continuum in turn.

Discrete–Embedded

This distinction addresses whether vocabulary is regarded as a separate construct with its own separate set of test items and its own score report, which is the discrete end of the continuum, or whether vocabulary is an embedded construct that contributes to, but is not regarded as separate from, the larger construct of text comprehension. All four of the assessments represented in Table 16.2 treat vocabulary as a discrete construct separate from comprehension. The PPVT-III is an entire test devoted to oral receptive vocabulary. The other three assessments each have a separate subtest or set of subtests devoted to vocabulary or, in the case of the WRMT-R, word comprehension. As is typical of norm-referenced reading tests, these subtests allow vocabulary to be reported both as a separate score or as a part of a combined reading score that is some aggregate of vocabulary plus some other reading subscores, most notably comprehension.

By contrast, the NAEP has traditionally taken an embedded stance to vocabulary assessment, being content to ensure that contextualized vocabulary items are a part of one or more of the stances assessed in creating aggregate comprehension scores for text genres. A typical item is immersed in a larger set of comprehension questions and queries the meaning of specific words as used in context, such as the following:

The word *misanthrope* on page 12 means

(a) an ill-intentioned person

(b) an ill person

(c) a person who reacts well to misery

(d) a person who mistrusts anthropology

In the 2009 NAEP Framework (NAGB, 2005; Salinger, Kamil, Kapinus, & Afflerbach, 2005), the goal is to report vocabulary separately, assuming that the construct, as measured, stands up to the psychometric validation of its statistical independence, and as a part of the overall comprehension score.

More often than not, if the option for a separate score is available, there will be a free-standing vocabulary section in the test battery, and it will have its own unique item format and separate time allotment. Conversely, when vocabulary items are included as a part of the overall comprehension score (i.e., embedded), they are most likely to be physically embedded within and distributed among the set of comprehension test items. Note, however, that one could report a separate vocabulary subtest score even if the vocabulary items were physically interspersed among comprehension items. That is exactly the approach that will be taken in the new NAEP assessment.

Inherently there is neither vice nor virtue in a separate vocabulary score; empirically, however, the case for reporting a separate score is strong. As far back as 1942, when Frederick Davis reported the first factor analysis of comprehension test items, he was able to extract a factor for word, along with factors for gist and reasoning. Further, again and again, analyses of the infrastructure of comprehension assessments implicate something independent about vocabulary knowledge (see Pearson & Hamm, 2005, for a summary of these studies). Hence, the decision by NAGB to report a separate score seems appropriate. As with other questions of vocabulary assessment, the wisdom of the new NAEP approach awaits empirical validation.

Selective–Comprehensive

This distinction refers to the relationship between the sample of items in a test and the hypothetical population of vocabulary items that the sample represents. Thus, if one assesses students' grasp of the allegedly new vocabulary in a story from an anthology or a chapter in a science text, the sample is inherently selective; one wants to know if the students learned the words in that particular sample. In general, the smaller the set of words about which we wish to make a claim, the more selective the assessment. We could, however, want to make a claim about students' mastery over a larger corpus of words, such as all of the words in the *American Heritage Dictionary* or the 2,000 most frequently occurring words in English, or all the words in Level 8 of a basal anthology, or all of the words in a science textbook. At the comprehensive end of the continuum, larger hypothetical corpora of words prevail.

This distinction is not just an idle mental exercise; it has enormous implications for the generalizations that can be made from assessments. Consider the items that assess vocabulary in Table 16.2. Because the items on real tests are copyrighted and cannot be shared publicly, we tried to convey the nature of the tests by creating items that paralleled what we saw on the actual assessments. The process of trying to identify parallel vocabulary to exemplify typical tests was both frustrating and instructive. What immediately struck us was that there were no guidelines, no theories, and no frameworks to guide our choices. We could not infer how or why particular words were chosen for these tests.

We ended up choosing our parallel words by matching the word frequency and decodability of the target words in the actual items. However, this information was not provided in the technical manuals of these assessments. Such a lack of clarity on the source of vocabulary in large-scale assessments is typical of current assessments. Most of our current vocabulary assessments have no theoretically defined population of words at all or, if they do, we have not been able to infer it from the materials they provide for test users. The core of the development process is psychometric, not theoretical. Test developers obtain a bunch of words, often by asking professionals in the field to tell them what words students at a particular grade level should know; then, they administer all the words to a sample of students at known levels of development or expertise (usually indexed by grade level). The words are sorted by their difficulty, expressed often as the percentage of students in a particular population who answered the question correctly. Ultimately, scores for individuals on such a test derive their meaning from comparisons with the population of students, not words, at large, which is why we call them norm-referenced tests. Under such circumstances, all we know is that a given student performed better, or worse, than the average student on the set of words that happened to be on the test. We know nothing about what the scores say about students' knowledge of any identifiable domain or corpus of words. Whether we want to possess information about domain mastery is, of course, a matter of policy and of educational values. Do we care about the terms in which we describe the vocabulary growth of individuals or groups? Will it suffice to know how a student or a group performed in relation to some other individuals or groups?

In analyzing assessment tasks in archival vocabulary studies, Scott et al. (2006) reported that most researchers had devised assessments that tested knowledge of the specific words that had been taught in an instructional intervention. The only common construct underlying word selection across a majority of studies was students' prior knowledge. That is, it was assumed that the words taught, or at least the majority of them, were unknown to the target students. This assumption was validated in one of three ways: (a) by using a pretest that tested each word directly, (b) by selecting words with a low *p* value (percent correct) from a source such as *The Living Word Vocabulary* (Dale & O'Rourke, 1981), or (c) by asking teachers or researchers to select words not likely to be known by the target population. The criterion of being likely known by the target age group provides little indication of what larger vocabulary students can access as a result of an intervention. For example, if students have learned *consume*, how likely is it that they will also learn something about members of its morphological family, such as *consumer* or *consumable*, or about words likely to be in a mental semantic network with consume, such as *eat* or *devour*?

Later in this essay, we review current proposals for theoretically grounded means of selecting words for instruction and assessment. Although none of these frameworks has yet been used for the design of an assessment, such frameworks suggest that it may be possible to move our assessments to the more comprehensive end of this continuum. Only then will we be able to make claims such as, "The average student in a given school exhibits basic mastery over X% of the words in a given corpus (e.g., the words encountered in a given curriculum in a given grade level)." One could even imagine a computerized assessment system in which all 200 students enrolled in 10th-grade biology took a different sample of 25 vocabulary items from the same corpus for purposes of estimating each student's mastery over that corpus. Given a corpus of, for example, 150 vocabulary items, there are an indefinitely large number of random samples of 25-word tests that could be generated by computer. One could also imagine a similar approach with smaller corpora within a course (e.g., all of the content vocabulary within a chapter, unit, or project). At the comprehensive end of this continuum, we can begin to think of domain-referenced assessment in the ways in which proponents such as Hively (1974) or Bock, Thissen, and Zimowski (1997) conceptualized the approach.

Contextualized–Decontextualized

This continuum refers to the degree that textual context is required to determine the meaning of a word. Any word can readily and easily be assessed in a decontextualized format. But simply assessing a word in a contextualized format does not necessarily mean that context is required to determine its meaning. In order to meet the standard of assessing students' ability to use context to identify word meaning, context must actually be used in completing the item. Table 16.3 details several examples to illustrate the continuum.

Item 1 falls firmly on the decontextualized side of the continuum. Even though context is provided for item 2, it is not needed if someone knows the meaning of *consume* as eat or drink. Because the context provides literally no clues about the meaning of *consume*, the item provides no information about a reader's ability to use context to infer the meaning of a word. In item 3,

because all four meanings denote one or another meaning of *consume*, context is essential for zeroing in on the meaning as used in the sentence. Item 4 is even trickier than item 3. Unlike item 3, which requires the selection of the most common meaning of *consume*, item 4 requires a student to reject the default (most common) meaning in favor of a more arcane sense of *consume*. Note also that a very fine semantic distinction is required in item 4 to select *spent wastefully* over *used up*. As a general rule, it is nearly impossible to assess vocabulary in context without reliance on polysemous words and distractor sets that reflect at least two of the meanings of each assessed word. In all fairness, we must admit that there are formats that do not require polysemous words or extremely rare words to assess contextual usage. For example, if one selects really rare, arcane words, the meanings of which can be derived from the textual context, then a straightforward format can be used. Also, one can argue that "picking a word"

Table 16.3   Degrees of Contextual Reliance

1. *consumed*
   a. ate or drank
   b. prepared
   c. bought
   d. enjoyed

2. The people consumed their dinner.
   a. ate or drank
   b. prepared
   c. bought
   d. enjoyed

3. The people consumed their dinner.
   a. ate or drank
   b. used up
   c. spent wastefully
   d. destroyed

4. The citizens consumed their supply of gravel through wanton development.
   a. ate or drank
   b. used up
   c. spent wastefully
   d. destroyed

that fits a blank space absolutely requires the systematic analysis of context. Even so, we like the polysemous format because of its emphasis on close reading of the surrounding context to make a selection from among a set of real meanings of real words.

WHAT COULD VOCABULARY ASSESSMENTS MEASURE?

To begin to answer the question of what vocabulary assessments could measure, we decided to look closely at research that had already been completed or was currently underway. Thus, we looked at existing reviews of research, current investigations, and current developments, particularly the new NAEP vocabulary assessment (Salinger et al., 2005). Our logic was that by looking broadly at extensive reviews of vocabulary and narrowly at cutting edge work, we would get a clear picture of the possible and the feasible.

Insights on Vocabulary Assessments From Reviews of Research

The RAND Reading Study Group (RRSG; 2002) was convened to examine what was known about comprehension, with the goal of formulating a plan for research and development. The resulting document includes an analysis of vocabulary research as well as questions in need of intensive research. RRSG acknowledged the strong link between vocabulary knowledge and reading comprehension and speculated that it is an especially important factor in understanding the reading problems experienced by second-language learners. However, RRSG cautioned that the relationship between vocabulary knowledge and comprehension is extremely complex, because of the relationships among vocabulary knowledge, conceptual and cultural knowledge, and instructional opportunities. Surely, as we look to the future, we will want to know more about whether there are any special considerations for assessing vocabulary for

students learning English as a second language.

What we know about the nature of instruction that influences vocabulary learning can aid in the design of assessments. The NRP (NICHD, 2000) reviewed 50 experimental and quasiexperimental studies published in English in refereed journals. One provocative finding from the NRP report is that students acquire vocabulary best when it is used in meaningful, authentic contexts; indeed, they are less able to remember words that are presented in isolated formats, such as lists. As was apparent in the analysis of the current assessments on the decontextualized–contextualized continuum, many current vocabulary assessments present words in a decontextualized context. Contrasting the power of isolated versus contextualized vocabulary assessments to predict both passage specific and general comprehension should be a priority.

Another critical finding in the NRP is that students often do not fully understand the task when asked to show evidence of vocabulary knowledge. If tasks are restructured so that students understand what is expected, students often do better. Restructuring seems to be particularly effective for low-achieving or at-risk students. Again, this conclusion has important implications for assessment, given the general difficulty of assessing skills and knowledge among low-achieving or at-risk students.

Two of the characteristics of vocabulary learning from Nagy and Scott's (2000) list of important characteristics of vocabulary acquisition have implications for assessment research: incrementality and heterogeneity. If a new word meaning is acquired incrementally rather than in an all-or-nothing fashion, it would seem useful to gauge students' developing depth of understanding of important words. There have been a few attempts to begin such an endeavor. For example, Stallman, Pearson, Nagy, Anderson, and García (1995) found a way to discriminate among levels of depth by manipulating the set of distractors from which a student was asked to select a correct response. Students encountered the same test item several times, as illustrated in Table 16.4. As one moves from one level to the next, the discrimination task

Table 16.4   Assessing Depth of Vocabulary Knowledge

1. A *gendarme* is a kind of
   a. toy
   b. person
   c. potato
   d. recipe

2. A *gendarme* is a kind of
   a. public official
   b. farmer
   c. accountant
   d. lawyer

3. A *gendarme* is a kind of
   a. soldier
   b. sentry
   c. law enforcement officer
   d. fire prevention official

4. One would most likely encounter a *gendarme* in
   a. New York
   b. Nice, France
   c. London, England
   d. New Orleans

becomes more refined and, presumably, more difficult. However, this represents only a beginning; much remains to be done to operationalize the construct of incrementality.

Heterogeneity in Nagy and Scott's (2000) view suggests that the more contexts in which a word is encountered, the greater the likelihood that its meaning will be acquired, or more precisely, the greater the likelihood that a precise, nuanced, and even sophisticated meaning will be acquired. To assess the influence of heterogeneity, we could assess word meaning across situations in which a new or rare word appeared in varying frequencies; say once, twice, and five times. In addition, of course, the quality of the context matters too; it may be that when a word is encountered in a highly supportive context (where the semantic relatedness of the surrounding words is high), students perform differently than in a less supportive context.

Insights on Assessment From Perspectives on Selecting Words for Instruction

Our previous discussion of the selective–comprehensive dimension of vocabulary selection emphasized the point that vocabulary on current assessments is not selected on the basis of any evident criteria. For all intents and purposes, any word in the English language could be found on a typical vocabulary test, provided that it discriminates across students. The question of interest is how *could* word choices be made in a more principled way. Three prominent perspectives on word selection offer underlying theoretical, or at least conceptually interesting, frameworks that could be translated into principles for selecting words to appear on a vocabulary test. To be clear, the scholars whose work we review have developed these frameworks as tools to select words for instruction. We are the ones who are extrapolating their potential as tools to select words for assessment; nonetheless, it may be a useful extrapolation.

The most prominent perspective on word selection at the present time is that of Beck, McKeown, and Kucan (2002). Beck and her colleagues view vocabulary as falling into three tiers. The first tier is comprised of high-frequency words (e.g., *come, go, happy, some*) that do not need to be taught, except perhaps to English learners, and the third tier is comprised of rare words that are specific to particular content domains (e.g., *chlorophyll, photosynthesis, xylum*). They believe that vocabulary instruction should focus on second-tier words. Words in that second tier characterize the vocabulary of mature language users when they read and write. They are best thought of as less common labels for relatively common concepts: *stunning* in place of *pretty*, *pranced* instead of *walked*, *astonished* but not *surprised*. As such, they constitute the language of sophisticated academic discourse, at least as it is represented in narrative fiction. In research and programs guided by the tier model, Beck and her colleagues have identified words from texts, mainly narrative, and either provided teachers with candidate words for Tier 2 instruction or taught them how to select Tier 2 words for their own lessons. The rules for selecting Tier 2 words are not precisely expressed in the Beck et al. research. This presents a problem for the development of vocabulary assessments. However, one could imagine a principle stipulating that only Tier 2 words (or perhaps Tier 2 words in a given frequency band—say English nouns, verbs, and adjectives that rank between 2,000 and 5,000 on a frequency count) are candidates for assessment at a given grade level and that the correct foil in a multiple-choice item is always the most common synonym (e.g., *pretty*) for any given Tier 2 target (e.g., *stunning*). The validity of such a rule would have to be established through research on the ultimate utility of such a definition of Tier 2 words.

There are other approaches to the selection of words. Biemiller (2005; Biemiller & Boote, 2006; Biemiller & Slonim, 2001) has identified a group of words judged to be worth teaching during the primary grades. These are words that are known by 40 to 80% of students at the end of grade 2. Such words might be thought of as a set of "Goldilocks" words—not too easy and not too hard (Stahl & Nagy, 2005). There is a deeper rationale behind Biemiller's work. He and his colleagues assume that, other things being equal, students are likely to acquire these words in roughly the order of their "knownness" by a large sample of students at the end of second grade, with the least commonly known words learned last. Equipped with such a hypothetical list, if we select and sequence words for instruction in descending order of how well they are known among end-of-year second-grade students, we can make it possible, at any given point in the school year, for students to be on track to learn the next set of words they are likely to need in their everyday reading. In this way, we could eliminate, or at least minimize, the vocabulary gap between various groups of students who, by virtue of differences in experience and instruction, differ markedly in their vocabulary knowledge. Biemiller found just such corpus of words in Dale and O'Rourke's (1981) *The Living Word Vocabulary* grade levels 2, 4, and 6. Level 2 words were considered easy and not recommended for teaching. Through testing approximately 2,870 *The Living Word Vocabulary* level 4 and level 6 root word meanings and rating

another 1,760 meanings, Biemiller has identified some 1,860 root-word meanings that are appropriate for instruction during the primary grades. These could easily become the corpus of words from which samples could be drawn for assessments of various sorts, including standardized assessments.

Hiebert's (2005, 2006) framework employs three elements as part of a principled vocabulary curriculum. The first principle—the richness of a word's semantic associations—builds on and extends the work of Beck et al. (2002). As new labels for already known concepts (Graves, 2000), the Tier 2 words are part of semantic networks with words that are similar in meaning. In the principled curriculum, the richness of a word's semantic network is established by reference to an analysis of semantic associations.

Hiebert has used Marzano and Marzano's (1988) semantic clusters to establish the richness of the semantic network of which a word is part. Marzano and Marzano classified 7,230 words from elementary school texts into three levels: superclusters (61), clusters (430), and miniclusters (1,500). Some superclusters have numerous clusters and these, in turn, have numerous miniclusters. For example, the word *hue* can be described as having a sparse set of semantic associations in that it is part of a minicluster with only two additional words (*color, tint*) and is part of the supercluster devoted to words about *color*, consisting of only 29 words. By contrast, *plunge* is part of the *descending motion* cluster with 19 words that, in turn, is part of the *types of motion* supercluster with 321 words.

To give a general indication of the opportunities that students have had with the semantic concept underlying a word, Hiebert (2006) has used the Marzano and Marzano (1988) categories to identify words as members of one of three different groups: (a) rich semantic connections (superclusters with 200 or more members), (b) moderate semantic connections (superclusters with 100–199 members), and (c) sparse semantic connections (superclusters with 21–99 members).

"Knownness" is the second principle of Hiebert's curriculum, and it builds directly on the work of Biemiller (2005; Biemiller & Boote, 2006) and Dale and O'Rourke (1981) described in a previous section of this essay. Knownness is operationally defined as those words that students at particular grade levels respond to correctly on the vocabulary assessments developed by Dale and O'Rourke and Biemiller and Boote.

The third principle, family frequency, combines the insights on the centrality of word frequency among second-language scholars such as Nation (1990, 2001) and the discoveries about the importance of the morphological families (Carlisle & Katz, 2006; Nagy, Anderson, Schommer, Scott, & Stallman, 1989). If one assumes that students are capable of recognizing common roots across instances of occurrence, then the notion of frequency must be modified dramatically from counts of the frequency of individual words. For example, although the word *consume* can be expected to appear 5 times per million words (Zeno, Ivens, Millard, & Duvvuri, 1995), members of its morphological family appear an additional 90 times per million words (*consumed*, 7; *consumer*, 37; *consumers*, 28; *consumers'*, 1; *consumes*, 1; *consuming*, 2; *consumption*, 14).

Hiebert (2006) has described how the words on four prominent vocabulary tests distributed themselves according to the three elements in her model—semantic connectedness, knownness, and frequency of morphological families. The analysis of words on vocabulary assessments used the third-grade forms of the same vocabulary tests for which items are illustrated in Table 16.2—the PPVT, WRMT, ITBS, and SAT. Table 16.5 presents the results of this analysis. It is relevant to our assessment concerns because it illustrates how the words on vocabulary assessments could be viewed in terms of Read's (2000) selective–comprehensive continuum.

Specifically, Table 16.5 portrays the distribution of one of Hiebert's (2005, 2006) elements, morphological families, across the four assessments.

The data in Table 16.5 show that the types of words on three of the four assessments, the WRMT-R, ITBS, and the SAT-10, were similar, with only a small percentage of the words in the rare category (8–20%). By contrast, the majority of the words (67%) on the PPVT-III fell into the rare zones. The pattern on this feature was similar to that for the other two features (semantic associations and knownness).

The PPVT-III is the outlier on these assessments. But why? One possibility is that the PPVT-III, as an individually administered, administrator-paced test, is designed to span a wide range of levels of vocabulary knowledge in a single text—thus it will necessarily require a large number of "obscure" words in order to be sensitive to individual differences at the high end of the vocabulary knowledge scale. But if range is responsible for differentiating the PPVT-III from the other assessments, then one would also expect the WRMT-R (another test with a wide range of items spanning various grades) to behave like the PPVT-III rather than like the other group reading tests. It doesn't. Another possibility is that the PPVT-III taps oral, not written, receptive vocabulary knowledge. Hence there is no need to worry about the decodability of words, making it possible to assess children's mastery over the conceptual knowledge of even orthographically rare words. In the final analysis, however, we admit that we are not sure what makes the PPVT-III behave so differently from other widely used, wide-range assessments.

Insights From New Assessments

Nowhere is a theory of contextualized vocabulary assessment more prominent than in the recent NAEP framework (NAGB, 2005; Salinger et al., 2005). In developing that framework, the Framework Committee took a new stance on the role of reading vocabulary assessment. In previous frameworks and assessments, vocabulary items were included, but only to ensure breadth of coverage of important aspects

Table 16.5   Target Words and Their Morphological Families in Particular Word Zones as Percentages of Total Words on an Assessment

	PPVT		WRMT		ITBS		SAT	
	Target word	Target word + morphological family	Target word	Target word + morphological family	Target word	Target word + morphological family	Target word	Target word + morphological family
Zones 0–2 (High: 100+)	6	14	39	48	36	57	49	7
Zones 3–4 (Moderate: 10–99.99)	27	36	41	37	46	33	43	24
Zones 5–6 (Rare: >1 –9.99)	67	50	20	15	18	10	8	4

Reprinted with permission from Hiebert (2006).

of the reading framework, and vocabulary items were folded into an overall comprehension score. In the previous model, a word was selected for two reasons: (a) because it was deemed important and (b) in order to assess whether a reader was able infer its meaning from context. In the new framework, the committee signaled an important shift: *"vocabulary items will function both as a measure of passage comprehension and as a test of readers' specific knowledge of the word's meaning as intended by the passage author"* (NAGB, p. iv, emphasis added). Thus, vocabulary takes on a more important role, with a hope that it will prove to be a sufficiently robust construct that it could be reported as a separate score in addition to serving as a part of the overall comprehension score.

In addition, the theory behind the role of vocabulary as a part of comprehension is quite different. In the new framework, the emphasis is "the meanings of the words that writers use to convey new information or meaning, not to measure readers' ability to learn new terms or words" (NAGB, 2005, p. 35). This principle is operationalized in a set of criteria for choosing words according to the following: (a) words that characterize the vocabulary of mature language users and written rather than oral language; (b) words that label generally familiar and broadly understood concepts, even though the words themselves may not be familiar to younger learners; (c) words that are necessary for understanding at least a local part of the context and are linked to central ideas such that lack of understanding may disrupt comprehension; and (d) words that are found in grade-level reading material (NAGB; Salinger et al., 2005). In short, the specified words are of the type that Beck et al. (2002) have called Tier 2 words—uncommon labels for relatively common concepts. As noted earlier, these words constitute the language of sophisticated academic discourse, particularly in literary text. In fact, in science and mathematics, much of academic discourse is new labels for new concepts—what Beck and her colleagues call Tier 3 words. The NAEP framework has emphasized information texts and recognizes the different vocabulary loads in information and literary text. We have limited knowledge of the generality of the "Tier" concept because the research of Beck and her colleagues has been focused on literary texts.

In order to achieve complete operationalization of this approach to vocabulary assessment, the committee has established a set of rules for generating items and distractors. A set of distractors may include (a) a word that has a more common meaning of a target word, but that must be ignored in favor of the meaning in context; (b) a word that presents correct information or content from the text that is not what is meant by the target word; (c) a word that has an alternative interpretation of the context in which the target word occurs; or (d) other words that look or sound similar to the target word (NAGB, 2005; Salinger et al., 2005). Distractors play an important role in operationalizing the underlying theory of vocabulary knowledge as key component of comprehension, especially in the requirement that students must reject an alternative, and presumably sometimes more common, sense of the word (e.g., ignore *stunning* as *bewildering* in favor of *stunning* as *splendid* or *beautiful*).

This development within NAEP would have a significant influence even if it had no interesting theoretical grounding simply because it is NAEP and therefore influential in shaping other assessments. Given the fact that the new assessment venture is both theoretically interesting and provocative (i.e., it takes a stand on which aspect of vocabulary acquisition is worth assessing), it is likely to be exceptionally influential in shaping a broader set of vocabulary assessment practices.

What Could Be the Research Agenda for the Next Decade?

The questions we have raised in this essay, where we have tried to draw inferences about vocabulary assessment issues from current efforts to understand or improve vocabulary instruction and assessment, would constitute an ambitious research agenda. However, we would certainly endorse such ambitious efforts. But we feel the need to raise additional assessment issues in closing, albeit without unpacking any of them in depth, just to make sure they get into the queue for future efforts.

1. A first priority should be to devote explicit research attention to the distinctions among various aspects of vocabulary that we have discussed in this essay, rather than simply using a global definition of vocabulary or some general concept of word meaning. One of the major issues is the type of vocabulary that is being taught and tested. For example, often reading vocabulary is intended to be assessed, although the instrument used might measure expressive vocabulary, or vice versa. Similarly, the term *vocabulary* is used almost interchangeably as we move between writing, listening, speaking and reading without making either conceptual or operational distinctions. We contend that these relatively simple changes would yield great dividends in our knowledge of the relationships between vocabulary knowledge, vocabulary instruction, and literacy. A simple example would be the targeted instruction of reading vocabulary based on a receptive vocabulary measure rather than an expressive vocabulary measure, which might be more important for speaking.

2. In order to conduct the research described in the preceding paragraph, much effort needs to be exerted in the development of assessments

that are clear about the components and types of vocabulary. Researchers need to focus on the components and formats of vocabulary assessment, particularly with regard to the selection of words, sampling procedures, and so forth as we have noted in this essay. That research is needed to determine whether any single assessments can represent the various aspects of vocabulary we have identified (and, perhaps, some we have not) or whether we need individual and targeted assessments for each of the types of vocabulary. Without that information, progress in vocabulary research will be limited.

3. It is clear that informational text typically carries a heavier vocabulary load than does literary text. Currently, that difference is a hidden variable in many studies. Research is needed to untangle the relationship between text genre and vocabulary variables such as how words are chosen for instruction and the vocabulary load of the text. Regardless of what the answers will be, they will have profound implications for vocabulary instruction and transfer. Because vocabulary is dealt with currently in a holistic fashion, one dividend might be to differentiate methods of instruction for vocabulary by text genre. Learning technical vocabulary from a biology text is clearly different from learning vocabulary in a story, where most of the word can be related to personal experiences.

4. The three preceding points all converge on the issue of transfer of vocabulary knowledge to other components of reading. The research alluded to here would almost certainly offer insights on the difficulties we have raised in this essay about issues of transfer and the specific effects of vocabulary instruction on comprehension. More important is the explicit attention to the issues of transfer, both near and far, for the tasks under investigation. In addition, the strength of transfer over time should be a part of

this effort, particularly given the relatively short duration of many vocabulary instruction interventions in the literature.

5. The NAEP venture bears close watching, to see whether it is capable of generating a new paradigm for conceptualizing and measuring vocabulary. In particular, we hope that someone undertakes some value-added studies to determine what the new paradigm adds above and beyond more prosaic and conventional approaches to vocabulary assessment. The first administration using this new paradigm will not occur until 2009, giving us some time to address some of these questions.

6. There is still a set of unanswered issues that were raised in the RRSG (2002) report about the conditions and effects of vocabulary and vocabulary instruction that would, if answered, provide quantum leaps in our knowledge base. Among the issues raised in the RRSG report is the relationship of vocabulary instruction to literacy for non-native speakers of English. At least a part of any research agenda should include an emphasis on the RRSG issues.

7. Finally, we need a serious attempt to implement computerized assessments of vocabulary domains, along the lines of those suggested in the section of this essay detailing the selective–comprehensive continuum. In a better world, we would not be limited to conventional norm-referenced assessments of vocabulary acquisition, where our only benchmark for gauging vocabulary growth is the average performance of other students. We could opt instead for estimates of mastery over particular domains of interest (e.g., all of the words in a given curriculum or a given frequency band) or estimates of control over other characteristics that might prove to be effective indexes of vocabulary learning (e.g., all words with a common morpheme, such as *spec*). Given the capacity

of computers to store and analyze large corpora and our recent advances in computer adaptive assessment, the time appears right for such an exploration.

As we said at the outset, it is our hope that this essay will help to fuel the recent enthusiasm in the field for vocabulary research, in particular research on vocabulary assessment. Only when we are sure about the validity and sensitivity of our assessments will we be able to determine the relations among various modes of vocabulary development and the relations between vocabulary knowledge and other aspects of reading development. This agenda, we believe, is a wise investment for the field.

P. David Pearson serves as Dean of the Graduate School of Education at the University of California, Berkeley and as a faculty member in the Language, Literacy, and Culture program. His current research focuses on issues of reading instruction and reading assessment policies and practices. Before coming to UC Berkeley, Pearson served on the reading education faculties at Minnesota, Illinois, and Michigan State. He can be contacted at the Graduate School of Education, 1501 Tolman Hall #1670, University of California, Berkeley, Berkeley, CA 94720-1670, USA, or by e-mail at ppearson@berkeley.edu.

Elfrieda H. Hiebert is an adjunct professor at the University of California, Berkeley. Her research interests focus on the effects of texts on the fluency, vocabulary, and comprehension of elementary-level students, especially English-language learners. She can be contacted at 106 Phelan Court, Santa Cruz, CA 95060, USA, or by e-mail at hiebert@berkeley.edu.

Michael L. Kamil is professor of psychological studies in education at the Stanford University School of Education. His research interests are in the intersection of literacy and technology and second language learners. He chaired the Vocabulary, Teacher Professional Development, and Technology subgroups of the National Reading Panel. He can be contacted at 123 Cubberley Hall, 485 Lasuen Mall, Stanford, CA 94305, USA, or by e-mail at mkamil@stanford.edu.

Article 17

Teacher Practices and Perspectives for Developing Academic Language

Jeff Zwiers

This study investigates the ways in which middle school teachers in the United States develop academic language in intermediate-level English learners who attend mainstream content classes. Analysis of field notes, transcripts, and student work show that (a) academic language and higher-order thinking skills are closely linked, and (b) classroom discourse patterns and activities both develop and impede language growth. The teachers used four principle communication strategies: questioning, gestures, connecting to background knowledge with examples and analogies, and personifying. The results suggest that students, despite growth in certain dimensions of cognition and language, also learn counterproductive "rules of school." This research is intended to benefit the millions of "non-mainstream" students worldwide who struggle in schools that have been created and shaped to serve mainstream purposes.

This article is available as a full-text PDF at http://www.sagepub.com/cappello/.

SOURCE: Zwiers, J. (2007). Teacher Practices and Perspectives for Developing Academic Language. *International Journal of Applied Linguistics, 17*(1), 93–116. Reprinted by permission.

Section VI

COMPREHENSION

OVERVIEW

Having a section that focuses on comprehension may seem like a contradiction to some readers, given that we have situated every prior section topic in a comprehension-centered idea of literacy. Indeed, all aspects of literacy lead to comprehension, the overriding goal. However, this section of the reader highlights explicit instruction for fiction and expository text comprehension.

STRATEGY

Use the "Cloze Procedure" to complete the following section description on comprehension. Cloze activities engage students in reading a passage where words have been omitted. The purpose of this strategy is to have students use semantic and syntactic context knowledge to make predictions about what words are missing from the passage and therefore make predictions about the text. Cloze may be used as an informal assessment as well as a strategy for building and monitoring comprehension.

There are many variations on the Cloze Procedure. Some suggest that every fifth word be deleted, or only the exact word should be considered a correct answer. Others suggest that Cloze may be used to emphasize the graphophonic cue as well, when teachers omit letters instead of whole words.

Cloze

(Tierney & Readence, 2005)

Directions

Read through the entire passage below. Then reread it and predict what words are missing from the passage. Remember, any word that makes sense in the blank is acceptable. Once you have completed the passage, write a brief paragraph that explains how you determined at least three omitted words.

Pardo (2004) begins this section, in "What Every Teacher Needs to Know About Comprehension," by helping readers understand comprehension as a complex process where "the reader, the text, and the context interact to create meaning." Her focus is on the many ways teachers can _____ this transaction. Throughout the article, Pardo proposes teacher support through a _____ of scaffolds. In "Scaffolding Students' Comprehension of Text," Clark and Graves (2005) also suggest _____ for explicit comprehension. Teachers create scaffolds to (temporarily) support student learning. While _____ scaffolds appear as many different activities and approaches, the goal of providing support for students remains the _____. Without a doubt, "scaffolding is a complex instructional _____ that takes many forms." Both of these articles position comprehension _____ and the use of scaffolds specifically, within the gradual release of responsibility model you read about in Fisher and Frey (2008, Article 3) because the supports should be modified and _____ as students take control of their own learning.

In "New Dimensions of Content Area Literacy," Wood (2003) focuses on exposition in her description and promotion of content area literacy. The author advocates _____ instruction for comprehending informational text across grade levels, including peer talk, Communal Writing, Story Impressions, and Think Pair Share. In her innovative article, "Teaching Expository Text Structures Through Information Trade Book Retellings," Moss (2004) describes how teachers may use retelling as a powerful ____ for improving understanding of expository text. Teachers helping students develop _____ comprehension have long used retellings, when students _____ information from listening to or reading a text. Acccording to Moss, "Reconstructing texts through retellings helps children develop reading flexibility as well as _____ of text forms, text conventions, and the processes involved in text construction." Expository text comprehension is important for _____ in our information era. In addition, many children are naturally drawn to expository texts and are therefore more engaged in the reading processes.

SOURCE: Tierney, R. J., & Readence, J. E. (2005). *Reading Strategies and Practices: A Compendium* (6th ed.). Boston: Allyn & Bacon.

Article 18

WHAT EVERY TEACHER NEEDS TO KNOW ABOUT COMPREHENSION

LAURA S. PARDO

Once teachers understand what is involved in comprehending and how the factors of reader, text, and context interact to create meaning, they can more easily teach their students to be effective comprehenders.

Comprehension is a complex process that has been understood and explained in a number of ways. The RAND Reading Study Group (2002) stated that comprehension is "the process of simultaneously extracting and constructing meaning through interaction and involvement with written language" (p. 11). Duke (2003) added "navigation" and "critique" to her definition because she believed that readers actually move through the text, finding their way, evaluating the accuracy of the text to see if it fits their personal agenda, and finally arriving at a self-selected location. A common definition for teachers might be that comprehension is a process in which readers construct meaning by interacting with text through the combination of prior knowledge and previous experience, information in the text, and the stance the reader takes in relationship to the text. As these different definitions demonstrate, there are many interpretations of what it means to comprehend text. This article synthesizes the research on comprehension and makes connections to classroom practice. I begin by introducing a model of comprehension.

SOURCE: Pardo, L. S. (2004). What Every Teacher Needs to Know About Comprehension. *The Reading Teacher, 58*(3), 272–280. Reprinted by permission of the International Reading Association.

HOW COMPREHENSION WORKS

Comprehension occurs in the transaction between the reader and the text (Kucer, 2001; Rosenblatt, 1978). The reader brings many things to the literacy event, the text has certain features, and yet meaning emerges only from the engagement of that reader with that text at that particular moment in time. Figure 18.1 presents a model of this process. Each of the elements in the model—reader, text, context, and transaction—is described in more detail later in this article, along with specific suggestions for how teachers can interact with the model to help children become strong comprehenders, beginning in kindergarten.

The Reader

Any literacy event is made up of a reader engaging with some form of text. Each reader is unique in that he or she possesses certain traits or characteristics that are distinctly applied with each text and situation (Butcher & Kintsch, 2003; Fletcher, 1994; Narvaez, 2002). The most important of these characteristics is likely the

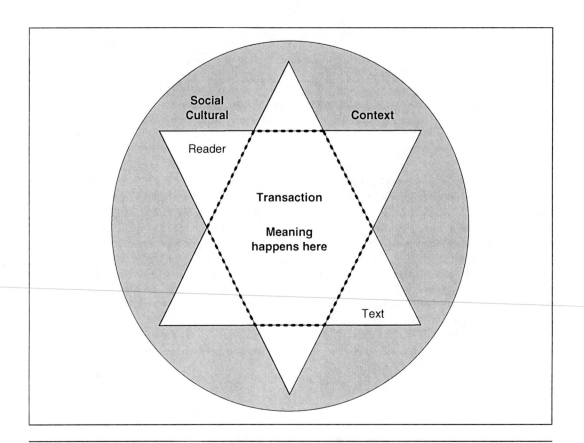

Figure 18.1   Model of comprehension

reader's world knowledge (Fletcher, 1994). The more background knowledge a reader has that connects with the text being read, the more likely the reader will be able to make sense of what is being read (Butcher & Kintsch, 2003; Schallert & Martin, 2003). The process of connecting known information to new information takes place through a series of networkable connections known as schema (Anderson & Pearson, 1984; Narvaez, 2002). In schema theory, individuals organize their world knowledge into categories and systems that make retrieval easier. When a key word or concept is encountered, readers are able to access this information system, pulling forth the ideas that will help them make connections with the text so they can create meaning. Schema theory involves the storage of various kinds of information in long-term memory. Because long-term memory appears to have infinite capacity (Pressley, 2003), it is likely that readers have many ideas stored in long-term memory. When a key word or concept is presented to the reader (through a title, heading, or someone who has recommended the text), some of this stored information is brought forward and temporarily placed into short-term memory so that the reader can return to it quickly as he or she reads. Short-term memory has limited capacity and often the information pulled from long-term memory prior to or during reading is only available for a short time and then is placed back in long-term memory. Short-term memory shifts and juggles information, using what is immediately pertinent and allowing less pertinent information to slip back into long-term memory (Schallert & Martin, 2003).

The amount and depth of a reader's world knowledge vary as do other individual characteristics. Readers vary in the skills, knowledge, cognitive development, culture, and purpose they bring to a text (Narvaez, 2002). Skills include such things as basic language ability, decoding skills, and higher level thinking skills. Knowledge includes background knowledge about content and text and relates to the available schema a reader has for a particular text. A reader's cognitive development causes that reader

to evaluate text in different ways—for example, to make moral judgments. Comprehension is affected by a reader's culture, based on the degree to which it matches with the writer's culture or the culture espoused in the text. Readers also read in particular ways depending on the purpose for reading. Another individual difference that exists in readers is motivation. Motivation can influence the interest, purpose, emotion, or persistence with which a reader engages with text (Butcher & Kintsch, 2003; Schallert & Martin, 2003). More motivated readers are likely to apply more strategies and work harder at building meaning. Less motivated readers are not as likely to work as hard, and the meaning they create will not be as powerful as if they were highly motivated.

Teachers Support Readers

If readers have all these individual differences, how do teachers best support elementary age readers to become competent comprehenders? They teach decoding skills, help students build fluency, build and activate background knowledge, teach vocabulary words, motivate students, and engage them in personal responses to text.

Teach decoding skills. In order to comprehend, readers must be able to read the words. Some level of automatic decoding must be present so that short-term memory can work on comprehending, not on decoding, words. Teachers help students get to this level of automatic decoding by providing instruction in phonemic awareness and phonics at all grade levels. If students put too much mental energy into sounding out the words, they will have less mental energy left to think about the meaning. While teachers in the primary grades work with phonemic awareness and phonics, teachers in the intermediate grades support students' continued development of automatic decoding through spelling, vocabulary, and high-frequency word activities.

Help students build fluency. As word reading becomes automatic, students become fluent and can focus on comprehension (Rasinski, 2003).

Teachers help students become more fluent by engaging them in repeated readings for real purposes (like performances and Readers Theatre). Teachers also model fluent reading by reading aloud to students daily so that they realize what fluent reading sounds like. Some research indicates that reading aloud to students is the single most effective way to increase comprehension (see Morrow & Gambrell, 2000, for a review of this literature).

Build and activate prior knowledge. Background knowledge is an important factor for creating meaning, and teachers should help students activate prior knowledge before reading so that information connected with concepts or topics in the text is more easily accessible during reading (Keene & Zimmermann, 1997; Miller, 2002). If students do not have adequate background knowledge, teachers can help students build the appropriate knowledge. Duke (2003) suggested that one way to add to world knowledge is to use informational books with all students, particularly very young students. By using information books, students build world knowledge so that they will have the appropriate information to activate at a later time. Teachers also support students' acquisition of world knowledge by establishing and maintaining a rich, literate environment, full of texts that provide students with numerous opportunities to learn content in a wide variety of topics.

Another way teachers help students build background knowledge is to create visual or graphic organizers that help students to see not only new concepts but also how previously known concepts are related and connected to the new ones (Keene & Zimmermann, 1997; Miller, 2002). Teachers teach students how to make text-to-text, text-to-self, and text-to-world connections so that readers can more easily comprehend the texts they read.

Reading aloud and teacher modeling show students how to activate schema and make connections. For example, a first-grade teacher read aloud from *Ira Says Goodbye* (Waber, 1991). She began the lesson by thinking aloud about the title and cover of the book. "Oh I see that the author is Bernard Waber and the title is *Ira Says Goodbye*. I think this book is about the same Ira as in *Ira Sleeps Over* (Waber, 1973). I can activate my schema from that book. I am making a text-to-text connection. I remember that. . . ." She continued modeling for her students how to activate schema and make connections that helped her make meaning from this text. As she read the book to her students, she stopped occasionally to model and think aloud how she activated her own schema to make connections.

Teach vocabulary words. If there are too many words that a reader does not know, he or she will have to spend too much mental energy figuring out the unknown word(s) and will not be able to understand the passage as a whole. Teachers help students learn important vocabulary words prior to reading difficult or unfamiliar texts. When teaching vocabulary words, teachers make sure that the selected words are necessary for making meaning with the text students will be reading and that they help students connect the new words to something they already know. Simply using the word lists supplied in textbooks does not necessarily accomplish this task (Blachowicz & Fisher, 2000). Many teachers consider the backgrounds and knowledge levels of their students and the text the students will be engaging in and then select a small number of words or ideas that are important for understanding the text. Once teachers have decided on the appropriate vocabulary words to use, students must actively engage with the words—use them in written and spoken language—in order for the words to become a part of the students' reading and writing vocabularies. For example, asking students to create graphic organizers that show relationships among new words and common and known words helps them assimilate new vocabulary. Asking students to look up long lists of unrelated, unknown words is unlikely to help students access the text more appropriately or to increase personal vocabularies.

Motivate students. Many individual reader factors (e.g., cognitive development, culture) are not within a teacher's control. However, teachers can motivate students by providing them with interesting texts, allowing them choices in reading and writing, and helping students set authentic purposes for reading (e.g., generating reports, writing letters, demonstrating some new ability or skill; Pressley & Hilden, 2002). Many teachers actively seek out students' interests so that they can select texts, topics, themes, and units that will more likely engage students. Teachers also provide and promote authentic purposes for engaging in reading and writing. Authentic literacy events are those that replicate or reflect reading and writing purposes and texts that occur in the world outside of schools. Some teachers do this by providing pen pals, using students' authentic questions for in-depth study, responding to community needs, or having students solve problems.

Engage students in personal responses to text. Teachers encourage students to read both efferently and aesthetically (Rosenblatt, 1978). Researchers (McMahon, Raphael, Goatley, & Pardo, 1997) building on the ideas of Rosenblatt developed a literature-based approach to teaching reading comprehension through the Book Club program. In this instructional approach students read authentic literature; write personal, critical, and creative responses; and talk about books with their classmates (Pardo, 2002). Teachers help students learn and apply comprehension strategies while reading, through writing, and during student-led discussion groups called Book Clubs, where students explore the individual meanings that have emerged as they engage with the text over a period of time. While this program initially focused on the intermediate grades, many teachers have found that students in first and second grades are successful comprehenders when they read and engage in Book Clubs (Grattan, 1997; Raphael, Florio-Ruane, & George, 2001; Salna, 2001).

The Text

Understanding the reader is one important piece of the comprehension puzzle, but features of the text also influence the transaction where comprehension happens. The structure of the text—its genre, vocabulary, language, even the specific word choices—works to make each text unique. Some would even argue that it is at the word or microstructure level that meaning begins (Butcher & Kintsch, 2003). How well the text is written, whether it follows the conventions of its genre or structure, and the language or dialect it is written in are all factors of the text. The content of a specific text, the difficulty or readability of it, and even the type font and size are factors of a text that can influence a reader's interaction. These features collectively are referred to as "surface feature," and studies have shown that the quality of the text at the surface level is important for readers to be able to make meaning effectively (Tracey & Morrow, 2002).

The author's intent in writing the text can influence how a reader interacts with that text, particularly if this intent is made known through a foreword, back-cover biography, or knowledgeable other (as in the case of teachers in schools). Some texts are promoted as carrying a certain message or theme by those who have encountered the book previously (Rosenblatt, 1978). The inherent message that some texts carry with them, often related to the author's intent, is referred to as *gist* and has been defined as "what people remember . . . the main ideas in the text" (Pressley, 1998, p. 46). Gist is frequently assessed through basal workbooks and standardized reading tests; therefore, the author's intent is a key feature of text.

Teachers Support Texts

Because certain features make some texts more easily comprehensible, teachers help young readers understand those features so they can comprehend effectively. Teachers teach text structures, model appropriate text selection, and provide regular independent reading time.

Teach text structures. Because features of the text are beyond a teacher's control, teachers select texts that have an obvious structure. They teach a variety of narrative genres and some expository text structures. With narrative works teachers help students understand basic story grammar, including the literary elements that are common across narrative pieces, such as plot, characters, and setting. They teach specific elements that make each genre unique (e.g., talking animals in folk tales). By doing this, students will be able to access a schema for a certain narrative genre when they begin to read a new text and can begin to make text-to-text connections for a particular story genre, which will help them more easily make meaning. Likewise, teachers share some common expository text structures with students, such as sequence, descriptions, comparison, and cause and effect. Teachers discuss the idea of "inconsiderate texts" (Armbruster, 1984) with students and show them how to use cues when reading nonfiction (such as reading tables, charts, graphs, and the captions under pictures; using bold print and italics to determine big or important ideas). Inconsiderate texts do not adhere strictly to one structure, but might be a combination of several structures, and teachers can address specific features and demands of informational text so that students are more likely to engage in informational text with a repertoire of strategies and schema to help them construct meaning (Duke, 2003).

Model appropriate text selection. Teachers teach students how to select appropriate texts by showing them what features to consider. Some teachers use the Goldilocks approach (Tompkins, 2003), while others suggest that teachers level books and tell students which level books they may select (Fountas & Pinnell, 1996). In the Goldilocks approach, readers look for books that are not too hard or too easy, but just right. Just-right books are those that look interesting, have mostly decodable words, have been read aloud previously, are written by a familiar author, or will be read with a support person nearby (Tompkins, 2003). Teachers have a wide variety of genres and levels of books available for students to select for independent reading, and they support students throughout the year with appropriate book selection.

Provide regular independent reading time. Teachers can make sure they provide students with time to read independently every day. Reading becomes better with practice, and comprehending becomes better with more reading practice (Pressley, 2003). Many teachers use programs such as DEAR (Drop Everything And Read) or SSR (Sustained Silent Reading) to ensure that students read independently every day.

Teachers Create and Support a Sociocultural Context

Reading takes place somewhere between a specific reader and a specific text. A sociocultural influence likely permeates any reading activity (Kucer, 2001; Schallert & Martin, 2003). Depending on the place, the situation, and the purpose for reading, the reader and the text interact in ways that are unique for that specific context. The same reading at another time or in a different place might result in a different meaning. The context also involves the activity that occurs around the transaction. If a teacher assigns his or her students to read a certain text for a specific reason, the transaction that occurs will be based on this context. If students are asked to discuss a text, generate questions from it, or come up with a big idea, these kinds of activities form a context within which the reader and text interact for a specific reason, one that is unlikely to occur in exactly the same manner ever again. Teachers create contexts and learning opportunities that will support the construction of meaning. Environments that value reading and writing, that contain a wide variety of texts, that allow students to take risks, and that find time for reading aloud and reading independently are contexts that effectively promote the construction of meaning (Keene & Zimmermann, 1997; Miller, 2002; Pardo, 2002).

The Transaction

As we consider the reader's individual and unique differences, the characteristics of the context, and the features of the text, we are left to wonder exactly what happens when these three come together. At the most basic level, microstructures (words, propositions) are being decoded and represented by mental images (Butcher & Kintsch, 2003). This is most likely happening quickly, automatically, and in short-term memory. These mental images are calling forth ideas and information stored in long-term memory to assist the reader in building a series of connections between representations (van den Broek, 1994). These connections occur between the reader and the text and between different parts of the text. This representation is fine-tuned by the reader as more information is encountered in the text and more connections are made. Readers exit the transaction maintaining a mental representation or gist of the text.

How do these connections lead to mental representations? One way is through making inferences. A reader is quite intentional as he or she engages with the text, asking, "What is it I'm looking at here?" Readers are searching for coherence and for a chain of related events that can lead them to infer or make meaning. As readers continue moving through the text, they continue to build inferences, drawing from long-term memory specific ideas that seem to create coherence and answer the question posed earlier. "What is it I'm looking at here?" As this answer emerges, meaning is realized. Inferencing is most likely done automatically and is one of the most important processes that occur during comprehension (Butcher & Kintsch, 2003; van den Broek, 1994).

The mental representation needs to make sense to the reader as it emerges; therefore, readers monitor the emerging meaning as they read, using metacognitive and fix-up strategies, sometimes discarding ideas in the text if they do not add to the coherence that the reader is trying to build (Pressley & Afflerbach, 1995). If the reader's background knowledge or personal experiences agree with the text, the reader assimilates this new information and creates new meaning. If, however, the reader's background knowledge and personal experiences do not agree with the new information presented in the text, readers either adjust the information to make it fit (accommodation), or they reject that

information and maintain their previous understanding (Kucer, 2001). Readers apply a variety of strategies throughout this process to support their construction of meaning such as summarizing, clarifying, questioning, visualizing, predicting, and organizing. It is through the application of these strategies at various moments throughout the interaction that meaning emerges.

Teachers Support Transaction

At this point, it seems fairly obvious that comprehension occurs in the transaction between a reader and a text within a sociocultural context. That makes the transaction crucial to comprehension and the teacher's role within this transaction very important. Teachers provide explicit instruction of useful comprehension strategies, teach students to monitor and repair, use multiple strategy approaches, scaffold support, and make reading and writing connections visible to students.

Provide explicit instruction of useful comprehension strategies. Good readers use strategies to support their understanding of text. Teachers help students become good readers by teaching them how to use the strategies or monitoring, predicting, inferring, questioning, connecting, summarizing, visualizing, and organizing (Keene & Zimmermann, 1997; Miller, 2002; Pardo, 2002). Teachers are explicit and direct in explaining what these strategies are and why good readers use them (Duffy, 2002; Pressley & McCormick, 1995). They model the strategies (often by thinking aloud) for the students and provide them with numerous opportunities to practice and apply the strategies. In order for strategies to transfer so that students use them on their own or in assessment situations, contexts need to remain similar. Therefore, teachers use texts and classroom structures that are easily maintained for teaching, practicing and applying independently, and assessing. Teachers help students think metacognitively about strategies, considering when and where to apply each strategy, how to use it, and the impact it can have. In addition, teachers occasionally provide students with difficult text. If students encounter only texts that they can read easily, there will be no reason to practice and apply strategies. It is when readers encounter challenging texts that they put strategies to use (Kucer, 2001).

Teach students to monitor and repair. Knowing what is understood and not understood while reading and then applying the appropriate strategy to repair meaning are vital for comprehension to occur. Good readers monitor while reading to see if things make sense, and they use strategies to repair the meaning when things stop making sense (Duke, 2003; Pressley & Hilden, 2002). While some studies support that monitoring is important (Baker, 2002; Pressley & Afflerbach, 1995), other studies indicate that readers often mismonitor (Baker, 1989; Baker & Brown, 1984; Kinnunen, Vauras, & Niemi, 1998). Readers have been found to both over- and underestimate their comprehension of text. So, while monitoring is important and good readers seem to monitor successfully, effective teachers realize that mismonitoring can affect meaning for less able students, and they provide additional support as needed so that all readers comprehend text successfully.

Use multiple strategy approaches. Researchers have found that teaching multiple strategies simultaneously may be particularly powerful (Trabasso & Bouchard, 2002; National Institute of Child Health and Human Development, 2002; Pressley, 2000).

There is very strong empirical, scientific evidence that the instruction of more than one strategy in a natural context leads to the acquisition and use of reading comprehension strategies and transfer to standardized comprehension tests. Multiple strategy instruction facilitates comprehension as evidenced by performance on tasks that involve memory, summarizing, and identification of main ideas (Trabasso & Bouchard, 2002, p. 184).

Perhaps the most frequently used multiple strategies approach is transactional strategy instruction (TSI), created and studied by Pressley and colleagues (Brown, Pressley, Van Meter, & Schuder, 1996; Gaskins, Anderson, Pressley, Cunicelli, & Satlow, 1993). TSI teachers encourage readers to make sense of text by using strategies that allow them to make connections between text content and prior knowledge. Teachers and students work in small reading groups to collaboratively make meaning using several teacher-identified strategies. Teachers model and explain the strategies, coach students in their use, and help students use them flexibly. Throughout the instruction, students are taught to think about the usefulness of each strategy and to become metacognitive about their own reading processes.

Scaffold support. When teaching strategies to elementary-age students, teachers gradually release responsibility for comprehending to students. An effective model that has been used by some teachers is the Gradual Release of Responsibility model (Pearson & Gallagher, 1983). In this model, teachers take all the responsibility for applying a newly introduced strategy by modeling, thinking aloud, demonstrating, and creating meaning. As time passes and students have more exposure to and practice with using the strategy, teachers scaffold students by creating activities within students' Zone of Proximal Development (Vygotsky, 1978) and slowly withdrawing more and more responsibility. Teachers work collaboratively with the students and the strategy, giving and taking as much as necessary to create meaning. Eventually, students take on more and more responsibility as they become more confident, knowledgeable, and capable. Finally, students are able to work independently. Teachers and students do not always progress in a linear way, but often slip back and forth between more and less responsibility depending on the task, the text, and the strategy. While adaptations may be made with students of different ages, teachers use this model with students in all elementary grades.

Make reading/writing connections visible. Teachers help students see that reading and writing are parallel processes and that becoming good writers can help them become good readers (Kucer, 2001). Composing a text can be thought of as writing something that people will understand. Writing can bring understanding about a certain topic to the writer, who will have to be clear about the topic he or she is writing about. Meaning matters in comprehending, and becoming a clear writer is all about how the reader will make meaning of the text that is being created. Recalling the earlier discussion of authentic purposes is important here as well; students will likely become engaged with the task of writing if asked to write for authentic and important purposes.

CLOSING COMMENTS

Comprehending is a complicated process, as we have discovered and explored in this article. Yet it is one of the most important skills for students to develop if they are to become successful and productive adults. Comprehension instruction in schools, beginning in kindergarten, is therefore crucial. Teachers use their knowledge and understandings of how one learns to comprehend to inform classroom practices so they can most effectively help readers develop the abilities to comprehend text. It is hoped that the discussion in this article can open a dialogue with teachers and teacher educators toward this end.

Laura S. Pardo is a doctoral candidate in Teaching, Curriculum, & Educational Policy at Michigan State University.

Article 19

SCAFFOLDING STUDENTS' COMPREHENSION OF TEXT

KATHLEEN F. CLARK AND MICHAEL F. GRAVES

Classroom teachers looking to improve students' comprehension should consider three general types of scaffolding.

In a first-grade classroom, the teacher carefully monitors students' responses as the class reads Ruth Krauss's *The Carrot Seed* (1945), an informational storybook about a boy planting a carrot seed. The teacher realizes that the children don't understand what the green, fern-like plant they see in the picture has to do with the orange carrots they sometimes have for dinner. She immediately intervenes and, through a series of skillfully chosen questions, leads students to a basic understanding of what growing carrots look like. In another classroom, a group of sixth-grade students is beginning to read Michael Cooper's *Indian School* (1999) as part of a social studies unit. The teacher recognizes that *Indian School* will be a challenge for some of her students and wants to be sure that they all get off to a good start with it. As students begin the first chapter, she provides them with a carefully crafted set of prereading, during-reading, and postreading activities to support their initial understanding of the book. In a third classroom, a fourth-grade teacher is using direct explanation to teach the comprehension strategy of predicting. In doing so, he describes the strategy and how it should be used, models its use and has some students model it, works with students as they begin using the strategy, gradually gives students more and more responsibility for using

Clark, K. F., & Graves, M. F. (2005). Scaffolding Students' Comprehension of Text. *The Reading Teacher, 58*(6), 570–580. Reprinted by permission of the International Reading Association.

the strategy independently, and reminds and prompts students to use the strategy over time.

The assistance the teachers provide to aid students' comprehension in these three instances is in some ways quite different. Yet in each case, the teacher relies heavily on the use of instructional scaffolding, one of the most recommended, versatile, and powerful instructional techniques of constructivist teaching. Recent studies of classroom reading instruction have found that, although scaffolding is widely used by some of the best teachers (Taylor, Pearson, Clark, & Walpole, 2000; Wharton-McDonald, Pressley, & Hampston, 1998), it is not characteristic of most teachers (Taylor et al.) and that, when employed, it is typically in support of word recognition (Clark, 2000). Comprehension instruction of any sort is much less frequent than it needs to be (Pressley, 2002a; RAND Reading Study Group, 2002), and agreement about just what we can do to best foster students' comprehension is far from complete (Institute of Education Sciences, 2003). However, there is virtually universal agreement that scaffolding plays an essential and vital role in fostering comprehension (Duffy, 2002; Duke & Pearson, 2002; Palincsar, 2003; Pressley, 2002b). We believe that, because scaffolding is a complex instructional concept and takes many forms, gathering together examples and explanations of various sorts of scaffolding will help to foster its more widespread use. Our purpose here is to give readers a broader perspective of the different roles they can play in using various forms of scaffolding by providing carefully selected examples and descriptions of the forms that scaffolding can take. By so doing, we hope to help teachers construct a deeper understanding of scaffolding, use it more frequently in their classrooms, and thereby improve students' comprehension.

We begin by considering several definitions of scaffolding, noting the foundations for it, and highlighting reasons why it is effective. Next, we describe three general types of scaffolding and teachers' roles therein and provide examples of each type. Finally, we offer some considerations for making decisions about scaffolding.

WHAT IS SCAFFOLDING?

Wood, Bruner, and Ross (1976) were the first to use the term *scaffolding* in its educational sense. They described scaffolding as a "process that enables a child or novice to solve a problem, carry out a task or achieve a goal which would be beyond his unassisted efforts" (p. 90). Since this initial work, scaffolding has been described as "supported situations in which children can extend current skills and knowledge to a higher level of competence" (Rogoff, 1990, p. 93), "what teachers say and do to enable children to complete complex mental tasks they could not complete without assistance" (Pearson & Fielding, 1991, p. 842), "a process whereby a teacher monitors students' learning carefully and steps in to provide assistance on an as-needed basis" (Wharton-McDonald et al., 1998, p. 116), and as "a temporary supportive structure that teachers create to assist a student or a group of students to accomplish a task that they could not complete alone" (Graves, Watts, & Graves, 1994, p. 44). One of us (Graves & Graves, 2003) has expanded that definition, noting that

> In addition to helping children complete tasks they could not otherwise complete, scaffolding can aid students by helping them to better complete a task, to complete a task with less stress or in less time, or to learn more fully than they would have otherwise. (p. 30)

Pressley (2002b) has provided a particularly rich description, explaining both the metaphor entailed in the term and its educational meaning.

> The scaffolding of a building under construction provides support when the new building cannot stand on its own. As the new structure is completed and becomes freestanding, the scaffolding is removed. So it is with scaffolded adult-child academic interactions. The adult carefully monitors when enough instructional input has been provided to permit the child to make progress toward an academic goal, and thus the adult provides support only when the child needs it. If the child catches on quickly, the adult's responsive instruction will be less detailed than if the child experiences difficulties with the task. (pp. 97–98)

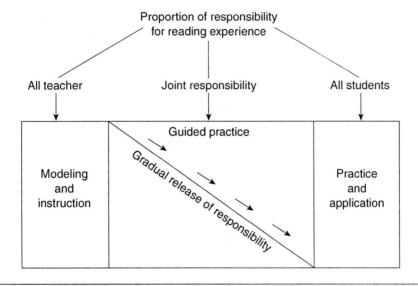

Figure 19.1 The Gradual Release of Responsibility for Reading Experience

Foundations of Scaffolding

The concept of scaffolding is grounded in Vygotsky's social constructivist view of learning. According to Vygotsky (1978), every mental function in a child's development first appears in collaboration with an adult. The collaboration occurs in what Vygotsky referred to as the zone of proximal development. This is the area between what children can do independently and what they can do with assistance. Over time, given repeated experiences, a child internalizes the collaborative form of the mental processes and is able to engage in them alone or in new contexts.

A related construct that is very helpful in understanding scaffolding is the gradual release of responsibility model (Pearson & Fielding, 1991), a version of which is shown in Figure 19.1. The model depicts a temporal sequence in which students gradually progress from situations in which the teacher takes the majority of the responsibility for successfully completing a reading task, to situations in which students assume increasing responsibility for reading tasks, and finally to situations in which students take all or nearly all the responsibility for reading tasks. At any point in time, teachers should scaffold students enough so that they do not give up on the task or fail at it but not scaffold them so much that they do not have the opportunity to actively work on the problem themselves.

An Effective Technique

What makes scaffolding so effective is that it enables a teacher to keep a task whole, while students learn to understand and manage the parts, and presents the learner with just the right challenge. Scaffolding integrates multiple aspects of a task into a manageable chunk and permits students to see how they interrelate (Rogoff, 1990). In so doing, it helps students to cope with the complexity of tasks in an authentic manner (Pearson, 1996). Of course, the way that scaffolding is implemented in the classroom depends on students' abilities. Varying levels of support are possible, and the more complex a task is, the more support students will need to accomplish it.

To provide some concrete examples of scaffolding that support students' comprehension and to illustrate the various types, we next describe three types of scaffolding and give two examples of each. These three types are moment-to-moment verbal scaffolding, instructional frameworks that foster content learning, and instructional procedures for teaching reading comprehension strategies.

MOMENT-TO-MOMENT VERBAL SCAFFOLDING

The teacher's role here is to prompt students, ask probing questions, and elaborate student responses in the course of instruction. To effectively scaffold in this way, teachers must call to mind their knowledge of students' instructional histories and ability to apply reading processes (Clark, 2004). In addition, they must consider two things: how their instructional talk moves students closer to the goal and how they can use students' responses to make them more aware of the mental processes in which they are engaged (Gaskins et al., 1997).

The Carrot Seed

In this example, we analyze the instructional scaffolding that a very accomplished teacher one of us observed (Clark, 2000) used with her first-grade students as they worked to make meaning when reading Ruth Krauss's *The Carrot Seed*. The teacher—we'll call her Mrs. Fry—monitors and prompts her students' thought processes and fosters their understanding as they proceed through the text, an informational storybook that complements the class's study of plants in the week's science curriculum. The story revolves around a young boy who plants a carrot seed. Family members repeatedly tell him that it will not come up. Nonetheless, the boy waters it daily. The story concludes with "And then one day a carrot came up." The accompanying illustration, however, is of a green, fern-like plant. There is no sign of a carrot as the students know it. In

light of this, the students are understandably confused about what's coming up. Mrs. Fry scaffolds their construction of meaning through careful questioning, and the students come to understand that the part of the carrot plant with which they are familiar, and that they eat, is the root that grows below the ground. In this dialogue, all names are pseudonyms.

Kim: [Reads] And then one day a carrot came up.

Mrs. Fry: [Holding up the picture] Where's the carrot?

Anna: Up?

David: I don't know.

Mrs. Fry: Where's the carrot? Do you see it? [Holds the picture up and points to the plant's sprouting leaves]

Anna: That's the big root.

Mrs. Fry: What's a carrot?

Students: [No response]

Mrs. Fry: Where's the carrot? [Points to the picture]

David: In the ground?

Mrs. Fry: So would a carrot be a root?

David: [Shakes head negative]

Mrs. Fry: Aren't roots in the ground?

Students: [Shake heads affirmative]

Students: [Emphatically] No!

Mrs. Fry: Do we eat carrots?

Students: Yes . . . yeah.

Mrs. Fry: Is a carrot a root?

Students: Yeah . . . yeah. [Heads nod affirmative]

Mrs. Fry: We must. The carrot came up.

In the dialogue, Mrs. Fry prompts students to think about the carrot in relation to what they see in the illustration. The first graders experience some confusion as they try to reconcile what they know about a carrot (that it is an orange vegetable) and what they see (the leafy shoots emerging from the ground). Mrs. Fry uses questions to engage their thought processes ("Where's the carrot? Do you see it?"). One child introduces the concept of a root. Building on this connection, Mrs. Fry poses the question "What's a carrot?" The students do not respond, so she points to the picture and refines her question: "Where's the carrot?" One child tentatively offers, "In the ground?" Mrs. Fry affirms this information and poses another question, one that connects the concept of root with that of carrot: "So would a carrot be a root?" One child voices hearty disagreement. Mrs. Fry asks, "Aren't roots in the ground?" The students respond affirmatively, and she pushes their thinking a step further: "So do we eat some roots?" In response to their emphatic negative response, Mrs. Fry asks whether they eat carrots and whether carrots are roots. In this way, through a series of carefully graded questions, students come to refine their understanding of how carrots grow.

The Popcorn Book

In this second example of moment-to-moment scaffolding, Carol Donovan, another very accomplished teacher, scaffolds first graders' efforts as they proceed through Tomie dePaola's *The Popcorn Book* (1978). As Smolkin and Donovan (2002) explained in the chapter from which the following example is taken, the scaffolding Donovan provides demonstrates a procedure they term an *Interactive Read-Aloud*. As they also explain, *The Popcorn Book* is a "dual-purpose book," one that presents two different texts:

> The first, a simple story displayed through cartoon-like characters with speech balloons, is about two brothers who decided to make popcorn. The second is informational; one of the boys wonders why their mother keeps popcorn in the refrigerator, and he reads aloud to his brother from a hefty, encyclopedic tome to find his answer. (p. 145)

Our example begins with the text, which the teacher reads aloud, and is followed by comments from the teacher and several students.

Teacher: [Reads] In 1612, French explorers saw some Iroquois people popping corn in clay pots. They would fill the pots with hot sand, throw in some popcorn and stir it with a stick. When the corn popped, it came to the top of the sand and made it easy to get.

Child: Look at the bowl.

Teacher: [Providing an oral commentary on the "story"] Okay, now it's hot enough [for the brothers] to add a few kernels.

Child: What's a kernel?

Child: Like what you pop.

Teacher: It's a seed.

Child: What if you, like, would you think [of] a popcorn seed? Like a popcorn seed. Could you grow popcorn?

Teacher: Oh, excellent, excellent question. Let's read and we'll see if this [book] answers that question, and if not, we'll talk about it at the end.

As you can see by comparing the two examples, Donovan's responses here are somewhat different from those of Mrs. Fry, whose scaffolding prompts were all questions. In this example of moment-to-moment verbal scaffolding, Donovan has just finished reading a segment of text in which the Iroquois procedure for popping corn is described. As the picture is displayed, a child directs the group's attention to the bowl. Donovan comments in a way that focuses readers' attention on a critical element of the popping procedure, the temperature of the sand: "Okay, now it's hot enough to add a few kernels." Then, a child asks the meaning of *kernel,* a word Donovan has used but the child does not understand. Donovan provides the meaning. Given that a kernel is a seed, another student asks if one

(Excerpt reprinted from Smolkin & Donovan, pp. 145–146, with permission of Guilford Press. Book quote, © 1978 by Tomie dePaola, reprinted from *The Popcorn Book* by permission of Holiday House, Inc.)

could grow popcorn. Rather than answer the question, Donovan affirms the question and uses it to set a purpose for reading the next segment of text. Finally, she identifies discussion as a strategy for meaning making following reading. Donovan's instructional actions, focusing attention on salient information, providing relevant information, and identifying a comprehension strategy, scaffold students' comprehension.

INSTRUCTIONAL FRAMEWORKS THAT FOSTER CONTENT LEARNING

Instructional frameworks that foster content learning are used to guide and improve students' understanding and learning as they read individual texts. The frameworks may or may not include moment-to-moment verbal scaffolding. In scaffolding of this sort, the teacher's role is to structure and orchestrate the reading experience so that students can optimally profit from it. Questioning the Author, or QtA (Beck, McKeown, Worthy, Sandora, & Kucan, 1996), the first framework we discuss, focuses on verbal scaffolding, while the Scaffolded Reading Experience, or SRE (Graves & Graves, 2003), the second framework we consider, includes a variety of types of scaffolding.

Questioning the Author

The intent of QtA is to help students to understand, interpret, and elaborate an author's meaning as they read the text. QtA enables teachers to guide and facilitate students' online or during-reading comprehension as they progress through successive sections of text. Teachers do so by posing certain sorts of questions, called queries. In contrast to more traditional questions that check for understanding of story elements (e.g., Who was involved? What happened first, next, last? How was the problem resolved?), queries enable students to cooperatively construct meaning as they read and reflect on ideas in text. Further, queries are open-ended, permitting multiple, divergent responses and allowing students

to participate at their evolving levels of understanding. For example, teachers might ask the following questions:

- What do you think the author means by that?
- How does that connect with what the author has already told us?
- How did the author work that out for us?
- Did the author explain it clearly?
- What's missing?
- What do we need to find out?

Teachers begin their use of QtA by explaining to students that texts are written by ordinary people who are not perfect and who create texts that are not perfect. Consequently, readers need to work hard to figure out what the authors are trying to say. Then members of the class read a text together, with the teacher stopping at critical points to pose queries that invite students to explore and grapple with the meaning of what is written.

The following QtA dialogue shows a fifth-grade social studies class studying U.S. history. The class had been working with QtA for some time and is quite skilled in grappling with text ideas. The class is discussing a text segment about the presidency of James Buchanan, a Pennsylvania native. The text indicated that many people believed that Buchanan liked the South better than the North because he believed that it was a person's choice whether or not to have slaves.

Teacher: All right. This paragraph that Tracy just read is really full of important information. What has the author told us in this important paragraph?

Laura: Um, they um think that Buchanan liked the South better because they, he said that it is a person's choice if they want to have slaves or not, so they thought um that he liked the South better than the North.

Teacher: Okay. And what kind of problem then did this cause President Buchanan when they thought that he liked the South better? What kind of problem did that cause?

Janet: Well, maybe um like less people would vote for him because like if he ran for President again, maybe less people would vote for him because like in Pennsylvania we were against slavery and we might have voted for him because he was in Pennsylvania, because he was from Pennsylvania. That may be why they voted for him, but now since we knew that he was for the South, we might not vote for him again.

Teacher: Okay, a little bit of knowledge, then, might change people's minds.

Jamie: I have something to add on to Janets 'cause I completely agree with her, but I just want to add something on. Um, we might have voted for him because he was from Pennsylvania so we might have thought that since he was from Pennsylvania and Pennsylvania was an antislavery state, that he was also against slavery. But it turns out he wasn't.

Angelica: I agree with the rest of them, except for one that um, like all of a sudden, like someone who would be in Pennsylvania you want to vote for them but then they, wouldn't they be going for the South and then you wouldn't want to vote for them after that.

(McKeown, Beck, & Sandora, 1996, pp. 112–113. Reprinted by permission of the publisher from Graves et al., *The First R: Every Child's Right to Read.* New York: Teachers College Press, © 1996 by Teachers College, Columbia University. All rights reserved.)

In this example, the teacher opens the discussion with the query "What has the author told us in this important paragraph?" Laura responds, and the teacher poses another query that furthers the discussion: "What kind of problem did that cause?" Janet contributes her developing understanding, and the teacher synthesizes her point: "Okay, a little bit of knowledge, then, might change people's minds." This scenario illustrates well the sort of scaffolding that takes place during a QtA discussion. The students are focused on the meaning of the text. In keeping with her role of structuring the reading experience, the teacher adroitly directs the discussion but does not dominate it. She leaves plenty of room for student input; the students are the ones who do most of the talking and thinking, and they respond at some length. Finally, they listen to one another and build on one another's responses as they jointly construct meaning for the text.

The Scaffolded Reading Experience

The SRE (Graves & Graves, 2003) is a flexible framework that teachers can use to assist students in understanding, learning from, and enjoying both narrative and expository texts. As in QtA, the teacher's role is to structure and orchestrate the reading experience so that students may optimally comprehend. The SRE has two phases: planning and implementation. During the planning phase, the teacher considers the students who will be doing the reading, the reading selection itself, and the purpose(s) of the reading. On the basis of these considerations, the teacher then creates a set of prereading, during-reading, and postreading activities designed to assist this particular group of students in reaching those purposes. Possible pre-, during-, and postreading activities to consider in creating an SRE are shown in Table 19.1 on the following page.

It is important to note that this is a list of *possible* components of an SRE. No single SRE includes all of these activities. As in all scaffolding, SREs should provide enough support that students succeed but not so much support that they do not put in the cognitive effort it takes to learn and grow as readers. SREs vary considerably, depending on the students, reading selections, and their purpose.

Consider as one example an SRE for Robert Coles's *The Story of Ruby Bridges* (1995). This picture-book biography tells the dramatic story of the first black student to attend Frantz Elementary School in New Orleans, Louisiana. The book is appropriate for many third graders and will certainly interest them, but some students will need more assistance in understanding it than others. We show a list of possible activities for the book in Figure 19.2.

Table 19.1   Possible Activities in a Scaffolded Reading Experience

Prereading	During Reading	Postreading
Relating the reading to students' lives	Silent reading	Questioning
Motivating	Reading to students	Discussion
Activating and building background knowledge	Supported reading	Writing
	Oral reading by students	Drama
Providing text-specific knowledge	Modifying the text	Artistic and nonverbal activities
Preteaching vocabulary		Application and outreach activities
Preteaching concepts		Building connections
Prequestioning, predicting, and direction setting		Reteaching
Suggesting stragegies		

Activities in regular type for students who will find the book relatively easy; those in **bold italic** are additional or alternative activities for students who will find the book more of a challenge.

Prereading	Motivating
	Building background knowledge
	Building text-specific knowledge
	Direction setting
During reading	***Reading to students***
	Silent reading
Postreading	Questioning and small-group discussion
	Writing
	Working with art

Prereading

- Motivate students by encouraging them to talk about problems they have encountered and how they solved them. They might also talk about some of the obstacles they encountered and what kept them going.

- Build relevant background knowledge by asking students to think about books they have read in which the characters faced a challenge they thought was difficult or impossible but were able to triumph in the end. Then, have students talk about the problems the characters encountered and how they overcame them. If necessary, you can share a few books that exemplify this theme.

- ***Build text-specific knowledge*** for students who need more assistance by previewing the biography. Begin by explaining what a biography is, emphasizing that this is a true story about something that happened to a real person. Introduce the setting, the main characters, and enough of the story line to whet students' appetite for the biography.

- Direction setting for stronger readers might consist of simply telling students to look for the challenges Ruby faces and how she handles them. Direction setting for less skilled readers might consist of asking them to look for one problem Ruby faces and her solution to that problem.

During reading

- *Reading some of the story aloud* can get less skilled readers off to a good start and leave them with a manageable amount of reading to do.
- Silent reading is appropriate for students who can successfully read the book on their own.

Postreading

- Answering questions that get at the essence of the biography in small groups will give all students an opportunity to review the book's important events and issues.
- Writing gives students an opportunity to solidify their understanding of the biography or to respond to it. You will probably want to suggest some topics—tell about the most challenging problem Ruby faced, tell what you admire most about Ruby, or tell how you would have reacted in Ruby's place.
- *Working with art* gives students who struggle with writing another way to solidify their understanding of the story or respond to it. Students might draw pictures illustrating significant events in the biography or make collages suggesting their responses to significant events. Of course, artistic activities are often appropriate alternatives for good writers, too.

Figure 19.2 Scaffolded Reading Experience Activities for *The Story of Ruby Bridges* (Coles, 1995).

Following are two more sets of activities that illustrate the range of options SREs provide. The first, a substantial SRE, was created for sixth graders studying the first chapter of Michael Cooper's *Indian School* as part of their social studies work and is designed to help them thoroughly understand the important information presented in the chapter.

SRE Activities for *Indian School*

Prereading	Motivating
Preteaching vocabulary	
Questioning	
During reading	Reading to students
Silent reading	
Postreading	Small-group discussion
	Answering questions
Large-group discussion	

The second, a much less substantial SRE, might be used with these same sixth graders

reading *Frindle* by Andrew Clements (1998) and is designed to help them enjoy this fast-paced and humorous tale.

SRE Activities for *Frindle*

Prereading	Motivating
During reading	Silent reading
Postreading	Optional small-group discussion

Again, it should be stressed that these are possible SREs. The scaffolding needed in one situation—what will be most helpful for a particular group of students, a particular text, and a particular purpose or purposes—will often be quite different from the scaffolding needed in another.

INSTRUCTIONAL PROCEDURES FOR TEACHING READING COMPREHENSION STRATEGIES

In addition to guiding their reading of individual texts, it is important to help students become independent readers by providing strategies for use as they read various texts over time. Scaffolding also plays a crucial role in these efforts: The teacher explicitly teaches strategies that foster reading independence, engages students in supported practice with multiple texts, and gradually transfers responsibility for strategy use as students become increasingly able. Here we consider two approaches to teaching comprehension strategies that are strongly supported by research and widely recommended: Direct Explanation of Comprehension Strategies (DECS) and Reciprocal Teaching (RT).

Direct Explanation of Comprehension Strategies

DECS (Duffy, 2002; Duffy et al., 1987) teaches individual strategies in an explicit and very straightforward way. Duke and Pearson (2002) listed the following five components of the procedure and gave a concrete example of the teacher's talk in scaffolding students' learning of the predicting strategy. We include parts of the teacher talk. At some points we have shortened and paraphrased, and, following the example of each component, we have added our comments in brackets.

1. An explicit description of the strategy and when and how it should be used.

"Predicting is making guesses about what will come next in the text you are reading. You should make predictions a lot when you read. For now, you should stop every two pages that you read and make some predictions."
[Note how the teacher greatly simplifies the initial task by telling students to make a prediction every two pages.]

2. Teacher and/or student modeling of the strategy in action.

"I am going to make predictions while I read this book. I will start with just the cover here. Hum . . . I see a picture of an owl. It looks like he—I think it is a he—is wearing pajamas, and

he is carrying a candle. I *predict* that this is going to be a make believe story because owls do not really wear pajamas and carry candles. I *predict* it is going to be about this owl, and it is going to take place at nighttime."
[Here the teacher strives to reveal the thought processes that he or she uses in predicting so that students can later use similar processes.]

3. Collaborative use of the strategy in action.

"So far, I've been doing all the predicting. Now, I want you to make predictions with me. Each of us should stop and think aloud about what might happen next. . . . Okay, let's hear what you think and why."
[At this point, the students begin to do some of the work but still have plenty of support from the teacher.]

4. Guided practice using the strategy with gradual release of responsibility.

[This first example is from an early session, and the teacher is still providing substantial scaffolding by reading along with students and telling them when to make predictions.]
"I have called the three of you together to work on making predictions while you read this and other books. After every few pages I will ask each of you to stop and make predictions. We will talk about our predictions and then read on to see if they come true."
[This second example is from a later session. Students still receive scaffolding, but now it comes from written directions rather than from the teacher, an appropriately less supportive form of scaffolding.]
"Each of you has a chart that lists different pages in your book. When you finish reading a page on the list, stop and make a prediction. Write the prediction in the column that says 'Predictions.' When you get to the next page on the list, check off whether your prediction 'Happened,' 'Will not happen,' or 'Still might happen.' Then make another prediction and write it down."
[Duke & Pearson attribute this technique to Mason & Au, 1986.]

5. Independent use of the strategy.

"It is time for silent reading. As you read today, remember what you have been working on—making predictions while you read. Be sure to make predictions every two or three pages. Ask yourself why you made the predictions you did—what made you think that. Check as you read to see whether your prediction came true. Jamal is passing out predictions bookmarks to remind you."

[Here, students are reading silently by themselves, without the teacher or a worksheet to prompt their predictions. But they are still receiving some scaffolding—the reminder to predict every two or three pages, to think about their predictions, and to check them as well as the bookmark.] (Adapted from Duke & Pearson, 2002, pp. 208–210)

At this point, students have received some excellent instruction and scaffolding and are well on their way to becoming competent with the predicting strategy. However, this should not be the end of the scaffolding. Over time, the teacher will continue to remind students of the importance of predicting, point out different and increasingly challenging texts where the predicting strategy is appropriate, and occasionally discuss with students how their efforts at predicting are progressing.

Reciprocal Teaching

RT (Palincsar & Brown, 1989) is a powerful technique for teaching a coordinated set of four comprehension strategies—questioning, summarizing, clarifying, and predicting. At the heart of RT is a series of dialogues in which the teacher and a small group of students read and discuss a text. Before beginning the dialogues, the teacher directly instructs students on each of the four strategies and evaluates individual students' proficiency with them so that she or he will know how to scaffold each student during the dialogues. Then, as the group progresses through the text segment by segment, the teacher models and guides students through the four strategies.

These strategies help students to understand the purposes of reading, activate prior knowledge, focus attention on important content, critically evaluate text, monitor comprehension, and draw and test inferences. The teacher's role in these dialogues is to assist students during reading as they work to comprehend text and to focus and direct the dialogue.

In the following example (see Palincsar & Brown, 1989, for full text), the teacher reads segments of a story about bear cubs to a group of six first graders and guides them through several of the components of RT.

[The teacher reads.] "Baby bear was bigger than his sister and he began to play too rough. His sister jumped onto a tree trunk and climbed quickly upward" (p. 33). One of the children interrupts to ask, "What's rough?" Other children come up with possible examples (one suggests something to do with texture; another says "like they beat you up"), then the teacher turns to the text for clarification. The children agree that the second suggestion is what is meant in the text. The teacher replies, "The pinching and hitting, playing too hard. Okay."

The teacher continues reading and comes to a portion of the text where a prediction would be appropriate. She asks the children to predict what happens next. They correctly predict that the tree limb will break and the bear will fall. The teacher reads to confirm the prediction. "He squalled for his mother. Now the mother splashed into the water. . . ." One of the children asks for the meaning of *squalled*. The teacher rereads the sentence, and then asks what the children think the little bear did when he fell. The child who asked the question replies, "Whining and crying," and the teacher confirms that this was a good guess.

In this example, the teacher has guided, modeled, and prompted students as they worked to understand the text. But—in keeping with the essence of scaffolding—she or he has not simply given students the answers. Students have had to do some of the work themselves—questioning, answering questions, and making a prediction—and by repeatedly doing such work, they become increasingly competent with the strategies. As students become more familiar with the strategies, they will take turns assuming the role of the teacher. While the classroom teacher will continue to model and prompt as necessary, he or she will gradually release responsibility for orchestrating and engaging in the strategies to students. Ultimately, the students will assume primary responsibility for employing the strategies as they read.

FLEXIBLE AND ADAPTABLE SUPPORT

As you consider the examples of scaffolding students' comprehension we have presented, you will recognize a lot of similarities as well as a number of differences. Both examples of moment-by-moment verbal scaffolding center on the dialogue between the teacher and a small group of students. Mrs. Fry, however, relied exclusively on asking questions, while Carol Donovan used various sorts of prompts, including focusing attention on critical aspects of text, giving information, using a student's question to set the purpose for reading, and directly identifying a simple comprehension strategy.

The next two examples we presented—the use of the Questioning the Author and Scaffolded Reading Experience instructional frameworks to foster content learning—are quite different from each other. QtA employs a set of queries to prompt students' thinking and discussion as they are reading a text, whereas the SRE gives students various supportive activities to do before, during, and after they read a text. In both cases, however, the goal is the same; to support and improve students' comprehension of a text.

The final two examples we presented—the use of Direct Explanation of Comprehension Strategies and Reciprocal Teaching to teach reading comprehension strategies—are again quite different. DECS teaches individual comprehension strategies through a multifaceted process

that includes describing the strategy, modeling it, using it collaboratively, guided practice, and independent use of the strategy. RT teaches the four strategies in a process that includes a relatively short period of instruction on them followed by many small-group dialogues in which the teacher guides students in their use as they collaboratively read segments of a text.

However, while the six examples have similarities and differences, all serve the function of scaffolding—"helping students complete tasks they could not otherwise complete, [and aiding] students by helping them to better complete a task, to complete a task with less stress or in less time, or to learn more fully than they would have otherwise" (Graves & Graves, 2003, p. 30).

In commenting on the sorts of evidence teachers can use in making educational decisions, Stanovich and Stanovich (2003) identified three standards: publication of findings in refereed journals, duplication of results by a number of investigators, and consensus from a body of studies. The use of scaffolding is strongly supported by evidence from all three of these sources. Our goal has been to help readers gain a broader perspective of the different roles they can play in using various forms of scaffolding, more frequently employ scaffolding in their classrooms, and thereby improve students' comprehension. We encourage teachers to add scaffolding to their instructional repertoire. It is a highly flexible and adaptable model of instruction that supports students as they acquire basic skills and higher order thinking processes, allows for explicit instruction within authentic contexts of reading and writing, and enables teachers to differentiate instruction for students of diverse needs. In summary, scaffolding invites students and teachers to collaborate as students become increasingly active readers and thinkers.

Kathleen F. Clark teaches in the Department of Reading in the School of Education at Marquette University.

Michael F. Graves teaches in the Department of Curriculum and Instruction at the University of Minnesota in Minneapolis.

Article 20

TEACHING EXPOSITORY TEXT STRUCTURES THROUGH INFORMATION TRADE BOOK RETELLINGS

BARBARA MOSS

Teachers can help students understand common expository text structures by having them retell information trade books.

During the past few years, teachers at all grade levels have become increasingly interested in developing student understanding of expository text. At least two factors have helped to drive this interest. First, teachers are well aware of the demands of living in an era when information is increasing at an alarming rate. They recognize that if today's students are to survive in the Information Age, they must develop greater familiarity with and understanding of expository text.

Second, mounting pressures for improved student standardized test performance have resulted in increased attention to exposition. Because 70–80% of standardized reading test content is expository (Daniels, 2002), it is essential to provide students with the tools necessary to develop understanding of this type of text.

Teachers, too, are discovering that the proliferation of excellent children's informational literature available today can provide a vehicle for teaching children about exposition. The authors

SOURCE: Moss, B. (2004). Teaching Expository Text Structures Through Information Trade Book Retellings. *The Reading Teacher, 57*(8), 710–718. Reprinted by permission of the International Reading Association.

of these books are experienced in making the most complex concepts comprehensible, and children have the opportunity to explore the real world through texts that are inviting, accurate, and accessible. Today's information books contain wonderful examples of well-written exposition and are ideal for exposing even the youngest children to common expository text structures such as description, sequence, comparison and contrast, cause and effect, and problem and solution.

While most teachers are very familiar with the power of narrative retellings to improve student comprehension, they are less experienced with expository retellings. Involving students in retelling information trade books represents a promising means not only for engaging students with outstanding literature but also for improving their understanding of expository text. This article describes how teachers can use information trade book retellings to improve student comprehension of expository text structures. First, I provide background information about retellings, expository text structure and teaching these text patterns through information trade books. In the second part of the article, I describe instructional strategies and procedures for teaching the various text structures through large-group, small-group, and paired retellings. In the final section of the article, I describe how teachers can assess individual student retellings.

WHY TEACH ABOUT EXPOSITORY TEXT?

Educators today are reexamining questions of what it means to be literate in the Information Age. Few would argue against the fact that technology is dramatically changing the way we live, and that the Internet, websites, e-mail, discussion boards, chat rooms, and other forms of communication have changed our views about what it means to be literate (Reinking, 1998). It is clear that the literacy demands of today's technological society require that students be able to read and write not only in the print world but also in the digital world (Schmar-Dobler, 2003).

The Internet arguably represents one of the most demanding forms of technology in terms of its literacy requirements. The ability to use the Internet to access information quickly, sift through volumes of text, evaluate content, and synthesize information from a variety of sources is central to success at school and in the workplace (Schmar-Dobler, 2003). All of these skills, however, require that students capably read the text found on Internet websites, most of which is expository (Kamil & Lane, 1997). For this reason, it is imperative that even young children begin to develop understanding of this text type.

For many years, experts assumed that children's ability to understand narrative text preceded the ability to comprehend exposition. Pappas's (1991) seminal study comparing 20 kindergartners' ability to retell information trade books with a fictional one called that assumption into question. She found that the children she studied were just as capable of retelling informational text as narrative. Even so, children have far less familiarity with expository texts and their underlying structures (Chambliss, 1995; Goldman, 1997) than with narrative. Knowledge of the structure of different text genres develops over time for children; older children have greater understanding of different text types than younger children (Goldman & Rakestraw, 2000). Despite this fact, students of all ages generally find reading expository text more difficult than reading narrative text (Langer, 1985).

There are at least two possible reasons for students' difficulty with this type of text. First, young children lack early exposure to exposition. Story continues to be the predominant genre in early elementary classrooms. Duke (2000), for example, found that very little informational text was available in the first-grade classrooms she studied, whether displayed on walls or in classroom libraries. Most important was that she found that students in these classrooms spent on average only 3.6 minutes with informational text per day.

The second possible reason is that in many cases students have not been taught how to read expository text. Children need more than exposure to informational texts; they need instruction that familiarizes them with its organization and structure. In a study involving more than 100 hours of observations in primary literacy classrooms, Fisher and Hiebert (1990) found there was not a single instance of teachers modeling strategies for reading expository text. Teaching common expository text structures such as description, sequence, comparison and contrast, cause and effect, and problem and solution facilitates reading and writing of exposition (Block, 1993; Goldman & Rakestraw, 2000; McGee & Richgels, 1985; Raphael, Kirschner, & Englert, 1988). Students who learn to use the organization and structure of informational texts are better able to comprehend and retain the information found in them (Goldman & Rakestraw, 2000; Pearson & Duke, 2002).

If today's students are to meet the literacy demands of the future, they need to engage in authentic literacy tasks with expository texts. Information trade book retellings can provide students rich opportunities for not only gaining exposure to expository text but also gaining expertise in understanding this text type.

WHAT ARE RETELLINGS?

Teachers and students often confuse retellings with summaries. Retellings are oral or written postreading recalls during which children relate what they remember from reading or listening to a particular text. Conversely, a summary represents a short, to-the-point distillation of the main ideas in the text. Retellings provide a holistic representation of student understanding rather than the fragmented information provided by answering comprehension questions (Bromley, 1998). When students retell, they attempt to recall as much of the information in the text as possible, not just the main points. Retellings are an important precursor to helping students develop summarization skills, both oral and written. Students who are unable to retell will find it difficult, if not impossible, to summarize effectively. As students gain facility in retelling in the

early grades, their recounts of expository texts will become increasingly sophisticated. Through these experiences they will be well prepared to develop skills in summarizing as they move beyond the primary grades.

Research (Gambrell, Koskinen, & Kapinus, 1991; Gambrell, Pfeiffer, & Wilson, 1985; Morrow, 1986) clearly supports the usefulness of retellings in improving student understanding of story. Reconstructing texts through retellings helps children develop reading flexibility as well as knowledge of text forms, text conventions, and the processes involved in text construction. Retellings provide insights about children's ways of constructing meaning from texts and their ability to organize information. When students share retellings, they "read, reread and reread again" and engage with text much more intensely than at other times (Brown & Cambourne, 1990, p. 11). In addition, retellings let teachers see *how* as well as *how much* information children retain after reading or listening to a text (Irwin & Mitchell, 1983).

By retelling the expository text in information trade books, students can sense text organization and identify relationships among pieces of information and develop their oral language abilities. English-language learners may particularly benefit from this strategy, because the concrete nature of informational text can help them build bridges between their first and second languages. Through oral retellings of information trade books, children can develop deeper understanding of the forms and functions of exposition—a critical component to comprehending nonnarrative material.

UNDERSTANDING EXPOSITORY TEXT STRUCTURES

Authors use different "tools" as they construct stories and information texts. Most of the time, stores are written in a narrative form, while information books are written in an expository one. Narrative and expository texts have different purposes. The main purpose of narrative texts is to tell a story, while expository text is intended to inform, describe, or report. Authors who create people and events from their imaginations use narrative structures to create stories. When authors write information books, they conduct research to gain information on the topic at hand. They organize the information as logically and interestingly as they can using various expository text structures.

Narrative texts have a specific, predictable structure that readers encounter over and over again. This structure, or story grammar, includes characters; a setting; a problem (or conflict); a climax, or high point to the action; and a resolution. Expository texts, like narrative ones, have their own structures. These structures provide students with a map that guides them through a text. The greater children's awareness of expository text structures and organizational patterns, the better they can follow the author's message.

The five most common expository text structures include description, sequence, comparison and contrast, cause and effect, and problem and solution (Meyer, 1985). Signal words (or cue words) alert readers to the presence of these patterns. Often, however, signal words are implied rather than stated. Figure 20.1 describes each of these text structures and their characteristics.

INFORMATION TRADE BOOKS THAT REFLECT EXPOSITORY TEXT PATTERNS

Today's information trade books are ideally suited for teaching expository text structures because, unlike textbooks, they contain well-organized and clearly written texts. Books used for this purpose should, however, be selected with care. First and foremost, texts should be selected on the basis of literary quality. Information books should be well written, accurate in terms of content and illustration, and appropriate to the age level of the child. They should not simply be "baskets of facts" but should be written in an engaging and appealing way. Second, teachers must choose books that don't overwhelm children with difficult technical

vocabulary and numerous complex concepts. The best informational books make even the most difficult terms and concepts comprehensible to children. Finally, teachers need to select books that clearly illustrate the text structure being taught. In many information trade books signal words are implied rather than explicitly stated. If this is the case, teachers should choose books with page layouts, headings, and table of contents that provide students with important clues about the pattern used.

Expository text structures work on two different levels. In books for younger children, these text patterns may provide the macrostructure, or overall structure for a particular book. Titles like *Amazing Snakes* (Parsons, 1990), for example, use a descriptive structure to teach children about different types of snakes.

At the microstructure, or paragraph level, however, authors may use many, or even all, of these structures within a given book or chapter, or even on a single page. Teachers might, then, select portions of text from such titles to illustrate particular text structures. Not every expository text uses these structures; some combine structures or incorporate features of narrative as well as exposition. As students increase their understanding, they can begin to identify texts illustrating a variety of structures, such as their textbooks. Figure 20.1 provides examples of high-quality information trade books illustrative of each type of text structure at the macrolevel.

INTRODUCING TEXT STRUCTURES THROUGH TRADE BOOKS

The teaching of expository text structures can begin as early as kindergarten and become increasingly sophisticated as students move through the grades. Each text structure should be taught individually; students need time to master one structure before leaning another. Structures like sequence and comparison and contrast tend to be easier for students to grasp, while description, cause and effect, and problem and solution

- *Description* presents a topic and provides details that help readers understand characteristics of a person, place, thing, topic, or idea. No specific signal words are typically associated with description. When authors delineate a topic they use description. Semantic maps (a graphic organizer that resembles a spider web and groups information by categories) provide a visual representation for this structure.

Trade book examples: *Bats* by Gail Gibbons, *Amazing Snakes* by Richard Parsons, and *Ant Cities* by Arthur Dorros

- The *sequence* structure involves putting facts, events, or concepts in their order of occurrence. Signal words like *first, second, third, then, next, last, before, after,* and *finally* indicate order of events. Authors use sequence when giving direction for an experiment or explaining the stages in an animal's life cycle. Series of events chains are visual organizers that use boxes and arrows to illustrate a sequence of events and the steps in that sequence.

Trade book examples: *My Puppy Is Born* by Joanna Cole, *How Kittens Grow* by Millicent Selsam, and *The Buck Stops Here* by Alice Provensen

- The *comparison and contrast* structure involves identification of similarities and differences between facts, concepts, people, and so forth. Signal words include *same as, alike, similar to, resembles, compared to, different from, unlike, but,* and *yet.* Authors use this structure to compare and contrast crocodiles and alligators or life in ancient times with life today. Venn diagrams use interlocking circles to illustrate similarities and differences between two things. Individual characteristics appear in the left and right sections, while common characteristics appear in the overlapping sections.

Trade book examples: *Fire, Fire* by Gail Gibbons, *Gator or Croc* by Allan Fowler, and *Outside and Inside You* by Sandra Markle

- The *cause and effect* structure includes a description of causes and the resulting effects. Cause and effect is often signaled by *if, so, so that, because of, as a result of, since, in order to,* and the words *cause* and *effect.* When authors explain the effects of an oil spill or the reasons for animal extinction they use this structure. Cause and effect maps use circles or squares with connecting arrows to illustrate relationships between causes and their resulting effects.

Trade book examples: *What Makes Day and Night?* by Franklyn Bramley, *What Happens to a Hamburger?* by Paul Showers, and *How Do Apples Grow?* by Guilio Maestro

- The *problem and solution* structure shows the development of a problem and its solution. Signal words include *problem, solution, because, cause, since, as a result,* and *so that.* Authors use this structure to explain why inventions are created, why money was invented, or why you should buy a particular product. Problem and solution outlines visually illustrate the problem-solving process by defining components of a problem and possible solutions.

Trade book examples: *A River Ran Wild: An Environmental History* by Lynn Cherry, *Cars and How They Go* by Joanna Cole, and *If You Traveled on the Underground Railroad* by Ellen Levine

Figure 20.1 Common Expository Text Structures

are more challenging. Figure 20.2 offers a clear sequence for teaching expository text structures through minilessons.

Teacher Alan Page wanted to teach his sixth graders the problem and solution text structure. His students were studying endangered animals.

---

1. Introduce the organizational pattern.

2. Explain the pattern and when writers use it. Point out the signal words associated with the structure and share an example.

3. Model ways students can determine text structures when signal words are not used. The table of contents and headings can help in this area.

4. Introduce a graphic organizer for the pattern.

5. Read aloud a trade book or a section of a book illustrating the appropriate text structure. Ask students to listen for signal words that can help them identify the structure.

6. Using the overhead projector, involve the group in completing a graphic organizer illustrating the text type.

7. Ask students to work in pairs to locate examples of the structure in information trade books. They can search for examples of the signal words, as well as use headings and other text features to guide their search.

8. Have students diagram these structures using a graphic organizer.

Figure 20.2   Sequence for Teaching Expository Text Structures

NOTE: Adapted from Tompkins (2002).

He introduced them to the problem and solution structure by asking, "What can we do to prevent endangered animals from disappearing from the planet?" Students then brainstormed solutions to the problem. After that, Alan explained that authors may use the problem and solution pattern when discussing world problems, scientific inventions, and so on. He pointed out the signal words often used with this pattern. At this point, he presented the following paragraph from *Ospreys* (Patent, 1993) on the overhead projector. He read the paragraph aloud and asked students to note signal words that could indicate this pattern. He then underlined the words "solve the problem" to emphasize their usefulness in identifying the pattern.

In some areas ospreys have become pests by nesting on power poles. Their large nests can damage the wires. Or even worse, the birds can touch their wings to two wires at once, killing themselves and shorting out the power. Some companies solve this problem putting up spiked poles where the birds can't nest. (p. 53)

He then distributed copies of the problem and solution outline. Students worked together to complete the outline (see Figure 20.3). Students later searched for examples of this pattern on selected pages of their science text.

TEACHING THE RETELLING PROCESS

After students understand a particular text structure, experience retelling texts that illustrate that structure can provide understanding of how these texts are constructed. A two-phase sequence can facilitate student development of expository retelling skills. During Phase 1, teachers need to

---

Problem

Who has the problem? The osprey.

What was the problem? They nest on power poles.

Why was it a problem? Their nests can damage the wires. Sometimes the birds touch their wings to the wires and kill themselves and short out the power.

Solution

Some companies put up spiked poles where birds can't nest.

Figure 20.3   Problem and Solution Outline for *Ospreys* (Patent, 1993)

model the retelling process. During Phase 2, students need opportunities to practice retellings, in small groups or pairs.

Phase 1: Teacher Modeling of Retellings

Because expository text may be unfamiliar to students, teacher modeling is a critical first step in involving students in expository retellings. Teachers need to provide extensive scaffolding for students as they develop understanding of the process. Teachers should model retelling books with structures like sequence or comparison and contrast first and then gradually move to more complex structures such as cause and effect. With younger children it is best to model the retelling process using a read-aloud; older students may read the text silently.

Step 1: Before reading a text, develop links between children's experiences and the text itself. Use prereading activities designed to activate prior knowledge and stimulate thinking about the content of the book, such as KWL (what I know, what I want to know, what I learned), brainstorming, or problem solving. Make book concepts more concrete by using props, pictures, or actual examples of things mentioned in the story.

Step 2: During reading of the text, point out specific text features that facilitate retelling, such as signal words, the table of contents, headings, bolded words, maps, charts, or diagrams. Instruct students to read or listen carefully to remember as much about the text as they can.

Step 3: After reading, retell the text as completely as possible. Ask students to add any missing information, and model "look backs" by reading or directing students to reread particular sections of the text that might have been missed during the retelling.

Step 4: Model more "embellished" retellings by including analogies, personal anecdotes, and imagery (Wood & Jones, 1998). This demonstrates to students that making the text their own is not only acceptable but desirable.

Phase 2: Students Practice Retelling

After students understand the concept of retelling, they need opportunities to practice. Involvement in large-group retellings allows students to experience the process again with peer support. Once students are comfortable with large-group retellings, they can begin to retell in pairs or small groups. To begin using large-group retellings, the following sequence may be useful:

Step 1: Involve students in before reading activities (see Step 1 of Phase 1) and then read the text aloud or ask students to read it. Encourage students to predict what the text might be about and to think about what the organization pattern of the text might be by previewing the text or the table of contents.

Step 2: Ask students what they can remember about the text. Record their responses on the whiteboard. Provide scaffolds and prompts that aid student recall, such as pictures from the text or questions such as the following: What did you find out first? What did you find out next? What did you learn after that?

Step 3: Reread the text or ask students to reread the text and encourage them to identify information missed during the first retelling. Add this information to what has already been recorded on the whiteboard.

Step 4: Encourage students to make personal connections between their lives and the text. Record these on the whiteboard as appropriate.

After reading *How Kittens Grow* (Selsam & Bubley, 1973), a sequential text, aloud to her first graders, teacher Andrea Craig engaged her class in a large-group retelling. To prompt students, as they retold for the first time, she mounted key photographs from the text onto the whiteboard. She also prompted the students by asking questions like "What did we find out first about kittens? What did we find out after that?" and so on, modeling important signal words associated with a sequential structure. After students retold, Andrea reread the text, and the students filled the gaps in their retelling by noting details they neglected the first time.

Once students have experience with large-group retellings, they can move to small-group or paired retelling. These smaller groups can provide students with more independent retelling experiences but still give them some degree of peer support. Cumulative retellings (Hoyt, 1999) are ideal for small-group retelling practice. After reading a text, the first student in the group retells the first events from the story. The second student retells the next series of events but repeats the earlier events. The third student relates the events provided by the first two and then adds the next set of events. The process continues until the entire text has been retold.

After practice with group retellings, students can retell in pairs. Here are steps to follow for paired retellings:

Step 1: Ask students to select a trade book to read on their own silently or through paired reading. Remind them that they will want to remember the big ideas from the text as well as the details.

Step 2: Have students work in pairs to reconstruct the text. Each child in the pair can retell half of the text. One child can be identified as the reteller and one as the listener. They can then switch roles.

Step 3: Instruct students to listen carefully to one another as they retell. With older children, the listener can record the ideas recounted by the reteller.

Step 4: After each pair of students has retold, they can look back at the text and compare it with the ideas that have been recorded to identify information missed during their retelling.

To teach her students about the sequential text structure, fifth-grade teacher Maria Gomez involved her students in paired retellings of a section of *Mummies, Tombs, and Treasures* (Perl, 1987), dealing with the sequence of events in an ancient Egyptian funeral procession. Maria began the lesson by reviewing sequential text signal words. She then asked her students to read the text silently. Following this, students completed series of events chains in pairs (see Figure 20.4). After that, students retold the information from the text in pairs, relying on their series of events chains as needed.

INDIVIDUAL RETELLINGS AND ASSESSMENT

While the focus of this article has been on using retellings as an instructional strategy, individual retellings represent a powerful means of assessment. Rubrics like the one adapted from Irwin and Mitchell (1983) provide a framework for

---

Event 1

The dead person was sent to be mummified.

Event 2

On the day of burial, a procession was formed starting at the house of the dead person. A new coffin was pulled on a wooden sled.

Event 3

Mourners and servants followed the coffin.

Event 4

The mummy was laid in its coffin.

Event 5

The procession continued into the foothills.

Event 6

At the tomb site, the mourners ate a funerary banquet.

Event 7

After the banquet, the mummy was sealed into its tomb.

Figure 20.4   Series of Events Chain for *Mummies, Tombs, and Treasures* (Perl, 1987)

---

teacher evaluation of student retellings (see Figure 20.5). This scale provides for holistic evaluation of retellings not unlike that used for evaluating writing samples. The scoring method acknowledges the child's response as a whole, with all its individual, unique features and richness. Moreover, it assesses a student's ability to identify main ideas, relevant details, and overall text structure, along with the ability to infer beyond the text, summarize, and relate text information to his or her own life.

The following steps can guide teachers as they use individual retellings for assessment.

Step 1: Before beginning the retelling assessment, ask the student to predict what a book might be about based upon the title. Ask the

child to read the book or read it to that child. Instruct the student to remember everything he or she has heard or read.

Step 2: Ask the child to tell you everything he or she can about what has been read. Use prompts such as "Can you tell me more about that?" or "What else do you remember?" to ensure that the student shares as much information as he or she can about the text without looking back at the book.

Step 3: At the end of the retelling, use follow-up questions to elicit additional information about the student's understanding. For example, assess ability to summarize by asking, "If you were going to tell a friend what this book was about in just a few words, what would you say?"

Level: Criteria for Establishing Level

5: *Very cohesive and complete retelling.*

Student includes all main ideas and supporting details, sequences material properly, infers beyond the text, relates text to own life, understands text organization, summarizes, gives opinion of text and justifies it, and may ask additional questions.

4: *Cohesive and complete retelling.*

Student includes most main ideas and supporting details, sequences material properly, relates text to own life, understands text organization, summarizes, and gives opinion of text and justifies it.

3: *Fairly complete retelling.*

Student includes some main ideas and details, correctly sequences most material, understands text organization, and gives opinion of text.

2: *Incomplete retelling.*

Student includes a few main ideas and details, has some difficulty putting material in sequence, may give irrelevant information, and gives opinion to text.

1: *Very incomplete retelling.*

Student gives details only, sequences material poorly, and gives irrelevant information.

Figure 20.5   Richness of Retelling Scale

NOTE: Adapted from Irwin & Mitchell (1983).

To learn about personal responses to the book, ask, "What was the most important thing you learned from this book? How did you feel about this book? Why did you like or dislike it? Would you tell a friend to read it, and why or why not?"

Step 4: Encourage students to relate these texts to their own lives and schema.

Students must draw connections between their own lives and the text in order to obtain higher scores on the rubric (see Figure 20.5). Students need to "personalize" their retellings by demonstrating their own interest in and questions about the text rather than by providing dry recitations of the facts. The following is an example of a fourth grader's retelling of an excerpt from *Storms* (Simon, 1992) relating to hailstorms and downdrafts. The student obviously felt comfortable embellishing her retelling in ways that made it personal for her. This retelling clearly indicates that the student is connecting the text to her own life and experiences:

It talked about hailstones and how they can harm you and other animals. I think that's pretty interesting, because they can kill chickens and rabbits and squirrels and I never knew that it could actually kill little animals. But if it hits you in the right way, it could kill you too. The hailstones are pretty interesting looking. They look like an onion. It's shaped like an onion. . . . It also talks about downdrafts and how they could hurt people in airplanes and how airplanes could crash in seconds because the downdrafts are so heavy. So if you ever go on an airplane and know that there are downdrafts—don't.

As this example indicates, it is possible for students to draw connections between expository text information and their own lives in many of the same ways they connect narrative text to their own experiences. As their comfort level with exposition increases, students will find it easier to move beyond the recitation of facts to more meaningful retellings.

CAPITALIZE ON ENTHUSIASM

Information trade book retellings can acquaint students with the expository text patterns most commonly found in their reading. By engaging students in retelling information trade books, teachers can capitalize on students' enthusiasm for nonfiction literature while providing rich experiences for engagement with nonnarrative texts. Through carefully sequenced instruction involving introduction of each text pattern; teacher modeling; and the use of large-group, small-group, and paired retellings, teachers can ensure that students increase their familiarity with and understanding of expository text. In addition, careful assessment of information trade book retellings can provide teachers with valuable information about each student's emerging abilities in comprehending nonnarrative text—an essential literacy skill for success in our technological world.

Barbara Moss teaches at San Diego State University.

Article 21

NEW DIMENSIONS OF CONTENT AREA LITERACY

Not Just for Secondary Teachers Anymore

KAREN D. WOOD

The promotion of content area reading, helping students comprehend the textbooks for their courses, has been taking place for decades. However, in recent years, the term content area reading has been supplanted by the term "content area literacy." This new concept involves integrating the communication processes (of reading, writing, listening, speaking and viewing) across all subject areas. With this new terminology comes a broader range of emphasis involving the following principles.

CONTENT AREA LITERACY IS NOT JUST FOR HIGH SCHOOLS

Mention the topic "content area literacy" and most people think of integrating literacy in middle and high school classrooms. Yet, familiarity with content area material should begin in the primary grades. Recent classroom observational research by Duke (2000) has shown that few informational text activities take place in the early grade curricula. Looking in several first grade classrooms, the researcher found a mean of only 3.6 minutes per day was spent reading or interacting with informational discourse. The amount of time engaged in informational texts was even less in low SES districts. These findings led the researcher to conclude that it may not be the difficulty of reading content area material that is causing low performance, but rather, a lack of experience with this form of discourse. It is essential to encourage more informational reading beginning in the primary grades. This means schools must provide numerous opportunities from Kindergarten and Grade 1 for beginning

SOURCE: K. D. Wood. (2003). New Dimensions of Content Area Literacy: Not Just for Secondary Teachers Anymore. *California Reader, 36,* 12–17. Reprinted by permission of the California Reading Association.

readers to become familiar with informational text. For example, read alouds can be taken from expository material and students can be asked to listen for details as the teacher records their responses on chart paper or the board. Classroom libraries can and should be stocked with expository literature as well as narrative material. In addition, students can be shown the differences in narrative and expository text in the primary grades and how to best approach the reading of each to maximize understanding.

CONTENT AREA LITERACY INVOLVES MORE THAN JUST READING

The primary goal of teachers is to communicate the content of their disciplines in a manner that addresses the needs of all levels of students. Consequently, content area literacy means drawing upon all of the communication processes including reading, writing, listening, speaking and viewing. Teachers can introduce, reinforce and review key concepts by engaging students in various individual and collaborative activities including discussion, problem-solving and presenting ideas, to name a few. Peer talk has been found to be an essential element in learning and has proven to be especially beneficial for students functioning below grade level to gain new information (Harmon, Hedrick, & Wood, in press; Vygotsky, 1978; Wells, Chang, & Mather, 1990).

CONTENT AREA LITERACY MEANS SUBJECT AREA INSTRUCTION THAT IS READING AND WRITING INTENSIVE

Since reading and writing are reciprocal processes, practice in either communication process has a positive effect on the other process (Tierney & Shanahan, 1991). Research has also indicated that the more quality time students

spend in reading and writing activities, the higher their achievement test scores (Gambrell, Morrow, Neuman, & Pressley, 1999; Greenwald, Persky, Campbell, & Mazzeo, 1998; Rhodes & Dudley-Marling, 1996; Routman, 1996; Wood & Algozzine, 1994). Students need opportunities to engage in all types of writing activities from informal, practice writing to formal, polished writing which may be evaluated by peers, self and the teacher as well (Wood, 2002). Writing activities can be "smuggled" into content area instruction in varied ways that are not overwhelming to students or teachers. For example, students can engage in "communal writing" where two to four students "put their heads together" in the composition of a single product (Wood, 2002). This could be using key terms to construct a passage predicting the selection to be read as in Exchange-Compare Writing (Wood, 2000) or McGinley and Denner's (1987) Story Impressions. Or, it could be two students writing down their thinking in response to a collaborative activity such as Kagan's (1994) "Think, Pair, Share."

CONTENT AREA LITERACY REQUIRES ACTIVE, STRATEGIC INSTRUCTION

While ensuring that students have more experiences reading information discourse is essential, content area literacy requires strategic instruction. Students need to be taught the skills and strategies that aid in understanding and recall. Instruction in how to read information text should begin in the primary grades and be reinforced, refined and extended to the intermediate, middle and high schools levels.

This instruction should include metacognitive strategies such as self-monitoring, thinking aloud and overcoming obstacles while reading. Likewise, retelling, creating images, inferring and summarizing are additional strategies that promote understanding (Block, Gambrell, & Pressley, 2002).

CONTENT AREA LITERACY REQUIRES HIGHER ORDER THINKING

The ability to engage in critical thinking involves a number of skills including: analyzing the author's purpose, reading between the lines, taking on a different perspective, engaging in self-reflection and being able to imagine and empathize is essential in the development of independent thinkers and strategic readers (Weaver & Alvermann, 2000). It is these higher-order thinking skills that students need as they engage in and prepare for post-school careers. The "read, listen to lecture and copy down" transmission model is simply not sufficient for today's learners (Bean, 2001, online document).

CONTENT AREA LITERACY IS "INFORMATION LITERACY"

Students in contemporary classrooms must know how to locate, interpret and synthesize information from a number of sources such as the Internet, email interviews, public television broadcasts, trade books, websites, journals, encyclopedias, to name a few (Elkins & Luke, 1999). This ability has been referred to in the professional literature as "information or multiple source literacy" (Breivik & Senn, 1994; Cohen 1995). Instruction in the content areas in today's classroom must provide experiences that incorporate all of these resources as well as training in how to sort out what is and is not relevant. Gone are the days of the single textbook as the sole source of information. Textbooks today come packaged with CD ROMs, access to online websites, magazines and other resources.

CONTENT AREA LITERACY IS "CRITICAL LITERACY"

Luke and Freebody (1999) describe four essential elements needed by readers in today's world.

These elements are: 1) code breaker; 2) meaning maker; 3) text user; and 4) text critic. The "text critic" element is tied to the thinking of reading as "critical literacy," the need to help students recognize the voices and agendas behind a text that are often not neutral and that frequently represent narrow viewpoints (Cervetti, Pardales, & Damico, 2001, online documents).

CONTENT AREA LITERACY IS "MEDIA LITERACY"

In a review by Mraz, Heron, and Wood (in press), media literacy is defined as a process of developing the ability to create personal meaning from the visual and verbal messages conveyed through television, radio, computers, newspapers, magazines, and advertising (Thomas, 1999). Critical media literacy encompasses understanding how both print and non-print media messages permeate everyday life and how those messages contribute to individuals' understanding of, positions held and perspective on the environment in which they operate (Alvermann, Moon, & Hagood, 1999; Baker & Luke, 1991).

Desmond (1997) identified two components of media literacy: 1) teaching students to be critical receivers of media messages by helping them become aware of their own media viewing habits, the conventions of television production, and the way in which media shape social stereotypes and attitudes; and 2) increasing students' ability to use media messages to gain insight from what is being observed by learning something from the media message being communicated.

Given that students in today's society are immersed in messages from the media, media literacy is a dimension of literacy that cannot be ignored by educators. Particularly in the form of popular culture, media literacy is a potential source for motivating student interest and eliciting their higher order thinking abilities (Mraz, Heron, & Wood, in press).

CONTENT AREA LITERACY MEANS PROMOTING A CONCEPTUAL UNDERSTANDING OF KEY CONCEPTS

The practice of giving students worksheets with fill in the blanks, seek and find or matching exercises has long been denounced as an inadequate means of developing students' conceptual understanding of key concepts in social studies and other subject areas. However, there is ample research in the literature that students of all ability levels greatly increase their understanding of vocabulary and concepts when teachers provide "rich" instruction (Beck & McKeown, 1991; Harmon, Hedrick, & Fox, 2000; Nagy, 1988). Rich instruction can involve teaching vocabulary terms in the context of the selection, not through drill and practice and rote memorizations activities. It can also mean allowing students to self-select some of the vocabulary they do not know and want to learn and engaging in the reading of easier material related to the content areas to build up a working knowledge of some key vocabulary terms. Another facet of rich instruction is to teach vocabulary explicitly, introducing the key terms in context, drawing attention to the words during the reading and reviewing, discussing and expanding upon their meanings and usage after reading. It is through meaningful, multiple exposures to these terms that students' understanding of key vocabulary is extended and enhanced (Harmon, Hedrick, & Wood, in press).

CONTENT AREA LITERACY BEGINS IN THE PRIMARY GRADES AND EXTENDS TO THE UPPER GRADES

The skills and strategies that make proficient readers should be modeled, demonstrated and practiced in their rudimentary forms in the early grades and extended across the grade levels and subject areas. This concept is not a new one. As early as the 1960's, Jerome Bruner described "the spiral curriculum" as one in which ideas, concepts and problem solving strategies can be geared to the child's predominant mode of representation and then re-introduced with more complexity as the child matures. The skills, strategies and concepts students will need throughout their school careers should be introduced early and reinforced throughout their school experiences.

Content area literacy requires standards-based content and strategies to provide a core curriculum. According to Marzano (2001, p. 14), "standards hold the greatest hope for significantly improving achievement." Standards are a means of keeping everyone, students, teachers and parents apprised of what students should learn each year. The path of content area instruction is not teaching what comes next in the textbook. Instead, content area literacy entails finding the most current, age-appropriate materials and methods to coordinate with and meet the requirements of state and local curricula.

CONTENT AREA LITERACY REQUIRES "STUDENT FRIENDLY" INSTRUCTIONAL MATERIAL

Armbruster and Anderson (1981) described content area text as either a) considerate, fitting a reader's prior knowledge and presented in an understandable format or b) inconsiderate, requiring maximum effort on the part of the reader and presented in a poorly organized manner. Textbooks and other material chosen for instruction should address readers' needs by having a more reasonable, more "considerate" amount of text on each page and using colorful, up to date pictures and graphics to motivate and entice students to want to read the material.

CONTENT AREA LITERACY IS REINFORCED THROUGH WIDE READING EXPERIENCES

It is a well-established fact that, in addition to broadening background knowledge, wide reading increases vocabulary knowledge (Nagy, 1988; Nagy & Anderson, 1984). Students need numerous opportunities each class day to read material they can handle with relative ease to enable them to increase their lexicon incidentally through recreational reading. Research has shown that having students read every day supplemented with skill and strategy instruction leads to significant increases in reading performance (Hiebert, 1996; Roller, 1996; National Reading Panel Report, 2000; Routman, 1996). Findings from the National Assessment of Educational Progress in Reading (Donahue, Voelkl, Campbell, & Mazzeo, 1999) indicate that students who reported more reading both in and outside of school had higher achievement test scores.

One suggestion to encourage reading is for classroom teachers to keep available trade books written below, on, and above grade level that are topically related to areas under study. A number of textbook publishers are providing easy read, fiction and non-fiction books on topics typically found on state courses of study in science, social studies and literature. Having students read trade books on a related topic study, for example, The Civil War, Volcanoes, etc., has shown promise as a means of helping students gain conceptual knowledge as a prelude to the more difficult textbook reading (Harmon & Wood, 2001; Harmon, Hedrick, & Wood, in press).

SUMMARY

Content area literacy was once thought of as a means of helping students gain information from course textbooks. Newer conceptions of content area literacy involve writing and all of the communication processes, critical thinking and discussion, multiple texts and resources, the integration of technology and the promotion of higher order thinking skills. Students today must be critical consumers of information sources, knowing not only how to locate information, but how to discern what is relevant. The promotion of content area literacy is no longer the exclusive responsibility of middle and secondary teachers, but instead must be a primary area of focus throughout all grades and subject areas.

Students need to be taught the skills and strategies that aid in understanding and recall. Instruction in how to read information text should begin in the primary grades and be reinforced, refined and extended to the intermediate, middle and high school levels.

The practice of giving students worksheets with fill in the blanks, seek and find or matching exercises has long been denounced as an inadequate means of developing students' conceptual understanding of key concepts in social studies and other subject areas.

Another facet of rich instruction is to teach vocabulary explicitly, introducing the key terms in context, drawing attention to the words during the reading and reviewing, discussing and expanding upon their meanings and usage after reading.

Karen D. Wood is Professor of Education at the University of North Carolina at Charlotte.

Section VII

ADOLESCENT LITERACY

OVERVIEW

Many students are not prepared for the changes in classroom instruction they encounter when they enter middle and high schools. Elementary literacy practices tend to overemphasize the narrative, a genre that often takes the backseat to exposition in content area classrooms. Complicating matters further, in "Rethinking Middle School Reading Instruction," Blanton, Wood, and Taylor (2007) state that "teachers at this level often lack the time and resources to provide both reading interventions and instruction on reading to learn from subject matter texts." Indeed, there is a "sense of crisis in adolescent literacy that begs for immediate solutions," according to Fisher and Ivey (2006) in "Evaluating the Interventions for Struggling Adolescent Readers." Both articles in this section offer guidelines and instructional alternatives to help teachers of adolescents better meet the needs of the literacy learners in their classrooms.

Why do many middle and high schools continue to utilize lecture, recitation, and round-robin reading in subject matter instruction when there is significant research to indicate that these methods do not meet students' complex literacy needs? This is one important question posed by Blanton et al. in their article. In answering this question, the authors propose an alternative view of middle school reading as well as specific options for subject matter classroom literacy instruction. Fisher and Ivey also question the current literacy interventions at work with adolescent youth and "worry that middle and high schools eager to see changes in achievement may overlook the most fundamental conditions for meeting the needs of struggling readers."

STRATEGY

The articles in this section focus on the complex needs of adolescent literacy learners. Use the "Save the Last Word for Me" strategy of Harste, Short, and Burke (1995) while reading the two articles in this section. As you independently read, use index cards to write any segments of the texts (words, phrases, or sentences) that particularly catch your attention.

On the reverse side of the card, write your response. Bring the cards back to the university classroom, where we will engage in small-group discussions of your quotes. The purpose of this strategy is to help you identify sections of the text you strongly connect with or find confusing, challenging, or especially interesting. By completing the Save the Last Word for Me strategy, you will have an opportunity to hear your peers' perspectives and gain deeper understanding of the text.

SAVE THE LAST WORD FOR ME

(Harste, Short, & Burke, 1995)

DIRECTIONS

1. Gather 6 index cards to complete this strategy. Independently read the articles in this section of your reader.

2. As you read, use the index cards to write any segments of the texts (words, phrases, or sentences) that particularly catch your attention. These segments may be items you strongly connect with or find confusing, challenging, or especially interesting. Record the page number of that segment.

3. On the reverse side of the cards, write what you want to say about each selected segment. Your responses may be points of agreement, disagreement, or connection, or they may be in the form of questions you want to pose to the group.

4. Bring the cards back to the university classroom. We will gather in small groups to share cards.

5. Before the discussion, organize your cards in the order you wish to share. During the discussion, place any similar quotes shared by peers in the back of your pile.

6. Each student takes a turn reading his or her quote to the group. The other members react to what was read. The student who read the quote then has the *last word* about why that segment of text was chosen.

SOURCE: Harste, J., Short, K. G., & Burke, C. (1995). *Creating Classrooms for Authors and Inquirers* (2nd ed.). Portsmouth, NH: Heinemann.

Article 22

RETHINKING MIDDLE SCHOOL READING INSTRUCTION

A Basic Literacy Activity

WILLIAM E. BLANTON, KAREN D. WOOD, AND D. BRUCE TAYLOR

Research on subject matter instruction across the 20th century (e.g., Stevens, 1912; Bellack, 1966; Hoetker & Ahlbrand, 1969; Gall, 1970; Langer, 1999; Mehan, 1979; Nystrand, 1997) reveals a preponderance of teacher-directed lecture, recitation, and round-robin reading of text in place of instruction that focuses on reading-to-learn, thinking, and transforming information into meaning and understanding (Durkin, 1978–79; Langer, 1999; Blanton & Moorman, 1990; Wood & Muth, 1991). This kind of instruction persists despite the fact that observations of higher performing schools indicated the tendency to organize instruction around meaningful learning communities with extensive interactive discussion of material read (Langer, 1999; Myers, 1996; Wenglinsky, 2000, 2004).

The purpose of this essay is twofold: (a) to argue that a great deal of reading instruction fails to meet the multiple and complex literacy needs of most middle school students, and (b) to propose

SOURCE: Blanton, W. E., Wood, K. D., & Taylor, D. B. (2007). Rethinking Middle School Reading Instruction: A Basic Literacy Activity. *Reading Psychology, 28*(1), 75–95. Reprinted by permission.

a new orientation for thinking about middle school reading instruction. We begin with a discussion of research findings on classroom reading instruction, followed by an exploration of issues central to the problem. Then we propose what we have titled the basic literacy activity, a conceptual tool for thinking about and arranging middle school reading instruction. We end with an overview of selected instructional strategies that exemplify the characteristics of basic literacy activity.

INTRODUCTION

In 1998, the National Assessment of Educational Progress (NAEP) reported that fewer than 7% of students in grades 4, 8, and 12 were able to comprehend, critically analyze, and apply information obtained by reading text at a proficient level (Donahue, Voelkl, Campbell, & Mazzeo, 1999). Other assessments have exposed deficiencies in the instruction of students on reading and thinking strategies (Campbell, Hombo, & Mazzeo, 2000) and revealed that only 24% of fourth-graders and 29% of eighth-graders were able to meet the standard for proficiency in reading (National Assessment of Educational Progress in Reading Report Card [NAEP], 2003). These results are disheartening. Students who fall behind in reading do not often catch up with their more successful peers, show lower self-esteem, and display less motivation for participating in reading and subject matter instruction.

By the end of the fourth grade, most readers have just accomplished the task of *learning to read* when they embark on *reading to learn*, as they encounter more varied forms of expository text. Many students have not received sufficient instruction for reading expository text to adequately prepare them for the tasks this type of reading requires (Duke, 2000; Newkirk, 1989; Pappas, 1993). Even students who read at grade level exhibit difficulties when asked to read expository text (Readence, Bean, & Baldwin, 1998). This period is often referred to as the "fourth-grade slump," the beginning of a decline in many students' performance and progress in reading (Chall, Jacobs, & Baldwin, 1990; Mullis,

Campbell, & Farstrup, 1993). At this point, many struggling readers begin a pattern of academic failure that continues through middle and high school.

As students move from elementary to middle school, most reading remediation instruction is presented in pullout programs. Instruction of this kind removes students from subject matter instruction (Irvin, 1990). Consequently, they miss the opportunity to participate in instruction that integrates comprehension, thinking, understanding, critical analysis, and meta-cognition with reading to learn from subject matter text.

The purpose of this essay is to argue that a great deal of reading instruction fails to meet the multiple and complex literacy needs of most middle school students and to propose a new orientation for thinking about middle school reading instruction. We begin with a discussion of research findings on classroom reading instruction, followed by an exploration of issues central to the problem. Then we propose what we have titled the *basic literacy activity*, a conceptual tool for thinking about and arranging middle school reading instruction. We end with an overview of selected instructional strategies that exemplify the characteristics of basic literacy activity.

Research on Classroom Reading Instruction

Research across the 20th century (e.g., Stevens, 1912; Bellack, 1966; Hoetker & Ahlbrand; 1969; Gall, 1970; Mehan, 1979; Nystrand, 1997; Langer, 1999) underscores the overreliance of subject matter instruction on teacher-directed lecture, recitation, and round-robin reading of text that reduces students' engagement with a wide range of texts and diminishes opportunities to participate in instruction that focuses on reading to learn, thinking, and transforming information into meaning and understanding (Durkin, 1978–79; Blanton & Moorman, 1990; Wood & Muth, 1991). In spite of changing demands, this kind of instruction persists (Myers, 1996). Recently, Nystrand (1997) reported that many teachers limit discussion of material read to an average of 50 seconds per lesson at the eighth-grade level and an even briefer 15 seconds at the ninth-grade level. These findings coordinate with the results of a large-scale study of high- and low-performing middle and secondary schools. Langer (1999) found that typical classroom instruction in low-performing schools failed to engage students in collaborative activities, provided few opportunities for group discussion, and failed to focus on developing understanding of material read. In contrast, higher performing schools tended to organize instruction around learning communities and promoted extended discussion of material read.

Issues Central to Middle School Reading Instruction

Three issues surround the problem of middle school reading instruction. First, teachers at this level often lack the time and resources to provide both reading interventions and instruction on reading to learn from subject matter text. This problem is further exacerbated by the climate of high-stakes testing. For example, teachers have been observed realigning curriculum and altering instructional methods in response to high-stakes testing (e.g., Barksdale-Ladd & Thomas, 2000; Haney, 2000; Hoffman, Assaf, Pennington, & Paris, 2001; Jones & Johnston, 2002; Yarbrough, 1999). Moreover, high-stakes testing has motivated a reduction of time allocated to reading and subject matter instruction and an increase in time for teaching test-taking skills that utilize materials formatted to resemble high-stakes tests (e.g., Ananda & Rabinowitz, 2000; International Reading Association, 1999; Johnston, 1998; Kohn, 2000; McColskey & McMunn, 2000). It is important to note that the research on whether these changes have positive (Borko & Elliot, 1999; Bridge, Compton-Hall, & Cantrell, 1997; Jones & Johnston, 2002) or negative (Calkins, Montgomery, & Santman, 1998; Gordon & Reese, 1997; Kohn, 2000; Passman, 2001; Wideen, O'Shea, Pye, & Ivany, 1997) effects on the quality of instruction is inconclusive.

Second, many teachers lack sufficient knowledge of reading instruction to provide necessary reading instruction or to support students' reading, comprehending, and understanding of diverse subject matter text. States and local education agencies require that prospective teachers who will be certified to teach at the middle school level receive minimum preparation in the areas of basic reading instruction and teaching reading in subject matter areas. University and college graduates taking alternative routes to certification receive even less preparation. The solution has been to step up professional development to assist practicing teachers in acquiring and applying the knowledge and skills needed to help struggling readers and to engage students in reading to learn from subject matter text. Unfortunately, the resources for professional development programs are scarce and compete with other high-priority needs, such as teaching an increasingly diverse range of students.

The reading ability of students can be substantially improved (Guastello, Beasley, & Sinatra, 2000; Montali & Lewandowski, 1996), and most teachers can learn to integrate reading and subject matter instruction successfully (Dupuis, Askov, & Lee, 1979; Wedman & Robinson, 1988). More than three decades of reading research documents a growing and diverse toolkit of research-based reading instruction strategies available for teachers to use (Alvermann, 2003; Kamil, 2003; Rand Reading Study Group, 2002; Snow & Biancarosa, 2003). However, faced with increasing pressure of high-stakes testing and local, state, and federal mandates for student achievement, school districts have increasingly turned to pre-packaged instructional materials, scripted instruction, and practice exercises to teach reading and its application to subject matter text.

Last, the decisions school districts are making about reading and subject matter instruction are being influenced by the anticipation that the NAEP and other standardized tests of reading may place a greater emphasis on measuring subskills in future assessments and reduce the emphasis placed on thinking, understanding, and application (Wenglinsky, 2004). We believe that this will further degrade the quality of instruction for middle school students. The research evidence (Wenglinsky, 2000) demonstrating that students in classrooms encouraging thinking and understanding perform significantly better than their counterparts who do not receive such instruction should not be overlooked.

Pre-packaged, scripted instruction and practice exercises are not an ideal approach for engaging middle school students in reading an increasing array of challenging texts, in or out of school. Most prepackaged scripted instruction is implemented as de-contextualized drill and practice and teacher-directed questioning that probes for the literal comprehension of text. While instruction of this kind may align with the demands of high-stakes tests, it creates nothing more than an *appearance* of learning. The development of students' ability to coordinate reading and thinking necessary for comprehending, interpreting, analyzing, and transforming complex information presented in subject matter text into meaning and understanding is constrained. It has been well established in the professional literature that students learn more from participatory models of teaching and learning where multiple sources of subject matter, rich discussions, and metacognitive conversations are encouraged (Bransford, Brown, & Cocking, 2000; Alvermann, 2002; International Reading Association, 1999; Schoenbach, Greenleaf, Cziko, & Hurwitz, 1999; Wade & Moje, 2000).

Reading ability and reading to learn from subject matter text are much more than the mastery of isolated skills. Reading to learn from text is a complex task that requires social interaction among teachers and students in order to understand *how reading works* and to successfully construct meaning and understanding. Reading to learn from text represents a unification of language to frame the learning task and its purpose, language to regulate the monitoring of reading, application of strategies, and selection of appropriate information. It also involves synthesizing interactions with others during discussion to construct a sense of meaning and understanding for further self-regulation and the generation of new knowledge.

Accomplished reading ability develops gradually through engagement in meaningful learning activity in which students receive explicit instruction, guided and independent practice, and assistance of teachers and more accomplished peers to support their gradual transition to independence in the self-regulation of reading (Pearson & Gallagher, 1983). Many times there is an expectation that students do not need continued social support once new knowledge and skill has been introduced, practiced a few times, and reviewed. This is especially true for students who have moved beyond the elementary school level. Readers *do* need social support until they have both mastered a skill and infused it with personal meaning and understanding. When social support is abruptly withdrawn or is not available, students' level of skill tends to drop sharply when they move to a new level of instruction or confront more complex text (Fischer & Farrar, 1987; Fischer & Granott, 1995).

Never has the need for students to develop a more robust understanding of discourse in all its forms been more essential than it is in today's society. Students need to develop skill to coordinate a complex set of literacy tasks, reading strategies, language, and thinking processes to negotiate a world that is becoming increasingly reliant on multiple sources of information, referred to as "*multiliteracies*" (Gee, 2003; New London Group, 2000; Rush, 2002) and "new literacies" (Lankshear & Knobel, 2003; Leu, 2002; O'Brien & Bauer, 2005). In what Luke and Elkins (1998) tag as "New Times," reading and reading to learn are viewed as multi-modal processes that include the reading of print-based and electronic texts, use of visual, spatial, gestural, and aural representations. Given the increasingly complex demands placed on readers in a multi-textual society, reading instruction should go beyond surface level recitation, lecture, and simple drill on skills. Prepackaged content, scripted instruction, information dumping, and repeated practice do not develop accomplished readers (Allington, 2002). Instruction of this kind leads students to develop what Perkins (1992) refers to as incomplete or "fragile knowledge." Fragile knowledge is inert, ritualistic, fraught with misconceptions, devoid of supportive thinking, and lacks understanding.

To address the need for an alternative view of reading instruction, we propose an instructional framework that we call the *basic literacy activity* as a heuristic for helping teachers address the complex literacy demands their students face in middle school classrooms. Reading and reading-to-learn instruction should be arranged in such a way that middle school students engage in a basic literacy activity (e.g., Blanton, Moorman, & Hayes, 1998; Griffin & Cole, 1987), which provides an alternative for integrating reading tasks with goal-oriented learning activity in which students have a personal interest. The reading knowledge and skill required for performing the reading tasks are subservient to the accomplishment of the goal of the activity and are used in its accomplishment. An example of a basic literacy activity is recruiting a student's interest in playing a computer game to learn a reading skill. Learning to follow written directions is subservient to the goal of playing the computer game.

We suggest the term "basic" to foreground the primacy of reading and literacy to learning in any subject area—that is, reading is a central or basic ingredient to learning. Also, we believe a pedagogic approach (the "activity") emphasizes teaching and learning specific content within the context or culture of a specific subject-area classroom. We expand upon the role of culture and context in the next section by grounding the basic literacy activity in four tenets of cultural-historical theory.

Cultural-Historical Theory and Basic Literacy Activity

The idea of basic literacy activity is influenced by cultural-historical theory founded by Vygotsky and his colleagues (Leontiev, 1978; Luria, 1979, 1985; Vygotsky, 1978). Cultural-historical theory describes the way in which human thinking is fundamentally the outcome of participation in cultural activity. Four key tenets of cultural-historical activity guide the development of basic literacy activity.

The first tenet is that psychological functions appear twice: first, on the social plane, and later on the personal plane. For example, students' ways of thinking, comprehending, and thinking about text are, first, located in the collective thinking of the group engaged in a reading lesson and later internalized by participants. The process of internalization transforms their thinking processes. The basic literacy activity seeks to provide students with a more active social environment, which helps create more active social and therefore cognitive learning. The 5th Dimension (Blanton, Greene, & Cole, 1999), an exemplar we will later describe, is an example of a basic literacy activity we believe scaffolds learning from the social to the cognitive domain.

The second tenet is that the use of psychological tools, such as language (discourse), concepts, and notational systems, and instrumental tools, such as books, computers, pencils, and cell phones, are used by humans to mediate their activities. Language (discourse) is the primary tool (Vygotsky, 1978). Discourse is used to mediate self-regulation, the regulation of others, the transformation of experience and information into public meaning and personal understanding, and the formulation and communication of one's thinking to self and others. For example, as a particular discourse approach is used to coordinate the discussion of material read, students internalize the discourse and patterns and ways of thinking that it privileges. In future reading and discussion, students use the discourse to mediate their synthesis of interactions among the collective group and transform it into meaning and understanding. As an instructional framework, the basic reading activity seeks to foreground the role of discourse and language as tools for learning. As we will suggest, think-alouds are one instructional vehicle for teachers and students to share and discuss specific subject-area discourses.

The third tenet is that learning occurs in the zone of proximal development (ZPD), "the distance between the actual developmental level as determined by independent problem solving and the level of potential development as determined through problem solving under adult guidance or in collaboration with more capable peers" (Vygotsky, 1978, p. 86). The ZPD is a socially organized activity motivated and organized around the interest and goals of students who receive guided assistance, as needed, but only as much as is needed, to gradually accomplish a task that they were unable to perform independently. There is no required or designated teacher; only one who is more expert in the task at hand is needed. Students work together, assisting one another and learning from the contributions of others. It is assumed that the task is just beyond the ability of the students and requires social support for its completion, providing an opportunity for the learner to develop new knowledge and understanding and to master new skills. The greater the difficulty that students experience, the more direct the assistance given from the more accomplished others. Reciprocal teaching (Palincsar & Brown, 1984) is an instructional strategy that aligns with the basic literacy activity and can help students to work in collaboration with more capable others to develop greater competence and subject area expertise.

The fourth tenet is that the structure of activity affects thinking. For example, the organization of reading a reading lesson, such as a directed reading-thinking activity (Stauffer, 1969a, 1969b) or information text reading activity (Moorman & Blanton, 1990), affects comprehending, thinking, and constructing meaning and understanding of material read. The tools used to mediate the lesson—such as discourse, kind of text used, rules for participation, division of labor and participant roles, focus of the lesson, intended outcome—all coordinate a lesson. The discourse approach used directs student attention to how reading works and the resources used to construct meaning and understanding. As pointed out earlier, the structure of the lesson is internalized. However, the process of internalization is not a carbon copy of the lesson structure. Rather, the process of internalization changes the thinking structures of students.

The fourth tenet is that tools, such as discourse and concepts, and skills are mastered. Mastery of a tool goes beyond 90 to 100% accuracy on practice sheets. Mastery of a tool involves learning to act with the tool, how it fits into particular activities, and how and in what context to use it. Mastery also embraces the idea of investing a tool with personal meaning (Wertsch, 1998). Literature circles (Daniels, 2002; Hill, Noe, & King, 2003) and book clubs (Raphael & McMahon, 1994) are forms of pedagogy we see as aligned with the basic literacy activity that help students to work towards a higher level of mastery with the many facets of literacy including reading, writing, talking, listening, and thinking.

In summary, the cognitive structures necessary for reading, comprehending, thinking about, and constructing meaning and understanding of text are, first, located in the structures of social interactions of reading lessons. As students participate in a reading lesson, the structure of the lesson is internalized and transforms students' thinking processes and how they read, think about, and understand what they have read. The zone of proximal development further explains how learners participate in activity along side of more accomplished others who provide guided assistance for accomplishing a task just beyond their reach but in reach with assistance.

Basic Literacy Activity

In the basic literacy activity, the reading knowledge and strategies students learn are embedded in and subservient to accomplishing reading tasks to attain a goal. As an illustration, students may enter the activity of playing a computer game, such as *Counting on Frank*, with limited reading ability. In the beginning, they may be unable to focus on comprehending written directions because they must direct their attention to decoding and word meaning. However, while engaging in game play with a more knowledgeable classmate or volunteer, who provides help with decoding, word meaning, and following written directions, students learn word recognition strategies and how to follow written directions in order to eventually play the game with a high level of skill. In doing so, they come to develop an understanding of the importance of following written directions and how they work in real activity that goes beyond the level of understanding reached through the completion of worksheet exercises.

Working cooperatively with others in basic reading activity assures that students will acquire the meta-language necessary for framing reading tasks, mediates the self-regulation necessary for monitoring reading and fixing problems when reading is disrupted, and synthesizing the contributions of others to a discussion. With guided assistance, students gradually learn to perform reading tasks they were unable to perform independently. The kinds of tools used to mediate basic literacy activity also transform how students think about what they do and how they do it.

Instructional Exemplars of Basic Literacy Activity

A great deal of successful reading instruction available for middle and secondary school students possesses the characteristics of basic literacy activity. In this section, we offer selected instructional approaches that express the characteristics of basic literacy activity.

5th Dimension

The 5th Dimension demonstrates how it is possible to arrange basic literacy activity by making reading and the use of technology subservient to accomplishing education goals (Blanton, Greene, & Cole, 1999). Participants

mediate their activity with multi-media, including print and electronic text, digital technology, and board games to engage in activity. By embedding basic reading knowledge and strategies in specific activities, desired mastery is reached during pursuit of a personally meaningful goal. Students get exposure to and practice reading in the context of meaningful activities, not separated drill and practice activity.

Activity in the 5th Dimension begins with trained adults and participants using an Adventure Guide that accompanies each activity to help participants get started, specify expected achievements, and provide the necessary information for reaching one of three levels of proficiency (beginner, good, expert) in each game. In essence, participants engage in reading, interpreting, and using text at two levels. At the macro level, they map out the possible directions for moving through the various activities. And they participate in the joint reading, interpretation, and implementation of the Adventure Guide directions for coordinating game play. At the micro level, they interpret and follow written directions in manuals accompanying the games and other activities. As students proceed from the beginning level of playing a game to the good and excellent levels, they gradually learn subject matter, new skills and extend their existing skills. The choice of which activity to engage in next is related to the level of mastery attained in playing the game.

The Adventure Guide also provides an Adventure Task, an obligation that must be completed before moving to the next activity. All Adventure Tasks require writing to others, writing in a personal journal, putting information in a hints book, making a video, or creating art work representing the strategies used and knowledge gained in the activity. These tasks require that students constantly formulate and reflect on what they are doing and communicate it to others.

The results of research on the effects of participation in the 5th Dimension demonstrate that participants spend a greater amount of time engaged in educational tasks and acquire proficiency in using computers and other technology. When 5th

Dimension participants are compared with their counterparts in control groups, significant effects are found on measures of near transfer, such as reading, comprehending, and following written directions (Blanton, Menendez, Moorman, & Pacifici, 2003) and state-wide measures of reading (Blanton, Moorman, & Hayes, 1998).

WebQuests

WebQuests are student-inquiry activities in which most of the sources used to obtain information are drawn from the Internet in a structured fashion. WebQuests allow students to access, organize, evaluate, and synthesize a large amount of information about a topic in a short amount of time. This shifts the focus of research from gathering information to analyzing and evaluating information. The WebQuest model was developed at San Diego State University (Dodge, 1995) and provides students with a task for using Internet resources. WebQuesting differs from more open-ended Internet research in which students often use search engines to "surf" for information about a topic. To direct students away from sources of questionable quality, WebQuests are typically designed with many of the Internet sources already embedded in their instructions. From a cultural-historical perspective, this allows the teacher to assist students through the seemingly boundless resources available on the Internet.

Reciprocal Teaching

Reciprocal Teaching (Brown, Palincsar, & Purcell, 1986; Palincsar & Brown, 1984; Palincsar & Klenk, 1992) aligns with the properties of the basic literacy activity. The teacher models strategies and then asks students to reciprocate in small peer groups, exchanging roles, taking turns leading discussions about segments, asking and answering questions, and sharing their thinking with one another. Four comprehension strategies are employed throughout the interactive process: prediction, clarification, summarization, and questioning.

The strength of reciprocal teaching is its focus on reading to learn. A meta-analysis of 16 studies

reveals that reciprocal teaching is a highly effective approach that enables students to internalize a meta-language that can be used for reading, comprehending, and understanding text (Rosenshine & Meister, 1994). It should be understood that students need opportunities to use this strategy regularly.

Question–Answer Relationships

Questioning is the most pervasive comprehension instructional activity. It provides students with a purpose for reading, a focus, a plan for selecting important information, and a reference point for reflecting on how well the purpose was attained (Armbruster, Lehrer, & Osborn, 2001; Duke & Pearson, 2002). Raphael's (1986) research revealed that students' answers to questions tend to fall in two groups: those that rely on their memory and prior knowledge and those that are in the text. As a result of these findings, she developed Question–Answer Relationships (QARs) as a means of helping students distinguish between answers to questions that are found "in the book," "between the lines," or "in my head." Students acquire a language to use to mediate thinking and processing of information related to the locations of answers. Students well trained in the QAR approach readily use phrases such as "I found the answer in the book and in my head," or "I had to put information from this page and this page together."

Think-Aloud

The ability to determine when and where comprehension is breaking down and to employ the necessary fix-up strategies, such as re-reading, self-questioning, or retelling has long been associated with successful, proficient reading (Block & Israel, 2004; Pressley, 2002; Walker, 2005). Think-alouds have been recommended for decades as a means by which readers can learn to regulate their own comprehension activities (Alvermann, 1984; Brown, Pressley, Van Meter, & Schuder, 1996; Davey, 1983; Nist & Kirby, 1986). The importance of thinking aloud is that it provides students with an opportunity to learn and understand the processes of thinking about and talking aloud with the language used to reveal the mental processes taking place while engaged in reading tasks.

Think-aloud techniques help students internalize language used to mediate essential comprehension strategies, such as predicting, verifying, inferring, and retelling. Research (Baumann, Seifert-Kessell, & Jones, 1992, 1993; Walker, 2005) reveals that students engage in more discussion of their strategy use with more proficient readers or a tutor. They also master a wider range of comprehension monitoring strategies. As a result, students are far better able to internalize the meta-language for directing their thinking aloud processes when they interact with others.

Literature Circles and Book Clubs

Literature circles (Daniels, 2002; Hill, Noe, & King, 2003; Noll, 1994; Short & Kauffman, 1995) and book clubs (Raphael & McMahon, 1994) are ways of organizing the reading of books and other texts in which students play a significant role in text selection and collective discussions. Typically, groups of four or five students read the same book or text and hold discussions about it. The text selected can be short or long, fiction or nonfiction, so long as it is of interest to the students and can stimulate meaningful discussion. Students may read in or out of class or meet periodically during class to discuss their reading. Students assume specific roles during the discussions (i.e., discussion leader, recorder, encourager, etc.) and may keep a journal or reader-response log.

Literature circles and similar instructional models allow students to read, collectively construct meaning, and develop an understanding of a topic or text. Through their discussions, they are able to interact with each other through sections of the text, through discussions of words, word meaning, concepts, and other content that they find challenging or unclear. Students can bring their questions to the group for discussion or recruit help from the teacher when necessary. However, the focus of the conversation typically remains among the students, with the teacher monitoring from the background.

Discussion Approaches

The main goal of discussion approaches is to assist students in comprehending text and constructing meaning and understanding. Discussion approaches and their discourse are important in mediating social interaction, direction of attention, tool use, self-regulation, and thinking. In order to comprehend and construct meaning and understanding of subject matter text, it is imperative that students master the *academic discourse* and the technical vocabulary of subject matter areas, such as earth science, biology, physics, law, literature, and literary criticism. Mastery of subject matter requires participation in learning activity arranged so that technical language and meaning are made public through technical vocabulary, symbols, graphs, text, and other tools specialized disciplines use. The meaning of technical vocabulary is more salient when it is learned in activity that leads students to "see" what the vocabulary means and how it is used to "fit" the subject matter area together. Otherwise, students simply remember de-contextualized definitions of vocabulary. The meaning of technical vocabulary, comprehension, and understanding of subject matter is attained as a student synthesizes the interactions among students and teachers.

Wilkinson and colleagues (Murphy & Edwards, 2005; Soter & Rudge, 2005; Wilkinson & Reninger, 2005) performed a meta-analysis of the research on discussion approaches. They determined that the most often used approaches could be categorized by three literary stances: *an expressive stance* that gives primacy to a reader's emotional response (e.g., literature circles, grand conversations, book club); an *efferent stance* that gives prominence to a reader acquiring information from text (e.g., questioning the author, instructional conversation, junior great books); and *a critical-analytic stance* (e.g., philosophy for children, collaborative reasoning, Paideia seminars) that gives primacy to evidence-based responses through the reader's questioning of text to determine underlying assumptions, beliefs, and arguments.

The effects of discussion approaches begin to take hold in approximately three weeks, effects begin to stabilize in a short time, and most approaches increase the level of student engagement and talk. The major effects tend to favor lower ability students, followed by average ability students, and less for higher ability students. It was also noted that commercial measures of comprehension tended not to be very sensitive to changes in student performance. Analysis of lesson transcripts further revealed that expressive approaches encourage students to actively participate in discussions, that there is a relationship between levels of student thinking and questions posed by teacher or students, students seem to recognize that their responses are central to constructing meaning and understanding, and that critical-analytical approaches seem to encourage students to probe both the text and each other's thinking.

SUMMARY

In this essay, we have argued that reading instruction is not meeting the complex literacy needs of today's adolescent readers and that alternative ways of thinking about instruction are needed to meet these needs. The basic literacy activity is a new orientation for thinking about middle school reading instruction. In basic literacy activity, the language and cognitive structures needed by students for mediating reading, comprehending, thinking, and constructing meaning and understanding of text are internalized through the social interactions promoted by the organization of reading lessons and, in particular, the discourse used. We provided familiar instructional approaches that characterize the learning interactions promoted by the basic literacy activity.

William E. Blanton, University of Miami, Coral Gables, Florida
Karen D. Wood, University of North Carolina at Charlotte
D. Bruce Taylor, University of North Carolina at Charlotte

Article 23

EVALUATING THE INTERVENTIONS FOR STRUGGLING ADOLESCENT READERS

DOUGLAS FISHER AND GAY IVEY

The authors assess current reading interventions for struggling readers and offer five guidelines for choosing an effective program.

Literacy educators across the grade levels are often asked for their opinions on the quality of particular reading programs. However, for researchers and teacher educators who study adolescent literacy, these questions are now coming more frequently and more urgently. The recent flood of information on later reading difficulties has received much attention in the United States and has created a sense of crisis in adolescent literacy that begs for immediate solutions. For instance, the United States Department of Education reports that more than 8 million students in grades 4–12 are struggling readers

(Grigg, Daane, Jin, & Campbell, 2003). National Assessment of Educational Progress data from 2002 indicate that 33% of the 8th-grade students and 36% of the 12th-grade students who were tested performed at or above a "proficient" level. These data mean that nearly 70% of the 8th graders tested could not describe the purpose of a practical passage and support their views with examples and details. We are also reminded that poor readers are at significant risk for dropping out of high school (Snow & Biancarosa, 2003). Over 3,000 students drop out of high school every school day (Alliance for Excellent Education, 2003).

SOURCE: Fisher, D., & Ivey, G. (2006). Evaluating the Interventions for Struggling Adolescent Readers. *Journal of Adolescent & Adult Literacy, 50*(3), 180–189. Reprinted by permission of the International Reading Association.

The federal government has responded to this issue by focusing funds on a "Striving Readers" initiative. According to the White House website at www.whitehouse.gov/infocus/education,

> The President's Striving Readers initiative provides a focus on improving the reading skills of high school students who read below grade level. This Presidential initiative, first funded in 2005, builds on the No Child Left Behind elementary school reading initiatives. The President's [fiscal year] 2006 budget will provide $200 million, an increase of $175 million, eight times the 2005 level to improve the reading skills of these high school students. (press release dated January 12, 2005)

Along with this federal focus, states are responding with funds for reading intervention programs for middle and high school students. For example, in California, funds are available for schools to adopt intervention programs. The purpose of the current middle school reading intervention, for example, is "to provide a comprehensive, intensive, accelerated reading/language arts program designed for students in grades four through eight whose reading achievement is significantly below grade level," as described on the Department of Education's website (www.cde.ca.gov/ci/rl/im/documents/ri.rtf).

Although we agree that far too many students do not read well and that reading and writing interventions are necessary to move students to proficient and advanced levels, we worry that middle and high schools eager to see changes in achievement may overlook the most fundamental conditions for meeting the needs of struggling readers. Few independent research studies have been conducted on popular commercial reading programs, but the use of such programs in secondary schools is burgeoning, and No Child Left Behind legislation threatens to seep into the upper grades. The merits and pitfalls of particular programs have been debated elsewhere (e.g., Biggers, 2001; Mallette, Henk, & Melnick, 2004; Pavonetti, Brimmer, & Cipielewski, 2002/2003).

WHEN IS INTERVENTION NECESSARY?

Our purpose in this article is to suggest some research-based principles for developing and evaluating instructional frameworks that can be used by literacy educators and secondary-level administrators faced with difficult but crucial decisions about how to help students in critical need.

Before describing these principles we would like to consider two assumptions about schools seeking an intervention involving "special" reading instruction for students. First, we assume that schools looking for intervention programs to supplement their efforts already provide students with significant opportunities for wide reading. By this, we mean that students have access to a substantial number of readable, interesting books that focus on the content they are studying. We also mean that students are provided the opportunity to "just read" books of their own choosing (Fisher, 2004; Worthy, Broaddus, & Ivey, 2001). The power of addressing such a fundamental condition for literacy development can be seen in the changes experienced by students and teachers at Mountain View High School (Brozo & Hargis, 2003). Assessments indicated that nearly 35% of all students at the school were reading one or more grade levels below their placement, so the school implemented four initiatives aimed at increasing the quantity and quality of wide reading for all students: sustained silent reading, reading young adult novels in content classrooms, offering alternative texts to struggling readers and advanced readers in content classrooms, and buddy reading with elementary-grade students. These initiatives alone yielded notable increases in students' achievement and motivation to read.

Second, we assume that the entire school is focused on literacy achievement and that teachers use content literacy approaches to ensure that their students are engaged in meaningful curriculum. By this, we mean that the history, science, math, English, art, music, and other teachers ensure that students are developing strategic reading skills as they read for information (Fisher &

Frey, 2004; Ivey, 2004). For instance, Tubman High School in San Diego (Fisher, 2001) experienced a 12% overall gain in statewide achievement tests over a two-year period as three trends took shape in classrooms across content areas. First, staff development for all teachers focused on specific instructional strategies (e.g., K–W–L [Ogle, 1986], writing to learn, concept mapping, reciprocal teaching) that students experienced consistently from content area to content area. Second, a daily independent reading time was created, and large quantities of books were purchased specifically for this initiative. Third, block scheduling was implemented to allow teachers substantial amounts of time to provide reading and writing opportunities and instruction across all content area classes.

Without these two nonnegotiable features of the learning environment—access to high-quality, readable texts and instruction in strategies to read and write across the school day—it is doubtful that a specific, limited intervention will make much of a difference. If a school has already made these fundamental changes and there are still students who struggle to read, it is likely that an intervention program or initiative is necessary (Ivey & Fisher, 2006). Although there are many programs that can be considered, we suggest that the people who have the power to purchase, implement, or develop a program consider the following five guidelines.

1. The Teacher Should Play a Critical Role in Assessment and Instruction

A key component in case studies of struggling readers who became better readers is lots of time spent with an expert teacher (e.g., McCormick, 1994; Morris, Ervin, & Conrad, 1996). In fact, it is difficult to find success stories that do not feature teacher involvement in a major way. When we refer to teacher involvement, we are suggesting something that extends far beyond the general notion of individualization. There are many programs that differentiate materials and assignments for students, but that does not mean instruction is personalized.

We know of many commercial programs that advertise individualized learning, but what does that mean? It might mean that students get texts at different levels, that they work alone at a computer at their own pace, or that they are grouped according to ability levels. But what is different about the teaching, and how is that connected to individual students? It is highly unlikely that a computer, for example, could accurately evaluate a student's strengths and needs or tend to the complexity of adolescents' motivations for reading and writing (Alvermann & Rush, 2004). Only expert teachers can make split-second decisions that facilitate students' understandings from text and knowledge about literacy processes (Johnston, 1987).

Consider 10th-grader Michael (student names are pseudonyms) during a one-to-one tutoring session with his teacher. Michael reads at roughly a first-grade level, and even at age 16, he still enjoys Dr. Seuss books. As he read *I Am Not Going to Get Up Today!* (Seuss, 1987), he came across the phrase "You are wasting your time" (p. 15). He became stuck on *wasting* and stopped reading, with no apparent strategies for moving on. His teacher advised that sometimes she skips the word, reads the next several words, and then makes a guess about the word in question using the meaning of the sentence and the first couple of letters of the unknown word. Before she could finish the explanation, Michael exclaimed, "Wasting!" They used this strategy successfully a few more times with this same passage. Without the teacher present and participating, it would be impossible to know where Michael is getting stumped and what needs to be explained to him (e.g., Duffy, 2003). When we implement programs that do not prominently feature the teacher's expertise, we are likely leaving students' learning up to chance.

2. The Intervention Should Reflect a Comprehensive Approach to Reading and Writing

We see an either/or theme in reactions to low reading achievement among older students. A common assumption is that persistent reading problems are either the result of deficiencies in word-level skills or deficiencies in comprehension skills. Certainly, we know of students with obvious problems in word recognition and others who can read every word but seem not to remember or understand what they read. If the reality were that simple, though, we would have solved the problem of persistent reading problems long ago, because for decades there has existed a plethora of programs aimed at "fixing" specific reading difficulties. Still, such programs seem to be rising in their popularity, despite a lack of solid evidence that they make much of a difference. Programs that focus on phonemic awareness and phonics instruction are particularly problematic because there is little reason to believe that emphasizing these fundamental skills would have any significant benefits for secondary students (Ivey & Baker, 2004).

One belief underlying the skill-by-skill approach to learning to read is that once students learn all the necessary skills for reading and writing, they will magically put it all together. You can find research showing that teaching a particular skill increases your aptitude with that skill, but does that make you a better or more motivated reader? Older students need to "see the big picture" when it comes to reading and writing, and good interventions should begin with reading, writing, listening to, and thinking about meaningful texts. Instruction in the processes of reading and writing (e.g., word recognition, comprehension strategies, vocabulary, fluency) ought to help facilitate student engagement and understanding with real texts rather than take center stage in the program.

3. Reading and Writing in the Intervention Should Be Engaging

It is easy to find a reading program for which even struggling or resistant students will sit still. After all, most programs are designed to offer instruction and materials that are much easier than grade-level, whole-class types of assignments, and for students who consistently struggle

with most school reading and writing experiences, this is a welcome relief. In other words, some reading programs get students who might be noncompliant in regular classroom activities to suddenly appear compliant. To see this kind of change in students may falsely lead an observer to believe that the intervention must be working and that students are learning.

In order to see gains in achievement and motivation outside of the intervention, instruction and materials need to be engaging, as Guthrie (1996) cautioned us:

> When children read merely to complete an assignment, with no sense of involvement or curiosity, they are being compliant. They conform to the demands of the situation irrespective of their personal goals. Compliant students are not likely to become lifelong learners. (p. 433)

When we inundate older struggling readers with superficial and lifeless reading and writing tasks that bear no resemblance to the reading and writing they encounter in the real world, we ensure their status as outsiders to the real literate community. We have a hard time finding studies of adolescent literacy these days that do not highlight the critical role of engagement and particularly the importance of using interesting reading materials (e.g., Ivey & Broaddus, 2001; Worthy, Moorman, & Turner, 1999). Effective instruction for all adolescents focuses on their personal interests and incorporates diverse reading materials such as trade books and the digital texts they read on their own (Alvermann, 2002), and this is no less true for inexperienced older readers and writers.

4. Interventions Should Be Driven By Useful and Relevant Assessments

How can we determine what students need from an intervention? Often, standardized tests are used to place students in special reading programs. Then, with commercial intervention programs, one of two scenarios may be encountered. The first is that the program is designed so that everyone starts at the same level, with an initial focus on fundamental skills followed by a progression toward more sophisticated skills. The second scenario is that the program comes with an assessment that places each student in a particular strand or level within it. Unfortunately, neither of these scenarios helps us to determine what students need to progress in real reading and writing.

Research studies and individual student descriptions of recent years (e.g., Alvermann, 2001; Ivey, 1999; Knobel, 2001; Rubenstein-Avila, 2003/2004) leave us with an instructional challenge that is difficult to ignore: Older struggling readers are extremely complex, and to meet their needs we must take a closer and more sophisticated look at their literate strengths, needs, and preferences. This means that in addition to good initial assessments (e.g., an informal reading inventory, spelling inventory, writing samples, interviews, observations), ongoing assessments will be necessary to determine students' purposes for reading and writing, what they already do, and where they could use some help.

To fully understand the needs of students within an intervention, we have to see them engaging in literate tasks in a variety of contexts, including diverse print and electronic reading materials, and for a variety of purposes, including reasons for reading and writing outside of school. It is doubtful that paying close and deliberate attention to students will result in the simplistic conclusion that students are simply poor decoders or poor comprehenders. In fact, purchasing, adopting, or designing an intervention without this kind of information would likely be a waste of teacher energy, student time, and fiscal resources.

5. The Intervention Should Include Significant Opportunities for Authentic Reading and Writing

We do not know of any cases of older struggling readers who became better readers by *not* reading. On the other hand, we have strong evidence to suggest that time spent reading separates good readers from poor readers (Allington, 2001). If we want low-achieving readers to become more like successful readers, any intervention ought to include many opportunities for students to actually read. In fact, it should be the focal point of the instructional time. Unfortunately, many middle and high school students who are still struggling may have been assigned to special reading programs in the elementary grades that focused on skill-and-drill activities to the exclusion of authentic reading and writing (Johnston & Allington, 1991).

Working on skills and strategies should facilitate real reading and writing. It should take place in the context of activities where students actually need to know how to use the skills and strategies and have purposes for using them. Furthermore, the amount of time students spend reading and writing (and here we mean *engaged* in reading and writing) ought to substantially outweigh the amount of time students spend considering skills and strategies related to literacy. For instance, during a 45-minute session, we imagine a student spending at least 30 minutes actually reading.

EXAMINING THE GUIDELINES IN CONTEXT

To help consider how these guidelines for intervention might apply in a real classroom, we offer two glimpses of instruction with students whose experiences and profiles probably resemble those of many struggling readers in secondary programs. Our first scenario demonstrates an intervention that likely has little productive impact on the student receiving it, while the second scenario includes characteristics of interventions that make a difference.

The Case of Anthony

Anthony is an African American male who attends a large urban school. He is 16 years old and has failed ninth grade. He has no identified disabilities. This high school is the third he has attended; he has attended a total of 12 schools between first and ninth grade. He lives with his mother and five siblings in a one-bedroom apartment. He saw his father get shot on the street during a drug-related transaction. Anthony consistently performs at the fourth-grade level on reading assessments. He writes sentence fragments and does not spell well. In fact, he often misspells common sight words such as *when*, *there*, and *once*.

The school Anthony attends has purchased a computerized reading intervention program and Anthony is scheduled into the computer room for intervention one period per day. He also has an English class in addition to his content area classes. The school provides 20 minutes per day of self-selected reading, and Anthony can often be found reading the sports page of the newspaper or one of the many sports magazines in the room. Using the five criteria outlined above as talking points, Anthony, the reading specialist, and an administrator discussed the reading intervention program.

The reading specialist noted that the web-based computer program did not require any support or time from an adult, but instead that "students just sit down at the computer and begin working." The administrator asked how the specialist knew Anthony was being challenged and how lessons were planned based on his skills. The reading specialist replied that there was a series of lessons through which all students had to progress.

Observing Anthony confirmed the reports from the school staff. He was engaged with the computer program and said, "Reading is easy." The computer program introduced him to three sight words—*I*, *you*, and *was*. He clicked on each word as the computer said that word, then he moved on to sentences. There were blank lines in the sentences and Anthony was asked to identify the missing word. The first sentence was "The cub gets a rug." The second sentence was "The cat gets a nap." The third sentence was "Ron has a dip in the _____." His choices were *van*, *fox*, and *tub*. We asked Anthony to select the wrong answer. He chose

van. The computer said, "Nope, that's not it," and read the sentence again. We did this 11 more times. The computer offered no assistance or guidance. The same sentence, with the same choices, was offered to Anthony over and over again. He would have to use process of elimination, and not reading, if he were to answer correctly and move on. The program did not require Anthony to use the sight words that were presented in the sentences he was reading.

Back in the office, we continued our conversation and our evaluation of this program. While we agreed that the text selections were not very engaging, the graphics, music, and voice on this particular program were very engaging for adolescents. Our conversation focused on the fact that students progress through the program in the same sequence, regardless of their current level of performance. Anthony's assessments indicated that he read at approximately the fourth-grade level but wrote very poorly. The intervention activities we observed were nowhere near his instructional level.

The reading specialist confirmed that the intervention was not driven by assessment data and that the program could not provide the instructional support Anthony needed when he did not answer correctly. She also noted that he was not required to read any authentic texts as part of this program.

Given this assessment of the intervention program, we had to ask ourselves what to do. While Anthony enjoyed his time on the computer and felt successful, we did not have any evidence that he was reading better or more as a result. The reading specialist noted that she would have to start by adding independent reading time to the class as well as providing some individual instruction in writing for Anthony. Clearly, much more thought would need to go into effective intervention for Anthony and his classmates.

The Case of Raquel

Raquel is a seventh grader who reads far below grade level. She has been in the United States since she was 6 years old, after crossing the border illegally. She has yet to be redesignated as fluent English proficient and has been identified as "intermediate" in her language proficiency for several years. She lives with her brother and his wife, as her parents did not make it across the border. She has attended two middle schools and four elementary schools thus far in her schooling experience. Her current middle school educates over 1,200 students in grades 6–8. The school operates on a 4 × 4 block schedule with each class lasting 90 minutes. This term, Raquel has English/genre, science, English language development, and math. She attends an after-school program funded by the U.S. Department of Education. The first 90 minutes of the after-school program focus on tutoring and homework assistance and the remaining two hours are designated for social and recreational activities. Raquel regularly selects music and art for her activities following tutoring.

Raquel receives 20–30 minutes per day of individualized instruction as part of her after-school program. In addition, she reads for 20–30 minutes of the period and completes center activities and tasks with a small group of students for the remaining time. During each school day, Raquel participates in 15 minutes of Silent Sustained Reading (SSR). Raquel likes to read series books and is currently on the fourth Series of Unfortunate Events book. She talks with her peers about these books and was overheard telling Zenaida that she practices reading the books at school so that she can read them at night at home.

In addition to the SSR time, part of Raquel's intervention time is devoted to independent reading. In both SSR and independent reading, students read books on their own. The difference is in the book selection. During SSR time, Raquel selects any reading material she wants. During independent reading, the teacher narrows the choices to texts that are at Raquel's independent reading level and that are based on the topics that Raquel is reading during her intervention. The books that Raquel reads during the after-school reading intervention program are often shorter and can be read in a single sitting.

Looking through the book bin at titles that have been set aside for Raquel, it is easy to see that she enjoys music and art. The books include *Lives of the Artists* (Krull, 1995), *Lives of the Musicians* (Krull, 1993), *Frida* (Winter, 2002), *My Name Is Georgia* (Winter, 1998), and *When Marian Sang* (Ryan, 2002). As Raquel stated when asked about the number of books chosen for her, "I didn't know they had so many girl artists . . . I didn't read books in my other school, only these papers the teacher gave us."

According to her intervention teacher, the center activities add to Raquel's understanding of language and focus on "the structure and function of the English language." This is part of the focused English-language development curriculum for the school (Dutro & Moran, 2003). There are a number of centers in the room, including word sorts, listening stations with books on CDs, and grammar games. As we entered the room, we noticed that Raquel was at a table with three other students. They were each reading picture books with Role, Audience, Format, Topic (RAFT) writing prompts written on the inside. RAFT writing prompts help writers take perspective and write to different audiences (Santa & Havens, 1995). Raquel was working on a RAFT that is written inside the wordless picture book *You Can't Take a Balloon Into the Metropolitan Museum* (Weitzman & Glasser, 1998) and read:

R - balloon

A - tourists

F - postcard

T - why you should visit the Metropolitan

Raquel worked busily, trying to fit her ideas into the space of a postcard. She rewrote her sentences to be as concise as possible until she was called by the teacher for her individualized instruction.

During the individualized reading intervention, Raquel practiced her part in a Readers Theatre script. Repeated readings, an integral part of the Readers Theatre experience, are an effective and purposeful means for building reading fluency (Worthy & Broaddus, 2001/2002). During this particular week, Raquel and a group of her classmates in the after-school program were preparing to present a portion of *Zin! Zin! Zin! A Violin* (Moss, 1995) to the other students and teachers. In this rhyming picture book, 10 instruments are introduced one by one in a musical performance. The performance will begin with one voice—the trombone—and a new voice will be added as the next instrument is described.

Before Raquel practiced her part, her teacher reads the entire book to her, modeling fluency and appropriate expression. Afterward, they talk about unfamiliar vocabulary (e.g., *valves, bleating, mournful*). In a second journey through the book, Raquel and her teacher take turns reading. Then they read the book in unison. During each successive reading, Raquel's confidence and fluency improve.

As Raquel began to practice her assigned part for the Readers Theatre, her teacher noted some ways she could read the passage to make it more engaging and comprehensible to the audience. For example, Raquel had to read, "Now, a mellow friend, the cello, neck extended, bows a hello" (p. 7). In her initial reading, Raquel read *cello* and *hello* with similar intonation. Her teacher pointed out to her that it would be more effective to read *hello* as if she were actually using it in a conversational greeting, with an emphasis on the final *o*. Raquel agreed and incorporated this into her performance.

Following our observation of the class and the systems of support provided to Raquel, we met with the school's reading specialist. While not a "perfect" intervention, the support provided to Raquel required significant teacher involvement—from selecting texts, to modeling, to providing feedback, to gradually releasing responsibility in reading to the student. Raquel received many opportunities for real reading and writing, and the texts used for instruction clearly interested Raquel and were often connected by

subject. Initial and ongoing assessments helped Raquel's teacher find materials that made sense to Raquel. Also, to a large degree, what we typically think of as "components" of the reading process were addressed within the context of more substantial, purposeful, and connected reading and writing experiences (e.g., fluency practice was embedded within a Readers Theatre activity).

Although it is likely that Raquel will need even more explanations and modeling from the teacher regarding vocabulary, fluency, and comprehension within the context of reading and writing, this time after school is well spent. The differences between Anthony's experiences and Raquel's experiences are substantial, and it is possible to predict that Raquel will make greater strides in literacy in terms of achievement and motivation.

KEEPING AN EYE ON QUALITY CONTROL

Having extra time set aside to focus on literacy is truly beneficial for older struggling readers and their teachers. Interventions that are antitheoretical or ineffective, however, may do more harm than good. When adolescents still learning to read and write show no real progress with program after program, it is tempting for us to sigh, "We've tried everything," and move on to students who seem more "teachable." Furthermore, students who experience no identifiable changes in their reading and writing despite the school's efforts begin to feel hopeless about becoming more literate (Kos, 1991).

In middle and high schools, we have somewhat of a "Catch-22." We know that when it comes to improving literacy, teachers—not methods or materials—make the most difference (Duffy & Hoffman, 1999). But how often do secondary teachers really get an opportunity to learn about supporting literacy development? Building teacher expertise is our most formidable long-term challenge, and that should be an ongoing process for schools.

As we think about our current students, however, good interventions *can* make a difference. If your school is presently looking to implement programs or frameworks for instruction, we hope you will consider the guiding principles we shared in this article as well as the rubric found in Figure 23.1. If you are currently using a program or if you must select from an approved list of programs, use the principles for assessment and decide what

kind of instruction you will need in addition to what you already have.

In our experiences as teachers of older struggling readers and as researchers, we have not yet come across students who absolutely could not grow as readers and writers. We are also certain that we have not "tried everything," as we continue to grow as teachers and as we encounter new adolescent learners who cause us to be more reflective and responsive.

Do the intervention initiatives cause students to read more and better?

	5	4	3	2	1
4.1 Level of teacher involvement	Significant teacher involvement in the design and delivery of the intervention		Some teacher oversight but the majority of the program is delivered by volunteers or paraprofessionals		Limited or no teacher involvement; intervention is delivered in the absence of a teacher (e.g., computer-only programs or take-home workbooks)
4.2 Intervention reflects a comprehensive approach to reading and writing	Intervention is comprehensive and integrated such that students experience reading and writing as a cohesive whole		Intervention includes important components of the reading processes but addresses them separately (e.g., 15 minutes of word study followed by an unrelated comprehension activity); either reading or writing are addressed, but not both		Intervention focuses on an isolated skill (e.g., topic sentence) or singular aspect of literacy development (e.g., phonics, phonemic awareness, fluency, vocabulary, comprehension)
4.3 Intervention reading and writing is engaging	Authentic children's and adolescent literature (fiction and nonfiction) are at the core of the intervention		Isolated paragraphs on topics selected by intervention program		Artificial text; no connected text; skills work

(Continued)

Figure 23.1 (Continued)

	5	4	3	2	1
4.4 Intervention instruction is driven by useful and relevant assessments	Teacher-administered assessments are ongoing and are used to tailor individual instruction; writing samples and text-based discussions are one type of assessment used		Uniform assessments are used for placement, program entry, and program exit		All students start at the same point and move through the intervention components regardless of their individual performance
4.5 Intervention includes significant opportunities for authentic reading and writing	The majority of intervention time is devoted to authentic reading and writing		Periodic opportunities are provided for students to read or write		No connected reading and writing is provided or required (e.g., sole focus on word-level activities or skills worksheets)

Figure 23.1   Intervention and Support for Struggling Readers

SOURCE: Ivey, G., & Fisher, D. (2006). *Creating Literacy-Rich Schools for Adolescents*. Alexandria, VA: Association for Supervision and Curriculum Development.

Douglas Fisher teaches at San Diego State University. He may be contacted at 4283 El Cajon Boulevard, #100, San Diego, CA 92105, USA. E-mail dfisher@mail.sdsu.edu. Ivey teaches at James Madison University.

Section VIII

WRITING

OVERVIEW

This section focuses on the trends in writing research and instruction during a time when "demand for written communication has never been higher," according to Juzwik et al. (2006), in their article "Writing Into the 21st Century: An Overview of Research on Writing, 1999 to 2004." In addition to an overview of the research literature, Cappello (2005) and Whitney et al. (2008) offer specific instructional recommendations to meet the multifaceted needs of literacy learners developing writing skills in your classrooms.

In "Supporting Independent Writing: A Continuum of Writing Instruction," Cappello (2005) situates writing instruction within the Gradual Release of Responsibility model you have read about in previous sections of this reader. She suggests specific instructional settings to meet individual learners' needs across the instructional continuum. In their article, "Beyond Strategies: Teacher Practice, Writing Process, and the Influence of Inquiry," Whitney and colleagues (2008) address the many variations in what teachers identify as "process writing" in their classrooms. The authors discuss the differences in two teachers' instructional practices regarding their methods for "preparing students to write, developing a piece of writing over time, and encouraging student investment and independence in writing."

Included in this section (available at http://www.sagepub.com/cappello/) is a survey on the research on writing. The article by Juzwik et al (2006) takes a broad look at the contemporary research literature on writing to determine the differences in the last decade of practice. Their analysis yielded several important categories that may suggest changes in the ways literacy researchers understand writing. Those dimensions include "problems studied, population age groups studied, and methods used."

STRATEGY

The articles in this section focus on writing research and instructional practice. Use the "Concept Guide" (Spencer & Guillaume, 2009) during and immediately after you read the articles. Content guides are usually used by teachers to support independent reading of content material and may have two or three parts, including true-false statements, cloze sentences, and a categorizing activity. The purpose of the Concept Guide is to help students organize information and illuminate the relationships between new words and concepts found in the text. Completing this strategy will encourage deeper idea development.

CONCEPT GUIDE

(Spencer & Guillaume, 2009)

DIRECTIONS

Part One: Indicate in the left column which of the following sentences are true. Create true statements from those you consider false.

Statements	True?
1. Writing process research dominates contemporary studies on writing pedagogy.	
2. A sociocultural view of writing considers the co-construction of texts.	
3. There is no need to differentiate writing in the ways we do reading instruction. The products created by students already differentiate.	
4. Patterned writing activities are student-responsible tasks.	
5. Writing pedagogy and practice has a long history in literacy research.	
6. Writing products make effective authentic assessments.	
7. Writing programs tend to construct their own understandings of what "writers' workshop" means.	
8. Research on composing and instruction cannot provide prescriptions of proven techniques that work for all learners.	

Statements	True?
9. Process-oriented approaches to writing emphasize invention and revision.	
10. There is still no research to show that process-oriented approaches to writing instruction benefit student achievement.	

Part Two: Reread all of the (now) true statements above. Decide which of the following categories the statements belong in:

Writing Research
Writing Pedagogy

Use a highlighter to indicate which category you feel each statement best belongs in.

SOURCE: Spencer, B. H., & Guillaume, A. M. (2009). *Thirty-Five Strategies for Developing Content Area Vocabulary.* Boston: Allyn & Bacon.

Article 24

SUPPORTING INDEPENDENT WRITING

A Continuum of Writing Instruction

MARVA CAPPELLO

Every teacher knows the ultimate goal of education is student independence. Contemporary understandings of the teaching and learning process highlight the multiple roles teachers enact in their classrooms to support their students' journey toward independence (e.g., coach, facilitator, model, informant). A major theoretical influence on our growing knowledge of the social nature of teaching/learning is the work of Lev Vygotsky. Most applicable to this paper is the zone of proximal development (ZPD). Vygotsky (1978) described the ZPD as "the distance between the actual development level as determined by independent problem solving and the level of potential development as determined through problem solving under adult guidance or in collaboration with more capable peers" (p. 86). Teachers frequently (though not exclusively) serve as the "more capable other" to

scaffold their students' efforts and approximations toward independence.

Many of the teachers I work with in an urban district-university partnership are focusing attention on classroom writing instruction, concerned that their students lack the necessary skills needed to be successful across curricular domains. Indeed, several of the schools in this partnership have decided to make writing their schoolwide focus. It is not just the teachers in this district that have shifted their thinking. "Professional insights into writing and its development may have produced one of the last century's most significant changes in primary pedagogy" (Roser and Bomer, 2005, p. 26).

The recent National Assessment of Educational Progress (NAEP) report confirms growing concerns regarding student writing. Although the 2002 data reported an increase in student performance

SOURCE: Cappello, M. (2005). Supporting Independent Writing: A Continuum of Writing Instruction. *California Reader, 39*(2), 38–46. Reprinted by permission of California Reading Association.

in grades 4 and 8, approximately two thirds of our nation's young writers performed below Proficient levels—defined as being able to write an "organized and cohesive response" (National Center for Education Statistics, 2002). In the state of California, average scores for fourth (146) and eighth (144) grades are lower than the national avenges (154 and 153 respectively). Contributing to the problem may be the reality that most credential programs in California do not offer writing methods courses, and many teachers were exempt from basic writing skill classes in their own undergraduate programs. Thus, teachers may be unfamiliar with best practices in writing and writing instruction.

The purpose of this paper is to present a structure to help teachers promote the writing independence of their students. The framework presented here organizes classroom-writing instruction to meet individual needs using varying degrees of teacher support. In the discussion that follows, each writing scaffold across the continuum is supported by a description, an explicit classroom scenario, and a rationale for use.

THE WRITING INSTRUCTION CONTINUUM

Pearson and Gallagher have stated that "any academic task can be conceptualized as requiring different proportions of teacher and student responsibility for successful completion" (1983, p. 337). Based upon the classic gradual release model introduced by Pearson and Gallagher

(1983), the continuum presented here organizes instructional approaches according to the degree of teacher support provided. Other models (Duke and Pearson, 2002; Fisher and Frey, 2003; Fountas and Pinnell, 1996) describe a shift of responsibility (or control) from the teacher to student. A predominant goal of each instructional approach is student independence; they result in children's ability to transfer skills to their independent writing. Researchers and teachers understand that students need different levels of support within a "region of shared responsibility" (Duke and Pearson, 2002, p. 210) toward children's application of new knowledge and skills, that is independent writing. The instructional situations presented in this paper collectively represent a "journey" from interdependence toward independence.

Table 24.1 visually displays the roles and responsibilities for teachers and students in a wide range of classroom writing experiences and provides teachers an organization that aids their decision making as they plan to help all students become independent writers. Examples where teachers take on roles where they are responsible for task completion are at one end of the continuum. At the other end of the continuum are instructional approaches that prompt students to primary responsibility toward their independent writing. In the middle of the continuum are ideas that share the responsibility between both teacher and student. All of the instructional approaches described are vehicles for helping students learn and practice the skills and strategies needed to become independent writers.

Table 24.1   Writing Instruction Continuum

Patterned Writing Given Word Sentences	Interactive Writing Guided Writing Dialogue	Drop Everything and Write (DEW Time)
Teacher-Responsible Tasks	Shared-Responsibility Tasks	Student-Responsible Tasks

Examples of Teacher-Responsible Tasks

On the far left of the continuum are instructional approaches that provide opportunities for teacher modeling. These instructional approaches demonstrate how "when the teacher is taking all or most of the responsibility for task completion, he is 'modeling' or demonstrating the desired application of some strategy" (Pearson and Gallagher, 1983, p. 337).

Patterned Writing

Books may also serve as models for developing writers. Patterned writing activities require students to follow a teacher-created template that is closely aligned with the original pattern in the book. Usually, students complete open sentences with words or phrases of their own choosing. Predictable, simple structures or patterned books provide a model that is easily emulated by young writers. For example, the following writing activity borrows a pattern from *It Looked Like Spilt Milk*, by Charles G. Shaw (1947). First, students create their own "spilt milk" using white paint on blue paper mimicking illustrations in the original text. After students decide what their "milk" painting resembles, they complete the teacher created sentence frame based on the original text.

Sometimes it looked like _____, but it wasn't _____.

Teacher may use patterned writing to teach text structures, parts of speech or a variety of other skills. In addition, pages may be assembled into a book for use in shared or independent reading.

Given Word Sentences

Recent research (Fearn and Farnan, 2001) points to effective instruction for the craft of writing. An excellent example from their book *Interactions: Teaching Writing and the Language Arts,* takes teachers through the steps of how to engage students in thinking about how to construct sentences. Sentence thinking is not intuitive, yet it is an essential element in becoming a writer. "The sentence is where writing begins. People who can write a sentence can write" (p. 82).

Sentence thinking can be a difficult task for students without explicit support from teachers. "The Given Word Sentence—a sentence that contains a given or dictated word—is a *deliberate* opportunity for young writers to think *deliberately* at the sentence level" (Fearn and Farnan, 2001, p. 87, italics in the original). For example, the students in one fourth grade class were asked to think of a sentence that contains the word *mountain* (a vocabulary word important to their unit on California geography). Students were given time to create deliberate sentences in their heads before I asked for their responses to transcribe on the board. This reinforces that writing is thinking. I repeated students' sentences, modeling what sentences sound like. Several students make contributions, all variations, yet all containing the given word. Two of their responses were: "I live near a mountain." "The mountain has snow on top."

Given Word Sentences may require more specifics such as sentence length or word placement. The same students were asked to create a five-word sentence that contains the word mountain. This time their responses included: "I see a big mountain." "I live near Cowles Mountain." Another possible variation would include asking students to create a five-word sentence that contains mountain in the third position. One appropriate response would be "The big mountain is snowy." Giving students a place to start allows young authors the necessary support for planning and writing sentences.

Examples of Shared Responsibility Tasks

Tasks found in the middle of the continuum are the instructional approaches that share the responsibility between both teacher and student. These variations on classroom writing offer hidden and diverse ways to offer students support within a "region of shared responsibility" (Duke and Pearson, 2002, p. 210). These approaches shift the responsibility for task completion from the teacher to the student. The overriding goal remains application of new knowledge and skills, that is, independent practice.

Dialogue Journals

Dialogue journals are written authentic conversations between students and teachers. Every student corresponds with the teacher in his or her own journal. Entries take the form of a friendly letter and may address personal or academic matters. Teachers reply without correcting student mistakes on their pages. Instead, they respond to the students' letters with praise and support, sometimes offering clarification and "indirect editing" (Bode, 1989, p. 570) as they model academic and conventional writing. Response length and complexity are dictated by student's needs and abilities. Indeed, dialogue journals provide personalized responses that enable teachers to subtly differentiate instruction for individual students. The dialogue journal in Table 24.2 illustrates one first grader's literacy abilities.

It is evident from this example that Mitchell is learning conversation skills and the basic format of a friendly letter. He benefited from having specific and individualized responses to his letters. His strengths and weaknesses could be assessed and addressed in the context of the dialogue journal. Teachers respond to students with varied levels of support.

Teachers may consider using dialogue journals when they want to build rapport, teach conversation skills, connect oral and written language, and meet children's individual needs by evaluating writing created in authentic situations. "How a teacher responds to students' journal letters is a key component of personalized learning" (Werderich, 2002, p. 753).

Interactive Writing

Like the language experience approach and shared writing, interactive writing uses transcriptions of students' oral compositions as materials for instruction (Aston-Warner, 1963; McKenzie, 1985; Snuffer, 1970). Shared writing takes a step toward independence when we include the students in the negotiation of the collectively composed text. Interactive writing moves us further along the continuum when we include the

Table 24.2   Dialogue Journals

1/16	1/20
Dear Mitchell,	Dear Mrs. L,
What are you going to do this weekend? How did you like the assembly? I think Mr. L and I are going to watch a movie this weekend.	What movie did you and Mr. L go to? I met an author at the bookstore. He talked about writing books. I played basketball.
Love, Mrs. L	Love, Mitchell
1/21	1/23
Dear Mitchell,	Dear Mrs. L,
Mr. L and I watched a movie called Good Will Hunting. It was about a guy who is a genius and about friendships. Do you want to write books when you are an adult? What would you write about?	When I grow up I would want to write a book after I do my basketball career. I would write about my basketball career. I would want to play on the LA LAKERS. What is your favorite team in the *NBA*?
Love, Mrs. L	Love, Mitchell

students in the transcription of the text. There is a physical difference in interactive writing; students share the pen (Pinnell & McCarrier, 1994). This instructional approach increases student responsibility for the writing process with the teacher facilitating the experience as she provides for individual needs.

As students write with the teacher, they make a wide range of contributions: a kindergartner may add the first letter in his name, a fourth grader may add a prefix or dialogue marker. The teacher continues to do some of the writing to help with lesson pacing and to provide a scaffold for students.

The text in Table 24.3 was created interactively with Mrs. L's first grade literacy learners. This text was composed after a series of literacy lessons linked by the common theme of "names."

Despite an earlier lesson on the apostrophe, the first grader who wrote "Mrs. L." did not make it a possessive. Another student was called to the chart to help correct and co-write the text. Students do not correct each other during interactive writing; they support each other as they take increasing responsibility for their writing. One student correctly contributed the word "people," another was able to write the number 6, and still another first grader served as the two-finger space holder between words. Whenever the task was beyond what the students could do, the teacher supported their writing efforts by guiding authors to the necessary information. This interactive writing experience provided different opportunities for students to participate at their own level.

One of the most significant benefits of interactive writing is that it "provides opportunities for teachers to engage in instruction precisely at the point of student need" (Button, Johnson, and Furgerson, 1996). With the help of the teacher,

students immediately repair mistakes using correction tape or fluid. The teacher may use the "teachable moment" to demonstrate a phonics principle, appropriate grammar, or comprehension skill for the class. As students construct texts, teachers use direct questioning to create specific situations for instruction.

Interactive writing may be used to demonstrate concepts about print and "how words work" (Fountas and Pinnell, 1996, p. 23). This instructional approach is also an effective way to teach and reinforce sound/print correspondences (phonics) and provides an authentic opportunity to assess children's writing skills and strategies. As children construct texts, the teacher records anecdotal notes that inform instructional plans for individual students. This method also provides two unique advantages for students and teachers. First, interactive writing models student generated academic writing. Students need to see capable writers in their peers and not just their teachers. Finally, while dialogue journals differentiate for all students by meeting individual children at their place of need, interactive writing meets them at the time of need.

Guided Writing

Some researchers use the term *guided writing* synonymously with writing workshop because the teacher's role is to guide writers through the process (Fountas and Pinnell, 1996). In this article, guided writing refers to the instructional approach where children borrow form or content from a piece of literature. Children respond to the literature by emulating the author's work. The broader goal of this imitative experience is the development of writing competencies for transfer to other writing contexts, in independent practice.

Table 24.3   Interactive Writing

Names

Most of our names in Mrs. L's class have six 6 letters. Nine students have Aa in their name. Four people have the letter D. We read Tikki Tikki Tembo.

Since one overriding goal of instruction is transfer, lesson topics always reflect the repeatable and reproducible aspects of text (Wertsch, 1998). Teachers must carefully coordinate literature to focus lessons on the salient text traits such as descriptive language, lead sentences, etc. Focus lessons resemble the traditional lesson models talked about by many writing researchers (Calkins, 1986; Graves, 1994; Atwell, 1987) but are always connected back to the piece of literature at the core of instruction.

The following lesson was taught in many primary classrooms throughout southern California after being shared in professional development through the California Reading and Literature Project. The samples in Table 24.4 were collected from one second/third grade combination class in urban Los Angeles where children were working on ways to make their writing more descriptive. Their appropriations are based on Sandra Cisneros' *Hairs/Pelitos* (1994).

These English Language Learners benefited from the models provided in the original text and wrote descriptive narratives, sometimes using similes, in response to the literature. Typically, teachers chose topics for guided writing lessons that were "craft" centered, focusing on stylistic attributes writers employ in communicating their message to readers (Giacobe, 1981). Activities may also focus on structural analysis, grammar or text conventions such as punctuation. Essentially, students respond to the literature in writing, trying to emulate the author's use of features highlighted during the lesson sequence.

Examples of Student-Responsible Tasks

Independent writing happens when children have the opportunity to make all the decisions about writing, including form, function and audience. Truly independent writing opportunities are rare in school settings. Here is one suggestion that provides time for students to be independent writers.

Drop Everything and Write (DEW Time)

Drop Everything and Write (DEW time) offers one way to focus on independent writing. During DEW time, students write for their own intentions. Some classrooms manage this brief writing time by enforcing a "pencil is going" rule but leave task decisions to the students. Students may choose to write whatever they want as long as the teacher sees a pencil or pen moving across the page (see Table 24.5).

Table 24.4   Guided Writing

Original Text Hairs/Pelitos	Student One's Response	Student Two's Response	Student Three's Response
My papa's hair is like a broom, all up in the air.	My dad's eyes sparkle like the beach water in the night.	My father's eyes are like almonds.	My father's eyes shine like glass. My brother's eyes are like sticky mud, they are very brown.
An me, my hair is lazy . . .	Me, my eyes are brown as a tree trunk		
And Kiki who is the youngest has hair like fur.		Gerald, who has eyes like a crow . . .	
But my mother's hair, my mother's hair, like little rosettes . . . like little candy circles . . .	But mom's eyes are cocoa brown like a coconut up, up in a tree		

Table 24.5 DEW Time

Dear M,

Will you meet me on the playground after school? Circle one.

Yes No

Love, J

Children may work in their journals, on stories started in workshop or may even be permitted to practice handwriting activities. Independent writing should be student generated.

One second/third grade combination class engaged in DEW time for approximately 15 minutes once or twice weekly. The favored writing activity during this time was note passing. The children wrote and responded to notes passed during DEW time after their teacher allowed it to become an official school activity. Students wrote short friendly letters to their classmates asking quick questions and getting quick responses. As they wrote, the students borrowed elements they learned from other classroom activities. They even appropriated elements from the standardized assessments they were practicing for.

The teacher's role in successful independent writing is to provide a range of resources and the time dedicated to engage in the activity. Independent writing should not comprise a large section of a writing instructional program,

however, it is important that it allows children to try out independent writing in school where it is safe and they know they can get support if needed.

DISCUSSION

Like practices advocated by Fisher and Frey (2003), the instructional continuum presented here advocates for a "connected and coordinated literacy curriculum—one that has significant emphasis on writing instruction" (p. 404) while at the same time varying the level of teacher support. The shifting responsibility represented in the Writing Instruction Continuum allows teachers a way to plan and differentiate instruction for all student writers. Teachers will want to develop the kinds of structures that create situations that provide the appropriate level of support for individual learners in their classrooms. As demonstrated by the examples above, writing instruction can be planned to provide individualized support leading toward independence in writing.

The instructional methods described here also provide products for use as assessments. By consistently supporting children's efforts along the writing continuum, teachers can easily track individuals' progress over time, establish goals for learning and effectively decide what to plan and teach.

Marva Cappello is Assistant Professor of Teacher Education at San Diego State University.

Article 25

BEYOND STRATEGIES

Teacher Practice, Writing Process, and the Influence of Inquiry

ANNE WHITNEY, SHERIDAN BLAU, ALISON BRIGHT, ROSEMARY CABE, TIM DEWAR, JASON LEVIN, ROSEANNE MACIAS, AND PAUL ROGERS

In 1982, Maxine Hairston claimed that a dozen years of research and development in the files of composition and rhetoric—most notably the development of a process-centered theory of teaching writing—were sufficiently revolutionary to mark the beginnings of what amounted to (citing Kuhn, 1962) "the first stages of a paradigm shift" (77) in which a current-traditional paradigm emphasizing style, organization, and correctness with respect to conventions was giving way to a process-oriented one emphasizing invention and revision. She cited factors propelling this shift, which included such events as the onset of open admission policies and their attendant sense of a "writing crisis," the success of the Bay Area Writing Project, and most particularly the emergence of research investigating writing processes as initiated by Emig (1971), Britton (1975), and Shaughnessy (1977) and, by 1982, carried on by the work of scholars like Perl (1979), Flower and Hayes (1980), Sommers (1980), Faigley and Witte (1981), and Pianko (1979). Hairston also noted the continuing development of research in composition, the emergence of graduate programs in rhetoric, and the increasing interest of textbook publishers in what this new scholarship had to offer as further evidence of a seismic change in the field of composition studies. She predicted too that "the change will even reach into some high schools because one large company has hired one of the country's leading rhetoricians"

SOURCE: Whitney, A., et al. (2008). Beyond Strategies: Teacher Practice, Writing Process, and the Influence of Inquiry. *English Education, 40*(3), 201–232. Copyright © 2008 by the National Council of Teachers of English. Reprinted by permission.

(87) to shape its high school texts, and she issued a challenge to the field to further this development so that a feasible and coherent approach to teaching writing would be available to the non-specialists who do the writing instruction in schools and colleges around the country.

Now, twenty-five years later, it is apparent that Hairston's vision of a dramatically changing academic field was entirely accurate. Composition has continued to develop as a distinct field of inquiry. It has developed graduate programs, writing departments, and a rich fabric of approaches to theorizing and researching writing and to practicing its teaching, all of which represent a departure from earlier knowledge and practices amounting to a virtual paradigm shift in the field. With respect to the writing process in particular, a new well-established body of research demonstrates that process-oriented writing instruction benefits student achievement in writing (for a recent review, see Pritchard & Honeycutt, 2006). Process-oriented terms and concepts have entered the material environment of America's schools, in textbooks and curricula even where the theoretical bases underlying those materials might appear to conflict with it, such as materials in which priority is placed on rhetorical modes, form, or grammatical correctness. Even in settings where no one would explicitly claim to embrace a "process pedagogy," classrooms exhibit some of its markers: students and teachers use words like "drafts," "prewriting," and "revision" in commonplace speech.

Yet, though it is now difficult to imagine any language arts teacher at any grade level not knowing about "the writing process," many of the teaching practices employed in classrooms in the name of "the writing process" suggest that teachers may have different understandings about what the writing process entails as a model of writing and learning to write, conceptually or epistemologically. What "prewriting" means in classrooms, for example, may differ. Most teachers know about different strategies for prewriting, but differences appear in how teachers and school programs construct their own understanding of what prewriting means. Thus in some classrooms prewriting represents a seemingly loose, exploratory period of ruminating and listing ideas, while in others it is the preparation of a formal outline for a grade. In one setting, the term "writing process" suggests a writer's workshop in which students choose topics and self-select writing tasks freely (e.g., Atwell, 1987); in other classrooms, it denotes a lockstep set of tasks to be completed on the way to an essay on a teacher-assigned topic. Thus "process" terminology and classroom practices can saturate many school settings, yet what these terms mean and the actual content and tenor of writing instruction in those settings vary widely, particularly in regard to the recursive nature of the writing process and the ways writing tasks are framed for students. "The writing process" is framed in some classrooms as a series of assignments or, in others, as a recursive, fluid activity in which writers engage differently as rhetorical situations vary.

The Bay Area Writing Project, though formally eschewing any endorsement of any particular approach to teaching or any theory of instruction, throughout the 1970s shaped the practices that came to represent the National Writing Project (NWP) model for professional development, strongly influenced both by the notion of "writing process" as articulated by Elbow and others and by a sociocultural view of writing: thinking of texts as co-constructed and of writers as the members of discourse communities or communities of practice. Vygotsky, Bruner, and Moffett's approaches (discussed in Blau, 2003) are often blended in "standard" Writing Project practice, but it is important to note that what is "standard" in Writing Project practice stems not from any official endorsement of an approach or theoretical stance but instead from a set of traditions and influences that are subtly changed from year to year by the teachers who may bring into the project ideas from their own classroom settings.

Our aim in this article is to present and discuss case studies of two teachers, drawn from a larger study, who represent different ways of envisioning and enacting a process-influenced pedagogy, one who worked with the South Coast Writing Project in an inquiry-oriented inservice program and one who did not. These two teachers work in similar school settings with similar kinds of students and similar (in some instances identical) district-provided writing curricula, yet their differing approaches to the "same" classroom strategies suggest how NWP-influenced professional development might continue to influence even basic practice in the teaching of writing.

BACKGROUND

The South Coast Writing Project (SCWriP) has been active in working with teachers in a three-county area in Southern California since 1979, serving over 500 area teachers in its Summer Institute and thousands more in its open institutes, classes, and school-based professional development programs. In addition to this direct influence on the professional development of teachers in the region, SCWriP also influences the credential program at the University of California, Santa Barbara. That program involves teacher candidates in workshops on the teaching of writing led by "SCWriP fellows" (teachers who have participated in a SCWriP-sponsored summer institute and have since conducted professional development activities in local schools). Thus most teachers in this region have at least heard of the writing project, and many have participated directly in its programs either as preservice or inservice teachers.

While SCWriP and writing projects generally are not explicitly committed to any one approach to teaching writing, at least in their early years they were influential in accelerating the spread of process ideas such as drafting and revising among K–12 teachers in the area. Site leaders recall that when theories about the writing process were introduced at SCWriP's first summer institute in 1979, those ideas seemed revolutionary, and many teachers went on to communicate those ideas to their colleagues with almost evangelical zeal. Yet SCWriP, like other writing project sites, embraces a variety of teaching approaches promoted by the expert teachers who are its fellows.

Further, teachers in this area encounter process approaches to the teaching of writing in a variety of venues other than SCWriP. The writing process is addressed, for example, in the major texts used in language arts credential programs (e.g., Burke, 2003; Christenbury, 2000) at area universities. It is addressed, with varying degrees of emphasis and integration, in all of the major language arts textbook series (e.g., Holt, Rinehart & Winston's *Elements of Language;* MacDougal Littell's *Language Network*). Moreover, members of a professional association like the National Council of Teachers of English or its California affiliate have the opportunity to read about process approaches in the journals of those organizations and see examples of writing process-influenced instruction at conferences.

Under the auspices of the National Writing Project's Local Sites Research Initiative, we undertook an evaluation of one of SCWriP's inservice programs using a comparative reference. In doing so, we experienced a tension between our work with teachers and our charge, specified by NWP in funding the study, to evaluate that work using a quasi-experimental design. Our goal for the study was to assess the effects of participation in a sustained, site-based inservice program, focusing on the influence of inquiry groups and work with classroom coaches on teachers and their classroom practices in the teaching of writing. The study was conceived as a program evaluation, in which we would first detect any differences in classroom practice between program and comparison classrooms and then, ultimately, examine whether those differences were reflected in differential outcomes in student performance (results of the larger study are reported in National Writing Project, 2006a). However, the central aims of the inservice program (explained in more detail in the program description below) were to influence the ways teachers thought about the teaching of writing in two ways: first, to help them see writing as a process of discovering and constructing meaning, to discover, refine, and articulate one's thinking, and second, to have teachers understand that writing is learned through participation in a community of writers with genuine uses for a real audience as part of an activity system. Thus implicit in the task of evaluating the program was not only an aim to identify the use of specific classroom practices by teachers but also to explore an interest in how teachers thought about those practices.

The research revealed that, in fact, teachers in both groups tended to use very similar classroom strategies, particularly those having to do with writing as a process. However, teachers differed in how they used those strategies, talked about them, and built opportunities for students to gain independence in navigating the writing process on their own. Teachers took from SCWriP's inservice program not simply a set of process strategies, but also a set of attitudes and stances with respect to writing that could be seen in the varying ways these "same" strategies were enacted. To understand the results, it helps to consider the program's goals of not only improving lesson design and classroom strategies but also supporting teachers in their own intellectual growth and professionalism; the program aims to develop teacher-leadership and to change the culture of the school, so that teachers can become more reflective, take an inquiry stance in their teaching, and claim professional authority. Our study is thus contextualized within research on developing an inquiry stance, the history of such work within NWP, and prevailing approaches to evaluating professional development programs.

Cochran-Smith and Lytle (1999, 2001) offer a vision of professional development as developing an inquiry stance. Understanding professional development as inquiry entails breaking the traditional distinction between formal knowledge and practical knowledge as separate; instead, "the knowledge teachers need to teach well is generated when teachers treat their own classrooms and schools as sites for intentional investigation at the same time that they treat the knowledge and theory produced by others as generative material for interrogation and interpretation" (Cochran-Smith & Lytle, 2001, 48). Engaging in inquiry means not only learning

practices recommended by others or perfecting the practical execution of a set of teaching strategies but, rather, theorizing about teaching and learning in a way that then frames future interpretation and decision-making. In an inquiry stance, teachers "make problematic their own knowledge and practice as well as the knowledge and practice of others and thus stand in a different relationship to knowledge" (Cochran-Smith & Lytle, 2001, 49). Professional development then positions teachers' learning as "challenging their own assumptions; identifying salient issues of practice; posing problems; studying their own students, classrooms, and schools; constructing and reconstructing curriculum; and taking on roles of leadership and activism in efforts to transform classrooms, schools, and societies" (Cochran-Smith & Lytle, 1999, 278).

As Cochran-Smith and Lytle point out, the kind of professional development programs that National Writing Project sites have offered over the past thirty years have invited teachers to adopt such a stance, both in Summer Invitational Institutes and in a variety of staff development programs conducted in schools during the academic year. NWP encourages teachers to interrogate their own and others' practices, to consider the implications of research and theory on their changing understandings of teaching and learning, and to articulate (either in their own writing, in discussion, or in presentations to colleagues) principles that underlie and unite a teacher's set of practices in a particular context (Bratcher & Stroble, 1994; Gomez, 1990; Lieberman & Wood, 2002, 2003; Pritchard & Marshall, 1994; Wood & Lieberman, 2000). Thus NWP has often been misunderstood as primarily a disseminator of "expressivist" practices; instead, NWP does not adhere to any one official curriculum but more generally embraces a process-oriented pedagogy that encourages teachers to work with their students on aspects of writing such as invention and revision. NWP's "core principles" are statements about the nature of teaching, writing, and learning: "The NWP model is based on the belief that teachers are the key to education reform, teachers make the best teachers of other teachers, and teachers benefit from studying and conducting research" (National Writing Project, 2006b). Thus, while teachers indeed are likely to come into contact with many process-oriented strategies in NWP professional development programs, simply transmitting a body of strategies for teachers to implement is not the goal of such programs.

The Study in Context

As part of the National Writing Project's effort to gather research data in support of its mission and activities, the NWP, beginning in 2003, sponsored the "Local Sites Research Initiative" (LSRI). The intent of the LSRI was to document the impact and effectiveness of the writing project model of professional development on students and teachers, in unique local contexts. LSRI research studies were designed by individual NWP sites in order to match their local professional development activities and needs, as well as to add definition to the national picture of NWP activities. In acknowledgment of the wide variety of contexts in which Writing Project sites operate, the requirements of LSRI were highly flexible; however, each site was required to include some form of comparative reference as well as a direct assessment of student writing performance.

As indicated previously, the South Coast Writing Project, located at the University of California, Santa Barbara, has conducted staff development programs for K–12 schools for 27 years in a three-county service area with a population of roughly one million people. This region, stretching 200 miles from the northern border of Santa Barbara County to the southern border of Ventura County at the Los Angeles County line, includes agricultural and ranching communities with large numbers of migrant laborers and farm workers, a number of wealthy suburban communities, and several smaller cities, including Santa Barbara, Santa Maria, Ventura, and Oxnard. Approximately 50% of all children in schools within the two-county region

are eligible for the federal free-lunch program, and approximately 50% of the children in public schools in the cities and in the rural communities are Mexican-American.

In recent years, in response to increasingly intense demands for the improvement of student achievement on district and state assessments and other forms of high-stakes testing, schools in this two county region have been particularly receptive to proposals for staff-development programs that hold some promise of improving instruction and student performance in the crucial testing areas of reading and writing. SCWriP's IIMPaC program responds to those needs by making long-term learning commitments at a single school site or within a consortium of schools, where groups of teachers volunteer to reflect on teaching practices and experiment with alternative practices supported by expert practitioners and informed by current theory and research.

The inservice program is carried out through five interrelated and mutually reinforcing activities:

Inquiry Groups: Teachers gather at least four times per academic year in groups consisting of 5 to 7 teachers from the same school. These groups examine student work together and discuss what they see, experiment with classroom strategies and meet to examine the results, wrestle with common challenges, and identify common goals.

Inservice Workshops: Teachers attend three full-day workshops conducted by teams of veteran teachers, expert practitioners, and teacher-consultants of the South Coast Writing Project who come from similar schools and grade levels as the participants.

Modeling: Participating teachers visit colleagues' classrooms to observe experienced, exemplary teachers of reading and writing who employ strategies introduced in IIMPaC. Modeling is also emphasized through an intensive program of coaching (see below) and through presentations at inservice workshops.

Practice: Participating teachers employ the teaching approaches and strategies introduced in the program in their own classrooms, then reflect on their teaching in teacher-research logs and discussions at inquiry-group and workshop meetings.

Coaching and Classroom Demonstrations: Teacher-consultants present demonstration lessons in the classroom of each participation teacher. This gives classroom teachers the opportunity to observe their own students engaged in the strategies presented in the three all-day workshops; consultants and teachers then meet to discuss what happened and consider implications.

METHODS

The overall study from which these two cases are drawn involved 15 teachers of grades 4–8 in 2004–2005 and 17 teachers of grades 3–8 in 2005–2006. Teachers volunteered to participate in the study and received modest stipends to compensate them for their time and effort. Half of these teachers were drawn from schools that had participated in the IIMPaC program (hereafter referred to as program schools), and the other half from schools that were similar based on student achievement, socioeconomic status, ethnicity, and English language status of students, but which had not participated in IIMPaC (hereafter referred to as comparison schools).

Data collection for both program and comparison groups included (a) classroom observations of writing-oriented instructional activities, conducted twice during the academic year, (b) interviews with teachers, and (c) a self-selected collection of documents from one week of classroom activity. The interviews and classroom observations were conducted by doctoral students in education who engaged in a six-hour training session focused on eliciting low-inference descriptions, writing fieldnotes, and learning interview strategies; they practiced observing classrooms using videotape, interviewing teachers using peer role-playing, and writing

consistent reports across researchers and across the two time periods.

Teachers were observed in their classrooms twice during the academic year. The observations focused on the resources available to students in the classroom and on teachers' classroom practices in the teaching of writing. Observations were designed to explore not only the extent to which teachers in the IIMPaC program engaged the specific strategies they had experienced in the program, but also the ways they contextualized and framed writing. Researchers observed classrooms on a teacher selected date, the only stipulation being that the observer have the opportunity to witness a writing-related lesson. Fieldworkers first recorded a running record, then prepared an analytic report addressing each of the concerns in more depth.

Direct observations of classroom practice were supplemented with the collection of classroom documents designed to reflect teachers' instructional support for and students' implementation of skills such as planning and revision. These collections included any one writing assignment or activity, along with any and all supporting documents (such as teacher lesson plans, handouts, or rubrics). They also included all the written work in response to that assignment produced by at least three students chosen by the teacher, using the criteria of one high-achieving, one average-achieving, and one lower-achieving student. Student samples included answers to classroom exercises, final copies of writing assignments, and rough drafts if such drafts had been assigned.

Interviews were conducted in the teacher's classroom using a protocol with questions focused on professional development activities and classroom strategies. Teachers were interviewed in fall and again in spring of the academic year. The protocol used in initial interviews focused on professional development experiences, the extent to which those experiences affected teaching (if at all), and classroom strategies related to writing instruction. Follow-up interviews focused on teachers' thinking behind classroom practices and assignments.

A research team of doctoral students in education and university researchers, along with two SCWriP co-directors, analyzed the body of qualitative data. In a series of analysis meetings as data was being collected, teams of three to four researchers analyzed interview and observation reports from which identifying information had been removed. Eventually, the team identified a list of salient areas for further analysis, areas in which practices discussed or observed were notable for their quality, frequency, or similarity or difference across programs and comparison groups. Relevant passages from each teacher's interviews and observation notes and collections of documents were coded and compiled using NVivo software, a tool for coding and retrieving qualitative data; the data were then partitioned into program and comparison groups and reanalyzed in depth to explore the nuanced ways in which the teachers' classroom practices might differ across groups and the potential implications of these differences.

RESULTS

Striking differences were found in the classroom practices of program and comparison teachers in the way they prepare students to write, develop a piece of writing, and promote student investment in writing. However, the differences were not simply that particular terms and strategies discussed in the professional development program appeared in one set of classrooms and not in another. Instead, while at times program teachers used strategies that comparison teachers did not use, more typically teachers in both groups used the same basic terms and strategies but used them in different ways or for different purposes. These differences in practice centered on three aspects of teaching writing: helping students as they prepared to write, helping students as they developed a piece of writing, and encouraging student investment in the writing process. Here we present examples drawn from two teachers in the study, which serve as illustrations of the trends in data as a whole; these vividly illustrate

the differences in ways teachers employed these "same" strategies.

TWO CASES: "MS. GONZALES" AND "MS. BARRERA"

The two teachers discussed in this article worked in similar schools with similar populations of students. Eucalyptus Elementary, a comparison school, is located in an agricultural community (population approximately 12,000) situated on the outskirts of a larger city in California's central valley. Dolores Huerta Elementary, a program school, is located in a small city (population approximately 100,000) in southern California also known primarily as an agricultural center. Both schools serve primarily low-income families, many of whom work as farm workers. The overwhelming majority of students are English language learners from Spanish-speaking backgrounds. Tables 25.1 and 25.2 list demographic and language data, respectively, for the two schools.

Ms. Gonzales at Eucalyptus Elementary (a comparison school) and Ms. Barrera at Huerta Elementary (a program school) both taught fifth grade and are Latinas who describe themselves as having strong commitments to working with English language learners. Their bachelor's degrees and teacher preparation came from peer institutions within the same state university system. At the time of the study, Ms. Gonzales had been teaching for four years and Ms. Barrera for seven. Both cited writing as a major concern in their teaching, and both sought out professional development in the teaching of writing beyond what the school or district required.

CASE STUDY: MS. GONZALES

We observed and interviewed Ms. Gonzales over the course of the 2005–2006 school year at Eucalyptus Elementary. Ms. Gonzales explained that the main thing she was trying to teach to her

Table 25.1   School Matching Data: Demographic

School		Eucalyptus Elementary (Comparison)		Huerta Elementary (Program)	
Enrollment		877		583	
Free and Reduced Price Meals		799	(91.5%)	508	(87.1%)
Ethnicity	African, not Hispanic	5	(0.6%)	1	(0.2%)
	American Indian or Alaskan Native	4	(0.5%)	0	(0.0%)
	Asian	6	(0.7%)	0	(0.0%)
	Filipino	1	(0.1%)	2	(0.3%)
	Hispanic or Latino	730	(83.2%)	568	(97.4%)
	Pacific Islander	5	(0.6%)	1	(0.2%)
	White, not Hispanic	118	(13.5%)	9	(1.5%)
	Multiple/No Response	8	(0.9%)	2	(0.3%)

Table 25.2   School Matching Data: Language and Achievement

School	Eucalyptus Elementary (Comparison)		Huerta Elementary (Program)	
English Learners	396	(45.2%)	397	(68.1%)
Fluent English-Proficient Students	145	(16.5%)	79	(13.6%)
Students Redesignated FEP	25	(6.8%)	17	(3.8%)
Language Arts Percent Proficient and Above	19%		10%	
Language Arts Percent Basic and Above	54%		43%	

fifth-grade students in writing was to complete all forms of writing required by the California State Standards: persuasive, descriptive, informative, and narrative. Ms. Gonzales hoped to "expose the kids to different types of the different forms of writing." Additionally, she worked to teach her students to self-correct, to use and understand rubrics, and to use peer-editing techniques that "really work." She summarized her goals for her students: "to produce more mature writing by self-correcting, and to use and know rubrics."

When asked to share a success in her teaching of writing, Ms. Gonzales recounted lessons where her instruction and her lesson plans have been "systematic," such as teaching her students "everything they need to know about what goes into a paragraph." She believed that "teaching explicitly, not implicitly" led to her success in teaching writing, "being very systematic and always going back to the basics." Asked to elaborate on what she meant by "basics," she listed paragraphs, grammar, and vocabulary. She believed that she could not "always assume that kids know how to write." Instead, Ms. Gonzales approached the task of teaching writing as though "kids do not know how to write."

Ms. Gonzales focused her instruction around the state standards, stating that "My students have to list the standard they're meeting for each assignment, but I also try to get them to apply it to real life to make it interesting." During one classroom observation, she began the lesson by writing the California standard on the board, Responding to Literature 3.0, and by telling students that the focus of this lesson was "retelling" a story with transition words. After defining transition words as words that "move from one sentence or idea to the next," Ms. Gonzales turned off the lights in the classroom and began to read the story of Amelia Earhart out loud to the students. After the reading, students were asked to "retell" the story, using a template provided on the overhead projector. Ms. Gonzales again noted afterward that their primary focus in "retelling" the story was for the children to understand transitions and use them correctly. Their overhead template looked like this (see Figure 25.1).

Ms. Gonzales modeled how students were to do the assignment by completing her own on the overhead with their help. The students were asked to listen carefully to Ms. Gonzales and participate by raising their hands when she asked them for more specific details about the story. Once Ms. Gonzales had completed her version on the overhead, which she referred to as an outline of the "details" of the story, the students were then asked to work with the student sitting next to them to complete a similar outline independently.

While the students worked, Ms. Gonzales circulated around the room to take questions from students, get off-task students back to work, and guide students toward the most important details in the story. Additionally, she frequently reminded students that since paying attention to detail was crucial when taking notes in junior high, the details they were finding in the text would be good practice for taking notes next year. Once students had completed filling in the outline, they turned in their papers to Ms. Gonzales.

In general, Ms. Gonzales described her teaching of writing as taking students through a distinct, explicit process with "a lot of steps." First, she liked to provide her students with a lot of "exposure" to the topic on which the student would be writing, so that they could approach the assignment "systematically." She noted, "I tell the students 'This is what we are going to be writing about' so that we can all organize our papers together." For instance, at the beginning of the year, Ms. Gonzales assigned a "descriptive experience." Topics for descriptive experiences included "a day at the beach," "a frightening experience," and "getting lost." When assigning

---

Retelling

Once there was a _____ who _____ in the _____.

_____ had a problem. To solve the problem _____. First,

_____. Second, _____. Third, _____. Finally, the problem

was solved by _____ and then _____.

Figure 25.1   Retelling Overhead

these topics, Ms. Gonzales liked to share her own experiences as models, "because you can not assume that students can relate to an experience, especially if they have never been to the beach . . . Students have to relate to what they write about and participate in the process. Kids have to write about an experience they know about." She reported being particularly aware of that necessity that academic year, when she asked them to write about a day at the beach, a place many of her students had never been to and could not write about. The result of this new-found understanding was that she altered the topics of her assignments so that her students would feel like they had something to say.

"All students have to do all prewriting," Ms. Gonzales explained. "Because I have a background in high school and in special education, I know that students have to see everything," so she teaches organization methods "over and over again." To support students in prewriting, she used a graphic organizer to generate ideas in class "together . . . We start with an idea someone has, and then I ask the kids, 'Would this go in the intro, is it a detail or a reason, does it go in the beginning, middle, or the end?'" Students must "stick to an order, don't jump around, and stick to the topic." The graphic organizers she used in such situations tended to be either "web diagrams," "clustering" of the parts of the essay, or "stoplight paragraph maps" that assist students in building paragraphs with a prescribed number of sentences, details, etc.

One observed lesson demonstrated how Ms. Gonzales' students engaged in prewriting together using a paragraph map. According to Ms. Gonzales, that lesson was designed to prepare students for the written test of "Standard 1.2" which focuses on transition words. Ms. Gonzales began this lesson by distributing a paragraph template to her students and displayed the same on the overhead projector at the front of the class. She reminded the students that the handout was their "plan" for the paragraph they would later write and then used the overhead to model their task for the morning, which was to use transition words in the creation of a set of

instructions for a recipe. She cued her students to offer their responses to the handout verbally, one step at a time, and then she would reveal the complementary step on her own model template. The topic of Ms. Gonzales' template, which she had prepared ahead of time, was "How to Make Pancakes," featuring different steps in pancake-making filled into a series of boxes on the hand-out. Next, different students were called upon to read aloud Ms. Gonzales' finished recipe paragraph, also titled "How to Make Pancakes," one sentence at a time. Ms. Gonzales then reminded her students of the steps they needed to include, the importance of using transition words, and the standard the assignment was meeting. At the end of whole-class modeling, the students were each given a recipe card and were instructed to use the next 25 minutes to first produce their own "plan" using the template to create a finished-product recipe (with a paragraph of instructions) complete with highlighted transition words, highlighted verbs, and the standard that the assignment addressed (written out on the bottom of the page).

Ms. Gonzales wanted her students to become more independent, and toward that end, she taught them how to peer edit. She emphasized constructive criticism in peer editing, because "writing is so personal." She also reminded students that their peers are "allowing you to read" their paper, and she did not want to hear negative peer comments such as "That is so dumb." Peer editing occurred before students turned in their work for grading. For instance, in the Amelia Earhart "retelling" activity described above, Ms. Gonzales asked the students to first fill in the template with their own words, then share these drafts with their peers. Peer-reviewers were encouraged to respond to the grammatical aspects of the exercise, based on what the students had learned in earlier Daily Oral Language exercises. Once the students made changes, they quickly turned in their exercises to the teacher. That sequence was pretty typical of the roles Ms. Gonzales asked peers to play in responding to one another's work; their role was to "catch any mistakes" in their partner's writing, assisting their peers in isolating grammatical errors.

Another important component of fifth grade writing in Ms. Gonzales' class was the state report, "a major project" on which students spent six to eight weeks, containing several parts related to one of the fifty U.S. states, "including the people of the state, its demographics, and population number." Students were required to create a bibliography of "both primary and secondary sources," and Ms. Gonzales lectured the students on "reputable sources." She asked her students to think, "Why are there different dates or different numbers?" in different sources, and why some sources may be more reliable than others, in essence encouraging her students to double-check their numbers and figures. She had the children write sections on the state's economy, agriculture, and manufacturing. By means of example, she asked the children, "What do we grow here in the Central Valley?" She then went on to bracket information on the board, either "grow" or "make," explaining later that "we grow corn" and that we "don't grow cars." She said that when using vocabulary like "grow" and "manufacture," Ms. Gonzales could not assume that the children "knew the meaning of the words." Ms. Gonzales told the children, "This is how you research," and "This is how you cite sources," because "the students are expected to know how to write in these ways" in junior high and high school. Several examples of state reports were displayed on the walls in the classroom, containing pictures, facts, and figures drawn from reference materials and websites along with small amounts of student writing. The student writing was focused primarily on the historical facts of a particular state and measured approximately a half of a page in length.

Ms. Gonzales explained that she usually asks her students to keep their work at school: "Kids with computers are hard to find. Only three or four students in my class will have parents with computers. Many parents are ELD [English language deficient] or have very little education," she said. For students to "do hard work at school, it depends on their parents and teachers. Students

need parents who want them to succeed." If students said they needed to take math notes home to study for a test, Ms. Gonzales explained that she "wanted them to keep their notebook at school," because she wanted students to "take good notes" and if students take their notebooks home, "they might be misinformed by their parents." For example, some parents did not know "to only capitalize mom and dad if it is a proper name," and Ms. Gonzales did not "want to get into a debate with the parents"; instead, she wanted students to "know the language convention right now." Thus students were urged to keep their work at school: "If students keep their work here, I will help [them] with it."

CASE STUDY: MS. BARRERA

We observed and interviewed Ms. Barrera in 2004–2005 and 2005–2006, the third and fourth years of her participation in the IIMPaC program at Huerta Elementary. Ms. Barrera explained that her goals for students in writing for the fifth grade were for the students to have "a basic understanding of what the traits for good writing are" and to "build an author within them." She said she has been trying to build a community of authors and wanted students to come to see themselves as authors. Her second goal was for her students to be successful in academic writing. She said, "I want them to be able to manipulate language so that it's communicated well in the community as well as the academic setting." Like Ms. Gonzales, Ms. Barrera was also attentive to state standards, but she tended to cite these overall goals first before mentioning specific standards or the specific genres (persuasive, descriptive, informative, and narrative) in which California fifth graders were asked to write.

Her objectives for specific activities and assignments followed from these larger goals. In general, Ms. Barrera said she was trying to teach her students the "solid traits of writing," which influenced her instructional and assessment focuses for each of the various assignments students wrote during the year: she wanted them to "manipulate words, ideas, sentences" and to feel comfortable and "fluid" with language. For instance, in a previous assignment, she was looking at word choice, if "they can play around with words." For another assignment, she was looking for sentence structure and if "they can play around with sentences, flip it back and forth and play around with clauses. Can they do sentence combining?"

Like Ms. Gonzales, Ms. Barrera often modeled prewriting and planned tasks for students as well as providing graphic organizers for students to plan their work. During one observed class, for example, Ms. Barrera asked students to work in groups to compose a persuasive essay about the need for physical education. (This topic evolved out of the school-wide preparation for state physical fitness testing that had been going on during students' usual writing class period all week.) She began the class by telling the students, "Writing affects every area of our life." She noted how writing is a part of many subjects, including physical education. Recalling that some of the students in the class had mentioned in the past that they wanted to be writers, she pointed out that there are many ways to write that take up the topic of physical fitness, including writing sports books, novels pertaining to health and fitness, or even instruction manuals for games.

Ms. Barrera then discussed with students different interpretations of "being physically fit." She told the students they could choose their own word that meant physically fit, and she instigated a whole-class conversation about ways to stay fit, including jogging and a healthy diet. Ms. Barrera also made sure students understood the difference between a healthy diet and dieting to lose weight. The class continued to discuss what it means to be physically fit and how different body types respond differently to diet and exercise. Students had learned to write persuasive essays about a month before, and the fitness activity served as a review of that genre. After the whole class brainstormed general ideas, students engaged in prewriting activities and drafting in groups. Ms. Barrera also gave the

groups of students the option of using a graphic organizer or immediately beginning to write.

One important project for Ms. Barrera's fifth-grade classroom was the research report. Ms. Barrera described in an interview how that process unfolded over time for her students, and she and the students were observed working on the reports at several stages in the process. On the first day of the unit, she worked on students' organizational skills and set expectations for the project as a whole. The class constructed writing folders, working portfolios where everything related to the project would be kept. That folder contained standards and rubrics and was divided into sections: one section contained models and activities that had been guided by Ms. Barrera, and the other contained "their stuff," independent work students accumulated toward a final product. Using this portfolio, students continually referred to models both of finished writing and of the various processes and steps along the way. Further, a clear and physical line was drawn between those activities which were completed as models (such as templates composed aloud as a class and then copied off the overhead) and the students' original thought (such as notes and drafts of an individual student's report)—in sharp contrast to many of the comparison classrooms, in which students' finished work was often essentially copied from whole-class models.

On the second day of the project, Ms. Barrera talked with students about the reason for writing a research report at all, which she described as "finding information and sharing it with other people." The writing task was framed as primarily communicative, and while Ms. Barrera did speak to specific skills and standards, they were treated as features of the writing task rather than as the purpose of the activity. Soon after the discussion, the students chose topics, which had to fall under the broad umbrella of ancient civilizations (the class' social studies focus). Ms. Barrera explained, "We try to look at the possible topics because not everything is going to be easy to research. I had two students pick Isaac from ancient Israel, and it was hard to find information about him." Once the students identified topics, Ms. Barrera conducted a workshop to narrow these topics and develop ideas for the project. She offered a graphic organizer students could use for the purpose and modeled how to use it on the overhead using Amelia Earhart, a topic students had studied previously, as an example. She first asked them to "skim" the selection they had previously read on Earhart in order to prepare for discussion; then she demonstrated how she would prepare for a research project on Earhart, using the graphic organizer to identify promising research ideas and gradually reach a specific focus. Students contributed ideas to the process along the way and copied the model onto the outside of their portfolios.

Students continued to work on their research reports as writing in Ms. Barrera's class was presented as a fluid and recursive process. Although there were tasks Ms. Barrera wanted each child to accomplish on the way to a finished product, students took up these tasks when they were ready to do so and were considered to be responsible for their own progress. Ms. Barrera's sense of writing as individually directed and process-based was dramatized through the pathway to the research report observed on her blackboard. The pathway consisted of 8½" by 11" sheets of colored paper marked with each step in the research report process which Ms. Barrera wanted the students to complete. These steps included selecting, narrowing, and researching a topic, as well as a variety of specific tasks in composing and revising. For example, students were to complete such activities as filling out a "fluency chart" for each paragraph of their paper, getting comments from their peers, and having a conference with Ms. Barrera—each one of these activities would represent one stage. As an individual student finished each of these activities, he/she or Ms. Barrera would move that student's name into the appropriate space on the board to indicate where he/she was in the process. Writing activities unfolded in that way over several days.

On the day of one observation, for example, stations were established and Ms. Barrera was located at the front of the class near the door at a circular table marked Revision/Teacher Conference. On the chart/pathway posted on the blackboard (described above), each student's name was posted on the wall, so each child was able to see where he or she stood in relation to: the entire task, their classmates, where they should be, and where they could be and still be current in their work. Students sat in different sections of the classroom based on their progress. The table closest to Ms. Barrera was where the students who were struggling the most sat. Some students used the computer stations throughout the class period. The pace of the project was flexible as students were at various places on the timeline without penalty. As students worked, they utilized their portfolios to collect drafts, consult models, and retrieve information they had gathered in other class sessions. In addition, they consulted models of finished pieces of the research report posted on the walls—models they had analyzed as a class during an earlier session with Ms. Barrera.

Ms. Barrera was also flexible with the time allotted for each part of the writing process. The pace for prewriting, discovering ideas, and drafting appeared to depend on students' skill and comfort level. She told the class, "I'd like to suggest a time; you can follow or not. You have a total of 7 minutes for the graphic organizer, and then I'll tell you how long for the writing." Later, after the students had spent some time on the graphic organizer, she told them, "I'd like to suggest you start writing."

Ms. Barrera explained that for most assignments, the audience for the students' writing was their peers. She admitted that the students may ultimately think it's for the teachers, but she said she works to make the case that "it's really so they can share it with their peers and get a rise or not out of them." In past years, Ms. Barrera was the only source of feedback for students, and she noted that students still tend to look to her first for feedback, but over time she has worked to change that dependence. "Little by little, they are doing the affirming of one another." During one observation, for instance, a student's work was used by the class as a whole to talk about the traits of a successful product, and peers offered suggestions to that student and made similar changes in their own work. Ms. Barrera frequently asked students to turn to a partner for a response, noting that she "sets up class so they immediately have a partner next to them." These partnerships varied according to the writing task: students usually worked with a partner to share work, but other times, such as when they began writing research reports, they were grouped according to topic in order to assist each other.

Parents also saw student work, as portfolios were used during parent conferences to help them understand the students' progress over the course of the year. That communication with parents was important to Ms. Barrera was further confirmed by her calling a parent on the phone during one observed lesson to let the parent know that a student had come to class without the day's homework.

DISCUSSION

These two fifth grade teachers worked with similar students under similar conditions: in addition to the demographic similarities noted earlier, they also worked with similar curricula (both working on Amelia Earhart around the same time, for example) and assigned similar types of writing (such as the research reports both teachers introduced in fifth grade). Perhaps more notably for our study, both Ms. Gonzales and Ms. Barrera talked about writing as a process and deployed a fairly sophisticated set of strategies to guide students through a writing task, such as whole-class modeling, graphic organizers and other planning tools, as well as work with peers. Yet each teacher used different approaches to three major areas: preparing students to write, developing a piece of writing over time, and encouraging student investment and independence in writing.

PREPARING TO WRITE

Ms. Gonzales and Ms. Barrera explicitly taught students approaches for planning their writing; in particular, they occasionally offered students models of finished writing and regularly asked students to brainstorm or use graphic organizers before drafting a piece of writing. However, Ms. Barrera's approach to before-writing activities explicitly helped students to make sense of models and draw upon them as resources. She also offered opportunities for students to develop their own topics and shared a range of prewriting tools while encouraging students to use those tools independently.

Both teachers were attentive to state standards and listed as goals the hope that students would be prepared for testing. Ms. Gonzales tended to begin by telling students what standard they would be addressing, writing the standard's name and number on the board and sometimes asking students to copy it down on to their own paper. Ms. Barrera also planned activities to address specific standards and sometimes discussed these standards with students; however, conversations about standards and testing occurred after the task had already been framed as a communicative one. For instance, when Ms. Barrera had students write about the importance of physical education (an activity explicitly tied to the upcoming P.E. testing and also in a genre, persuasive writing, on which students would be tested), she opened by discussing the pervasiveness of writing in all areas of life and by having the students brainstorm genres in which they might write about fitness outside of school.

Ms. Gonzales and Ms. Barrera either showed samples of finished work or modeled how to approach assignments before asking students to write. But in Ms. Barrera's classroom, the models provided were usually student-written or written on the spot, in front of students, for the assignment in question (as in the case of the research report, in which she spontaneously created an example on Earhart), whereas Ms. Gonzales was more likely to use models that came with the text book or would pre-make models before presenting them to students (as in the case of the pancake recipe).

Ms. Barrera posted models of recent, successful student writing around the room from an assignment about tsunamis. Classroom discussion frequently referenced the specific traits that made such pieces successful, such as word choice or sentence fluency. In another instance, when Ms. Barrera's students were working on a research report, models of finished sections of the research report were available on the walls as students drafted those sections. In contrast, Ms. Gonzales' room also had student research reports on the walls, but they were not referred to in the course of instruction or examined by students. Ms. Gonzales tended to provide models of specific steps students were to complete on the way to a finished product (such as graphic organizers for planning). She did not share or discuss student-authored models and only occasionally showed a model of finished writing that she had created herself.

In Ms. Gonzales' class, topic selection was rarely discussed in observed classes or mentioned in interviews, and in the cases in which it was discussed, topics were assigned by the teacher. On the other hand, Ms. Barrera was frequently observed teaching topic selection and discussed it in interviews, and in all of these cases, the topics were at least to some degree student-selected.

Ms. Gonzales, for example, assigned specific topics for her students to use in writing a descriptive piece, such as "a day at the beach" or "getting lost." When the beach topic proved inappropriate for her students, Ms. Gonzales devised a different topic but still retained control over topics. In Ms. Barrera's classroom, topics were occasionally assigned (such as in the case of the persuasive essay about physical education), but other times they were left for students to choose and develop. Further, Ms. Barrera taught explicitly about topic selection and development, as observed for example in her teaching of the research report. Her explicit teaching of topic selection seemed to better prepare her students for writing outside the classroom and

school setting, where writers rarely find themselves writing to an entirely pre-set prompt. When students participate in choosing topics and in generating the ideas on those topics which will be included in a piece, they can gain experience in shaping and developing ideas rather than simply writing down the ideas of others.

Both Ms. Gonzales and Ms. Barrera devoted class time to presenting and guiding students in using prewriting tools such as graphic organizers on a regular basis. However, differences emerged in the types of strategies used, the way these activities were presented, and the extent to which students applied these strategies in their writing. Ms. Gonzales, for example, offered a "paragraph map" that students used to compose paragraphs. After writing sentences into the map, students simply recopied those sentences onto fresh paper to make a final draft. Prewriting of this type was most often completed as a whole class, with Ms. Gonzales filling in a template on the overhead with ideas the students contributed. When students were then directed to fill in their own templates, several students were observed directly copying down what had been written on the overhead, while other students took those same ideas and cast them into their own words.

Ms. Barrera also offered organizers for students to use in planning their writing. Like Ms. Gonzales, Ms. Barrera often composed a model for students aloud and on the overhead, explaining what she was doing and asking students to contribute to the ideas as she worked, as seen when students were preparing to write their research reports. However, Ms. Barrera's model used not the students' assigned topic (after all, these varied significantly among the various students) but a topic the class had studied earlier. Thus the modeling demonstrated *how* to use the planning tool but not *what* exactly to write. Students copied down the model much as they had in Ms. Gonzales' class, but in Ms. Barrera's class students then attached the model to the front of their working portfolios and were observed referring to it as they worked on their own pieces. In Ms. Gonzales' class, "all students have to do all prewriting," and each student's prewriting takes the same form for each assignment, but in Ms. Barrera's class, prewriting is still required but self-managed (as in the case of the research report) or is offered as a tool that students may or may not take up (as in the P.E. essay).

These differences in how teachers approach samples, topics, and prewriting are important in that they help to frame writing tasks as governed by communicative needs rather than classroom needs. In classrooms such as Ms. Barrera's, rhetorical situations presented themselves much as they do in the world outside the classroom, and it was up to students (with the teacher's support) to navigate those situations by developing ideas, choosing tools for invention and planning, and making all of the other decisions writers must make. In Ms. Gonzales' classroom, writing was usually framed as necessary for school assignments more than for communication, and tools and support were made available to assist students in meeting the requirements of these school assignments. We have found that when models of writing are available and include not only professional examples but also locally produced examples and examples written by students of similar age and skill level, students more easily imagine how to craft a product incorporating similar features. When students participate in the selection and development of topics, they are usually better able to develop ideas within the eventual product, for they have a stake in the writing's purpose. Further, when students possess experiences with a range of prewriting strategies, those strategies are often more portable. If they have experimented with several strategies, students in a new writing situation can select from their toolkit of the possible approaches, whereas if students have practiced prewriting as the filling out of forms, they may be at a loss in writing situations where no form is provided. Thus, Ms. Barrera seemed to better support her students in planning to write effectively on independent writing tasks and tasks occurring outside the context of that one classroom or that one assignment.

DEVELOPING A PIECE OF WRITING

The two classrooms also differed in a second major area: their approach to helping students develop a piece of writing once a first draft has begun. Both teachers used "process terms" such as "editing" or "revision." Both Ms. Gonzales and Ms. Barrera, for example, took students through a series of steps toward a final product, including prewriting, drafting, and revision and/or editing. However, in Ms. Barrera's class, those terms took on nuanced, open meanings, denoting moves a writer might make rather than rigid sets of procedures, stages of the development of writing rather than components of an assignment. For instance, students in Ms. Barrera's class had more flexibility in how they used graphic organizers for planning. Further, they had more flexibility in the timeline on which they completed various parts of the writing process, as seen in the pathway chart that Ms. Barrera kept on her blackboard when students were working on their research reports. While students in her class were all expected to engage in certain activities on the way to a product, the class structure implied that different students or different pieces of writing might require that time be allocated in many ways.

"Revision" activities in Ms. Gonzales' classroom (many of which were actually editing activities) seemed geared toward moving pieces as quickly as possible toward a correct final draft; rarely if ever did pieces get longer, more complex, or change direction between the first and final draft. For example, Ms. Gonzales offered her students a list of "proofreading marks," a "proofreading checklist," and an opportunity to work with a peer to "catch any mistakes." For one assignment, students were also asked to complete a self-assessment sheet in which they identified strong and weak points of their paper as a whole (which might be interpreted as promoting revision of content), but these self-assessments were not used as tools for changing or improving the writing (instead, they were simply completed and turned in after the writing was complete). In Ms. Barrera's classroom, a series of revision activities was geared toward improving a piece along a variety of lines, including making the piece longer or more detailed, clarifying confusing passages, varying word choice, and improving sentence variety. Students' goals in changing drafts included not only making writing more correct but also making it more complete, more clear, or more effective in achieving its rhetorical purpose. Editing for mistakes was also encouraged, but it was done after these other activities had been completed.

ENCOURAGING STUDENT INVESTMENT IN WRITING

The third major area in which the classroom practices of these two teachers differed was in promoting student investment in writing. Both teachers expressed interest in engaging students, and both program and comparison classrooms were generally positive, learning-focused environments. Both Ms. Gonzales and Ms. Barrera, for instance, offered frequent praise for students and their writing, tried to set writing tasks that students would be interested in, and celebrated student writing by posting it on the walls of the classroom. Ms. Barrera, however, tended not only to emphasize fun and hard work, but also to encourage students to think of their writing as their own, consider themselves as authors, and take an active role in their own development as writers. In fact, Ms. Barrera explicitly named this aim as one of her main goals for students: to "build an author within them."

Ms. Gonzales and Ms. Barrera frequently had students work together to complete tasks, and in fact both teachers had desks arranged to facilitate working with a partner. However, the nature of the collaboration was somewhat different across the two classrooms: Ms. Gonzales' students collaborated primarily for the purpose of editing, whereas Ms. Barrera's students collaborated on brainstorming, planning, and revision in addition to editing. Thus students in Ms. Barrera's class were consistently expected to use one another as resources, and written pieces were crafted to meet the needs of an audience of students rather than solely a teacher who would assign a grade. A reorientation of audience away from the traditional single teacher/evaluator shifts writing tasks from low-investment activities for school requirements to high-investment activities which improves communication within a real social context.

In Ms. Gonzales' class, peers helped one another with editing, but not with ideas; writing was framed primarily as an activity where correctness was prized over ideas. In that scenario, the teacher gave ideas to the students, and the students' job was to present those ideas correctly. The student got good grades and was prepared for junior high by doing the assignment the way the teacher deemed correct, and other students' role in the process was to help identify errors for which the teacher might later deduct points. In Ms. Barrera's class, on the other hand, students became a roomful of authors who could freely turn to each other for help not only with editing but with ideas, understanding the social nature of composition. Students in Ms. Barrera's classroom did help one another find and correct mechanical errors, but assistance was usually provided more in the spirit of helping to make the piece of writing more effective for communication rather than as a way of avoiding lost points. These divergent paths for positioning students as authors or as the completers of assignments were further evidenced in the ways students amassed a body of written work into portfolios over time. Both teachers kept portfolios of a sort, but for dramatically different purposes. The purpose for collecting student work in Ms. Gonzales' room was partly to keep it from being lost or corrupted at home and partly to send home at the end of the year. Ms. Barrera's students kept two portfolios: one was a collection of finished work, to be used in parent conferences as a record of students' growth, and the other was a working writing folder in which models, drafts, and notes were stored during a writing project. In the first case, students rarely if ever accessed the collected material; in the second case, students frequently consulted the collection and participated in its construction, using portfolios much as authors might.

IMPLICATIONS

While both teachers used similar terms and strategies when they taught writing, such as having students prewrite, showing models, taking pieces of writing through multiple drafts, and having students work together, they framed these practices in strikingly different ways, beyond instrumental knowledge of possible teaching practices that teachers are aware of or the degree to which a single set of "desirable" strategies is implemented. Instead, these differences speak to the ways in which generally accepted classroom practices relate to writing as a process. The nuts and bolts of these teachers' materials and strategies were not especially different, but there were considerable differences in the framing of the purposes and processes of writing and what students' relationships to writing were imagined to be.

These data suggest the potential for inquiry-oriented professional development to influence more sophisticated enactments of the teaching practices such as prewriting, peer review, portfolios, and other elements which have in some regions become standard. The differences seen here follow at least in principle from the IIMPaC program's emphasis on inquiry, and these teachers' anecdotal comments in interviews support the notion that IIMPaC's opportunities for in-depth discussion and for supported experimentation contribute to a more nuanced understanding of issues in the teaching of writing.

They suggest that program teachers find an increased sense of responsibility for improving instruction and an increased desire to interrogate received curricula and practices—to question and reevaluate even those practices which have become so standard in today's classrooms as to seem unremarkable. Any time particular classroom strategies are modeled, recommended, or discussed in the IIMPaC program, they are interrogated and reflected upon by the teachers. Thus teachers in the program have an opportunity to understand not only the procedures of instructions (as might typically be emphasized in any programs recommending practices to teachers) but also the principles that underlie those procedures—and to consider how those principles align with their own existing knowledge.

Professional development can promote the adoption of an inquiry stance from which teachers examine and manipulate both existing practices (in our case, the features of process-oriented writing instruction that have, at least nominally, become standard practice in the region) and formal knowledge (in our case, knowledge about writing presented in inservice presentations and readings). It dramatizes the difference between teachers who have been invited to "implement" what they learned in inservice programs and teachers who have been invited to understand, to inquire, and to develop (where we see some of the same strategies, but framed in a way that promotes student learning and eventual independence beyond testing/school writing). Thus our findings make a case for future research examining whether (and, if so, how) specific existing practices get adjusted and revised over the course of a teacher's participation in an inquiry program. For instance, research might trace one teacher's iterations of a single strategy over a period of months or years and connect that to what teachers say in their inquiry meetings and the teacher's own sense of the strategy as changing over time. Our findings also raise questions about the impact of different teachers' approaches on student achievement in writing and in patterns of growth across an academic year or set of years; and highlight the potential for differences in student attitudes toward writing in the two environments. We have begun research on the relationships between teachers' professional development, student attitudes, and student achievement (e.g., National Writing Project, 2006a), but that work is far from complete.

Our study also has implications for the way we think about evaluating professional development when programs attempt to influence not just strategies used but also the thinking behind those strategies. While the IIMPaC program's organizers have long thought of their work in inquiry terms, our first impulse upon beginning evaluation research was, however unintentionally, to move back toward an "implementation" concept of professional development, in which we would visit classrooms to discover the extent to which teachers were using "our" practices. While powerful exceptions exist (see for example Lieberman & Wood, 2003), prevailing approaches to evaluation research have usually emphasized the extent to which teachers adopt and implement content presented in workshops. It is generally posited, for instance, that professional development can be evaluated on four levels including (a) teachers' reactions to or satisfaction with programs, (b) the knowledge teachers acquire, (c) transfer of that knowledge or how it is enacted in behavior, and (d) outcomes for students (Guskey, 2000; Kirkpatrick, 1998). These schema maintain a divide between knowledge and practice, making it difficult to examine changes in knowledge which are connected to changes in practice or to examine how knowing and doing both construct and are constructed through teacher inquiry.

The problems inherent in this approach to studying teacher knowledge are particularly important when professional development occurs in a local context like ours, in which the markers for instrumental learning about process

pedagogy (such as using common "process terms") are commonplace. The program, then, is less about presenting teachers with a new set of strategies than it is about encouraging them to interrogate and modify strategies; in turn, our evaluation had to look not only at what strategies were used, but also how they were used and why. In other words, our inquiry needed to be sufficiently sensitive to shed light on the subtle differences in teachers' classroom practices that might result from their adopting an inquiry stance. While a range of research in this area has been done from a variety of theoretical and methodological perspectives, in the main, typical studies of professional development in the context of inservice have been of two types: (1) designs showing depth and complexity but not using a comparative reference, or (2) comparative designs which are evaluations of "implementation" of a set of strategies. Increasingly, comparative designs are the coin of the realm (our own decision to use one, for instance, was an outcome of design constraints imposed by the National Writing Project on behalf of the federal sources funding the research). Rich portraits of this kind of learning in a few teachers, without comparative reference, are extremely helpful and a necessary part of the research basis for professional development work, but they do not really resolve questions about what that program offers that another program wouldn't. A program like IIMPaC, which is sustained, long term, and not a quick fix takes time; the effects on teacher practice and student achievement may take years to accrue; in addition, the research designs best suited to capture those effects are by necessity time-consuming and costly to execute. Asking school administrators to sponsor an inquiry-based program such as SCWriP's IIMPaC program means investing very limited resources in something that may in the long run affect test scores but won't have the immediate effect on test scores that they're under such pressure to produce, and it is asking them to do so without a great deal of research-based evidence of effectiveness that administrators now must demand. Thus thoughtful examinations of professional development that illustrate not only how teachers learn from inquiry programs but also how that learning leads to improved classroom practice and, ultimately, differences in student learning are essential.

AUTHORS' NOTE: This research was funded by the Local Sites Research Initiative of the National Writing Project. The work could not have been undertaken without the contributions of a research team, including (along with the authors of this article) Monica Bulger, Eddi Christensen, Sarah Hochstetler, Henny Kim, Chia-Chen Lai, Suzanne Null, Nada Rayyes, Jennifer Scalzo, and Zandree Stidham. We are also indebted to the Research Unit of the National Writing Project and the anonymous reviewers of English Education for their invaluable support and feedback.

Anne Whitney is on the faculty at the Pennsylvania State University in the department of Curriculum and Instruction.

Sheridan Blau is on the faculty at the University of California, Santa Barbara in the departments of English and Education and is director of the South Coast Writing Project.

Alison Bright is in the doctoral program in education at the University of California, Santa Barbara.

Rosemary Cabe is co-director of the South Coast Writing Project.

Tim Dewar is on the faculty at the State University of New York at New Paltz in the department of Secondary Education.

Jason Levin is in the doctoral program in Education at the University of California, Santa Barbara.

Roseanne Macias is in the doctoral program in Education at the University of California, Santa Barbara.

Paul Rogers is on the faulty at George Mason University in the Department of English.

Article 26

Writing Into the 21st Century

An Overview of Research on Writing, 1999 to 2004

Mary M. Juzwik, Svjetlana Curcic, Kimberly Wolbers, Kathleen D. Moxley, Lisa M. Dimling, and Rebecca K. Shankland

This study charts the terrain of research on writing during the 6-year period from 1999 to 2004, asking "What are current trends and foci in research on writing?" In examining a cross-section of writing research, the authors focus on four issues: (1) What are the general problems being investigated by contemporary writing researchers? Which of the various problems dominate recent writing research, and which are not as prominent? (2) What population age groups are prominent in recent writing research? (3) What is the relationship between population age groups and problems under investigation? and (4) What methodologies are being used in research on writing? Based on a body of refereed journal articles (N = 1,502) reporting studies about writing and composition instruction that were located using three databases, the authors characterize various lines of inquiry currently undertaken. Social context and writing practices, bi- or multilingualism and writing, and writing instruction are the most actively studied problems during this period, whereas writing and technologies, writing assessment and evaluation, and relationships among literacy modalities are the least studied problems. Undergraduate, adult, and other postsecondary populations are the most prominently studied population age group, whereas preschool-aged children and middle and high school students are least studied. Research on instruction within the preschool through 12th grade (PreK–12) age group is prominent, whereas research on genre, assessment, and bi- or multilingualism is scarce within this population. The majority of articles employ interpretive methods. This indicator of current writing research should be useful to researchers, policymakers, and funding agencies, as well as to writing teachers and teacher educators.

This article is available as a full-text PDF at http://www.sagepub.com/cappello/.

SOURCE: Juzwik, M. M., et al. (2006). Writing Into the 21st Century: An Overview of Research on Writing, 1999 to 2004. *Written Communication*, 23(4), 451–476. Reprinted by permission of Sage Publications, Inc.

Section IX

WORKING WITH ENGLISH LANGUAGE LEARNERS

OVERVIEW

According to Verdugo and Flores (2007) in their article "English Learners: Key Issues," although it is very clear that "the challenges posed by ELL students are significant, it is less clear what strategies and programs educators can use to improve the educational experiences of this population." To better explore these challenges, we include articles in this section that represent an overview of the research literature and address many of the questions we face when deciding how to best support our students who are learning English, one of the most important challenges we face in schools today.

Krashen (2008) opens this section of the reader by contextualizing research in language education. In "Language Education: Past, Present, and Future," he urges educators to move from the Skill-Building Hypothesis to take advantage of the "Comprehension Hypothesis, the view that we acquire language when we understand messages." In his article, "Teaching English Language Learners: What the Research Does—and Does Not—Say," Goldenberg (2008) urges us to "move beyond charged debates and all-too-certain answers" to look at the major findings in recent reviews of the research. Manyak (2007), in "A Framework for Robust Literacy Instruction for English Learners," offers practical advice for teachers working with English learners by helping teachers "translate the relevant research insights into practice." To better guide our English learners, Manyak suggests a framework that includes "explicit code and comprehension instruction, language-rich instruction, socio-culturally informed instruction, and additive literacy instruction."

Verdugo and Flores (2007) (available at http://www.sagepub.com/cappello/) frankly address researchers and policymakers as they sift through the debates to focus on the key issues surrounding our work with ELLs in schools. The authors focus on "four important topics affecting the education of the ELL student population: language acquisition, testing, school capacity, and teacher preparation."

STRATEGY

The articles in this section focus on the many challenges we face helping the English learners in our classrooms. Use the "Herringbone Strategy" (Wood, 2001) to negotiate this section of the reader. The Herringbone Strategy is a structured note-taking activity that engages the learner in identifying significant information in the texts. The purpose of the Herringbone Strategy is to help you attend to, remember, and organize important information in the text. Completing the graphic organizer will help you summarize the text content.

HERRINGBONE STRATEGY

(Wood, 2001)

DIRECTIONS

Step One: After you have read the articles in this section, use the following guiding questions to complete the herringbone graphic organizer.
Feel free to return to the articles when needed.

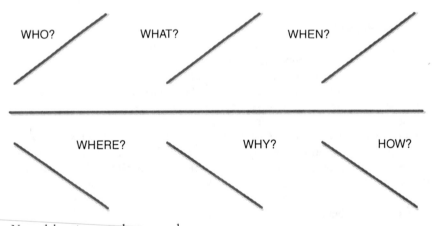

Step Two: Now elaborate on each answer above:

Who?
What?
When?
Where?
Why?
How?

Step Three: Use the statements above to create a summary of the section on "Working With English Language Learners" in the reader.

SOURCE: Wood, K. D. (2001). *Literacy Strategies Across the Subject Areas.* Boston: Allyn & Bacon.

Article 27

LANGUAGE EDUCATION

Past, Present, and Future

STEPHEN KRASHEN

Abstract The recent past in language teaching has been dominated by the Skill-Building Hypothesis, the view that we learn language by first learning about it, and then practicing the rules we learned in output. The present is marked by the emergence of the Comprehension Hypothesis, the view that we acquire language when we understand messages, and is also characterized by the beginning stages of its applications: comprehensible-input based teaching methods, sheltered subject matter teaching, and the use of extensive reading for intermediate language students. My hope is that the future will see a clearer understanding of the Comprehension Hypothesis, and the profession taking more advantage of it.

Keywords Comprehension Hypothesis, free voluntary surfing, Skill-Building Hypothesis

THE PAST: THE SKILL-BUILDING HYPOTHESIS

Approaches to language teaching in the recent past have been based on "skill-building." The hypothesis that we develop competence in language and literacy by first "learning about" language, that is, consciously learning the rules, and by deliberately studying vocabulary. We practice using the rules and new words in output (speaking and writing) again and again until they become "automatic." Correction helps us, it is claimed, by forcing us to reformulate our rules, to change our idea of the rules until we get them right.

The Skill-Building Hypothesis is a delayed-gratification hypothesis. It says that we must first study rules and learn vocabulary, and then

SOURCE: Krashen, S. (2008). Language Education: Past, Present, and Future. *RELC Journal, 39*(2), 178–187. Reprinted by permission of Sage Publications Ltd.

someday, after lots of hard work, we can actually use the language.

For the public, the Skill-Building Hypothesis is not an hypothesis: it is an axiom. For many people, it is the only way they can imagine language and literacy development taking place. Nearly all texts in foreign language education are based on skill-building, with presentations of grammar and vocabulary followed by very short texts and exercises designed to help the student "automatize" the rules. Real language use is delayed until the rules are "mastered."

Most approaches to literacy development are also based on skill-building. They assume that children must first consciously learn all sound-spelling correspondences (phonics), and then practice applying the rules of phonics in reading simple texts. Real reading is delayed until phonics is mastered.

Skill-building cannot be the major means of producing competence in language and literacy.

First, the system to be consciously learned is simply too complex and has not even been completely described. In fact, expert linguists admit that they have not succeeded in fully describing the grammatical rules of any language or the rules of phonics, and those they have come up with are often forbiddingly complicated. In fact, teachers have told me that they have to review the rules before coming to class! There are also far too many vocabulary words for language students to memorize one at a time.

Second, there are abundant cases of those who have acquired all or nearly all of a second language but who do not have conscious knowledge of more than a handful of rules (for cases, see Krashen 1981, 2000, 2004).

Third, the effect of error correction on language development has thus far been shown to be weak or nonexistent (Truscott 1996).

I have argued that conscious knowledge of language plays a very small role in language production; it is available only as a monitor, or editor. We can appeal to our conscious knowledge of language to correct ourselves before or after we speak or write something, but only if certain conditions are met, and the conditions are severe. We have to know the rule, be thinking about correctness, and have time to retrieve and apply the rule. For most people, this happens only when they take grammar tests (Krashen 1981).

THE PRESENT: THE COMPREHENSION HYPOTHESIS

Newer approaches to language teaching do not rely on painful "skill-building" but are based on the idea that we acquire language when we understand what we hear and read. They are based on the Comprehension Hypothesis.

According to the Comprehension Hypothesis, most of our language competence is the result of what we have subconsciously acquired, or absorbed, not what we have learned consciously, and real language competence is stored in the brain subconsciously. We are not aware we are acquiring when we are acquiring, and after we acquire, we are not aware that anything has happened.

The Comprehension Hypothesis has had several inventors and has been known by several different names. I have referred to it as the Input Hypothesis in previous publications. Well before my work began, Frank Smith and Kenneth Goodman hypothesized that "we learn to read by reading," by understanding what is on the page. James Asher and Harris Winitz, among others, also hypothesized that comprehension is the mechanism underlying language acquisition in publications that predate mine.

The manifestation of the Comprehension Hypothesis in literacy is the Reading Hypothesis, the claim that we learn to read by reading, as well as the claim that reading is the source of much of our vocabulary and spelling competence, our ability to handle complex grammatical structures, and to write with an acceptable writing style.

The Comprehension Hypothesis and the Skill-Building Hypothesis have squared off in a number of direct confrontations and the Comprehension Hypothesis has been a consistent winner. (It may be impossible to test pure forms of these hypotheses: while traditional methods are based on Skill-Building, they will inevitably contain some comprehensible input. Also, students in classes using methods based on the Comprehension Hypothesis may engage in self-study. But there is no doubt that traditional methods involve more skill-building than those based on the Comprehension Hypothesis.)

For beginning language teaching, methods based on the Comprehension Hypothesis, such as TPR, the Natural Approach, and Focal Skills have been shown to be more effective than traditional methods on tests of communication, and at least as effective on tests of "skills" (Krashen 1981, 2003a; Hastings 1997).

For intermediate language teaching, methods involving teaching content (sheltered subject matter teaching) have been shown to be just as effective or more effective than traditional intermediate methods (Krashen 1991).

For beginning literacy development in the first language, students in classes in which more real reading is done outperform those in classes in which less reading is done (Krashen 1999).

In both first and second language development, students who participate in classes that include in-school self-selected reading programs (known as sustained silent reading) typically outperform comparison students, especially when the duration of treatment is longer than an academic year (reviews include Krashen 2003a, 2004; Renandya 2007).

The case for reading has been strengthened by a new wave of research from Asia, studies demonstrating the efficacy of in-school for elementary school children in Korea (K.-S. Cho and H. Kim 2004; K.-S. Cho and H.-J. Kim 2005), college students in Japan (Mason and Krashen 1997), and high school and college students in Taiwan (Smith 2006, 2007; S.-Y. Lee 2007; C.-K. Liu 2007).

Correlational studies also support the Comprehension Hypothesis (e.g. S.-Y. Lee 2005; Witton-Davies 2006; Gradman and Hanania 1991; Constantino, S.-Y. Lee, K.-S. Cho and Krashen 1997; Stokes, Krashen and Kartchner 1998): Those who get more comprehensible

input in the form of reading do better on a variety of measures, a result that holds when other possible confounds are controlled.

A number of short-term comparisons have been done that claim to compare the impact of grammar instruction and comprehensible input, and the results have been interpreted as support for grammar, or the Skill-Building Hypothesis. Not so. The "comprehensible input" treatment in these studies has always been an impoverished version of comprehensible input, subjects in every study were experienced "learners" who valued conscious learning of language, and in all studies the conditions for the use of conscious learning were met. Nevertheless, in general, the impact of grammar study was surprisingly small (Truscott 1998; Krashen 2003a).

THE FUTURE

The future of language education, in my view, will, I hope, include at least two steps forward:

1. Distinguishing between the Comprehension Hypothesis and the Communicative Approach

Communicative language teaching has been defined as an approach that "makes use of real-life situations that necessitate communication. The teacher sets up a situation that students are likely to encounter in real life" (Galloway 1993).

According to this definition, the Communicative Approach is implicitly based on the Comprehensible Output Hypothesis (Swain 1985), the view that we acquire language when we try to produce it, fail to make ourselves understood, and keep trying until we achieve communicative success when we finally get it right. (A more subtle version of the Comprehensible Output Hypothesis maintains that the "need" to use certain structures in production makes acquirers more sensitive to these structures when they occur in input.)

I have presented arguments against the strong form of the Comprehensible Output Hypothesis (i.e. the view that it is the primary mechanism for language development). Briefly, instances of comprehensible output are too rare for it to make any substantial contribution to language competence and language acquisition is possible without output of any kind. Evidence against the weak form, that comprehensible output contributes to language development, is the fact that there is no clear empirical evidence supporting it (Krashen 2003b).

The Communicative Approach (again, as I understand it) is thus not only not the same as the Comprehension Hypothesis, it is the opposite. (Of course, "real-life situations" entail input as well as output, but nearly all manifestations of the Communicative Approach I have seen focus on the output side.)

2. Taking Full Advantage of the Comprehension Hypothesis in Language Education

The second step forward I hope for is for the language teaching profession to take full advantage of the Comprehension Hypothesis. Thus far, the language teaching profession has not come close to applying the Comprehension Hypothesis with full force. In my view, the most under-utilized application is the easiest one to use: extensive reading.

The first sub-step in applying this aspect of the Comprehension Hypothesis is to simply make good reading material available, the establishment of super-libraries, filled with good books, magazines, and comics, with a selection wide enough to ensure that each student of English can read for pleasure in a variety of areas for hours at a time and for years, if desired. Funding for such an enterprise is modest, compared to the millions we are willing (and eager) to spend on computer technology, despite the fact that there is no solid evidence that computer-aided instruction helps language development (but see below).

The second sub-step in applying the Reading Hypothesis is to give students some time to read. This is important for two reasons: first, it signals

to students how important self-selected reading is; second, a small amount of daily regular reading will stimulate more reading outside of school (Sims 1996).

The third sub-step is to inform students how language and literacy are acquired. If we want our students to be autonomous, to be independent language acquirers, able to continue to make progress after the school program is finished, they need to know how. If the Comprehension Hypothesis is correct, students need to know about it, and not devote their time to vocabulary flash cards and extensive grammar review. They need to know that a reading habit will guarantee continuing growth in English.

I am also hoping that in the future we will no longer reward students for reading with prizes or names on a public list. There is no empirical evidence supporting this practice (Krashen 2003b, 2005), and there is the danger that if we reward a pleasurable activity we send the message that the activity is not really pleasant and that nobody would do it without a bribe (Kohn 1999).

The methodology of the future will, I hope, include sheltered popular literature, an introduction to what is available in the target language, taught in a way to reveal aspects of current culture in other countries, and to stimulate interest in reading.

The Computer in the Future. Of course, no discussion of the future of language education would be complete without some discussion of the potential of the computer. Nearly all pedagogical applications of the computer to language education have assumed the correctness of the Skill-Building Hypothesis, and experiments in Computer-Assisted Instruction typically compare one form of skill-building with another and are therefore of peripheral value.

How can the computer be used to deliver comprehensible input? Fortunately, the future is already here. For aural input, students of English as a foreign or second language, *eslpod.com* provides free listening experiences on a wide variety of topics (*eslpod.com* also has some materials for sale; I am enthusiastic about their material, and I have no financial interest in this enterprise).

In terms of reading, the Internet has a wide selection of pedagogical texts in English, but they are inevitably followed by exercises and comprehension questions. And of course, the Internet is filled with authentic English reading, but much of it is too difficult for most language students.

The best way to use the Internet as a source of reading may be "free voluntary surfing," or FVS. In FVS, as in free voluntary reading, students read what they want to read (within reason), with no accountability, no follow-up exercises, no assigned topics, and no vocabulary list that they must try to remember.

Evidence so far suggests that surfing is beneficial to first language development. Jackson, von Eye, Biocca, Barbatsis, Zhao and Fitzgerald (2006) provided computers with Internet access to 140 children from low-income families who previously did not have access and reported that more Internet use resulted in improved reading, as reflected by grades and standardized tests. The improvements were present after six months of Internet use for test scores and after one year for grades. There was no impact on mathematics test scores, and the data did not support the hypothesis that better readers used the Internet more; rather, Internet use improved reading.

There is no need to fear that surfing will take the place of reading: in fact, studies show that it results in more reading (for adolescents in the Netherlands; de Haan and Huysmans 2004; for adults in Taiwan; Liu, Day, Sun and Wany 2000).

The Popularity of the Internet and Surfing. Most students already know all about the Internet and many are dedicated surfers. In the US, for example, it has been estimated that 42% of the entire population uses the Internet (Horrigan 2006). More interesting is the fact that 81% of high school students use the Internet, which indicates that Internet use among the general population will continue to increase (DeBell and Chapman 2006).

Not only do many people use the Internet, many surf: Fallows (2006) reported that "surfing for fun" is the second most popular online activity,

behind using email. Zhu and He (2002) reported that 52% of the 1007 Hong Kong residents they interviewed were connected to the Internet at home, averaging 350 minutes per week on the net at home. About 30% of total home-use time was devoted to "searching for personal Internet information." In addition, the children studied by Jackson et al. clearly liked web-surfing: when asked what their main activity on the computer was, 33% said it was "web search" (Jackson, von Eye, Biocca, Barbatsis, Zhao and Fitzgerald 2005: 263).

Problems and Solutions. Few language students take advantage of the Internet for free voluntary surfing. In Taiwan, for example, over 90% of Internet use is in Chinese (Liu, Day, Sun and Wany 2000), and I suspect that the few who are reading texts in other languages are already highly proficient in these languages. Why is this so?

First, few language teaching programs mention the use of the Internet for simply reading. Second, just as is the case with free voluntary reading, few have any idea that surfing would be good for them, having only been presented with the Skill-Building point of view. For most language students, if they try the Internet at all in another language, the temptation is to do intensive reading, making sure they understand every word and focusing on form.

The cure may be wandering through the Internet and finding reading material that is truly compelling, so compelling that the reader is absorbed in the message and matters of form become irrelevant. Ironically, this will result in more acquisition of the language and literacy development (Krashen 2004).

CONCLUSION

Humans are not very good at predicting the future. So much of what science-fiction writers have predicted, in both technology and political events, has turned out to be wrong. (Back in the 1950s, we were sure that by 2000 we would have colonies on Mars, we would be free of most diseases, and we would have world peace.) So instead of predicting the future, I have made up a wish-list, but of course we know from experience that sometimes we are better off when not all of our wishes come true. I have therefore restricted my discussion of the future to the near future, to hopes and wishes that are, I think, already in the process of happening and that have a good chance to continue to develop. Even so, next week's research breakthrough might change everything.

Stephen Krashen, University of Southern California (Emeritus)

Article 28

TEACHING ENGLISH LANGUAGE LEARNERS

What the Research Does—and Does Not—Say

CLAUDE GOLDENBERG

Should students who are learning English spend the school day in classes where only English is spoken? Or should they be taught reading and other academic skills and content in their native language? Or should their classes be primarily in English, but include some explanations or materials in their native language? If their native language is to be used, how much native language instruction should they receive and for what purposes? And aren't there other issues we need to consider, aside from language of instruction? These are important questions, and anyone who can provide a quick answer is surely oversimplifying the issues. Some English language learners (ELLs) do not speak a word of English and are not literate in their native language. Others have some conversational English, but are not yet fluent, and in their native language they are not only literate, but have mastered a great deal of academic content. There will probably never be a formula for educating ELLs, just as there is no formula for educating students who already know English. What we can do is provide guidelines based on our strongest research about effective practices for teaching ELLs.

It's time to move beyond charged debates and all-too-certain answers. What students need is for educators and policymakers to take a more in-depth look, starting with what existing research does—and

SOURCE: Teaching English Language Learners: What the Research Does—and Does Not—Say, by Claude Goldenberg. Reprinted by permission from the Summer 2008 issue of *American Educator*, the quarterly journal of the American Federation of Teachers, AFL-CIO.

does not—say. In this article, Claude Goldenberg walks us through the major findings of two recent reviews of the research on educating ELLs. Given all the strong opinions one sees in newspaper op-eds, readers may be surprised to discover how little is actually known. What's certain is that if we conducted more research with ELLs, and paid more attention to the research that exists, we would be in a much better position.

And so, we bring you this article with four goals in mind. First, we hope that everyone who engages in debates about educating ELLs will become a little more knowledgeable and, therefore, will start taking a little more nuanced positions. Second, we wish to spur more research (and more funding for more research). Third, to keep the snake-oil salesmen at bay, we think it's best for educators to know what existing research cannot support. And fourth, we believe that what has been reasonably well established is worth knowing.

—EDITORS

Imagine you are in second grade. Throughout the year you might be expected to learn irregular spelling patterns, diphthongs, syllabication rules, regular and irregular plurals, common prefixes and suffixes, antonyms and synonyms; how to follow written instructions, interpret words with multiple meanings, locate information in expository texts, use comprehension strategies and background knowledge to understand what you read, understand cause and effect, identify alliteration and rhyme, understand structural features of texts such as theme, plot, and setting; read fluently and correctly at least 80 words per minute, add approximately 3,000 words to your vocabulary, read tens if not hundreds of thousands of words from different types of texts; and write narratives and friendly letters using appropriate forms, organization, critical elements, capitalization, and punctuation, revising as needed.

And that's just before recess.

After recess you will have a similar list for math. And if you are fortunate enough to attend a school where all instruction has not been completely eclipsed by reading and math, after lunch you'll be tackling such things as motion, magnetism, life cycles, environments, weather, and fuel; interpreting information from diagrams, graphs, and charts; comparing and contrasting objects using their physical attributes; tracing your family history, comparing the lives of your parents and grandparents to your life; putting important events in a timeline; labeling the countries, the state where you live, mountain ranges, major rivers, and lakes on a map of North America; and learning how important historical figures such as Martin Luther King, Jr., Albert Einstein, Abraham Lincoln, Cesar Chavez, and Sally Ride made a difference in the lives of others. The expectations created by state and district academic standards can be a bit overwhelming—for students and for teachers.[1]

Now, imagine that you don't speak English very well. Your job is to learn what everyone else is learning, plus learn English. And it's not sufficient to learn English so you can talk with your friends and teacher about classroom routines, what you are having for lunch, where you went over the weekend, or who was mean to whom on the playground. You have to learn what is called "academic English," a term that refers to more abstract, complex, and challenging language that will eventually permit you to participate successfully in mainstream classroom instruction. Academic English involves such things as relating an event or a series of events to someone who was not present, being able to make comparisons between alternatives and justify a choice, knowing different forms and inflections of words and their appropriate use, and possessing and using content-specific vocabulary and modes of expression in different academic disciplines such as mathematics and social studies. As if this were not enough, you eventually need to be able to understand and produce academic English both orally and in writing.[2] If you don't, there is a real chance of falling behind your classmates, making poorer grades, getting discouraged, falling further behind, and having fewer educational and occupational choices.

Sound intimidating?

This is the situation faced by millions of students in U.S. schools who do not speak English fluently. Their number has grown dramatically just in the past 15 years. In 1990, one in 20 public school students in grades K–12 was an English language learner (ELL), that is, a student who speaks English either not at all or with enough limitations that he or she cannot fully participate in mainstream English instruction. Today the figure is 1 in 9. Demographers estimate that in 20 years it might be 1 in 4. The ELL population has grown from 2 million to 5 million since 1990, a period when the overall school population increased only 20 percent.[3] States not typically associated with non-English speakers—Indiana, North Carolina, South Carolina, and Tennessee—each saw an increase in the ELL population of at least 300 percent between 1994–95 and 2004–05.[4]

ELL students in the U.S. come from over 400 different language backgrounds. What may come as a surprise to many readers is that most ELLs were born in the United States. Among elementary-age ELLs, 76 percent were born in the U.S. Among middle- and high-school students, 56 percent were born in this country. However, about 80 percent of ELLs' parents were born outside of the U.S.[5]

By far, the majority of ELLs—80 percent—are Spanish speakers. This is an important fact to bear in mind, since Spanish speakers in the U.S. tend to come from lower economic and educational backgrounds than either the general population or other immigrants and language minority populations.[6] For example, nearly 24 percent of immigrants from Mexico and Central America are below the poverty level, compared with 9 to 14 percent of immigrants from other regions of the world (and 11.5 percent of the U.S. native-born population). Fewer than 40 percent of immigrants from Mexico and Central America have the equivalent of a high school diploma, in contrast to between 80 and 90 percent of other immigrants (and 87.5 percent of U.S.-born residents). Consequently, most ELLs are at risk for poor school outcomes not only because of language, but also because of socioeconomic factors.

Speakers of Asian languages (e.g., Vietnamese, Hmong, Chinese, Korean, Khmer, Laotian, Hincli, Tagalog) comprise the next largest group—about eight percent of the ELL population. Students of Asian origin tend to come from families with higher income and education levels than do other immigrant families. For example, among immigrants from the major world regions, the poverty rate of Asian immigrants is the second lowest (at 11.1 percent); only immigrants from Europe have a lower poverty rate. Over 87 percent of Asian immigrants have the equivalent of a high school diploma, the highest among immigrants from major world regions.[7] But these figures hide the tremendous diversity within the Asian populations in the U.S. For example, 50 percent or fewer Cambodian, Laotian, and Hmong adults in the U.S. have completed the equivalent of high school and fewer than 10 percent have a college degree. In contrast, Filipinos, Indians, and Japanese in the U.S. have high school completion rates around 90 percent. Over 60 percent of Taiwanese and Indians in the U.S. have college degrees.[8]

What sort of instructional environments are ELLs in? This question is difficult to answer, partly because of definitional and reporting inconsistencies from state to state.[9] The most recent national data come from a 2001–02 school year survey.[10] To the extent the portrait is still accurate six years later, a majority of English learners—approximately 60 percent—are in essentially all-English instruction: one-fifth of these students—about 12 percent of all ELLs—apparently receive no services or support at all related to their limited English proficiency;[i] the other four-fifths—nearly 50 percent of all ELLs—receive all-English instruction, but with some amount of "LEP services." (ELLs were formerly called "LEP" or limited English proficient; the term is sometimes still used.) "LEP services" can include aides or resource teachers specifically for ELLs, instruction in English as a second language (ESL), and/or content instruction specially designed for students with limited English proficiency. The remaining ELLs—about 40 percent—are in programs that make some use of their home language, but it is impossible to say what is typical. In some cases, students receive one of several forms of bilingual education, a term that describes any instructional approach that teaches at least some academic content (e.g., reading or science) in the native language in addition to teaching students academic content in English. Sometimes teaching academic content, such as reading, is just for a year or two as students transition to all-English instruction; sometimes it is for several years (e.g., through the end of elementary school or into middle school) to develop bilingualism and biliteracy. In other cases, students are taught academic content in English, but their primary language is used for "support" such as translations by an aide, explanations during or after class, or to preview material prior to an all-English lesson.[11] Currently, there is no way to know the amount of support students receive or, most critically, the quality of the instruction and whether or not it is helpful for student achievement.

What we do know is that on average, ELLs' academic achievement tends to be low. On the 2007 National Assessment of Educational Progress (NAEP), fourth-grade ELLs scored 36 points below non-ELLs in reading and 25 points below non-ELLs in math. The gaps among eighth-graders were even larger—42 points in reading and 37 points in math. Those are very large gaps. In fact, the gaps between ELLs and non-ELLs are 3 to 18 points larger than the gaps between students who are and are not eligible for free or reduced-price lunch.[12]

These discrepancies should be no surprise since ELLs are limited in their English proficiency, and the tests cited here are in English. But there is no way to know whether ELLs tested in English score low because of lagging content knowledge and skills, or because of limited English proficiency, or because of other factors that interfere with their test performance—or some combination. Whatever the explanation for these achievement gaps, they bode ill for English learners' future educational and vocational options. They also bode ill for society as a whole, since the costs of large-scale underachievement are very high.[13] Teachers of ELLs are thus under tremendous pressure. It is imperative that they, as well as administrators and other school staff, understand the state of our regarding how to improve the achievement of these students. Unfortunately, the state of our knowledge is modest. But what is known offers some useful guidance for educators to improve the academic success of English language learners.

My aim in this article is to summarize key findings of two major reviews of the research on educating English learners that were completed in 2006—one by the National Literacy Panel, or NLP,[14] the other by researchers associated with the Center for Research on Education, Diversity, and Excellence, or CREDE.[15] These reviews represent the most concerted efforts to date to identify the best knowledge available and set the stage for renewed efforts to find effective approaches to help English learners succeed in school. As needed, I will also reference additional research that appeared after the years covered by the NLP and CREDE reviews.

---

[i]This figure might be an underestimate. It comes from school and district officials who could be reluctant to report that ELLs receive "no services," which is likely to be a violation of the 1974 Supreme Court decision in *Lau v. Nichols* (414) U.S. No. 72-6520, pp. 563–572) requiring schools to teach ELLs so that they have "a meaningful opportunity to participate in the public education program" (p. 563).

As companion to this article on what we do know about educating ELLs, a section at the end of this article explores critical questions that have yet to be answered (see "Critical Questions" box) and possible instructional modifications that might help ELLs achieve at levels more comparable to that of their English-speaking peers. I encourage educators to read this as carefully as they read this article—especially before adopting programs that promise extraordinary results.

The NLP comprised 18 researchers with expertise in literacy, language development, the education of language minority students, assessment, and quantitative and qualitative research methods. The NLP, whose work took nearly three years, identified over 3,000 reports, documents, dissertations, and publications produced from approximately 1980 to 2002 as candidates for inclusion in its review. Fewer than 300 met the criteria for inclusion: they were empirical (that is, they collected, analyzed, and reported data, rather than stated opinions, advocated positions, or reviewed previous research), dealt with clearly identified language minority populations, and studied children and youth ages 3–18.

The CREDE report was produced over two years by a core group of four researchers (and three co-authors), all of whom had been engaged in language minority and language research for many years. As did the NLP, the CREDE panel conducted literature searches to identify candidate empirical research reports on language minority students from preschool to high school, but their searches were not as extensive as the NLP's. Approximately 200 articles and reports comprised the final group of studies the CREDE panel reviewed and upon which they based their conclusions. The studies the CREDE panel reviewed were published during approximately the same period as the studies the NLP reviewed.

Although they covered a lot of the same terrain, the CREDE and NLP reports differed in some ways. For example, the CREDE report only examined research conducted in the U.S. and only took into consideration outcomes in English; the NLP included studies conducted anywhere in the world (as long as they were published in English) and took into consideration outcomes in children's first or second language. The CREDE panelists included quantitative studies (experiments or correlational research) almost exclusively, whereas the NLP also included a large number of qualitative studies.[ii] The CREDE panel reviewed research that addressed children's English language development, literacy development, and achievement in the content areas (science, social studies, and mathematics). In contrast, the NLP only looked at influences on literacy development (and aspects of oral language that are closely related to literacy, such as phonological awareness and vocabulary). A final and very important difference between the two reports was the criteria used to determine which studies of bilingual education to include. The NLP used more stringent criteria, resulting in a difference in the two reports' findings regarding the effects of different lengths of time in bilingual education on ELLs' academic achievement. I describe this difference in the "Critical Questions" box.

In doing their reviews, both sets of panelists paid particular attention to the quality of the studies and the degree to which reported findings were adequately supported by the research undertaken. The goal of both reviews was to synthesize the research and draw conclusions that would be helpful to educators and that would

---

[ii]Experimental studies are considered the "gold standard" if one wants to determine the effect of a particular program or type of instruction. Experiments use treatment and comparison groups, as well as other controls designed to ensure that any impacts found can be attributed to the treatment (as opposed to differences, for example, between two groups of students). Correlational studies can establish that there is a relationship between two things (like an instructional method and student achievement), but they cannot be used to demonstrate that one thing caused another. Qualitative studies generally attempt to describe and analyze rather than measure and count. Precise and highly detailed qualitative studies can establish causation (e.g., a part of a lesson that led to the student learning), but because the number of subjects in a qualitative study is typically low, they are not good for establishing generalizability.

also identify areas for additional future study. Readers should be aware of the dramatic discrepancy between the research base for English speakers and English learners. For example, eight years ago the National Reading Panel (which excluded studies of language learners) synthesized findings from over 400 experimental studies of instruction in phonological awareness, phonics, vocabulary, reading fluency, and reading comprehension.[16] In contrast, the NLP could identify only 17 experimental studies of instructional procedures, even though the NLP considered more topics and used looser inclusion criteria. The amount of research with ELLs has increased greatly, even in the two years since these reports were published. However, more research on educating ELLs is clearly needed.

It would be impossible to fully summarize the reports here, and educators are encouraged to obtain and study them. But their key conclusions can help us forge a new foundation for improving the education of children from non-English-speaking homes. The findings can be summarized in three major points:

- Teaching students to read in their first language promotes higher levels of reading achievement *in English*;

- What we know about good instruction and curriculum in general holds true for English learners as well; but

- When instructing English learners in English, teachers must modify instruction to take into account students' language limitations.

Let's take a closer look at each point.

I. Teaching Students to Read in Their First Language Promotes Higher Levels of Reading Achievement in English

Whether English learners should be instructed exclusively in English or in their native language and English has been, without question, the single most controversial issue in this area.[17] Dozens of studies and evaluations have been conducted and reported over the past 35 years comparing reading instruction that uses students' first and second languages with second language immersion (which in the U.S. would, of course, be English). The NLP conducted a meta-analysis[iii] with 17 of these studies—the others did not meet the panel's stringent methodological criteria. The analysis concluded that teaching ELLs to read in their first language and then in their second language, or in their first and second languages simultaneously[18] (at different times during the day), compared with teaching them to read in their second language only, boosts their reading achievement in *the second language*. And the higher-quality, more rigorous studies showed the strongest effects.

For example, five of the most rigorous studies the NLP reviewed involved random assignment of Spanish-speaking students either to English-only instruction or to instruction that was in both English and Spanish. The five studies were varied in terms of students who participated and the use of Spanish for academic instruction. Of these five studies, three were with elementary-age students (including one study with special education ELLs), one was with middle-school

---

[iii]A meta-analysis is a statistical technique that allows researchers to combine data from many studies and calculate the average effect of an instructional procedure. It is useful because studies often come to conflicting conclusions. Some find positive effects of a program, others find negative effects of the same type of program, and yet others find no effects. Even among studies that report positive findings, the effects can be small or large. The questions a meta-analysis addresses are these: Taking into account all the relevant studies on a topic, overall, is the effect positive, negative, or zero? And if it is overall positive or negative, what is the magnitude of the effect—large, and therefore meaningful; small, and therefore of little consequence; or something in between? Are there additional factors, e.g., student characteristics, that influence whether effects are large or small?

students, and one was with high-school students. In one of the elementary studies, students in grades one through three received all their academic instruction (reading, math, writing, science, social studies) in Spanish until they knew enough English to "transition" to English instruction. Students in the control condition received no instruction or support in Spanish. In the study with special education students, second- and third-graders received reading instruction either in English only or in Spanish combined with English as a second language instruction for one year, followed by gradually more instruction in English and less in Spanish over the next two years. The middle-school study included two groups of low-achieving seventh-graders who received equivalent English instruction, but one group received additional instruction in Spanish that focused on reading skills. And the high-school study involved students with low reading achievement who received either English-only instruction or instruction in English and Spanish. All five studies found positive effects of bilingual education on students' reading achievement on various measures of reading in English.

This consistent finding might surprise some readers. But the NLP was the latest of five meta-analyses that reached the same conclusion: learning to read in the home language promotes reading achievement in the second language.[19] Readers should understand how unusual it is to have five meta-analyses on the same issue conducted by five independent researchers or groups of researchers with diverse perspectives. The fact that they all reached essentially the same conclusion is worth noting. No other area in educational research with which I am familiar can claim five independent meta-analyses based on experimental studies—much less five that converge on the same basic finding.

To some people this finding might seem counterintuitive. A few years ago a fair-minded colleague expressed disbelief: "Doesn't it just make sense," she asked, "that the earlier and more intensively children are placed in all-English instruction at school the better their English achievement will eventually be?" That's when it hit me: when the goal is English proficiency, delivering any instruction in the first language probably does *not* make sense to some people. But this is why we do scientific research: common sense does not always turn out to be the truth. If we only relied on common sense, we would still think the sun revolves around a flat earth.

How does learning reading skills in their first language help students read in their second language? Although several explanations are possible, a likely one is based on what educational psychologists and cognitive scientists call "transfer." Transfer is one of the most venerable and important concepts in education. With respect to English learners, a substantial body of research reviewed by both CREDE and NLP researchers suggests that literacy and other skills and knowledge transfer across languages. That is, if you learn something in one language—such as decoding, comprehension strategies, or a concept such as democracy—you either already know it in (i.e., transfer it to) another language or can more easily learn it in another language.

We do not have a very precise understanding of exactly what transfers across languages, but there are numerous candidates. Phonological awareness might transfer—once you know that words are made up of smaller constituent sounds, you can probably apply that understanding to any language. Decoding skills, as well as knowledge of specific letters and sounds, probably transfer also. The letter *m,* for example, represents the same sound in many languages. But while the concept of decoding probably transfers across alphabetic languages, students will need to learn which rules should transfer and which should not. Spanish, for instance, has no final silent *e* that makes a preceding vowel long. Thus, a Spanish speaker applying Spanish orthographic rules to English words would think the word "tone" has two syllables (since he would pronounce the *e*). In all likelihood, English learners are helped by instruction that points out both what does and does not transfer from their home language to English.[iv] Numerous other aspects of reading probably transfer, for example, comprehension skills and knowledge of concepts (background knowledge) that are essential for comprehension.

Transfer of reading skills across languages appears to occur even if languages use different alphabetic systems, although the different alphabets probably diminish the degree of transfer. For example, studies of transfer between English and Spanish find relatively high correlations on measures of word reading, phonological awareness, and spelling. Some studies of English and non-Roman alphabets (e.g., Arabic), in contrast, find much lower correlations. However, comprehension skills appear to transfer readily between languages with different alphabets such as English and Korean.

Teachers cannot assume that transfer is automatic. Students sometimes do not realize that what they know in their first language (e.g., cognates such as *elefante* and *elephant,* or *ejemplo* and *example;* or spelling and comprehension skills) can be applied in their second. One researcher puts it this way: "Less successful bilingual readers view their two languages as separate and unrelated, and they often see their non-English language backgrounds as detrimental."[20] Ideally, teachers should be aware of what students know and can do in their primary language so they can help them apply it to tasks in English.

Let's be clear: the effects of primary language instruction are modest—but they are real. Researchers gauge the effect of a program or an instructional practice in terms of an "effect size" that tells us how much improvement can be expected from using the program or practice. The average effect size of primary language reading instruction over two to three years (the typical length of time children in the studies were followed) is around .35 to .40; estimates range from about .2 to about .6, depending on how the

calculation is done. What this means is that after two to three years of first and second language reading instruction, the average student can expect to score about 12 to 15 percentile points higher than the average student who only receives second language reading instruction. That's not huge, but it's not trivial either. These effects are reliable and, as mentioned previously, have been found with secondary as well as elementary students, and special education as well as general education students. Primary language reading instruction is clearly no panacea, but relatively speaking, it makes a meaningful contribution to reading achievement *in English.* We are less clear, however, on the effects of different lengths of time in bilingual education; that is, do more years of bilingual education produce higher levels of English achievement? (See the "Critical Questions" box for more on this.)

In addition, the meta-analyses found that bilingual education helps ELLs become bilingual and biliterate. The NLP, whose criteria for including studies were very strict, concluded that "children in the bilingual programs studied . . . also developed literacy skills in their native language. Thus, they achieved the advantage of being bilingual and biliterate."[21] Knowing two languages confers numerous obvious advantages—cultural, intellectual, cognitive,[22] vocational, and economic (some studies have found increased earnings for bilingual individuals[23]).

In many schools, instruction in the primary language is not feasible, because there is no qualified staff or because students come from numerous language backgrounds or, sadly, because of uninformed policy choices or political decisions. English learners can still be helped to achieve at higher levels. Although the research here is not as solid as the research on primary language instruction in reading, educators have two other important principles, supported by research to varying degrees, on which to base their practice. We turn to them now.

[iv]See http://coe.sdsu.edu/people/jmora/MoraModules/MetaLingResearch.htm for a helpful document identifying elements of English and Spanish spelling that do and do not transfer.

II. WHAT WE KNOW ABOUT GOOD INSTRUCTION AND CURRICULUM IN GENERAL HOLDS TRUE FOR ELLs

Both the CREDE and NLP reports conclude that ELLs learn in much the same way as non-ELLs (although instructional modifications and enhancements are almost certainly necessary, as discussed in the next section). Good instruction for students in general tends to be good instruction for ELLs in particular. If instructed in the primary language, the application of effective instructional models to English learners is transparent; all that differs is the language of instruction. But even when instructed in English, effective instruction is similar in important respects to effective instruction for non-ELLs.

As a general rule, all students tend to benefit from clear goals and learning objectives; meaningful, challenging, and motivating contexts; a curriculum rich with content; well-designed, clearly structured, and appropriately paced instruction; active engagement and participation; opportunities to practice, apply, and transfer new learning; feedback on correct and incorrect responses; periodic review and practice; frequent assessments to gauge progress, with reteaching as needed; and opportunities to interact with other students in motivating and appropriately structured contexts. Although these instructional variables have not been studied with ELLs to the degree they have been with English speakers, existing studies suggest that what is known about effective instruction in general ought to be the foundation of effective teaching for English learners. There are, of course, individual or group differences: some students might benefit from more or less structure, practice, review, autonomy, challenge, or any other dimension of teaching and learning. This is as likely to be true for English learners as it is for English speakers.

The NLP found that ELLs learning to read in English, just like English speakers learning to read in English, benefit from explicit teaching of the components of literacy, such as phonemic awareness, phonics, vocabulary, comprehension, and writing. The NLP reviewed five studies that as a group showed the benefits of structured, direct instruction for the development of literacy skills among ELLs. A study in England, for example, found that a structured program called Jolly Phonics had a stronger effect on ELLs' phonological awareness and alphabet knowledge, and their application to reading and writing, than did a Big Books approach.[24] Other studies also showed similar effects of directly teaching the sounds that make up words, how letters represent those sounds, and how letters combine to form words. More recent studies[25] continue to provide evidence of the benefits of directly teaching phonological and decoding skills to English learners, particularly as part of comprehensive approaches to boost early literacy among children at risk for reading problems.[v]

Studies of vocabulary instruction also show that ELLs are more likely to learn words when they are directly taught. Just as with English speakers, ELLs learn more words when the words are embedded in meaningful contexts and students are provided with ample opportunities for their repetition and use, as opposed to looking up dictionary definitions or presenting words in single sentences. For example, a study[26] reviewed by the NLP involving fifth-graders showed that explicit vocabulary instruction, using words from texts appropriate for and likely to interest the students, combined with exposure to and use of the words in numerous contexts (reading and hearing stories, discussions, posting target words, and writing words and definitions for homework), led to improvements in word learning and reading comprehension.[vi] These are principles of effective vocabulary instruction

[v]For more information, see "Enhanced Proactive Reading" at http://ies.ed.gov/ncee/wwc/reports/english_lang/topic/taabfig.asp

[vi]For more information, see "Vocabulary Improvement Program for English Language Learners and Their Classmates, VIP" at http://ies.ed.gov/ncee/wwc/reports/english_lang/topic/taabfig.asp

that have been found to be effective for English speakers.[27] Similarly, a preschool study too recent to be included in the NLP or CREDE reviews showed that explaining new vocabulary helped Portuguese-speaking children acquire vocabulary from storybook reading.[28] Although children with higher initial English scores learned more words, explaining new words was helpful for all children, regardless of how little English they knew.

Other types of instruction that the NLP review found to be promising with ELLs, especially for increasing their reading comprehension, include cooperative learning (students working interdependently on group instructional tasks and learning goals), encouraging reading in English, discussions to promote comprehension ("instructional conversations"), and mastery learning (which involves precise behavioral objectives permitting students to reach a "mastery" criterion before moving to new learning).[vii] One mastery learning study reviewed by the NLP was particularly informative because the researchers found this approach more effective in promoting Mexican-American students' reading comprehension than an approach that involved teaching to the students' supposed "cultural learning style."

The CREDE report reached similar conclusions, which it summarized this way: "The best recommendation to emerge from our review favors instruction that combines interactive and direct approaches."[29] "Interactive" refers to instruction with give and take between learners and teacher, where the teacher is actively promoting students' progress by encouraging higher levels of thinking, speaking, and reading at their instructional levels. Examples of interactive teaching include structured discussions ("instructional conversations"), brainstorming, and editing/discussing student or teacher writing. "Direct approaches" emphasize explicit and direct teaching of skills or knowledge, for example, letter-sound associations, spelling patterns, vocabulary

words, or mathematical algorithms. Typically, direct instruction uses techniques such as modeling, instructional input, corrective feedback, and guided practice to help students acquire knowledge and skills as efficiently as possible. The CREDE report notes that direct instruction of specific skills is important in order to help students gain "mastery of literacy-related skills that are often embedded in complex literacy or academic tasks."[30]

In contrast to interactive and direct teaching, the CREDE report found at best mixed evidence supporting what it termed "process approaches." These are approaches where students are exposed to rich literacy experiences and literacy materials, but receive little direct teaching or structured learning. In one study, for example, students were exposed to alternative reading and writing strategies on wall charts, but this was insufficient to ensure that students would use the strategies. In another study, Spanish-speaking ELLs who received structured writing lessons outperformed students who received extended opportunities to do "free writing." The CREDE report concludes that process approaches are "not sufficient to promote acquisition of the specific skills that comprise reading and writing.... [F]ocused and explicit instruction in particular skills and sub-skills is called for if ELLs are to become efficient and effective readers and writers."[31]

III. WHEN INSTRUCTING ENGLISH LEARNERS IN ENGLISH, TEACHERS MUST MODIFY INSTRUCTION TO TAKE INTO ACCOUNT STUDENTS' LANGUAGE LIMITATIONS

Although many aspects of effective instruction apply across the board for learners in general, for English learners, instructional modifications are almost certainly necessary. A very important

viiFor more information, see "Bilingual Cooperative Integrated Reading and Composition, BCIRC," "Peer-Assisted Learning Strategies (PALS)," "Instructional Conversatons and Literature Logs," and "Reading Mastery" at http://ies.ed.gov/ncee/wwc/ reports/english_lang/topic/taabfig.asp finding that emerged from the NLP's review was that the impact of instructional practices or interventions tends to be weaker for English learners than for English speakers.

For example, the National Reading Panel identified eight types of reading comprehension strategy instruction that had reliable positive effects on the reading comprehension of English-speaking students, such as comprehension monitoring, question asking, and summarization. The effect sizes of some of these were as high as 1.0, meaning that the average student who received this type of instruction scored 34 percentile points higher than the average student who did not receive this instruction. In contrast, the NLP found the effects of comprehension strategy instruction in English with ELLs so weak that there is a real question as to whether there were any effects at all. There was only one study specifically targeted at improving ELLs' reading comprehension that produced statistically reliable results, and it wasn't even a study of comprehension strategies—it was a study of the effects of simplifying a text. But its implications are a bit ambiguous: although using simplified texts can help ELLs access content that they would not otherwise have, clearly we can't (and wouldn't want to) limit ELLs' reading to simplified texts. To be clear: the NLP did find studies that demonstrated effects of reading instruction on reading comprehension among ELLs, as discussed previously, e.g., cooperative learning, instructional conversations, and mastery learning. But the effects of teaching reading comprehension *strategies* per se was not nearly as strong for ELLs as it has been shown to be for English speakers. In fact, it might have had no effect at all.

Why might this be so? And what are some special considerations for promoting comprehension with ELLs? There are probably many factors that influence the effects of comprehension instruction on English learners, some possibly having to do with these children's out-of-school experiences. But an undoubtedly important factor is the double challenge ELLs face: learning academic content and skills *while* learning the language in which these skills are taught and practiced. Reading comprehension requires not only the skills of reading—accurate and fluent word recognition, understanding how words form texts that carry meaning, and how to derive meanings from these texts—but it also requires fundamental language proficiency—knowledge of vocabulary, syntax, and conventions of use that are the essence of "knowing" a language. Learners who have the basic reading skills and know the language can concentrate on the academic content. But learners who do not know the language, or do not know it well enough, must devote part of their attention to learning and understanding the language in which that content is taught. It's an enormous challenge that most ELLs probably have difficulty meeting without additional instructional supports.

In the earliest stages of learning to read, however, when the focus is on sounds, letters, and how they combine to form words that can be read, English learners can make progress in English that is comparable to that of English speakers, provided the instruction is clear, focused, and systematic. In other words, when the language requirements are relatively low—as they are for learning phonological skills (the sounds of the language and how words are made up of smaller constituent sounds), letter-sound combinations, decoding, and word recognition—ELLs are more likely to make adequate progress, as judged by the sort of progress we would expect of English speakers. They still probably require some additional support due to language limitations.

As content gets more challenging and language demands increase, more and more complex vocabulary and syntax are required, and the need for instructional modifications to make the content more accessible and comprehensible will probably increase accordingly. The NLP concluded that high-quality reading instruction alone will be "insufficient to support equal academic success" for ELLs, and that "simultaneous efforts to increase the scope and sophistication of these students' oral language proficiency" is also required.[32] Our knowledge of how to accelerate this development of oral English proficiency, however, is unfortunately quite limited (see "Critical Questions" box).

Nonetheless, it is evident that improving oral English proficiency is a must. ELLs' language limitations begin to impede their progress most noticeably as they move beyond the early stages of reading, and vocabulary and content knowledge become increasingly relevant for continued reading (and general academic) success—usually around third grade. This is why it is critical that teachers work to develop ELLs' oral English, particularly vocabulary, and their content knowledge from the time they start school, even as they are learning the reading "basics." Vocabulary development is, of course, important for all students, but it is particularly critical for ELLs. There can be little doubt that explicit attention to vocabulary development—everyday words as well as more specialized academic words—needs to be part of English learners' school programs.

So, how should instruction be modified to help ELLs develop oral English proficiency? And how should it be modified to take into account their language limitations and ensure that they have access to the academic content? Several instructional modifications for ELLs have been proposed. Some have support from research; others seem like common sense but have not yet been validated empirically. . . .

The instructional modifications students need will probably change as children develop English proficiency and in relation to what they are being expected to learn. Students who are beginning English speakers will need a great deal of support, sometimes known as "scaffolding," for learning tasks that require knowledge of English. For example, at the very beginning levels, teachers will have to speak slowly and somewhat deliberately, with clear vocabulary and diction, and use pictures, other objects, and movements to illustrate the content being taught. They should also expect students to respond either nonverbally (e.g., pointing or signaling) or in one- or two-word utterances. As they gain in proficiency, students will need fewer modifications—for example, teachers can use more

complex vocabulary and sentence structures and expect students to respond with longer utterances; when possible, information can be presented both in pictures and in writing. On the other hand, even fairly advanced ELLs might require modifications when completely new or particularly difficult topics are taught. It might also be that some students in some contexts will require more modifications than others. We are utterly lacking the data necessary to offer such guidelines. But it is likely that ELLs will need some additional instructional support for much of their schooling. Conversational English can be learned to a reasonably high level in just two to three years, but proficiency in academic English can require six, seven, or more years.[33]

* * *

Although there are numerous areas in which there is insufficient research to guide policy and practice, we can lay claim to some things that matter for the education of ELLs. Chief among these is that 1) teaching children to read in their primary language promotes reading achievement in English; 2) in many important respects, what works for learners in general also works for ELLs; and 3) teachers must make instructional modifications when ELLs are taught in English, primarily because of the students' language limitations.

Practically, what do these findings and conclusions mean? In spite of the many gaps in what we know, the following is the sort of instructional framework to which our current state of knowledge points:

- If feasible, children should be taught reading in their primary language. Primary language reading instruction a) develops first language skills, b) promotes reading in English, and c) can be carried out as children are also learning to read, and learning other academic content, in English.

- As needed, students should be helped to transfer what they know in their first language to learning tasks presented in English; teachers should not assume that transfer is automatic.

- Teaching in the first and second languages can be approached similarly. However, adjustments or modifications will be necessary, probably for several years and at least for some students, until they reach sufficient familiarity with academic English to permit them to be successful in mainstream instruction; more complex learning might require more instructional adjustments.

- ELLs need intensive oral English language development (ELD), especially vocabulary and academic English instruction. However, as the sidebar on critical unanswered questions explains (see "Critical Questions"), we have much to learn about what type of ELD instruction is most beneficial. Effective ELD provides both explicit teaching of features of English (such as syntax, grammar, vocabulary, pronunciation, and norms of social usage) and ample, meaningful opportunities to use English—but we do not know whether there is an optimal balance between the two (much less what it might be).

- ELLs also need academic content instruction, just as all students do; although ELD is crucial, it must be in addition to—not instead of—instruction designed to promote content knowledge.

Local or state policies, such as in California, Arizona, and Massachusetts, that block use of the primary language and limit instructional modifications for English learners are simply not based on the best scientific evidence available. Moreover, these policies make educators' jobs more difficult, which is unconscionable under any circumstance, but especially egregious in light of the increased accountability pressures they and their students face. Despite many remaining questions, we have useful starting points for renewed efforts to improve the achievement of ELLs—the fastest growing segment of the school-age population. Given all the challenges that ELLs (and their teachers) face, policy and practice must be based on the best evidence we have.

Critical Questions

What the Research Does Not Say—Yet

As discussed throughout the main article, current research offers some solid information that should help educators increase English learners' achievement. But many critical questions remain unanswered. What follows is in no way an exhaustive list. Rather it is a brief look at three groups of questions that educators and others frequently ask, and that need to be answered.

Bilingual Reading Instruction Helps, but in What Settings? With Which Students? For How Long?

Beyond the finding that primary language reading instruction promotes reading achievement in English (and in the primary language), there are more questions than answers. The NLP and CREDE syntheses should be catalysts to untangling the role of primary language instruction in ELLs' education and serve as the platform from which to ask important questions. Is primary language instruction more beneficial for some learners than for others? For example, those with weaker or stronger primary language skills? Weaker or stronger English skills? Is it more effective in some settings and with certain ELL populations than others? What should be the relative

(Continued)

(Continued)

emphasis between promoting knowledge and skills in the primary language and developing English language proficiency? What level of skill in the students' primary language does the teacher need to possess in order to be effective? In an English immersion situation, what is the most effective way to use the primary language to support children's learning? We presently cannot answer these questions with confidence. Individual studies might point in certain directions, but we lack a body of solid studies that permits us to go beyond the general finding about the positive effects of primary language instruction on reading achievement in English.

We also cannot say with confidence how long students should receive instruction in their primary language. This is a key difference between the NLP and CREDE reports. The CREDE synthesis concluded that more primary language instruction over more years leads to higher levels of ELL achievement in English. This conclusion was strongly influenced by studies and evaluations of "two-way bilingual education," in which children from two language groups (e.g., Spanish and English) participate in a program designed to develop bilingualism and biliteracy in *both* groups. There are different two-way models, but they all involve some combination of first and second language instruction throughout elementary school; some go through middle and high school. Evaluations have been very positive, and ELLs in these programs seem to do very well, possibly better than students in shorter-term bilingual programs (three or fewer years).[1] Thus, CREDE researchers concluded that the longer ELLs received instruction in a mix of their first language and English, the better their achievement in English.

The NLP, however, did not include these longer term studies because they did not have adequate experimental controls. The problem is that these studies did not make sure that the achievement of children in contrasting programs (e.g., two-way bilingual, transitional bilingual education, or English immersion) was equivalent at the start of the study or that children in different programs had the same demographic characteristics (e.g., parental education and level of English use in the home). Pre-existing differences could create the false impression that one program is better than another. For this reason, the NLP only included well-controlled studies in its meta-analysis; and because the well-controlled studies were relatively short term, the NLP reached no conclusions about the impact of length of time students are in primary language instruction.

Can ELLs' Oral English Development Be Accelerated? How?

The NLP and CREDE reports reached similar conclusions regarding effective instructional practices for ELLs. This is good news. We need to find points of agreement in this complex and contentious field. But there is still a great deal that we do not know. There is one area in particular in which more research is desperately needed: oral English development, and specifically, whether and how it can be accelerated. It should be apparent that providing ELLs with English language development instruction is critically important. There are some studies that have looked at promoting various aspects of oral language, such as vocabulary or listening comprehension (both of which can be enhanced through instruction), but the CREDE review did not find any studies that addressed how or even whether progress in the acquisition of English can be accelerated. (The NLP did not address this issue.)

ELLs are thought to progress through a series of levels of English proficiency. The exact nature of this progression has not been fully mapped out, but generally we think of four or five levels of English language development (ELD), from total lack of English to native-like proficiency. In one influential conceptualization, there are three phases in the beginner to early intermediate period: preproduction (sometimes called the "silent period"), early production (students can say one- or two-word utterances), and speech emergence (longer phrases and sentences). In the scheme used by California and other states, there are five levels—beginning, early intermediate, intermediate, early advanced, and advanced.

Progress from the beginning (or preproduction) stage to the point where students are approaching native-like proficiency seems to take at least six years for most students (e.g., from kindergarten to grade 6 or later; there is variability from one person to the next, so these numbers represent general trends). ELLs seem to progress from beginning to intermediate levels more rapidly (in roughly two to three years) than they do from intermediate to full proficiency, which can take an additional three, four, or more years. In other words, students beginning to learn the language can make what appears to be fairly rapid progress, but then slow down once they reach intermediate proficiency. According to the CREDE report, even students who are in all-English instruction do not begin to show higher intermediate levels of English proficiency for at least four years (i.e., grade 3 or later). The idea that children (at least those represented by studies done to date) will quickly become fluent in English if immersed in all-English instruction is contradicted by the research literature, yet some states' language policies (for example, California's and Arizona's) require that students enter mainstream English instruction after a year of school. Certainly individual exceptions can be found, but fluency within a year of English immersion in school is not the norm.

Why does gaining full proficiency take so much longer than intermediate proficiency? There are probably two reasons. First, the vocabulary and sentence patterns required to be an intermediate speaker of English are simpler than those required for advanced proficiency levels. Second, intermediate speakers can rely on the immediate context of a conversation where gestures, pointing, intonation, and other nonlinguistic cues assist communication. Intermediate proficiency likely means that the student has sufficient command of the language to engage effectively in familiar situations, such as play, daily activities, and normal conversations with friends. Such language situations are highly contextualized, fairly recurrent and familiar, and supported by gestures, intonation, and shared references. They therefore require less precise vocabulary and sentence structures.

Full proficiency likely means that a student has sufficient command of the language to engage effectively in more complex interactions that involve abstract concepts and references to things that are not in the immediate vicinity. In these situations, the vocabulary and sentence structures required for adequate communication will be more challenging. In addition, pointing and gesturing will help much less, if at all. Linguistic demands are, therefore, far greater once a speaker tries to get beyond an intermediate proficiency level. The speaker and listener must know the meaning of the words and understand the sentence structures and other nuances that communicate the intended message. Academic situations (e.g., lectures, discussions, and group work) are often like this, but so are many conversations about movies, political events, or a complex personal situation. Such language situations tend to be less contextualized by the social and pragmatic circumstances and more focused on abstract ideas and concepts that we are less likely to come across in our everyday affairs.

(Continued)

(Continued)

Students must learn and study many of these concepts, and the *language* needed to talk about them, in school. Academic English—the type of language that is essential for school success—is particularly difficult to master because it is generally not used outside of the classroom and it draws on new vocabulary, more complex sentence structures, and rhetorical forms not typically encountered in nonacademic settings. Knowing conversational English undoubtedly helps in learning academic English, but the latter is clearly a more challenging task that requires more time.

What Is the Best Way to Teach English Language Development?

This is another area about which there is little agreement. In fact until fairly recently, researchers were divided on the question of whether a second language could even be taught directly, as opposed to being acquired through meaningful interactions with other speakers. However, we now are pretty confident that teaching the language directly helps learners learn the language, but learners also need to be in situations where they can use the language for genuine communication. Several publications have appeared since the CREDE report was completed that support this perspective.[2] Effective second language instruction provides a combination of a) explicit teaching that helps students directly and efficiently learn features of the second language such as syntax, grammar, vocabulary, pronunciation, and norms of social usage and b) ample opportunities to use the second language in meaningful and motivating situations. We do not know whether there is an "optimal" balance, much less what it might be. But there is every reason to believe that successful second language instruction comprises elements of both. What we need is a new generation of second language research that examines the nature of this balance and addresses whether, and what kind of, instruction can shorten the time required for ELLs to gain native or near-native English proficiency.

A final point. Educators often wonder whether English language development (ELD) should be taught as a separate subject at a distinct time in the day or if it should be "integrated" throughout the day, taught alongside the regular curriculum. A recent study suggests that ELD probably benefits from a separate period.[3] Researchers found that when a separate ELD block was used, students scored higher on a standardized measure of English oral language. Teachers spent more time on oral English and were more efficient and focused in their use of time. The ELD block was, by design, targeted at oral English language development, and teachers taught accordingly. In contrast, when there was no ELD block, less time was spent focusing on English per se and more on other language arts activities such as reading. This study was limited to kindergarten, and the effect was small. But if the findings are accurate, the cumulative effect of a separate block of ELD instruction over many years could be substantial. At the moment, however, this is speculation.

ELLs' language needs are complex, and while they benefit from ELD instruction per se, they also need instruction in the use of English in the content areas (math, history, science, etc.). Teaching both content and language is a challenge for teachers; this is currently also an area of active research.[4] But whether we isolate and teach explicitly the language and vocabulary of academic subject areas in ELD instruction or integrate the teaching of language within content lessons, we should recognize that doing either or both requires very careful planning and effective instructional practices in order to achieve the desired language and content objectives.

Claude Goldenberg is professor of education at Stanford University. Previously, at California State University, Long Beach, he was associate dean of the College of Education and executive director of the Center for Language Minority Education and Research. He served on the National Research Council's Committee for the Prevention of Early Reading Difficulties in Young Children and on the National Literacy Panel, which synthesized research on literacy development among language minority children and youth. This article is adapted with permission from "Improving Achievement for English Language Learners," a chapter in Educating the Other America: Top Experts Tackle Poverty, Literacy, and Achievement in Our Schools, *edited by Susan B. Neuman, forthcoming in August 2008, Paul H. Brookes Publishing Co., Inc. The author wishes to thank Rhoda Coleman, Ronald Gallimore, Patricia Gándara, Fred Genesee, Michael Graves, Peggy McCardle, Patricia Mathes, Michael Kamil, Bill Saunders, Timothy Shanahan, Jessie Sullivan, Robert Rueda, and Sharon Vaughn for their helpful comments.*

Article 29

A FRAMEWORK FOR ROBUST LITERACY INSTRUCTION FOR ENGLISH LEARNERS

PATRICK C. MANYAK

For the last 16 years, I have been a teacher and researcher of young English learners (ELs) and thus immersed in the issues surrounding the language and literacy instruction of these children. My years as a bilingual teacher in southern California taught me about the great privilege and the tremendous challenge of teaching ELs. I was surrounded by bright, respectful children who earnestly applied themselves to the task of learning in two languages. At the same time, while my colleagues and I worked hard to help our Latina/o students, they lagged far behind our native English speakers (NS) in reading and writing. Thus, my own teaching experience mirrored what years of results from the National Assessment of Educational Progress reveal: A significantly lower percentage of Latina/o ELs reach proficiency in reading than their white NS peers. Nevertheless, during the last decade, I have come to believe that our current research base offers important guidance that could dramatically improve the literacy achievement of all ELs. It will not be simple, however, to translate the relevant research insights into practice; it will require a multifaceted form of classroom instruction that addresses the cognitive challenges of literacy, accounts for ELs' special language needs and abilities, and includes their unique cultural experiences. In this column, I outline a framework for this kind of robust literacy instruction for ELs. The framework consists of four complementary elements: (1) explicit code and comprehension instruction, (2) language-rich instruction, (3) socioculturally informed instruction, and (4) additive literacy instruction. Drawing on key research findings and successful classroom interventions, I provide a brief rationale for each of these elements.

SOURCE: Manyak, P. C. (2007). A Framework for Robust Literacy Instruction for English Learners. *The Reading Teacher, 61*(20), 197–199. Reprinted by permission of the International Reading Association.

Explicit Code and Comprehension Instruction

Recent research demonstrates that explicit instruction in phonemic awareness and phonics is very beneficial for ELs learning to read in English. Consider the findings from two important studies. First, Lesaux and Siegel (2003) examined the reading development of 978 NS and 188 ELs from a variety of language backgrounds from kindergarten to the end of 2nd grade. The study took place in a Canadian school district that provided explicit instruction in phonemic awareness and phonics within a balanced approach to literacy and intervention for struggling beginning readers. At the end of second grade, the ELs performed equal to or better than the NS on assessments of a variety of reading skills, including comprehension. Second, Vaughn, Mathes, Linan-Thompson, and Francis (2005) studied the effects of a code-based early reading intervention program on struggling first-grade Spanish-speaking ELs in Texas. The intervention program included explicit, systematic instruction in phonemic awareness, letter knowledge, word recognition, decodable text reading, basic comprehension processes, and vocabulary. Students made dramatic gains in decoding and comprehension, scoring on par with NS in these areas. Together, these two studies suggest the value of explicit, systematic code-based instruction as a part of a comprehensive literacy program for ELs. However, while such instruction may provide ELs with an excellent start in English reading, it does not ensure long-term reading achievement. A recent review of research found that ELs generally experience more difficulty in reading comprehension than their NS peers (Lesaux, Koda, Siegel, & Shanahan, 2006). Given that ELs regularly face texts with more unfamiliar content and vocabulary than NS, ELs must be particularly strategic in activating background knowledge, inferring meanings of words, and monitoring their comprehension. Thus, the need for high-quality instruction in comprehension strategies is especially acute for ELs.

Language-Rich Instruction

Language-rich instruction aims to accelerate ELs' oral language and academic vocabulary development in English. With regard to oral language development, longstanding principles of English as a second language stress the critical nature of providing ample access to competent speakers of and comprehensible input in the target language, a comfortable atmosphere for experimenting with the new language, frequent modeling, and feedback that prompts elaboration. Building on these principles, Mohr and Mohr (2007) have developed a valuable tool that provides specific guidance to teachers seeking to extend ELs' engagement in classroom interactions. Their Response Protocol details possible teacher responses—each aimed at valuing contributions and prompting elaboration—to a wide variety of student utterances and should help any teacher improve the language-acquisition climate of their classroom. In addition to promoting ELs' participation in everyday activities, language-rich instruction also must address the large and persistent English vocabulary gap between NS and ELs. Research has established the strong relationship between vocabulary knowledge and reading comprehension (Cunningham & Stanovich, 1997), and Saville-Troike (1984) demonstrated that English vocabulary was strongly associated with the performance on a standardized test of English reading by ELs in second through sixth grade. In light of these findings, I believe that explicit, intensive academic vocabulary instruction represents a particularly critical dimension of robust literacy instruction for ELs.

Socioculturally Informed Instruction

A common folk theory in schools holds that many culturally and linguistically diverse families deprive their children of experiences that form a foundation for school learning. In contrast, research reveals that many diverse children possess a broad range of cultural knowledge, linguistic abilities, and problem-solving skills that represent important resources for literacy learning (Moll, Amanti, & Gonzalez, 2005; Vasquez, Pease-Alvarez, & Shannon, 1994). For instance, in research conducted in a Mexicano community in northern California, Vasquez et al. (1994) found that children engaged in numerous "intercultural transactions," such as acting as translators for their parents during visits to the doctor, that prompted the children to develop as "language and cultural brokers" (p. 13). With regard to literacy, the authors described how a family collaboratively interpreted tax and immigration documents across languages. Socioculturally informed instruction entails teachers recognizing these valuable cultural experiences and resources and finding ways to incorporate them in classroom activities. Research has demonstrated that connecting literacy activities to ELs' out-of-school lives can lead to meaningful, engaging, and sophisticated literate activity (Dworin, 2006; Moll et al., 2005). In one recent example, Dworin (2006) described a classroom project in which fourth-grade Latina/o students read and discussed family memoirs; interviewed their own family members about their lives; and wrote, revised, and translated a memoir based on the interviews. While such projects are not sufficient to ensure ELs' successful literacy development, they play a critical role in making literacy meaningful to diverse students and creating a space in the classroom for their out-of-school lives.

ADDITIVE LITERACY INSTRUCTION

The previous three elements that I have discussed primarily address ELs' development of English literacy. However, research demonstrates that young ELs can and do develop literacy skills in two languages (Moll & Dworin, 1996) and that when bilingual children develop literacy skills in either of their two languages, this development positively contributes to the growth of their literacy skills in the other language (Verhoeven, 1994). In light of such findings, I believe that any framework for robust literacy instruction for ELs must consider biliteracy as its ultimate goal and that teachers should actively advocate for some form of consistent native language literacy instruction in their schools or communities. While effective bilingual education programs represent a time-honored path to biliteracy, such programs may not be practical or even permitted in many settings. As a consequence, I consider it critical that teachers committed to serving ELs consider alternative ways to support their students' biliteracy development. For instance, I have observed schools that cannot provide full bilingual programs offer primary-language literacy instruction as a regular special or after-school enrichment class for ELs. In addition, teachers might also encourage, advise, or collaborate with parents and other community members to develop community-based programs aimed at teaching native language literacy skills to young ELs.

MORE TO COME . . .

In this column, I have outlined a framework for robust literacy instruction for ELs. By necessity, I have only touched briefly on each of its four elements. In later columns, I plan to discuss these elements in greater depth, offering more specific guidance in translating them into effective classroom instruction. However, I hope that this overview will challenge teachers of ELs to examine their current instruction and consider general ways that it might be enhanced.

Patrick C. Manyak teaches at the University of Wyoming, Laramie.

Article 30

ENGLISH LEARNERS

Key Issues

RICHARD R. VERDUGO AND BRITTNEY FLORES

Since its inception, America's system of public education has faced many challenges. One of its more important challenges has been how to teach children from diverse backgrounds and cultures. As a society that prides itself on a democratic ideology, cultural diversity and schooling are not trivial issues. One of the more significant diversity topics has been the presence of English-language learners (ELL) in American public schools. This article introduces the topic of ELL students and the education and education-related issues surrounding ELL students. For researchers and policymakers deeply steeped in the issues surrounding ELL students, the issues and concerns raised in this article are familiar. However, for the vast majority of other researchers and policymakers, these issues are not familiar and may have an important impact on their own research agendas.

This article is available as a full-text PDF at http://www.sagepub.com/cappello/.

SOURCE: Verdugo, R. R., & Flores, B. (2007). English Learners: Key Issues. *Education and Urban Society,* *39*(2), 167–193. Reprinted by permission of Sage Publications, Inc.

Section X

DIFFERENTIATING INSTRUCTION/UNIVERSAL ACCESS

OVERVIEW

"The central job of schools is to maximize the capacity of each student," as stated by Tomlinson (2000) in "Reconcilable Differences? Standards-Based Teaching and Differentiation." This section of the reader highlights the many classroom influences that are relevant for individualized instruction, including student needs, pacing, and the range of teacher support. In her article, Tomlinson situates the need for differentiation in a mandated, standards-based curriculum. She discusses this tension because "by definition, differentiation is wary of approaches to teaching and learning that standardize." However, Tomlinson does not see standards and differentiation as a contradiction and remains hopeful that differentiation and standards-based instruction can be compatible.

In their article "Differentiating Standards-Based Education for Students With Diverse Needs," Hoover and Patton (2004) elaborate on the seeming dichotomy of standards and differentiation in a post–No Child Left Behind era in education. The authors pay special attention to providing universal access to curricula for students with disabilities, yet their suggestions are nonetheless relevant for all teachers who differentiate standards-based curriculum and instruction.

STRATEGY

This section in the reader helps you make decisions when planning for meeting the needs of *all* students in your classroom. Use the "Exclusion Brainstorming Strategy" (Tompkins, 2009) to activate your background knowledge and prepare to read about differentiating instruction. This strategy is to be used before and after reading the text. Before you read this section, review the words below and decide which of them relate to the topic. After reading, go back and review your choices to see whether they remain consistent. The purpose of Exclusion Brainstorming is to activate and expand background knowledge as well as introduce some key vocabulary.

EXCLUSION BRAINSTORMING

(Tompkins, 2009)

DIRECTIONS

- Review the word box below. Decide which words are important to "Section X: Differentiating Instruction/Universal Access" and which are not. Circle words you do not believe are related to this section in the reader.

- Read the articles and notice whether these words appear in the text.

- After you finish reading, return to the word box to make corrections. Put a checkmark by related words. Cross out unrelated words regardless of whether they were circled earlier.

WORD BOX FOR DIFFERENTIATING INSTRUCTION/UNIVERSAL ACCESS

variance	refinement	prescribed	skills	groups
assessments	philosophy	individual	choice	pacing
expectations	flexibility	opportunities	inclusion	uniform
strategy	scripted	gradual release	distinguish	community

SOURCE: Tompkins, G. E. (2009). *Fifty Literacy Strategies: Step by Step.* Boston: Allyn & Bacon.

Article 31

RECONCILABLE DIFFERENCES?

Standards-Based Teaching and Differentiation

CAROL ANN TOMLINSON

Standards-based instruction and differentiated learning can be compatible approaches in today's classrooms.

Recent demands for more standards-based teaching can feel like a huge impediment to encouraging differentiated instruction, especially for teachers and principals who recognize student variance and want to address it appropriately. A relatively new phenomenon (at least in its current form), standards-based instruction dominates the educational terrain in a time of great academic diversity in contemporary classrooms. In fact standards-based instruction and the high-stakes testing that drives it can often feel like a locomotive rolling over everything in its path, including individualized learning.

When any phenomenon in education suggests that we may have to jettison common sense and good pedagogy, we must first examine it in light of what we know about high-quality instruction. In other words, if we understand how standards-based teaching does or does not align with sound teaching and learning practices, we can then approach what look like barriers to differentiation. In truth, the conflict between focusing on standards and focusing on individual learners' needs exists only if we use standards in ways that cause us to abandon what we know about effective curriculum and instruction.

SOURCE: From "Reconcilable Differences? Standards-Based Teaching and Differentiation," by Carol Ann Tomlinson. In the September 2000 issue of *Educational Leadership, 58*(1), 6–13. © 2000 by ASCD. Used by permission. Learn more about ASCD at www.ascd.org.

DIFFERENTIATION: A WAY OF THINKING ABOUT THE CLASSROOM

What we call *differentiation* is not a recipe for teaching. It is not an instructional strategy. It is not what a teacher does when he or she has time. It is a way of thinking about teaching and learning. It is a philosophy. As such, it is based on a set of beliefs:

- Students who are the same age differ in their readiness to learn, their interests, their styles of learning, their experiences, and their life circumstances.

- The differences in students are significant enough to make a major impact on what students need to learn, the pace at which they need to learn it, and the support they need from teachers and others to learn it well.

- Students will learn best when supportive adults push them slightly beyond where they can work without assistance.

- Students will learn best when they can make a connection between the curriculum and their interests and life experiences.

- Students will learn best when learning opportunities are natural.

- Students are more effective learners when classrooms and schools create a sense of community in which students feel significant and respected.

- The central job of schools is to maximize the capacity of each student.

By definition, differentiation is wary of approaches to teaching and learning that standardize. Standard-issue students are rare, and educational approaches that ignore academic diversity in favor of standardization are likely to be counterproductive in reaching the full range of learners.

Differentiation must be a refinement of, not a substitute for, high-quality curriculum and instruction. Expert or distinguished teaching focuses on the understandings and skills of a discipline, causes students to wrestle with profound ideas, calls on students to use what they learn in important ways, helps students organize and make sense of ideas and information, and aids students in connecting the classroom with a wider world (Brandt, 1998; Danielson, 1996; Schlechty, 1997; Wiggins & McTighe, 1998).

Differentiation—one facet of expert teaching—reminds us that these things are unlikely to happen for the full range of students unless curriculum and instruction fit each individual, unless students have choices about what to learn and how, unless students take part in setting learning goals, and unless the classroom connects with the experiences and interest of the individual (Tomlinson, 1995, 1999). Differentiation says, "Building on core teaching and learning practices that are solid, here's what you do to refine them for maximum individual growth."

We first need to ask, Is a given teaching or learning approach likely to have a positive impact on the core of effective teaching and learning? When we are content with the answer, we can ask further, What is the effect of the practice on individuals in an academically diverse population? The latter question always helps us refine the effectiveness of the former but cannot substitute for it.

STANDARDS-BASED TEACHING

For many teachers, curriculum has become a prescribed set of academic standards, instructional pacing has become a race against a clock to cover the standards, and the sole goal of teaching has been reduced to raising student test scores on a single test, the value of which has scarcely been questioned in the public forum. Teachers feel as though they are torn in opposing directions: They are admonished to attend to student differences, but they must ensure that every student becomes competent in the same subject matter and can demonstrate the competencies on an assessment that is differentiated neither in form nor in time constraints.

To examine the dichotomy between standards-based teaching and differentiation, we must ask questions about how standards influence the quality of teaching and learning. What is the impact of standards-based teaching on the quality of education in general? Then we can assess ways in which standards-based approaches make an impact on gifted or academically challenged students whose abilities are outside the usual norms of achievement.

- Do the standards reflect the knowledge, understandings, and skills valued most by experts in the disciplines that they represent?

- Are we using standards as a curriculum, or are they reflected in the curriculum?

- Are we slavishly covering standards at breakneck pace, or have we found ways to organize the standards within our curriculum so that students have time to make sense of ideas and skills?

- Does our current focus on standards enliven classrooms, or does it eliminate joy, creativity, and inquiry?

- Do standards make learning more or less relevant and alluring to students?

- Does our use of standards remind us that we are teaching human beings, or does it cause us to forget that fact?

If we are satisfied that our standards-based practices yield positive answers, we can look fruitfully at how to make adaptations to address the needs of academically diverse learners. If our answers are less than satisfactory, we should address the problems. Such problems inevitably point to cracks in the foundation of quality teaching and learning, and we diminish our profession by failing to attend to them. Differentiating curriculum and instruction cannot make up for ill-conceived curriculum and instruction.

NEGATIVE CASES

The following examples are recent and real. Sadly, they are not rare. They also show how good intentions can go awry.

- In one standards-driven district, primary grade teachers attended a staff development session that they had requested and in which they had high interest. The staff developer asked them to list some concepts that they taught so that the session would be linked to what went on in their classrooms. When—even with coaching and examples—no one was able to name the concepts they taught, the staff developer asked for the topics they taught. More awkward silence followed. A few teachers said that they sometimes took a day or two to talk about holidays, such as Halloween, Christmas, or Kwanza, because young students were excited about special occasions. Other teachers explained that they no longer taught units or topics (and certainly not concepts). Their entire curriculum had become a list of skills that students learned out of context of any meaning or utility—except that the test was coming, and all 6- through 8-year-olds were expected to perform.

- A highly successful elementary school was started two decades ago to serve a student population that speaks more than 25 languages and whose homes are often marked by economic stress. The librarian in the school recently remarked,

This has always been the best place in the world to teach. The students have loved it. Their parents have trusted it. Our students have done well. The teachers have always been excited to come to work. It has been a place of energy and inspired teaching. In the last two years [since the inception of a standards-based program and high-stakes testing], I've watched us become what we were created to avoid. We are telling instead of teaching. We fight to find time to reach out to the kids. Joy in classrooms has been replaced by fear that is first felt by the teachers and then by the students. We're trying hard to keep alive what we believe in, but I'm not sure we can.

- In another standards-driven district, middle school teachers listed student names in one of three columns: *Definitely, Maybe,* and *No Hope.* The designations showed who would surely pass the standards tests, who might pass, and who had no chance of passing. The teachers separated the students into columns because, they said, there was no point in worrying about students who already knew enough to pass the test, and there was no point in wasting time on students who could not be raised to the standard. "It's the only way to go," said one teacher. "It's what we have to do to get the points on this year's test."

In all these places, teachers feel torn between an external impetus to cover the standards and a desire to address the diverse academic needs. In truth, the problem is not a contradiction between standards and appropriately responsive instruction. The problem lies in an ill-conceived interpretation and use of standards that erode the underpinnings of effective teaching and learning. The problem is not that we can't attend to the needs of individual learners, but rather that we've lost the essential frameworks of the disciplines in addition to the coherence, understanding, purpose, and joy in learning. Our first obligation is to ensure that standards-based teaching practice does not conflict with best teaching practice. Once those are aligned, differentiation—or attention to the diverse needs of learners—follows naturally.

STANDARDS AND DIFFERENTIATION

There is no contradiction between effective standards-based instruction and differentiation. Curriculum tells us *what* to teach: Differentiation tells us *how*. Thus, if we elect to teach a standards-based curriculum, differentiation simply suggests ways in which we can make that curriculum work best for varied learners. In other words, differentiation can show us how to teach the same standard to a range of learners by employing a variety of teaching and learning modes.

Choose any standard. Differentiation suggests that you can challenge all learners by providing materials and tasks on the standard at varied levels of difficulty, with varying degrees of scaffolding, through multiple instructional groups,

and with time variations. Further, differentiation suggests that teachers can craft lessons in ways that tap into multiple student interests to promote heightened learner interest in the standard. Teachers can encourage student success by varying ways in which students work: alone or collaboratively, in auditory or visual modes, or through practical or creative means.

POSITIVE CASES

• Science teachers in one small district delineated the key facts, concepts, principles, and skills of their discipline for K–12. Having laid out the framework, they examined the state-prescribed standards for science and mapped them for K–12. They found that the standards in their state did a pretty good job of reflecting the facts and skills of science but did a poor job of making explicit the concepts and principles of science. With the two frameworks in front of them, the teachers could fill in gaps—and more important, could organize their curriculum in ways that were coherent and manageable. Their work helped their colleagues see the big picture of science instruction for K–12 over time, organize instruction conceptually, and teach with the essential principles of science in mind. The result was a district-wide science curriculum that made better sense to teachers and students alike, helped students think like scientists, reduced the teachers' sense of racing to cover disjointed information, and still attended to prescribed standards.

• In a high school Algebra II class, the teacher acknowledged that some of her students lacked prerequisite skills, whereas others learned as rapidly as she could teach or even without her help. At the outset of each chapter, the teacher delineated for students the specific skills, concepts, and understandings that they needed to master for that segment of the curriculum—both to have a solid grasp of mathematics and to pass the upcoming standards exam. She helped students make connections to past concepts, understandings, and skills. She divided each week into segments of teacher-led instruction, whole-class instruction, and small-group work.

For group-work sessions, she sometimes met with students who were advanced in a particular topic to urge on their thinking, to help them solve problems in multiple ways, and to apply their understandings and skills to complex, real-life problems. Sometimes she met with students who needed additional instruction or guided assistance in applying what they were learning. Sometimes she created mixed-readiness teams of students whose goal was solving a problem in the most effective way possible. The teacher randomly called on students to present and defend their team's approach, thus maximizing the likelihood that every student had a model for solving an important problem and was able to explain the reasoning behind the solution. These problem-solving groups often evolved into teacher-created study groups that worked together to ensure that everyone had his or her questions answered. Not only did the teacher provide some class time for the study groups, but she also encouraged regular after-school meetings in her room, where she was able to monitor group progress and assist if needed. She recalls:

> The hardest thing for me was learning to teach a class where I wasn't always working with the class as a whole, but that has been rewarding too. I know my students better. They know Algebra II better—and I think I probably understand it better, too. I haven't made a math prodigy out of everyone, of course, but I can honestly say the students like algebra better and are more confident in their capacity to learn. Their scores on the standards test improved, even though I targeted some ideas and skills more than others. I think what that fact tells me is that if I help students organize their mathematical knowledge and thinking, they can fare better in unfamiliar territory.

• In an elementary classroom, a teacher organized many of her standards around three key concepts—connections, environments, and change—and their related principles; for example, living things are changed by and change their environments. She used them to study history, science, language-arts, and sometimes mathematics. Although she generally taught each of the three subjects separately, she helped students make links among them; she created activities for the students that called for reading skills in social studies. for example, and social studies skills in science, That approach, she said, allowed everyone to work with the same big ideas and skills in a lesson while she could adjust materials, activities, and projects for varied readiness levels, diverse interests, and multiple modes of learning. Bringing the students together for class discussions was no problem, she reflected, because everyone's work focused on the essentials—even though students might get to those essentials in different ways. "It took me some time to rethink the standards and how I taught them," she recalled.

> But I feel as if I'm a better teacher, I understand what I'm teaching better, and I certainly have come to understand the students I teach more fully. I no longer see my curriculum as a list to be covered, and I no longer see my students as duplicates of one another.

In these settings, teachers have retained—or, in some cases, have discovered for the first time—the essential frameworks of the disciplines and the coherence, understanding, purpose, and joy in learning. The teachers have struggled to meet their first obligation—to ensure that standards-based teaching practice is not in conflict with best teaching practice. Once the teachers aligned standards with high-quality instruction, differentiation followed naturally.

QUALITY AND PERSONALIZATION

Overwhelmed by the task, a teacher recently pleaded, "I have all these students with all these different needs; how can anyone expect me to differentiate in my classroom?" Odd as the comment sounds, she spoke for many of us. The more complex the task, the more inviting it is to retreat to the familiar—to find a standardized—approach and cling to it.

Thus, we find ourselves saying, "I know I'm missing lots of my students, but if I don't hurry to cover all the standards, how will they succeed on the test?" Or, "I know it would be good to involve students in thinking and problem solving, but there's just no time. The deeper issue is about what happens when we use any approach that allows us to lose sight of the soul of teaching and learning. A secondary factor is that such approaches make it difficult to attend to individual differences.

Do standardizing practices fail academically diverse learners? Of course they do. Whatever practices invite us to be paint-by-number teachers will largely fail students who do not fit the template. Paint-by-number approaches will fall short for all of us—teachers and students alike— because they abandon quality. Paint-by-number approaches will fail teachers because they confuse technical expedience with artistry. They will fail students because they confuse compliance with thoughtful engagement. Any educational approach that does not invite us to teach individuals is deeply flawed.

Teaching is hard, teaching well is fiercely so. Confronted by too many students, a schedule without breaks, a pile of papers that regenerates daily, and incessant demands from every educational stakeholder, no wonder we become habitual and standardized in our practices. Not only do we have no time to question why we do what we do, but we also experience the discomfort of change when we do ask the knotty questions. Nonetheless, our profession cannot progress and our increasingly diverse students cannot succeed if we do less.

Grading Practices

The following questions help ensure that grading practices are productive for all students.

- How do learners benefit from a grading system that reminds everyone that students with disabilities or who speak English as a second language do not perform as well as students without disabilities or for whom English is their native tongue?

- What do we gain by telling our most able learners that they are "excellent" on the basis of a standard that requires modest effort, calls for no intellectual risk, necessitates no persistence, and demands that they develop few academic coping skills?

- In what ways do our current grading practices motivate struggling or advanced learners to persist in the face of difficulty?

- Is there an opportunity for struggling learners to encounter excellence in our current grading practices?

- Is there an opportunity for advanced learners to encounter struggle in our current grading practices?

—Carol Ann Tomlinson

Carol Ann Tomlinson is Associate Professor of Educational Leadership, Foundations, and Policy at the Curry School of Education at the University of Virginia.

Article 32

DIFFERENTIATING STANDARDS-BASED EDUCATION FOR STUDENTS WITH DIVERSE NEEDS

JOHN J. HOOVER AND JAMES R. PATTON

Abstract The need to differentiate or adapt curriculum and instruction to meet special needs continues to challenge educators of students with high-incidence disabilities. The current emphasis on teaching and assessing standards requires knowledge and skills to differentiate standards-based education to successfully meet diverse needs in the classroom.

In January of 2002, the act commonly known as "No Child Left Behind" (NCLB; Elementary and Secondary Education Act, 2001) became law. Its overall purpose is to ensure that all children meet state educational standards. As a result, standards-based education and associated assessment are of particular significance to educators of students with special needs. Specifically, curricula must reflect state standards, and all students must be taught the information and skills associated with those standards. Because of these changes mandating use of curricula to meet standards-based initiatives, the task of adapting instruction (i.e., *differentiation*) for students with special needs has become increasingly more important. Currently, most states have adopted some form of standards-based education, and both the 1999 amendments to the Individuals with Disabilities Education Act and NCLB require that all students be provided the opportunity to learn in the state-mandated curricula.

SOURCE: Hoover, J. J., & Patton, J. R. (2004). Differentiating Standards-Based Education for Students With Diverse Needs. *Remedial and Special Education, 25*(2), 74–78. Reprinted by permission of Sage Publications, Inc.

The importance of differentiating education for students with learning and behavior problems has been recognized for many years. Since the early 1980s, inclusion efforts have challenged all educators to modify curriculum and instruction to meet diverse learning and behavior needs in the classroom. Although specific terminology may vary (e.g., *adaptation, differentiation, modification*), the underlying constant for students with learning and behavior problems is that curricula, including standards-based curricula, must meet diverse educational needs. This includes differentiation or adaptation on an ongoing basis in the classroom. Gartin, Murdick, Imbeau, and Perner (2002) described differentiated instruction as "using strategies that address student strengths, interests, skills, and readiness in flexible learning environments" (p.8). In addition, Tomlinson (2000) emphasized that teachers must possess a solid understanding of a curriculum and its components to successfully differentiate instruction to meet diverse needs.

This perspective addresses several interrelated aspects associated with standards-based curricula and adaptations necessary to meet the diverse needs of students, including an overview of standards-based curricula, aligning a curriculum with standards, adapting or differentiating a standards-based curriculum, and achieving competence in abilities to differentiate curricula and instruction. Specific components of a curriculum are also discussed to assist educators in making informed decisions regarding differentiating instruction.

STANDARDS-BASED CURRICULUM

A standards-based curriculum offers direction as to what students should learn. Teachers must adapt specific instruction to ensure that all students are given opportunities to acquire content and skills associated with each standard (Quenemoen, Lehr, Thurlow, & Massanaair, 2001). According to Glatthorn (1998) and McLaughlin and Shepard (1995), a standards-based curriculum is composed of three interrelated areas:

1. Content standards—Subject area skills and knowledge

2. Performance standards—Proficiency levels required

3. Opportunity to learn standards—Materials, strategies, and structure necessary for successful learning

All three types of standards must be emphasized to successfully teach and adapt a standards-based curriculum for students with learning and behavior problems. Creators of standards-based curricula typically avoid mandating specific curriculum methods or instructional strategies; instead, they offer clear expectations for learners and suggested options available to teachers to help meet state-mandated standards (Education Commission of the States, 2003). This facilitates opportunity and support for teachers in differentiating a curriculum and instruction to meet special learning and behavior needs.

Initially, the standards-based curriculum was developed during the reform efforts of the 1970s in the form of "minimum competencies." Although current reform efforts reflect previous accomplishments, the assessment of the proficiency levels associated with the standards has changed from multiple-choice or pass/fail assessment into multiproficiency levels (e.g., Not Proficient, Partially Proficient, Proficient; Linn & Herman, 1997). Also, educational standards must be written in a manner understandable to all individuals involved, including parents, and must clearly state what students are expected to learn along with the specified levels of proficiency (Education Commission, 2003).

Hoover and Patton (in press) and Linn and Herman (1997) identified several key aspects of standards-based education:

1. linking assessment closely to instruction,

2. comparing students' results to standards, not to results of other students,

3. using alternative assessments and applying the assessment results, and

4. challenging all students to meet high expectations.

These key components provide a framework for successfully implementing standards-based education to meet diverse needs.

Alignment of Standards and Curriculum

Currently, standards-based education is requiring school districts nationwide to align their curricula with mandated district, state, and/or national standards. Alignment procedures follow steps, or phases, similar to other curriculum development and reform efforts, as illustrated in Table 32.1.

Knowledge of the process for aligning standards with a curriculum provides educators valuable insight into how to differentiate curricula for students with high-incidence disabilities (Hoover & Patton, in press). Specifically, experiences with alignment efforts, especially field tests and revisions, are reflected in the curriculum. Particular strengths of the curriculum are determined through the alignment process, and adaptations should build upon these strengths to meet students' needs.

Differentiating Standards-Based Curriculum and Instruction

One significant result of standards-based reform is that educators have a greater opportunity to reverse the trend of lowered standards for students with learning and behavior problems. Educators are being challenged to do what is necessary to help students achieve proficiency in the standards. In other words, educators should be raising their expectations and associated

Table 32.1 Phases in the Alignment of Standards With Curriculum

Phase	Description
I	*Plan*—Identify needs, resources, and skills needed to effectively align curriculum with standards. This phase includes determining which standards should be included in the alignment, procedures for alignment, and the timelines.
II	*Needs Assessment*—Complete a needs assessment of the existing curriculum to determine to what extent it currently addresses standards in the alignment.
III	*Development*—Infuse new standards into the curriculum. This includes developing performance standards and ensuring that students have sufficient opportunities to acquire, master, and generalize knowledge and skills associated with each aligned standard.
IV	*Pilot*—Field-test the newly revised curriculum to ensure that all standards to be included in the alignment have been infused into the curriculum. Evaluation of the pilot should address the extent to which the content, performance, and opportunity-to-learn standards are being met by students and teachers.
V	*Revise*—Identify and incorporate any necessary revisions to the newly aligned curriculum, based on feedback obtained from the pilot.
VI	*Implementation*—Full-scale implementation of the newly aligned curriculum. Evaluate the implementation similar to efforts completed during the piloting of the curriculum.
VII	*Adaptations*—Adapt curricular elements for students with learning and behavior problems to address the three standards (content, performance, opportunity to learn).

NOTE: From *Curriculum Adaptations for Students With Learning and Behavior Problems: Principles and Practices for Differentiating Instruction* (3rd ed.), by J. J. Hoover and J. R. Patton, in press, Austin, TX: PRO-ED. Copyright by PRO-ED. Adapted with permission. Austin, TX: PRO-ED.

teaching competence to meet standards rather than lowering the standards for students with special needs.

Hoover and Patton (in press) identified four necessary elements for addressing effective implementation and differentiation of curriculum and instruction:

1. *Content*—specific subject-area skills and knowledge associated with each curriculum standard (i.e., content standards)

2. *Instructional strategies*—various techniques or methods used to assist students in acquiring content and managing behavior

3. *Instructional settings*—includes small groups, independent work, paired learning, and large groups

4. *Student behaviors*—students' abilities to manage and control their own behaviors within a variety of learning situations and groupings in the classroom

Each of these four curricular elements contributes to the overall process of implementing standards-based curricula.

In addition, the interrelationship among these four elements is the basis for successful implementation and adaptation or differentiation of a total curriculum. As Hoover and Patton (in press) noted, "As the curricular elements of Content, Instructional Strategies, Instructional Settings, and Behavior Management are adapted, all learners have the best chance to succeed with their education within the broader context of standards-based education and assessment." These four elements must be modified to effectively help students with learning and behavior problems to meet the three standards (content, performance, opportunity) that are the foundation for the standards-based curriculum illustrated in Figure 32.1.

When differentiating a standards-based curriculum for students with learning and behavior problems, the educator must address each of the

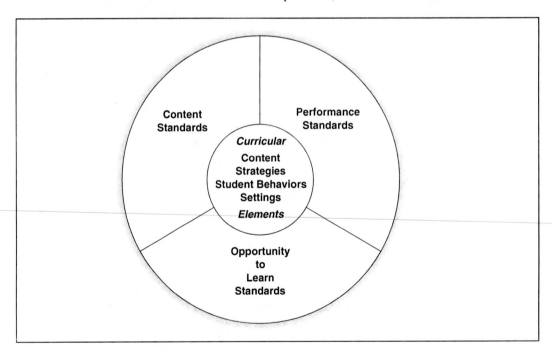

Figure 32.1　Adaptations of standards-based curriculum.

NOTE: From *Curriculum Adaptations for Students With Learning and Behavior Problems: Principles and Practices for Differentiating Instruction* (3rd ed.), by J. J. Hoover and J. R. Patton, in press, Austin, TX: PRO-ED. Copyright by PRO-ED. Reprinted with permission.

four specific curricular elements—content, instructional strategies, instructional settings, and student behaviors—relative to the three broad areas (content, proficiency, opportunity to learn) to ensure comprehensive and interrelated adaptations. Table 32.2 further illustrates this process.

As shown in Table 32.2, specific decisions for each curriculum element must be made relative to each of the three broad areas. Recognizing the relationships among the standards and the curricular elements will help ensure that educators adapt a standards-based curriculum in comprehensive ways.

Curriculum Differentiation Competence

Educators of students with special needs must regularly adapt curricula to provide differentiating instruction to successfully meet educational needs in the classroom (Hoover, 2001). Differentiating curricula is a skill requiring understanding of the process and the potential benefits to students. Table 32.3 summarizes key abilities important to providing differentiated learning to students with special needs.

Developing effective curriculum differentiation skills is an ongoing process as the educator applies the competencies. Teacher competence

Table 32.2 Adapting Standards With Curricular Elements

Curricular Element	Standards	Differentiation Considerations
Content	Content standards	Specific benchmarks should be reviewed and adapted as necessary
	Performance standards	Identify optimum levels of proficiency necessary to master content
	Opportunity to learn	Ensure that adequate materials and hands-on activities exist to support content
Instructional strategies	Content standards	Identify strategies that facilitate mastery and generalization of content
	Performance standards	Consider compatibility between teaching and learning styles used
	Opportunity to learn	
		Ensure that strategies used facilitate effective use of materials/resources
Instructional settings	Content standards	Determine which setting(s) best facilitate mastery of content
	Performance standards	Ensure that the setting(s) facilitate mastery and generalization of skills
	Opportunity to learn	Setting(s) must allow for quality and effective learning to occur
Student behaviors	Content standards	Student behaviors must help learners acquire and master content
	Performance standards	Acceptable levels of self-management should be identified and monitored
	Opportunity to learn	Overall class management must facilitate safe/effective learning environment

NOTE: From *Curriculum Adaptations for Students With Learning and Behavior Problems: Principles and Practices for Differentiating Instruction* (3rd ed.), by J. J. Hoover and J. R. Patton, in press, Austin, TX: PRO-ED. Copyright by PRO-ED. Reprinted with permission.

Table 32.3   Skills to Achieve Competence in Differentiating Curriculum and Instruction

Development competencies (knowledge of)	Implementation competencies (knowledge of)
• Process for curriculum development • Curricular issues and their implications for students with disabilities • Appropriate curriculum by age, grade, and learning strengths • Topics taught, how they are taught, and the class settings used • Least intrusive adaptations • Interrelatedness of the content, materials, instructional strategies, and instructional settings • Value of culture and language diversity in teaching and learning • Impact of language development on academic and social development	• Curricular strategies to match student's learning styles • Various classroom-based assessments to monitor progress with adaptations • Instructional materials most relevant to the learner • Strategies for differentiating the learning environment to reflect implementation of adaptations, strategies, learning styles, and curricular needs • Modifications to facilitate maintenance and generalization of knowledge and skills • Cognitive learning strategies and study skills and their uses in curriculum to maximize learning • Collaboration skills to facilitate adaptations in the inclusive education setting • Professional advocacy for all students to differentiate curriculum and setting

NOTE: Adapted from *Curriculum Adaptations for Students With Learning and Behavior Problems: Principles and Practices for Differentiating Instruction* (3rd ed.), by J. J. Hoover and J. R. Patton, in press, Austin, TX: PRO-ED. Copyright by PRO-ED. Adapted with permission. Austin, TX: PRO-ED.

and flexibility increase the potential success for all students, providing them with sufficient opportunities to meet the current demands placed upon them in regard to the mandated standards-based curriculum.

CONCLUSION

Both the NCLB and the 1999 amendments to IDEA have brought to the forefront the importance of meeting diverse needs while implementing and assessing the procedures of a standards-based education. Because all students must be included in state-mandated assessments, they must also be included in the implementation of the standards-based curriculum. As a result, curriculum differentiation or adaptation for students with learning and behavior problems must occur more frequently within the guidelines established by standards-based teaching.

John J. Hoover, PhD, is an associate director of the BUENO Center and an adjunct faculty member in special education at the University of Colorado at Boulder. His research interests include curriculum differentiation/ adaptation and study skills education to meet diverse needs in the classroom.

James R. Patton, EdD, is affiliated with PRO-ED in Austin, Texas, and is an adjunct faculty member in special education at The University of Texas at Austin. His research interests include transition and implications for meeting diverse needs in education. Address: John J. Hoover, School of Education, UCB 247, University of Colorado, Boulder, CO 80309.

Trends: New Literacies/ Multiple Literacies

Overview

Our societies are rapidly changing, dynamic, and increasingly global. Communication systems are also quickly changing to keep up. These differences impact our everyday life as well as our school life. Indeed, these "new developments within everyday literacy practices" beg for our attention, as noted by Knobel and Lankshear (2006) in "Discussing New Literacies." Knobel and Lankshear are pioneers in thinking about the ways media and technology influence literacy and the ways of knowing in our world today. In their article, the authors elaborate on their research, ideas, and issues surrounding new literacy practices.

Because globalization impacts our new definitions of literacy, Hassett and Schieble urge teachers to include the visual in literacy instruction where traditional texts still dominate. The authors encourage teachers to learn "how images and text work together in multiple ways." Their article, "Finding Space and Time for the Visual in K–12 Literacy Instruction" (2007), suggests several updates on accepted reading strategies that reflect new literacies. In "Literacy Inquiry and Pedagogy Through a Photographic Lens," Cappello and Hollingsworth (2008) also make specific recommendations for embedding the visual in literacy instruction. They explore the many ways photography may be used for teaching and learning literacy in elementary schools.

Jewitt's (2008) article, "Multimodality and Literacy in School Classrooms" (available at http://www.sagepub.com/cappello/), explores what these changes in societies and communication "mean for being literate in this new landscape of the 21st century" (p. 241). In this review, literacy is seen as more than a linguistic engagement; literacy demands to be considered alongside images and multiple ways representing knowledge.

Strategy

Since this section of your text focuses on expanded definitions of literacy that include and emphasize the visual, we wanted to offer readers a visually based literacy companion

313

strategy. The Open-Mind Portrait (Tompkins, 2009) strategy is traditionally used to broaden and deepen students' understanding of a character from a story or history. However, we encourage you to use the Open-Mind Strategy to visually represent your thoughts on new literacies. The purpose of this strategy is to help you focus on important elements in the text. By completing this strategy, you will experience one way to incorporate visuals in your literacy instruction.

OPEN-MIND STRATEGY

(Tompkins, 2009)

DIRECTIONS

Fill this open-mind graphic with words and images that reflect your thoughts on new literacies.

SOURCE: Tompkins, G. E. (2009). *Fifty Literacy Strategies: Step by Step.* Boston: Allyn & Bacon.

Article 33

DISCUSSING NEW LITERACIES

MICHELE KNOBEL AND COLIN LANKSHEAR

IDEAS AND EXPERIENCES

We met in 1992, coming from very different backgrounds so far as literacy is concerned. Michele had worked as a primary school teacher; Colin had never taught in a school or even trained as a teacher. Michele had always been interested in what was then referred to in Australia as the "language arts," a field that, until the 1990s, had been framed mostly by psychological and cognitive theories of reading and writing. Her master's dissertation, written in 1992, built on reader response theory and the work of Lawrence Kohlberg and Carol Gilligan. Her schooling had surfed early waves of digital technology in Australia and included learning BASIC programming language in high school, as well as LOGO programming at teachers' college. Colin arrived at literacy via the study of philosophy of language (through such scholars as Frege, Russell, Wittgenstein, Sustin) and through Paulo Freire's philosophy of culture, education and freedom. In the 1980s, he did fieldwork in Nicaragua following the Nicaraguan Literacy Crusade, while also reading early works in sociocultural studies of literacy, like Silvia Scribner and Michael Cole's *The Psychology of Literacy* (1981) and Brian Street's *Literacy in Theory and in Practice* (1984). This generated his first (coauthored) literacy book, *Literacy, Schooling, and Revolution* (1989), born at precisely the wrong time. It celebrated classic modernist radical and revolutionary initiatives in literacy at the very moment the world was officially abandoning left-wing modernism. He saw his first modem in Nicaragua when British health researchers he was working with brought one to Managua to dial up England and exchange files related to a project investigating adult female literacy and infant morbidity.

Three key influences shaped our work through the 1990s. One was the sea change in people's working lives. A second was the explosion of new technologies, especially the Internet. The third was our meetings with Jim Gee, with whom we began to work collegially—initially around shared interests in the genre of "fast capitalist texts." Jim, Colin, and Glynda Hull wrote

SOURCE: Knobel, M., & Lankshear, C. (2006). Discussing New Literacies. *Language Arts, 84*(1), 78–86.

The New Work Order: Behind the Language of the New Capitalism (1996). Michele's doctoral thesis drew strongly on Jim's work, notably on *Social Linguistics and Literacies: Ideology in Discourses* (1996). His D/discourse construction framed her investigation of four young adolescents and their literacy practices in and out of school, affording an analytic perspective that took into account ways of knowing, doing, and using language (Knobel, 1999).

The "cyberian" experience became paramount and brought our respective literacy trajectories together into a shared project that is ongoing. This project is partly academic and research-oriented, but is mainly an existential project. We were—and are—conscious of living at a defining moment in history—when massive changes occur routinely in technologies, institutional life, everyday social practices, and configurations that are often bundled together under the umbrella of "globalisation." We wanted to understand these changes as deeply as we could.

We spent as much time as possible in the second half of the 1990s coming to grips with successive waves of innovation in computing and communications technologies—especially the Internet—and pondering how these waves of innovation were associated with trends in cultural practices, economic life, and global communications. We resorted to stealth to get ourselves online at home via the university (when commercial providers were expensive and unreliable) and then spent as much time as possible online. We often recall our first online forays using Lynx, a text-based Internet interface that predated graphic browsers, sensing that something seismic was underway as we accessed texts using online indices, downloaded files using FTP programs and Kermit protocols, participated in MUDs and MOOs, subscribed to email lists, and began telecommuting to work whenever we could. Coming to grips with these new developments also involved reading eclectically. We devoured academics who were theorizing patterns and trends from a sociological perspective and trade book authors writing about technology development and innovation, cyberculture, Gen X, pioneers of digital remix, and the like.

RESEARCH MOVES

Towards the second half of the 1990s, Michele was investigating young people's in-school and out-of-school literacy practices (cf. Knobel, 1999), and Colin was spearheading a national project on new technology uses in schools (cf. Lankshear, C., Bigum, C., Durrant, C., Green, B., Honan, E., Morgan, W., 1997; Lankshear & Snyder with Green, 2000). Combining insights from both projects was a logical step, and our research interest in investigating children's and young people's literacy practices and uses of new digital technologies became a central motif in our collaborative research (cf. Lankshear & Knobel, 1997a, 1997b). Our other work at the time also focused very much on critical literacy and pedagogy, and this, too, found its way into our growing focus on new technologies. Among other things, this convergence produced a book chapter written collaboratively with Michael Peters that was among the first works in education to focus on critical pedagogy and cyberspace (Lankshear, Peters, & Knobel, 1996).

In 1999, we moved to Mexico, and experienced firsthand the extent to which the Internet made it possible to live and work outside conventional academic settings while still remaining in touch with new developments within literacy education. It also saw us spending even more time online and documenting different practices we saw there, or participating ourselves (see our work in netgrrrl * (12) & chicoboy21 * (32), 2002 [our eBay aliases], though it may be easier to find under Knobel & Lankshear, 2002). We first spoke formally about "new literacies" as a distinct and important field warranting serious research attention during a conference organized by Jim Gee at the University of Wisconsin (see Lankshear & Knobel, 2000). A conference hosted by Donna Alvermann at the University of Georgia in January, 2001, provided another important forum for us to discuss with others new developments within everyday literacy practices (see Alvermann, 2002).

We consolidated our thinking about new literacies and new technologies in our 2003 book, *New Literacies: Changing Knowledge and*

Classroom Learning, and have continued this in the new edition of this book (2006).

What Do We Mean by New Literacies?

In the new edition of *New Literacies* (2006), we argue that what makes a literacy "new" has to do with two kinds of "stuff," which we call "technical stuff" and "ethos stuff," respectively. The more that a literacy is constituted by both new technical stuff and new ethos stuff, the more it can be considered a "new" literacy.

The new technical stuff is *digitality.* Paradigm or prototypical instances of new literacies involve the use of digital electronic apparatuses, like computers. Much of what is important for literacy about the new technical stuff has been neatly captured by Mary Kalantzis (Cope, Kalantzis, & Lankshear, 2005): "You click for 'A' and you click for 'red.'" Basically, programmers write source code as binary code (combinations of 0s and 1s) that drives different kinds of applications (for text, sound, image, animation, communications functions, etc.) on digital-electronic apparatuses (computers, games hardware, CD and MP3 players, etc.). For networked computers, this means that anybody with access to a machine and an Internet connection, and who has fairly basic knowledge of standard software applications, can, say, create a multimodal text (such as a Photoshopped image posted to Flickr.com; an animated Valentine's Day card; a short animated film sequence, complete with music soundtrack, using toys and objects found at home; a slide presentation of images of an event that includes narrated commentary; remixed clips from a video game that spoof some aspect of popular culture or retell literary works) and send it to a person, group, or an entire Internet community in next to no time and at next to no cost. All this work is done using a strictly finite set of physical operations or techniques (keying, clicking, cropping, dragging) in a tiny space, with just one or two (albeit complex) "tools."

The ethos stuff has to do with the kind of mindset informing a literacy practice. We distinguish between two broad mindsets that people use to understand and orient themselves toward the world. One mindset approaches the contemporary world as being much the same now as it has been in the past, only a bit more "technologized"—it has had digital technologies added to it, but is nonetheless to be understood and related to more or less as we have done for the past 200 to 300 years. This involves approaching the world from the standpoint of what may be called a "physical–industrial mindset" (Lankshear & Bigum, 1999; Lankshear & Knobel, 2006). The other mindset sees the world as having changed very significantly from how it was, necessitating a different approach from the one used in the past. This second mindset can be thought of as a kind of post-physical and post-industrial mindset. It recognizes cyberspace as a fact of the new world, to be taken into account along with the physical world, but believes that cyberspace operates on the basis of different assumptions and values from physical space. It also operates from very different procedural assumptions and values as those associated with a "physical-industrial" orientation toward the world. Germane to this discussion is Negroponte's well-known example of the hotel clerk who assessed the value of his laptop for insurance purposes at $2000, conceiving it as "atoms," whereas Negroponte assessed it at $2 million, conceiving it as "bits" and evaluating the project proposals and concepts stored on the hard disk.

We cannot go into the difference between the two mindsets in detail here, but Table 33.1 below summarizes some key dimensions.

For us, new literacies are informed by the second mindset and reflect the kinds of assumptions and values that define this second mindset. They do not *have* to involve the use of digital-electronic apparatuses such as computers or the Internet, although they mostly do. They *must* however, be imbued with the second mindset. The key point here is that we see nothing especially new about doing the same familiar things in pretty much the same familiar ways, just with digital technologies (e.g., there's not much new

Table 33.1   Some Dimensions of Variation Between the Two Mindsets on Knowledge Production

Mindset 1	Mindset 2
The world is much the same as before, only now it is more technologized, or technologized in more sophisticated ways.	The world is very different from before, largely as a result of the emergence and uptake of digital electronic inter-networked technologies.
The world is appropriately interpreted, understood, and responded to in broadly physical-industrial terms (e.g., truth values are considered paramount).	The world cannot adequately be interpreted, understood, and responded to in physical-industrial terms (e.g., "true/not true" is considered open to interpretation and reinvention).

• Value is a function of scarcity (e.g., diamonds)
 	
• An "industrial" view of production
 	
  - Products as material artifacts (e.g., a firm or company)
 	
  - A focus on infrastructure and production units (e.g., a firm or company)
 	
  - Tools for producing (e.g., lathes, sewing machines)
 	
• Focus on individual intelligence (e.g., individual test scores as markers of knowledge/proficiency)
 	
• Expertise and authority "located" in individuals and institutions (e.g., university degrees, teaching certification)
 	
• Space as enclosed and purpose-specific (e.g., schools, grade levels, subject area boundaries in education)
 	
• Social relations of "bookspace"; a stable "textual order"
	• Value is a function of dispersion (e.g., open source software development)
	
	• A "post-industrial" view of production
	
	  - Products as enabling services (e.g., Google.com)
	
	  - A focus on leverage and non-finite participation (e.g., the Internet)
	
	  - Tools for mediating and relating (e.g., Flickr.com, MySpace.com)
	
	• Focus on collective intelligence (e.g., Wikipedia.org)
	
	• Expertise and authority are distributed and collective; hybrid experts (e.g., Citizen journalism blogs)
	
	• Space as open, continuous, and fluid (e.g., massive multiplayer online games)
	
	• Social relations of emerging "digital media space"; texts in change (e.g., fanfiction, machinima, and other remixing practices)

in retelling narratives by way of presentation software like PowerPoint). Rather, we think that the history of the contemporary world is a history that is moving more and more in the direction of the second mindset. The second mindset will not *displace* the first one because the world will always have its physical component and will need to be addressed as such. But we see an historical drift toward the second mindset, and believe that in time, more and more of what we do and how we "be" will reflect the working out of a dialectic, or productive, set of tensions between the mindsets. Hence, in the future, much of *what* literacies will be and much

of *how* literacies will be are going to reflect the working out in practice of this second mindset: the realization in practice of a very different kind of "ethos stuff" from the literate world of the physical-industrial order (i.e., bookspace).

Consequently, we see new literacies in terms of practices like fanfiction, fan manga, fan anime, weblogging, podcasting, Photoshopping, "flickr-ing," "memeing," participating in "writing" collective works like *Wikipedia,* online gaming, and the like. This is because these are collaborative practices, involving distributed participation and collaboration, where rules and procedures are flexible and open to change, and soon. In terms of current jargon, there is a great deal about new literacies that is captured in the concept of "Web 2.0" as distinct from "Web 1.0," and in practices like "tagging" and their affiliation with "folksonomies" rather than "taxonomies."

This means that new literacies are better understood in terms of an historical trend rather than in terms of technical specifics. The fact that email has been a large-scale practice for almost 20 years now does not make it an "old new literacy." Some emailing was *always* "old"—just "letters done on a new machine." When emailing became a truly collaborative practice, underpinning listservs and the like, *that* was new because that bespoke collaboration and participation on a scale and within a timeframe that was more or less impossible to achieve under older media. There is nothing interesting that is new about doing narrative recounts as PowerPoint presentations or as web pages: it's just the same old same old classroom practice in digital "drag." Likewise, there is not much of interest that is new in just using the Internet as a huge reference book to be held hostage to familiar canons of credibility. That's not to say that subjecting Internet information to scrutiny is not *important*. It's just to say that it is not especially new in the terms we recognize. On the other hand, going nuts in terms of participating on Flickr by spending hours uploading photos, commenting on other people's photos, joining and contributing to special interest groups, etc. has a lot of "new" about it, although it may not be especially "deep" in highbrow terms.

We think that for the foreseeable future, the people who are best equipped in literacy terms will be those who can draw appropriately from *both* mindsets and, moreover, who can move between conventional epistemologies and what we call "digital epistemologies" (Lankshear, Peters, & Knobel, 2000). In digital epistemologies, the conventional epistemological emphasis on "truth" and "justified belief" will often be overshadowed by an emphasis on knowing how to gain or structure attention, how to make novel "moves," or innovate successfully in contexts where there are few or no established rules and procedures, and how to break rules creatively or invent new rules and conventions.

TENSIONS OPERATING IN TEACHING AND LEARNING CONTEXTS

Something we wrestle with in our research and writing is the tension we and many other researchers observe between the facility and sensibilities many young people have with digital media and new literacies and the circumstances they often encounter within formal learning settings. This can be a tension for teachers as well, when they want to support and promote students' agency but at the same time feel bound by curricular and reporting requirements that define *literacy* as encoding, decoding, and comprehension of conventional texts and *curriculum delivery* as an orderly progression through an official program of topics and tasks.

For example, within the traditional view of formal education, learning space is bordered by the classroom walls, lesson space by the 40- to 60-minute class period, and curriculum and timetable space by the grid of subjects to be covered and the time allocations assigned to them. Space tends to be strongly centered around the teacher and/or architectural features, like the chalkboard, electronic whiteboard, or the layout of computers or desks. Tasks tend to be singular and confined to a given time, during which all learners are doing the same task; not being on that task is seen as being disengaged from learning. By contrast, learners who have grown up "digital" often have a very different view and approach to learning. The very notion of dealing with one task at a time or operating in one "place" at a time when engaged in learning (or entertainment or recreation) is foreign to these students. Rather, "multitasking"—often extending to several simultaneous engagements—is the norm for digital youth.

The traditional view of learning as described above is not necessarily well adapted to classrooms. Kevin Leander and colleagues observed lessons in a school that was experimenting with mobile computing within a wireless environment. Not surprisingly, they witnessed students spending considerable time in class engaged in self-selected purposes: gaming, shopping, downloading music, emailing, chatting online, and instant messaging (IMing). For example, during one English class, Zoe moved between reading aloud passages from a Robert Frost poem at the behest of her teacher (using a book borrowed from a friend because Zoe had left hers at home), offering comments and interpretations in response to the teacher's questions, all the while pulling up different friends' blogs on her computer screen and reading, laughing, and responding to what she found there, as well as updating her own blog. Zoe remained engaged in the class at hand, but got on with doing other tasks as well. The project field notes (Leander, 2005) record a typical instance as follows:

Zoe opens her laptop and logs into the network. She accesses Xanga.com—a popular weblog hosting service—and begins reading a weblog. The title of the weblog is, "Thank God I'm an Atheist," and Zoe laughs while reading the latest entry on this blog.

The teacher asks, "Is there anybody who doesn't understand imagery?" She walks close by Zoe, who quickly opens a blank Word document and keys in "Imagery" before flipping back to her web browser and reading a different weblog.

Teacher: *"Who can describe an image from 'After Apple Picking' by Frost?"*

Zoe keeps the weblog she was reading open on her laptop, but looks at Alana's book and gives the first answer of the day: "In the first four lines you get an image of an apple in an apple tree."

Teacher: *"Good, a very realistic one. Read those lines again because they are interesting lines."*

The blog in front of Zoe reads: "There is nothing more foul than dissecting a fetal pig."

Teacher: *"Frost especially likes to use the seasons of the year."*

Zoe opens her own blog and begins working on an entry for that day.

Students who engaged most in pursuing self-selected purposes during class time did not believe they were learning less than they otherwise would as a result of this. Two claimed that being able to go to other places during time in class when they already knew about the matters under discussion alleviated boredom. Their capacity for multitasking seemingly allowed them to maintain one eye on the task while going about other business.

Contrary to such self-appraisals on the part of students, however, some teachers in this school limited students' use of laptops to specific points in the lessons. Under current policy and reporting conditions, the teachers' imposition of "appropriate limits" does not constitute *unreasonable* behavior. Indeed, given the extent to which schools are under constant reporting surveillance and subject to the logic of "performativity" (Lyotard, 1984), this behavior could be considered necessary for self-preservation. We think, however, that at this historical juncture, it is an educationally inappropriate response. We make sense of and comment on such tensions by analyzing the two mindsets we have previously mentioned.

In formal and informal settings beyond the school, including workplaces, the capacity to multi-task fluently is often highly valued and sometimes serves as a status marker. Effective multitasking is associated with greater efficiency, as well as with being digitally proficient. From the insider perspective (the second mindset), there is no conception of "disrespect" or of paying insufficient attention to a task if one is multitasking, whereas from the "one space–one task" perspective, such connotations often apply. The insider moves fluently between tasks, seeing them as equally important and viewing this more-or-less simultaneous online attention as efficient and advantageous. As workplace competition intensifies, efficient multitasking will undoubtedly become an important part of the competitive edge. In fact, it seems very likely that the social, cultural, and economic value and esteem associated with multitasking will increase to the point of becoming the default mode. To this extent, responses like those of the teachers in Leander's study who limited possibilities for multitasking might well prove to be on the wrong side of history. So far as Zoe (and students like her) is concerned, it appears that even under conditions of extreme multitasking, she was able to provide at least as much attention to the tasks specifically associated with the official learning of the classroom to perform them adequately. That may well say something about formal classroom tasks, but it does not provide a basis for preemptive strikes against multitasking in class.

ISSUES CONCERNING PREDATORS, HYPERSEXUALISED IMAGERY, AND OTHER POTENTIAL DAMAGE ONLINE

Data collection is inevitably influenced by researcher standpoint. What does one see when one goes looking at young people's encounters with online content, other people online, and so on? Our interests are in young people's social and cultural practices online, and we investigate young people who seem to us to be interesting. What *we* find when *we* go looking are young people who are engaging in the pursuits we more or less expected, because we have chosen to research them on the basis of information we already have. These young people tend to be quite savvy about keeping themselves safe online. For example, we sought permission from a youngster to use some excerpts from her fanfiction, promising her a copy of the book in which it would appear when it was published. We said nothing more and nothing less. Our informant said to stay in touch and something could be arranged, but she was not giving her address out on the Internet. Another participant in our fanfic research said she likes to include romance

in her narratives, but not sex, because she wants to keep a "general audience" rating for her stories in order to reach as wide an audience as possible. Our colleagues who research young people tend to have much the same experience; their subjects are savvy young people who are more interested in designing their avatars than going after hypersexualised images for gaming; kids who value online role-play gaming because it teaches them "honor, courage and loyalty"; kids who know how to keep themselves safe online (cf. Leander, 2005; Thomas, 2005). So the images that we present of young people are the ones we think we can responsibly report; that is, the ones we encounter. And the ones we encounter are not a full spectrum sample—we don't claim they are. And we don't go looking for "negative" instances, either. Instead, we look for "constructive typicality."

On the other hand, many people have very strong interests in reporting other kinds of cases, whether they have witnessed them or not. Let's not mince words here: there are very powerful corporate forces emphasizing the risks and the potential aberrations involved with having young people spending a lot of time online. A lot of these interests, not surprisingly, are bound up with education and, especially, with schooling. Imagine the enormous challenge to curricular, social, and political authority in schools if creative and effective ways of integrating the Internet into young people's education suddenly appeared overnight, and imagine the challenge to the many adults who need to believe that they know more than the students they teach.

This relates to what we think is a key educational issue around literacy. Like a lot of educational researchers and writers who have reasonably rich experiences with computing and communications technologies, we are distressed by the extent to which schooling has been reduced to the task of ensuring that all young people master "literacy," narrowly defined as encoding and decoding alphabetic script for the purposes of accessing information (reliable, "true" information, of course). We think that this emphasis has a lot to do with the fact that the "core business" is now widely construed as "teaching and learning" rather than as "educating." Teaching and learning, in our view, are compatible with grinding away at "literacy" in a very minimal sense. One of our young research participants exemplifies what is at stake here. "Rikku-chan" is an African American attending an urban public high school. At school, Rikku-chan receives low or failing grades for English. Online, she writes fanfic that draws on Greek and Roman myths as well as on different elements of contemporary popular culture. Her spelling and grammar and plot construction receive supportive attention from peers online. In other words, Rikku-chan gets her language education online, whereas at school, she gets "remediation"—this, in spite of her mother showing Rikku-chan's fanfics to the English teacher.

Rikku-chan has not fallen prey to porn peddlers, pedophiles, password stealers, or identity thieves when she is online at home. This is not to say that she cannot, any more than the rest of us are immune to such things online. But her mother, who is around and about when Rikku-chan is online, has chatted openly with Rikku-chan about the importance of not divulging too much about herself online and is certainly not keeping Rikku-chan from using the Internet. On the contrary, she grasps the importance of Rikku-chan having every opportunity for a full and rich online experience to the extent that she seeks it. This is how "netizens" approach the Internet. Are we going to stop buying books on Amazon.com or plane tickets to conferences on Expedia.com for fear that someone might steal our identities? Not likely. For Rikku-chan as much as for us, the Internet is the key portal for our ongoing *education.* Continuing to educate ourselves and evolve as human beings is definitely worth some risk. Rikku-chan's mother keeps in touch with her interests. Michele and Colin do what they can to keep tabs on the credit card statements, on new scamming strategies, and on the reputation of sites and providers. This takes some work, some effort, and some responsibility, but it is integral to our ongoing education. Why wouldn't we take these risks while at the same time taking care to educate ourselves about the nature of these risks and how to defend against them?

This is a positive orientation, an educational orientation, a labor-intensive orientation, and a "will to be more" orientation—with respect to ourselves and on behalf of others. We have found that people who emphasize negative images about the use of the Internet for in-class and at-home purposes are almost universally those whose personal experience with computing and communications technologies is limited. Conversely, those with rich online lives are aware of the risks and informed about how to protect themselves and others. This, we suggest, constitutes an educational orientation. Although the finite group of people who tend toward the negative on this subject are not typically people we associate with strong investments in *education,* they do often have strong interests in maintaining schooling as a system of cautions and controls.

A LIGHT EDUCATIONAL WALK THROUGH A NEW LITERACY: MEMES

Among Internet insiders, "meme" (pronounced "meem") is a popular term for the rapid uptake and spread of a particular idea presented as a written text, image, language "move," or some other unit of cultural "stuff." Memes are often defined as contagious patterns of cultural ideas, information, knowledge and/or values, etc. that are passed from mind to mind and directly shape and generate key actions and mindsets of a social group. Memes include popular tunes, catchphrases, clothing fashions, architectural styles, ways of doing things, and so on. There is a technical science of memes—Memetics—that has built on seminal work by geneticist Richard Dawkins. Internet memes, however, opt out of this discourse. "Hatching" memes and participating in memes as a popular online pursuit is about "dropping" something into net-space that captures a lot of attention very fast, spreads rapidly by gathering recruits who "build" the meme, and lasts as long as it may. Some memes are quirky, even absurd. Others are serious. Some are hoaxes, others are constructive attempts to recruit people to worthy causes. Many are simply jokes.

Our own research interest has documented and analyzed successful online memes of all kinds as a way of understanding an aspect of popular online culture that mobilizes considerable energy. A good example of an absurdist meme is the Lost Frog meme (c. 2004 and onwards). This alludes to a range of popular culture phenomena as it remixes the text of a flier for a lost pet named Hopkin Green Frog. The original flier was found posted along Seattle streets. A member of a popular image-sharing forum scanned the found text and uploaded it to the forum archive. Group members quickly picked up on the pathos and determination in the child's language (e.g., "If I looking for frog" and "P.S. I'll find my frog") and the hand-drawn images. They used image editing software to "photoshop" the original image, and the results—both by this group, and later, by others around the world—are always humorous and often touching. Collectively, they narrate massive, albeit fictional, citizen mobilization in the ongoing search for Hopkin Green Frog and include typical "missing persons" announcement vehicles (e.g., broadcast media news, milk cartons, road signs), crowd scenes seemingly devoted to spreading the news about the lost frog (e.g., "lost frog" banners at a street march and a crowded soccer match), and a host of other "remember Hopkin" scenarios (e.g., lost frog scratch-it lottery tickets, Hopkin's ID on someone's instant message buddy list, Hopkin as a "not found" Internet file image).

Successful social critique memes online tend to carry biting commentary on some social practice or event. The Nike Sweat Shop Shoes meme is a good example of this. In January 2001, Jonah Perretti forwarded to friends a series of email exchanges he had had with the Nike company concerning Nike's iD campaign that allows customers to customize their shoes. Perretti's request to have "sweatshop" embroidered on his new shoes (at a time when Nike was under fire for exploiting workers in underdeveloped countries) had been denied by the company. Despite persistent questions on Perretti's part, the company hid behind company policy statements and did not provide a logical rationale for the cancelled order. Perretti gathered these exchanges together in a single email and sent it off to a few friends. The satiric humour and social commentary contained in the set of email correspondence caught popular attention and soon reached thousands of people via email networks, ultimately arousing the interest of broadcast news networks.

Meming may be a fruitful practice to focus on when thinking about new forms of social participation and civic action in the wake of widespread access to the Internet and involvement in increasingly dispersed social networks. Meme analysis can include tracing where or how certain memes (or mind viruses) were most likely acquired; what effects these memes have on decision-making, mindsets, and actions; the effects these memes may have on other people; and what ethical decisions must be made with respect to passing on, or *not* passing on, certain memes.

Not all the memes we have studied contribute positively to human well-being. The "Dog Poop Girl" meme, for example, generated intense public criticism. It seems a woman in Korea refused to clean up after her dog had fouled a train carriage. After a disgruntled fellow traveler posted a camera phone image of her to the Internet, the woman was identified and subjected to a "vigilante" response: within a very short time, her personal details and address were posted to the Internet and the woman was hounded publicly online and offline until she apologized. The power of this meme to mobilize public censure of this woman is patent. It has raised issues concerning the use of memes for redress and by what authority this is done. Participating in this meme by passing the woman's picture and personal details to others is not an innocent, playful, or morally clear-cut act. It presents educators with a potential catalyst for discussing the moral and civic dimensions of participating in certain memes.

It may be constructive, as part of revising critical literacy practices in classrooms, to analyze meme processes and effects as new forms of social influence. In doing so, students may come to understand new literacy practices and the consequences of transmitting healthy or toxic ideas rapidly and extensively. Ultimately, such an analysis might enable educators and students to recognize or develop strategies for identifying memes that infect minds and evaluating their effects on one's (ethical) decision making, actions, and relations with others.

Counter-meming is a well-established practice online, and refers to the deliberate generation of a meme that aims at neutralizing or eradicating potentially harmful ideas. This phenomenon offers a range of models for working with memes within classroom spaces. For example, the nonprofit group Adbusters (adbusters.org) models the kinds of memes that offer students a means of resisting corporate-manufactured identities and consumption mindsets (see, for example, unbrandamerica.org) via their critiques of mainstream media, marketing, and consumption memes. Nonprofit community groups are also looking to the grassroots mobilization that occurs around remixed or evolving multimedia memes as a viable model for mobilizing commitment to social causes (e.g., Surman & Reilly, 2003). Teachers should be aware that well-informed and savvy online meming may provide students with a fruitful and accessible practice for bringing about positive social changes.

EDITORS' NOTE: As the Language Arts editors considered how best to address the rapid technological and conceptual changes related to language arts education and new media, we returned again and again to the ideas and research of Colin Lankshear and Michele Knobel. Their research explores and analyzes youth practices with new media, and their vision of new literacies offers educators and researchers unprecedented pathways for thinking about texts, media, youth, and relations of power in the 21st century. The format for this article grew out of a set of questions posed to Colin and Michele via email.

We asked them to:

  describe the ideas that have informed their thinking over the past decade;

  elaborate on their definition of new literacies;

  discuss tensions between new media experimentation and learning contexts;

  address the concerns adults and youth might have about the content and potentially predatory nature of online voices and images;

  and walk readers through an example of the social networking possibilities of meaning making with new media.

Their thoughtful explorations of these questions were adapted and excerpted for this profile.

Michele Knobel is associate professor at Early Childhood, Elementary Education, and Literacy Education, Montclair State University.

Colin Lankshear is visiting scholar, Faculty of Education, McGill University.

Article 34

FINDING SPACE AND TIME FOR THE VISUAL IN K–12 LITERACY INSTRUCTION

DAWNENE D. HASSETT AND MELISSA B. SCHIEBLE

awnene D. Hassett and Melissa B. Schieble contend that literacy instruction must include attention to the multiple ways in which print and visual images work together. They propose ways to update accepted reading strategies with visual texts and new literacies in mind. Using examples from picture books and graphic novels, they expand our understanding of how readers extend three cueing systems—graphophonic, semantic, and syntactic—to negotiate multiple levels of meaning in visual texts.

The social, cultural, and political environment shaped by globalization has seen an emergence of greater reliability on visual modes of communication. Television, film, and the Internet have become major sources of public information and communication. In addition, the texts students encounter today embody cues for reading that extend beyond the letters and words on the page, requiring readers to actively focus on textual elements beyond the decoding of print (Hammerberg [Hassett], "Reading" 207). The computerization of type design and the photomechanical printing technologies available today make it possible for alphabetic text to intermingle with graphics, extending the ways in which thought may be represented. New technologies make it possible to provide interactive, nonlinear, and hypertextual forms of communication that rival the printed word, thus expanding and challenging notions of representation and interpretation commonly associated with traditional printed texts. Gunther Kress asserts that "the potentials of electronic technologies will entrench visual modes of communication as a rival to language in many domains of public life" ("Visual" 55).

SOURCE: Hassett, D. D., & Schieble, M. B. (2007). Finding Space and Time for the Visual in K–12 Literacy Instruction. *English Journal, 97*(1), 62–68. Copyright © 2007 by the National Council of Teachers of English. Reprinted by permission.

Meanwhile, back at the school, literacy instruction is dominated by traditional texts and alphabetic print. Visual modes of communication are seen as secondary to print, technology instruction is placed alongside or separate from literacy instruction, and new technologies are often used to teach traditional, print-based concepts. Yet, if the visual is to be entrenched or saturated to the point of rivalry with the verbal as a primary mode of communication, what does this mean for education?

One implication is that we need to understand and teach how images and printed text work together in multiple ways. Following Carolyn Handa, who states that "finding space for the visual in the curriculum is possible without sacrificing the course goals of developing careful thinkers and thoughtful writers" (9), we suggest ways to find space for the visual within existing methods of literacy instruction so that new literacies and new texts can be used in the classroom without sacrificing curricular goals. Specifically, we look at accepted reading strategies for the purpose of updating them with visual texts and new literacies in mind.

New Literacies: From Theory to Practice

Colin Lankshear and Michele Knobel offer us two different ways of thinking about "new literacies," one ontological and one paradigmatic (16–17). First, an ontological shift means that texts have changed because they look different from traditional print-based texts where graphemes are the primary carrier of meaning.[1] In part a product of new technologies, such as photomechanical printing technologies or digital technologies that allow combinations of sound, print, and images, texts for children today produce a situation where alphabetic print must be understood as only a partial transporter of meaning. These kinds of texts require new ways of reading, writing, interpreting, and interacting, and they also indicate the possibility for a shift in

the ways we might think about literacy as a school subject (Bearne 14).

For example, in Jules Feiffer's *Meanwhile,* a text that borrows a comic book style, a mother (we presume) is screaming (we presume), "Raymond!" (1), but in the book itself, there are no quotation marks around "Raymond," and there is no signifying trailer, such as, "Mom yelled." Instead, the size and placement of his name on the page, shaped in a megaphone kind of configuration with "noise" lines running through it, are signs that let us "know" that Raymond's mom is yelling his name. So, using this example, we can define text as the cohesive whole of a document, including words, images, design, and their relations.

Second, sociocultural theories of language and literacy, such as those developed and explained by James Paul Gee, Shirley Brice Heath, Bertha Pérez, and Brian V. Street, provide a paradigmatic shift to the ways we can think about literacy learning. This means that our models of thinking about literacy learning (our paradigms) have moved away from psychological theories, where learning to read is thought to happen in the head, to an understanding of literacy as always embedded within a social context and purpose for meaning-making. In sociocultural theories, the sense that readers are able to make out of a text is shaped by the experiences, background knowledge, and social/cultural identities that they bring to a reading. Where visual/text relations are concerned, we would add that the makeup of the text itself, and what the reader is to do with it, helps to shape the meaning that the reader takes away as well. The text as a whole, with images, graphics, placement of print, and so on, helps to shape the sociocultural plane on which readers are situated when they make sense of a text.

Sociocultural theories become an important tool for thinking about the role of the reader in constructing meaning out of visual/text relations. When we understand that "comprehension" involves social and cultural practices (Hammerberg [Hassett], "Comprehension"), we can also recognize that there are new social and cultural practices at play when new forms of text are used. Charles A. Hill notes that "comprehending and interpreting any image . . . requires an active mental process that is driven by personal and cultural values and assumptions" (113); in texts where images carry a great deal of meaning, the meaning at large may shift and change depending on each individual's interpretation. The paradigmatic shift for education, then, is about leaving behind the idea that texts "contain" information that readers "receive" and moving toward an understanding that meaning is produced through active negotiation, conversation, and communication of individual values and thoughts. Sociocultural forms involve an understanding that specific codes, such as an alphabetic sign system, don't mean anything outside of the context of the text, including its images, or the social and cultural practices that the readers bring.

For Kress, the complexity of text/image relations lies in the fact that images afford different ways of shaping knowledge, imagination, and design, rather than functioning simply as an illustrative feature for the written text. He articulates this point by stating, "the assumption is that some things are best done by using writing, and others are best done by using images" ("Visual" 63). We would add to this that some things are best done by combining print and image (the verbal and the visual), because, as Handa notes, "today's documents are increasingly hybrids of words, images, and design" (9). Rather than drawing a division in instruction between understanding the visual and the verbal, this relationship should be considered as epistemologically interconnected. Instruction ought to "[require] readers and writers to have a richer understanding of how words and images work together to produce meaning" (Stroupe and Welch 109).

In the remainder of this article, we employ these understandings of new literacies—both ontological and paradigmatic—to examine images as "complex texts in their own right" (Hill 121). While current research and pedagogy in reading have been built on a traditional notion of text that leads to a particular notion of good reading instruction, we wish to build on existing reading research, especially the theories that highlight the active role of the reader in making meaning out of text, to update reading instruction to include new forms of texts and new literacies. To that end, we consider how reading strategies can be applied when various text/image affordances are in play, and we analyze how images and print work together to scaffold meaning-making in a sociocultural sense.

SPACE FOR THE VISUAL IN READING STRATEGIES

Carrie Rood notes that "in the age of the visual image," students must be able to implement "a set of skills in order to interpret the content of these visual images, their social impact, and their ownership" (111). We heartily agree, but the skill set that readers must employ to interpret the visual might begin with an updated notion of traditional reading strategies. In traditional reading theory, readers gain meaning from print by coordinating three basic cueing systems: graphophonic cues, or the print within the words and sentences; semantic cues, or the meaning; and syntactic cues, or the grammatical language structure.[2] A strategic reader searches for information from these cueing systems and deciphers the meaning by thinking about what the print looks like (graphophonic), whether it makes sense (semantic), and whether it sounds right (syntax).

With texts that combine print and images, all three cueing systems are also available, but there are more cues to negotiate—some in print, some in images, some from the readers' backgrounds and sociocultural identities. This sets up a new context for making sense of text.

Graphophonic (Visual) Cues

Graphophonic cues are visual to the extent that readers must pay attention to the symbols of written language. In early literacy instruction, young readers are taught to pay attention to directionality, letters, beginning and ending sounds, words, spaces, and punctuation (Hassett, "Signs"). However, reading from left to right and top to bottom is not always possible in texts that combine print and images to convey meaning.

For example, in *The Stinky Cheese Man and Other Fairly Stupid Tales,* by Jon Scieszka and Lane Smith, half of the dedication page is written in huge, block print upside down, with a note right side up saying the following:

> I know. I know. The page is upside down. I meant to do that. Who ever looks at that dedication stuff anyhow? If you really want to read it—you can always stand on your head. (1)

The upside-down block print carries meaning and direction outside of the dedication message. The text, right side up, demands to be read: The image of the little character, Jack, holding the loud dedication page upside down, is a direct address to the reader to turn the book around (or else stand on your head). It is up to the reader, not the author, to decide how (or whether) to engage with particular textual aspects. This type of text contains signs to consider beyond the print itself: ways of knowing what to do with the text and ways of understanding its demanding, yet humorous, meaning.

Print-image relations also add an additional level of information to be "decoded" through graphics, color, size, and shape, as in the example of Raymond's mom yelling his name in *Meanwhile*. In Jonathan London's *Froggy Gets Dressed,* Froggy's mom yells his name, too, in large, capital, purple letters across page 8, in orange letters on page 14, and in red later on (London 17). Emotion is carried in these color changes, and the *idea* of yelling is carried throughout. Comprehending Mom's meaning requires more than decoding: it requires drawing on one's own knowledge of color, placement, and yelling moms.

While we have been using examples of picture books for children to illustrate the types of visual cues available beyond letters and words on a page, these same cueing systems are available

in picture books for secondary students. In other words, this is not just an issue for elementary literacy instruction. Anne Burke and Shelley Stagg Peterson argue that "[m]any picture books today explore complex themes and address topics appropriate for secondary school students" and that "picture books offer a medium for teaching visual and critical literacy across the curriculum in secondary classrooms" (74). Likewise, Elizabeth Schmar-Dobler notes that reading on the Internet requires students to effectively "use links, headings, graphics, and video and audio clips" to gather information (80). Thus, visual cues are not just for beginning readers.

Semantic Cues

Readers use semantic cues to determine what makes sense. Traditionally, this means that as readers decode print from left to right, they check to see whether what they are reading makes sense. However, with texts that combine images and print, the meaning must be constructed by paying attention to both words and pictures. For example, David Macaulay's *Black and White* contains four stories occurring on the page all at once, mostly through illustrations but also through accompanying print for each story. A "warning" on the title page reads, "This book appears to contain a number of stories that do not necessarily occur at the same time. Then again, it may contain only one story. In any event, careful inspection of both words and pictures is recommended" (1). The reader, not the author, decides how to proceed and where to focus attention. Readers can choose to follow one story through the whole book, look at the stories simultaneously, compare similar images in all stories, compare continuities among stories, or follow the story or stories in other ways. Interestingly, a main character in each story is a robber, who is never referred to in the text alone. The presence of the robber, though, helps to scaffold an understanding of the print—without the robber, the text makes no sense.

Graphic novels for adolescents also necessitate a reading of print and images to create meaning because much of the meaning is carried in the image itself. The print becomes a tool or a scaffold for making meaning of the image, versus the traditional notion of images illustrating print. Graphic novels are best understood as "a language, [whose] vocabulary is the full range of visual symbols" (McCloud 1).

For example, in *Persepolis: The Story of a Childhood* by Marjane Satrapi, the shading of Marjane's face shows her internal conflict. She is torn from within about the freedoms that she has within her household versus the oppression she faces outside of the home or at school, and this anguish is represented by the images more than the print. To demonstrate this point, on page 25, Marjane's face is shaded (showing conflict) even when she is verbally not talking about conflict. In fact, she says she wants to take a bath. Yet in earlier frames, her mother discussed her own fears growing up that her father would be taken to prison for his communist views, how prison destroys, and so forth. Marjane carries this with her (represented visually) even when saying something relatively mundane and everyday. This demonstrates that the visual does carry more information than the print alone, and in this case, it provides a semantic cue for interpreting meaning. "I want to take a bath" here can mean "I want to cleanse myself of these thoughts," but only in combination with the image.

The text-image relationship, then, requires an active reader to make meaning using his or her sociocultural knowledge and background to make the images come alive in relation to the print. In reading graphic novels, semantic cues include the image itself as a carrier of meaning, and the image becomes a significant way to check whether one's interpretations of the text are acceptable and consistent.

Syntactic Cues

Syntax in linguistic terms is typically the study of the rules of a language (e.g., grammatical structures); syntactic cues embedded in various language patterns and genres help to inform the reader about word meaning. However, in logical terms, syntax is also a branch of study that looks at how various signs are arranged or can be arranged. With texts that use the visual as a primary carrier of meaning, images can also be seen as a sign system, and syntactic cues for the interpretation of text-image relations are also held in the arrangement and tone (e.g., color, design layout, harshness of line) of the image itself.

The relationship between images and printed text can be synergistic, where the message must be read through images-as-text in ways that make it difficult to say where meaning lies, in the words or in the images. Eliza T. Dresang describes synergy this way: "In the most radical form of synergy, words and pictures are so much a part of one another that it is almost impossible to say which is which" (88). Text becomes a conglomeration of both. Words appear *in* pictures and *over* pictures in ways that require a nonliteral reading of the printed text, for to only read the words for their literal meaning would be to leave with no meaning whatsoever. One example of this is a photo of an attorney in Virginia Walter's *Making Up Megaboy,* on whose face is superimposed a series of printed sentences, not in lines but contoured to the face, that ramble in pointless concern over a serious juvenile crime:

> Mr. Jones does not realize the seriousness of Robbie's situation. His son committed a capital crime, a felony, to which there was a witness and to which he has confessed. There are no facts in dispute about his actions. It is just fortunate that he hadn't turned fourteen; I don't think I could have prevented his being tried as an adult if he had been a year older. I think I might have been more effective in securing an alternative treatment facility for Robbie if his father had been cooperative with the social workers and probation officers who were investigating his case. We were unable to establish any motive for the crime. To this day, I don't know why Robbie Jones killed Jae Lin Koh. I wonder if Robbie even knows why he did it. He'll have a lot of time to think about it. He won't be released until he is twenty-five. (57)

There is noise in the graphic, layered words contoured on a face, but the words mean nothing compared to the synergy between photo and text, which says how nobody can explain, how nobody knows why, how in the end there is no answer. The words babble with no new information: "this attorney . . . talks a lot but knows nothing" (Dresang 88). Thus, the syntactic cues for reading this synergistic image include the design and layout of the text, where the reader makes meaning out of the "grammatical" placement of the images as combined and integrated with print.

In graphic novels, syntactic cues for making meaning lie in abundance in the image itself. A frame from *Maus I: A Survivor's Tale/My Father Bleeds History* by Art Spiegelman contains print that is limited, stating above the image, "Anja and I didn't have where to go," and below the image, "We walked in the direction of Sosnowiec—but where to go?!" The literal meaning of the print is clear. The characters are without a place to seek refuge and safety. However, the power and emotion of this frame lies in how the text and the image work together.

Scott McCloud comments on the inaccurate public perception that comics offer "a *linear, plot driven form,* lacking prose's ability to handle *layers of meaning—subject*—within a story" (31; italics in original). Clearly, *Maus I* contains layers of subtexual meaning that may not be possible to re-create in print alone. In this frame, the couple is portrayed as small and in shadow, before a crossroads path that is configured as the Nazi swastika. The trees alongside the path are empty and dismal, emphasizing the desolate future ahead for Vladek and his wife. The layout of the path and the cold, empty landscape foreshadow the events that this couple face later in the novel: at this stage in the novel, the Nazis are so prolific in this region that any path the couple follows will lead to an eventual concentration camp (hence the swastika). Perhaps the leafless, rail-thin trees symbolize the extreme hunger and fatigue that Vladek and Anja will face. In the horizon of this image lies an industrial-looking building, with smoke rising from one of its stacks; the subtext of this particular part of the

image may also foreshadow the gas chambers that await them in the camp.

Syntactically, the spatial arrangement of this image carries almost the entire meaning in this frame. The smoke-billowing building is projected with distance from the couple, yet within sight, much like the actual events as the novel unfolds. The cues for making meaning lie almost entirely in the image; the print works as a scaffold for relaying that the couple have nowhere to go, but the power of this frightening truth lies in the image and its spatial arrangement.

CONCLUSION

New forms of texts, which do not rely primarily on alphabetic print, require readers to negotiate multiple levels of meaning while constructing connections within and across various textual elements. In hybrid texts, the visual takes on a distinct role. It carries information differently than alphabetic print by calling on emotional and affective associations in the reader's/viewer's mind. Unlike writing, which depicts "*[t]he world told*" through arguments sequentially arranged with logic and evidence, the visual evokes "*the world shown*" (Kress, *Literacy* 1; italics in original) through spatial arrangement and display.

To help students negotiate this "world shown," we might begin by updating our reading cueing systems to encompass a greater scope. For example, visual cues clearly extend beyond the sign systems of print and now include images, graphics, and the look of the word on the page. Likewise, meaning and structural cues can now be derived from textual placement, image/text relations, and the synergy between words and pictures. Teachers can explore with their students the multiple layers in a text: many sources of information to draw on, many possible interpretations, and many choices for interacting with the text.

Our students encounter new forms of text that indicate new ways of reading, interpreting, interacting, and thinking in their everyday lives; yet, literacy instruction is currently dominated by traditional texts in schools. However, finding space and time for the visual in K–12 literacy instruction is not only possible when new literacies and new texts can be used in the classroom without sacrificing curricular goals, it is also necessary in a world influenced by changing forms of communication, information, and mass media.

Dawnene D. Hassett is assistant professor at the University of Wisconsin–Madison in the Department of Curriculum and Instruction. Her research examines new literacies in curriculum and instruction, especially sociocultural literacies, new technologies, and new forms of text. email: ddhassett@wisc.edu.

Melissa B. Schieble is a doctoral candidate at the University of Wisconsin–Madison in the Department of Curriculum and Instruction. Her research interests include adolescent literacies, computer-mediated communication, and exploring technology as a tool for learning in English education. email: mbschieb@wisc.edu.

Article 35

LITERACY INQUIRY AND PEDAGOGY THROUGH A PHOTOGRAPHIC LENS

MARVA CAPPELLO AND SANDRA HOLLINGSWORTH

Photography becomes an effective tool for teaching, learning, and studying literacy in elementary school classrooms as students' photographs and the act of photographing provide new ways to problem solve and create more complex texts.

Hollingsworth: Wow! Your story on monster trucks really changed from your first draft. Why?

Alex: Well, we had to take pictures without any real monster trucks around to show, except we took pictures from books . . . [that] sort of make me think what we wanted to tell about in the story.

Hollingsworth: Did the Author's Chair feedback help?

Christian: Oh, yeah, because they asked us what we were trying to say in the writing. "Monster trucks are big trucks, or what?" I said, "Yeah, but that's not the point I was trying to make. I wanted to tell about . . . It's how you feel when you go to a monster truck show and see those trucks smashing cars and stuff . . . that's the important part."

Hollingsworth: Read me your opening paragraph.

Alex: "There is a monster truck named Bigfoot. It splashes through mud piles and roars down the dirty tracks. It drops all over junk cars, smashing them to smither lens [sic] before the crowd goes wild, it's the star of many performances on planet Earth."

For Alex and Christian, the ability to move between communication systems (photography, oral language, and writing) helped construct and interpret meaning. The composing process was enhanced through transmediation, when "learners retranslate their understanding of an idea, concept, or text through another medium" (Albers, 2006, p. 90). In the students' transmediation between sign symbols, the photographs served as process and product. The images were not substitutes for the written texts; they "enlarged and expanded meaning" (Seigel, 2006, p. 67). Integrating visual knowledge helped Alex and Christian problem solve and "think what [they] wanted to tell about in the story."

The writing changed from a description of the monster trucks to "how you feel when you go to a monster truck show and see those trucks smashing cars and stuff . . . that's the important part." The semiotic process energized their writing. The young writers focused on their narrowed subject (how you feel at a show) and demonstrated verbal acuity when composing "it's the star of many performances on planet Earth."

PHOTOGRAPHY IN EDUCATION

Since the 1980s, qualitative research has gained respect in educational circles, albeit not without criticism. We are aware that the form of data representation affects what is communicated. Eisner reminds us that "there is an intimate relationship between our conception of what the products of research are to look like and the way we go about doing research" (1997, p. 5). Even so, researchers in education have not been quick to accept visual methodologies as tools for inquiry. In fact, use of still photography in educational settings has been limited (Allen et al., 2002; Bintz, 1997; Cappello, 2005, 2006; Dempsey & Tucker, 1994; English, 1988; Orellana, 1999; Orellana & Hernandez, 1999; Preskill, 1995). We believe photography has the potential to "enhance what is possible by amplifying what teachers are able to do . . . [and] by

extending what students are able to produce as a result of their investigations." Photography has the potential to help "change the ways in which students learn" (Schiller & Tillet, 2004, p. 401).

There are few notable models of photography in education. Bintz's (1997) teacher research of the nature of curriculum at an alternate school included conversation and photographs as guiding data. He invited students to photograph what they thought was "most significant" (p. 35) about their school. Bintz used photography as a way for his students to "participate vicariously" in the research process (p. 34). Students were typically enthusiastic about participating and created images that confirmed the school's overriding goal of providing a safe and supported learning environment. Orellana and Hernandez (1999) offered cameras to first-graders during neighborhood literacy walks that focused on environmental print. Students used the cameras to read their world and composed images that captured places of significance to them. Later, these photographs were used in the classroom to generate new literacy events through writing and dictation. Building on the work of Prosser (1998), Hollingsworth used visual images to document the quality of changes in an urban school Professional Development School (PDS) focused on literacy development. When quantitative reading scores placed the school at the bottom of the district's assessments, Hollingsworth and colleagues introduced data that visually documented the confidence, spirit, and resilience of the teachers and students. Those data earned the school a grant to design and implement a new literacy program that eventually raised test scores (see Gallego, Hollingsworth, & Whitenack, 2001). Since the field of education lacks a rich photographic tradition, one purpose of this paper is to build the theoretical foundation for other educational researchers and to provide an example in literacy where we feel visual research is especially well suited. Specifically, we will explore the role photography plays in mediating and representing meaning in classroom literacy experiences.

THEORETICAL FRAMEWORK

The Nature of Photography

Sontag (1977) reminds us that when we photograph, we "confer importance" (p. 28). Regardless of the reason we choose to create an image, it has relevance or importance, and except in the case of art, is used for another purpose. However, importance as portrayed through the lens of the camera is not an objective idea. For many, photography still carries positivist notions that it depicts an objective reality. Collier and Collier (1986) praise the camera as an "instrumental extension of our senses, one that can record on a low scale of abstraction" (p. 7).

If we begin by thinking there is one objective reality to represent, then exercises in photography are not helpful for inquiry in education. However, Eisner pointed out that alternative forms of data representation might provide "productive ambiguity . . . more evocative than denotative . . . [I]n its evocation, it generates insight and invites attention to complexity" (1997, p. 8). Photography offers students an alternative way to respond to text, moving beyond positivist notions of photography depicting a literal truth.

Indeed, photography is best used where there is an understanding that reality is perceived or constructed (English, 1988), and that photographs reflect, in some ways, the person behind the camera lens. Like researcher-writers, researcher-photographers make decisions, based on experience and theoretical perspectives, that influence the outcome of their reports. The image cannot be separated from its creator. English, like Lincoln and Guba (1985), recognizes that "generalizations cannot be freed from the human context from which they sprang" (English, 1988, p. 9). Furthermore, English acknowledges this connectedness as an asset of the medium.

Walker (1993) offers another advantage of visual information. He described the medium as a "silent voice" for the researcher: another language we can employ in constructing understandings and communicating them to others. Photography is offered as a researcher's dialect for discussing complexities that cannot be sufficiently captured in oral or written language. By acknowledging a "vision" or a "voice," Walker includes the photographer in the photograph. The photographer remains in the tones of a black-and-white image, in the deliberate framing, in the choice of the exact moment to release the shutter. Sometimes the image of its creator may lie latent, but it is there nonetheless.

Becker, who has been writing about photography for over 20 years, emphasizes that our understandings of photographs are situated. "Photographs get meanings, like all cultural objects, from their context" (Becker, 1995, p. 8). Photographs have no meaning in and of themselves. What helps us understand them more than content alone is context (Becker, 1995). Another way of looking at context is to examine the situations where we study. Elementary classrooms, for example, are layered with activity in geography and discourse, but their nature makes them difficult to observe. Looking at multiple activities with multiple participants over time is very difficult for the classroom ethnographer, yet that is precisely what we must do to capture some essence of the classroom culture under study. "The unique agility and flexibility of the still camera in revealing a rich fabric and texture of complexity in one brief moment, which can then be examined again and again, exceeds the ability to commit the moment to paper during or after studying a social setting" (English, 1988, p. 14). This additional data source allows us to take our inquiry further. Secondulfo (1997) tells us, "This ability to 'freeze' pieces of reality in forms to which other, subsequent, methods of research can easily be applied is an advantage of photography which cannot be renounced" (p. 34). He also discusses ways to use photographs with participants as a way to elicit data. One method he illustrates, which will be fully developed later in the paper, is the photo-interview—an interview process that uses images to guide conversations and elicit data. We believe one of photography's greatest strengths is this ability to be a source of data as well as a tool for eliciting data when employed as a stimulus.

Transmediation: Moving Between Sign Symbols

Transmediation, the process of interpreting meaning from one sign system to another, is central to understanding the possibilities of photography in classrooms. This shifting or spiraling between communication systems "increases students' opportunities to engage in generative and reflective thinking because learners must invent a connection between the two sign systems" (Seigel, 1995). Students mediate between the signs to make sense and represent meaning. When students are given opportunities to represent meaning semiotically, their literacy skills, including thinking, are enhanced (Albers, 2001). However, this is not a simple process. It is not translation; it is transformation. We wanted to know if photography is an effective communication system for transmediation within a semiotic classroom curriculum.

The classrooms where we studied provided a range of sign systems, including written and visual "texts" (Alvermann & Hagood, 2000) for students to use in meaning making. This was important to us because, like Short and Kauffman (2000), we believe "students need to have many ways of thinking and sharing available to them in order to engage more fully in pursuing questions within the classroom that are significant in their own lives" (p. 43). The sign systems (writing, oral language, and photography) and the way students moved between them were interesting because they are distinct tools for communication with different potentials for meaning (Eisner, 1994).

THE RESEARCH STORY

Photography seemed a natural approach to use in the classrooms because of our backgrounds. Cappello has a Bachelor of Fine Arts in photography and worked in the field as a camera assistant, photo-librarian, and photographic fine art collection consultant. Hollingsworth's interest in photography is more experiential: her father was a photographer and her first job as a teenager was in a photo lab that processed black-and-white film. Later she acquired her own lab and used photographs to illustrate her academic texts (see Hollingsworth 1978 and 1994). Our photographic knowledge helped us be successful with the medium because the more we know about any communication, the easier it is to use it for mediating and representing meaning. "When constructing multimodal texts, meaning makers intentionally choose media with which they are familiar, and/or the media that will enable them to say what they want to say" (Albers, 2006, p. 78). However, extensive knowledge of photography is not necessary in order to use it for literacy instruction. Indeed, even with our grounding in photographic arts, we noticed our own perceptions evolve as we utilized these new approaches.

Our studies were situated in similar California classrooms. Cappello studied a combined second- and third-grade classroom at the Bridge School, a unique public school located in urban southern California. The ethnically and economically diverse student body was divided into multi-age classes guided by two teachers. Randolph Elementary School, where Hollingsworth studied, was very similar to the Bridge School, except that it was comprised of stand-alone grades and single teachers. Located in an economically disadvantaged part of a northern California city, the students were African American, Pacific Islander, White, and Latino. Seventy percent of them had first languages other than English.

Participant-Made Images

In Worth and Adair's (1977) now classic anthropological film footage, researchers trained seven Navajo men and women on the workings of a 16 mm camera and sent them off to photograph life on their reservation. These were the first images created from the insider's perspective. They "produce[d] images of their own conception of their world and their place in it" (Collier & Collier, 1986). Those of us concerned with representing participants' ideas through their own voice find the idea of participant-generated images very exciting. By allowing the participants the tools they need for expression, researchers are offering them another language to convey their ideas (Walker, 1993). This approach can be just as powerful with still cameras, in that they also allow the researchers an opportunity to see the insiders' view and (in our story) learn how young writers see their literacy practice and their world at school.

Building on Walker's (1993) ideas and Bintz's (1997) seminal study, Cappello offered students disposable cameras as a tool to discover what the students see in their classroom literacy practices. The cameras provided an alternate means for students to express important ideas about the writing process, free from the constraints of typical school participation structures. In addition, Cappello noticed that when composing written text, some students struggled for expression through limited language development, searching for words to suitably match their ideas. The photographs spoke for these students.

Cappello asked students to photograph "important" writing while she was away from the classroom at a professional conference. She assumed the students would create images of important writing processes such as conferences, research, and Author's Chair. These are elements of classroom writing *she* considered important and portrayed as important to the students. Instead, the students created image after image of their own written products, reminding us of Sontag's notion that simply by photographing, we make something important. The students also photographed images of the work hanging in the classroom, thus capturing the artifacts the teachers deemed important enough to display proudly.

These unexpected results challenged Cappello's perceptions about classroom writing and reminded her how students' perceptions were at the center of this research. The students' photographs also taught her that it is not enough to provide classroom literacy experiences where students construct meaning across sign systems. Students must be taught about the new modes of communication. Indeed, "the more learners understand the tools, techniques, and language of a sign system, the better they are able to integrate

it with the texts that they produce" (Cowen & Albers, 2006, p. 125). The student-generated photographs, along with researcher-generated images, were later used to further clarify perceptions in a series of photo-interviews.

Hollingsworth had a different purpose for offering cameras to her students. She asked students to take photographs to visually represent their perceptions of the meaning behind their writing: ideas they wanted to share with others using images instead of words. At the time Hollingsworth overviewed the setting,[1] it became clear that the students had already chosen topics and were engaged in the writing process. Final published papers were anticipated after 2 or 3 weeks of writing and revising. Hollingsworth thought this was an ideal time to give students cameras; she hoped the pictures students took would help them turn their intended meaning into written meaning.

The excited students exercised patience as Hollingsworth took the "Author's Chair" to explain the procedure. With their teacher's guidance, they role-played the kind of things they might photograph—"since my real little sister isn't here, you play her part like this . . . [demonstrates] and I'll take your picture." When students were stumped about what to shoot, suggestions were plentiful. For instance, one student commented, "I don't think I can photograph my story, because it's about a very rare car, the Lamborghini. . . . there are few left." Other students suggested: "You could take a picture of a Mustang and show how it's different." "You could take a picture of someone pretending to drive a Lamborghini . . . what they'd be wearing, and how they would look." Hollingsworth interjected at that point, "What is it you want the readers of your paper to know?" The student responded: "How sporty and fast it [the Lamborghini] was. How only rich people could have it." Hollingsworth asked, "How could you do that?" By the end of their conversation, the students had their questions about the task answered and were able to repeat the directions for operating the cameras and photographing their ideas.

This conversation began the transmediation process. Students used oral language to mediate meaning and clarify ideas they wanted to represent in their texts. The discussions prepared students for work with another communication system (photography) and facilitated problem solving in more complex ways. "Semiotic texts are always generative; that is, they have the potential to extend the initial meaning of the sign-maker (Kress, 1996).

Students worked in pairs (determined by similar topics) to photograph perceived "meanings" of their work inside and outside of the classroom. Hollingsworth also photographed students as they worked, noting how their original topics changed shape because of their visual explorations. By compiling the photos with their developing drafts over time, she was able to determine how the photographs changed their perceptions of the writing task. One example came from a pair of boys whose topic was "Squash Ball." The initial draft before the photography sessions included just the rules. After reenacting the game to photograph it, the writing became more spirited. "When it is time for recess somebody grabs the ball and speed out the door because he or she is so excited for squash ball. I jammed my finger once, but I still like squash ball." Author's Chair followed, and the students pressed the authors to talk about their perceptions of the meaning in their stories, as well as how to expand on the work. This spiraling between written, visual, and oral sign systems continued over the next two weeks as students made additional revisions to their work and circled back through Author's Chair for more feedback. The transmediation process informed and amplified students' texts. Like Cappello, Hollingsworth used the student-made and researcher-made photographs for photo-interviews conducted to clarify and expand on research understandings.

The Photo-Interview

The photo-interview is one of the most widespread uses of photography for qualitative

inquiry (Bunster, 1977; Cappello, 2005; Collier & Collier, 1986; Dempsey & Tucker, 1994; Preskill, 1995; Secondulfo, 1997; Wagne, 1979), yet it has not been well developed in the field of education. Photographs prompt participants to attend to ideas they might not have talked about (Bunster, 1977; Dempsey & Tucker, 1994; Orellana, 1999; Orellana & Hernandez, 1999; Secondulfo, 1997), focus the interview (Collier & Collier, 1986; Wagner, 1979), serve as a memory check (Bunster, 1977; Collier & Collier, 1986; Wagner, 1979), and a member check for researchers drawing conclusions from data (Bunster, 1977).

The idea of photo-elicitation is especially useful when interviewing students who have preset ideas about the dynamics of interacting with adults (Cappello, 2005; Dempsey & Tucker, 1994; Preskill, 1995). Interviews are complicated by the school setting where students perceive the researcher in a teacher-like fashion and the interview as part of "doing school." In this context, it is not uncommon for researchers to report difficulty in interviewing for significant information. Students are quick to feed researchers responses they think are the "best answers" at school or the answer they believe their teacher would most like to hear from them.

Cappello used photographs to structure her conversations about literacy. Indeed, the images led the discussions and engaged the students in the interview process while she used an open-ended protocol. The photographs helped put the students at ease. Cappello used the participants' pictures (both depicting the students and created by the students) to initiate the interviews and establish immediate rapport, making it possible for the students to challenge traditional school discourses. For example, when Cappello asked one student if he thought any of the pictures were important, instead of repeating the expected school discourse ("Yes, the ones that [the teacher thought] were important"), he responded, "No, do you?"

The photographs also acted as tools to understand student learning. For example, when Cappello asked another student why he picked one specific image of a writing sample as important over another, he responded, "Here's one of my first stories; you can see about a million mistakes and eighteen staples. . . . this [photo of the final draft] shows how much I learned since the beginning of the year." During the 20–30-minute interviews, Cappello asked students to select, sort, and rank the photographs. This process enabled students to engage in preliminary analysis with the researcher, providing a means for getting to a deeper view of the participant's perspectives.

Once the students had completed their written texts, Hollingsworth scheduled photo-interviews with eight students representing the demographics and writing abilities of the class. Students were able to express their perceptions and ideas more clearly than they had before Hollingsworth introduced the experiment.

Hollingsworth: I thought you were writing about great monuments in the U.S. Why did you take this picture of your teacher writing on the board?

Student: Because we couldn't do this writing without her help.

Hollingsworth: So after you took the picture, you revised the story to include that.

Student: Yes.

****

Hollingsworth: Tell me about these pictures of your friend playing like she's a dog, then putting her head on your shoulder.

Student: Well, I was just going to write about how my dog looked and what he ate, but taking the pictures made me remember how my dog also makes me feel. So I asked the dog [her partner] to snuggle close with me while someone else took the picture.

****

Hollingsworth: Your story changed from writing about Lamborghinis to stories about your friends from Nicaragua and India and the cars they liked. Why?

Student: Well, we looked for cars to photograph around the school, and we just started talking and found out that cars were different in the places we came from. So we changed it to that.

****

Previous perceptions about pets, Lamborghinis, and the writing task were all challenged through the semiotic process. In the students' transmediation between sign symbols, the photographs were both process and product. Photographs and the photographic process provided the stimulus for writing, extended the meaning of the original texts (drafts), and encouraged complex thinking. "Knowledge about language was reconsidered in light of knowledge about image" (Cowen & Albers, 2006, p. 135). Participating as photographers in preparing their drafts led to deeper perspectives about their topics. In other words, giving students cameras and asking them to visually show what they really wanted to express in their writing enriched the results. "Learners used one sign symbol to mediate another," thus achieving generative and reflective power (Seigel, 2006, p. 70). Revisions of initial topics that took place *after* making decisions as a photographer helped students go much deeper to represent meaning. Their teacher was amazed.

****

Teacher: In this set, I can see where [student x] started with just a description/list of what national monuments were, to incorporating the process of how they came to know what the monuments meant . . . they apparently got that from my lessons!!! . . . and how they really felt about the monuments . . . In that team, one student posed as the statue of liberty, while the other photographed. The photographer kept directing the pose: "torch [upside down plastic cone] needs to go higher up . . . up like when you think about what that statue meant to all the new people coming to this country. . . . their feelings got higher and higher." "Fascinating! I can see how I was really promoting shallow or superficial writing before!! Never again!!"

DISCUSSION

In this study, photography served as a research tool for getting an insider's view of the classroom writing community in two ways: through participant-made images and photo-interviews. While there are many methods for tapping participants' understandings, cameras allowed the young students another language for conveying their ideas. In other words, photography was an effective communication system for transmediation in a semiotic literacy curriculum. Students' photographs and the act of photographing enabled them to problem solve in new ways and to create more complex texts. Literacy thinking and writing was enhanced when students engaged in experiences that encouraged them to translate meaning across sign systems. Photo-elicitation was especially useful for interviewing young students. The photographs helped students create narratives about their writing process and products, including ranking images systematically by their perceived importance. As the students reflected, they told stories about their own relationship to what was in the images and what was left out of them. Photographs cannot be separated from the photographers who create them.

The advantages of employing visual methodologies cannot be denied. "There is little doubt that photography can enhance students' (and teachers') responses to the demands of learning" (Ewald & Lightfoot, 2001, p. 119). Considering the impact of visuals in our students' worlds and the potential for teaching and learning, using photography (and other visuals) in classrooms is clearly important and beneficial. We encourage educators at all levels to exploit the utility of the photographic medium for expression across educational contexts.

Tips for Teachers

- Disposable cameras are good for beginners but are very expensive to process. A couple of inexpensive digital cameras can serve the same audience as 10–15 disposables.

- Use a cart similar to the one your overhead projector is on. Keep cameras charged so they can be used for teachable moments in the classroom.

- Digital photography teaches critical composition and allows more freedom to "shoot away."

- Allow students to make editing decisions. Just like writing, teach students *how* to revise, and then trust them to make decisions that will demonstrate their voice or vision.

- Establish common vocabulary. As Cowen and Albers (2006) say, "The more learners understand the tools, techniques, and language of a sign system, the better they are able to integrate it with the texts that they produce" (p. 15). To understand photography tools and techniques, start with these:

Vantage Point: bird's-eye view, long shot, close-up, etc.
Framing: foreground, background, etc.
Composition and Elements of Design: line, shape, pattern, color, contrast, scale

—Marva Cappello and Sandra Hollingsworth

Marva Cappello is associate professor of teacher education at San Diego State University, San Diego, CA.

Sandra Hollingsworth is professor of education at San José State University, San Jose, CA.

Article 36

MULTIMODALITY AND LITERACY IN SCHOOL CLASSROOMS

CAREY JEWITT

The characteristics of contemporary societies are increasingly theorized as global, fluid, and networked. These conditions underpin the emerging knowledge economy as it is shaped by the societal and technological forces of late capitalism. Such developments have significantly affected the communicational landscape of the 21st century. A key aspect of this is the reconfiguration of the representational and communicational resources of image, action, sound, and so on in new multimodal ensembles. The terrain of communication is changing in profound ways and extends to schools and ubiquitous elements of everyday life, though to different degrees and at uneven rates. Against this backdrop, this critical review explores school multimodality and literacy and asks what these changes mean for literacy in this new landscape of the 21st century.

The two key arguments in this article are that it is not possible to think about literacy solely as a linguistic accomplishment and that the time for the habitual conjunction of language, print literacy, and learning is over. This review, organized in three parts, does not provide an exhaustive overview of multimodal literacies in and beyond classrooms. Instead, it sets out to highlight key definitions in an expanded approach to new literacies, then to link these to emergent studies of schooling and classroom practice. The first part outlines the new conditions for literacy and the ways in which this is conceptualized in the current research literature. In particular, it introduces three perspectives: New Literacies Studies, multiliteracies, and multimodality. Contemporary conceptualizations of literacy in the school classroom are explored in the second part of the chapter. This discussion is organized around themes that are central to multimodality and multiliteracies. These include multimodal perspectives on pedagogy, design, decisions about connecting with the literacy worlds of students, and the ways in which representations shape curriculum knowledge and learning. Each theme is discussed in turn, draw-

SOURCE: Jewitt, C. (2008). Multimodality and Literacy in School Classrooms. *Review of Research in Education, 32,* 241–267. Reprinted by permission of Sage Publications, Inc.

ing on a range of examples of multimodal research. The third and final part of the article discusses future directions for multiple literacies, curriculum policy, and schooling.

This article is available as a full-text PDF at http://www.sagepub.com/cappello/.

REFERENCES AND ENDNOTES

Article 1 Endnotes

1. Some of the arguments in this article first appeared in a chapter titled "Reclaiming the Center" (Pearson, 1996); others first appeared in Pearson's *Reading in the 20th Century* (2000).

2. Perhaps the most compelling sign of the backgrounding of skills was their systematic removal from the pupil books. In the mid- and even late 1980s, basal companies featured skills lessons in the pupil books on the grounds that even teachers who chose not to use the workbooks would have to deal with skills that were right there in the student materials. By the early 1990s, as I noted earlier, they were out of the student books.

3. Perhaps the best documentation for the resistance to, or at least a more critical acceptance of, whole-language practices comes from studies of exemplary teachers who, it appears, never bought into whole language lock, stock, and barrel but instead chose judiciously those practices that helped them to develop rich, flexible, and balanced instructional portfolios (Wharton-MacDonald, Pressley, & Hampton, 1998).

4. An analysis by Hiebert, Martin, and Menon (in press) of the basals adopted in the early 1990s in California suggests that the vocabulary load of many of these basals was so great that most first graders could gain access to them only if they were read to them by a teacher.

5. For a compelling account of this "no-text" phenomenon, see Schoenbach, Greenleaf, Cziko, and Hurwitz (2000). In this account, the staff developers and teachers of a middle school academic literacy course document the role of (or lack of a role for) text in middle school as well as attempts to turn the tide to help students tackle the texts that so often serve as their nemeses.

6. In 1989, a special interest group with the apocryphal label of Balanced Reading Instruction was organized at the International Reading Association. The group was started to counteract what they considered the unchecked acceptance of whole language as the approach to use with any and all students and to send the alternate message that there is no necessary conflict between authentic activity (usually considered the province of whole language) and explicit instruction of skills and strategies (usually considered the province of curriculum-centered approaches). For elaborate accounts of balanced literacy instruction, see McIntyre and Pressley (1996); Gambrell, Morrow, Newman, and Pressley (1999); and Pearson (1996).

7. As early as 1965, Kenneth Goodman had popularized the use of miscues to gain insights into cognitive processes. The elaborate version of miscue analysis first appeared in Y. Goodman and Burke (1970).

8. See Guthrie and Hall (1984) and Bloome and Greene (1984) for in-progress indices of the rising momentum of qualitative research in the early 1980s.

9. As a way of documenting this change, examine the *Handbook of Reading Research*, Volume I (Pearson, Barr, Kamil, & Mosenthal, 1984) and Volume II (Barr, Kamil, Mosenthal, & Pearson, 1991). Volume I contains only two chapters that could be construed as relying on some sort of interpretive inquiry. Volume II has at least eight such chapters. For an account of these historical patterns in nonquantitative inquiry, see Siegel and Fernandez (2000).

10. Starting in the mid-1980s and continuing until today, the pages of *Educational Researcher* began to publish accounts of the qualitative-quantitative divide. It is the best source to consult in understanding the terms of the debate.

11. At least until it was brought into question by professional critics (see B. Taylor, Anderson, Au, & Raphael, 2000), the most highly touted pedagogical experiment supported by the National Institute for Child Health and Human Development (NICHD) was published by Foorman, Francis, Fletcher, Schatschneider, and Mehta (1998). The NICHD work in general and the Foorman et al. piece in particular have been cited as exemplary in method and as supportive of a much more direct code emphasis, even in the popular press (e.g., Bowler, 1998; Mills, 1998; Strauss, 1997).

12. Much, for example, is made in this new work of the inappropriateness of encouraging young readers to use context clues as a way of figuring out the pronunciations of unknown words. The data cited are eye-movement studies showing that adult readers appear to process each and every letter in the visual display on the page and most likely, to then recode those visual symbols into a speech code prior to understanding.

13. Allington and Woodside-Jiron (1998) documented the manner in which an unpublished manuscript, *30 Years of Research: What We Now Know About How Children Learn to Read* by Bonnie Grossen (1997), which is an alleged summary of the research sponsored by NICHD, was used in several states as the basis for reading policy initiatives.

14. One entire issue of *American Educator* (1995) was devoted to the phonics revival; authors of various pieces would generally be regarded as leaders in moving phonics back onto center stage—Marilyn Adams, Isabel Beck, Connie Juel, and Louisa Moats. A second issue of *American Educator* (1998) was also devoted entirely to reading. The piece by Adams and Bruck (1995) is the clearest exposition of the modern phonics-first position I can find.

15. One of the reasons for the continuation of the debate is that few people seek common ground. Researchers who come from the whole-language tradition, were they to read Adams and Juel openly, might find much to agree with—privileging of big books, writing, invented spelling, and the like. They would not even disagree with them about the critical role that phonemic awareness or knowledge of the cipher plays in early reading success. They would, however, disagree adamantly about the most appropriate instructional route to achieving early success; phonics knowledge and phonemic awareness are better viewed, they would argue, as the consequence of, rather than the cause of, success in authentic reading experiences.

16. These and other reading policy matters have been well documented in a series of pieces in *Education Week* by Kathleen Kennedy Manzo (1997, 1998a, 1998b).

17. Allington and Woodside-Jiron (1998) conducted a thorough analysis of the genesis of this "research-based" policy and concluded that it all goes back to an incidental finding from a study by Juel and Roper-Schneider (1985). They could find no direct experimental tests of the efficacy of decodable text. Interestingly, the National Reading Panel report (2000) is moot on the issue of decodable text.

18. See Pearson, DeStefano, and García (1998) for an account of the decrease in reliance on portfolio and performance assessment.

19. An interesting aside in all of the political rhetoric has been the question of who is de-skilling teachers. As early as the 1970s, whole-language advocates were arguing that canned programs and basal-reader manuals were de-skilling teachers by providing them with preprogrammed routines for teaching. Recently, whole language has been accused of the de-skilling by denying teachers access to technical knowledge needed to teach reading effectively (see McPike, 1995).

20. I am grateful to Richard Allington and Alfie Cohn for bringing this vivid example to my attention.

21. The *balance* label comes with excess baggage. I use it only because it has gained currency in the field. Balance works for me as long as the metaphor of ecological balance, as in the balance of nature, is emphasized and the metaphor of the fulcrum balance beam, as in the scales of justice, is suppressed. The fulcrum, which achieves balance by equalizing the mass on each side of the scale, suggests a standoff between skills and whole language—one for skills, one for whole language. By contrast, ecological balance suggests a symbiotic relationship among elements within a coordinated system. It is precisely this symbiotic potential of authentic activity and explicit instruction that I want to promote by using the term *balance*.

Article 1 References

Adams, M. J. (1990). *Beginning to read: Thinking and learning about print.* Cambridge, MA: MIT Press.

Adams, M. J., & Bruck, M. (1995). Resolving the great debate. *American Educator, 19*(7), 10–20.

Allington, R. (2002). *Big brother and the national reading curriculum: How ideology trumped evidence.* Portsmouth, NH: Heinemann.

Allington, R., & Woodside-Jiron, H. (1998). Decodable texts in beginning reading: Are mandates based on research? *ERS Spectrum, 16*(2), 3–11.

Allington, R., & Woodside-Jiron, H. (1999). The politics of literacy research: How "research" shaped educational policy. *Educational Researcher, 28*(8), 4–13.

American Educator. (1995). *19*(2).

American Educator. (1998). *22*(1, 2).

Anderson, R. C., Hiebert, E. H., Scott, J., & Wilkinson, I. (1984). *Becoming a nation of readers.* Champaign, IL: Center for the Study of Reading.

Anderson, R. C., & Pearson, P. D. (1984). A schema-theoretic view of basic processes in reading comprehension. In P. D. Pearson, R. Barr, M. Kamil, & P. Mosenthal (Eds.), *Handbook of reading research* (Vol. 1, pp. 255–291). New York: Longman.

Anderson, R. C., Wilson, P. T., & Fielding, L. G. (1988). Growth in reading and how children spend their time outside of school (1988). *Reading Research Quarterly, 23*(3), 285–303.

Barr, R., Kamil, M., Mosenthal, P., & Pearson, P. D. (Eds.). (1991). *Handbook of reading research* (Vol. 2). New York: Longman.

Berliner, D. (2002). Educational research: The hardest science of all. *Educational Researcher, 31*(8), 18–20.

Bloome, D., & Green, J. (1984). Directions in the sociolinguistic study of reading. In P. D. Pearson, R. Barr, M. Kamil, & P. Mosenthal (Eds.), *Handbook of reading research* (Vol. 1, pp. 394–421). New York: Longman.

Bowler, M. (1998, August 9). Experts' bias complicates lesson debate. *Baltimore Sun,* p. 2B.

Brown, D. (2002, September 12). Prostate cancer therapies about equal: Having surgery may extend patient's life. *Washington Post,* p. A2.

Brown, R. (1970). *Psycholinguistics.* New York: Macmillan.

California Assembly Bill 1086. (1997). *Reading instruction.* Available from http://www.leginfo.ca.gov/pub/97-98/bill/asm/ab_1051-1100/ab_1086_bill_19970818_ chaptered.html

Campbell, D. T. (1984). Can we be scientific in applied social science? In R. E. Conner, D. G. Altman, & C. Jackson (Eds.), *Evaluation studies: Review annual* (Volume 9, pp. 85–97). Beverly Hills, CA: Sage.

Campbell, D. T., & Stanley, J. C. (1963). *Experimental and quasi-experimental designs for research.* Boston: Houghton Mifflin.

Chall, J. (1967). *Learning to read: The great debate.* New York: McGraw-Hill.

Clarke, L. K. (1988). Invented versus traditional spelling in first graders' writings: Effects on learning to spell and read. *Research in the Teaching of English, 22*(3), 281–309.

Elley, W. (1998). *Raising literacy levels in third world countries: A method that works.* Culver City, CA: Language Education Associates.

Firestone, W. (1987). Meaning in method: The rhetoric of quantitative and qualitative research. *Educational Researcher, 16*(7), 16–21.

Fletcher, J., & Lyon, G. R. (1998). Reading: A research based approach. In W. Evers (Ed.), *What's gone wrong in America's classrooms* (pp. 49–90). Stanford, CA: Hoover Institution Press.

Foorman, B. R., Francis, D., Fletcher, J. M., Schatschneider, C., & Mehta, P. (1998). The role of instruction in learning to read: Preventing reading failure in at-risk children. *Journal of Educational Psychology, 90,* 37–55.

Gambrell, L. B., Morrow, L. M., Newman, S. B., & Pressley, M. (Eds.). (1999). *Best practices in literacy instruction.* New York: Guilford.

Garan, E. M. (2001). Beyond the smoke and mirrors: A critique of the National Reading Panel report on phonics. *Phi Delta Kappan, 82*(7), 500–506.

Garan, E. M. (2002). *Resisting reading mandates: How to triumph with the truth.* Portsmouth, NH: Heinemann.

Gee, J. P. (1989). The legacies of literacy: From Plato to Freire through Harvey Graff. *Journal of Education, 171*(1), 147–165.

Goals 2000: Education America Act of 1994, H.R. 1804. Available from http://www.ed.gov/legislation/GOALS2000/TheAct/index.html

Good, T., & Braden, J. (2000). *Reform in American education: A focus on vouchers and charters.* Mahweh, NJ: Lawrence Erlbaum.

Goodman, K. S. (1965). A linguistic study of cues and miscues in reading. *Elementary English, 42,* 639–643.

Goodman, K. S. (1969). Analysis of oral reading miscues: Applied psycholinguistics. *Reading Research Quarterly, 5,* 1.

Goodman, Y. (1989). Roots of the whole-language movement. *Elementary School Journal, 90,* 113–127.

Goodman, Y. M., & Burke, C. L. (1970). *Reading miscue inventory manual procedure for diagnosis and evaluation.* New York: Macmillan.

Gough, P. B., & Hillinger, M. L. (1980). Learning to read: An unnatural act. *Bulletin of the Orton Society, 30,* 179–190.

Grossen, B. (1997). *30 years of research: What we now know about how children learn to read.* Santa Cruz, CA: The Center for the Future of Teaching and Learning. Retrieved from http//www.cftl.org/30years/30years

Guthrie, L. F., & Hall, W. S. (1984). Ethnographic approaches to reading research. In P. D. Pearson, R. Barr, M. Kamil, & P. Mosenthal (Eds.), *Handbook of reading research* (Vol. 1, pp. 91–110). New York: Longman.

Hartshorne, C., Weiss, P., & Burks, A. (1931–1958). *Collected papers of Charles Sanders Peirce* (Volumes 1–8). Cambridge, MA: Harvard University Press.

Heath, S. B. (1983). *Ways with words: Language, life and work in communities and classrooms.* Cambridge, UK: Cambridge University Press.

Hiebert, E. H., Martin, L. A., & Menon, S. (in press). Are there alternatives in reading textbooks? An examination of three beginning reading programs. *Reading Writing Quarterly.*

Hiebert, E. H., & Taylor, B. M. (Eds.). (1994). *Getting reading right from the start: Effective early literacy intervention.* Boston: Allyn & Bacon.

Hoffman, J. V., McCarthey, S. J., Abbott, J., Christian, C., Corman, L., Dressman, M., et al. (1995). So what's new in the "new" basals. *Journal of Reading Behavior, 26,* 47–73.

Holdaway, D. (1984). *The foundations of literacy.* Portsmouth, NH: Heinemann.

Howe, K. R., & Eisenhart, M. (1990). Standards for qualitative (and quantitative) research: A prologomenon. *Educational Researcher, 9*(4), 2–9.

Juel, C. (1988). Learning to read and write: A longitudinal study of 54 children from first through fourth grades. *Journal of Educational Psychology, 80*(4), 437–447.

Juel, C. (1991). Beginning reading. In R. Barr, M. Kamil, P. Mosenthal, & P. D. Pearson (Eds.), *Handbook of reading research* (Vol. 2, pp. 759–788). New York: Longman.

Juel, C., & Roper-Schneider, D. (1985). The influence of basal readers on first grade reading. *Reading Research Quarterly, 20,* 134–152.

Kolata, G. (2002, September 12). Prostate cancer surgery found to cut death risk. *New York Times,* p. A16.

Luke, A. (1995). The social practice of reading. In J. Murray (Ed.), *Celebrating differences: Confronting literacies* (pp. 167–187). Sydney: Australian Reading Association.

Lyon, G. R. (1995). Research initiatives in learning disabilities: Contributions from scientists supported by the National Institute of Child Health and Human Development. *Journal of Child Neurology, 10,* 120–126.

Lyon, G. R. (1999, October 26). *Statement of Dr. G. Reid Lyon.* Presented to the House Science Committee, Subcommittee on Basic Research, U.S. House of Representatives, Washington, DC. Retrieved May 31, 2000, from http://web .lexis-nexis.com/congcomp

Lyon, G. R. (2003, May). *Keynote address.* Presented to the Urban Dean's Network, International Reading Association, New Brunswick, NJ.

Lyon, G. R., & Chhaba, V. (1996). The current state of science and the future of specific reading disability. *Mental Retardation and Developmental Disabilities Research Reviews, 2,* 2–9.

Manzo, K. K. (1997). Study stresses role of early phonics instruction. *Education Week, 16*(24), 1, 24–25.

Manzo, K. K. (1998a). New national panel faulted before it's formed. *Education Week, 17*(23), 7.

Manzo, K. K. (1998b). NRC panel urges end to reading wars. *Education Week, 17*(28), 1, 18.

McIntyre, E., & Pressley, M. (Eds.). (1996). *Balanced instruction: Strategies and skills in whole language.* Boston: Christopher-Gordon.

McPike, E. (1995). Learning to read: The school's first mission. *American Educator, 19,* 4.

Mills, K. (1998, October 11). Duane Alexander: Catching kids who can't read, a guardian extends his reach. *Los Angeles Times,* p. M3.

Mosteller, F., & Baruch, R. (Eds.). (2002). *Evidence matters: Randomized trials in education research.* Washington, DC: Brookings Institution.

National Reading Panel. (2000). *Teaching children to read: An evidence-based assessment of the scientific research literature on reading and its implications for reading instruction* (National Institute of Health Pub. No. 00-4769). Washington, DC: National Institute of Child Health and Human Development.

No Child Left Behind Act of 2001, Pub. L. No. 107-110 (2002). Available from http://www.ed.gov/policy/elsec/leg/ esea02/index.html

Pearson, P. D. (1989). Reading the whole-language movement. *Elementary School Journal, 90*(2), 231–241.

Pearson, P. D. (1992). RT remembrance: The second 20 years. *The Reading Teacher, 45,* 378–385.

Pearson, P. D. (1996). Reclaiming the center. In M. Graves, P. van den Broek, & B. M. Taylor (Eds.), *The first R: Every child's right to read* (pp. 259–274). New York: Teachers College Press.

Pearson, P. D. (1999). Essay book reviews: A historically based review of "Preventing Reading Difficulties in Young Children." *Reading Research Quarterly, 34*(2), 231–246.

Pearson, P. D. (2000). Reading in the 20th century. In T. Good (Ed.), *American education: Yesterday, today, and tomorrow* (Yearbook of the National Society for the Study of Education, pp. 152–208). Chicago: University of Chicago Press.

Pearson, P. D., Barr, R., Kamil, M., & Mosenthal, P. (Eds.). (1984). *Handbook of reading research* (Vol. 1). New York: Longman.

Pearson, P. D., DeStefano, L., & García, G. E. (1998). Ten dilemmas of performance assessment. In C. Harrison & T. Salinger (Eds.), *Assessing reading 1, theory and practice* (pp. 21–49). London: Routledge & Kegan Paul.

Pearson, P. D., & Stephens, D. (1993). Learning about literacy: A 30-year journey. In C. J. Gordon, G. D. Labercane, & W. R. McEachern (Eds.), *Elementary reading: Process & practice* (pp. 4–18). Boston: Ginn Press.

Pressley, M., Wharton-MacDonald, R., Allington, R., Block, C. C., Morrow, L., Tracey, D., et al. (2001). A study of effective first-grade literacy instruction. *Scientific Studies of Reading, 5,* 35–58.

Reading Excellence Act of 1998, Pub. L. No. 105-227. Available from http://www.ed.gov/offices/OESE/REA/index.html

Richardson, V., & Placier, P. (2002). Teacher change. In V. Richardson (Ed.), *Handbook of research on teaching* (4th ed., pp. 905–947). Washington, DC: American Educational Research Association.

Salkind, N. J. (2000). *Exploring research.* Upper Saddle Creek, NJ: McGraw-Hill.

Schoenbach, R., Greenleaf, C., Cziko, C., & Hurwitz, L. (2000). *Reading for understanding in the middle and high school.* San Francisco: Jossey-Bass.

Schoenfeld, A. H. (2004). The math wars. *Educational Policy, 18*(1).

Shavelson, R. J., & Towne, L. (Eds.). (2002). *Scientific research in education*. Washington, DC: National Academy Press.

Siegel, M., & Fernandez, S. L. (2000). Critical approaches. In M. Kamil, P. Mosenthal, P. D. Pearson, & R. Barr (Eds.), *Handbook of reading research* (Vol. 3, pp. 141–152). Mahwah, NJ: Erlbaum.

Smith, F. (1971). *Understanding reading: A psycholinguistic analysis of reading and learning to read*. New York: Holt, Rinehart & Winston.

Smith, F. (1983). Reading like a writer. *Language Arts, 60,* 558–567.

Snow, C. E. (2001). Preventing reading difficulties in young children: Precursors and fallout. In T. Loveless (Ed.), *The great curriculum debate* (pp. 484–504). Washington, DC: Brookings Institution.

Snow, C. E. (2002). *Reading for understanding: Toward an R&D program in reading: The report of the Rand Reading Study Group*. Washington, DC: RAND.

Snow, C., Burns, S., & Griffin, P. (Eds.). (1998). *Preventing reading difficulties in young children*. Washington, DC: National Academy Press.

Spiro, R., & Jehng, J. (1990). Cognitive flexibility and hypertext: Theory and technology for the linear and nonlinear multidimensional traversal of complex subject matter. In D. Nix & R. Spiro (Eds.), *Cognition, education, and multimedia: Exploring ideas in high technology* (pp. 163–205). Hillsdale, NJ: Lawrence Erlbaum.

Stauffer, R. G. (1980). *The language experience approach to the teaching of reading*. New York: Harper & Row.

Strauss, S. (1997, February 18). Phonics reading method best, study finds: Whole language approach significantly less effective, Houston research shows. *The Toronto Globe and Mail*, p. A1, A9.

Taylor, B., Anderson, R. C., Au, K. H., & Raphael, T. E. (2000). Discretion in the translation of research to policy: A case from beginning reading. *Educational Researcher, 29*(6), 16–26.

Taylor, B., Frye, B., & Maruyama, G. (1990). Time spent reading and reading growth. *American Educational Research Journal, 27,* 351–362.

Taylor, B. M., Pearson, P. D., Clark, K., & Walpole, S. (2000). Effective schools and accomplished teachers: Lessons about primary-grade reading instruction in low-income schools. *Elementary School Journal, 101*(2), 121–165.

Taylor, B. M., Pearson, P. D., Peterson, D. S., & Rodriguez, M. C. (2003). Reading growth in high-poverty classrooms: The influence of teacher practices that encourage cognitive engagement in literacy learning. *Elementary School Journal, 104*(1), 3–28.

Taylor, D. (1998). *Beginning to read and the spin doctors of science: The political campaign to change America's mind about how children learn to read*. Urbana, IL: National Council of Teachers of English.

Veatch, J. (1959). *Individualizing your reading program*. New York: G. P. Putnam.

Wharton-MacDonald, R., Pressley, M., & Hampton, J. M. (1998). Literacy instruction in nine first-grade classrooms: Teacher characteristics and student achievement. *Elementary School Journal, 99,* 101–128.

Whitehurst, G. R. (2001, December). *Evidence-based education* [PowerPoint presentation]. Retrieved from http://www.ed.gov/offices/IES/speeches/evidencebase.html

Wilson, S. M., & Berne, J. (1999). Teacher learning and the acquisition of professional knowledge: An examination of research on contemporary professional development. In A. Iran-Nejad & P. D. Pearson (Eds.), *Review of research in education* (pp. 173–209). Washington, DC: American Educational Research Association.

Winsor, P., & Pearson, P. D. (1992). *Children at-risk: Their phonemic awareness development in wholistic instruction* (Tech. Rep. No. 556). Urbana: University of Illinois, Center for the Study of Reading.

Article 2 References

Allington, R. L., Johnson, P. H. and Day, J. P. (2002) 'Exemplary Fourth-Grade Teachers', *Language Arts* 79(6): 462–6.

Anyon, J. (1996) 'Social Class and the Hidden Curriculum of Work', in E.R. Hollins (ed.) *Transforming Curriculum for a Culturally Diverse Society*, pp. 179–203. Mahwah, NJ: Erlbaum.

Baker, L., Dreher, M. J. and Guthrie, J. T. (2000) 'Why Teachers Should Promote Reading Engagement', in L. Baker, M. J. Dreher and J. T. Guthrie (eds) *Engaging Young Readers: Promoting Achievement and Motivation*, pp. 1–16. New York: Guilford.

Baldwin, J. (1988) 'A Talk to Teachers', in R. Simonson and S. Walker (eds) *Multicultural Literacy: Opening the American Mind*, pp. 3–12. St Paul, MN: Graywolf.

Bohn, C. M., Roehrig, A. D. and Pressley, M. (2004) 'The First Days of School in the Classrooms of Two More Effective and Four Less Effective Primary-Grades Teachers', *The Elementary School Journal* 104(4): 269–87.

Broughton, M. A. and Fairbanks, C. M. (2002) 'Stances and Dances: The Negotiation of Subjectivities in a Reading/Language Arts Classroom', *Language Arts* 79(4): 288–96.

348 Contemporary Readings in Literacy Education

Cazden, C. (1988) *Classroom Discourse: The Language of Teaching and Learning*. Portsmouth, NH: Heinemann.

Cotton, K. (2001) *Educational Time Factors*. School Improvement Research Series, Close-Up no. 8, Northwest Regional Educational Laboratory. Retrieved 19 September 2004 from http://www.nwrel.org/scpd/sirs/4/cu8.html.

Deyhle, D. (1996) 'Navajo Youth and Anglo Racism: Cultural Integrity and Resistance', in T. Beauboeuf-Lafontant and D. S. Augustine (eds) *Facing Racism in Education*, 2nd edn, pp. 23–67. Cambridge, MA: Harvard Educational Review.

Edelsky, C. (1991) *With Literacy and Justice for All: Rethinking the Social in Language and Education*. Bristol, PA: Falmer, Taylor and Francis.

Edelsky, C. (ed.) (1999) *Making Justice Our Project*. Urbana, IL: NCTE.

Finn, P. J. (1999) *Literacy with an Attitude*. Albany: SUNY Press.

Freppon, P. A. and McIntyre, E. (1999) 'A Comparison of Young Children Learning to Read in Different Instructional Settings', *The Journal of Educational Research* 92(4): 206–17.

Gambrell, L. B. and Almasi, J. F. (eds) (1996) *Lively Discussions: Fostering Engaged Reading*. Newark, DE: International Reading Association.

Gambrell, L. B., Mazzoni, S. A. and Almasi, J. F. (2000) 'Promoting Collaboration, Social Interaction, and Engagement with Text', in L. Baker, M. J. Dreher and J. T. Guthrie (eds) *Engaging Young Readers: Promoting Achievement and Motivation*, pp. 119–39. New York: Guilford.

Guthrie, J. T. and Anderson, E. (1999) 'Engagement in Reading: Processes of Motivated, Strategic, Knowledgeable, Social Readers', in J. T. Guthrie and D. E. Alvermann (eds) *Engaged Reading: Processes, Practices, and Policy Implications*, pp. 17–45. New York: Teachers College Press.

Guthrie, J. T., Schafer, W. and Huang, C. W. (2001) 'Benefits of Opportunity to Read and Balanced Instruction on the NAEP', *Journal of Educational Research* 94(3): 145–62.

Kohl, H. R. (1995) *'I Won't Learn from You': And Other Thoughts on Creative Maladjustment*. New York: New Press.

Kohn, A. (1993) 'Choice for Children: Why and How to Let Students Decide', *Phi Delta Kappan* 75(1): 8–20.

McCarthey, S. J., Hoffman, J. V. and Galda, L. (1999) 'Readers in Elementary Classrooms: Learning Goals and Instructional Principles That Can Inform Practice', in J.T. Guthrie and D.E. Alvermann (eds) *Engaged Reading: Processes, Practices, and Policy Implications*, pp. 46–80. New York: Teachers College Press.

McCombs, B. L. (1996) 'Alternative Perspectives for Motivation', in L. Baker, P. Afflerbach and D. Reinking (eds) *Developing Engaged Readers in School and Home*, pp. 67–87. Mahwah, NJ: Erlbaum.

McNeil, L. M. (1988) *Contradictions of Control: School Structure and School Knowledge*. New York: Routledge.

Meyer, R. J. (2002) *Phonics Exposed: Understanding and Resisting Systematic Direct Intense Phonics Instruction*. Mahwah, NJ: Erlbaum.

Miles, M. B. and Huberman, M. (1994) *Qualitative Data Analysis: An Expanded Source Book*. London: Sage.

Moll, L. C. (2001) 'The Diversity of Schooling: A Cultural-Historical Approach', in M. de la Luz Reyes and J.J. Halcón (eds) *The Best for Our Children: Critical Perspectives on Literacy for Latino Students*, pp. 13–28. New York: Teachers College Press.

Morrow, L. M. and Tracey, D. H. (1997) 'Strategies Used for Phonics Instruction in Early Childhood Classrooms', *The Reading Teacher* 50(8): 2–9.

Oldfather, P. (1993) 'What Students Say about Motivating Experiences in a Whole Language Classroom', *The Reading Teacher* 46: 672–81.

Paris, S. G. and Paris, A. H. (2001) 'Classroom Applications of Research on Self-Regulated Learning', *Educational Psychologist* 36(2): 89–101.

Peshkin, A. (1997) *Places of Memory: Whiteman's Schools and Native American Communities*. Mahwah, NJ: Erlbaum.

Powell, R. (1999) *Literacy as a Moral Imperative: Facing the Challenges of a Pluralistic Society*. Lanham, MD: Rowman and Littlefield.

Pressley, M., Wharton-McDonald, R., Allington, R., Block, C. C. and Morrow, L. (1998) *The Nature of Effective First-Grade Literacy Instruction*. CELA Research Report 11007. National Center on English Learning and Achievement. Albany: SUNY. http://cela. Albany.edu/1stgradelit/index.html.

Report of the National Reading Panel (2000) *Teaching Children to Read: Report of the Subgroups*. Washington, DC: National Institute of Child Health and Human Development.

Shannon, P. (ed.) (1992) *Becoming Political: Readings and Writings in the Politics of Literacy Education*. Portsmouth, NH: Heinemann.

Shannon, P. (1998) *Reading Poverty*. Portsmouth, NH: Heinemann.

Shor, I. and Freire, P. (1987) *A Pedagogy for Liberation: Dialogues on Transforming Education*. Granby, MA: Bergin and Garvey.

Spaulding, A. (2000) Micropolitical Behavior of Second Graders: A Qualitative Study of Student Resistance in the Classroom. *The Qualitative Report* 4(1/2). Retrieved 28 August 2005 from http://www.nova.edu/ssss/QR/QR4-1/spaulding.html.

Taylor, B. M., Pearson, P. D., Peterson, D. S. and Rodriquez, M. C. (2003) 'Reading Growth in High-Poverty Classrooms: The Influence of Teacher Practices That Encourage Cognitive Engagement in Literacy Learning', *The Elementary School Journal* 104(1): 3–28.

Taylor, B. M., Strait, J. and Medo, M. A. (1994) 'Early Intervention in Reading: Supplementary Instruction for Groups of Low Achieving Students Provided by First Grade Teachers', in E.H. Hiebert and B.M. Taylor (eds) *Getting Reading Right from the Start: Effective Early Literacy Interventions*. Needham, MA: Allyn and Bacon.

Tharp, R. G. and Gallimore, R. G. (1993) *Rousing Minds to Life: Teaching, Learning, and Schooling in Social Context*. New York: Cambridge University Press.

Tracey, D. H. and Morrow, L. M. (1998) 'Motivating Contexts for Young Children's Literacy Development: Implications for Word Recognition', in J. L. Metsala and L. C. Ehri (eds) *Word Recognition in Beginning Reading*, pp. 341–56. Mahwah, NJ: Erlbaum.

Turner, J. C. (1995) 'The Influence of Classroom Contexts on Young Children's Motivation for Literacy', *Reading Research Quarterly* 50(3): 410–41.

Turner, J. and Paris, S. G. (1995) 'How Literacy Tasks Influence Children's Motivation for Literacy', *The Reading Teacher* 48(8): 662–73.

Valenzuela, A. (1999) *Subtractive Schooling: U.S.–Mexican Youth and the Politics of Caring*. Albany: SUNY Press.

Wigfield, A. (2000) 'Facilitating Children's Reading Motivation', in L. Baker, M. J. Dreher and J. T. Guthrie (eds) *Engaging Young Readers: Promoting Achievement and Motivation*, pp. 140–58. New York: Guilford.

Willis, P. (1977) *Learning to Labor*. New York: Columbia University Press.

Article 3 References

Dong, Y. R. (2004/2005). Getting at the content. *Educational Leadership, 62*(4), 14–19.

Fisher, D., & Frey, N. (2008). *Better learning through structured teaching: A framework for the gradual release of responsibility.* Alexandria, VA: ASCD.

Fisher, D., Frey, N., & Lapp, D. (2008). Shared readings: Modeling comprehension, vocabulary, text structures, and text features for older readers. *The Reading Teacher, 61,* 548–557.

Hill, J., & Flynn, K. (2006). *Classroom instruction that works with English language learners.* Alexandria, VA: ASCD.

Markow, D., Kim, A., & Liebman, M. (2007). *The Metlife survey of the American teacher: The homework experience.* New York: Metropolitan Life Insurance Company.

Summers, J. J. (2006). Effects of collaborative learning in math on sixth graders' individual goal orientations from a socioconstructivist perspective. *Elementary School Journal, 106,* 273–290.

Totten, S., Sills, T., Digby, A., & Russ, P. (1991). *Cooperative learning: A guide to research.* New York: Garland.

Winerman, L. (2005). The mind's mirror. *Monitor on Psychology, 36*(9), 48–49.

Article 4 References

Barton, P. E. (2002). *Staying on course in education reform.* Princeton, NJ: Statistics & Research Division. Policy Information Center, Educational Testing Service.

Bloom, B. S. (1968). Learning for mastery. *Evaluation Comment (UCLA-CSEIP), 1*(2), 1–12.

Bloom, B. S. (1971). Mastery learning. In J. H. Block (Ed.), *Mastery learning: Theory and practice.* New York: Holt, Rinehart & Winston.

Guskey, T. R. (1997). *Implementing mastery learning* (2nd ed.). Belmont, CA: Wadsworth.

Guskey, T. R. (1998). Making time to train your staff. *The School Administrator, 55*(7), 35–37.

Guskey, T. R. (2000a). Twenty questions? Twenty tools for better teaching. *Principal Leadership, 1*(3), 5–7.

Guskey, T. R. (2000b). *Evaluating professional development.* Thousand Oaks, CA: Corwin Press.

Kifer, E. (2001). *Large-scale assessment: Dimensions, dilemmas, and policies.* Thousand Oaks, CA: Corwin Press.

Sternberg, R. J. (1994). Allowing for thinking styles. *Educational Leadership, 52*(3), 36–40.

Stiggins, R. J. (1999). Evaluating classroom assessment training in teacher education programs. *Educational Measurement: Issues and Practice, 19*(1), 23–27.

Stiggins, R. J. (2002). Assessment crisis: The absence of assessment for learning. *Phi Delta Kappan, 83*(10), 758–765.

Whiting, B., Van Burgh, J. W., & Render, G. F. (1995). *Mastery learning in the classroom*. Paper presented at the annual meeting of the American Educational Research Association, San Francisco.

Wiggins, G. (1998). *Educative assessment*. San Francisco: Jossey-Bass.

Article 5 References

Allington, R. L. (Ed.). (2002). *Big brother and the national reading curriculum: How ideology trumped evidence*. Portsmouth, NH: Heinemann.

Allington, R. L., & Johnston, P. H. (Eds.). (2002). *Reading to learn: Lessons from exemplary fourth grade classrooms*. New York: Guilford.

Allington, R. L., & McGill-Franzen, A. (1989). Different programs, indifferent instruction. In A. Gartner & D. Lipsky (Eds.), *Beyond separate education* (pp. 75–98). Baltimore: Brookes.

Allington, R. L., & McGill-Franzen, A. (1995). Flunking: Throwing good money after the bad. In R. L. Allington & S. A. Walmsley (Eds.), *No quick fix: Rethinking literacy programs in America's elementary schools* (pp. 45–60). New York: Teachers College Press.

Allington, R. L., & Woodside-Jiron, H. (1999). The politics of literacy teaching: How "research" shaped educational policy. *Educational Researcher, 28*(8), 4–13.

Argyris, C. (1990). *Overcoming organizational defenses: Facilitating organizational learning*. Boston: Allyn & Bacon.

Arya, P. (2003). Influences of reading group experiences on second graders' perceptions of themselves as readers. *Literacy Teaching and Learning, 8*(1), 1–18.

Barrs, M., Ellis, S., Hester, H., & Thomas, A. (1989). *The primary language record: Handbook for teachers*. London: Inner London Education Authority/Centre for Language in Primary Education.

Baudanza, L. (2001). *Disabilities of a child or disabilities of the system?* Unpublished manuscript, University at Albany, Albany, NY.

Black, P., & Wiliam, D. (1998a). Assessment and classroom learning. *Assessment in Education: Principles, Policy & Practice, 5*(1), 7–74.

Black, P., & Wiliam, D. (1998b, October). Inside the black box: Raising standards through classroom assessment. *Phi Delta Kappa International*, pp. 139–148.

Bourdieu, P. (1991). *Language and symbolic power* (J. B.Thompson, Ed.; G. Raymond & M. Adamson, Trans.). Cambridge, MA: Harvard University Press.

Brandt, D. (2001). *Literacy in American lives*. Cambridge, UK: Cambridge University Press.

Broadfoot, P. (2002). Editorial. Assessment for lifelong learning: Challenges and choices. *Assessment in Education, 9*(1), 5–7.

Broikou, K. (1992). *Understanding primary grade classroom teachers' special education referral practices*. Unpublished doctoral dissertation, State University of New York at Albany, Albany, NY.

Carr, M., & Claxton, G. (2002). Tracking the development of learning dispositions. *Assessment in Education, 5*(1), 9–37.

Claxton, G. (1999). *Wise up: The challenge of lifelong learning*. New York: Bloomsbury.

Clay, M. M. (1987). Learning to be learning disabled. *New Zealand Journal of Educational Studies, 22*, 155–173.

Clay, M. (1991). *Becoming literate: The construction of inner control*. Portsmouth, NH: Heinemann.

Clay, M. M. (1993). *An observation survey of early literacy achievement*. Portsmouth, NH: Heinemann.

Collins, J., & Blot, R. K. (2003). *Literacy and literacies: Texts, power and identity*. New York: Cambridge University Press.

Comeyras, M. (1995). What can we learn from students' questions? *Theory Into Practice, 34*, 101–106.

Crooks, T. (2001, September). *The validity of formative assessments*. Paper presented at the annual meeting of the British Educational Research Association, Leeds, UK.

Crooks, T. J. (1988). The impact of classroom evaluation practices on students. *Review of Educational Research, 58*, 438–481.

Darling-Hammond, L. (2004). Standards, accountability, and school reform. *Teachers College Record, 106*, 1047–1085.

Deci, E. L., Siegel, N. H., Ryan, R. M., Koestner, R., & Kauffman, M. (1982). Effects of performance standards on teaching styles: Behavior of controlling teachers. *Journal of Educational Psychology, 74*, 852–859.

Delandshere, G. (2001). Implicit theories, unexamined assumptions and the status quo of educational assessment. *Assessment in Education, 8*, 113–133.

Dweck, C. S. (1999). *Self-theories: Their role in motivation, personality, and development*. Philadelphia: Psychology Press.

Fairclough, N. (1992). *Discourse and social change*. London: Longman.

Falk, B. (1998). Using direct evidence to assess student progress: How the Primary Language Record supports teaching and learning. In C. Harrison & T. Salinger (Eds.), *Assessing reading 1: Theory and practice: International perspectives on reading assessment* (pp. 152–165). London: Routledge.

Falk, B. (2001). Professional learning through assessment. In A. Lieberman & L. Miller (Eds.), *Teachers caught in the action: Professional development that matters* (pp. 118–140). New York: Teachers College Press.

Falk, B., & Darling-Hammond, L. (1993). *The Primary Language Record at P.S. 261: How assessment transforms teaching and learning.* New York: The National Center for Restructuring Education, Schools, and Teaching, Teachers College, Columbia University.

Fennimore, B. S. (2000). *Talk matters: Refocusing the language of public school.* New York: Teachers College Press.

Flockton, L., & Crooks, T. (1996). *National Education Monitoring Project: Reading and speaking: Assessment results: 1996* (No. 6). Dunedin, New Zealand: Educational Assessment Research Unit.

Gee, J. P. (1996). *Social linguistics and literacies: Ideology in discourses* (2nd ed.). London: Falmer.

Gee, J. P. (2000). Discourse and sociocultural studies in reading. In M. L. Kamil, P. B. Mosenthal, P. D. Pearson, & R. Barr (Eds.), *Handbook of reading research* (Vol. 3, pp. 195–207). Mahwah, NJ: Erlbaum.

Gilmore, A. (2002). Large-scale assessment and teachers' assessment capacity: Learning opportunities for teachers in the National Education Monitoring Project in New Zealand. *Assessment in Education, 9,* 343–361.

Goodman, Y. (1978). Kidwatching: Observing children in the classroom. In A. Jagger & M. T. Smith-Burke (Eds.), *Observing the language learner* (pp. 9–18). Newark, DE: International Reading Association.

Greenberg, K. H., & Williams, L. (2002). Reciprocity and mutuality in dynamic assessment: Asking uncomfortable questions. In G. M. v. d. Aalsvoort, W. C. M. Resing, & A. J. M. Ruijssenaars (Eds.), *Learning potential assessment and cognitive training* (Vol. 7, pp. 91–110). Amsterdam: JAI.

Greene, M. (1985). The role of education in democracy. *Educational Horizons, 63,* 3–9.

Harlen, W., & Crick, R. D. (2003). Testing and motivation for learning. *Assessment in Education: Principles, Policy & Practice, 1*(2), 169–207.

Hill, C. (2004). Failing to meet the standards: The English language arts test for fourth graders in New York State. *Teachers College Record, 106,* 1086–1123.

Himley, M., & Carini, P. F. (Eds.). (2000). *From another angle: Children's strengths and school standards: The Prospect Center's descriptive review of the child.* New York: Teachers College Press.

International Reading Association and National Council of Teachers of English Joint Task Force on Assessment. (1994). *Standards for the assessment of reading and writing.* Newark, DE: International Reading Association.

Johnson, D., & Kress, G. (2003). Globalisation, literacy and society: Redesigning pedagogy and assessment. *Assessment in Education, 10*(1), 5–14.

Johnston, P. H. (1989). Constructive evaluation and the improvement of teaching and learning. *Teachers College Record, 90,* 509–528.

Johnston, P. H. (1993). Assessment as social practice. In D. Leu & C. Kinzer (Eds.), *42nd yearbook of the National Reading Conference* (pp. 11–23). Chicago: National Reading Conference.

Johnston, P. H. (1997). *Knowing literacy: Constructive literacy assessment.* York, ME: Stenhouse.

Johnston, P. H. (1999). Unpacking literate achievement. In J. Gaffney & B. Askew (Eds.), *Stirring the waters: A tribute to Marie Clay* (pp. 17–25). Portsmouth, NH: Heinemann.

Johnston, P. H. (2003). Assessment conversations. *The Reading Teacher, 57,* 90–92.

Johnston, P. H. (2004). *Choice words: How our language affects children's learning.* York, ME: Stenhouse.

Johnston, P. H., Afflerbach, P., & Weiss, P. (1993). Teachers' evaluation of teaching and learning of literacy. *Educational Assessment, 1*(2), 91–117.

Johnstzis, P. H., Jiron, H. W., & Day, J. P. (2001). Teaching and learning literate epistemologies. *Journal of Educational Psychology, 93*(1), 223–233.

Johnston, P. H., & Rogers, R. (2001). Early literacy assessment. In S. B. Neuman & D. K. Dickenson (Eds.), *Handbook of early literacy research* (pp. 377–389). New York: Guilford.

Kalantzis, M., Cope, B., & Harvey, A. (2003). Assessing multiliteracies and the new basics. *Assessment in Education: Principles, Policy & Practice, 10,* 15–26.

Learning, S. (2002). Retrieved August 3, 2002, from http://www.scilearn.com.

McDermott, R. P. (1993). The acquisition of a child by a learning disability. In S. Chaiklin & J. Lave (Eds.), *Understanding practice: Perspectives on activity and context* (pp. 269–305). Cambridge, UK: Cambridge University Press.

McDonald, B., & Boud, D. (2003). The impact of self-assessment on achievement: The effects of self-assessment training on performance in external examinations. *Assessment in Education: Principles, Policy & Practice, 10*(2), 209–220.

McNeil, L. M. (2000). *Contradictions of school reform: Education costs of standardized tests.* New York: Routledge.

Mehan, H. (1993). Beneath the skin and between the ears: A case study in the politics of representation. In S. Chaiklin & J. Lave (Eds.), *Understanding practice: Perspectives on activity and context* (pp. 241–268). Cambridge, UK: Cambridge University Press.

Messick, S. (1994). The interplay of evidence and consequences in the validation of performance assessments. *Educational Researcher, 23*(2), 13–23.

Morrison, K., & Joan, T. F. H. (2002). Testing to destruction: A problem in a small state. *Assessment in Education, 9,* 289–317.

Moss, P., & Schutz, A. (2001). Educational standards, assessment and the search for consensus. *American Educational Research Journal, 38*(1), 37–70.

Moss, P. A. (1998). The role of consequences in validity theory. *Educational Measurement: Issues and Practice, 17*(2), 6–12.

Niemi, P., & Poskiparta, E. (2002). Shadows over phonological awareness training: Resistant learners and dissipating gains. In E. Hjelmquist & C. V. Euler (Eds.), *Dyslexia and literacy* (pp. 84–99). London, UK: Whurr.

No Child Left Behind Act Of 2001, Pub. L. No. 107-110, 115 Stat. 1425 (2002).

Nystrand, M., Gamoran, A., Kachur, R., & Prendergast, C. (1997). *Opening dialogue: Understanding the dynamics of language and learning in the English classroom.* New York: Teachers College Press.

Paris, S. G. (2002). Measuring children's reading development using leveled texts. *The Reading Teacher, 55,* 168–170.

Pradl, G. M. (1996). Reading and democracy: The enduring influence of Louise Rosenblatt. *The New Advocate, 9*(1), 9–22.

Pressley, M., Allington, R. L., Wharton-MacDonald, R., Collins-Block, C., & Morrow, L. (2001). *Learning to read: Lessons from exemplary first-grade classrooms.* New York: Guilford.

Rex, L. A., & Nelson, M. C. (2004). How teachers' professional identities position high-stakes test preparation in their classrooms. *Teachers College Record, 106,* 1288–1331.

Rodgers, C. (2002). Defining reflection: Another look at John Dewey and reflective thinking. *Teachers College Record, 106*(4), 842–866.

Rogers, R. (2002). Between contexts: A critical analysis of family literacy, discursive practices, and literate subjectivities. *Reading Research Quarterly, 37,* 248–277.

Rogers, R. (2003). *A critical discourse analysis of family literacy practices: Power in and out of print.* Mahwah, NJ: Erlbaum.

Roskos, K., & Neuman, S. B. (1993). Descriptive observations of adults' facilitation of literacy in young children's play. *Early Childhood Research Quarterly, 8,* 77–97.

Rueda, R., & Mercer, J. (1985, June). *Predictive analysis of decision-making practices with limited English proficient handicapped students.* Paper presented at the Third Annual Symposium: Exceptional Hispanic Children and Youth. Monograph series, Denver, CO.

Russell, M., & Abrams, L. (2004). Instructional uses of computers for writing: The effect of state testing programs. *Teachers College Record, 106,* 1332–1357.

Sadler, R. R. (1987). Specifying and promulgating achievement standards. *Oxford Review of Education, 13,* 191–209.

Scanlon, D. M., Vellutino, F. R., Small, S. G., & Fanuele, D. P. (2000, April). *Severe reading difficulties—can they be prevented? A comparison of prevention and intervention approaches.* Paper presented at the American Educational Research Association, New Orleans, LA.

Schaffer, H. R. (1996). Joint involvement episodes as context for development. In H. Daniels (Ed.), *An introduction to Vygotsky* (pp. 251–280). London: Routledge.

Shavelson, R. J., Baxter, G. P., & Pine, J. (1992). Performance assessments: Political rhetoric and measurement reality. *Educational Researcher, 21*(4), 22–27.

Shepard, L. A. (1991). Psychometricians' beliefs about learning. *Educational Researcher, 20*(7), 2–16.

Shepard, L. A., Taylor, G. A., & Kagan, S. L. (1996). *Trends in early childhood assessment policies and practices.* Washington, DC: Office of Educational Research & Improvement.

Smith, M. L. (1991). Put to the test: The effects of external testing on teachers. *Educational Researcher, 20*(5), 8–11.

Smith, M. L., & Rottenberg, C. (1991). Unintended consequences of external testing in elementary schools. *Educational Measurement: Issues and Practice, 10*(4), 7–11.

Smith, P. (1997). *A third chance to learn: The development and evaluation of specialized interventions for young children experiencing difficulty with learning to read* (No. 13227). Wellington, New Zealand: National Council for Educational Research.

Stallman, A. C., & Pearson, P. D. (1991). Formal measures of early literacy. In L. M. Morrow & J. K. Smith (Eds.), *Assessment for instruction in early literacy* (pp. 7–44). Englewood Cliffs, NJ: Prentice Hall.

Teale, W. (1991). The promise and the challenge of informal assessment in early literacy. In L. M. Morrow & J. K. Smith (Eds.), *Assessment for instruction in early literacy* (pp. 45–61). Englewood Cliffs, NJ: Prentice Hall.

Torgeson, J. K. (2000). Individual differences in response to early interventions in reading: The lingering problem of treatment resisters. *Learning Disabilities Research and Practice, 15*(1), 55–64.

Tudge, J., & Rogoff, B. (1989). Peer influences on cognitive development: Piagetian-Vygotskian perspectives. In M. H. Bornstein & J. S. Bruner (Eds.), *Interactions in human development* (pp. 17–40). Hillsdale, NJ: Erlbaum.

Wixson, K. K., & Pearson, P. D. (1998). Policy and assessment strategies to support literacy instruction for a new century. *Peabody Journal of Education, 74,* 202–227.

Yalom, I. D. (1989). *Love's executioner and other tales of psychotherapy.* New York: Basic Books.

Article 6 References

Adams, M. J. (1990). *Beginning to read: Thinking and learning about print.* Cambridge, MA: MIT Press.

Aldenderfer, M., & Blashfield, P. (1984). *Cluster analysis.* Beverly Hills, CA: Sage.

Allington, R. L. (2001). *What really matters for struggling readers.* New York: Longman.

Allington, R. L., & Johnston, P. H. (2001). What do we know about effective fourth-grade teachers and their classrooms? In C. M. Roller (Ed.), *Learning to teach reading: Setting the research agenda* (pp. 150–165). Newark, DE: International Reading Association.

Antunez, B. (2002, Spring). Implementing reading first with English language learners. *Directions in Language and Education, 75.* Retrieved October 15, 2003, from http://www.ncela.gwu/ncbepubs/directions

Black, P., & Wiliam, D. (1998). Assessment and classroom learning. *Assessment in Education, 5*(1), 7–74.

Block, C. C., & Pressley, M. (2002). *Comprehension instruction: Research-based best practices.* New York: Guilford.

Cummins, J. (1991). The development of bilingual proficiency from home to school: A longitudinal study of Portuguese-speaking children. *Journal of Education, 173,* 85–98.

Cunningham, P. M., & Allington, R. L. (1999). *Classrooms that work* (2nd ed.). New York: Longman.

Duke, N. K., & Pearson, P. D. (2002). Effective practices for developing reading comprehension. In A. E. Farstrup & S. J. Samuels (Eds.), *What research has to say about reading instruction* (pp. 9–129). Newark, DE: International Reading Association.

Echevarria, J., Vogt, M. E., & Short, D. (2000). *Making content comprehensible for English language learners: The SIOP model.* Boston: Allyn & Bacon.

Edmondson, J., & Shannon, P. (2002). The will of the people. *The Reading Teacher, 55,* 452–454.

Elmore, R. F. (2002, Spring). *Unwarranted intrusion.* Education Next. Retrieved March 21, 2003, from http://www.education-next.org

Goodnough, A. (2001, May 23). *Teaching by the book, no asides allowed. The New York Times.* Retrieved March 21, 2003, from http://www.nytimes.com

Harris, A. J., & Sipay, E. R. (1990). *How to increase reading ability* (9th ed.). New York: Longman.

Helfland, D. (2002, July 21). *Teens get a second chance at literacy. Los Angeles Times.* Retrieved March 21, 2003, from http://www.latimes.com

Hiebert, E. H., Pearson, P. D., Taylor, B. M., Richardson, V., & Paris, S. G. (1998). *Every child a reader: Applying reading research to the classroom.* Ann Arbor, MI: Center for the Improvement of Early Reading Achievement, University of Michigan School of Education. Retrieved March 21, 2003, from http://www.ciera.org

Klein, S. P., Hamilton, L. S., McCaffrey, D. F., & Stecher, B. M. (2000). What do test scores in Texas tell us? *Education Policy Analysis Archives, 8*(49). Retrieved March 21, 2003, from http://epaa.asu.edu/eppa/v8n49

Kuhn, M. R., & Stahl, S. A. (2000). *Fluency: A review of developmental and remedial practices* (CIERA Rep. No. 2-008). Ann Arbor, MI: Center for the Improvement of Early Reading Achievement, University of Michigan School of Education. Retrieved March 21, 2003, from http://www.ciera.org

Linn, R. L. (2000). Assessments and accountability. *Educational Researcher, 29*(2), 4–16.

Linn, R. L. (n.d.). *Standards-based accountability: Ten suggestions.* CRESST Policy Brief 1. Retrieved March 21, 2003, from http://www.cse.ucla.edu

Lipson, M. Y., & Wixson, K. K. (2003). *Assessment and instruction of reading and writing difficulty: An interactive approach* (3rd ed.). Boston: Allyn & Bacon.

McNeil, L. M. (2000). *Contradictions of school reform: Educational costs of standardized testing.* New York: Routledge.

Nagy, W. E. (1988). *Teaching vocabulary to improve reading comprehension.* Urbana, IL: ERIC Clearinghouse on Reading and Communication Skills and the National Council of Teachers of English.

National Institute of Child Health and Human Development. (2000). *Report of the National Reading Panel. Teaching children to read: An evidence-based assessment of the scientific research literature on reading and its implications for reading instruction* (NIH Publication No. 004 769). Washington, DC: U.S. Government Printing Office. Retrieved March 21, 2003, from http://www.nationalreadingpanel.org

Olson, L. (2001). Overboard on testing. *Education Week, 29*(17), 23–30.

Opitz, M. F. (1998). *Flexible grouping in reading.* New York: Scholastic.

Paterson, F. R. A. (2000). The politics of phonics. *Journal of Curriculum and Supervision, 15,* 179–211.

Pinnell, G. S., Pikulski, J. J., Wixson, K. K., Campbell, J. R., Gough, P. B., & Beatty, A. S. (1995). *Listening to children read aloud.* Washington, DC: U.S. Department of Education.

Place, N. A. (2002). Policy in action: The influence of mandated early reading assessment on teachers' thinking and practice. In D. L. Schallert, C. M. Fairbanks, J. Worthy, B. Malock, & J. V. Hoffman (Eds.), *Fiftieth yearbook of the National Reading Conference* (pp. 45–58). Oak Creek, WI: National Reading Conference.

Riddle Buly, M., & Valencia, S. W. (2002). Below the bar: Profiles of students who fail state reading tests. *Educational Evaluation and Policy Analysis, 24,* 219–239.

Samuels, S. J. (2002). Reading fluency: Its development and assessment. In A. Farstrup & S. J. Samuels (Eds.), *What research has to say about reading instruction* (pp. 166–183). Newark, DE: International Reading Association.

Shepard, L. A. (2000). The role of assessment in a learning culture. *Educational Researcher, 29,* 4–14.

Snow, C. E., Burns, M. S., & Griffin, P. (Eds.). (1998). *Preventing reading difficulties in young children.* Washington, DC: National Academy Press.

Stahl, S. A., & Kapinus, B. A. (2001). *Word power: What every educator needs to know about vocabulary.* Washington, DC: National Education Association Professional Library.

Stanovich, K. E. (1986). Matthew effects in reading: Some consequences of individual differences in the acquisition of literacy. *Reading Research Quarterly, 27,* 360–407.

Stanovich, K. E. (1988). Explaining the difference between the dyslexic and garden-variety poor reader: The phonological-core variable-difference model. *Journal of Learning Disabilities, 21,* 590–612.

Stanovich, K. E. (1994). Romance and reality. *The Reading Teacher, 47,* 280–290.

Article 7 References

Brabham, E. G., & Villaume, S. K. (2002). Leveled text: The good news and the bad news. *The Reading Teacher, 55,* 438–441.

Clark, K. F. (2000). Instructional scaffolding in reading: A case study of four primary grade teachers. *Dissertation Abstracts International, 61,* 06A.

Clay, M. M. (1991). *Becoming literate: The construction of inner control.* Auckland, New Zealand: Heinemann.

Clay, M. M. (2001). *Change over time in children's literacy development.* Portsmouth, NH: Heinemann.

Cunningham, P. M., & Allington, R. L. (2003). *Classrooms that work: They can all read and write.* Boston: Allyn & Bacon.

Ehri, L. C. (1991). Development of the ability to read words. In R. Barr, M. L. Kamil, P. B. Mosenthal, & P. D. Pearson (Eds.), *Handbook of reading research* (Vol. 2, pp. 383–417). Mahwah, NJ: Erlbaum.

Glaser, B. G., & Strauss, A. L. (1967). *The discovery of grounded theory: Strategies for qualitative research.* New York: Aldine Press.

Graves, M. F., Juel, C., & Graves, B. B. (2001). *Teaching reading in the 21st century.* Boston: Allyn & Bacon.

Hiebert, E. H., & Taylor, B. M. (2000). Beginning reading instruction: Research on early interventions. In M. L. Kamil, P. B. Mosenthal, P. D. Pearson, & R. Barr (Eds.), *Handbook of reading research* (Vol. 3, pp. 455–482). Mahwah, NJ: Erlbaum.

Juel, C. (1991). Beginning reading. In R. Barr, M. L. Kamil, P. B. Mosenthal, & P. D. Pearson (Eds.), *Handbook of reading research* (Vol. 2, pp. 759–788). Mahwah, NJ: Erlbaum.

Lipson, M. Y., & Wixson, K. K. (2003). *Assessment & instruction of reading and writing difficulty: An interactive approach.* Boston: Allyn & Bacon.

Pressley, M. (1998). *Reading instruction that works: The case for balanced teaching.* New York: Guilford.

Pressley, M., Wharton-McDonald, R., Allington, R., Block, C. C., Morrow, L., Tracey, D., et al. (2001). A study of effective first-grade literacy instruction. *Scientific Studies of Reading, 5*(1), 35–58.

Rodgers, E. M. (2000). Language matters: When is a scaffold really a scaffold? In T. S. Shanahan & F. V. Rodriquez-Brown (Eds.), *49th yearbook of the National Reading Conference* (pp. 8–90). Chicago: National Reading Conference.

Stahl, S. A. (2002). Saying the "p" word: Nine guidelines for exemplary phonics instruction. In International Reading Association (Ed.), *Evidence-based reading instruction: Putting the National Reading Panel report into practice* (pp. 61–68). Newark, DE: International Reading Association.

Strickland, D. S. (2002). The importance of effective early intervention. In A. E. Farstrup & S. J. Samuels (Eds.), *What research has to say about reading instruction* (pp. 69–86). Newark, DE: International Reading Association.

Taylor, B. M., Pearson, P. D., Clark, K. F., & Walpole, S. (2000). Effective schools and accomplished teachers: Lessons about primary-grade reading instruction in low-income schools. *Elementary School Journal, 101*(2), 121–165.

Van den Broek, P., & Kremer, K. E. (2000). The mind in action: What it means to comprehend during reading. In B. M. Taylor, M. F. Graves, & P. van den Broek (Eds.), *Reading for meaning: Fostering comprehension in the middle grades* (pp. 1–31). New York: Teachers College Press.

Children's Books Cited

Aliki. (1992). *My visit to the aquarium.* New York: HarperCollins.

Brenner, B. (1989). *The color wizard.* New York: Bantam.

Dodds, D. A. (1996). *Where does everybody go?* St. Charles, IL: Houghton Mifflin.

Dubowski, C. E. (1988). *Cave boy.* New York: Random House.

Krauss, R. (1945). *The carrot seed.* New York: HarperCollins.

Marshall, J. (1987). *Red Riding Hood.* New York: Dial.

Oppenheim, J. (1989). *"Not now!" said the cow.* New York: Bantam.

Young, E. (1989). *Lon Po Po: A Red-Riding Hood story from China.* New York: Penguin Putnam.

Article 8 References

Aaron, P. G., & Joshi, R. M. (1992). *Reading Problems: Consultation and remediation.* New York: Guilford Press.

Adams, M. J., & Henry, M. K. (1997). Myths and realities about words and literacy. *School Psychology Review, 26,* 425–436.

Bear, D. R., Invernizzi, M. A., Templeton, S., & Johnston, F. (1996). *Words their way: Word study for phonics, vocabulary, and spelling.* Englewood Cliffs, NJ: Prentice Hall.

Clay, M. (1993). *Reading Recovery: A guidebook to teachers in training.* Portsmouth, NH: Heinemann.

Greenwood, C. R. (1991). Longitudinal analysis of time, engagement, and achievement in at-risk versus non-risk students. *Exceptional Children, 57,* 521–535.

Greenwood, C. R., Delquadri, J. C., & Hall, R. V. (1984). Opportunity to respond and student academic performance. In W. L. Heward, T. E. Heron, D. S. Hill, & J. Trap-Porter (Eds.), *Focus on behavior analysis in education* (pp. 53–88). Columbus, OH: Charles E. Merrill.

Levy, B. A., & Carr, T. H. (1990). Component process analysis: Conclusions and challenges. In T. H. Carr & B. A. Levy (Eds.), *Reading and its development: Component skills approaches* (pp. 460–468). New York: Academic Press.

Stahl, S. A. (1998). Teaching children with reading problems to decode: Phonics and "not-phonics" instruction. *Reading & Writing Quarterly: Overcoming Learning Difficulties, 14,* 165–188.

Article 9 References

Ball, E., & Blachman, B. (1991). Does phoneme awareness training in kindergarten make a difference in early word recognition and developmental spelling? *Reading Research Quarterly, 26*(1), 49–66.

Bear, D., Invernizzi, M., Templeton, S., & Johnston, F. (2003). *Words their way: Word study for phonics, vocabulary, and spelling instruction* (3rd ed.). Upper Saddle River, NJ: Pearson.

Blachman, B., Ball, E., Black, R., & Tangel, D. (2000). *Road to the code: A phonological awareness program for young children.* Baltimore: Paul Brookes.

Castiglioni-Spalten, M. L., & Ehri, L. C. (2003). Phonemic awareness instruction: Contribution of articulatory segmentation to novice beginners' reading and spelling. *Scientific Studies of Reading, 7*(1), 25–52.

Ehri, L. (1998). Grapheme-phoneme knowledge is essential for learning to read words in English. In J. Metsala & L. Ehri (Eds.), *Word recognition in beginning literacy* (pp. 3–40). Mahwah, NJ: Erlbaum.

Gaskins, I., Ebri, L., Cress, C., O'Hara, C., & Donnelly, K. (1996/1997). Procedures for word learning: Making discoveries about words. *The Reading Teacher, 50*(4), 312–327.

Liberman, A. (1998). Why is speech so much easier than reading? In C. Hulme & J. Joshi (Eds.), *Reading and spelling: Development and disorders* (pp. 5–17). Mahwah, NJ: Erlbaum.

National Institute of Child Health and Human Development. (2000). *Report of the National Reading Panel. Teaching children to read: An evidence-based assessment of the scientific research literature on reading and its implications for reading instruction* (NIH Publication No. 00-4769). Washington, DC: U.S. Government Printing Office.

Richgels, D. (2001). Invented spelling, phonemic awareness, and reading and writing instruction. In S. Neuman & D. Dickinson (Eds.), *Handbook of early literacy research* (pp. 142–155). New York: Guilford.

Article 11 References

Adams, M. J. (1990). *Beginning to read: Thinking and learning about print.* Cambridge, MA: MIT Press.

Adams, M. J., Foorman, B. R., Lundberg, I., & Beeler, T. (1998). *Phonemic awareness in young children.* Baltimore: Paul Brookes.

Anderson, R. C., Hiebert, E. H., Scott, J. A., & Wilkinson, I. A. G. (1985). *Becoming a nation of readers: The report of the commission on reading.* Washington, DC: The National Institute of Education.

Bear, D. R., Invernizzi, M., Templeton, S., & Johnston, F. (1996). *Words their way.* Columbus, OH: Merrill.

Beck, I. L., McKeown, M. G., & Kucan, L. (2002). *Bringing words to life.* New York: Guilford.

Blachowicz, C., & Fisher, P. J. (2002). *Teaching vocabulary in all classrooms.* Columbus, OH: Merrill.

Chard, D. J., Vaughn, S., & Tyler, B. J. (2002). A synthesis of research on effective interventions for building fluency with elementary students with learning disabilities. *Journal of Learning Disabilities, 35,* 386–406.

Cunningham, A. E., & Stanovich, K. E. (1998). What reading does for the mind. *American Educator, 22*(1), 8–15.

Cunningham, P. M. (2000). *Phonics they use.* New York: Longman.

Ehri, L. C. (1995). Stages of development in learning to read words by sight. *Journal of Research in Reading, 78,* 116–125.

Ehri, L. C. (1998). Grapheme-phoneme knowledge is essential for learning to read words in English. In J. L. Metsala & L. C. Ehri (Eds.), *Word recognition in beginning literacy* (pp. 3–40). Mahwah, NJ: Erlbaum.

Fountas, I. C., & Pinnell, G. S. (1996). *Guided reading: Good first teaching for all children.* Portsmouth, NH: Heinemann.

Greene, F. P. (1979). Radio reading. In C. Pennock (Ed.), *Reading comprehension at four linguistic levels* (pp. 104–107). Newark, DE: International Reading Association.

Harris, T. L., & Hodges, R. E. (1995). *The literacy dictionary: The vocabulary of reading and writing.* Newark, DE: International Reading Association.

Hasbrouck, J. E., & Tindal, G. (1992). Curriculum-based fluency norms for grades 2 through 5. *Teaching Exceptional Children, 24,* 41–44.

Heckelman, R. G. (1969). A neurological-impress method of remedial-reading instruction. *Academic Therapy, 4,* 277–282.

Hiebert, E. H., & Fisher, C. W. (in press). A review of the National Reading Panel's studies on fluency: On the matter of text. *Elementary School Journal.*

Houghton Mifflin. (2001). *Leveled reading passages.* Boston: Author.

Huey, E. B. (1968). *The psychology and pedagogy of reading; with a review of the history of reading and writing and of methods, texts, and hygiene in reading.* Cambridge, MA: MIT Press. (Originally published 1908)

Kuhn, M. R., & Stahl, S. A. (2000). *Fluency: A review of developmental and remedial practices.* Ann Arbor, MI: Center for the Improvement of Early Reading Achievement.

LaBerge, D., & Samuels, S. J. (1974). Towards a theory of automatic information processing in reading. *Cognitive Psychology, 6,* 293–323.

Mathes, P. G., & Fuchs, L. S. (1993). Peer-mediated reading instruction in special education resource rooms. *Learning Disabilities Research & Practice, 8,* 233–243.

Nagy, W. E. (1988). *Teaching vocabulary to improve reading comprehension.* Newark, DE: International Reading Association.

Nathan, R. G., & Stanovich, K. E. (1991). The causes and consequences of differences in reading fluency. *Theory Into Practice, 30,* 176–184.

National Institute of Child Health and Human Development. (2000). *Report of the National Reading Panel. Teaching children to read: An evidence-based assessment of the scientific research literature on reading and its implications for reading instruction* (NIH Publication No. 00-4769). Washington, DC: U.S. Government Printing Office.

O'Connor, R. E., Notari-Syverson, A., & Vadasy, P. F. (1998). *Ladders to literacy: A kindergarten activity book.* Baltimore: Paul Brookes.

Pinnell, G. S., Pikulski, J. J., Wixson, K. K., Campbell, J. R., Gough, P. B., & Beatty, A. S. (1995). *Listening to children read aloud.* Washington, DC: Office of Educational Research and Improvement, U.S. Department of Education.

Rasinski, T. V. (2003). *The fluent reader.* New York: Scholastic.

Reitsma, P. (1983). Printed word learning in beginning readers. *Journal of Experimental Child Psychology, 75,* 321–339.

Reutzel, D. R. (1996). Developing at-risk readers' oral reading fluency. In L. Putnam (Ed.), *How to become a better reader: Strategies for assessment and intervention* (pp. 241–254). Englewood Cliffs, NJ: Merrill.

Samuels, S. J. (1979). The method of repeated readings. *The Reading Teacher, 32,* 403–408.

Samuels, S. J. (2002). Reading fluency: Its development and assessment. In A. E. Farstrup & S. J. Samuels (Eds.), *What research has to say about reading instruction* (3rd ed., pp. 166–184). Newark, DE: International Reading Association.

Stanovich, K. E. (1986). Matthew effects in reading: Some consequences in individual differences in the acquisition of literacy. *Reading Research Quarterly, 21,* 360–407.

Stecker, S. K., Roser, N. L., & Martinez, M. G. (1998). Understanding oral reading fluency. In T. Shanahan & F. V. Rodriquez-Brown (Eds.), *47th yearbook of the National Reading Conference* (pp. 295–310). Chicago: National Reading Conference.

Strickland, D. S., & Schickedanz, J. (2004). *Learning about print in preschool: Working with letters, words, and links with phonemic awareness.* Newark, DE: International Reading Association.

Topping, K. (1987). Paired reading: A powerful technique for parent use. *The Reading Teacher, 40,* 608–614.

Article 12 References

Adams, M. J. (1990). *Beginning to read: Thinking and learning about print.* Cambridge, MA: MIT Press.

Bryant, D. P., Vaughn, S., Linan-Thompson, S., Ugel, N., Hamff, A., & Hougen, M. (2000). Reading outcomes for students with and without reading disabilities in general education middle-school content area classes. *Learning Disability Quarterly, 23,* 238–252.

Carnine, D. W., Silbert, J., Kame'enui, E. J., & Tarver, S. G. (2004). *Direct instruction reading* (4th ed.). Upper Saddle River, NJ: Prentice Hall/Merrill.

Dahl, P. R. (1977). An experimental program for teaching high speed word recognition and comprehension skills. In J. E. Burton, T. Lovitt, & T. Rowland (Eds.), *Communications research in learning disabilities and mental retardation* (pp. 33–65). Baltimore: University Park Press.

Dowhower, S. L. (1987). Effects of repeated reading on second-grade transitional readers' fluency and comprehension. *Reading Research Quarterly, 22*(4), 389–406.

Freeland, J. T., Skinner, C. H., Jackson, B., McDaniel, C. E., & Smith, S. (2000). Measuring and increasing silent reading comprehension rates: Empirically validating a repeated reading intervention. *Psychology in the Schools, 37*(5), 415–429.

Fuchs, L. S., Fuchs, D., & Hosp, M. K. (2001). Oral reading fluency as an indicator of reading competence: A theoretical, empirical, and historical analysis. *Scientific Studies of Reading, 5*(3), 239–256.

Gilbert, L. M., Williams, R. L., & McLaughlin, T. F. (1996). Use of assisted reading to increase correct reading rates and decrease error rates of students with learning disabilities. *Journal of Applied Behavior Analysis, 29*(2), 255–257.

Hasbrouck, J. E., & Tindal, G. (1992). Curriculum-based oral reading fluency norms for students in grades 2 through 5. *Teaching Exceptional Children, 24*(3), 41–44.

Homan, S. P., Klesius, J. P., & Hite, C. (1993). Effects of repeated readings and nonrepetitive strategies on students' fluency and comprehension. *The Journal of Educational Research, 87*(2), 94–99.

Kamps, D. M., Barbetta, P. M., Leonard, B. R., & Delquadri, J. (1994). Classwide peer tutoring: An integration strategy to improve reading skills and promote peer interactions among students with autism and general education peers. *Journal of Applied Behavior Analysis, 27*(1), 49–61.

Koenig, A. J., & Layton, C. A. (1998). Increasing reading fluency in elementary students with low vision through repeated reading. *Journal of Visual Impairment and Blindness, 92*(5), 276–292.

Kuhn, M. R., & Stahl, S. A. (2003). Fluency: A review of developmental and remedial practices. *Journal of Educational Psychology, 95*(1), 3–21.

Mathes, P. G., & Fuchs, L. S. (1993). Peer-mediated reading instruction in special education resource rooms. *Learning Disability Research and Practice, 8*(4), 233–243.

Mercer, C. D., Campbell, K. U., Miller, M. D., Mercer, K. D., & Lane, H. B. (2000). Effects of a reading fluency intervention for middle schoolers with specific learning disabilities. *Learning Disability Research and Practice, 15*(4), 179–189.

Mercer, C. D., & Mercer, A. R. (2001). *Teaching students with learning problems* (6th ed.). Upper Saddle River, NJ: Prentice Hall/Merrill.

Miller, A. D., Barbetta, P. M., & Heron, T. A. (1994). START tutoring: Designing, training, implementing, adapting, and evaluating tutoring programs for school and home settings. In R. Gardner, D. Sainato, J. Cooper, T. Heron, W. Heward, J. Eshleman, & T. Grossi (Eds.), *Behavior analysis in education: Focus on measurably superior instruction* (pp. 265–282). Belmont, CA: Brooks-Cole.

Moats, L. C. (1999). *Teaching reading is rocket science: What expert teachers of reading should know and be able to do.* Washington, DC: American Federation of Teachers.

National Reading Panel. (2000). *Report of the National Reading Panel: Teaching children to read* [Online]. Available: http://www.nichd.nih.gov/publications/nrp-pubskey.cfm [2000, November, 10].

O'Shea, L. J., Sindelar, P. T., & O'Shea, D. J. (1985). The effects of repeated readings and attentional cues on reading fluency and comprehension. *Journal of Reading Behavior, 17*(2), 129–141.

O'Shea, L. J., Sindelar, P. T., & O'Shea, D. J. (1987). The effects of repeated reading and attentional cues on the reading fluency and comprehension of learning disabled readers. *Learning Disabilities Research, 2*(2), 103–109.

Rashotte, C. A., & Torgesen, J. K. (1985). Repeated reading and reading fluency in learning disabled children. *Reading Research Quarterly, 20,* 180–188.

Rasinski, T. V. (2000). Speed does matter in reading. *The Reading Teacher, 54*(2), 146–151.

Rasinski, T., Padak, N., Linek, W., & Sturtevant, E. (1994). Effects of fluency development on urban second-grade readers. *The Journal of Educational Research, 87*(3), 158–165.

Samuels, S. J. (1979). The method of repeated readings. *The Reading Teacher, 41,* 756–760.

Simmons, D. C., Fuchs, L. S., Fuchs, D., Mathes, P., & Hodge, J. P. (1995). Effects of explicit teaching and peer tutoring on the reading achievement of learning-disabled and low-performing students in regular classrooms. *The Elementary School Journal, 95*(5), 387–408.

Sindelar, P. T., Monda, L. E., & O'Shea, L. J. (1990). Effects of repeated readings on instructional- and mastery-level readers. *The Journal of Educational Research, 83*(4), 220–226.

Stoddard, K., Valcante, G., Sindelar, P. T., O'Shea, L., & Algozzine, B. (1993). Increasing reading rate and comprehension: The effects of repeated readings, sentence segmentation, and intonation training. *Reading Research and Instruction, 32*(4), 53–65.

Therrien, W. J. (2004). Fluency and comprehension gains as a result of repeated reading: A meta-analysis. *Remedial and Special Education, 25*(4), 252–261.

Vaughn, S., Chard, D. J., Bryant, D. P., Coleman, M., & Kouzekanani, K. (2000). Fluency and comprehension interventions for third-grade students. *Remedial and Special Education, 21*(6), 325–335.

Weinstein, G., & Cooke, N. L. (1992). The effects of two repeated reading interventions on generalization of fluency. *Learning Disability Quarterly, 15,* 21–28.

Article 14 References

Allington, R. (2006). *What really matters for struggling readers: Designing research-based programs* (2nd ed.). Boston: Allyn & Bacon.

Basurto, I. (2004). Teaching vocabulary creatively. In G. E. Tompkins & C. L. Blanchfield (Eds.), *Teaching vocabulary: 50 creative strategies, grades K–12* (pp. 1–4). Upper Saddle River, NJ: Pearson Education.

Baumann, J. F., & Kame'enui, E. J. (1991). Research on vocabulary instruction: Ode to Voltaire. In J. Flood, J. M. Jensen, D. Lapp, & J. R. Squire (Eds.), *Handbook of research on teaching the language arts* (pp. 602–632). New York: Macmillan.

Blachowicz, C., & Fisher, P. (2004). Vocabulary lessons. *Educational Leadership, 61*(6), 66–69.

Broaddus, K., & Ivey, G. (2002). Taking away the struggle to read in the middle grades. *Middle School Journal, 34*(2), 5–11.

Bromley, K. (2002). *Stretching students' vocabulary, grades 3–8.* New York: Scholastic.

Davis, F. B. (1972). Psychometric research on comprehension in reading. *Reading Research Quarterly, 7,* 628–678.

Graves, M. F., & Watts-Taffe, S. M. (2002). The place of word-consciousness in a research-based vocabulary program. In A. E. Farstrup & S. J. Samuels (Eds.), *What research has to say about reading instruction* (3rd ed., pp. 140–165). Newark, DE: International Reading Association.

Greenwood, S. (2004). Content matters: Building vocabulary and conceptual understanding in the subject areas. *Middle School Journal, 35*(3), 27–34.

Hahn, M. L. (2002). *Reconsidering read-aloud.* Portland, ME: Stenhouse.

Juel, C., & Deffes, R. (2004). Making words stick. *Educational Leadership, 61*(6), 30–34.

Lederer, R. (1991). *The miracle of language.* New York: Pocket Books.

Merriam-Webster's collegiate dictionary (11th ed.). (2005). Retrieved November 7, 2005, from http://www.m-w.com/info/new_words.htm

Moats, L. C. (2005/2006). How spelling supports reading: And why it is more regular and predictable than you think. *American Educator, 29*(4), 12–22, 42–43.

Nagy, W. E. (1988). *Teaching vocabulary to improve reading comprehension.* Urbana, IL: National Council of Teachers of English; Newark, DE: International Reading Association.

Nagy, W., & Scott, J. (2000). Vocabulary processes. In M. L. Kamil, P. B. Mosenthal, P. D. Pearson, & R. Barr (Eds.), *Handbook of reading research* (Vol. 3, pp. 269–284). Mahwah, NJ: Erlbaum.

Ogle, D. (1986). K-W-L: A teaching model that develops active reading of expository text. *The Reading Teacher, 39,* 564–570.

Paivio, A. (1990). *Mental representations: A dual coding approach.* New York: Oxford University Press.

Pressley, M. (2002). Comprehension instruction: What makes sense now, what might make sense soon. *Reading Online, 5*(2). Retrieved November 7, 2005, from http://www.readingonline.org/articles/art_index.asp?HREF=/articles/handbook/pressley/index.html

Robb, L. (2000). *Teaching reading in middle school.* New York: Scholastic.

Rupley, W. H., Logan, J. W., & Nichols, W. D. (1999). Vocabulary instruction in a balanced reading program. *The Reading Teacher, 52,* 336–346.

Samuels, S. J. (2002). Reading fluency: Its development and assessment. In A. E. Farstrup & S. J. Samuels (Eds.), *What research has to say about reading instruction* (3rd ed., pp. 166–183). Newark, DE: International Reading Association.

Stahl, S. A., & Fairbanks, M. M. (1986). The effects of vocabulary instruction: A model-based meta-analysis. *Review of Educational Research, 56*(1), 72–110.

Tompkins, G., & Blanchfield, C. L. (Eds.). (2004). *Teaching vocabulary: 50 creative strategies, grades K–12*. Upper Saddle River, NJ: Pearson.

Trelease, J. (2001). *The read-aloud handbook* (5th ed.). New York: Penguin.

Vacca, J. L., Vacca, R. T., Gove, M. K., Burkey, L., Lenhart, L. A., & McKeon, C. (2005). *Reading and learning to read* (6th ed.). Boston: Allyn & Bacon.

Watts, S. (1995). Vocabulary instruction during reading lessons in six classrooms. *Journal of Reading Behavior, 27,* 399–424.

Selected Professional Resources on Vocabulary Teaching

Allen, J. (1999). *Words, words, words: Teaching vocabulary in grades 4–12*. Portland, ME: Stenhouse.

Beck, I. L., McKeown, M. G., & Kucan, L. (2002). *Bringing words to life: Robust vocabulary instruction*. New York: Guilford.

Blachowicz, C., & Fisher, P. J. (2002). *Teaching vocabulary in all classrooms* (2nd ed.). Upper Saddle River, NJ: Merrill.

Brand, M. (2004). *Word savvy: Integrating vocabulary, spelling, and word study, grades 3–6*. Portland, ME: Stenhouse.

Brand, M. (2005). *A day of words: Integrating word work in the intermediate grades* (VHS or DVD). Portland, ME: Stenhouse.

Bromley, K. (2002). *Stretching students' vocabulary, grades 3–8*. New York: Scholastic.

Ganske, K. (2000). *Word journeys: Assessment guided phonics, spelling, and vocabulary instruction*. New York: Guilford.

Literacy study group: Vocabulary module. (2002). Discussion guide, articles, and books on vocabulary. Newark, DE: International Reading Association.

Murray, M. (2004). *Teaching mathematics vocabulary in context*. Portsmouth, ME: Heinemann.

Nagy, W. E. (1988). *Teaching vocabulary to improve reading comprehension*. Urbana, IL: National Council of Teachers of English; Newark, DE: International Reading Association.

Article 15 References

Baumann, J. F., Kame'enui, E. J., & Ash, G. E. (2003). Research on vocabulary instruction: Voltaire redux. In J. Flood, D. Lapp, J. R. Squire, & J. M. Jensen (Eds.), *Handbook of research on teaching the English language arts* (2nd ed., pp. 752–785). Mahwah, NJ: Erlbaum.

Beck, I. L., & McKeown, M. G. (1991). Conditions of vocabulary acquisition. In R. Barr, M. L. Kamil, P. Mosenthal, & P. D. Pearson (Eds.), *Handbook of reading research* (Vol. 2, pp. 789–814). White Plains, NY: Longman.

Beck, I. L., McKeown, M. G., & Kucan, L. (2002). *Bringing words to life: Robust vocabulary instruction*. New York: Guilford.

Biemiller, A. (1999). *Language and reading success*. Cambridge, MA: Brookline Books.

Blachowicz, C. L. Z., & Fisher, P. J. (2006). *Teaching vocabulary in all classrooms* (3rd ed.). Upper Saddle River, NJ: Merrill.

Chall, J. S., & Conard, S. S. (1991). *Should textbooks challenge students? The case for easier or harder textbooks*. New York: Teachers College Press.

Cunningham, A. (2005). Vocabulary growth through independent reading and reading aloud to children. In E. H. Hiebert & M. L. Kamil (Eds.), *Teaching and learning vocabulary: Bringing research to practice* (pp. 45–68). Mahwah, NJ: Erlbaum.

Hayes, D. P., & Ahrens, M. (1988). Vocabulary simplification for children: A special case of "motherese"? *Journal of Child Language, 15,* 395–410.

Hiebert, E. H. (2005). In pursuit of an effective, efficient vocabulary curriculum for elementary students. In E. H. Hiebert & M. L. Kamil (Eds.), *Teaching and learning vocabulary: Bringing research to practice* (pp. 243–263). Mahwah, NJ: Erlbaum.

Kamil, M. L., & Hiebert, E. H. (2005). Teaching and learning vocabulary: Perspectives and persistent issues. In E. H. Hiebert & M. L. Kamil (Eds.), *Teaching and learning vocabulary: Bringing research to practice* (pp. 1–23). Mahwah, NJ: Erlbaum.

National Institute of Child Health and Human Development. (2000). *Report of the National Reading Panel. Teaching children to read: An evidence-based assessment of the scientific research literature on reading and its implications for reading instruction* (NIH Publication No. 00-4769). Washington, DC: U.S. Government Printing Office.

Scott, J. A., & Nagy, W. E. (2004). Developing word consciousness. In J. F. Baumann & E. J. Kame'enui (Eds.), *Vocabulary instruction: Research to practice* (pp. 201–217). New York: Guilford.

Yopp, H. K., & Yopp, R. H. (2003). Ten important words: Identifying the big ideas in informational text. *Journal of Content Area Reading, 2,* 7–13.

Literature Cited

Berger, M. (1995). *Germs make me sick!* New York: HarperCollins.

Wallace, M. (1999). *The Inuksuk book*. Toronto, ON: Owl.

Article 16 References

Anderson, R. C., & Freebody, P. (1985). Vocabulary knowledge. In H. Singer & R. B. Ruddell (Eds.), *Theoretical models and processes of reading* (3rd ed., pp. 343–371). Newark, DE: International Reading Association.

Armstrong, J. E., & Collier, G. E. (1990). *Science in biology: An introduction.* Prospect Heights, IL: Waveland.

Beck, I. L., McKeown, M. G., & Kucan, L. (2002). *Bringing words to life: Robust vocabulary instruction.* New York: Guilford.

Biemiller, A. (2005). Size and sequence in vocabulary development: Implications for choosing words for primary grade vocabulary instruction. In E. Hiebert & M. Kamil (Eds.), *Teaching and learning vocabulary: Bringing research to practice* (pp. 223–242). Mahwah, NJ: Erlbaum.

Biemiller, A., & Boote, C. (2006). An effective method for building vocabulary in primary grades. *Journal of Educational Psychology, 98,* 44–62.

Biemiller, A., & Slonim, N. (2001). Estimating root word vocabulary growth in normative and advantaged populations: Evidence for a common sequence of vocabulary acquisition. *Journal of Educational Psychology, 93,* 498–520.

Bock, R. D., Thissen, D., & Zimowski, M. F. (1997). IRT estimation of domain scores. *Journal of Educational Measurement, 34,* 197–211.

Bravo, M. A., & Tilson, J. L. (2006, April). *Assessment magazines: Gauging students' depth of reading comprehension and science understanding.* Paper presented at the annual meeting of the American Educational Research Association, San Francisco, CA.

Carlisle, J. F., & Katz, L. A. (2006). Effects of word and morpheme familiarity on reading of derived words. *Reading and Writing, 19,* 669–693.

Dale, E., & O'Rourke, J. (1981). *The living word vocabulary: A national vocabulary inventory.* Chicago: World Book/Childcraft International.

Davis, F. B. (1942). Two new measures of reading ability. *Journal of Educational Psychology, 33,* 365–372.

Flexner, S. B. (Ed.). (2003). *Random House Webster's unabridged dictionary* (2nd ed.). New York: Random House.

Graves, M. F. (2000). A vocabulary program to complement and bolster a middle-grade comprehension program. In B. M. Taylor, M. F. Graves, & P. van den Broek (Eds.), *Reading for meaning: Fostering comprehension in the middle grades* (pp. 116–135). New York: Teachers College Press.

Hiebert, E. H. (2005). In pursuit of an effective, efficient vocabulary curriculum for elementary students. In E. H. Hiebert & M. L. Kamil (Eds.), *Teaching and learning vocabulary: Bringing research to practice* (pp. 243–263). Mahwah, NJ: Erlbaum.

Hiebert, E. H. (2006, April). *A principled vocabulary curriculum.* Paper presented at the annual meeting of the American Educational Research Association, San Francisco, CA.

Hively, W. (1974). Introduction to domain-reference testing. *Educational Technology, 14,* 5–10.

Johnston, P. H. (1984). Assessment in reading. In P. D. Pearson, R. Barr, M. L. Kamil, & P. Mosenthal (Eds.), *Handbook of reading research* (pp. 147–184). New York: Longman.

Just, M. A., & Carpenter, P. A. (1987). *The psychology of reading and language comprehension.* Boston: Allyn & Bacon.

Kame'enui, E. J. (2002). *An analysis of reading assessment instruments for K–3.* Eugene, OR: Institute for the Development of Educational Achievement, University of Oregon.

Marzano, R. J., & Marzano, J. S. (1988). *A cluster approach to elementary vocabulary instruction.* Newark, DE: International Reading Association.

Nagy, W., Anderson, R. C., Schommer, M., Scott, J., & Stallman, A. (1989). Morphological families in the internal lexicon. *Reading Research Quarterly, 24,* 262–282.

Nagy, W. E., & Scott, J. A. (2000). Vocabulary processes. In M. L. Kamil, P. Mosenthal, P. D. Pearson, & R. Barr (Eds.), *Handbook of reading research* (Vol. 3, pp. 269–284). Mahwah, NJ: Erlbaum.

Nation, I. S. P. (1990). *Teaching and learning vocabulary.* Boston: Heinle & Heinle.

Nation, I. S. P. (2001). *Learning vocabulary in another language.* Cambridge, England: Cambridge University Press.

National Assessment Governing Board. (2005). *Reading framework for the 2009 National Assessment of Educational Progress.* Washington, DC: American Institutes for Research.

National Institute of Child Health and Human Development. (2000). *Report of the National Reading Panel. Teaching children to read: An evidence-based assessment of the scientific research literature on reading and its implications for reading instruction* (NIH Publication No. 00-4769). Washington, DC: U.S. Government Printing Office.

No Child Left Behind Act of 2001, Pub. L. No. 107-110, 115 Stat. 1425 (2002).

Pearson, P. D., & Hamm, D. N. (2005). The history of reading comprehension assessment. In S. G. Paris & S. A. Stahl (Eds.), *Children's reading comprehension and assessment* (pp. 13–70). Mahwah, NJ: Erlbaum.

Rand Reading Study Group. (2002). *Reading for understanding: Toward an R&D program in reading comprehension.* Santa Monica, CA: RAND.

Read, J. (2000). *Assessing vocabulary*. Cambridge, England: Cambridge University Press.

Resnick, D. P., & Resnick, L. (1977). The nature of literacy: An historical exploration. *Harvard Educational Review, 47*, 370–385.

Salinger, T., Kamil, M. L., Kapinus, B., & Afflerbach, P. (2005). Development of a new framework for the NAEP reading assessment. In C. M. Fairbanks, J. Worthy, B. Maloch, J. V. Hoffman, & D. L. Schallert (Eds.), *54th yearbook of the National Reading Conference* (pp. 334–349). Oak Creek, WI: National Reading Conference.

Scott, J. A., Lubliner, S., & Hiebert, E. H. (2006). Constructs underlying word selection and assessment tasks in the archival research on vocabulary instruction. In J. V. Hoffman, D. L. Schallert, C. M. Fairbanks, J. Worthy, & B. Maloch (Eds.), *55th yearbook of the National Reading Conference* (pp. 264–275). Oak Creek, WI: National Reading Conference.

Stahl, S. A., & Nagy, W. E. (2005). *Teaching word meanings*. Mahwah, NJ: Erlbaum.

Stallman, A. C., Pearson, P. D., Nagy, W. E., Anderson, R. C., & García, G. E. (1995). *Alternative approaches to vocabulary assessment* (Tech. Rep. No. 607). Urbana-Champaign, IL: Center for the Study of Reading, University of Illinois.

Whipple, G. (Ed.). (1925). *The 24th yearbook of the National Society for the Study of Education: Report of the National Committee on Reading*. Bloomington, IL: Public School Publishing.

Zeno, S., Ivens, S., Millard, R., & Duvvuri, R. (1995). *The educator's word frequency guide*. Brewster, NY: Touchstone Applied Science Associates.

Article 18 References

Anderson, R. C., & Pearson, P. D. (1984). A schema-thematic view of basic processes in reading comprehension. In P. D. Pearson, R. Barr, M. L. Kamil, & P. Mosenthal (Eds.), *Handbook of reading research* (pp. 255–291). New York: Longman.

Armbruster, B. B. (1984). The problem of "inconsiderate texts." In G. G. Duffy, L. R. Roehler, & J. Mason (Eds.), *Theoretical issues in reading comprehension* (pp. 202–217). New York: Longman.

Baker, L. (1989). Metacognition, comprehension monitoring, and the adult reader. *Educational Psychology Review, 1*, 3–38.

Baker, L. (2002). Metacognition in comprehension instruction. In C. C. Block & M. Pressley (Eds.), *Comprehension instruction: Research-based best practices* (pp. 77–95). New York: Guilford.

Baker, L., & Brown, A. L. (1984). Metacognitive skills and reading. In P. D. Pearson, R. Barr, M. Kamil, & P. Mosenthal (Eds.), *Handbook of reading research* (pp. 353–394). New York: Longman.

Blachowicz, C. L. Z., & Fisher, P. (2000). Vocabulary instruction. In M. L. Kamil, P. B. Mosenthal, P. D. Pearson, & R. Barr (Eds.), *Handbook of reading research* (Vol. 3, pp. 503–523). Mahwah, NJ: Erlbaum.

Brown, R., Pressley, M., Van Meter, P., & Schuder, T. (1996). A quasi-experimental validation of transactional strategies instruction with low-achieving second-grade students. *Journal of Educational Psychology, 88*(1), 18–37.

Butcher, K. R., & Kintsch, W. (2003). Text comprehension and discourse processing. In A. F. Healy & R. W. Proctor (Vol. Eds.) & I. B. Weiner (Ed.-in-Chief), *Handbook of psychology, Volume 4, Experimental psychology* (pp. 575–595). New York: Wiley.

Duffy, G. G. (2002). The case for direct explanation of strategies. In C. C. Block & M. Pressley (Eds.), *Comprehension instructions: Research-based best practices* (pp. 28–41). New York: Guilford.

Duke, N. (2003, March 7). *Comprehension instruction for informational text*. Presentation at the annual meeting of the Michigan Reading Association, Grand Rapids, MI.

Fletcher, C. R. (1994). Levels of representation in memory for discourse. In M. A. Gernsbacher (Ed.), *Handbook of psycholinguistics* (pp. 589–607). San Diego: Academic Press.

Fountas, I. C., & Pinnell, G. S. (1996). *Guided reading: Good first teaching for all children*. Portsmouth, NH: Heinemann.

Gaskins, I. W., Anderson, R. C., Pressley, M., Cunicelli, E. A., & Satlow, E. (1993). Six teachers' dialogue during cognitive process instruction. *The Elementary School Journal, 93*, 277–304.

Grattan, K. W. (1997). They can do it too! Book Club with first and second graders. In S. I. McMahon, T. E. Raphael, V. J. Goatley, & L. S. Pardo (Eds.), *The Book Club connection: Literacy learning and classroom talk* (pp. 267–283). New York: Teachers College Press.

Keene, E. O., & Zimmermann, S. (1997). *Mosaic of thought: Teaching comprehension in a reader's workshop*. Portsmouth, NH: Heinemann.

Kinnunen, R., Vauras, M., & Niemi, P. (1998). Comprehension monitoring in beginning readers. *Scientific Studies of Reading, 2*, 353–375.

Kucer, S. B. (2001). *Dimensions of literacy: A conceptual base of teaching reading and writing in school settings*. Mahwah, NJ: Erlbaum.

McMahon, S. I., Raphael, T. E., Goatley, V. J., & Pardo, L. S. (1997). *The Book Club connections: Literacy learning and classroom talk*. New York: Teachers College Press.

Miller, D. (2002). *Reading with meaning: Teaching comprehension in the primary grades.* Portland, ME: Stenhouse.

Morrow, L. M., & Gambrell, L. B. (2000). Literature-based reading instruction. In M. L. Kamil, P. B. Mosenthal, P. D. Pearson, & R. Barr (Eds.), *Handbook of reading research* (Vol. 3, pp. 563–586). Mahwah, NJ: Erlbaum.

Narvaez, D. (2002). Individual differences that influence reading comprehension. In C. C. Block & M. Pressley (Eds.), *Comprehension instruction: Research-based best practices* (pp. 158–175). New York: Guilford.

National Institute of Child Health and Human Development. (2000). *Report of the National Reading Panel: Teaching children to read: An evidence-based assessment of the scientific research literature on reading and its implications for reading instruction* (NIH Publication No. 00-4769). Washington, DC: U.S. Government Printing Office.

Pardo, L. S. (2002). Book Club for the twenty-first century. *Illinois Reading Council Journal, 30*(4), 14–23.

Pearson, P. D., & Gallagher, M. (1983). The instruction of reading comprehension. *Contemporary Education Psychology, 8,* 317–344.

Pressley, M. (1998). *Reading instruction that works: The case for balanced teaching.* New York: Guilford.

Pressley, M. (2000). What should comprehension instructions be the instruction of? In M. L. Kamil, P. B. Mosenthal, P. D. Pearson, & R. Barr (Eds.), *Handbook of reading research* (Vol. 3, pp. 545–561). Mahwah, NJ: Erlbaum.

Pressley, M. (2003, March 7). *Time to revolt against reading instruction as usual: What comprehension instruction could and should be.* Presentation at the annual meeting of the Michigan Reading Association, Grand Rapids, MI.

Pressley, M., & Afflerbach, P. (1995). *Verbal protocols of reading: The nature of constructively responsive reading.* Hillsdale, NJ: Erlbaum.

Pressley, M., & Hilden, K. (2002). How can children be taught to comprehend text better? In M. L. Kamil, J. B. Manning, & H. J. Walberg (Eds.), *Successful reading instruction: Research in educational productivity* (pp. 33–51). Greenwich, CT: Information Age.

Pressley, M., & McCormick, C. (1995). *Advanced educational psychology for researchers, educators, and policymakers.* New York: HarperCollins.

RAND Reading Study Group. (2002). *Reading for understanding: Toward a research and development program in reading comprehension.* Santa Monica, CA: Office of Education Research and Improvement.

Raphael, T. E., Florio-Ruane, S., & George, M. (2001). Book Club Plus: A conceptual framework to organize literacy instruction. *Language Arts, 79,* 159–168.

Rasinski, T. (2003, March 7). *Fluency: Chasing the illusive reading goal.* Presentation at the annual meeting of the Michigan Reading Association, Grand Rapids, MI.

Rosenblatt, L. R. (1978). *The reader, the text, the poem: The transactional theory of the literary work.* Carbondale: Southern Illinois University Press.

Salna, K. (2001). Book Clubs as part of a balanced curriculum. *Illinois Reading Council Journal, 29*(4), 40–47.

Schallert, D. L., & Martin, D. B. (2003). A psychological analysis of what teachers and students do in the language arts classroom. In J. Flood, D. Lapp, J. R. Squire, & J. M. Jensen (Eds.), *Handbook of research of teaching the English language arts* (pp. 21–45). Mahwah, NJ: Erlbaum.

Tompkins, G. E. (2003). *Literacy for the 21st century: Teaching reading and writing in pre-kindergarten through grade 4.* Upper Saddle River, NJ: Merrill Prentice Hall.

Trabasso, T., & Bouchard, E. (2002). Teaching readers how to comprehend text strategically. In C. C. Block & M. Pressley (Eds.), *Comprehension instruction: Research-based best practices* (pp. 176–200). New York: Guilford.

Tracey, D. H., & Morrow, L. M. (2002). Preparing young learners for successful reading comprehension. In C. C. Block & M. Pressley (Eds.), *Comprehension instruction: Research-based best practices* (pp. 319–333). New York: Guilford.

Van den Broek, P. (1994). Comprehension and memory of narrative texts: Inferences and coherences. In M. A. Gernsbacher (Ed.), *Handbook of psycholinquistics* (pp. 539–588). San Diego, CA: Academic Press.

Vygotsky, L. S. (1978). *Mind in society.* Cambridge, MA: Harvard University Press.

Waber, B. (1973). *Ira sleeps over.* Boston: Houghton Mifflin.

Waber, B. (1991). *Ira says goodbye.* Boston: Houghton Mifflin.

Article 19 References

Beck, I. L., McKeown, M. G., Worthy, J., Sandora, C. A., & Kucan, L. (1996). Questioning the author: A year-long classroom implementation to engage students with text. *The Elementary School Journal, 96,* 385–414.

Clark, K. F. (2000). *Instructional scaffolding in reading: A case study of four primary grade teachers* (Doctoral dissertation, University of Minnesota, 2000). Dissertation Abstracts International, 61, 06A.

Clark, K. S. (2004). What can I say besides "sound it out"? Coaching word recognition in beginning reading. *The Reading Teacher, 57,* 440–449.

Duffy, G. G. (2002). The case for direct explanation of strategies. In C. C. Block & M. Pressley (Eds.), *Comprehension instruction: Research-based best practices* (pp. 28–41). New York: Guilford.

Duffy, G. G., Roehler, L. R., Sivan, E., Rackliffe, G., Book, C., Meloth, M., et al. (1987). Effects of explaining the reasoning associated with using reading strategies. *Reading Research Quarterly, 22,* 347–368.

Duke, N. K., & Pearson, P. D. (2002). Effective practices for developing reading comprehension. In A. E. Farstrup & S. J. Samuels (Eds.), *What research has to say about reading instruction* (3rd ed., pp. 205–242). Newark, DE: International Reading Association.

Gaskins, I. W, Rauch, S., Gensemer, E., Cunicelli, E., O'Hara, C., Six, L., et al. (1997). Scaffolding the development of intelligence among children who are delayed in learning to read. In K. Hogan & M. Pressley (Eds.), *Scaffolding student learning: Instructional approaches and issues* (pp. 43–73). Cambridge, MA: Brookline.

Graves, M. F., & Graves, B. B. (2003). *Scaffolding reading experiences: Designs for student success.* Norwood, MA: Christopher-Gordon.

Graves, M. F., Watts, S., & Graves, B. B. (1994). *Essentials of classroom teaching: Elementary reading.* Boston: Allyn & Bacon.

Institute of Education Sciences. (2003, October 23). *Reading comprehension and reading scale-up research grants* (CEDA No. 84.305). Washington, DC: Author. Retrieved November 15, 2003, from http://ed.gov/programs/edresearch/applicant.html#read04

Mason, J. M., & Au, K. (1986). *Reading instruction for today.* Glenview, IL: Scott, Foresman.

McKeown, M. G., Beck, I. L., & Sandora, C. A. (1996). Questioning the author: An approach to developing meaningful classroom discourse. In M. F. Graves, P. van den Broek, & B. M. Taylor (Eds.), *The first R: Every child's right to read* (pp. 97–119). New York: Teachers College Press.

Palincsar, A. S. (2003). Collaborative approaches to comprehension instruction. In A. P. Sweet & C. E. Snow (Eds.), *Rethinking reading comprehension* (pp. 99–114). New York: Guilford.

Palincsar, A. S., & Brown, A. L. (1989). Instruction for self-regulated learning. In L. B. Resnick & L. E. Klopter (Eds.), *Towards the thinking curriculum: Current cognitive research* (pp. 19–39). Washington, DC: Association for Supervision and Curriculum Development.

Pearson, P. D. (1996). Reclaiming the center. In M. S. Graves, P. van den Broek, & B. M. Taylor (Eds.), *The first R: Every child's right to read* (pp. 259–274). New York: Teachers College Press.

Pearson, P. D., & Fielding, L. (1991). Comprehension instruction. In P. Barr, M. L. Kamil, P. Mosenthal, & P. D. Pearson (Eds.), *Handbook of reading research* (Vol. 2, pp. 815–860). Mahwah, NJ: Erlbaum.

Pearson, P. D., & Gallagher, M. C. (1983). The instruction of reading comprehension. *Contemporary Educational Psychology, 8,* 317–344.

Pressley, M. (2002a). Comprehension strategies instruction: A turn-of-the-century status report. In M. Pressley & C. C. Block (Eds.), *Comprehension instruction: Research-based best practices* (pp. 11–27). New York: Guilford.

Pressley, M. (2002b). *Reading instruction that works: The case for balanced teaching* (2nd ed.). New York: Guilford.

RAND Reading Study Group. (2002). *Reading for understanding: Toward an R & D program in reading comprehension.* Santa Monica, CA: RAND Education.

Rogoff, B. (1990). *Apprenticeship in thinking.* New York: Oxford University Press.

Smolkin, L. B., & Donovan, C. A. (2002). "Oh excellent, excellent question!" Developmental differences in comprehension acquisition. In C. C. Block & M. Pressley (Eds.), *Comprehension instruction: Research-based best practices* (pp. 140–157). New York: Guilford.

Stanovich, P. J., & Stanovich, K. E. (2003). *Using research and reason in education: How teachers can use scientifically based research to make curricular decisions.* Washington, DC: National Institute for Literacy.

Taylor, B. M., Pearson, P. D., Clark, K. F., & Walpole, S. (2000). Effective schools and accomplished teachers: Lessons about primary-grade reading instruction in low-income schools. *Elementary School Journal, 101,* 121–165.

Vygotsky, L. S. (1978). *Mind in society: The development of higher psychological processes.* Cambridge, MA: Harvard University Press.

Wharton-McDonald, R., Pressley, M., & Hampston, J. M. (1998). Literacy instruction in nine first-grade classrooms: Teacher characteristics and student achievement. *Elementary School Journal, 99,* 101–128.

Wood, D., Bruner, J. S., & Ross, G. (1976). The role of tutoring in problem solving. *Journal of Child Psychology and Psychiatry, 17,* 89–100.

Children's Books Cited

Clements, A. (1998). *Frindle.* New York: Aladdin.

Coles, R. (1995). *The story of Ruby Bridges.* New York: Scholastic.

Cooper, M. L. (1999). *Indian school: Teaching the white man's way.* New York: Clarion.

dePaola, T. (1978). *The popcorn book.* New York: Holiday House.

Krauss, R. (1945). *The carrot seed.* New York: Harper & Row.

Article 20 References

Block, C. C. (1993). Strategy instruction in a student-centered classroom. *Elementary School Journal, 94,* 137–153.

Bromley, K. (1998). *Language arts* (3rd ed.). Needham Heights, MA: Allyn & Bacon.

Brown, H., & Cambourne, B. (1990). *Read and retell: A strategy for the whole-language/natural learning classroom.* Portsmouth, NH: Heinemann.

Chambliss, M. (1995). Text cues and strategies successful readers use to construct the gist of lengthy written arguments. *Reading Research Quarterly, 30,* 778–807.

Daniels, H. (2002). Expository text in literature circles. *Voices From the Middle, 9,* 7–14.

Duke, N. K. (2000). 3.6 minutes per day: The scarcity of informational texts in first grade. *Reading Research Quarterly, 35,* 202–224.

Fisher, C. W., & Hiebert, E. H. (1990, April). *Shifts in reading and writing tasks: Do they extend to social studies, science, and mathematics?* Paper presented at the annual meeting of the American Educational Research Association, Boston, MA.

Gambrell, L. B., Koskinen, P. S., & Kapinus, B. A. (1991). Retelling and the reading comprehension of proficient and less-proficient readers. *Journal of Educational Research, 84,* 356–363.

Gambrell, L. B., Pfeiffer, W., & Wilson, R. (1985). The effects of retelling upon reading comprehension and recall of text information. *Journal of Educational Research, 78,* 216–220.

Goldman, S. R. (1997). Learning from text: Reflections on the past and suggestions for the future. *Discourse Processes, 23,* 357–398.

Goldman, S. R., & Rakestraw, J. A. (2000). Structural aspects of constructing meaning from text. In M. Kamil, P. B. Mosenthal, P. D. Pearson, & R. Barr (Eds.), *Handbook of reading research* (Vol. 3, pp. 311–336). Mahwah, NJ: Erlbaum.

Hoyt, L. (1999). *Revisit, reflect, retell.* Portsmouth, NH: Heinemann.

Irwin, P. A., & Mitchell, J. N. (1983). A procedure for assessing the richness of retellings. *Journal of Reading, 26,* 391–396.

Kamil, M., & Lane, D. (1997, May). *Using information text for first grade reading instruction: Theory and practice.* Paper presented at the National Reading Conference, Scottsdale, AZ.

Langer, J. A. (1985). Children's sense of genre: A study of performance on parallel reading and writing tasks. *Written Communication, 2,* 157–187.

McGee, L., & Richgels, D. (1985). Teaching expository text structure to elementary students. *The Reading Teacher, 38,* 739–748.

Meyer, B. J. F. (1985). Prose analysis: Purposes, procedures, and problems. In B. K. Britton & J. B. Black (Eds.), *Understanding expository text* (pp. 11–64). Hillsdale, NJ: Erlbaum.

Morrow, L. M. (1986). Effects of structural guidance in story retelling on children's dictation of original stories. *Journal of Reading Behavior, 28,* 135–152.

Moss, B. (2003). *Exploring the literature of fact: Children's nonfiction trade books in the elementary classroom.* New York: Guilford.

Pappas, C. C. (1991). Fostering full access to literacy by including information books. *Language Arts, 68,* 449–462.

Parsons, A. (1990). *Amazing snakes.* New York: Knopf.

Patent, D. H. (1993). *Ospreys.* New York: Clarion.

Pearson, P. D., & Duke, N. K. (2002). Comprehension instruction in the primary grades. In C.C. Block and M. Pressley (Eds.), *Comprehension instructions: Research-based best practice* (pp. 247–258). New York: Guilford.

Perl, L. (1987). *Mummies, tombs, and treasures: Secrets of ancient Egypt.* New York: Clarion.

Raphael, T. E., Kirschner, B. W., & Englert, C. S. (1988). Expository writing programs: Making connections between reading and writing. *The Reading Teacher, 41,* 790–795.

Reinking, D. (1998). Introduction: Synthesizing technological transformations of literacy in a post-typographic world. In D. Reinking, M. C. McKenna, L. D. Labbo, & R. D. Kieffer (Eds.), *Handbook of literacy and technology: Transformation in a post-typographic world* (pp. xi–xxx). Mahwah, NJ: Erlbaum.

Schmar-Dobler, E. (2003). Reading on the Internet: The link between literacy and technology. *Journal of Adolescent & Adult Literacy, 47,* 80–85.

Selsam, M. E., & Bubley, E. (1973). *How kittens grow.* New York: Scholastic.

Simon, S. (1992). *Storms*. New York: Mulberry

Tompkins, G. (2003). *Language arts: Content and teaching strategies*. Saddle River, NJ: Merrill Prentice Hall.

Wood, K. D., & Jones, J. (1998). Flexible grouping and group retellings include struggling learners in classroom communities. *Preventing School Failure, 43,* 37–38.

Article 21 References

Alvermann, D. E., Moon, J. S., & Hagood, M. C. (1999). *Popular culture in the classroom: Teaching and researching critical media literacy*. Newark, DE: IRA.

Armbruster, B. B., & Anderson, T. H. (1981). *Content area textbooks*. Reading Education Report No. 23. Urbana: University of Illinois Center for the Study of Reading.

Baker, C. C., & Luke, A. (Eds.). (1991). *Towards a critical sociology of reading pedagogy*. Philadelphia, PA: John Benjamin.

Bean, T. W. (2001, December/January). An update on reading in the content areas: Social constructionist dimensions. *Reading Online, 5*(5).

Beck, I. L., & McKeown, M. G. (1991). Conditions of vocabulary acquisition. In R. Barr, M. L. Kamil, P. Mosenthal, & P. D. Pearson (Eds.), *Handbook of reading research* (Vol. 2, pp. 789–814). White Plains, NY: Longman.

Block, C. C., Gambrell, L. B., & Pressley, M. (Eds.). (2002). *Improving comprehension instructions: Rethinking research, theory and classroom practice*. San Francisco, CA: Jossey-Bass.

Breivik, P. S., & Senn, J. A. (1994). *Information literacy: Educating children for the 21st century*. New York: Scholastic.

Cervetti, G., Pardales, M. J., & Damico, J. S. (2001, April). A tale of differences: Comparing the traditions, perspectives, and educational goals of critical reading and critical literacy. *Reading Online, 4*(9).

Cohen, P. (1995). Putting resource-based learning to work. *Education Update, 37,* 6.

Desmond, R. (1997). TV viewing, reading, and media literacy. In J. Flood, S. B. Heath, & D. Lapp (Eds.), *Handbook of research on teaching literacy through the communicative and visual arts* (pp. 23–30). New York: Simon & Schuster.

Donahue, P. L., Voelkl, K. E., Campbell, J. R., & Mazzeo, J. (1999). *National assessment of educational progress, 1998 reading report card for the nation and the states*. Washington, DC: NAEP.

Duke, N. K. (2000). 3.6 minutes per day: The scarcity of informational texts in first grade. *Reading Research Quarterly, 35,* 202–225.

Elkins, J., & Luke, A. (1999). Redefining adolescent literacies. *Journal of Adolescent & Adult Literacy, 43,* 212–215.

Gambrell, L. B., Morrow, L. M., Neuman, S. B., & Pressley, M. (Eds.). (1999). *Best practices in literacy instruction*. New York: Guilford Press.

Greenwald, E. A., Persky, H. R., Campbell, J. R., & Mazzeo, J. (1999). *NAEP 1998 writing report card for the nation and the states*. Washington, DC: U.S. Department of Education.

Harmon, J. M., Hedrick, W. B., & Fox, E. A. (2000). A content analysis of vocabulary instruction in social studies textbooks for grades 4–8. *The Elementary School Journal, 100,* 253–271.

Harmon, J. M., Hedrick, W. B., & Wood, K. D. (in press). Research on vocabulary instruction in the content areas: Implications for struggling readers. *Reading and Writing Quarterly.*

Harmon, J. M., & Wood, K. D. (2001). The TAB Book Club Approach: Talking (T) about (A) books (B) in content area classrooms. *Middle School Journal, 32*(3), 51–56.

Hiebert, E. H. (1996). Revisiting the question: What difference does reading recovery make to an age cohort? *Educational Researcher, 25*(7), 26–28.

Kagan, S. (1994). *Cooperative learning*. San Juan Capistrano, CA: Kagan Cooperative Learning.

Luke, A., & Freebody, P. (1999, August). Further notes on the four resources model. *Reading Online.*

McGinley, W. J., & Denner, P. R. (1987). A prereading/writing activity. *Journal of Reading, 31,* 248–253.

Mraz, M., Heron, A., & Wood, K. (in press). Media literacy, popular culture and the transfer of higher order thinking abilities. *Middle School Journal.*

Nagy, W. E. (1988). *Teaching vocabulary to improve reading comprehension*. Newark, DE: International Reading Associates.

Nagy, W., & Anderson, R. C. (1984). How many words are there in printed school English? *Reading Research Quarterly, 19,* 304–330.

National Reading Panel. (2000). *Teaching children to read: An evidence-based assessment of the scientific research literature on reading and its implications for reading instruction.* Washington, DC: National Institute of Child Health and Human Development.

Rhodes, L. K., & Dudley-Marling, C. (1996). *Readers and writers with a difference: A holistic approach to teaching struggling readers and writers* (2nd ed.). Portsmouth, NH: Heinemann.

Roller, C. M. (1996). *Variability not disability: Struggling readers in a workshop classroom.* Newark, DE: International Reading Association.

Routman, R. (1996). *Literacy at the crossroads: Critical talk about reading, writing and other teaching dilemmas.* Portsmouth, NH: Heinemann.

Thomas, E. (1999). Skills and strategies for media education. *Educational Leadership, 56, 5,* 50–54.

Tierney, R. J., & Shanahan, T. (1991). Research on the reading-writing relationship: Interactions, transactions and outcomes. In R. Bart, M. L. Kamil, P. Mosenthal & P. D. Pearson (Eds.) *Handbook of reading research* (Vol. 2, pp. 246–280). New York: Longman.

Vygotsky, L. S. (1978). *Mind in society.* Cambridge, MA: Harvard Press.

Weaver, D., & Alvermann, D. (2000). Critical thinking and discussion. In K. D. Wood & T. S. Dickinson (Eds.), *Promoting literacy in grades 4–9: A handbook for teachers and administrators* (pp. 344–351). Boston: Allyn & Bacon.

Well, G., Chang, G. L. M., & Maher, A. (1990). Creating classroom communities of literate thinkers. In S. Shara (Ed.), *Cooperative learning* (pp. 95–121). New York: Praeger.

Wood, K. D. (2000). *Literacy strategies across the subject areas.* Boston: Allyn & Bacon.

Wood, K. D. (2002) .Differentiating content reading and writing experiences to promote learning. In C. C. Block, L. B. Gambrell, & M. Pressley (Eds.), *Improving comprehension instruction* (pp. 155–180). San Francisco, CA: Jossey-Bass.

Wood, K. D., & Algozzine, B. (1994). *Teaching reading to high-risk learners: A unified perspective.* Boston: Allyn & Bacon.

Article 22 References

Allington, R. L. (2002, June). What I've learned about effective reading instruction from a decade of studying exemplary elementary classroom teachers. *Phi Delta Kappan, 83*(10), 740–747.

Alvermann, D. E. (1984). Second graders' strategic reading preferences while reading basal stories. *Journal of Educational Research, 77,* 184–189.

Alvermann, D. E. (Ed.). (2002). *Adolescents and literacies in a digital world.* New York: Lang.

Alvermann, D. E. (2003, November). Seeing themselves as capable and engaged readers: Adolescents and re/medial instruction. *Learning Point,* 1–19. Retrieved February 16, 2005, from http://www.ncrel.org/litweb/readers/readers.pdf

Ananda, S., & Rabinowitz, S. (2000). *The high stakes of HIGH-STAKES testing.* San Francisco, CA: WestEd. (ERIC Document Reproduction Service No. ED455254).

Armbruster, B. B., Lehrer, F., & Osborn, J. (2001). *Put reading first: The research building blocks for teaching children to read.* Washington, DC: National Institute for Literacy.

Barksdale-Ladd, M. A., & Thomas, K. F. (2000). What's at stake in high-stakes testing: Teachers and parents speak out. *Journal of Teacher Education, 51*(5), 384–397.

Bauman, J. F., Seifert-Kessell, N., & Jones, L. A. (1992). Effect of think-aloud instruction on elementary students' comprehension monitoring abilities. *Journal of Reading Behavior, 24,* 143–172.

Bauman, J. F., Seifert-Kessell, N., & Jones, L. A. (1993). *Monitoring reading comprehension by thinking aloud* (Instructional Resource No. 1). Athens, GA: University of Georgia, National Reading Research Center.

Bellack, A. (1966). *The language of the classroom.* New York: Teachers College Press.

Blanton, W. E., Greene, M. W., & Cole, M. (1999). Computer mediation for learning and play. *Journal of Adolescent & Adult Literacy, 43,* 272–278.

Blanton, W., Menendez, R., Moorman, G., & Pacifici, L. C. (2003). Effects of participation in technology rich environments on understanding written directions. *Early Education & Development, 14*(3), 313–333.

Blanton, W., & Moorman, G. (1990). The presentation of reading lessons. *Reading Research and Instruction, 29,* 35–55.

Blanton, W., Moorman, G., & Hayes, B. (1998). Effects of participation in the fifth dimension on far transfer. *Journal of Computing Research, 16,* 371–396.

Block, C., & Israel, S. (2004). The ABCs of performing highly effective thinkalouds. *The Reading Teacher, 58,* 154–167.

Borko, H., & Elliott, R. (1999). Hands-on pedagogy versus hands-off accountability: Tensions between competing commitments for exemplary math teachers in Kentucky. *Phi Delta Kappan, 80,* 394–400.

Bransford, J. D., Brown, A. L., & Cocking, R. R. (2000). *How people learn: Brain, mind, experience, and school.* Washington, DC: National Academy Press.

Bridge, C. A., Compton-Hall, M., & Cantrell, S. C. (1997). Classroom writing practices revisited: The effects of statewide reform on writing instruction. *The Elementary School Journal, 98*(2), 151–170.

Brown, A. L., Palincsar, A. S., & Purcell, L. (1986). Poor readers: Teach, don't label. In U. Neisser (Ed.), *The school achievement of minority children: New perspectives* (pp. 105–143). Mahwah, NJ: Lawrence Erlbaum.

Brown, R., Pressley, M., Van Meter, P., & Schuder, T. (1996). A quasi-experimental validation of transactional strategies instruction with low-achieving second grade readers. *Journal of Educational Psychology, 88*, 18–37.

Calkins, L., Montgomery, K., & Santman, D. (1998). *A teacher's guide to standardized reading tests: Knowledge is power.* Portsmouth, NH: Heinemann.

Campbell, J. R., Hombo, C. M., & Masseo, M. (2000, August). *NAEP 1999 trends in academic progress: Three decades of student performance.* Retrieved from http://nces.ed.gov/naep/pdf/main1999/200049pdf

Chall, J. S., Jacobs, V. A., & Baldwin, L. E. (1990). *The reading crisis: Why poor children fall behind.* Cambridge, MA: Harvard University Press.

Daniels, H. (2002). Expository text in literature circles. *Voices From the Middle, 9*(4), 7–14.

Davey, B. (1983). Think aloud—Modeling the cognitive processes of reading comprehension. *Journal of Reading, 27*, 44–47.

Dodge, B. (1995). WebQuests: A technique for Internet-based learning. *Distance Educator, 1*(2), 10–13.

Donahue, P. L., Voelkl, K. E., Campbell, J. R., & Mazzeo, J. (1999). *NAEP 1998 reading report card for the nation and the states* (NCES 1999-500). Retrieved May, 2005, from http://nces.ed.gov/naep

Duke, N. K. (2000). 3.6 Minutes per day: The scarcity of informational texts in first grade. *Reading Research Quarterly, 35*(2), 202–225.

Duke, N. K., & Pearson, P. D. (2002). Effective practices for developing reading comprehension. In A. E. Farstrup & S. J. Samuels (Eds.), *What research has to say about reading instruction* (3rd ed., pp. 205–242). Newark, DE: International Reading Association.

Dupuis, M. M., Askov, E. N., & Lee, J. W. (1979). Changing attitudes toward content area reading: The content area reading project. *Journal of Educational Research, 73*(2), 65–74.

Durkin, D. (1978–79). What classroom observations reveal about reading comprehension instruction. *Reading Research Quarterly, 14*, 481–533.

Fischer, K., & Farrar, M. J. (1987). Generalizations about generalization: How a theory of skill development explains both generality and specificity. *International Journal of Psychology, 22*, 643–677.

Fischer, K. W., & Granott, N. (1995). Beyond one-dimensional change: Parallel, concurrent, socially distributed processes in learning and development. *Human Development, 38*, 302–314.

Gall, M. (1970). The use of questions in teaching. *Review of Educational Research, 40*, 707–720.

Gee, J. P. (2003). *What video games have to teach us about literacy and learning.* New York: Palgrave MacMillan.

Gordon, S. P., & Reese, M. (1997). High stakes testing: Worth the price? *Journal of School Leadership, 7*, 345–368.

Griffin, P., & Cole, M. (1987). New technologies, basic skills, and the underside of education: What's to be done? In J. Langer (Ed.), *Language, literacy, and culture: Issues of society and schooling* (pp. 199–231). Norwood, NJ: Ablex.

Guastello, E. F., Beasley, T. M., & Sinatra, R. C. (2000). Concept mapping effects on science content comprehension of low-achieving inner-city seventh graders. *Remedial & Special Education, 21*(6), 356–364.

Haney, W. (2000). The myth of the Texas miracle in education. *Education Policy Analysis Archives, 8*(41). Retrieved March 14, 2003, from http://epaa.asu.edu/epaa/v8n41/

Hill, B. C., Noe, K. L. S., & King, J. A. (2003). *Literature circles in the middle school: One teacher's journey.* Norwood, MA: Christopher-Gordon Publishers.

Hoetker, J., & Ahlbrand, W. P., Jr. (1969). The persistence of the recitation. *American Education Research Journal, 6*, 145–167.

Hoffman, J. V., Assaf, L., Pennington, J., & Paris, S. G. (2001). High stakes testing in reading: Today in Texas, tomorrow? *The Reading Teacher, 54*(5), 482–492.

International Reading Association. (1999). *High-stakes assessment in reading: A position statement of the International Reading Association.* Newark, DE: Author.

Irvin, J. (1990). *Reading in the middle grades.* Boston, MA: Allyn & Bacon.

Johnston, P. (1998). The consequences of the use of standardized tests. In Murphy, S., Shannon, P., Johnston, P., & Hansen, J. (Eds.), *Fragile evidence: A critique of reading assessment* (pp. 89–101). Mahwah, NJ: Lawrence Erlbaum.

Jones, B. D., & Johnston, A. F. (2002, April). *The effects of high-stakes testing on instructional practices.* Paper presented at the 2002 annual meeting of the American Educational Research Association, New Orleans, LA.

Kamil, M. L. (2003). *Adolescents and literacy: Reading for the 21st century.* New York: Alliance for Excellent Education.

Kohn, A. (2000). *The case against standardized testing: Raising the scores, ruining the schools.* Portsmouth, NH: Heinemann.

Langer, J. A. (1999). *Beating the odds: Teaching middle and high school students to read and write well* (Research Rep. No. 12014). Albany, NY: National Research Center on English Learning & Achievement.

Lankshear, C., & Knobel, M. (2003). *New literacies: Changing knowledge and classroom teaching.* Philadelphia: Open University Press.

Leontiev, A. N. (1978). *Activity, consciousness, personality.* Englewood Cliffs, NJ: Prentice-Hall.

Leu, D. J., Jr. (2002). The new literacies: Research on reading instruction with the Internet and other digital technologies. In J. Samuels & A. E. Farstrup (Eds.), *What research has to say about reading instruction* (pp. 310–336). Newark, DE: International Reading Association.

Luke, A., & Elkins, J. (1998). Reinventing literacy in "new times." *Journal of Adolescent & Adult Literacy, 42*(1), 4–7.

Luria, A. R. (1979). *The making of mind.* Cambridge, MA: Harvard University Press.

Luria, A. R. (1985). *Cognitive development: Its cultural and historical foundations.* Cambridge, MA: Harvard University Press.

McColskey, W., & McMunn, N. (2000). Strategies for dealing with high-stakes state tests. *Phi Delta Kappan, 82*(2), 115–120.

Mehan, H. (1979). *Learning lessons: Social organization in the classroom.* Cambridge, MA: Harvard University Press.

Montali, J., & Lewandowski, L. (1996). Bimodal reading: Benefits of a talking computer for average and less skilled readers. *Journal of Learning Disabilities, 29*(3), 271–279.

Moorman, G., & Blanton, W. (1990). The Information Text Reading Activity (ITRA): Engaging students in meaningful learning. *Journal of Reading, 34*, 174–193.

Mullis, I. V., Campbell, J. R., & Farstrup, A. E. (1993). *Reading report card for the nation and the states* (NCES 93269). Washington, DC: U.S. Department of Education, Office of Educational Research and Improvement.

Murphy, P. K., & Edwards, M. E. (2005, April). *What the studies tell us: A meta-analysis of discussion approaches.* Paper presented at the annual meeting of the American Educational Research Association, Montreal, Canada.

Myers, M. (1996). *Changing our minds: Negotiating English and literacy.* Urbana, IL: National Council of Teachers of English.

National Assessment of Educational Progress in Reading Report Card. (2003). http://nces.ed.gov/nationalreportcard/naepdata/search.asp

Newkirk, T. (1989). *Critical thinking and writing: Reclaiming the essay* (Monograph No. 3). Bloomington, IN: ERIC Clearinghouse on Reading and Communication Skills. (ERIC Document Reproduction Service No. ED 309 457).

New London Group. (2000). A pedagogy of multiliteracies: Designing social futures. In B. Cope & M. Kalantzis (Eds.), *Multiliteracies: Literacy learning and the design of social futures* (pp. 9–38). New York: Routledge.

Nist, S. L., & Kirby, K. (1986). Teaching comprehension and study strategies through modeling and thinking aloud. *Reading Research and Instruction, 25*, 256–264.

Noll, E. (1994). Social issues and literature circles with adolescents. *Journal of Reading, 38*(2), 88–93.

Nystrand, M. (with Gamoran, A., Kachur, R., & Prendergast, C.). (1997). *Opening dialogue: Understanding the dynamics of language and learning in the English classroom.* New York: Teachers College Press.

O'Brien, D. G., & Bauer, E. (2005). New literacies and the institution of old learning. *Reading Research Quarterly, 40*, 120–131.

Palincsar, A. S., & Brown, A. L. (1984). Reciprocal teaching of comprehension-fostering and comprehension-monitoring activities. *Cognition and Instruction, 2*, 117–175.

Palincsar, A. S., & Klenk, L. (1992). Fostering literacy learning in supportive contexts. *Journal of Learning Disabilities, 25*(4), 211–225, 229.

Pappas, C. C. (1993). Is narrative primary? Some insights from kindergarteners' pretend readings of stories and information books. *Journal of Reading Behavior, 25*(1), 97–129.

Passman, R. (2001). Experiences with student-centered teaching and learning in high-stakes assessment environments. *Education, 122*(1), 189–211.

Pearson, P., & Gallagher, M. (1983). The instruction of reading comprehension. *Contemporary Educational Psychology, 8*, 317–344.

Perkins, D. (1992). *Smart schools.* New York: The Free Press.

Pressley, M. (2002). *Reading instruction that works: The case for balanced teaching* (2nd ed.). New York: Guilford.

Rand Reading Study Group. (2002). *Reading for understanding: Toward an R&D program in reading comprehension.* Santa Monica, CA: Rand.

Raphael, T. (1986). Teaching question–answer relationships. *Reading Teacher, 39*, 516–520.

Raphael, T. E., & McMahon, S. I. (1994). Book club: An alternative framework for reading instruction. *The Reading Teacher, 48*, 102–117.

Readence, J. E., Bean, T. W., & Baldwin, R. S. (1998). *Content area literacy: An integrated approach* (6th ed.). Dubuque, IA: Kendall/Hunt.

Rosenshine, B., & Meister, C. (1994). Reciprocal teaching: A review of the research. *Review of Educational Research, 64*(4), 479–530.

Rush, L. S. (2002). Taking a broad view of literacy: Lessons from the Appalachian Trail thru-hiking community. Retrieved April 22, 2004, from http://www.readingonline.org/newliteracies/lit

Schoenbach, R., Greenleaf, C., Cziko, C., & Hurwitz, L. (1999). *Reading for understanding*. San Francisco: Jossey-Bass.

Short, K., & Kauffman, G. (1995). So what do I do? The role of the teacher in literature circles. In N. Roser & M. Martinez (Eds.), *Book talk and beyond: Children and teachers respond to literature* (pp. 140–149). Newark, DE: International Reading Association.

Snow, C. E., & Biancarosa, G. (2003). *Adolescent literacy and the achievement gap: What do we know and where do we go from here?* New York: Carnegie Corporation.

Soter, A. O., & Rudge, L. (2005, April). *What the discussions tell us: Talk and indicators of high-level comprehension.* Paper presented at the annual meeting of the American Educational Research Association, Montreal, Canada.

Stauffer, R. G. (1969a). *Teaching reading as a thinking process*. New York: Harper & Row.

Stauffer, R. G. (1969b). *Directing reading maturity as a cognitive process*. New York: Harper & Row.

Stevens, R. (1912). *The question as a measure of efficiency in instruction: A critical study of classroom practice*. New York: Columbia University.

Vygotsky, L. S. (1978). *Mind in society*. Cambridge, MA: Harvard University Press.

Wade, S. E., & Moje, E. B. (2000). The role of text in classroom learning. In M. L. Kamil, P. B. Mosenthal, P. D. Pearson, & R. Barr (Eds.), *Handbook of reading research, Vol. 3* (pp. 609–627). Mahwah, NJ: Erlbaum.

Walker, B. (2005). Think aloud: Struggling readers often require more than a model. *The Reading Teacher, 58*, 688–692.

Wedman, J. M., & Robinson, R. (1988). Effects of an extended in-service program on secondary teachers' use of content reading instructional strategies. *Journal of Research and Development in Education, 21*(3), 65–70.

Wenglinsky, H. (2000). *How teaching matters: Bringing the classroom back into discussions of teacher quality*. Princeton, NJ: Educational Testing Service.

Wenglinsky, H. (2004). Facts or thinking skills? What NAEP results say. *Educational Leadership, 62*(1), 32–35.

Wertsch, J. V. (1998). *Mind in action*. New York: Oxford University Press.

Wideen, M. F., O'Shea, T., Pye, I., & Ivany, G. (1997). High-stakes testing and the teaching of science. *Canadian Journal of Education, 22*(4), 428–444.

Wilkinson, I. A. G., & Reninger, K. B. (2005, April). *What the approaches look like: A conceptual framework for discussions.* Paper presented at the annual meeting of the American Educational Research Association, Montreal, Canada.

Wood, K., & Muth, D. (1991). The case for improved instruction in the middle grades. *Journal of Reading, 35*(2), 84–90.

Yarbrough, T. L. (1999). *Teacher perceptions of the North Carolina ABC Program and the relationship to classroom practice.* Unpublished doctoral dissertation, University of North Carolina at Chapel Hill.

Article 23 References

Alliance for Excellent Education. (2003). *Progress report on American high schools*. Washington, DC: Author.

Allington, R. L. (2001). *What really matters for struggling readers: Designing research-based programs*. New York: Longman.

Alvermann, D. E. (2001). Reading adolescents' reading identities: Looking back to see ahead. *Journal of Adolescent & Adult Literacy, 44*, 676–690.

Alvermann, D. E. (2002). Effective literacy instruction for adolescents. *Journal of Literacy Research, 34*, 189–208.

Alvermann, D. E., & Rush, L. S. (2004). Literacy intervention programs at the middle and high school levels. In T. L. Jetton & J. A. Dole (Eds.), *Adolescent literacy research and practice* (pp. 210–227). New York: Guilford.

Biggers, D. (2001). The argument against Accelerated Reader. *Journal of Adolescent & Adult Literacy, 45*, 72–75.

Brozo, W. G., & Hargis, C. H. (2003). Taking seriously the idea of reform: One high school's efforts to make reading more responsive to all students. *Journal of Adolescent & Adult Literacy, 47*, 14–23.

Duffy, G. G. (2003). *Explaining reading*. New York: Guilford.

Duffy, G. G., & Hoffman, J. V. (1999). In pursuit of an illusion: The flawed search for a perfect method. *The Reading Teacher, 53*, 10–16.

Dutro, S., & Moran, C. (2003). Rethinking English language instruction: An architectural approach. In G. G. Garcia (Ed.), *English learners: Reaching the highest level of English literacy* (pp. 227–258). Newark, DE: International Reading Association.

Fisher, D. (2001). "We're moving on up": Creating a school-wide literacy effort in an urban high school. *Journal of Adolescent & Adult Literacy, 45*, 92–101.

Fisher, D. (2004). Setting the "opportunity to read" standard: Resuscitating the SSR program in an urban high school. *Journal of Adolescent & Adult Literacy, 48*, 138–150.

Fisher, D., & Frey, N. (2004). *Improving adolescent literacy: Strategies at work*. Englewood Cliffs, NJ: Merrill.

Grigg, W. S., Daane, M. C., Jin, Y., & Campbell, J. R. (2003). *The nation's report card 2002*. Washington, DC: National Center for Educational Statistics.

Guthrie, J. T. (1996). Educational contexts for engagement in literacy. *The Reading Teacher, 49*, 432–445.

Ivey, G. (1999). A multicase study in the middle school: Complexities among young adolescent readers. *Reading Research Quarterly, 34*, 172–192.

Ivey, G. (2004). Content counts with urban struggling readers. In D. Lapp, C. C. Block, E. J. Cooper, J. Flood, N. Roser, & J. V. Tinajero (Eds.), *Teaching all the children: Strategies for developing literacy in an urban setting* (pp. 316–326). New York: Guilford.

Ivey, G., & Baker, M.I. (2004). Phonics instruction for older readers? Just say no. *Educational Leadership, 61*, 35–39.

Ivey, G., & Broaddus, K. (2001). "Just plain reading": A survey of what makes students want to read in middle school classrooms. *Reading Research Quarterly, 36*, 350–371.

Ivey, G., & Fisher, D. (2006). *Creating literacy-rich schools for adolescents*. Alexandria, VA: Association for Supervision and Curriculum Development.

Johnston, P. H. (1987). Teachers as evaluation experts. *The Reading Teacher, 40*, 744–748.

Johnston, P. H., & Allington, R. L. (1991). Remediation. In R. Barr, M. L. Kamil, P. Mosenthal, & P. D. Pearson (Eds.), *Handbook of reading research* (Vol. 2, pp. 984–1012). New York: Longman.

Knobel, M. (2001). "I'm not a pencil man": How one student challenges our notions of literacy "failure" in school. *Journal of Adolescent & Adult Literacy, 44*, 404–414.

Kos, R. (1991). Persistence of reading disabilities: The voices of four middle school students. *American Educational Research Journal, 28*, 785–895.

Krull, K. (1993). *Lives of the musicians: Good times, bad times (and what the neighbors thought)*. San Diego, CA: Harcourt.

Krull, K. (1995). *Lives of the artists: Masterpieces, messes (and what the neighbors thought)*. San Diego, CA: Harcourt.

Mallette, M. H., Henk, W. A., & Melnick, S. A. (2004). The influence of Accelerated Reader on the affective literacy orientations of intermediate grade students. *Journal of Literacy Research, 36*, 73–84.

McCormick, S. (1994). A nonreader becomes a reader: A case study of literacy acquisition by a severely disabled reader. *Reading Research Quarterly, 29*, 157–176.

Morris, D., Ervin, C., & Conrad, K. (1996). A case study of middle school reading disability. *The Reading Teacher, 49*, 368–377.

Moss, L. (1995). *Zin! Zin! Zin! A violin*. New York: Simon & Schuster.

Ogle, D. (1986). K–W–L: A teaching model that develops active reading of expository text. *The Reading Teacher, 39*, 564–570.

Pavonetti, L. M., Brimmer, K. M., & Cipielewski, J. F. (2002/2003). Accelerated Reader: What are the lasting effects on the reading habits of middle school students exposed to Accelerated Reader in elementary grades? *Journal of Adolescent & Adult Literacy, 46*, 300–311.

Rubenstein-Avila, E. (2003/2004). Conversing with Miguel: An adolescent English language learner struggling with later literacy development. *Journal of Adolescent & Adult Literacy, 47*, 290–301.

Ryan, P. M. (2002). *When Marian sang*. New York: Scholastic.

Santa, C., & Havens, L. (1995). *Creating independence through student-owned strategies: Project CRISS*. Dubuque, IA: Kendall/Hunt.

Seuss, Dr. (1987). *I am not going to get up today!* New York: Random House.

Snow, C. E., & Biancarosa, G. (2003). *Adolescent literacy and the achievement gap: What do we know and where do we go from here?* New York: Carnegie Corporation of New York.

Weitzman, J. P., & Glasser, R. P. (1998). *You can't take a balloon into the Metropolitan Museum*. New York: Dial Books for Young Readers.

Winter, J. (1998). *My name is Georgia*. San Diego, CA: Harcourt.

Winter, J. (2002). *Frida*. New York: Arthur A. Levine Books.

Worthy, J., & Broaddus, K. (2001/2002). Fluency beyond the primary grades: From group performance to silent, independent reading. *The Reading Teacher, 55*, 334–343.

Worthy, J., Broaddus, K., & Ivey, G. (2001). *Pathways to independence: Reading, writing, and learning in grades 3–8*. New York: Guilford.

Worthy, J., Moorman, M., & Turner, M. (1999). What Johnny likes to read is hard to find in school. *Reading Research Quarterly, 34*, 12–27.

Article 24 References

Aston-Warner, S. (1963). *Teacher.* New York: Doubleday.

Atwell, N. (1987). *In the middle: Writing, reading and learning with adolescents.* Portsmouth, NH: Boynton/Cook.

Bode, B. A. (1989). Dialogue journal writing. *The Reading Teacher, 42,* 568–571.

Button, K., Johnson, M. J., & Furgerson, P. (1996). Interactive writing in a primary classroom. *The Reading Teacher, 49,* 446–454.

Calkins, L. M. (1986). *The art of teaching writing.* Portsmouth, NH: Heineman.

Cisneros, S. (1994). *Hairs/Pelitos.* New York: Alfred A. Knopf.

Clay, M. M. (1975). *What did I write?* Portsmouth, NH: Heinemann.

Duke, N. K., & Pearson, P. D. (2002). Effective practices for developing reading comprehension. In A. Farstrup & J. Samuels (Eds.), *What research has to say about reading instruction* (3rd ed., pp. 205–242). Newark, DE: International Reading Association.

Fearn, L., & Farnan, N. (2001). *Interactions: Teaching writing and the language arts.* Boston: Houghton Mifflin Company.

Fisher, D., & Frey, N. (2003). Writing instruction for struggling adolescent readers: A gradual release model. *Journal of Adolescent & Adult Literacy, 48,* 396–405.

Fountas, I. C., & Pinnell, G. S. (1996). *Guided reading: Good first teaching for all children.* Portsmouth, NH: Heinemann.

Giacobbe, M. E. (1981). Who says children can't write the first week? In R. D. Walshe (Ed.), *Donald Graves in Australia.* Rozelle, New South Wales: Primary English Teaching Association.

Graves, D. H. (1994). *A fresh look at writing.* Portsmouth, NH: Heinemann.

McKenzie, M. G. (1985). Shared writing: Apprenticeships in writing. *Language Matters, 1,* 1–5.

National Center for Educational Statistics. (2002). *NAEP reports: The nation's report card.* Retrieved February 4, 2005, from http://nces.ed.gov/nationsreportcard

Pearson, P. D., & Gallagher, M. C. (1983). The instruction of reading comprehension. *Contemporary Educational Psychology, 8,* 317–344.

Pinnell, G. S., & McCarrier, A. (1994). Interactive writing: A transition tool for assisting children in learning to read and write. In E. Heibert & B. Taylor (Eds.), *Getting reading right from the start: Effective early literacy interventions* (pp. 149–170). Boston, MA: Allyn & Bacon.

Roser, N. L., & Bomer, K. (2005). Writing in primary classrooms: A teacher's story. In R. Indrisano & J. R. Paratore (Eds.), *Learning to write, writing to learn: Theory and research in practice.* Newark, DE: International Reading Association.

Shaw, C. G. (1947). *It looked like spilt milk.* New York: HarperCollins.

Stauffer, R. (1970). *The language experience approach to the teaching of reading.* New York: Harper & Row.

Vygotsky, L. S. (1978). *Mind in society: The development of higher psychological processes.* Cambridge, MA: Harvard University Press.

Werderich, D. E. (2002). Individualized responses: Using journal letters as a vehicle for differentiated reading instruction. *Journal of Adolescent & Adult Literacy, 45,* 746–754.

Wertsch, J. V. (1991). *Voices of the mind: A sociocultural approach to mediated action.* Cambridge, MA: Harvard University Press.

Article 25 References

Atwell, N. (1987). *In the middle: Writing, reading, and learning with adolescents.* Portsmouth, NH: Heinemann.

Blau, S. (2003). *The literature workshop: Teaching texts and their readers.* Portsmouth, NH: Heinemann.

Bratcher, S., & Stroble, E. J. (1994). Determining the progression from comfort to confidence: A longitudinal evaluation of a National Writing Project site based on multiple data sources. *Research in the Teaching of English, 28,* 66–88.

Britton, J. N. (1975). *The development of writing abilities.* London: Macmillan.

Burke, J. (2003). *The English teacher's companion* (2nd ed.). Portsmouth, NH: Heinemann.

Christenbury, L. (2000). *Making the journey: Being and becoming a teacher of English language arts* (2nd ed.). Portsmouth, NH: Heinemann.

Cochran-Smith, M., & Lytle, S. (1999). Relationships of knowledge and practice: Teacher learning in communities. *Review of Research in Education, 24,* 249–305.

Cochran-Smith, M., & Lytle, S. (2001). Beyond certainty: Taking an inquiry stance on practice. In A. Lieberman & L. Miller (Eds.), *Teachers caught in the action: Professional development that matters.* New York: Teachers College Press.

Emig, J. (1971). *The composing processes of twelfth graders. NCTE research report #13.* Urbana, IL: National Council of Teachers of English.

Faigley, L., & Witte, S. (1981). Analyzing revision. *College Composition and Communication, 32,* 400–414.

Flower, L., & Hayes, J. (1980). Identifying the organization of the writing processes. In L. W. Gregg & E. R. Steinberg (Eds.), *Cognitive processes in writing.* Hillsdale, NJ: Lawrence Erlbaum.

Gomez, M. L. (1990). The National Writing Project: Staff development in the teaching of composition. In G. E. Hawisher, A. O. Soter, & A. C. Purves (Eds.), *On literacy and its teaching: Issues in English education* (pp. 68–83). Albany: SUNY Press.

Guskey, T. R. (2000). *Evaluating professional development.* Thousand Oaks, CA: Corwin.

Hairston, M. (1982). The winds of change: Thomas Kuhn and the revolution in the teaching of writing. *College Composition and Communication, 33,* 76–88.

Kirkpatrick, D. L. (1998). *Evaluating training programs: The four levels* (2nd ed.). San Francisco: Berrett-Koehler.

Kuhn, T. S. (1962). *The structure of scientific revolutions.* Chicago: University of Chicago Press.

Lieberman, A., & Wood, D. R. (2002). The National Writing Project. *Educational Leadership, 59*(6), 40–43.

Lieberman, A., & Wood, D. R. (2003). *Inside the National Writing Project. Connecting network learning and classroom teaching.* New York: Teachers College Press.

National Writing Project. (2006a). *Local site research initiative report, Cohort II.* Available at http://www.writingproject.org/cs/nwpp/print/nwpn/21. Berkeley, CA: National Writing Project.

National Writing Project. (2006b, May 14). *What is the National Writing Project?* Retrieved May 14, 2006, from http://www.writingproject.org/About/nwpitour1.html

Perl, S. (1979). The composing processes of unskilled college writers. *Research in the Teaching of English, 13,* 317–336.

Pianko, S. (1979). A description of the composing processes of college freshman writers. *Research in the Teaching of English, 13,* 5–22.

Pritchard, R. J., & Honeycutt, R. L. (2006). The process approach to teaching writing: Examining its effectiveness. In C. A. MacArthur, S. Graham, & J. Fitzgerald (Eds.), *Handbook of research on writing* (pp. 275–290). New York: Guilford.

Pritchard, R. J., & Marshall, J. C. (1994). Evaluation of a tiered model for staff development in writing. *Research in the teaching of English, 28,* 259–285.

Shaughnessy, M. (1977). *Errors and expectations.* New York and London: Oxford University Press.

Sommers, N. (1980). Revision strategies of student writers and experienced adult writers. *College Composition and Communication, 31,* 378–388.

Wood, D. R., & Lieberman, A. (2000). Teachers as authors: The National Writing Project's approach to professional development. *International Journal of Leadership in Education, 3,* 255–273.

Article 27 References

Cho, K.-S., and H. Kim. (2004). 'Recreational Reading in English as a Foreign Language in Korea: Positive Effects of a 16-Week Program', *Knowledge Quest* 32(4): 36–38.

Cho, K.-S., and H.-J. Kim. (2005). 'Using the Newspaper in an English as a Foreign Language Class', *Knowledge Quest* 34(4): 47–49.

Constantino, R., S.-Y. Lee, K.-S. Cho and S. Krashen. (1997). 'Free Voluntary Reading as a Predictor of TOEFL Scores', *Applied Language Learning* 8: 111–18.

DeBell, M., and C. Chapman. (2006). *Computer and Internet Use by Students in 2003* (Washington: US Department of Education NCES 2006-065).

De Haan, J., and F. Huysmans. (2004). 'IT/Media Use and Psychological Development among Dutch Youth', *IT&Society* 1(7): 44–58.

Fallows, D. (2006). Pew Internet Project Data Memo, February, 2006.

Galloway, A. (1993). *Communicative Language Teaching: An Introduction and Sample Activities.* http://www.cal.org/resources/digest/gallow01.html

Gradman, H., and E. Hanania. (1991). 'Language Learning Background Factors and ESL Proficiency', *Modern Language Journal* 75: 39–51.

Hastings, A. (1997). 'Focal Skills: A Brief Sketch', in N. Bochorishvili, L. Gorodetskaya, M. Greene and E. Carmack (eds.), *TESOL Russia 1996 Conference Proceedings: Global Community: EFL in an Evolving World* (Moscow State University, Faculty of Foreign Languages): 34–37.

Horrigan, J. (2006). *Home Broadband Adoption* (Pew Report May 28, 2006).

Jackson, L., A. von Eye, F. Biocca, G. Barbatsis, Y. Zhao and H. Fitzgerald. (2005). 'How Low-income Children Use the Internet at Home', *Journal of Interactive Learning Research* 16(3): 259–72.

———. (2006). 'Does Home Internet Use Influence the Academic Performance of Low-income Children?', *Developmental Psychology* 42(3): 429–33.

Kohn, A. (1999). *Punished by Rewards* (New York: Houghton Mifflin).

Krashen, S. (1981). *Second Language Acquisition and Second Language Learning* (New York: Prentice Hall). (Available at http://www.sdkrashen.com)

———. (1991). 'Sheltered Subject Matter Teaching', *Cross Currents* 18: 183–88.

———. (1999). *Three Arguments against Whole Language and Why They Are Wrong* (Portsmouth: Heinemann).

———. (2000). 'What Does It Take to Acquire Language?', *ESL Magazine* 3(3): 22–23.

———. (2003a). *Explorations in Language Acquisition and Use* (Portsmouth: Heinemann).

———. (2003b). 'The (Lack of) Experimental Evidence Supporting the Use of Accelerated Reader', *Journal of Children's Literature* 29(2): 9, 16–30.

———. (2004). *The Power of Reading* (Portsmouth, NH: Heinemann, 2nd edn).

———. (2005). 'Accelerated Reader: Evidence Still Lacking', *Knowledge Quest* 33(3): 48–49.

Lee, S.-Y. (2005). 'Facilitating and Inhibiting Factors in English as a Foreign Language Writing Performance: A Model Test with Structural Equation Modeling', *Language Learning* 55(2): 335–74.

———. (2007). 'Revelations from Three Consecutive Studies on Extensive Reading', *RELC Journal* 38(2):150–70.

Liu, C.-C., W.-W. Day, S.-W. Sun and G. Wang. (2002). 'User Behavior and "Globalness" of the Internet: From a Taiwan Users' Perspective', *Journal of Computer-Mediated Communication* 7(2). http://jcmc.indiana.edu/vol7/issue2/taiwan.html

Liu, C.-K. (2007). 'A Reading Program that Keeps Winning', in *Selected Papers from the Sixteenth International Symposium on English Teaching* (Taipei: Crane Publishing Company): 634–36.

Mason, B., and S. Krashen. (1997). 'Extensive Reading in English as a Foreign Language', *System* 25: 91–102.

Renandya, W. (2007). 'The Power of Extensive Reading', *RELC Journal* 38(2): 133–49.

Sims, J. (1996). 'A New Perspective: Extensive Reading for Pleasure', in *Proceedings of the Fifth International Symposium on English Teaching* (Taipei: Crane Publishing Company): 137–44.

Smith, K. (2006). 'A Comparison of "Pure" Extensive Reading with Intensive Reading and Extensive Reading with Supplementary Activities', *International Journal of Foreign Language Teaching* 2(2): 12–15.

———. (2007). 'The Effect of Adding SSR to Regular Instruction', in *Selected Papers from the Sixteenth International Symposium on English Teaching* (Taipei: Crane Publishing Company): 625–29.

Stokes, J., S. Krashen and J. Kartchner. (1998). 'Factors in the Acquisition of the Present Subjunctive in Spanish: The Role of Reading and Study', *ITL: Review of Applied Linguistics* 121–122: 19–25.

Swain, M. (1985). 'Communicative Competence: Some Roles of Comprehensible Input and Comprehensible Output in its Development', in S. Gass and C. Madden (eds.), *Input in Second Language Acquisition* (New York: Newbury House): 235–56.

Truscott, J. (1996). 'The Case against Grammar Correction in L2 Writing Classes', *Language Learning* 46(2): 327–69.

———. (1998). 'Noticing in Second Language Acquisition: A Critical Review', *Second Language Research* 14(2): 103–35.

Witton-Davies, G. (2006). 'What Does It Take to Acquire English?', *International Journal of Foreign Language Teaching* 2(2): 2–8.

Zhu, J., and He, Z. (2002). 'Diffusion, Use and Impact of the Internet in Hong Kong: A Chain Process Model', *Journal of Computer-Mediated Communication* (January) 7(2) at http://jcmc.indiana.edu/vol7/issue2/hongkong.html

Article 28 Endnotes

Throughout the article, individual studies discussed but not cited are included in either the NLP report or the CREDE report and often in both.

1. Most of the preceding list is derived from content standards for second grade adopted by the California State Board of Education, available at www.cde.ca.gov. Reading fluency figure from Behavioral Research and Teaching 2005. *Oral Reading Fluency 90 Years of Assessment* (BRT Technical Report No. 33), Eugene, OR: Author (available at www.jhasbrouck.com). Vocabulary from Lehr, F., Osborn, J., and Hiebert, E. (n.d.). *A Focus on Vocabulary*. Honolulu: Pacific Resources for Education and Learning; and from Nagy, W. E. and Herman, P. A. 1987. Breadth and depth of vocabulary knowledge: Implications for acquisition and instruction. In *The Nature of Vocabulary Acquisition*, eds. McKeown, M. and Curtis, M., 19–35. Hillsdale, NJ: Lawrence Erlbaum Associates.

2. Scarcella, R. 2003. *Academic English: A Conceptual Framework* (Technical report 2003-1). Santa Barbara, CA: Linguistic Minority Research Institute (available at http://lmri.ucsb.edu).

3. NCELA 2006. *How Has the English Language Learner Population Changed in Recent Years?* Washington, DC: NCEI; available online at www.ncela.gwu.edu/expert/faq/08 leps.html.

4. NCELA retrieved April 2008. *ELL Demographics by State.* Washington, DC: NCELA. Available online at www.ncela.gwu.edu/stats/3_bystate.htm

5. Capps, R., Fix, M., Murray, J., Passel, J. S., and Herwantoro, S. 2005. *The New Demography of America's Schools: Immigration and the No Child Left Behind Act.* Washington, DC: The Urban Institute.

6. Capps, R., Fix, M., Murray, J., Passel, J. S., and Herwantoro, S. 2005. *The New Demography of America's Schools: Immigration and the No Child Left Behind Act.* Washington, DC: The Urban Institute. Also: Larsen, L.J. 2004. The foreign-born population in the United States: 2003. *Current Population Reports,* P20-551. Washington, DC: U.S. Census Bureau.

7. Larsen, L. J. 2004. The foreign-born population in the United States: 2003. *Current Population Report,* P20-551. Washington, DC: U.S. Census Bureau.

8. U.S. Census Bureau, retrieved April 2008. *Fact Sheet for a Race, Ethnic, or Ancestry Group.* Washington, DC: U.S. Census Bureau; available online at http://factfinder.census.gov/servlet/SAFFFactsCharlteration?_submenuld=factsheet_ 2&_sse=on.

9. U.S. Department of Education 2005. *Biennial Evaluation Report to Congress on the Implementation of the State Formula Grant Program, 2002–2004: English Language Acquisition, Language Enhancement and Academic Achievement Act (ESEA, Title III, Part A).* Washington, DC: U.S. Department of Education. Also: Zehler, A. M., Fleischman, H. L., Hopstock, P. J., Stephenson, T. G., Pendzick, M. L., and Sapru, S. 2003. *Descriptive Study of Services to LEP Students and LEP Students with Disabilities. Volume I: Research Report.* Arlington, VA: Development Associates, Inc.

10. Zehler, A. M., Fleischman, H. L., Hopstock, P. J., Stephenson, T. G., Pendzick, M. L., and Sapru, S. 2003. *Descriptive Study of Services to LEP Students and LEP Students with Disabilities. Volume I: Research Report.* Arlington, VA: Development Associates, Inc.

11. Ibid.

12. U.S. Department of Education 2008. *National Assessment of Educational Progress in Reading and Mathematics, 2007.* Washington, DC: U.S. Department of Education.

13. Natriello, G., McDill, E., and Pallas, A. 1990. *Schooling Disadvantaged Students: Racing Against Catastrophe.* New York: Teachers College Press.

14. August, D. and Shanahan, T., eds. 2006. *Developing Literacy in Second-Language Learners: Report of the National Literacy Panel on Language-Minority Children and Youth.* Mahwah, NJ: Lawrence Erlbaum.

15. Genesee, F., Lindholm-Leary, K., Saunders, W., and Christian, D. 2006. *Educating English Language Learners.* New York: Cambridge University Press.

16. National Reading Panel 2000. *Report of the National Reading Panel—Teaching Children to Read: An Evidence-Based Assessment of the Scientific Research Literature on Reading and Its Implications for Reading Instruction* (Report of the subgroups). Washington, DC: National Institute of Child Health and Human Development.

17. Crawford, J. 1999. *Bilingual Education: History, Politics, Theory, and Practice* (4th edition). Los Angeles: Bilingual Education Services.

18. This finding was first reported in Slavin, R., and Cheung, A. 2005. A synthesis of research on language of reading instruction for English Language Learners, *Review of Educational Research* 75:247–281. Robert Slavin was a member of the NLP and was working on the meta-analysis of instructional language. He resigned in order to publish his review before the Panel's work was completed.

19. The CREDE report also reached the same conclusion, but it was a narrative review, not a meta-analysis. The other four meta-analyses are as follows: Greene, J. 1997. A meta-analysis of the Rossell and Baker review of bilingual education research. *Bilingual Research Journal* 21:103–122. Rolstad, K., Mahoney, K. and Glass, G. 2005. The big picture: A meta-analysis of program effectiveness research on English Language Learners. *Educational Policy* 19:572–594. Slavin, R. and Cheung, A. 2005. A synthesis of research on language of reading instruction for English Language Learners. *Review of Educational Research* 75:247–281. Willig, A. 1985. A meta-analysis of selected studies on the effectiveness of bilingual education. *Review of Educational Research* 55:269–317.

20. Jiménez, R. 1997. The strategic reading abilities and potential of five low-literacy Latina/o readers in middle school. *Reading Research Quarterly,* 32:224–243; quote from p. 227.

21. August, D. and Shanahan, T., eds. 2006. *Developing Literacy in Second-Language Learners: Report of the National Literacy Panel on Language-Minority Children and Youth.* Mahwah, NJ: Lawrence Erlbaum; quote from p. 398.

22. See, for example, Bialystok, E. 2001. *Bilingualism in Development: Language, Literacy, and Cognition.* New York: Cambridge University Press.

23.   Saiz, A. and Zoido, E. 2005. Listening to what the world says: Bilingualism and earnings in the United States. *Review of Economics and Statistics* 87 (3):523–538.

24.   Stuart, M. 1999. Getting ready for reading: Early phoneme awareness and phonics teaching improves reading and spelling in inner-city second language learners. *British Journal of Educational Psychology* 69:587–605.

25.   See, for example, Vaughn, S., Cirino, P. T., Linan-Thompson, S., Mathes, P. G., Carlson, C. D., Cardenas-Hagan, E., et al., 2006. Effectiveness of a Spanish intervention and an English intervention for English-language learners at risk for reading problems. *American Educational Research Journal* 43 (3):449–487; Vaughn, S., Mathes, P. G., Linan-Thompson, S., Cirino, P. T., Carlson, C. D., Pollard-Durodola, S. D., et al. 2006. Effectiveness of an English intervention for first-grade English language learners at-risk for reading problems. *Elementary School Journal* 107 (2):153–180.

26.   Carlo, M. S., August, D., McLaughlin, B., Snow, C. E., Dressler, C., Lippman, D. N., Lively, T. J., and White, C. E. 2004. Closing the gap: Addressing the vocabulary needs of English-language learners in bilingual and mainstream classrooms. *Reading Research Quarterly* 39 (4:188–215).

27.   See, for example, Beck, I., McKeown, M., and Kucan, L. 2002. *Bringing Words to Life: Robust Vocabulary Instruction.* New York: Guilford.

28.   Collins, M. 2005. ESL preschoolers' English vocabulary acquisition from storybook reading. *Reading Research Quarterly* 40:406–408.

29.   Genesee, B., Lindholm-Leary, K., Saunders, W., and Christian, D. 2006. *Educating English Language Learners.* New York: Cambridge University Press; quote from p. 140.

30.   Genesee, F., Lindholm-Leary, K., Saunders, W., and Christian, D. 2006. *Educating English Language Learners.* New York: Cambridge University Press; quote from p. 140.

31.   Genesee, F., Lindholm-Leary, K., Saunders, W., and Christian, D. 2006. *Educating English Language Learners.* New York: Cambridge University Press; quote from p. 139–140.

32.   August, D. and Shanahan, T., eds. 2006. *Developing Literacy in Second-Language Learners: Report of the National Literacy Panel on Language-Minority Children and Youth.* Mahwah, NJ: Lawrence Erlbaum; quote from p. 448.

33.   Genesee, F., Lindholm-Leary, K., Saunders, W., and Christian, D. 2006. *Educating English Language Learners.* New York: Cambridge University Press.

"Critical Questions" Endnotes

1.   Readers interested in finding out more about two-way bilingual education should consult: Lindholm-Leary, K. J. 2001. *Dual language education.* Avon, United Kingdom: Multilingual Matters; Lindholm-Leary, K. J. 2003. Dual language achievement, proficiency, and attitudes among current high school graduates of two-way programs. *NABE Journal* 26:20–25; Lindholm-Leary, K. J. 2005. The rich promise of two-way immersion. *Educational Leadership* 62:56–59; Lindholm-Leary, K. J. 2007. *Effective Features of Dual Language Education Programs: A Review of Research and Best Practices* (2nd ed.). Washington, DC: Center for Applied Linguistics.

2.   Ellis, R. 2005. Principles of instructed language learning. *System,* 33:209–224. Norris, J. and Ortega, L. 2006. *Synthesizing Research on Language Learning and Teaching.* Philadelphia, PA: John Benjamins. Lyster, R. 2007. *Learning and Teaching Languages through Content: A Counterbalanced Approach.* Philadelphia, PA: John Benjamins.

3.   Saunders, W., Foorman, B., and Carlson, C. 2006. Do we need a separate block of time for oral English language development in programs for English learners? *Elementary School Journal* 107:181–198.

4.   See, for example, Lyster, R. 2007. *Learning and Teaching Languages through Content: A Counterbalanced Approach.* Philadelphia, PA: John Benjamins.

Article 29 References

Cunningham, A., & Stanovich, K. (1997). Early reading acquisition and its relation to reading experience and ability 10 years later. *Developmental Psychology, 33,* 934–945.

Dworin, J. (2006). The Family Stories Project: Using funds of knowledge for writing. *The Reading Teacher, 59,* 510–520.

Lesaux, N., Koda, K., Siegel, L., & Shanahan, T. (2006). Development of literacy. In D. August & T. Shanahan (Eds.), *Developing literacy in second-language learners: Report of the National Literacy Panel on language-minority children and youth* (pp. 75–122). Mahwah, NJ: Erlbaum.

Lesaux, N. K., & Siegel, L. S. (2003). The development of reading in children who speak English as a second language. *Developmental Psychology, 39,* 1005–1019.

Mohr, K. A. J., & Mohr, E. S. (2007). Extending English-language learners' classroom interactions using the Response Protocol. *The Reading Teacher, 60,* 440–450.

Moll, L. C., Amanti, C., & Gonzalez, N. (2005). *Funds of knowledge: Theorizing practices in households and classrooms.* Mahwah, NJ: Erlbaum.

Moll, L. C., & Dworin, J. E. (1996). Biliteracy development in classrooms: Social dynamics and cultural possibilities. In D. Hicks (Ed.), *Discourse, learning, and schooling* (pp. 221–246). New York: Cambridge University Press.

Saville-Troike, M. (1984). What really matters in second language learning for academic achievement? *TESOL Quarterly, 17,* 199–219.

Vasquez, O. A., Pease-Alvarez, L., & Shannon, S. M. (1994). *Pushing boundaries: Language and culture in a Mexicano community.* New York: Cambridge University Press.

Vaughn, S., Mathes, P. C., Linan-Thompson, S., & Francis, D. J. (2005). Teaching English language learners at risk for reading disabilities to read: Putting research into practice. *Learning Disabilities Research and Practice, 20*(1), 58–67.

Verhoeven, L. T. (1994). Transfer in bilingual development: The linguistic interdependence hypothesis revisited. *Language Learning, 44,* 381–415.

Article 31 References

Brandt, R. (1998). *Powerful teaching.* Alexandria, VA: ASCD.

Danielson, C. (1996). *Enhancing professional practice: A framework for teaching.* Alexandria, VA: ASCD.

Schlechty, P. (1997). *Inventing better schools: An action plan for educational reform.* San Francisco: Jossey-Bass.

Tomlinson, C. (1995). *How to differentiate instruction in mixed-ability classrooms.* Alexandria, VA: ASCD.

Tomlinson, C. (1999). *The differentiated classroom: Responding to the needs of all learners.* Alexandria, VA: ASCD.

Wiggins, G., & McTighe, J. (1998). *Understanding by design.* Alexandria, VA: ASCD.

Article 32 References

Education Commission of the States. (2003). *No Child Left Behind issue brief: A guide to standards-based assessment.* Denver: Author. Elementary and Secondary Education Act of 2001, Pub. Law No. 107-110 (2002).

Gartin, B. C., Murdick, N. L., Imbeau, M., & Perner, D. E. (2002). *How to use differentiated instruction with students with developmental disabilities in the general education classroom.* Arlington, VA: Council for Exceptional Children.

Glatthorn, A. A. (1998). *Performance assessment and standards-based curricula: The achievement cycle.* Larchmont, NY: Eye on Education.

Hoover, J. J. (2001). *Class management* (CD-ROM). Boulder: University of Colorado at Boulder, BUENO Center.

Hoover, J. J., & Patton, J. R. (in press). *Curriculum adaptations for students with learning and behavior problems: Principles and practices* (3rd ed.). Austin, TX: PRO-ED.

Individuals with Disabilities Education Act Amendments of 1999.

Linn, L. R., & Herman, J. L. (1997). *A policymaker's guide to standards-led assessment.* Denver: Education Commission for the States.

McLaughlin, W. W., & Shepard, L. A. (1995). *Improving education through standards-based reform.* Stanford, CA: The National Academy of Education.

Quenemoen, R. F., Lehr, C. A., Thurlow, M. L., & Massanaair, C. B. (2001). *Students with disabilities in standards-based assessment and accountability systems: Emerging issues, strategies, and recommendations.* Minneapolis: National Center on Educational Outcomes.

Tomlinson, C. A. (2000). Reconcilable differences: Standards-based teaching and differentiation. *Educational Leadership, 58*(1), 6–11.

Article 33 References

Alvermann, D. (Ed.). (2002). *Adolescents and literacies in a digital world.* New York: Peter Lang.

Cope, B., Kalantzis, M., and Lankshear, C. (2005). A contemporary project: An interview. *E-Learning, 2*(2), 192–201.

Gee, J., Hull, G., & Lankshear, C. (1996). *The new work order: Behind the language of the new capitalism.* Boulder, CO: Westview.

Knobel, M. (1999). *Everyday literacies: Students, discourses, and social practice.* New York: Peter Lang.

Knobel, M., & Lankshear, C. (a.k.a. netgrrrl * [12] and chicoboy21 * [32]). (2002). What am I bid? Reading, writing and ratings and eBay.com. In I. Snyder (Ed.), *Silicon literacies* (pp. 15–30). London: Routledge-Falmer.

Lankshear, C., & Bigum, C. (1999). Literacies and new technologies in school settings. *Pedagogy, Culture, and Society* (formerly *Curriculum Studies;* special issue guest edited by E. Millard), *7*(3), 241–261.

Lankshear, C., Bigum, C., Durrant, C., Green, B., Honan, E., Morgan, W., Murray, J., Snyder, I., Wild, M., et al. (1997). *Digital rhetorics: Literacies and technologies in classrooms—current practices and future directions.* Canberra: Department of Employment, Education, Training, and Youth Affairs.

Lankshear, C., & Knobel, M. (1997a). Literacies, texts, and difference in the electronic age. In C. Lankshear (Ed.), *Changing literacies* (pp. 149–188). Buckingham, UK: Open University Press.

Lankshear, C., & Knobel, M. (1997b). Different worlds: Technology-mediated classroom learning and students' social practices with new technologies in home and community settings. In C. Lankshear (Ed.), *Changing literacies* (pp. 149–188). Buckingham, UK: Open University Press.

Lankshear, C., & Knobel, M. (2000). Mapping postmodern literacies: A preliminary chart. *Journal of Literacy and Technology, 1*(1). Retrieved June 14, 2006, from www.literacyandtechnology.org/v1n1/lk.html.

Lankshear, C., & Knobel, M. (2003). *New literacies: Changing knowledge and classroom learning.* Buckingham, UK: Open University Press.

Lankshear, C., & Knobel, M. (2006). *New literacies: Everyday practices and classroom learning* (2nd ed.). Maidenhead and New York: Open University Press.

Lankshear, C., & Lawler, M. (1987). *Literacy, schooling, and revolution.* London: Falmer.

Lankshear, C., Peters, M., & Knobel, M. (1996). Critical pedagogy in cyberspace. In C. Lankshear, H. Giroux, P. McLaren, and M. Peters, *Counternarratives: Cultural studies and critical pedagogies in postmodern spaces* (pp. 149–188). New York: Routledge.

Lankshear, C., Peters, M., & Knobel, M. (2000). Information, knowledge and learning: Some issues facing epistemology and education in a digital age. *Journal of Philosophy of Education, 34*(1), 17–40.

Lankshear, C., & Snyder, I., with Green, B. (2000). *Teachers and technoliteracy.* Sydney: Allen and Unwin.

Leander, K. (2005). *Fieldnote excerpts from the SYNchrony project.* Nashville: Vanderbilt University.

Lyotard, J.-F. (1984). *The postmodern condition: A report on knowledge* (G. Bennington & B. Massumi, Trans.). Minneapolis: University of Minnesota Press.

Scribner, S., and Cole, M. (1981). *The psychology of literacy.* Cambridge, MA: Harvard University Press.

Street, B. (1984). *Literacy in theory and practice.* Cambridge: Cambridge University Press.

Surman, M., & Reilly, K. (2003). Chapter 5: Mobilization. In *Appropriating the Internet for social change* (Report commissioned by the Social Sciences Research Council, Canada). Accessed March 7, 2005, at commons.ca/articles/fulltext.shtml?x=336.

Thomas, A. (2005). Children online: Learning in a virtual community of practice. *E-learning, 2*(1), 27–38, http://www.wwwords.co.uk/elea/content/pdfs/2/issue2_1.asp.

Article 34 Endnotes

1. See Bolter; Burbules and Callister; Dresang; Kress; Landow; Lanham; or Snyder for a full description of how texts have changed ontologically.

2. See for example, Adams; Allington; Pressley.

Article 34 References

Adams, Marilyn Jager. *Beginning to Read: Thinking and Learning about Print.* Cambridge: MIT, 1990.

Allington, Richard L. *What Really Matters for Struggling Readers: Designing Research-Based Programs.* New York: Longman, 2001.

Bolter, Jay David. *Writing Space: The Computer, Hypertext, and the History of Writing.* Hillsdale: Erlbaum, 1991.

Burbules, Nicholas C., and Thomas A. Callister. "Knowledge at the Crossroads: Some Alternative Futures of Hypertext Environments for Learning." *Educational Theory* 46.1 (1996): 23–50.

Burke, Anne, and Shelley Stagg Peterson. "A Multidisciplinary Approach to Literacy through Picture Books and Drama." *English Journal* 96.3 (2007): 74–79.

Dresang, Eliza T. *Radical Change: Books for Youth in a Digital Age.* New York: Wilson, 1999.

Feiffer, Jules. *Meanwhile.* New York: Harper, 1997.

Gee, James Paul. *Social Linguistics and Literacies: Ideology in Discourses.* 2nd ed. Bristol: Taylor and Francis, 1996.

———. "Socio-Cultural Approaches to Literacy." *Annual Review of Applied Linguistics* 12 (1992): 31–48.

Handa, Carolyn. "Introduction to Part One." *Visual Rhetoric in a Digital World: A Sourcebook.* Ed. Carolyn Handa. Boston: Bedford, 2004.

Hammerberg [Hassett], Dawnene D. "Comprehension Instruction for Socioculturally Diverse Classrooms: A Review of What We Know." *The Reading Teacher* 57.7 (2004): 2–12.

———. "Reading and Writing 'Hypertextually': Children's Literature, Technology, and Early Writing Instruction." *Language Arts* 78.3 (2001): 207–16.

Hassett, Dawnene D. "Signs of the Times: The Governance of Alphabetic Print Over 'Appropriate' and 'Natural' Reading Development." *Journal of Early Childhood Literacy* 6.1 (2006): 77–103.

———. "Technological Difficulties: A Theoretical Frame for Understanding the Non-Relativistic Permanence of Traditional Print Literacy in Elementary Education." *Journal of Curriculum Studies* 38.2 (2006); 135–59.

Heath, Shirley Brice. "Sociocultural Contexts of Language Development." *Beyond Language: Social and Cultural Factors in Schooling Language Minority Students.* Los Angeles: Evaluation, Dissemination, and Assessment Center, California State U, 1986. 143–86.

———. *Ways with Words: Language, Life, and Work in Communities and Classrooms.* New York: Cambridge UP, 1983.

Hill, Charles A. "Reading the Visual in College Writing Classes." *Visual Rhetoric in a Digital World: A Sourcebook.* Ed. Carolyn Handa. Boston: Bedford, 2004. 107–30.

Kress, Gunther. *Literacy in the New Media Age.* New York: Routledge, 2003.

———. "Visual and Verbal Modes of Representation in Electronically Mediated Communication: The Potentials of New Forms of Text." *Page to Screen: Taking Literacy into the Electronic Era.* Ed. Ilana Snyder. St. Leonards, Australia: Allen, 1997. 53–79.

Landow, George P. *Hypertext: The Convergence of Contemporary Critical Theory and Technology.* Baltimore: Johns Hopkins UP, 1992.

Lanham, Richard. "What's Next for Text?" *Education Communication and Information* 1.1(4 Jan. 2002). 22 May 2007 <http://www.open.ac.uk/eci/lanham/femoset.html>.

Lankshear, Colin, and Michele Knobel. *New Literacies: Changing Knowledge and Classroom Learning.* Philadelphia: Open UP, 2003.

London, Jonathan. *Froggy Gets Dressed.* New York: Puffin, 1992.

Macaulay, David. *Black and White.* Boston: Houghton, 1990.

McCloud, Scott. *Understanding Comics: The Invisible Art.* New York: Harper, 1993.

Pérez, Bertha, ed. *Sociocultural Contexts of Language and Literacy.* Mahwah: Erlbaum, 1998.

Pressley, Michael. *Reading Instruction That Works: The Case for Balanced Teaching.* 3rd ed. New York: Guilford, 2006.

Rood, Carrie. "Critical Viewing and the Significance of the Emotional Response." *Eyes on the Future: Converging Images, Ideas and Instruction.* Ed. Robert E. Griffin, Darrell G. Beauchamp, J. Mark Hunter, and Carole B. Schiffman. Chicago: International Visual Literacy Assn., 1996. 111–17.

Satrapi, Marjane. *Persepolis: The Story of a Childhood.* New York: Pantheon, 2003.

Schmar-Dobler, Elizabeth. "Reading on the Internet: The Link between Literacy and Technology." *Journal of Adolescent and Adult Literacy* 47.1 (2003): 80–85.

Scieszka, Jon, and Lane Smith. *The Stinky Cheese Man and Other Fairly Stupid Tales.* New York: Viking, 1992.

Snyder, Ilana. "Beyond the Hype: Reassessing Hypertext." *Page to Screen: Taking Literacy into the Electronic Era.* Ed. Ilana Snyder. St. Leonards, Australia: Allen, 1997. 125–43.

Spiegelman, Art. *Maus I: A Survivor's Tale/My Father Bleeds History.* New York: Pantheon, 1986.

Street, Brian V. *Literacy in Theory and Practice.* Cambridge: Cambridge UP, 1984.

Walter, Virginia. *Making Up Megaboy.* New York: DK, 1998.

Article 35 Endnote

1. Early stages of ethnographic research usually include an orientation to the study setting. When a researcher overviews the setting, she or he becomes familiar with its physical characteristics and geography. The researcher may also identify interaction patterns of various sorts and survey the community's artifacts and tools that are readily displayed.

Article 35 References

Albers, P. (2001). Literacy in the arts. *Primary Voices K–6, 9*(4), 3–9.

Albers, P. (2006). Imagining the possibilities in multimodal curriculum design. *English Education, 38,* 75–101.

Allen, J., Fabregas, V., Hankins, K. H., Hull, G., Labbo, L., Spruill, H., et al. (2002). PhOLKS lore: Learning from photographs, families, and students. *Language Arts, 79,* 312–322.

Alvermann, D. E., & Hagood, M. C. (2000). Critical media literacy: Research, theory, and practice in "new times." *Journal of Educational Research, 93,* 193–205.

Becker, H. S. (1995). Visual sociology, documentary photography, and photojournalism: It's (almost) all a matter of context. *Visual Sociology 10*(1–2), 5–14.

Bintz, W. P. (1997). Seeing through different eyes: Using photography as a research tool. *Teacher Research, 5,* 29–46.

Bunster, X. B. (1977). Taking pictures: Field method and visual mode. In Wellesley Editorial Committee (Eds.), *Woman and national development: The complexities of change.* Chicago: University of Chicago Press.

Cappello, M. (2005). Photo interviews: Eliciting data through conversations with students. *Field Methods, 17,* 170–182.

Cappello, M. (2006). Under construction: Voice and identity development in writing workshop. *Language Arts, 83,* 478–487.

Collier, J., Jr., & Collier, M. (1986). *Visual anthropology: Photography as a research method.* Albuquerque: University of New Mexico Press.

Cowen, K., & Albers, P. (2006). Semiotic representations: Building complex literacy practices through the arts. *The Reading Teacher, 60,* 124–137.

Dempsey, J. V., & Tucker, S. A. (1994). Using photo-interviewing as a tool for research and evaluation. *Educational Technology, 34*(4), 55–62.

Eisner, E. W. (1994). *Cognition and curriculum reconsidered.* New York: Teachers College Press.

Eisner, E. W. (1997). The promise and perils of alternative forms of data representation. *Educational Researcher, 26*(6), 4–10.

English, F. (1988). The utility of the camera in qualitative inquiry. *Educational Researcher, 19*(4), 8–15.

Ewald, W., & Lightfoot, A. (2001). *I wanna take me a picture: Teaching photography and writing to children.* Boston: Beacon Press.

Galleqo, M., Hollingsworth, S., & Whitenack, D. (2001). Relational knowing in the reform of educational cultures. *Teachers College Record, 103*(2), 240–266.

Hollingsworth, S. (1978). *The Atlantic Copper and community south of Portage Lake.* Hancock, MI: John H. Forster Press.

Hollingsworth, S. (1994). *Teacher research and urban literacy education: Lessons and conversations in a feminist key.* New York: Teachers College Press.

Housen, A. C. (2002). Aesthetic thought, critical thinking, and transfer. *Arts and Learning Journal, 18*(1), 99–132.

Kress, G. (1996). *Reading images: The grammar of visual design.* New York: Routledge.

Lincoln, Y. S., & Guba, E. G. (1985). *Naturalistic inquiry.* Beverly Hills, CA: Sage.

Orellana, M. F. (1999). Space and place in an urban landscape: Learning from children's views of their social worlds. *Visual Sociology, 14,* 73–89.

Orellana, M. F., & Hernandez, A. (1999). Taking the walk: Students reading urban environmental print. *The Reading Teacher, 52,* 612–619.

Preskill, H. (1995). The use of photography in evaluating school culture. *Qualitative Studies in Education, 8,* 183–193.

Prosser, J. (1998). *Image-based research: A sourcebook for the qualitative researcher.* London: Falmer.

Schiller, J., & Tillet, B. (2004). Using digital images with young children: Challenges of integration. *Early Child Development and Care, 174,* 401–414.

Secondulfo, D. (1997). The meaning of things: A working field for visual sociology. *Visual Sociology, 12*(2), 33–45.

Seigel, M. (1995). More than words: The generative power of transmediation for learning. *Canadian Journal of Education, 20,* 455–475.

Seigel, M. (2006). Reading the signs: Multimodal transformations in the field of literacy education. *Language Arts, 84,* 65–77.

Short, K. G., & Kauffman, G. (2000). Exploring sign systems within an inquiry system. In M. A. Gallego & S. Hollingsworth (Eds.), *What counts as literacy* (pp. 42–61). New York: Teachers College Press.

Sontag, S. (1977). *On photography.* New York: Farrar, Straus and Giroux.

Wagner, J. (1979). Introduction: Information in and about photographs. In J. Wagner (Ed.), *Images of information: Still photography in the social sciences* (pp. 11–22). Beverly Hills, CA: Sage.

Walker, R. (1993). Finding a silent voice for the researcher: Using photographs in evaluation and research. In M. Schratz (Ed.), *Qualitative voices in educational research* (pp. 72–92). London: Falmer.

Worth, S., & Adair, J. (1977). *Through Navajo eyes: An exploration in film communication and anthropology.* University of New Mexico Press.

INTERNET RESOURCES

LITERACY INSTRUCTION

Center of the Improvement of Reading Achievement

http://www.ciera.org/

The Center for the Improvement of Early Reading Achievement (CIERA) is a national center for research on early reading, representing a consortium of educators from five universities (the University of Michigan and Michigan State University, with the University of Southern California, the University of Minnesota, and the University of Georgia); teacher educators; teachers; publishers of texts, tests, and technology; professional organizations; and schools and school districts across the United States. CIERA is supported under the Educational Research and Development Centers Program, PR/Award Number R305R70004, as administered by the Office of Educational Research and Improvement, U.S. Department of Education.

Colorín Colorado

http://www.colorincolorado.org/educators/teaching

Colorín Colorado is a free web-based service that provides information, activities, and advice for educators and Spanish-speaking families of English language learners (ELLs).

A Compendium of Children's Literature Resources

http://edweb.sdsu.edu/bmoss/index.html

The site is divided into sections related to traditional genres of children's literature including folktales, fairy tales and fantasy, historical fiction, poetry, multicultural literature, picture books, young adult books, and informational texts. In addition, other sections of this website focus on ways that teachers can evaluate and use literature in the classroom.

Edutopia

http://www.edutopia.org/best-site-download-free-lessons-2008

Edutopia is published by The George Lucas Educational Foundation, founded in 1991 by filmmaker George Lucas as a nonprofit operating foundation that documents, disseminates, and advocates for innovation and the redesign of K–12 learning environments, including how technology can transform teaching and learning. Through Edutopia.org, Edutopia magazine, Edutopia video, Edutopia e-newsletters, and a growing online community, the Foundation is building a movement to stimulate education reform with a special focus on core concepts of project learning, integrated studies, social and emotional learning, comprehensive assessment, and teacher development. For more information about Edutopia, visit Edutopia.org, one of the leading education sites on the Internet.

Literacy and Learning

http://www.litandlearn.lpb.org/strategies.html

Literacy & Learning involves a cooperative effort between Southeastern Louisiana University and Louisiana Public Broadcasting to develop and deliver, via satellite, a professional development series whose purpose is to enhance reading skills in grades 5 through 8. This five-year project is funded through a grant from the National Educational Telecommunications Association. The focus of the project is to provide support by developing special video materials for staff development addressing classroom instructional strategies for reading across the curriculum, including the major content areas of language arts, mathematics, science, and social studies. The series of 16 videos will include instructional information, illustrated with actual classroom vignettes.

Literacy Leader

http://www.literacyleader.com/?q=literacywebsites

A website devoted to providing online literacy content.

Literacy Matters

http://www.literacymatters.org/lessons/content.htm

This site provides teacher resources and lesson plans for language arts, English, mathematics, science, and social studies. It also includes the following sections: Instructional Strategies Resources, References and Resources, and WebQuests.

Literacy Strategies

http://literacystrategies.org/

Literacy strategies are used in strategic teaching to maximize the understanding and retention of content material. Strategic teaching incorporates pre-reading, during, and after reading strategies as well as a variety of vocabulary development and writing strategies. The strategies a teacher chooses will depend on the purpose of the lesson and the nature of the material being studied.

National Writing Project

http://www.nwp.org/cs/public/print/resource/922

The National Writing Project's *30 Ideas for Teaching Writing* offers successful strategies contributed by experienced writing project teachers. Since NWP does not promote a single approach to teaching writing, readers will benefit from a variety of eclectic, classroom-tested techniques.

Reading Online

http://www.readingonline.org

This website, provided by the International Reading Association, offers hundreds of articles on a range of topics in reading education. To find articles that match your particular interests, simply search or browse the author, title, and subject indexes.

Read.Write.Think

http://www.readwritethink.org

ReadWriteThink, established in April of 2002, is a partnership between the International Reading Association (IRA), the National Council of Teachers of English (NCTE), and the Verizon Foundation. NCTE and IRA are working together to provide educators and students with access to the highest-quality practices and resources in reading and language arts instruction through free, Internet-based content.

NEW/MULTIPLE LITERACIES

Collaborative Arts Resources for Education

http://www.carearts.org/home.html

The Collaborative Arts Resources for Education (CARE) website consists of California standards-aligned arts-based lesson plans and resources for K–12 educators. CARE is a unique arts education initiative offered by the Museum of Contemporary Art San Diego, the Museum of Photographic Arts, and the San Diego Museum of Art.

New Literacies

http://www.newliteracies.uconn.edu

The New Literacies Research Lab at the University of Connecticut is the most widely recognized center in the world for conducting research on the new reading comprehension and learning skills required by the Internet and other emerging information and communication technologies. Our work develops research-based evidence to prepare students for their literacy and learning future.

Visual Literacy Toolbox

http://www.arhu.umd.edu/vislit/

Visual literacy is a multifaceted subject matter, and faculty wishing to include images in their curricula can quickly find themselves overwhelmed by the prospect of addressing visual literacy.

PROFESSIONAL LITERACY ORGANIZATIONS

International Reading Association

http://www.reading.org

Since 1956, IRA has been a nonprofit global network of individuals and institutions committed to worldwide literacy. More than 85,000 members strong, the Association supports literacy professionals through a wide range of resources, advocacy efforts, volunteerism, and professional development activities.

International Visual Literacy Association

http://www.ivla.org

IVLA was formed for the purpose of providing a forum for the exchange of information related to visual literacy. They are also concerned with issues related to education, instruction, and training in modes of visual communication and their application through the concept of visual literacy to individuals, groups, organizations, and the public in general.

National Reading Conference

http://www.nrconline.org

NRC is a professional organization for individuals who share an interest in research and the dissemination of information about literacy and literacy instruction.

National Council of Teachers of English

http://www.ncte.org

The National Council of Teachers of English is devoted to improving the teaching and learning of English and the language arts at all levels of education. This mission statement was adopted in 1990: "The Council promotes the development of literacy, the use of language to construct personal and public worlds and to achieve full participation in society, through the learning and teaching of English and the related arts and sciences of language."

INDEX

ABOUT THE EDITORS

Marva Cappello, PhD, is an Associate Professor of Teacher Education at San Diego State University, where she teaches courses in literacy and coordinates a district/university partnership at a Professional Development School. Her recent research focuses on young children's writing and the use of photography for teaching and learning literacy in elementary schools. Cappello is a coeditor of *Literacy Teaching and Learning: An International Journal of Early Reading and Writing*. Her articles have appeared in *Language Arts* and the anthropology journal *Field Methods*.

Barbara Moss, PhD, Professor of Education in the Department of Teacher Education at San Diego State University, has taught English and language arts in elementary, middle, and high school and has worked as a reading supervisor and a reading coach. Her research interests focus on issues surrounding the teaching of informational texts at the elementary and secondary levels, especially student access to informational texts and the uses of informational texts in the classroom. She has served as editor of *The Ohio Reading Teacher* and has assumed leadership roles in the International Reading Association as a local chapter president, as a committee member, and as a coeditor of *The Reading Teacher*. She has also authored and coauthored numerous columns, book chapters, and journal articles, which have appeared in *The Reading Teacher, Reading Research and Instruction,* and *The Journal of Literacy Research*. She has authored and coauthored several books, including *25 Strategies for Guiding Readers Through Informational Texts* and *Exploring the Literature of Fact: Children's Nonfiction Trade Books in the Elementary Classroom*.

CPSIA information can be obtained
at www.ICGtesting.com
Printed in the USA
FFOW01n0003140917
39915FF